Books by Allan W. Eckert

THE WINNING OF AMERICA SERIES

THE FRONTIERSMEN

WILDERNESS EMPIRE

THE CONQUERORS

THE WILDERNESS WAR

OTHER BOOKS

THE GREAT AUK

A TIME OF TERROR

THE SILENT SKY

WILD SEASON

THE CROSSBREED

BAYOU BACKWATERS

THE KING SNAKE

THE DREAMING TREE

IN SEARCH OF A WHALE

BLUE JACKET

INCIDENT AT HAWK'S HILL

THE OWLS OF NORTH AMERICA

THE COURT-MARTIAL OF DANIEL BOONE

THE HAB THEORY

THE WADING BIRDS OF NORTH AMERICA

TECUMSEH! (DRAMA)

THE LEGEND OF KOO-TAN (SCREENPLAY)

BLUE JACKET (SCREENPLAY)

THE FRONTIERSMEN (SCREENPLAY)

The Wilderness War

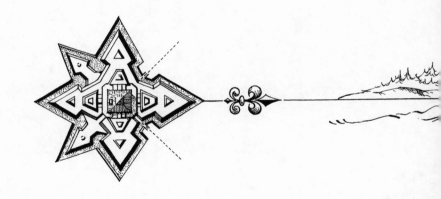

The Wilderness War

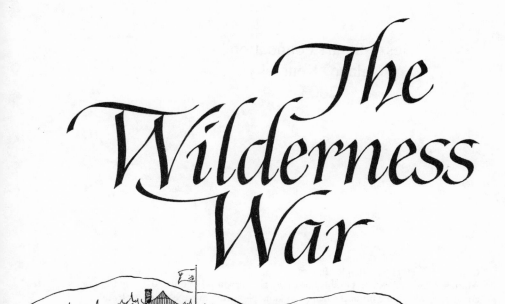

A NARRATIVE

By

ALLAN W. ECKERT

Jesse Stuart Foundation
Ashland, Kentucky
2003

Jesse Stuart Foundation
Ashland, Kentucky
2003

Library of Congress Cataloging-in-Publication Data

Eckert, Allan W.
 the wilderness war : a narrative / by Allan W. Eckert.
  p. cm.
 Originally published: Boston : Little, Brown, c1978.
 Includes bibliographical references and index.
 ISBN1-931672-13-X -- ISBN 1-931672-14-8 (pbk.)
  1. Sullivan's Indian Campaign, 1779. 2. Sullivan, John, 1740-1795. 3. Brant,
Joseph, 1742-1807. I. Title.

E235 .E26 2003
973.3'35--dc21

             2002040612

Jacket Design by Brett Nance
Original Art by John Alan Maxwell

Published by:
Jesse Stuart Foundation
1645 Winchester Avenue • P.O. Box 669
Ashland, Kentucky 41105
(606) 326-1667

To
the man who has worked
with me over the years
and whose assistance and advice
are so invaluable

MY EDITOR
LARNED G. BRADFORD

AUTHOR'S NOTE

T*he Wilderness War* is fact, not fiction. Every incident herein described actually occurred; every date is historically accurate; every character, regardless of how major or how minor, actually lived the role in which he is portrayed.

This book is meant to provide an accurate and comprehensive, yet swiftly paced and dramatic picture of the events and people of the time period it covers. It is the result of extended and intensive research through a great multitude of original documents, including many hundreds of personal letters and notes, memoranda, diaries, legal papers, journals, deeds, military records, depositions, tribal records where they exist, governmental reports, logbooks, newspapers and magazines of the time, and other sources. Modern books covering the period have not been excluded as source material, but a much greater reliability has been placed upon the original material written at the time of the occurrence.

Within the text there are occasional numbered notes keyed, through consecutive numbering, to a section entitled Amplification Notes at the back of the book. These notes provide material that is essentially tangential to the subject under discussion, but nevertheless of added interest and value in providing the reader with an increased understanding of the events portrayed and a stronger sense of orientation where geographic locales are concerned.

Unfortunately, the greater majority of Indians written about in history are referred to by nicknames or clumsy translations of the actual meaning of their Indian names. As a result, there are literally hundreds of Indians who were known as Joe or Billy, Captain Jack or Big George, Colonel Bull or Platkopff or other such appellations. Sometimes, as in the case of Chief Joseph Brant of this book, his English name is far more familiar and has more historical significance than his Indian name, which in Brant's case was Thayendanegea. In such cases the English name has been used, with only occasional reference to the Indian name. In other cases, however, there is a tendency for the translated name to be insulting or at least not as dignified or not having quite the charm and musical ring of the Indian name. Thus, Brant's grandfather Tiyanoga was long known by the name Hendrik; Kanonaron of the Mohawks was called Aaron, or Little Aaron; Logan's real name was Tal-ga-yee-ta; the Wampanoag chief Metacomet was called King Philip and his brother, Wamsutta, was dubbed Alexander. Catahecassa, of the Shawnees, became known as Black Hoof, and his predecessor as the tribe's principal chief, Hokolesqua, is more familiar as Chief Cornstalk. I have endeavored, wherever possible in this volume, and where the Indian name is practicably pronounceable, to refer to the Indians by their true names.

Certain techniques normally associated with the novel form have been utilized in this book, as in the other books in this series, in order to help provide continuity and maintain a high degree of reader interest, but in no case has this been at the expense of historical accuracy. Where dialogue occurs in this volume it is actual quoted conversation from a historical source or reconstructed from historically recorded interchange between individuals, but not written then as dialogue. In a few scattered instances historical fact has been utilized in the form of conversation to maintain the dramatic narrative pace, but always in keeping with the character and the fundamental leanings of the individual speaking the words.

As a further aid there is, at the back of the book, a chapter-by-chapter listing of the principal sources for the facts, dialogue and possibly controversial information contained in the text. There is also a complete index.

The Wilderness War is the fourth volume in the author's in-progress series entitled The Winning of America. Other volumes in the series are *The Frontiersmen*, *Wilderness Empire* and *The Conquerors*. The individual books do not depend upon one another, yet they strongly complement each other. All of them contribute to the principal theme of the series, which is precisely how the white man took North America from the Indians. In point of time *The Wilderness War* picks up the narrative thread where it left off in *Wilderness Empire*, but it is not necessary to have read one in order to appreciate the other.

Step by step this series moves across the continent, showing clearly and in the most fundamentally human terms how the land was won — through encroachment, trickery, warfare, grant, treachery, purchase, alliance, deceit, theft and treaty. Too often with such a theme the cause is overshadowed by the act and the act thereupon overemphasized. As a result, history can — and often has — become distorted. It is the purpose of this series to penetrate wherever possible to the initial and most basic causes; the simple meetings between individuals, along with their thoughts and aspirations and speech as these have been ferreted out from the original documents; the things — often seemingly very insignificant at the time — that were said and done that resulted in events of great historical import.

As in the past volumes — and those yet to come in The Winning of America series — it is neither the intention nor desire of the author to champion either the cause of the Indians or that of the whites; there were heroes and rascals on both sides, humanity and atrocity on both sides, rights and wrongs on both sides. The facts are presented chronologically, just as they occurred, and with the greatest possible degree of accuracy. There has been little author intrusion, editorializing, or moralizing. It has not been necessary. The facts speak amply for themselves and whatever conclusions are drawn must be drawn solely by the reader.

Barrington, Illinois　　　　　　　　　　　　　　　　ALLAN W. ECKERT
June 22, 1978

MAPS

Lake Ontario

Irondequoit Bay

■ FORT NIAGARA

NIAGARA FALLS

Tonawanda Cr.

Buffalo Cr.

L. Erie

Cattaraugus Cr.

CANAWAUGUS ▲

CHENUSSIO ▲

CANANDAIGUA ▲

CONESUS ▲

Genesee R.

Canisteo R.

KANASTIO ▲

SKOYASE ▲

KANADASAGA ▲

CANOG

KASHONG ▲ ▲ KENDAIA

Seneca Lake

Cayuga Lake

SHEQUAGA ▲

N

Conocton R.

KANAWAHOLLA ▲ ▲

TEAOGO ▲

CHEMUNG ▲

NEWT

QUEEN ESTHER'S TOWN ▲

OV

O

P E N N S Y L L

West Branch

■ FORT FREELAND

● SUNB

The Wilderness War

SCALE IN MILES

0 5 10   20   30

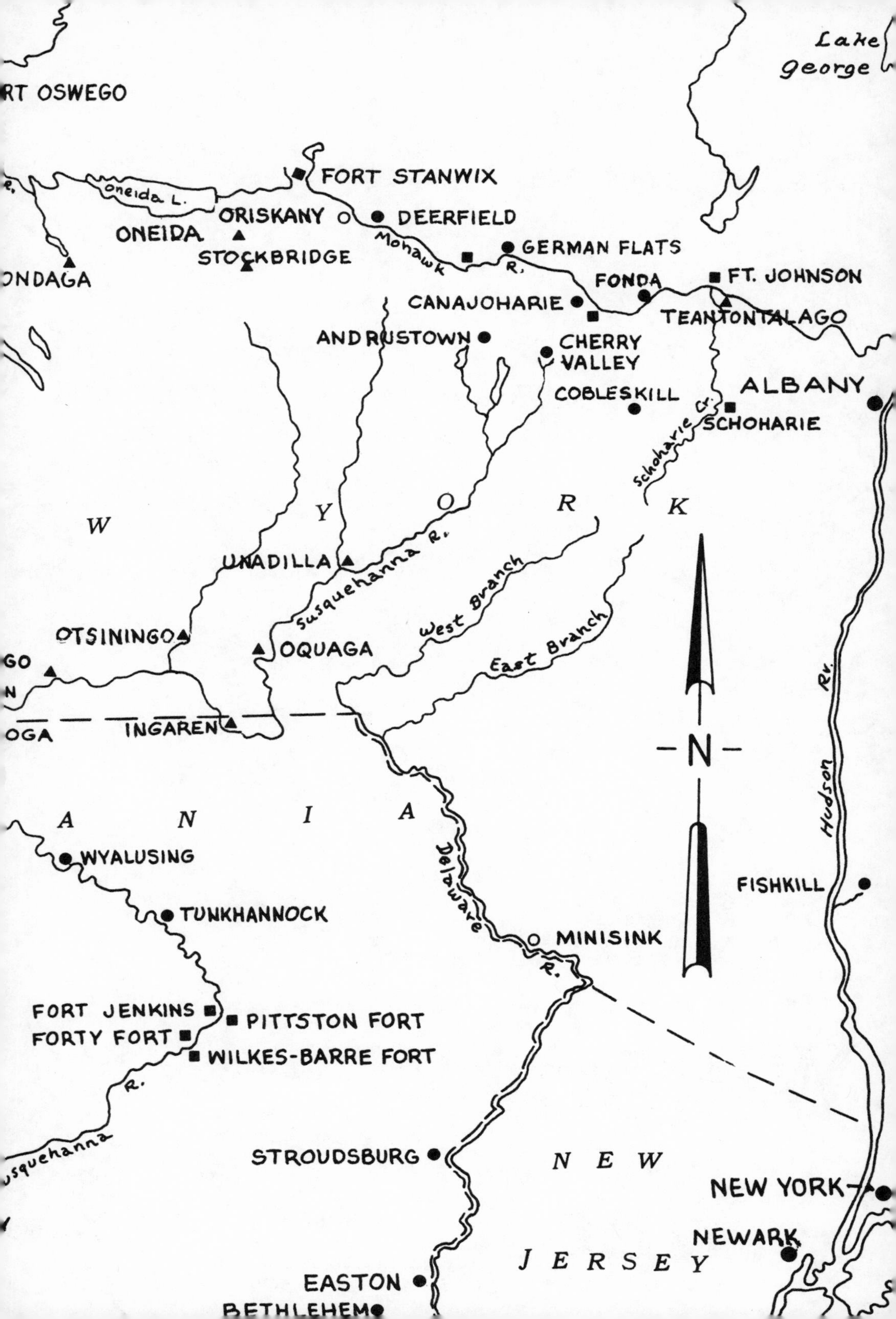

Lake George
RT OSWEGO
FORT STANWIX
Oneida L.
ORISKANY
DEERFIELD
ONEIDA
Mohawk R.
STOCKBRIDGE
GERMAN FLATS
ONDAGA
FONDA
FT. JOHNSON
CANAJOHARIE
TEANTONTALAGO
ANDRUSTOWN
CHERRY VALLEY
ALBANY
COBLESKILL
SCHOHARIE
Schoharie Cr.
W
Y
O
R
K
UNADILLA
Susquehanna R.
West Branch
East Branch
OTSININGO
OQUAGA
GO
N
OGA
INGAREN
N
A
N
I
A
Delaware R.
Hudson Rv.
WYALUSING
FISHKILL
TUNKHANNOCK
MINISINK
FORT JENKINS
PITTSTON FORT
FORTY FORT
WILKES-BARRE FORT
R.
usquehanna
STROUDSBURG
N E W
NEW YORK
NEWARK
J E R S E Y
EASTON
BETHLEHEM

The Wilderness War

PROLOGUE

[*October*, 1740]

AS yet, no tracks except those of a dog marred the stark, smooth surface of the two-inch blanket of snow that had fallen during the night and that now reflected the brightness of the newly risen sun. There were no more than twenty structures in the Indian village, all of which were well frosted with a heavy white layer from the unseasonably early snowfall. Wisps of blue-white wood smoke rose from most of them, and from the lengthy, slightly peaked roof of the central longhouse alone, four separate plumes of smoke wafted gently upward in the motionless air.

The village was Shenango[1] and it was situated on a point of land where a small stream entered the Ohio River from the northeast. Only fourteen miles upstream the mighty Ohio itself was formed by the convergence of two great rivers — the Monongahela from the south and the Allegheny from the north — and here at the village it hissed faintly as it slid past the whitened shores. At the water's edge half a dozen or more bark and log canoes, upside down on shore, were also heavily mantled with snow.

Shenango was not a well-known village[2] and certainly there was no awareness among its inhabitants that this was the most important day of its existence. From within the longhouse there was a faint sound and a dog lying outside the heavy door flap suddenly cocked his head, stood and shook himself and then began a vague wagging of his tail. The sound came again, the brief, faint cry that was the utterance of a newborn baby. Inside there were murmurs of approval and smiles among the score or more Indians assembled. A moment later, when the word passed among them that the birth was a boy-child, their eyes, which had for such a long while been on the young Mohawk woman Owandah during her labor, turned now to her husband, Teho-wa.[3] He was a heavy man, chunky and rather short. His round face widened with his own

broad grin and he nodded his head in acknowledgement of the silent praise. A
son! The Great Spirit too, must be smiling.

Teho-wa moved closer, the midwives parting to let him pass, and he looked
down at the fur-swaddled figure beside Owandah. The baby was no longer crying and there was a light of pride in the mother's eyes. She watched Teho-wa's
movements as his hand came out and gently pulled the fur partially aside so his
own eyes could confirm what had been said. Once more his head bobbed when
he saw the tiny penis and he tucked the swaddling back in place before the infant could become chilled.

"You said it would be a son, Owandah. It is. When the naming time comes
he will have the name of my father." [4]

Owandah nodded, pleased that her baby would bear the name of his paternal
grandfather Thayendanegea, but she was aware as well that the child would
have yet another name. Her eyes met Teho-wa's momentarily and she knew
the same thought was in his mind. Both she and Teho-wa had previously lived
in the Mohawk River valley and there, under the persuasive influence of missionaries from England, they had become Christians. That was long before
their first child, a daughter, had been born two years ago. In addition to naming her Degonwadonti, they had also christened her Mary. Now this newborn
boy-child, as well as being called Thayendanegea, would be called Joseph. [5]

Joseph and Mary. It was good. God would be pleased. Jesus would be
pleased. And the Great Spirit wouldn't mind at all.

[*November 5, 1742 — Monday*]

For Owandah, the year had started well but then was jarred with tragedy for her
and the children. Now, the difficult spring and summer well behind and winter
in the offing, fortune seemed once again on the upswing.

In the years she had been the wife of Teho-wa she had been very happy. He
had been a good man, devoted to her and the children and a reasonably good
provider for all of them. It was true, there were times when it had been difficult
being near him, but usually this was only when he had had access to the liquor
of the white man. Apart from the fact that he sometimes traded for rum the
furs that he had gathered for the support of his family, and that he grew increasingly sullen and morose the harder he drank, he had still been basically
dependable. In her way, she had grown to love him after they were married.
More than that, she had come to depend upon him.

His death had been wholly unexpected.

In late February he had gone downriver from Shenango a day's journey to
hunt deer, along with two other men from the village. He had hidden near an
area where a deer might be expected to pass and the other two had made a wide
circle and then come back toward him, hoping to drive a deer before them

within range of his bow. Teho-wa was not any sort of outstanding marksman with the weapon since he'd never had the determination to excel with it, as many of his companions during his youth had wished to do. Nevertheless, he could generally hit a stationary mark at thirty paces and had slain a number of standing or walking deer within that distance. He had never been able to hit a running animal.

Shortly after his companions left him to start their circular passage he decided that another area he could see some hundred yards distant might make a better stand for him, so he moved there. This was a mistake.

His companions had noted well where they left him and this was where they expected he would be when they returned. One of them, also armed with a bow, saw the faintest suggestion of a movement in the bushes somewhat in advance of where Teho-wa had been left. He stopped and slowly pulled an arrow to full draw and when the movement in the bushes came again he released the missile. It disappeared into the brush and, while there was no vocal sound, there was a brief thrashing and then silence. It was an exceptional shot. The arrow had taken Teho-wa in the inside corner of one eye and emerged just above the opposite ear.

After a period of mourning only partly understood by Degonwadonti and not at all by Thayendanegea, Owandah bundled up the infant boy and strapped him to a papoose-board to be carried on her back. She fixed a small pack for Degonwadonti to carry and a much larger one for herself to pull on a travois and set off through the wilderness for Canajoharie, the capital of the Mohawk nation, where she had been born. It took eight weeks to complete the journey, during which she often not only carried the baby and pulled the heavy travois, but also sometimes carried Degonwadonti and her pack. There was no one to complain to about the difficulty of the task, but even if there had been she would not have done so. It was something that needed to be done. She did it.

Canajoharie[6] was located on the south bank of the Mohawk River at the mouth of Canajoharie Creek. It was a large village with not only scores of fine wigwams, but also no less than thirty excellent homes of hewn timbers built in the fashion of the whites, with windows and doors, but without either floors or chimneys. Flooring was uncomfortable to feet accustomed to the feel of Mother Earth and, for the fire that burned almost constantly in the middle of the floor, a simple hole in the roof served admirably as a chimney, even as a hole in the top of each wigwam served the same function.

Owandah had returned to Canajoharie not only because it was the only other place she had ever lived, but because her father still lived there and he had not seen his grandchildren and would probably help her care for them in those areas where they would require the guidance of a man. But her father, too, was dead. A minor outbreak of smallpox had struck last winter and eight or ten of the villagers had died of it. Her father had been one of them.

That was when Nichus Brant, a strong and prominent man of the village, had taken the family under his wing and helped. Owandah's father had been a friend of Nichus's own father, so it was a matter of family honor to help. Actually, it was even more than that. Nichus had known Owandah before she had become the wife of Teho-wa and he was much taken by her then. Now that she was a widow he more than willingly helped her and the children and was quickly and deeply smitten by her.

So now, only a little over eight months following the death of Teho-wa, she was married to Nichus Brant and finding that she loved him with a greater depth than she had ever felt for Teho-wa. She was also greatly impressed with him, for he was not only the son of one of the most powerful chiefs in the history of the Iroquois League — the remarkable Brant,[7] who had died only four years ago — he was himself a noted sachem of the Mohawks. His father had helped to make his Mohawks the most feared tribe of the Six Nations — even more feared than the mighty Senecas, who were the guardians of the westernmost domain of the Iroquois League. When he died the chieftainship of the tribe did not devolve to Nichus, but rather to Brant's close friend and companion Tiyanoga, who had gone to England with him in 1710. As Brant had been, Tiyanoga was a great power in the Iroquois League and it was he who was still principal chief of the Mohawks and who resided here at Canajoharie. And Tiyanoga was very close to his old friend's son, Nichus.

Like his father, Nichus was also called Brant, though as a surname instead of just one name. To Indians and whites both he was known as Nichus Brant and the fact that he was proud of the surname was obvious, for he now quickly bestowed it upon his two new stepchildren, Joseph and Mary.[8]

For the two children, Canajoharie had decidedly become home and Nichus Brant became father. The valley of the Mohawk River was a beautiful country and the Mohawks loved it with a fierce pride and possessiveness. Yet, little by little over the years it was being nibbled away from them; peacefully, true, but disappearing into the possession of whites nonetheless, and a mounting concern was in the Mohawks. They needed a champion to represent them among the whites, to protect their rights and their lands. They found him in the person of a man named William Johnson, who was unlike any other white man ever known to them.

Johnson had come to America from Ireland when he was fifteen and had quickly imbued himself with a knowledge of the land and its people. He loved the Indians and their ways and adopted them as his own and quickly became known throughout the entire Iroquois League as a real friend. He was more than that: He had become what they needed — a champion, a man who understood the white world as none of them could and who could represent them in it; a man in whom they could have faith that he was truly representing their interests and not merely feathering his own nest. When at last they became convinced that William Johnson was indeed such a man they were swift to act. Johnson and Tiyanoga had become firm friends and remained so even now, and so, early last month in a ceremony extremely rare among the Mohawks, William Johnson was adopted into the tribe and became the official representative of the Iroquois League.[9] That ceremony had taken place right here at Canajoharie and had been witnessed by Nichus Brant and his new wife, Owandah, and afterward Johnson, who had now been given the name Warraghiyagey — The-Man-Who-Undertakes-Great-Things — came to the well-built hewn-log home of Nichus Brant and, as he had done many times in the past, ate with him as a friend and brother. But never before had the occasion been as ceremonious as this.

Just as William Johnson had that day received a new name, he also inadvertently bestowed one. The graying Chief Tiyanoga, intensely proud of his newly adopted twenty-seven-year-old white son, accompanied him to Nichus Brant's house and it was an afternoon filled with laughter and warmth. It was the first time Johnson had met Owandah and they were pleased with his courtly manners and the way he kissed the back of her hand when introduced to her. They smiled and nodded in tacit agreement when he observed the concentration with which two-year-old Joseph Brant was arranging some sticks on the floor and remarked that such concentration in one so young denoted great things for him in the future. They laughed aloud when he bounced the pretty little four-year-old Degonwadonti on his knee and called her Miss Molly, their politeness inhibiting them from pointing out the error, that her name was Mary, not Molly. In that moment, not even realizing that he had done so, William Johnson had renamed her.[10]

Now, just over a month since that day of adoption, Johnson's woman, Catherine Weisenberg — Catty — who had already borne him a daughter a couple of years ago whom they'd named Ann, today bore him a son. They named him John.

The baby was born early in the morning and so swiftly had word of it spread that by late afternoon Tiyanoga and Nichus Brant had arrived at the Johnson home on horseback bearing gifts and good wishes. Before they left Nichus placed his hand on Johnson's shoulder and spoke earnestly:

"We now both have sons. My son Joseph and your son John will be close in their lives. The two years of difference in their age is great when they are very young, but it becomes as nothing with the passage of years. They will grow up together and become brothers, as you and I are brothers, Warraghiyagey."[11]

Neither man doubted for an instant the truth of that declaration.

CHAPTER I

[*July 6, 1763 — Wednesday*]

AT twenty-two years of age, Joseph Brant was tall and rather spare, the last couple of years having eroded away all vestige of the tendency toward heaviness that had dominated his physical aspect since boyhood. He was now a man and his bearing exuded confidence and grace and even a degree of hauteur. Though he was approximately the same height and weight as the white man who rode beside him this morning, it was Brant who was the more impressive. Perhaps it was the nonchalance with which he sat astride his saddleless horse, flowing smoothly with the movements of the animal rather than bouncing choppily in a saddle as his companion was doing; perhaps it was in the penetration of his gaze, the dark eyes constantly roving, collecting, assimilating and cataloguing the multiplicity of things encountered, as compared to Smith, who rode with tunneled vision; perhaps it was the fiber of character that kept him from turning to take one last look at the place that had been his school and residence for so long — a temptation his companion could not resist.

Charles Jeffrey Smith turned in his saddle and looked at the school in the close distance behind them. Only last week he had been ordained as a minister of the gospel and now all the struggle of education and the accompanying discipline was being left behind. Smith had not yet managed to adopt the decorum proper to his new station in life and he giggled.

"We're leaving it behind, Joseph," he said. He repeated himself, as if unable to believe it fully even now. "We really are. Don't you want to take a last look?"

Brant shook his head. "As you say, it is behind us. For me, that is where it will stay."

Smith frowned. "You're really not coming back? It's a shame, Joseph. You should. You've been Dr. Wheelock's most promising pupil. You shouldn't let it go to waste."

Brant looked at him and smiled faintly. "No learning is ever wasted, nor is learning itself ever ended, but this *sort* of learning is over. I value what I've learned here, but I won't miss the school or Dr. Wheelock."

The school to which these two were referring was known as Moore's Charity School, after its chief benefactor. More correctly, it was the Charity School of Lebanon, Connecticut, which had been established just two years ago, in 1761.[12] The motivating force had been the Reverend Dr. Eleazar Wheelock, who had applied for and been granted by the General Assembly of the Province of Massachusetts Bay the right to set up a school where he could "teach, clothe and board six children of the Six Nations." For that purpose he was to be allotted £12 per child per year.

The term "child" was misleading, for what the Reverend Dr. Wheelock proposed to do was educate some Indian youths in their late teens and early twenties. It was only natural that he contact, as a first step, the white man most knowledgeable about the Indians, especially the Six Nations Indians. William Johnson was ideal for suggestions as to who might be promising candidates for training at the school.

The years had been good to Johnson. His fortunes had increased pro-digiously, as had his prestige and power among both the Indians and whites. He had become Superintendent of Indian Affairs for North America's Northern District by order of the King and then, in 1755, not too unexpectedly he was knighted. No other man in America was so well versed in Indian knowledge, but Sir William went even further than merely being adopted into the Mohawk tribe. Three years after the death of Catty, Sir William took the beautiful Molly Brant as his Indian wife and Molly, shrewd as she was, realized with great clar-ity the value that an English education could have for her brother and to his future in both the tribe and the Iroquois League. When the request came from Dr. Wheelock, Johnson's number one recommendation in return just hap-pened to be Joseph Brant.[13]

On arrival at the Reverend Dr. Wheelock's school on August 1, 1761, Joseph could speak only a few words of English and he was immediately placed under the personal tutelage of the Reverend Samuel Kirkland, who was to teach him English while at the same time learning the Mohawk tongue from him. It was a good arrangement and Joseph proved to be an exceptional student. Not only did he learn very quickly to read and write English, he also made consid-erable progress with Latin and Greek. However, there were many things about the school that were galling to Joseph. Though there were many students other than Indians at the school, only the Indians were obliged to hoe corn and per-form other agricultural chores for the benefit of the school. Without pay, of course. There was also the daily necessity of attending morning and evening prayers in the hallway of Dr. Wheelock's dwelling and woe betide the youth who exhibited a less than devout mien in this pursuit.

Only once during his two years at Wheelock's did Joseph leave the school and that was for a three-week period in November of that first year when, in the company of the Reverend Kirkland, he returned to Sir William Johnson to see about bringing back to the school another group of Indian youths to be educated.[14]

When Brant and Kirkland returned to the school, arriving there with two Mohawk youths whom Wheelock called Moses and Johannes, they bore with them a letter from Sir William in which he said he expected *"to send the rest of the boys when they come in from hunting."* Joseph bore up well under his schooling but he never really liked it. He chafed at the time it consumed and felt left out of the many things that were happening in his home territory.

In these years since his mother had moved back to Canajoharie and married Nichus Brant, a whole world of things had occurred. Owandah had died only a few years after that, but Nichus continued to raise Molly and Joseph. In 1747 Nichus was captured, along with some other Mohawks and British soldiers, and imprisoned by the French in Canada. It was two years before he was released, but that by no means ended the friction between the French and English. The Iroquois League was alternately wooed and castigated by both sides as each tried to win Indian alliance for its cause. Finally, though the Senecas supported the French, the Mohawks and the remainder of the Iroquois League, under the influence of Sir William, supported the British.[15]

The fact that Joseph Brant disliked school does not mean he disliked education, especially the sort he received from Chief Tiyanoga. Even now, the thought of the grand old leader of the Mohawks could bring a lump to Joseph's throat and dampen the corners of his eyes. It was Tiyanoga who had taught him the history of his tribe and that of the Iroquois League; and it was he who had taught Joseph the art of war.

In his deeply resonant baritone voice, Tiyanoga had spoken of how the Iroquois were proud people, but that before the League was formed the Five Nations[16] had been separate, unallied tribes constantly fighting one another. So terrible was the carnage that it became necessary to erect strong palisades around each village for protection. Among their chief villages the remnants of these fortifications yet remained, and when the white men first saw these they called them castles.[17]

At last, Tiyanoga had told him, some two and a half centuries ago, a remarkable thing occurred. A being from the skies came to the earth and spoke to them, telling them to cease their fighting and unite themselves in a league for both defense and attack. Another being was there, too — a man called Ato-tarho, a great Onondaga chief. Both an astounding warrior and great magician, he was bound in some indefinable way to the unnamed being from above. Finally there came a third being, again a man and a chief and yet somehow supernatural, who appeared to various influential tribesmen in their dreams and bade them form this League. His name was Taounyawatham; he was also known to his people as Hiawatha. For a long time he traveled among the five tribes, explaining in detail to their leaders the idea of the League. It was not, he told them, a league that would prevent them from being warriors and waging war, but merely one that would prevent them from destroying themselves, as they were on the brink of doing. And should any one of them be attacked, they would all rise as a single body to beat off and destroy the attackers.

Pride in their own individuality still kept the tribes from agreeing to the formation of a league, but gradually the reluctance wore away and the plan of federation was accepted. The government thereby established was a very strong one. It was so indestructible that it still survived now, after over two hundred and fifty years. Everyone believed it would last many times that much longer.

Then, in the year 1715, the Tuscaroras from the South[18] had been adopted by the Oneidas, to whom they had come and appealed for protection from their enemies, the Creeks. For seven years the Tuscaroras were kept on probation and then, in 1722, they were accepted into the League as members without voting rights in the League councils — which was still their status — and with this the Five Nations became the Six Nations.

"When our tribes joined as one at Hiawatha's bidding," Tiyanoga told Joseph, "our tribes were in a line from the rising sun to the setting sun. The Mohawks were the farthest east and then came the Oneidas. In the middle were the Onondagas and next in line were the Cayugas. Farthest west were the Senecas."[19]

Tiyanoga had paused, conjuring in his mind an image of the majesty of the Iroquois League. "We picture the League," he told Joseph, "as being like one of our longhouses, with a door at each end. The Senecas are the guardians of the western door, while the Mohawks are both guardians of the eastern door and the receivers of tribute. Because of their position in the middle, the Onondagas are the keepers of the council fire and the wampum.[20] The village of Onondaga is the League's seat of government,[21] where all official councils of the League are held.

"Our government," the old chief had continued, "operates in this manner: By law, the tribes elect their representatives and special rules are used for calling these chiefs into congress. On all matters of importance to the League as a whole, the tribal representatives must vote, becoming the voice of their individual tribes, whose will they have determined in previous council. If war is to be declared, the vote must be all one, with none opposed. Disputes between ourselves must be arbitrated before the council and never, under any provocation, be settled through violence. The number of chiefs who sit in this council as representatives of their people varies from tribe to tribe and village to village, depending upon numbers and strength. Some have as few as eight representatives, while others have as many as fourteen. In all, there are fifty principal chiefs of the five tribes which sit as equals in council."[22]

Tiyanoga had told Joseph when the boy was only ten years old that in the Iroquois country there was a great and inexhaustible silver mine on a tributary of a tributary of the Susquehanna River. The Indians who controlled it were called Tyadaghtons. They were not League members, but they were a protectorate of the League and provided, as a tribute, all the silver the Iroquois needed. The amount was prodigious. Then a great tragedy came one day and the earth opened up and swallowed the little isolated tribe completely, and they disappeared to the last individual without a trace. At the same time the shifting of the earth sealed the mouth of the mine that produced the silver and the tools of the Iroquois were never sufficient to reopen it.[23]

It was in the matter of training for warfare that Tiyanoga had made the strongest impression upon Joseph. Although the French and Indian War was as yet undeclared between the English and the French, battles were being fought. A very significant conflict was the one in which Tiyanoga indoctrinated Joseph Brant into the principles and practices of war. This was on September 8, 1755, and Joseph was but a month away from his fifteenth year. A major battle was shaping up at the head of Lake George, and though hundreds of Iroquois fought in that battle under Tiyanoga and Sir William against the French, and many of the warriors and chiefs wished to ride into that battle beside the great Chief Tiyanoga, it was Joseph Brant whom Tiyanoga chose to ride beside him. It was a tremendous honor for Joseph and as they rode, he listened with great attention to the words of Tiyanoga as he spoke softly and at length, sometimes with sorrow, often with pride. What he said had etched itself permanently in the young warrior's mind.

"My son," Tiyanoga had told him, "you see us now fighting for the British against the French. This is not because we are forced to do so by the British, but because we consider them our friends and have *agreed* to do so. The Six Nations have no dictator among the nations of the earth. We are not the wards of England. We are a free commonwealth."

Tiyanoga had then lapsed into such a long silence that Joseph thought he would speak no more, but he was wrong. As they neared the area where battle was expected, he spoke again:

"We Indians go forth to battle — to war — smarting under a sense of repeated injuries and indignities that we have suffered. We resort to stratagems that are praiseworthy. The very bravest warriors know it is no disgrace to lurk in silence and take every advantage of your foe, and we always triumph in the superior craft and sagacity by which we are enabled to surprise and destroy our enemy. The natural principle of war is to inflict the most injury to our enemy and the least harm to ourselves. As our tribes are sharply limited in the numbers of warriors and the weapons with which we must fight, we therefore resort to every stratagem to save our numbers. We do not ever consider even our lowliest warrior expendable and to trade a life for a life in the matter of war is a fool's bargain. We, the Iroquois — and especially the Mohawks, Joseph — have the most lofty contempt of death, but for the benefit of our nation and our League, we preserve our lives for the common good."

Those were the last words that Chief Tiyanoga ever spoke to him. The rush of battle pulled them somewhat apart and Joseph, experiencing for the first time the horror of violent death on all sides and the fragility of life in such a situation, abruptly found himself clinging to a sapling to remain upright, for his legs were trembling so badly he would have fallen had it not been for the tree. A devastating terror swept him and he closed his eyes and shook. Although the din of battle — the crashing of guns and clashing of weapons and screamings of the dying and injured — abated not at all, the terror gradually passed and soon he was able to break his tortured grip on the sapling, raise his own tomahawk in one hand and scalping knife in the other and sally forth into the thick of the fighting. There he vindicated himself well indeed. More important, he knew with an utter sureness that come what may, this form of terror would never again touch him.

With his composure recovered, Joseph looked for Tiyanoga but could not find him. He never did. For the great chief, it was the last battle. During the fighting he had become separated from his warriors and suddenly found himself where there was no fighting. An old man with now too much weight, he paused a moment to rest. Incredibly, as he did so, he was unexpectedly attacked by three small Caughnawaga Indian boys with crude little weapons not much more than toys, yet enough to kill him.[24]

The loss of Tiyanoga was devastating, but for Joseph Brant life went on and he was involved in many more battles, always with increasing skill on his own part as a warrior. He could not now recall when and where he had first killed a man in battle, only that he had killed many and that he would probably kill many more.

So many things for a young Mohawk to learn! So few of those lessons to come from the books and training at the Indian school. Just as he learned from Nichus Brant and Tiyanoga and Molly, so too he learned from the incredible Warraghiyagey — Sir William Johnson. Over the years his closeness to the Indian supervisor became ever greater, partly because of the relationship between the man and Joseph's sister.

There was not, as had been expected by Nichus, the development of a strong bond of brotherhood between Joseph Brant and John Johnson. They knew one another and were reasonably cordial to each other, but there was really no outstanding affinity. That was the fault of John, not Joseph. John lived in another world and in general preferred not to associate with either the Indians or what he contemptuously referred to as "the low Dutch of our valley." In recent years Johnny, as he was called, had begun overcoming his imperiousness and, to his father's satisfaction, took more of an interest in the work of Indian affairs, although it was obvious he would never be able to give it the dedication his father did. Also, his mind was much on other things; having been attending school in Philadelphia, he had been introduced to the social whirl there and he truly loved it.

Much more interested in William Johnson's work — which did not escape the notice of Johnson himself — was the Indian superintendent's nephew Guy Johnson. Their association began in a less than auspicious manner. One of seven sons of John, Sir William's brother, Guy was an opportunist and very early decided to latch onto the coattails of his illustrious uncle. Arriving in America from Ireland in 1757 without funds, the seventeen-year-old immediately located a gullible merchant and borrowed money from him on the basis that his uncle was the famous Sir William, who would underwrite the loan. He did not clarify that he'd never even met his uncle yet. When the merchant tried to collect his debt, the letters sent to Guy went unanswered, and so he finally wrote in exasperation to Sir William, who repaid him. To Johnson's credit, the incident amused rather than angered him and he sought out the youth and paved the way for him to get a commission in a Ranger Company under Sir Jeffrey Amherst.

For the past several years now, Guy Johnson had been working closely with Sir William, learning the intricacies of handling Indian affairs. He'd become reasonably fluent in the Mohawk language and the Indians themselves seemed to like his bluff and hearty ways. He did at times, like his cousin John, exhibit a rather grating haughtiness, but for the most part he kept it well under control. He was not a Warraghiyagey, of course, but then no one but Sir William Johnson could ever be that.

While becoming involved with Indian affairs, Guy Johnson was also becoming deeply involved with another cousin — Polly.[25] She was the younger and favorite daughter of Sir William, a bright and effusive young lady who quickly fell in love with her dashing cousin. They were married in the spring of 1763 and took up residence close to Johnson's baronial estate, Johnson Hall, in the excellent stone house Sir William had ordered built for them. It was near the Mohawk River east of Fort Johnson on part of the one hundred thousand acres north of the Mohawk River that the King had awarded to Johnson for his services. As both nephew and son-in-law of Sir William, Guy Johnson's own prestige increased.

For the past eight or ten months he had been working in the official capacity of deputy agent for Sir William and had come to the point where he was taking over full responsibility of Indian affairs during the absences and illnesses of Sir William. Like his uncle, he was adopted by the Iroquois and given the name of Uraghquadirha, meaning The-Rays-of-the-Sun-Enlightening-the-Earth.

Joseph Brant was himself deeply interested in Indian affairs and had already attended treaties of various types with both Sir William and Guy Johnson. He and Guy were the same age and though Guy was in many ways likable, Joseph never found in him a kindred spirit. Also, there were a few things about the deputy agent that he very much *dis*liked. In addition to drinking to excess far too often, Guy Johnson had both a short memory and a short temper.

The initial terror that Joseph had experienced at Lake George never repeated itself, though since then he had been exposed to battle several times and had even commanded parties of Indians. He was with Sir William for the campaign against Fort Niagara and in command of six hundred Indians when it fell to Johnson in 1759. It was there that he became exposed for the first time to a serious and growing rift in the Iroquois League. The Senecas on hand for that battle had, after the capitulation of the fort, demanded that the garrison be turned over to them for various and sundry torturings at which they were adept and which they considered their due for having participated. When William Johnson refused to allow it, their animosity for him in particular and the English in general grew apace. Since that time, even though the French had capitulated in 1760 and England had taken possession of previously French Canada, the Senecas had been aligning themselves with the tribes of the western Great Lakes against the British. The Mohawks on the other hand, being closest to the British settlements in America and most deeply involved with them, allied themselves to the newly enthroned King George III. The remainder of the Six Nations — the Onondagas, Cayugas, Oneidas and Tuscaroras — being pulled in both directions, were happy enough to follow Sir William's advice and remain neutral. How long that situation could last was anyone's guess.

Even though he was very close to Sir William since the Indian superintendent had taken Joseph's sister as his woman and had already sired two children through her,[26] as well as by being Joseph's benefactor in sending him to school, the young Mohawk nevertheless was becoming increasingly alarmed at what was occurring in his beloved Mohawk valley. Settlement was increasing prodigiously and land friction rising between the Indians who had always inhabited the land and the developers who coveted it. In addition, English traders among the Indians were becoming as avaricious as the land-grabbers and there was much anger being fomented. The Senecas since the French and Indian War, which had caused the deaths of so many Mohawk warriors, were now the most powerful tribe in the Iroquois League, mustering nearly as many warriors as the remainder of the Six Nations combined.[27]

A letter Joseph received from Molly, which she had written in the middle of

April, was the determining factor for Joseph leaving Dr. Wheelock's school now. Molly had urged him to come home at once because there was growing disfavor among the Mohawks at his continuing any longer in the white man's school. This placed Joseph in a dilemma because he had promised to guide Charles Jeffrey Smith into the Iroquois country and act as his interpreter, but Smith could not leave Connecticut until after his ordination in New York. As he had frequently done in past situations where it was difficult to reach a decision, Joseph depended upon the wisdom and advice of Sir William. Explaining the situation to the Reverend Dr. Wheelock, Joseph asked him to solicit his mentor's wishes in the matter. Wheelock agreed.

Sir William responded that he thought it would be a very good idea for Joseph to delay his return to the Mohawk Valley until young Smith came back to the school and then return with him. Johnson assured Joseph that he had spoken with Molly and a number of the Mohawks and, in explaining the situation to them, had gained their concurrence in his delaying his return.

So now they were on their way. Charles Smith had been ordained on the last day of June in New York and now, as a bona fide man of the cloth, was moving into his first station.

Smith, who was still turned in his saddle, looking at the dwindling form of the school behind them, straightened and then spoke earnestly to Brant.

"Joseph, I do hope your delay in returning home has not caused any problems for you. Also, I hope whatever required your return was not something serious."

"The delay has caused me no problems," Brant replied, "but I'm afraid the situation is serious."

He did not explain his comment and Smith did not press him to do so, which was just as well, since Brant would not have spoken of it. Since that initial letter from Molly in April, Joseph had learned only sketchy details of what was occurring, but that was enough. The friction between the tribes of the western Great Lakes and the British government had reached a point where it was no longer possible to keep it contained.[28] The Ottawa chief Pontiac had formed a confederation of tribes — Ottawas, Chippewas, Potawatomies, Hurons, and others — and on May 9 had laid siege to the British fortifications at Detroit. Simultaneously he had parties attack various other British posts throughout the western wilderness. Within weeks every British post west of Niagara, with the exception of Detroit itself, had been taken, usually with the destruction of the fort and its garrison. Of itself, that was news of the most serious nature, but to make it even more unsettling was the word Joseph had received from Molly only this morning. On June 16 a large body of Senecas had gained entry to British Fort Venango on the Allegheny River near its junction with French Creek.[29] At once they had butchered every soldier of the gar-

tion with French Creek.[29] At once they had butchered every soldier of the garrison except the commanding officer, a Lieutenant Gordon. He was forced to write, at their dictation, a statement of grievances against the Crown, after which he was tortured for three successive days until he died. What it all betokened was the unnerving possibility of a war of great consequence — the British against the Indians.

For a long while Joseph Brant rode quietly, steeped in thought.

[*May 10, 1764 — Thursday*]

It was nearly a year since Joseph Brant had left school in Connecticut, and a very eventful one. Immediately following his guiding of Charles Smith through the territory of the Iroquois, where the young minister was greeted with varying degrees of friendship and acceptance but then decided against becoming a permanent missionary among them, Joseph resumed his residence at Canajoharie.

Hardly had he settled in, however, when a call from Molly brought him to Johnson Hall and from there he was sent by the Indian superintendent to Detroit as part of a special deputation of Mohawks. Their mission was to convince the tribes that had allied themselves under Pontiac that they had made a mistake. Learning of the approach of the Mohawks, Pontiac had them kidnapped and held in a Huron village for some days while he continued to lay siege against the fort.

Relenting after a bit, Pontiac had let them address the Indians assembled there, knowing his hold on them was so great and they were so committed to his course of action at this point that they could not withdraw from him. They didn't. They listened to what the deputation had to say and then sent them away with word to the effect that if the Mohawks returned, it would only be for the purpose of leaving their bones to bleach in the sun.

The Mohawks were not merely Mohawks, they were official representatives of the Iroquois League. At any other time in the past such a response to the powerful Iroquois would have been cause for immediate retaliation, but this time there was none. Pontiac had correctly read the temper of the Iroquois and recognized that since the Senecas were definitely sympathetic and supportive to him, the rest of the League would be disinclined to launch any sort of attack.

The Seneca warriors were indeed a problem. Their support of the Lenni Lenape — the tribe the whites called Delaware Indians — against the settlers of western Pennsylvania had increased to such proportions that Sir William finally knew there was no recourse but to send out parties of the Mohawks to disrupt the Delawares in their depredations and perhaps in this way help convince the Senecas they had made a serious error. He sent out three parties to destroy the principal Delaware towns on the West Branch of the Susquehanna and to kill or capture the Delaware chiefs. These expeditions were headed by Henry Montour, John Johnson and Joseph Brant and they were very successful.

When Brant returned, he brought with him three prisoners and the scalp of a chief who was the nephew of a powerful Delaware sachem named Squash Cutter.

This brought Brant a great deal of renown throughout the Indian nations. Although a number of Delaware towns were destroyed, including the two most important — Kanastio and Kanaughton — it was the capture of the powerful Delaware chief Teedyscung[30] and the death of Squash Cutter's nephew, who had been considered invincible, that suddenly caused a very real fear to blossom among both Senecas and Delawares. The Delawares abruptly left their country and fled to the wilderness of the Ohio country, taking refuge among the Miamis and Shawnees while the Senecas did an about-face and begged for peace. With Brant at his side, Sir William Johnson held a huge congress at Niagara and these Senecas turned over to the Indian superintendent fourteen English prisoners, along with several deserters and runaway slaves, and promised to cease their harassment of the British. It was an easy promise to make, now that the Delawares had been driven away and Pontiac's confederation had collapsed, but this time the Senecas meant it. They would hereafter be supportive of the British.[31] To prove it they ceded to the Crown a four-mile strip of land on either side of the Niagara River from Lake Erie to Lake Ontario.

[*March 5, 1770 — Monday*]

The pressure being placed on the American colonies through both taxation and the restriction of liberties that the colonists considered their right had reached dangerous levels. Confronted with a breakdown of law and order, two regiments of the King's troops landed in Boston in 1768, allegedly to keep the peace. Their presence had an opposite effect. Discipline and comportment were poor among the redcoats, whom the colonials called "lobster-backs." A too-large percentage of the officers were pompous and disdainful and their soldiers were generally drunk, profane and bullying.

It was on the evening of this fifth day of March that the whole matter came to a head. A group of about sixty Bostonians, smarting under an insult that was a final straw, vented their spleen on a squad of ten soldiers in King Street.[32] One of the redcoats was struck with a stick and suffered a split in his brow that bled profusely and looked terrible but that was actually a very minor wound. Another soldier was knocked down. At this the squad leveled its muskets and fired into the crowd. Eleven of the citizens were killed or wounded and the event quickly became known throughout the Colonies as the Boston Massacre.[33]

With the spreading of the news of the clash between the King's soldiers and the people of Boston, the Indians were suddenly extremely keyed up and there was a strong belief that a full-scale revolution was breaking out. Even though the Mohawk River valley was far removed from the incident on King Street, a thrill of war fever was spreading. Joseph Brant, now a very close aide to Sir William Johnson and, in essence if not in legal fact, Johnson's brother-in-law, began taking steps under Sir William's direction to defend the King's authority in this quarter in the event of civil war.

From this time forward, so far as Brant was concerned, the Americans who supported rebellious inclinations were known as Bostonians, even though affairs in the East settled down and assumed a more favorable aspect. On another plane, one of great subtlety and discretion, both the Americans and the British began their first vague negotiations with the Indians for their services if war came.

It might be a long way off, but revolution was definitely in the wind.

[January 20, 1772 — Sunday]

With the world seeming to be in slightly less of a turmoil than it had been almost two years ago immediately following the so-called Boston Massacre, Joseph Brant's existence had become surprisingly sedentary. Everything and everyone seemed poised at a point of desperate balance, with utmost chaos just a hair's breadth away on the left and total catastrophe no farther away on the right. Practically everyone was certain that "something" was going to happen. No one knew precisely when or what and so everyone waited without realizing he was waiting.

The occurrences during this period involving Joseph Brant were very personal matters. After his period of helping Sir William with the chastisement of the Delawares, as a result of which he was being called Captain Brant, Joseph had returned to his childhood home at Canajoharie and, with Molly's approval, refused to return to the Reverend Wheelock's school. Instead he became employed by Sir William in the public business, learning a variety of important procedures and being especially helpful in regard to Indian affairs. Sir William came to depend upon him considerably.

During this time, Joseph married the pleasant, soft-spoken daughter of Gecoagh, an Oneida chief. Her name was Sasaya and she lived happily in the shadow of her husband — obedient to his wishes and providing him, within the first three years, with a son and a daughter. With Joseph's full approval before the birth of the children, Sasaya became a Christian and put aside her Oneida name, which meant Chosen-of-a-Grandmother. She was baptized Margaret and when the children came they in turn were christened in the church as Isaac and Christina. [34] At this same ceremony Margaret's half sister Wonagh was also baptized and took the name Susanna.

Brant himself was very actively supporting the church and even considered for a while becoming a Christian missionary to his own people. His home at Canajoharie, built with the help of Sir William, was a large frame house with a fireplace and windows and even two things uncommon in Indian houses —

hardwood floors and chimneys. Guests, both Indian and white, constantly stopped by and always were treated with generous cordiality. For the occasional travelers going up the Mohawk, Joseph Brant's home was becoming known as a fine overnight stop. No one was ever turned away.

A missionary who had been one of Joseph's first teachers at Wheelock's school had been coming for some time on a periodic basis to Canajoharie and he, as other travelers, lodged with the Brants. The Reverend Samuel Kirkland was an intense, strong-minded man who was impressed with Joseph, remembering with pleasure how they had taught one another their languages. At times now he encouraged Joseph to assist him with the Christian singing school for the Indians and in preparing his sermons for the Mohawks. In writing about Brant to a friend Kirkland remarked that *"Joseph endeavors to teach his poor brethren the things of God; those things in which his own heart seems much engaged. His house is an asylum for the missionaries in that wilderness."*

Another man of the cloth also stepped into Brant's life just about then. A devout young man not quite Brant's age, John Stuart had received his holy orders in London from the Church of England and was sent as a missionary to the Mohawks under the auspices of the Society for the Propagation of the Gospel. His base of operations became Fort Hunter at the Lower Mohawk Castle, Teantontalago, late in December, 1770.

By the middle of January, Stuart had become acquainted with Joseph and, as Kirkland had been, was very impressed by him. He began learning the Mohawk language from Joseph and soon was asking Joseph's assistance in a number of matters, not the least of which was establishing the "Form of Prayer" of the Church of England in the Mohawk language.

When Stuart met Joseph he was dismayed at the condition of the Mohawk's wife. Margaret — Sasaya — was wasting away rapidly, coughing blood almost constantly and obviously in the last stages of consumption.[35] Within the month she died, leaving Joseph alone with Isaac, now three years old, and Christina, eighteen months old. Immediately their aunt Susanna — Wonagh — took on the job of helping to raise them.

By the end of February, Joseph had moved away from Canajoharie temporarily, leaving the children in the care of their aunt. He took up residence with John Stuart and now plunged into the work of translating the Gospel of St. Mark, the Acts of the Apostles and more of the Indian Prayer Book into the Mohawk language. He also helped Stuart write a short history of the Bible, along with a concise explanation of the church catechism. The Society for the Propagation of the Gospel was greatly impressed and they authorized Stuart to go to New York and, at their expense, to have the entire work printed in the Mohawk language.

Joseph was very serious about religion and longed to do even more than he was doing. He promised himself to be greatly beneficial to the Iroquois League by helping to pave the way for even more proselytizing of the Indians. Because of his evident sincerity in this respect and in view of what he had already done to help the church among his people, great hopes were entertained by the elders for his future usefulness to the church. Almost certainly they would have had it, except for a serious blunder made by John Stuart.

During the year that Joseph extended himself enormously to help Stuart translate the Bible and other related works, the young clergyman had applied himself well and by the end of December, ten months after Joseph began working with him, he could read the liturgy in Mohawk, baptize and marry in the Mohawk tongue and converse with considerable fluency. But while he was a good student, Stuart was also an Episcopalian of extremely narrow perspective.

Only a few days away from the first anniversary of Sasaya's death, Joseph was absent for about a week and when he returned he brought Wonagh back with him. He introduced her to Stuart as Susanna, explained how for a year she had been caring for his children and that he now wished Stuart to join them in holy matrimony.

John Stuart was appalled.

"You can't be serious, Joseph!" he said, his manner suddenly stiff and righteously indignant. "Don't you realize that such a relationship is an abomination in the eyes of God?"

Joseph frowned. He saw nothing of the sort and, under the impression he may accidentally have misconstrued the relationships in Stuart's mind, slowly and patiently explained again.

"Susanna," he said, "is not *my* half sister. She is Wonagh, half sister to my wife, Margaret, who died a year ago. There is no blood relationship between us, only one of love. Wonagh has already cared for Isaac and Christina for this year and she has grown to love them, and they her. My marrying her will secure an even greater degree of love and tenderness for the children at a time when they need it most."

"That," said Stuart flatly, shaking his head, "is a disgusting concept." His manner became even more arch and unbending. "It is a relationship forbidden by God. It is tantamount to incest!"

Unfamiliar with the words in Stuart's final sentence, which was perhaps fortunate for the missionary, Joseph shook his head, still perplexed, and protested, "But she is the children's aunt!"

Stuart put up a hand, cutting off further comment. "No more, Joseph. You've said quite enough. I'm *very* disappointed in you. I can understand now why Dr. Wheelock has come to the sad conclusion that white men alone can be depended upon to conduct the work of Christianizing and civilizing the savages!"

Joseph's nostrils flared and his brows pinched together. For a long moment he stared at Stuart and then spun around and left the house, knowing he would never return. Only vaguely understanding what had occurred, Wonagh followed him outside without expression.

When the door had closed behind them, Stuart walked to the three-drawered desk in which he took such pride and opened the middle compartment. For a moment he rummaged through some papers there and then withdrew a printed sheet — a newspaper account in which the Reverend Dr. Eleazar Wheelock had made the comment he had alluded to a moment ago. Reading through it, he slowly and carefully digested the remainder of Wheelock's remarks:

The most melancholy part of the account which I have to relate and which has occasioned me the greatest weight of sorrow, has been the bad conduct and behavior of such as have been educated here after they have left the school. Among those whom I have educated here have been near 40, who were good readers and writers, and were instructed in the principles of the Christian religion, and were sufficiently masters of English grammar and arithmetic; and others carried through a course of learning with not less expense for each of them than would have been necessary to have supported an English youth through a course of collegiate studies; and they have generally behaved well while they were with me, and left my school with fair and unblemished characters, and under the influence of every motive I could set before them and enforce upon them to a good improvement of their talents; and many of them have gone immediately from my school into good and reputable business and nothing has prevented their being usefully and reputably employed in various capacities till this day except their own want of fortitude to resist the power of those fashionable vices which are rampant among all their tribes. I don't hear of more than half who have preserved their characters unstained, and some, who on account of their parts and learning bade the fairest for usefulness, are sunk down into as low, savage and brutish a manner of living as they were in before our endeavors were used with them. And six of those who did preserve a good character are dead.[36]

John Stuart slowly folded the paper and replaced it in the drawer, nodding as he did so. He considered it a vindication of his stance with Joseph and now he became no little irritated at the way Joseph had stormed off after trying to involve him in so nefarious a plan. Yes, even Dr. Wheelock had had to admit it: once a savage, always a savage.

Four hours later, across the Mohawk River at the home of the German minister Pyet Halenbeeck, Joseph Brant and Susanna — Thayendanegea and Wonagh — were united in a quiet little ceremony. There was no indication whatever that God was displeased.

[*April 11, 1773 — Sunday*]

Joseph Brant, for perhaps the hundredth time since last July when Sir William Johnson left for England, fervently wished that the Indian superintendent would hurry home. Even when conditions were good on the whole, there was a pervasive sense of unease among the Six Nations when Johnson was absent. At times such as this, when revolutionary talk was rife and neighbors had begun barring their doors to one another, the uneasiness became acute. Johnson alone seemed to have the power to ameliorate relationships between the tribes within the Iroquois League, between the Indians and the whites and between the rapidly diverging white factions.

Guy Johnson took over, of course, while Sir William was away, and Joseph helped him all he could, but Guy was not Sir William and he had not the experience, the skill nor the power of manipulation and mediation that made and kept Sir William so influential here. Sir William seemed to be the only one who had the ability to keep the lid on an increasingly volatile situation.

Brant had never ceased admiring the incredible abilities of the Superintendent of Indian Affairs and made a concerted effort to learn all he could from him. Ever since that first great congress he had attended at Sir William's side at Fort Niagara in June, 1764, when nearly single-handedly Warraghiyagey had brought the arrogant Senecas into line, Brant had been attending congresses and witnessing treaties with him. And, as Brant had learned ever more from Johnson, so the Indian superintendent had increasingly placed his reliance on Joseph.

Joseph Brant was not a chief, but his own sphere of influence was growing apace with the increased responsibilities Sir William was giving him. This influence was not confined to the Iroquois League but encompassed far distant tribes as well, to which Brant was sent as agent or ambassador. The Mohawk was turning out to be a surprisingly good diplomatist.

Still, Brant had not spoken to any extent in the congresses that had been held, content to provide the assistance and advice that Johnson required. In 1768 he had been a tremendous asset at the grand council at Fort Stanwix on the upper Mohawk River. Here gathered thirty-two hundred Indians in the greatest Indian assemblage ever held on this continent to date. Also in attendance were Governor William Franklin of New Jersey and the commissioners from Virginia, Pennsylvania and New York, as well as a multitude of other influential whites. The upshot was one of the most significant agreements consummated with the Indians to this time — the Fort Stanwix Treaty.[37]

Brant was close enough to Sir William to observe, as no other Indian could, the frustrations Johnson faced in trying to protect the rights of the Indians. Numerous congresses with the Indians were held at Johnson Hall and some in Albany or at German Flats,[38] but no matter what concessions the tribes won, they never seemed to last. Despite treaty lines and orders of the King to the contrary, the American colonists were continually pushing westward and the tribes were becoming uprooted. Even now the Mohawks were sharing their own territory of the Mohawk Valley with a growing multitude of settlers and relationships with them were steadily degenerating.

It was on the eve of William Johnson's departure for England last July that Brant had addressed the Indian congress at Johnson Hall generally and the New York governor William Tryon specifically, speaking on behalf of the young warriors of his tribe and of the Iroquois League.[39] Sir William was impressed and pleased with what Brant had said. Just before setting off for England, he talked with Brant earnestly.

"I will be gone for nearly a year, Joseph, hopefully to return with concessions from His Majesty which will be of benefit to the Iroquois. Before I leave there, the Crown will fully realize the immense importance of obtaining and thereafter maintaining a full alliance with the League."

Johnson seemed troubled as he continued: "Every day the Colonies are pulling further away from the Crown and one day they will try to stand alone. There is no way the King can permit this to happen. Until I return, I leave in your charge all of the Indians under my management. I have told them this in council, as you know. You are to keep them prepared to act, in event of any emergency, in support of the Crown, which is concerned with your welfare."

And so he had gone and the months since had dragged by interminably. The sense of unrest increased along with a mounting and more vocal outrage by the colonists against the strictures being placed on their freedoms by the Crown. And above all, expansion continued in the Mohawk Valley and elsewhere. Proclamations by the King had made it clear that the British governmental policy was to maintain the Indian lands for the Indians, but the American colonists were disobeying the edicts at every turn. The interior tribes of the Iroquois League — the Oneidas and Onondagas, Cayugas and Tuscaroras and Senecas — had not yet been strongly touched by the encroachment of the Americans. The Mohawks had, and within them there was a growing resentment.

If a rupture were to occur between the Crown and its colonies in America, it seemed rather apparent which way the Mohawks would go; but the Mohawks alone could do little. They needed the support of the entire League. Perhaps with the concessions Warraghiyagey would bring back from the Crown an alliance would be established.

Now at last had come a letter from Sir William stating that he would be leaving England very soon and would arrive at Johnson Hall in June. For the first time in many months Joseph Brant breathed a little easier.

[*February* 11, 1774 — *Friday*]

Throughout the frontier, unrest continued to mount. As much as Sir William Johnson attempted to maintain peace between the Indians and whites, his efforts continually were being undermined. The concessions he had brought back from King George III largely boiled down to the sovereign's solemn promise of even greater efforts to be made in stemming the westward encroachment of the settlers. In this respect the colonial governors were instucted to enforce the Royal Proclamations toward that end faithfully and to maintain a peaceful neighboring coexistence with the Indians.

Instead, virtually the opposite occurred. For long years the Pennsylvanians had been demanding greater protection by the government, or at least the leeway to better protect themselves. The expeditions Sir William had sent against the Delawares and Senecas, causing the removal of the former and the acquiescence of the latter, seemed to make little difference. Incredibly, on the very heels of it, the Pennsylvania governor issued a proclamation that promised a healthy bounty to be paid for any Indian prisoner or scalp. Overnight it became open season on Indians.

Recoiling deeper into their own territories to escape the onslaught of bounty-hunters, the Indians left their borders open and immediately a new wave of frontier settlement began. Once again bloody Indian war threatened and in the depths of his agitation and frustration Sir William Johnson wrote to the Lords of Trade:

Everywhere on the frontier is found new encroachment by our people as cabins are being built on Indian lands beyond the established white limitations. Worse, they abuse and maltreat the Indians at every meeting. It seems as if the people are determined to bring on a new war, though their own ruin may be the consequence.

One of the principal new settlement areas of the whites in Pennsylvania was along the banks of the main branch of the Susquehanna River in the area that had been given the name of Wyoming.[40] A small settlement had been laid out under that name and the bare trickle of settlers became almost a flood. The Wyoming Valley area was fertile and therefore desirable. Even so, life there was difficult in the extreme. The past year had been bad for crops and a very real famine threatened until now, when provisions were so exhausted that it became necessary to send a party of five men, led by Colonel Nathan Denison, fifty miles through the wilderness to the frontier town of Stroudsburg[41] for supplies. There was no road and no packhorses available to carry the supplies. The men returned almost dead of exhaustion, each man having carried on his back across half-frozen streams and along an extremely difficult foot trail one hundred pounds of flour. They returned in time to save the settlement and also in time for Denison to be on hand with his wife for the birth of their first child.

Denison was a strong young Pennsylvania Militia officer who had been one of the first residents of the Wyoming Valley. His marriage to the exceptionally beautiful Jane Sill in 1769 was the first marriage ever to occur there.[42] Now the birth of their son was the first birth there of a white child. Denison very proudly named him Lazarus, after his good friend Lazarus Stewart,[43] a crusty forty-year-old Indian fighter who himself had just recently settled in the Wyoming Valley with his wife, Martha.[44]

Denison admired Stewart because of his directness and his total lack of sympathy for the Indians. Stewart's hatred for the Quakers, who advocated treating the Indians with kindness, was almost as virulent as that which he harbored for the Indians themselves, and Denison, for the most part, had to agree. He was painfully aware, as were all the other Wyoming settlers, of what had happened a decade ago. A host of Delawares and Senecas had swept down on these Connecticut settlers who had only recently sunk their roots here at Wyoming, butchered many of them and took into captivity another twenty. Only a few had managed to escape in terror into the mountains. Lazarus Stewart was one of a party that came to help but arrived two days too late and found only death and destruction. It had taken a long while after that for the second Wyoming settlement to get established and the settlers all lived in fear to this day, only too aware of the precariousness of their existence, yet unwilling to abandon their claims.

Nevertheless, though Wyoming's troubles were not unique, in bits and pieces, from western Virginia through western Pennsylvania and New York, the frontier was becoming settled by whites, in many cases illegally. The Indians morosely watched it happen and there were those who sometimes wished that, despite how well he understood them and represented their interests, Sir William was not around, because then they could do what it was their natural inclination to do — fall upon and destroy every settlement and cabin in their territory. But they were tied to a giant who, on the one hand, provided them with what they needed and, on the other, devoured them.

Just recently another great chunk of the Iroquois lands had changed designation. A brand-new county had been formed in New York, carved from the impractical, almost province-sized county of Albany. Named Tryon County after the governor, it stretched from close to the Hudson River in the east to the Niagara River in the west.[45] Johnstown, just two miles from William Johnson's impressive mansion, Johnson Hall, was named the new county seat. The county was divided into five districts. These were, beginning in the east, the Mohawk District, which embraced Fort Hunter, Caughnawaga, Johnstown and Kingsborough; the south-of-the-river Canajoharie District, including the town of that name, plus all the country southward, including Cherry Valley and

Harpersfield; the north-of-the-river Palatine District, embracing the country known by that name as well as Stone Arabia; and finally the two westernmost districts, Kingsland and German Flats.

Tryon County was said to contain a population of 38,829 inhabitants, of which only 10,000 were whites. Although few cared to voice the thought, just about everyone was uncomfortably aware of a fundamental fact: The majority of the residents of Tryon County strongly and favorably influenced the sense of revolutionary unrest becoming so widespread. If, in fact, a revolution were to break out, then it was anticipated that the Indians, through Sir William's influence, would be prevailed upon to support the Crown. And if and when that occurred, there was going to be a hell on earth in the Mohawk Valley.

[*March 12, 1774 — Saturday*]

Although only twenty-two years old, Otetiana had just talked his way into becoming one of the leading sachems of the Seneca tribe, if not in the entire Iroquois League. It had not been an easy task. Otetiana was tall and thin, his sinews and muscles like wires and ropes beneath the coppery skin. He was extremely fleet of foot and could run faster for longer periods than anyone else in the tribe and so it was natural that he began as a runner of messages. But Otetiana had always seen himself as far more than that. The message-running he did for his own people and sometimes for the red-coated soldiers at Fort Niagara was only a temporary thing, a mere game to play while he waited for his great talents to be recognized.

For most of his life he had lived in the village where he had been born in 1752. This was Canoga[46] on the northwestern shore of Cayuga Lake. It was located in the border country of the Senecas and Cayugas, which was appropriate, because his father was Cayuga and his mother Seneca. The beautifully decorated wigwam in which he had been born stood then beneath a huge oak tree growing near a substantial bubbling spring that never ran dry in summer. The spring was named Otetiana, meaning "Always Ready." It was altogether fitting that the baby be named after the spring.

By 1764, when he was twelve, Otetiana had considered himself set apart from his contemporaries, better than they and destined for greater things. His contemporaries did not think so and his aloofness impressed them not at all. They were inspired by the things that impressed Indian youths generally — the abilities to fish and hunt and track and become a great warrior. These were things that did not interest Otetiana at all. His interest lay in expressing himself with novel ideas, which he did constantly. At first no one had listened to him. Yet, by the time he was sixteen, they had begun to do so.

Four years ago he began referring to himself as a sachem, although he had no right to the honor, either by birth or by vote of his people. Nevertheless, his ideas in respect to the Iroquois League and its form of government, his comments in regard to the League's relationship with the whites and his speculations concerning the future of the Six Nations were all causing many in the Iroquois to listen more closely to what he had to say.

It was a custom among the Iroquois that when a man had a prophetic dream it was partly the responsibility of those to whom he repeated the particulars to help that dream become reality. Oddly enough, though tremendous personal advantage could be taken under such a premise, abuse of the custom was rare. Otetiana took advantage. A dream thrice repeated was great medicine and in 1771 at the grand council of the Iroquois League at Onondaga, he rose and told the assemblage he dreamed he had been made a sachem. Though some were immediately in favor of making him just that, those more influential hesitated.

A year later he again told of his dreams, once more thrice in succession. The reaction was the same and so last year he spoke similarly, but this time adding that the Great Spirit was displeased at their failure to accept him as sachem and that if they did not do so, the displeasure would manifest itself in a tragic manner.

Now, in March of 1774, the League was just recovering from a tragedy attributable to none but the Great Spirit. Here and there throughout the entire League there had been, over the past two months, a serious outbreak of smallpox. Many had recovered after being smitten, but many had died and the mournful death song had been sung again and again in practically every village. Today when Otetiana had addressed the council, every head nodded when he pointed out that the epidemic had been the Great Spirit's way of showing her displeasure. And when he said a final time that it was the will of the Great Spirit that he should be considered a sachem, there was immediate and virtually unanimous assent. They recognized him at once in this role — one of the youngest sachems in the League's history — and now they changed his name, calling him Sagoyewatha, meaning He-Keeps-Them-Awake in reference to his pronounced powers of oratory and the fact that no one ever fell asleep through boredom when he spoke.

Only one influential man in the League did not believe in the dreams allegedly had by Otetiana nor in the smallpox epidemic as being a manifestation of the Great Spirit's displeasure, and he refused to call him Sagoyewatha. That man, who was not hesitant about letting his disbelief be known, was also not listened to by many because he was not a chief. But he did incur the immediate enmity of the newly named sachem.

That disbeliever was Thayendanegea — Joseph Brant.

Sagoyewatha was far more proud of his new name than he had been of the name Otetiana and he knew he would never use the latter again. But there was another name that had been given to him over a year ago that brought him almost as much pride as the name Sagoyewatha, even though its bestowal had not been as ceremonious as this name given to him today.

The other was an English name and it had been given to him by the officers of Fort Niagara. Because of the speed and reliability with which he ran messages for them, they had presented to him the gift of a fine British officer's scarlet coat. To the Seneca this was without doubt the greatest tribute that until now had ever been paid him; perhaps even more than the one now, for this tribute today had been gained, as Brant suspected, through a degree of deception, but the one from the British officers had been awarded for an ability he truly possessed.

Sagoyewatha knew that one of the names would eventually eclipse the other and he also knew which one it would be. Though he was deeply proud to be called Sagoyewatha, he knew that he would be called by the name he himself liked best and by which he referred to himself, the name they had given him at Fort Niagara:

Red Jacket.

[April 1, 1774 — Friday]

Sir William Johnson had not, except in the most subtle manner, articulated the general disappointment he felt in his son John. The very best of schooling and social upbringing had been provided for him and he had been given every opportunity to be at his father's side to learn Indian affairs from the absolute master, taught to him as they could have been taught by no other.

John Johnson was simply not all that interested. He never had been and it seemed apparent that he never would be. Thus, the great reliance that Sir William would have placed in John was diluted and spread out among others. Guy Johnson, with his analytical mind and his talent for business, became his foremost assistant in dealings with the whites and, to a lesser extent, the Indians on Indian affairs, but Guy had a drinking problem. Joseph Brant had become Sir William's foremost aide in dealings with the Mohawks and the Iroquois League, but he was neither skilled enough nor "white" enough to fill Johnson's shoes. Daniel Claus, another son-in-law,[47] was exceptionally good in dealing with the Canadian Indians and better than Guy in dealing with the Six Nations Indians, but his heavy German accent was a handicap, especially since he was nowhere near as skilled as Guy in his dealings with the bureaucratic figures in colonial government either in America or in England. Finally, there was George Croghan, whose skill in dealing with the western tribes from the Great Lakes in the north to the Ohio River in the south and westward to the Mississippi was prodigious. He was decidedly a very rough frontiersman type and his very uncouthness prevented his being useful in direct dealings with His Majesty or the members of the Royal Court. Furthermore, his grammar and spelling were atrocious and this was a job that required a pronounced command of both.

That Sir William did not chide his son John for his lack of interest showed remarkable restraint, because it placed him in this difficult position of trying to groom someone who might eventually become his successor from a collection in which each individual suffered drawbacks. This problem of his father's did not impinge on John's complacency. He was perfectly content to slide through life on the coattails of his father and at the elder Johnson's largess. In the autumn of 1765, when John was twenty-three, he went to England. Shortly after his arrival, under the guidance and sponsorship of a friendly lord, Adam Gordon, who had made Sir William's acquaintance in the land business, he became a knight and was thereafter Sir John Johnson.[48]

It was not until 1767 that John Johnson finally came home again and almost at once became captain of a troop of horse in the militia, but somehow he never quite succeeded in finding his niche. He was generally tolerated by those around him but never fully accepted and he made no close friendships, at least not among his fellow men. Where women were concerned it was different.

In September, 1772, he had gone to New York City for the social season and he took along with him for entry into a boarding school his two nieces, Catherine Claus and Polly Johnson. He then occupied himself for a good while with a buxom young lady named Clara Putnam, who became his mistress but whom he knew would never become his wife. During the winter, while still in New York, he met the daughter of a New York banker and merchant named John Watts, became engaged to her and not quite a year ago, on June 29, Mary Watts became his wife. All this had little effect on the relationship Sir John had with Clara Putnam. He continued to maintain their close friendship every time he went to New York.

It was clearly apparent that, at a time when civil unrest was reaching a peak, one man only was capable of holding the New York frontier together and that man was Sir William Johnson. Still, he had to have someone to pick up the reins if necessary, and who could it be? Again the possible choices paraded through his mind: Joseph Brant, the Mohawk Indian? George Croghan, the crude frontiersman? Daniel Claus, the heavily German-accented assistant who was his son-in-law? John Johnson, his own son, whom he loved as he loved no other yet whose limitations he knew so well? No, realist that he was, Johnson knew it could be none of these because for each the reason against it was very strong. Yet a successor had to be recommended without any further delay.

Johnson knew he was a much sicker man than anyone around him realized, which was the reason he had made out his very detailed last will and testament the past January 27. He wasn't really figuring on dying very soon, but it was well to be prepared for such an eventuality. Much more likely, he would soon be unable any longer to carry out his duties as Superintendent of Indian Affairs and he was deeply concerned lest such great responsibility fall into incompetent or uncaring hands. The King's minister must know his recommendation and so now, having made every possible consideration in the matter, he came to his decision. He nodded briskly, dipped the quill pen into the black ink and set about completing the letter he had begun an hour ago to Lord Dartmouth, the British Secretary of Colonial Affairs and president of the Board of Trade:

. . . and, Your Lordship, the duties and fatigues growing out of my civil and military employments have drawn upon me a train of infirmities which have often threatened my life and, at best, have rendered it precarious. With the Indians, I have often carried the most important points merely through personal influence, when all other means have failed. If, therefore, I have the least claim to indulgence in support of the application of the Indians, I cannot withhold my warmest recommendation in favor of the gentleman they wish for — Colonel Guy Johnson — and whilst I assure Your Lordship that I rate my present reputation and future fame too highly to prostitute it for interest or partiality. I would rather hazard the imputation of both than refuse my testimony towards a measure that may benefit the public when I am no more. . . .

[July 11, 1774 — Monday]

Sir William Johnson, at age fifty-nine, was not a well man. A variety of fevers and sundry diseases, not the least of which was syphilis, had taken their toll of him. Yet he refused to slow down, to take care of himself or even let his beloved Molly take care of him if it entailed what he considered to be molly-coddling — an unfortunately inappropriate term under the circumstances. It was not mollycoddling now that made her beg him to consider his health and postpone the council with the Iroquois, which was to take place today outside Johnson Hall, but he would not hear of it.

In the twenty years they had lived together, Sir William and Molly had remained very close and their love, while perhaps not as passionate as it had been when they were both much younger, had nonetheless mellowed into a strong solidarity, cemented by the bond of the eight children Molly had borne during this time.[49]

Throughout those years Molly had acquired the dignity and comportment of an English lady while at the same time never losing her Indian ties. She remained as close to her younger brother, Joseph, as she had ever been and equally close to the Mohawks and the Iroquois League. As a behind-the-scenes force, she obviously had been very useful to her own people.

The council that convened on the broad expanse of grounds before Johnson Hall today was comprised largely of Iroquois from all six tribes. As usual, their chief concern was the disappearance of their territory through the encroachment of the whites and their only hope for curtailment of it rested in Sir

William. It was a bad time for Indians everywhere, but especially for those whose lands abutted that of the white man. In the fourteen years since the English had won the war and taken over Canada from the French, it seemed that everything the French had warned them of had come true: The Indians on all fronts had been cheated outrageously, exploited wherever possible and had had their lands stripped away bit by bit until there was now very little left. An unfortunate truism was established: Treaties made with the English lasted only so long as the English cared to abide by them.

William Johnson carried within him a deep sorrow and a sense of guilt where the Iroquois were concerned. He knew he had done for them all that he could and that no other man could have done more, or even as much — a fact of which they, too, were well aware — but he also knew that it had never been enough and never could be. There was no solution to the dilemma the Iroquois were in and their only hope was an unrealistic dream of some future time when justice would prevail and the lands that had been taken from them would be returned; that the cities and towns of the English that were now on lands that had once belonged to them would return to their rightful owners. Somehow, the dream remained merely a dream and the nibbling away of the lands went on, sometimes rapidly, sometimes slowly, but always continuing.

Exploitation of the Indians and theft of their lands were, as usual, a part of this present council at Johnson Hall. The incident being complained of this time, however, involved Joseph Brant directly and he, realizing more clearly than others how Johnson was often hamstrung by his own white people in attempting to get a fair shake for the Indians, had taken matters into his own hands.

A young Mohawk named Kadagwha had, the year before, been tricked into going to London with a Mohawk Valley resident, George Klock, with the understanding that Kadagwha would make a great deal of money for a few months of his time. Instead, Klock had exhibited Kadagwha in a sort of freak show and then, on the way home earlier this year, had not only cheated him out of all the money he was supposed to have earned but also got him drunk and then had him sign away ownership to certain Mohawk lands that Klock had long coveted.

An overwhelming anger had risen in Brant when he learned all the facts and so on May 23 he had gone to the house of Klock with nineteen of his fellow Mohawks, including Kadagwha, forced his way in, took from him the exact amount of cash Kadagwha was supposed to have earned, tore up the deeds that the young Mohawk had signed in his drunkenness and then forced Klock to sign a release. After this was completed and Klock, furious, was ranting about how he would have Brant's scalp for this, Brant waved his men back and then worked Klock over as a lesson for what he had done and with a promise of much worse if he ever again attempted to bilk the Indians.

Klock had complained bitterly of his treatment to the governor and council of New York, who ordered that an inquiry be made, and this was part of what Sir William was investigating today. With Guy Johnson taking down his remarks as an official report and after listening closely to testimony from both sides, Sir William declared that Klock had gotten only what he deserved and that he was fortunate the party of Mohawks under Brant had so restrained themselves in their dealings with him.[50]

Now, with the six hundred Iroquois spread out before him, Johnson had moved into the shade of a large arbor from which he would be able to address them without standing in the sweltering July sun. Hardly had he begun to speak, however, when he abruptly broke off and swayed, grasped the upright of the arbor and clung there. The Indians stared at him in alarm and several got to their feet. Guy Johnson and Brant moved at once to help him, but he waved them off for the moment and straightened. He spoke loudly then, and immediately the murmuring throughout the assemblage died away.

"My Brothers, I am not able to go on at this time. Pipes, tobacco and liquor will be brought out now. I will —" He broke off again, his eyes widening, and would have pitched forward onto the ground if Guy and Joseph had not caught his arms on each side. They began walking him toward the house at once, but as they were doing so, Johnson called loudly to his audience:

"Brothers! Whatever may happen, you must not be shaken out of your shoes!"

Joseph and Guy were joined now by Molly, her expression taut. They took Sir William to his spacious bedroom in Johnson Hall and by the time they arrived there he was so recovered that he refused to lie down on the bed, even though he was still breathing in a rasping manner. Instead, he had them seat him in a comfortable armchair and called for wine and water. When these were brought by Molly, he drank a little of each, leaned his head back and closed his eyes. His face was ashen. Molly stroked his brow and dabbed away the perspiration. With the three attending him closely, he remained this way for nearly two hours, mostly with his eyes closed. Near the end of that time he opened his eyes and reached out to place his hand on Brant's arm. He spoke softly, looking at the younger man intently:

"Joseph, control your people. I am going away." He leaned his head back and once again closed his eyes, but now his breathing was becoming erratic.

Outside, amid the hubbub of Indian voices, there came the sound of a horse approaching at a gallop. In a few minutes more, booted feet pounded up the broad main staircase and then came running down the carpeted hallway. John Johnson, who had ridden as rapidly as possible from Fort Johnson on getting word of the seizure, burst into the room and immediately moved to his father without a glance at the others.[51] He took Sir William's hand and in a quavering voice told him he was here now, but there was no response nor any indication that Johnson had heard. The Indian superintendent's head remained back against the chair with eyes closed and the ghastly pallor had worsened. For a few minutes more the raspy breathing continued and then suddenly there was silence.

Sir William Johnson — Warraghiyagey — was dead.

Immediately the Mohawk death cry sprang from the lips of Molly Brant and was echoed by Joseph. Almost at once a similar death wail erupted from the six hundred Indians assembled outside. It was more than a tribute, more than an expression of immeasurable grief.

It was an omen for the Iroquois League.

[*August 15, 1774 — Monday*]

In the glow of the lanterns that filled the large room with a warm yellow light, Guy Johnson set his glass of brandy back on the desk and regarded his visitor with a vague smile. He took a few steps toward the man, shook his hand in welcome and indicated a deep comfortable chair.

Joseph Brant, clad in simple, unadorned buckskin, sat instead on a hard, straight-backed chair nearby, his level gaze on Johnson. Although he had many times passed Guy Park Manor, this was his first time inside. It was not so expansive as Sir William's great mansion, but it was grand in its own way and its furnishings were hardly less elegant.

Johnson returned to the desk and picked up the decanter by its neck. He held it up in silent question. Brant shook his head and Johnson shrugged faintly and refilled his own glass to the lip. Brant watched without expression as Johnson rolled a sip of the liquid in his mouth and then swallowed with obvious relish. The Mohawk was not opposed to liquor — he liked it in fact — but he knew that only a very little of it affected his judgment and so he was wise enough to avoid it except on rare occasions.

With the customary directness that whites had always found disconcerting but that made him rather well liked by the Indians, Johnson got right to the point. He sat in the desk chair and tapped a neat pile of paperwork with a long index finger.

"You're aware that Sir William had made preparations for his demise if it should occur and that he recommended to the House of Lords and specifically to the Board of Trade that in such case I should assume the superintendency?"

Brant nodded. He was not altogether overjoyed with the choice Warraghiyagey had made, but he knew of no one else more qualified than Guy Johnson to take control. The gap left by the great man's death last month could never adequately be filled and Brant knew he personally would not have been fully pleased with anyone named to the position.

"Provisional confirmation came today from Lord Dartmouth in England," Johnson continued.[52] "He does not as yet know of the superintendent's demise, but in response to a communiqué Sir William sent in April, the Board of Trade has agreed to his recommendation for a successor. Needless to say, I am pleased to be the one. There were those," he added meaningfully, "who thought Sir John would automatically succeed him."

Again Brant nodded. That Sir John Johnson had not succeeded Sir William was a relief. Much less popular among the Indians, Sir John had little real knowledge or understanding of human nature in general and certainly no pronounced degree of empathy with the Indians. Besides, he was essentially a morose individual with an irascible disposition — a temperament he was unlikely to overcome. Even worse, he was imperious in his manner, as was so apparent immediately after Sir William's death.

For two days the body had lain in state in the great drawing room of Johnson Hall. During that period hundreds had filed past the bier upon which the coffin rested, paying last respects to the man who lay there clad in beautifully embroidered frock and waistcoat, the whiteness of his high-collared silk shirt emphasizing the pallor that death had fixed. When, on the afternoon of July 13, the coffin had been closed and carried outside to the carriage and transported to St. John's Church in Johnstown, more than two thousand mourners followed on foot, including over a thousand Indians, whose genuine grief was far greater than realized by practically any of the whites on hand. Johnson Hall stood on an eminence overlooking Johnstown and the long, imposing funeral cortege was unbroken from the mansion to the mile-distant church.

The attitude of Sir John Johnson had manifested itself only too clearly from the moment of his father's death. He had immediately taken over, virtually excluding Molly from anything. In all the years of his father's association with Molly and through her giving birth to eight Johnson children, Sir John had maintained a cool aloofness, tolerating but never really accepting the fact of his father's love for a Mohawk woman.

Even while Sir William lay in state in the drawing room, Sir John addressed himself to Molly only to the extent of telling her to leave the residence, that he and his wife, Mary, would be moving from Fort Johnson into Johnson Hall at once. Because of Guy Johnson's insistence — Guy knew he would need both Molly and Joseph — Sir John had then relented a bit and magnanimously offered to Molly and her children the use of Fort Johnson as their new residence as soon as he moved out. Numbed by her grief almost beyond understanding, Molly had merely nodded in acceptance and the day after the Johnson coffin had been placed in the family vault, Molly and her brood were reestablished.

It had become common knowledge by then that Guy Johnson had been Sir William's choice as successor and, though the appointment had not been confirmed, the general assumption was that it would be. Thus, on the day after the funeral, following a special ceremony of condolence by the Indians assembled at Johnson Hall, the Indians gravely placed their trust in Guy Johnson.

"We wish you, Uraghquadirha," they said through their spokesman, Rozinoghyata, principal chief of the Onondagas and titular head of the entire
Iroquois League, "to rekindle the council fires at Johnstown and Onondaga.
Continue to give good advice to the young men, as your father did. Follow in
his footsteps. You know very well his ways and his transactions with us. Follow
these and continue to imitate them for the good of the Iroquois. As Warraghiyagey did for us for so many years, Uraghquadirha, take due care of our
affairs."

Guy Johnson promised in all sincerity that he would do so, but in his own
mind he was uncertain. While Sir William had recommended him as successor, there was yet no Crown approval and he wondered if it would come. The
responsibility was tremendous and the position one of great power. For the first
time he feared that his drinking habits might be held against him, but in this
respect he was wrong. Though many people knew he drank a lot, no one, not
even the late Sir William, had any conception of how much.

In other areas, Johnson had a good bit going for him. He was sharp in business dealings and had a natural ability to deal with people pleasantly. These
were the reasons he had progressed so well since his brashness at age seventeen
had first attracted Sir William's attention. One by one, positions of importance
and prestige had opened to him. As Sir William had been general of the militia
of Tryon County, Guy Johnson had become a colonel of that body. In rapid
succession he had then become a representative in the New York Provincial
Assembly, adjutant general of the militia and, finally, judge of the Common
Pleas Court. His credentials for being named Sir William's successor were obviously good, so now the appointment had been provisionally confirmed, and
abruptly Guy Johnson found himself to be one of the most influential and powerful men in North America, having under his control approximately one
hundred and thirty thousand Indians. Of these, over twenty-five thousand were
men who could fight.[53]

Guy Johnson now took another sip of his brandy and spoke to Brant more
briskly. "The resentment of the Colonies against the King is increasing. You
should know that my loyalty to the Crown is every bit as firm as was Sir
William's and that it will not waver, come what may. From my knowledge of
you, Joseph, yours is the same." He glanced up and, at Brant's confirming
nod, continued: "What about your people? How do they stand?"

Brant took his time in answering, choosing his words carefully. "The Mohawks are mostly of the same mind as I. A few, perhaps no, such as our old
chief, Steyawa. There are not many Mohawks who feel as he does, so I would
say yes, the Mohawks favor the King. This is because we all loved Warraghiyagey very much and knew of his love for the King and so we share that
love still, as he asked us to. As for the others of the Six Nations, it is difficult to
read their hearts. Ten years ago, through his strength and courage and wisdom,

Warraghiyagey turned our brother Senecas away from their love for the French and the western tribes and brought them under his wing until they were fully devoted to the English. The Senecas never change their minds easily and having done so, I know there is not any way now that they will turn their backs to the King. Where the others are concerned . . ." He shrugged.

"They're aware of the unrest? Aware that there might actually be an uprising against the Crown?"

"They are."

"Then which way will they go if it happens? They must have talked of it."

"They have. Their minds are teased by it and many of them are uncertain. They feel if it occurs, then it is a family affair, an argument between the father in England and his children here. As a family affair, they feel they should stay free of it and not interfere one way or another."

Guy Johnson started to say something but then stopped and sipped more of his brandy as the Mohawk continued.

"This is what they feel, but I do not think it will stay that way. Many of them do not like the British very well but they like even less the ones living here, like the Bostonians,[54] who have little regard for either the King or the Indians. These, I think, would eventually stay with the King, if they were sure that the King would support them."

"That includes the remaining four tribes of the League, apart from the Mohawks and Senecas?"

Brant shook his head. "No, not all. The Onondagas, probably. Also the Cayugas. The Tuscaroras . . ." He shrugged again. "They will no doubt go the way of their uncles, the Oneidas."

"And how will they go — the Oneidas?"

Brant's expression had become bleak. "They lean heavily toward the Americans and might even support them in opposition to the wishes of the League."

Guy Johnson's jaw fell open and he stared at Brant. That was unexpected, unheard of. It would be tantamount to the dissolution of the Iroquois League, which no one believed could ever really occur. It opened the virtually inconceivable possibility of Iroquois fighting Iroquois. With an intuitive sense that had served him well in the past, Johnson immediately pinpointed the cause of such a possibility.

"Kirkland?"

Brant nodded, impressed with the new superintendent's perspicacity. Samuel Kirkland was at the root of it, the man who had taught Brant the English language at Wheelock's school and the man to whom Brant had taught the Mohawk tongue and various dialects of the Iroquois tribes; Kirkland, who had become a missionary among the Senecas first and then among the Cayugas and now among the Oneidas, where his influence was greater than it had been with the former two; Kirkland, whom the Oneidas had grown to love and trust almost to the point of deification; Kirkland, whose own strong feelings about God and politics they accepted as their own; Kirkland, who was himself fundamentally a peace-loving man but whose antipathy toward the Crown was well known and his outspoken preachings about freedoms frequent. If revolution were to come, there was no doubt that the Reverend Samuel Kirkland would fully support the Rebels and probably convince the Oneidas to do the same.

Guy Johnson sat quietly for a moment, turning the stem of his glass between his fingers. Abruptly he quaffed the remainder of the brandy and then held up two fingers.

"Two things," he said. "First, I need both you and Molly to work closely with me. Ostensibly, you would be a natural choice as my secretary and this would be your title. You would also ostensibly serve as liaison with the tribes. Molly would be an assistant without particular title, but helping me with the business of Indian affairs through the experience acquired from her many years with my uncle. In point of fact, both of you would promote His Majesty's welfare among your people. You would also provide me with information in any way helpful to the League and to His Majesty, as well as anything else which might be used to put down disturbances by any possible enemies of His Majesty, present or future. This is no less than Sir William would have asked and expected of you were he here."

Without the exact words being said, it was an invitation to become confidential agents for the British as well as helping to settle Indian affairs and preserve the Six Nations for the British interest should a conflict erupt. The final remark of Johnson had hit home: It was true, Warraghiyagey would have asked and expected the same.

"I know the heart of my sister," he replied, "so I speak for Degonwadonti as well as for myself. We will do as you ask."

With a broad smile, Guy Johnson came to his feet and shook Brant's hand firmly. "Then that takes us to the second matter. It may be too late already," he said, "but if there is any possibility of making it happen, we must start at once to reverse the efforts of Kirkland among the Oneidas. If certain prejudices could be fomented against him, at least with the others of the Six Nations if not the Oneidas, and this could be followed with accusations, then as Indian superintendent it would naturally become obligatory upon me to remove him from his missionary position and discredit him. With the influence of his presence no longer on hand, is it not possible that the Oneidas might be brought about to accept, even if begrudgingly, the decision of the Iroquois League?"

"It is possible," Brant admitted.

The political intrigues had begun.

[*August 27, 1774 — Saturday*]

So strong had William Johnson been as a guiding and controlling power in the politics and policies of New York Province that more reliance had been placed on his holding things together than anyone had actually realized. With Johnson gone, there was a sense of being cast adrift and left to one's own devices and while previously convictions of the populace had been largely private in regard to where loyalties lay, now they were becoming vociferous about it. Those in the higher echelons — the judges and doctors, lawyers and military and politicians — were mostly Loyalists, adhering to the policies and dictates of the Crown. The greater majority, essentially in the lower and middle echelons — the farmers, small businessmen, settlers, general workers — liked referring to themselves as Americans. As often occurs at the outset of differences between political viewpoints, each party began calling the other by derogatory names. There were many of these, some of them vile, but the two that took on the greatest permanency were four-letter words that were not profane but carried indelible stigma.

For the loyal supporters of His Majesty, King George III, there was the term "Tory," which the Americans gleefully dubbed them, as a fitting epithet. It derived from the Irish word *toraidhe*, meaning "pursuer," and had been applied by the Irish in the previous century to a class of their dispossessed citizens, nominally royalists, who were noted for their outrages and cruelties. [55]

For those who called themselves Americans rather than colonists and who had begun taking stands against the strictures of taxation and embargo being placed against them by the mother country, the Loyalists had an epithet of their own to bestow: "Whig," a shortened form of Whiggamores — that body of rebels that had marched on Edinburgh in 1648.

The lines were being drawn and it was no longer fashionable — or very wise — to attempt to straddle the lines or keep one's political leanings a secret. Those who tried to do so were suspect by both sides and that was an untenable stance to maintain.

The Americans in Tryon County had been alarmed and indignant about the oppressive acts being committed against the Colonies by the English Parliament ever since the blockade of Boston Harbor had taken place in June. They warmly sympathized with the Bostonians and applauded the proposed Continental Congress. As a culmination of this feeling and with Sir William's settling influence absent, a large number of Palatine District citizens met and with an unabashed sense of bravado put into writing a remarkable set of resolves:

This meeting, looking with concern and heartfelt sorrow on the alarming and calamitous condition which the inhabitants of Boston are in, in consequence of

the act of Parliament blocking up the Port of Boston, and considering the ten-
dency of the late acts of Parliament, for the purpose of raising a revenue in
America, as to the abridging of the liberties and privileges of the American colo-
nies, do resolve:

I. That King George the Third is lawful and rightful Lord and Sovereign of
Great Britain, and the dominions thereunto belonging, and that, as part of his
dominions, we hereby testify that we will bear true faith and allegiance unto
him, and that we will with our lives and fortunes support and maintain him
upon the throne of his ancestors, and the just dependence of these his Colonies
upon the Crown of Great Britain.

II. That we think and consider it as our greatest happiness to be governed by
the laws of Great Britain and that with cheerfulness we will always pay submis-
sion thereunto as far as we consistently can with the security of the constitu-
tional rights and liberties of English subjects, which are so sacred that we cannot
permit the same to be violated.

III. That we think it is our undeniable privilege to be taxed only at our con-
sent, given by ourselves or our representatives; that taxes otherwise laid and ex-
acted are unjust and unconstitutional; and that the late Acts of Parliament,
declarative of their right on laying internal taxes on the American Colonies, are
obvious encroachments on the rights and liberties of the British subjects in
America.

IV. That the act for blocking up the Port of Boston is oppressive and arbi-
trary, injurious in its principles and particularly oppressive to the inhabitants of
Boston, whom we consider brethren suffering in the common cause.

V. That we will unite and join with the differing districts of this county, in
giving whatever relief it is in our power, to the poor distressed inhabitants of
Boston; and that we will join and unite with our brethren of the rest of this col-
ony in anything tending to support and defend our rights and liberties.

VI. That we think the sending of delegates from the different colonies to a
general Constitutional Congress is a salutary measure and absolutely necessary
at this alarming crisis, and that we entirely approve of the five gentlemen chosen
delegates for this colony by our brethren of New York, hereby adopting and
choosing the same persons to represent this colony in the Congress.

VII. That we hereby engage faithfully to abide by and adhere to such regula-
tions as shall be made and agreed upon by the said Congress. . . .

· [October 13, 1774 — Thursday]

The time of the harvest moon was also the time of the annual congress of the
Six Nations at the seat of government of the Iroquois League in Onondaga.
Here for over two hundred and fifty years the council fire had been burning.
Never before had Thayendanegea — Joseph Brant — been permitted to speak

here, since he was not a chief nor even a representative of the Mohawks to this congress. This time was different, as he was now here as an official representative of Colonel Guy Johnson, Superintendent of Indian Affairs.

There were many in attendance who thought that, because of his closeness to the Johnsons and the Johnsons' closeness to the British government, Thayendanegea would advocate the League's allying itself to the British in the event of a showdown between the mother country and the Colonies. That was not the case.

"I do not pretend to know which is the wisest course for us," he told the assemblage. "There are many things to consider before so grave a step should be made. In all matters, our chief concern must be our own future as six individual nations and as a great League. We are no longer as numerous or as powerful as we once were. The reason is partly that so many of our brave warriors and chiefs were killed when once before we found ourselves between two white forces bent upon one another's destruction.

"Some of us then" — he looked at the Seneca contingent — "supported the French and others of us supported the English. It makes no difference now which of those white factions was right or wrong or even who won. What is important is that during the progress of that war into which we were drawn, many hundreds of our people died. We, the Iroquois League, could at no time in our history afford such a loss. We could less afford it then and even less than that can we afford it now.

"Should war break out again among the whites, we may be drawn into it whether or not we desire to be. We need therefore to study the strengths and weaknesses of those whites who would war against one another and, if we must fight, then choose, for the sake of the perpetuation of our nations, the side which will win. In whatever decision is made we must, above all else, remain united."

There were others who spoke, some for the individual tribes, some for the entire League. There were harangues in favor of declarations of war and declarations of neutrality; for alliance with the British and alliance with the Americans. At one point the new young sachem of the Senecas, Sagoyewatha, wearing his fine red jacket, spoke a stirring speech, and although he did not refer to Brant by name, he spoke of him indirectly.

"We must always beware," he said, "of those with certain powers and influence, even if they have no real authority among us, who lay before us their thoughts in a very convincing manner. Might not they be, for all we know, the tools of a very powerful faction of the whites? Might not they be willing to risk destroying the unity of our League for personal gain from the whites, or for recognition among us here? We must beware!"

It was one of the most inconclusive congresses ever held by the Iroquois and few as they left were not ridden by a sense of dissatisfaction and a faint stirring of fear. It was as if for the first time in such a congress too many things were said that should have been left unsaid and too many things were left unspoken that had needed to be aired.

Brant was taking back to the Mohawk Valley with him the only conclusion of any significance made by the congress, a conclusion that was itself paradoxical in its inconclusiveness. The final decision of the chiefs had been not for war, nor for peace, nor even for neutrality. As its official stance for now, the Six Nations had declined to promise to help the King. Accustomed to Iroquois League congresses that made direct, strong and definitive decisions, Brant was deeply disappointed.

Guy Johnson too was going to be very disappointed.

[March 31, 1775 — Friday]

Colonel Guy Johnson's arbitrary removal of the Reverend Samuel Kirkland as missionary to the Oneidas created a great howl of protest through the valleys of the Mohawk and Hudson rivers. There was no argument that he, as Superintendent of Indian Affairs, had no right to take such action, but only that he had no right to do so without positive cause. In this matter there simply wasn't cause enough.[56]

Everyone had heard the whispers and rumors about the missionary: about how he was a poor example for carrying the word of the Lord to the heathens; of how he bedded with Indian women constantly and frequently beat them; of how he cheated the Indians; of how he induced them to work for him without payment; of how he was inciting them toward taking up the hatchet against those who supported the authority of the Crown. But they were just that — whispers and rumors, devoid of any solid substantiation and certainly not adequate grounds for removal from so important an office.

Johnson staunchly maintained that he was not responsible to the whims of popular sentiment and that enough evidence had come to him of the missionary's misconduct that he had no other course than to remove him. The Indian superintendent stated that he should have removed Kirkland long before this and only his sense of justice had prompted him to wait this long before taking his action.

In point of fact, he *had* waited too long. Even more than the whites of the Mohawk Valley, the Oneidas were furious over the removal of Kirkland and they let it be known that they would continue to be guided by what their beloved Kirkland had taught them and would be supportive of his views, even should such views be apart from those of the Iroquois League.

Throughout the Mohawk Valley a great sense of tension was growing, with neighbor suspicious of neighbor, with occasional fistfights breaking out and with more and more meetings being held at night in taverns or halls or in the homes of the most vociferous of the Whigs, at which the policies of the King, the Parliament and what they called the henchmen of the Crown in America were decried.

Guy Johnson was noted for the ease with which he could lose his temper, especially when in his cups, and he was maintaining his even keel now only with the greatest of effort. Yet the lies — and the truths — about him and his motives in the position of superintendent were getting under his skin and he had begun building a strong group of men in the area — primarily Irish and Scots — whose loyalties were in tune with his own.

A couple of weeks ago he had written to Lord Dartmouth asking for instructions on what he should do and just how far he should go at this point in winning the Indians over to support of the King. He also pointed out that matters were rapidly coming to a head and that until certain orders were received from Dartmouth he would be guided by past policy and in all matters be totally supportive of the Crown.

He was more than merely supportive. Two nights ago a meeting of the Rebels in a tavern at Caughnawaga in the Mohawk District of Tryon County was suddenly interrupted by the appearance of Guy Johnson and Sir John Johnson at the head of about thirty club-wielding Tories. The colonel ordered the Rebels to end their meeting and go home and, when they refused, a severe brawl broke out and a dozen or more people were hurt, some of them pretty badly.

The fury of the populace at this flared instantly to a high pitch and threats of a very serious nature were made. Without delay, Guy Johnson organized a corps of one hundred and fifty Scots Highlanders armed with muskets, had them surround and guard his house on a twenty-four-hour basis, announced his intention of using them to suppress any further exhibition of disaffection to the Crown, gave them orders to shoot and kill any interlopers and even took it upon himself to have travelers on the nearby King's Highway stopped and searched.

Tempers were set on hair trigger and the situation was extremely volatile. A hot war had not yet broken out between the British and the Americans, but the Hudson and Mohawk valleys were poised for it. The balance was delicate and it was obvious that such a condition could not be maintained for very long.

It wasn't.

[*April 19, 1775 — Wednesday*]

War!

No longer any doubt whether it would eventually happen or where. Today was the day and the place was Lexington and Concord and the sixteen miles in between.

Lieutenant General Thomas Gage, commander in chief of all His Majesty's armed forces in America and governor of the Province of Massachusetts Bay, was in no degree anticipating the outbreak of war when he ordered out a detachment to confiscate stores of gunpowder supposedly stockpiled by the rabble-in-arms at Lexington and Concord. If those two ringleaders of the discontent here could be seized — Samuel Adams and John Hancock — so much the better.

The alarm went out, thanks to Paul Revere and others, and sixty or seventy minutemen under Captain Jonas Parker formed at Lexington Green to face odds of about ten to one in the form of Lieutenant Colonel Francis Smith's 10th Regiment of Foot, preceded by Major John Pitcairn's advance marines.

It all happened quickly. A confrontation. A shot. A volley. Jonas Parker dead, along with seven other minutemen. Ten wounded and in wild retreat with the rest of the minutemen toward Concord. For the British, one private with a minor wound in the leg. Hardly an auspicious beginning for the Americans.

A march continued. Another confrontation, this time at Concord Bridge. A flurry of shots lasting only two or three minutes. A better showing for the Americans this time. For the British, three dead, nine wounded; for the Americans, two dead, four wounded.

It could have ended there. It should have ended there.

It didn't.

The British commenced a retreat, heading back to Charlestown, sixteen miles away, and with that all hell broke loose. By sunset they had crossed the isthmus connecting Charlestown with the mainland and at last were rid of their pursuers, but the day's totals were a grim catapult into a harsh new era. British casualties were two hundred and seventy-three; American casualties, ninety-five.

The War of the Revolution had begun.[57]

[*May 1, 1775 — Monday*]

In every district, precinct, hamlet and village in the Hudson and Mohawk River valleys, meetings were being held, inflammatory speeches were being given, views were being stated, positions were being declared, stands were being made. Everyone, it seemed, was angry and ready to fight. But for now they were like belligerent dogs walking stiff-legged around one another, trying to sniff out one another's weaknesses and strengths, measuring and weighing and growling before leaping for the throat.

At a court held in Johnstown, over five hundred Tories — mostly Roman Catholic Scottish Highlanders[58] — assembled under Colonel Guy Johnson and Sir John Johnson and drew up and circulated an address that avowed their strong opposition to the revolutionary measures adopted by the Congress hastily assembled in Philadelphia in the wake of the Massachusetts conflict. Not all in attendance at that Johnstown meeting were in agreement and a series of warm debates and even a few altercations occurred, but the address was at last signed by most of the grand jury and by nearly all the magistrates.

Immediately an opposition meeting was held in the church at Cherry Valley by the Palatine District residents and an article of association was drawn up approving of and upholding the articles of the Continental Congress against the specific wishes of the magistrates. It was significant that one of the foremost speakers at this meeting was Thomas Spencer, a principal chief of the Oneidas who had several years ago set himself up as a blacksmith in the Mohawk Valley.

Johnson Hall became the center of Loyalist activities and a rendezvous for Tories and Indians leaning toward British allegiance. Everyone everywhere was maneuvering for position and advantage and one of the immediate principal goals was an effort on each side to woo the Indians into an alliance against the enemy.

As secretary to Guy Johnson, Brant was extremely busy carrying messages and information back and forth between the Six Nations and Guy Park Manor, where Johnson was still headquartered. The superintendent felt frustrated and, without having received specific instructions from England, was marking time. Sir William in this position would have lost no time in personally visiting all the tribes, holding major councils with them and inciting them to fever pitch for defense of the Crown. Guy Johnson had neither that ability nor the courage to initiate such a step without direct orders from his immediate superior, Lord Dartmouth. And while he marked time and eased his frustration with liberal doses of alcohol in various forms, agents for the Americans already had begun moving among the Indians.

[*May 10, 1775 — Wednesday*]

Jehoiakim Mothskin hated the Mohawks with a depth of feeling that precluded any possibility of reconciliation. That he was himself an Indian and principal chief of his own small tribe made no difference. Long ago he had solemnly vowed in his own heart that no matter what the issue, whichever way the Mohawks went, he would lead his people in the opposing direction.

Jehoiakim was a chunky man of medium height in his late forties. He had been chief of his people for a quarter of a century, ever since the death of their previous principal chief, the venerable Chief Stockbridge. Where the old man had gotten the English name of Stockbridge no one seemed to know, but if he'd ever had another one it was lost to memory. It was here, just seven miles south of the village of Oneida, the principal village of that tribe, that Stockbridge had established his town and settled his people one hundred and eleven years ago. The town had been named after him and even the Indians of that town were now known as Stockbridge Indians.

Early in their history they had been a proud race which called themselves Mahicans,[59] a name meaning "The Wolf." They had occupied both sides of the upper Hudson River from Catskill Creek to Lake Champlain and eastward into the valley of the Housatonic,[60] with their capital at Schodac, near Albany. For years they had been at war with the Mohawks and finally had been forced to move to this present village of Stockbridge in 1664. Because of the intervention of the Oneidas on their behalf, an uneasy truce was arranged with the Mohawks and this had been the situation ever since. But Jehoiakim Mothskin, deeply steeped in the tradition of his tribe, passionately hated the Mohawks for what they had done. The Mahicans had once been numerous and powerful. Now, decimated by the Mohawks, ousted from their own territory and, under the name of Stockbridge Indians, forced to live as wards of the Oneidas, the total population of their tribe was only three hundred. Of these, ninety-two were able warriors, the remainder being women, children and old people.

Ties with the Oneidas had remained strong because of the favor they had done them in preventing the Mohawks from exterminating them. Thus, as the Oneidas went, so too ordinarily went the Stockbridges. That was very important, in consideration of the letter that was now being shown to Jehoiakim by Chief Hanyerry of the Oneidas.

"A runner brought this to us yesterday," Hanyerry said. "The contents have touched some of our people and they are inclined to lend their strength, as requested. Many of us, however, are not."

"Who is it from?" Jehoiakim asked. "What does it say?"

"It is signed by Thayendanegea — who calls himself Brant — and four other chiefs." Hanyerry was aware of the manner in which Jehoiakim stiffened beside him at the mention of the Mohawk, but he went on: "Brant signs it as secretary to Uraghquadirha, the nephew of Warraghiyagey. He writes: 'This is your letter, Oneida sachems, written at Guy Johnson's, May, 1775. Guy Johnson wishes you Oneidas to know what is happening now. He is much more certain now of the bad designs of the Americans. He is in fear of being taken prisoner by them. We Mohawks are obliged to watch him constantly to protect him. Therefore we send you this news so you will know it. Guy Johnson depends upon your assistance too and is convinced it will come. He does not believe you would knowingly see him suffer. We therefore expect you in a few days' time. So much at present. Thus far we send this only to you Oneidas but afterward perhaps to all the other nations. We close now and expect that you will be concerned about our superintendent, Guy Johnson, because we are all united.' "

Hanyerry remained silent when he finished, watching the Stockbridge chief. Jehoiakim's expression was fixed in harsh lines. Abruptly he hawked loudly and spat a great glob of phlegm onto the ground and then mashed it into the earth with his heel. Instantly Hanyerry burst into laughter and slapped his companion on the back.

"My feeling, too!" he said. "As I say, there are some of my people who are ready to help, but not many. Mostly they wish to have nothing to do with it. For myself, I will be opposite. I have never had any love for Uraghquadirha. Since he took Brother Kirkland from us, whom we loved, we will do nothing for him. And I, and whomever will follow me, will oppose him."

Jehoiakim smiled and put his hand on Hanyerry's shoulder. "I am with you, but you must know that it means we may find ourselves going against what the League decides."

"I will face up to my own choice and take the consequences of it. I am not speaking for the Oneidas, only for myself."

"Will your own choice mean making yourself an ally to those who oppose Uraghquadirha?"

Hanyerry nodded and now Jehoiakim chuckled. "Hanyerry, you and I are like the tiny bee who flies around the head of the great giant. We are but a little annoyance, even if we sting, at which time the hand of the giant might slap and crush us. But every now and then," he added, "the poison of the tiny bee's sting becomes more deadly than the bite of the snake which rattles and he who is stung dies."

Hanyerry grunted. "I do not think our stings can ever be that bad, but our buzzing about can be a great annoyance." He glanced at his companion and added, "I think part of that annoyance might be if the enemies of Uraghquadirha were to find along one of their roads a letter that had been 'accidentally' dropped by a messenger. This letter." He tapped the folded paper still in his hand. "Can you think of a way that might happen?"

Jehoiakim took it from him. "I will try," he said.

They laughed together and parted then. When Jehoiakim returned to Stockbridge later in the day, he found two men awaiting him on the path at the edge of the village. One he recognized as the Oneida chief who had taken up living with the whites. His name was Ahnyero, but among the whites he was called Thomas Spencer and he had become well known for the way he had learned to swiftly and expertly put iron shoes on the feet of horses. The other was a man he did not know, but whom Ahnyero now introduced to him as Colonel John Patterson.

The officer dipped his head toward Jehoiakim as he heard his own name mentioned and then shook the chief's hand warmly. Though Jehoiakim could speak English slightly and understand it somewhat better, he gave no indication of it as he listened first to Patterson's brief speech, obviously rehearsed, which was then interpreted by Ahnyero.

"I come to Chief Jehoiakim Mothskin and the rest of our brethren, the Indians of Stockbridge, with a message from the Second Provincial Congress. That Congress, in your behalf as well as its own, urges you and your people to take up the hatchet in the cause of liberty and justice against the representatives and soldiers of the King of England in these colonies. In this respect I am empowered to present each of you who have enlisted in this service with a blanket and a ribbon as testimony of our affection."

Obviously, while Guy Johnson was simmering in the juices of his own frustration and indecision, fearful of acting without orders, the Americans were taking the initiative in seeking Indian alliances.

"We will talk," Jehoiakim said. He began leading them toward his house and then abruptly paused and stooped over and seemed to pick up a folded piece of paper beside the path.

"This is strange," he murmured in the Oneida tongue to Ahnyero. "It would appear that some messenger may have become careless and dropped what he was carrying. I wouldn't think to read it, since it is not mine, but perhaps Ahnyero would do me the favor of determining where it should go and taking it there?"

Frowning slightly, Spencer took the letter from him and read it swiftly. Without change of expression he refolded it and then placed it carefully inside his belt.

"I will try to see that it reaches the proper hands," he said.

The two Indians smiled at one another and continued leading Colonel Patterson into the village of Stockbridge.

[*June 11, 1775 — Sunday*]

The progression of events over the past several weeks had been as unstoppable as an avalanche. Now, seated at a desk in his less than elegant quarters at Fort Oswego on Lake Ontario, Colonel Guy Johnson began a new page in the voluminous report he was preparing for Lord Dartmouth.

Johnson had become rather gaunt, his eyes burning with an unnatural luster brought about by too much drink and not enough sleep, his cheeks and chin scraggly with what was for him an uncommon four-day growth of whiskers.

He wrote a few lines at the head of the page, his hand not so bold and sure as in previous writings, and then he stopped and dropped the pen and rubbed his eyes. How in God's name could all this have occurred? How was it possible that he, one of the most influential of the King's men in America, had been forced to flee from his own home as if he were a criminal, leaving behind to God knows what fate the accumulation of a lifetime of personal goods?

He sighed deeply and picked up the papers, skimming through them, here and there rereading what he had written, here and there making a correction or addition in the margin. He was not always entirely sure of his chronology of events, but certainly it would be close enough.

THE MOHAWK RIVER VALLEY

SCALE

10 miles

Hudson R.

SARATOGA

BEMIS HEIGHTS

HALF MOON

SCHENECTADY

ALBANY

SCHOHARIE (FT. DEFIANCE)

FT. JOHNSON

Mohawk R.

TEANTONTALAGO

Schoharie Cr.

JOHNSTOWN

CAUGHNAWAGA

FT. HUNTER

COBLESKILL

SCHOHARIE

STONE ARABIA

CHERRY VALLEY

Schenevus Cr.

FT. PLAIN

CANAJOHARIE

ANDRUSTOWN

Cherry Valley Cr.

LITTLE FALLS

FT. HERKIMER (FT. DAYTON)

HERKIMER HOUSE

Otsego Lake

Oaks Cr.

Susquehanna R.

GERMAN FLATS

Mohawk R.

Canadarago Lake

DEERFIELD

ORISKANY

FT. STANWIX

Unadilla R.

N

He had written first of the flurry of correspondence that had occurred between him and the Palatine Committee and of that body's contact with the New York Provincial Congress in Albany, as had been reported to him by his spies. The Palatine Committee had become outrageous in their manners toward him and in their comments, both written and vocal. They had insinuated many things that were wholly untrue and hinted at knowledge of things that Johnson was sure could not possibly be known to them. And when he had finally been forced to resort to veiled threat, it had not at all had the desired effect. In a letter to the magistrates and committees of the western districts he had written:

I have lately had repeated accounts that a body of New Englanders, or other men, were to come and seize and carry away my person and attack our family under cover of malicious insinuations — these being that I intended to set the Indians upon the people. Men of sense and character know that my office is of the highest importance to promote peace amongst the Six Nations, and to prevent their entering any such disputes. . . . All men must allow that if the Indians find their council fire disturbed and their superintendent insulted, they will take a dreadful revenge. It is therefore the duty of all people to prevent this, and to satisfy any who may have been injured, and that their suspicions and the allegations they have collected against me are false and inconsistent with my character and office. I recommend this to you as highly necessary at this time, as my regard for the interest of the country, and self-preservation has obliged me to fortify my house and keep men armed for my defense till these idle and malicious reports are removed. . . .

The Palatine Committee, Johnson reported, had not replied with the anticipated grace and courtesy but had instead become insulting and reiterated vague threats, ending with the comment that they would not stand by and in any way see their liberties abridged or their freedom endangered. They realized, they had written to him,

very truly we have an open enemy before our faces and treacherous friends at our backs, but we resolve that your conduct, Colonel Johnson, is alarming, arbitrary, and unwarrantable, inasmuch as you are stopping and searching travelers upon the King's Highway, and we must assure you that we will defend our freedom with our lives and fortunes.

Worse, there was the certain knowledge delivered to him by his spies that the Palatine Committee had somehow come into possession of the letter written by Brant on his behalf to the Oneidas, asking for Indians to defend him. This letter, along with Johnson's, they had sent on to the Albany committee. That body thereupon wrote a more subtle but no less pointed missive to Johnson, saying:

We are not ignorant of the importance of your office as Superintendent, and have been perfectly easy with respect to any suspicions of the Indians taking a part in the present dispute between Great Britain and her Colonies, knowing them to be a people of too much sagacity to engage with the whole continent in a controversy that they can profit nothing by. . . . we hope that you will use all possible means in your power to restore peace and tranquility among the Indians and assure them that the report propagated, prejudicial to you or to them, is totally groundless of any just foundation, and that nothing will afford His Majesty's subjects in general a greater satisfaction than to be, and continue with them, on the strictest terms of peace and friendship. . . .

In an effort to mollify the fears of the various district representatives, Johnson convened an Indian congress at Guy Park on May 25, attended by some delegates from both Albany and Tryon counties. Supposedly all six Iroquois tribes were to be on hand, but only the Mohawks were there in force or with leadership, headed by their principal chief, the aged Steyawa, brother of Tiyanoga who had been killed so long ago at Lake George. Close at hand, too, was Brant, who was functioning as both secretary to Guy Johnson and interpreter. The congress was short, constrained, stiffly polite, ominously filled with things unsaid and largely disappointing to all concerned except Johnson, who had anticipated exactly what would occur.

The delegates spoke first, explaining that somehow false stories had begun circulating that Guy Johnson was to be taken prisoner and this would then leave the Indians without representation among the whites. They denied all of this, along with the report that their regular dole of gunpowder from the colony was being withheld from them, stating that the latter was only delayed.

It was the delegate from Schenectady who homed in on the matter of most immediate concern to the white inhabitants of New York Province. After some preliminary discussion during which the Indians denied contemplating alliance with the King, he addressed his remarks to Steyawa, calling him Little Abraham, by which name he was more familiar to most of the whites.

"Brothers, we are extremely satisfied to hear that you do not propose and are not inclined to interfere in the dispute between Old England and America. You must understand," he added with a certain sharpness, "that this dispute is not with Boston alone. It is between Old England and all her colonies. The people here are oppressed by Old England and the King sends over troops among us, to destroy us. This is the reason our people are all in arms to defend themselves. The arms they are gathering are intended for defense; they indicate no hostile intentions against you. If you continue in your peaceable way, as you say you intend doing, then you need apprehend no danger."

The speaker raised a hand and now emphasized his final remark by making jabbing motions in the air with his index finger at nearly every word. "Ours is a dispute which does not involve you and should not concern you. Have *nothing* to do with it! Do not disturb any of our people and, you can depend on it, they will leave you in peace."

Steyawa had difficulty rising from where he sat on the ground and Brant helped him get to his feet and readjusted the light ceremonial blanket over his shoulders. Steyawa was easily an octogenarian and growing feeble, yet his voice was clear and strong, his delivery without hesitation.

"We are glad to meet you here," he told them, "and to learn that the stories of men coming to take Uraghquadirha, our superintendent, are nothing but the false stories of bad birds who fly between us to cause trouble. We do not wish to have any trouble with the white people here. We have no quarrel with them. During the lifetime of Warraghiyagey and since, we have always been peaceably disposed toward you.

"Lately," he went on, his old eyes moving slowly across the provincial delegates, "we have become alarmed on account of the reports that our allotment of gunpowder was stopped. We get our things from the superintendent. If we lived as you do, the stopping of the powder would not be so great a loss, but we must have it whereby we can hunt our meat. If our ammunition is stopped . . ." He paused for a long while, allowing Brant to finish interpreting, and then, maintaining the pause uncomfortably longer, he continued: ". . . we will distrust you. We are happy that you indicate this will not happen."

Again he was silent a long while and when he continued it was with unmistakable hardness. "It is well that you understand that we cannot spare Uraghquadirha. The love we have for the memory of Warraghiyagey and the obligation that the whole Six Nations are under to him must make us regard and protect every branch of his family. All of the Six Nations know this and it is important to them. It is our wish that you explain this to your people and make them understand."

Had the meeting been attended by more than just the Mohawks, Steyawa's words would have carried greater weight. As it was, the delegation took the words into advisement but they were not very concerned and not at all convinced that Steyawa spoke for the Iroquois League.

A sizable number of whites whose loyalties remained with the King had also attended the council and, as a result of Johnson's forewarning to them to remain silent so as not to cause possibly uncontrollable difficulties, they had stood by silently, their expressions grim, having difficulty containing their animosity toward these delegates who were so openly rebellious to the King's authority.

Guy Johnson's remarks had been brief in the extreme. An express received the previous evening had caused him to forgo much of what he had intended saying. He concluded the congress by simply remarking that because not all of the Six Nations had been represented in this council, he felt it would be important in keeping the Indians quiet and peaceful while the problem between England and her colonies was resolved for him to hold another council as soon as possible in the far western part of Tryon County, where the more distant members of the Iroquois League would be able to attend. There, he promised, he would quiet the fears and pacify their intentions.

Among Johnson's group at this first council were a father and son who had a fine estate near Caughnawaga, only a few miles from Johnstown. They were the forty-seven-year-old Colonel John Butler[61] and his hotheaded, bellicose, twenty-six-year-old son, Walter N. Butler. The elder Butler and Sir William had been close friends for many years and, not surprisingly, both Butler and his son remained unswervingly allegiant to the King and ready to use whatever means was in their power to protect the Crown's interests in America. Both, in meetings with Guy Johnson, had already pledged themselves to support him and only Johnson's earlier warning to curb their reactions to this council kept them under control.

It was just prior to that council, Johnson's report to Lord Dartmouth continued, that he had received secret instructions from Thomas Gage that ordered that he take with him only those possessions of his he could carry and, on the pretext of conducting business elsewhere with the Indians and thus refraining from exciting suspicions, immediately leave the Mohawk Valley. The British commander in chief, too, had felt sure that the Rebel forces in the valley would very soon decide that it would be in their own best interests to arrest and incarcerate Johnson as a political prisoner to prevent his possibly agitating the Indians against the citizens. The possibility of such an arrest of Johnson was very real, Gage had pointed out, as the revolutionary sentiment in the Mohawk Valley was strong and proponents of it far outnumbered those whose inclinations were Loyalist.

The rapidity with which events followed had shown that Gage was correct in his assessment of the situation. Sir John Johnson declined Guy's invitation to go along, feeling his own situation was secure, so Guy had moved out with his wife and two daughters and a number of servants. He also took friends along, including John and Walter Butler, as well as a large contingent of other influential men of the valley generally considered to be Tories. Joseph Brant, with a large retinue of Indians, also accompanied him. Johnson took along only what baggage and equipment he could carry under the pretext that he had laid the groundwork for in the council, that he was going to hold a large Indian congress in the far western part of Tryon County to put down unrest among the tribes, as the Albany committee had wished him to do.

At the same time the county residents, emboldened by the actions of the Palatine Committee and the committee of Albany, held a mass meeting and included, for the first time, members from the Mohawk District who had previously been prevented by Johnson from attending such gatherings. This was the first united meeting of the Tryon County district representatives and, flushed with excitement and a sense of strength, they created the Tryon County Committee of Safety, choosing as chairman Christopher P. Yates. He had been chairman of the Palatine District and had drafted most of the previous correspondence.

Not yet realizing that Guy Johnson was in actuality fleeing this county, the Committee of Safety drafted a letter to him that was given to two of the attendees to carry to Johnson, who had thus far traveled up the Mohawk to the settlement of Cosby's Manor, a little distance above German Flats. One of these two was Edward Wall, chairman of the German Flats District. The other was Nicholas Herkimer, who was not only chairman of the Canajoharie District, but who, since William Johnson's death and the elevation of Sir John Johnson to brigadier general of the Tryon County Militia, had become colonel of that body.

Herkimer and Wall found Guy Johnson where he and his group had stayed over at the home of William Thomson and presented him with the Tryon County letter, telling him they would await his reply, to return with it. The letter left no doubt as to which way the populace of Tryon County was leaning in its sentiments:

To Colo. Guy Johnson
    SIR: —
According to the example of the counties in this and neighboring colonies, the people of the district we represent have met in a peaceable manner to consider of the present dispute with the mother country and the colonies, signed a general association, and appointed us a committee to meet in order to consult the common safety of our rights and liberties, which are infringed in a most enormous manner, but enforcing oppressive and unconstitutional acts of the British Parliament, by an Armed Force, in the Massachusetts Bay.

We have been deeply disturbed at the intelligence received through the recovery of a letter, purportedly written to the Oneidas in your behalf by five Mohawks, these being four chiefs and the man called Joseph Brant, who is presently in your employ as a secretary. The letter, by its nature, is conceived to instigate unrest and upset among the tribes and especially to turn aside the loyalties of the Oneidas, who have long been our friends. We cannot believe that you have had any part in this and would like your assurances to that head.

We are met because it is now evident that certain loyalties must be declared and certain rights must, if necessary, be defended with all that it is in the power and fortune of oppressed people to defend. Was it any longer a doubt that we are opposed by the mother country and that it is the avowed design of the ministers to enslave us, we might perhaps be induced to use argument to point out in what particulars we conceive that it is the birthright of English subjects to be exempted from all taxes, except those which are laid on them by their representatives, and think we have a right, not only by the laws and constitution of England, to meet for the purpose we have done. Which meeting we probably would have postponed for a while had there been the least kind of probability that the petition of the general assembly would have been noticed more than the united petition of almost the whole continent of America, by their delegates in Congress. Which, so far from being in any ways complied with, was treated with superlative contempt by the ministry and fresh oppressions were, and are, daily heaped upon us. Upon which principles — principles which are undeniable — we have been appointed to consult methods to contribute what little lies in our power to save our devoted country from ruin and devastation; which, with the assistance of Divine Providence, it is our fixed and determined resolution to do; and if called upon we shall be foremost in sharing the toil and danger of the field. We consider New England suffering in the common cause, and commiserate their distressed situation; and we should be wanting in our duty to our country and to ourselves, if we were any longer backward in announcing our determination to the world.

We know that some of the members of this committee have been charged with compelling people to come into the measures which we have adopted, and with drinking treasonable toasts. But as we are convinced that these reports are false and malicious, spread by our enemies with the sole intent to lessen us in the esteem of the world, and as we are conscious of being guilty of no crime, and of having barely done our duty, we are entirely unconcerned as to anything that is said of us, or can be done with us. We should, however, be careless of our character did we not wish to detect the despicable wretch who could be so base as to charge us with things which we never entertained the most distant thoughts of. We are not ignorant of the very great importance of your office as superintendent of the Indians, and therefore it is no more our duty than inclination to protect you in the discharge of the duty of your proper province, and we meet you with pleasure in behalf of ourselves and our constituents, to thank you for meeting the Indians in the upper parts of the country, which may be the means of easing the people of the remainder of their fears on this account, and preventing the Indians committing irregularities on their way down to Guy Park. And we beg of *you to use your endeavors with the Indians to dissuade them from interfering in the dispute with the mother country and the colonies. We cannot think that, as you and your family possess very large estates in this county, you are unfavorable to American freedom, although you may differ with us in the mode of obtaining redress of grievances. Permit us further to observe that we cannot pass over in silence the interruption which the people of the Mohawk District met in their meeting; and the inhuman treatment of a man whose only crime was being faithful to his employers, and refusing to give an account of the receipt of certain papers to persons who had not the least color of right to demand anything of that kind. We assure you that we are much concerned about it, as two important rights of English subjects are thereby infringed, to wit, a right to meet, and to obtain all the intelligence in their power. . . .*

Outwardly calm but seething inside after reading the letter, Guy Johnson had immediately penned his reply:

Cosby's Manor, June 6th, 1775

Sirs:

I have received the paper signed Chris. P. Yates, chairman on behalf of the district therein mentioned, which I am now to answer; and shall do it briefly in the order you have stated matters. As to the letter of some Indians to the Oneidas, I really knew nothing of it till I heard such a thing had been by some means obtained from an Indian messenger, and from what I have heard of its contents I can't see anything material in it, or that could justify such idle apprehensions, but I must observe that these fears among the people were talked of long before and were, I fear, propagated by some malicious persons for a bad purpose.

As to your political sentiments, on which you enter in the next paragraph, I have no occasion to enter on the justness or the merits of the cause. I desire to enjoy liberty of conscience and the exercise of my own judgment, and that all others should have the same privilege; but with regard to your saying that you might have postponed the affair if there had been the least kind of probability that the petition of the General Assembly would have been noticed more than that of the delegates, I must, as a true friend to the country in which I have a large interest, say that the present dispute is viewed in different lights according to the education and principles of the parties affected, and that however reasonable it may appear to a considerable number of honest men here, that the petition of the delegates should merit attention, it is not viewed in the same light in a country which admits of no authority that is not constitutionally established; and I persuade myself that you have that reverence of his Majesty that you will pay due regard to the Royal assurance given in his speech to Parliament, that whenever the American grievances should be laid before him by their constitutional assemblies, they should be fully attended to. I have heard that compulsory steps were taken to induce some persons to come into your measures and treasonable toasts drunk; but I am happy to hear that you disavow them.

I am glad to find my calling a congress on the frontiers gives satisfaction; this was principally my design, though I cannot sufficiently express my surprise at those who have, either through malice or ignorance, misconstrued my intentions and supposed me capable of setting the Indians on the peaceable inhabitants of this county. The interest our family has in this county, and my own, is considerable; and they have been its best benefactors; and malicious charges, therefore, to their prejudice, are highly injurious and ought to be totally suppressed.

The office I hold is greatly for the benefit and protection of this country, and on my frequent meetings with the Indians depends their peace and security; I therefore cannot but be astonished to find the endeavors made use of to obstruct me in my duties, and the weakness of some people in withholding many things from me, which are indispensably necessary for rendering the Indians contented; [62] and I am willing to hope that you, gentlemen, will duly consider this and discountenance the same.

You have been much misinformed as to the origin of the reports which have obliged me to fortify my house and stand on my defense. I had it, gentlemen, from undoubted authority from Albany, and since confirmed by letters from one of the committee at Philadelphia, that a large body of men were to make me prisoner. As to the effect this must have on the Indians, it might have been of dangerous consequences to you, (a circumstance not thought of) I was obliged at great expense to take these measures. But the many reports of my stopping travelers were false in every particular, and the only instance of detaining anybody was in the case of two New England men, which I explained fully to those of your body who brought your letter, and wherein I acted strictly agreeable to law, and as a magistrate should have done.

I am very sorry that such idle and injurious reports meet with any encouragement. I rely on you, gentlemen, to exert yourselves in discountenancing them, and am happy in this opportunity of assuring the people of a county I regard, that they have nothing to apprehend from my endeavors, but I shall always be glad to promote their true interests. . . .

GUY JOHNSON

Johnson folded and sealed the letter and took it outside. He handed it to Nicholas Herkimer who, with Edward Wall, was talking with Joseph Brant. Herkimer and Brant had been acquainted for many years. The militia colonel looked at Johnson in a penetrating manner and then dipped his head.

"I will see to it the committee gets this at once. I trust you will be successful in convincing your Indians to remain neutral during the settlement of our difficulties." Without shaking hands, he turned his glance back to Brant. "I am sure I will be seeing you again." There was no warmth in the remark.

Brant's reply was equally flat. "I'm sure you will, Colonel."

Herkimer and Wall returned to their horses and Wall hissed in an undertone, "Goddammit, we should arrest Johnson and his Tory friends while they're still here in the valley and within reach! Once they get beyond Fort Stanwix they'll be gone for good. We'll *never* get another chance like now."

Herkimer grunted sympathetically. "I broached the same possibility with the committee. I don't think there's any doubt what'll happen when he gets out there." He inclined his head westward. "The committee made two points with which we have to agree, whether or not we like it. We're basically unarmed and they're not. They wouldn't be apt to let themselves be taken, and Brant's savages would almost certainly interfere. More important, the committee says that whatever suspicions we may have of Johnson's ultimate designs, as yet he's committed no act of hostility and such a step by us is neither warranted nor justifiable."[63]

Shortly after the departure of Herkimer and Wall, Johnson and his retinue had packed up and left. Their final stop in the Mohawk Valley had been an overnight stay at Fort Stanwix,[64] on the carrying place between the eastward-flowing Mohawk and the northwestward-flowing Wood Creek. That creek led them into Oneida Lake and then out at the foot of the lake into the Oneida River, which subsequently emptied into the Onondaga River[65] and finally into Lake Ontario. That was the location of Fort Oswego.[66]

Now, stacking the papers of his report to one side, Guy Johnson bent again to his writing. He informed Lord Dartmouth that since his arrival here with Brant and his Mohawks, along with the Butlers and other friends, many hundreds of Indians had assembled and that a grand council was scheduled for the morrow. He would, he wrote, choosing his words very carefully, attempt to determine the temper of the Indians and, if they were of such a mind, to hold them in readiness to raise the hatchet in the King's interest, providing this met with the approval of his Lordship.

Guy Johnson did not normally pussyfoot in his dealings, but he was doing so now and he didn't appreciate the taste of it. He finished the contents of his glass, finding that taste much more to his liking, and decided that henceforth he would be a little stronger in his efforts to lead the Iroquois to a firm commitment of alliance with the Crown. For a little while they would probably accept vague promises, but he really wished that he knew to what degree he could commit the Crown to establish such an alliance. Abruptly he found himself thinking of Sir William Johnson and wondered if he would have approved of how matters had progressed or if he would have handled things differently.

With something of a start he realized that exactly a year ago today Sir William had died.

Guy Johnson sighed deeply and, having completed all he could do tonight, scuffed into the bedroom of his quarters to prepare for bed. Both his daughters had been sleeping poorly since the exodus from Guy Park Manor and he was relieved to find them sleeping soundly. His wife was lying quietly on her back, her eyes closed, and he was glad she was resting. The cross-country journey had been hard on her and the illness that had struck her early during the trip had worsened the farther they traveled. Now he stepped over to her and placed his hand on her brow, then instantly recoiled, shocked. Her flesh was cold. He leaned closer and realized she wasn't breathing.

Mary Johnson — called Polly — the wife of Guy Johnson and daughter of Sir William, was dead.

[*June 12, 1775 — Monday*]

Fourteen hundred and fifty-five Indians, including a majority of the most powerful chiefs of the Iroquois League, listened silently to the words that the various speakers were saying. Considering that Brant was not himself a chief, they paid great heed to what he said, sometimes murmuring or nodding in approval. They digested carefully the comments made by Colonel Butler and Guy Johnson as both men made an effort to explain what the problem was that presently existed between England and her colonies, painting the Whigs as black as they reasonably could and picturing them on the one hand as a mob of unruly children defying a parent and, on the other, as land-hungry speculators who would not be content until they had gobbled up all of the territory of the Iroquois.

"I have heard that they have begun coming among you now, these Rebels," Johnson said, "making great promises of what they will give you and how they will help if you join them against their father, the King. But I ask you to think back: Who has given you what you needed in the past and even up until now, until the Rebels have stopped you from receiving what it is your due to receive? Who has seen to your need for food and weapons, for powder and ball, for cloth and blankets and all the other things so necessary to you? You have seen with your own eyes and heard with your own ears, even felt with your own skins, how these others have treated you in trade, so that you come away without what you need for yourselves and your families.

"What do you think they would do for you if you were to support them in this conflict and they were to win?" he asked. "Do you think they would then remember you and the blood you had shed for them? Do you think they would then reach into their purse and give you what you had bargained to receive?

No! They will give you a bit of bread and a swallow of rum and then they will make horses and oxen of you. With their clever promises they will put you into wheelbarrows with your own consent and roll you away into slavery. Is this what you want?"

The loud negative response had filled the air for a long while and when it died away, it was Brant who spoke to them again.

"I have no rightful tongue to speak for you," he said, "but I can speak for myself. I know in my heart that if Warraghiyagey could be here, even more than Uraghquadirha has done, he would have led you to see that we must honor the covenant we have for so many years had with the King. For myself, I know that now is not the time to break that covenant, but to remain under the King's protection and stand forward and help him in his difficulties, for the war has begun. Just as Warraghiyagey would have assured us, so too has Uraghquadirha assured us that in addition to the King's possessions, our *own* possessions, including our very lands, are in jeopardy, and that we must fight for them and that whatever we lose as a result, the King will make up to us."

Guy Johnson inwardly winced at this. He had not quite gone that far out on a limb with his promises and he wished Joseph had not done so, but he held his tongue because it seemed that Brant was convincing them.

There were some who were not convinced at all. A few of the Oneida chiefs agreed to support the League in its decision if it went against the Rebels, but others were for neutrality. More than half refused to respond at all, maintaining that this was not a proper League council, which, by their laws, must be held at Onondaga where the council fire for the entire League always burned. The small contingent of Tuscaroras on hand said little, but it was clear that when a final decision came, they would lean in the direction the Oneidas took.

A surprise came when Steyawa, the principal chief of the Mohawks, flatly refused to agree to fight the Americans.

"I do not need to tell you, Thayendanegea," he told Brant before the others, "that we Mohawks are closest to the Americans; they are among us and our castle is surrounded by them. Our home is in Canajoharie and that is where I and those of our tribe who will go with me will return to. We will live there in peace."

"My heart hopes you are right, Steyawa," Brant replied, "but my mind says you are wrong. You may return to Canajoharie, but eventually they *will* raise their hands against you and it will be when you are most unable to defend yourself or be helped by the League."

Despite these disappointments, the council was a success. On a tentative basis, contingent on the official League decision that would ultimately be made at Onondaga, the Senecas, Cayugas, Onondagas and Mohawks agreed to fight the Americans on behalf of the English. It was the most unprepossessing declaration of war ever made by these tribes but it was, at least for now, a real commitment.

The great surprise was when the principal chief of the Onondagas, Rozinoghyata,[67] came to his feet, moved with great dignity to the front of the assemblage and then spoke. He said that the chiefs of the Six Nations had long been considering the filling of an office in the League that had been vacant. There were two candidates for this office. One of them was a powerful but sometimes impetuous chief of the Senecas. His name was Gu-cinge[68] and his bravery was unquestioned, his leadership qualities were considerable, his experience was exceptional and his sagacity was consistent except in cases where the very thrill of battle and of death hovering close drove him to take unnecessary risks. But the other candidate had these same qualities without the flaw of impetuosity. In addition, he had a great knowledge of the whites — their ways, their language, their written word — that Gu-cinge did not have. Finally, he was also extremely close to the most important family of whites that had ever dealt with the Iroquois — the Johnsons. The man was, of course, Thayendanegea — Joseph Brant.

The office to which he was now unanimously appointed in the Iroquois League was the second most important office that could be attained. The first was principal chief. The second was war chief.

CHAPTER II

[*July 24, 1775 — Monday*]

IN his elegantly appointed office in London, with here and there religious paintings on the walls and crucifixion icons on bookshelves and desks, the British Secretary of Colonial Affairs and Board of Trade leaned his elbows on his desk, folded his hands in a prayerful attitude, bowed his head and prepared to address God, as he did every morning before beginning his work.

"After all," he had once told his assistant secretary when the matter of piety was under discussion, "how better to commence one's day than to know that God is at one's elbow? How better to make decisions than to decide in the sure knowledge that it has been at the direction of God?"

The Earl of Dartmouth wore his own righteousness as an impregnable suit of armor. Devout Methodist that he was, so great was his evangelical fervor that the King's advisers actually feared letting him too often have audience with the King lest his forceful preachments undermine His Majesty's adherence to the Church of England. No man not himself a clergyman in all of Parliament or the King's court was so pious in his ejaculations, so devout in his conversations with the Almighty.

Now, his day beginning, he uttered the incantation that he knew would make God his ally in all matters to be considered for the good of the empire.

"Heavenly Father," he said, "touch me, Thy servant, with the ability to move all matters before me in honor to Thy grace. Let me today and always be no more than the expression of Thy will. Amen."

Having thus, in a manner of speaking, absolved himself of any guilt for his own decisions, he set about putting into motion the wheels that would light the fires of distrust, hatred, atrocity and murder. He did this in one simple letter to the Superintendent of Indian Affairs for the Northern District in America, Guy Johnson.

Only nineteen days ago he had written a letter to Johnson that laid the foundation for the one he began to write now in swift, sure strokes across the crisp pages of foolscap. That earlier letter had been brief and carried little of the material support Johnson had needed:

Whitehall, July 5th, 1775

Sir,

I have received your letter of the 17th of March, No. 7, and have laid it before the King. The present state of affairs in His Majesty's colonies, in which an unnatural rebellion had broken out, that threatened to overturn the constitution, precludes all immediate consideration in the domestic concerns of the Indians under your protection. Nor is it to be expected that any measure that the King would think fit to take, for redressing the injuries they complain of, respecting their lands, can in the present moment be attended with any effect.

It will be proper, however, that you should assure them in the strongest terms of His Majesty's firm resolution to protect them and preserve them in all their rights, and it is more than ever necessary that you should exert the utmost vigilance to discover whether any artifices are used to engage them in the support of the rebellious proceedings of His Majesty's subjects, to counteract such treachery, and to keep them in such a state of affection and attachment to the King, as that His Majesty may rely upon their assistance in any case in which it may be necessary to require it. . . .

DARTMOUTH

That, of course, had been written when Lord Dartmouth had known of the April 19 affairs at Lexington and Concord but considered them as being rabble-inspired rebellious sentiment easily put down by the strong application of subsequent doses of the King's troops. It was before he learned of the capture of Fort Ticonderoga on Lake Champlain by General Benedict Arnold and Colonel Ethan Allen on May 10 and then the incredible battle of Bunker Hill on June 17. The latter was being called a British victory, but as one member of Parliament had noted sourly, "Any more victories like that and we won't have any men left to carry the news of victory home."

Now, having come to the conclusion that the uprising in the Colonies was not to be a matter simply and quickly put down, Dartmouth had conferred with the King and, as a result of those conferences concluded yesterday, the secretary was now writing to Guy Johnson again in a much more supportive manner and providing the authority needed by Johnson to act. Several pages of the crisp paper were filled with the secretary's bold hand when he set his pen aside, blotted the final page and then reread what he had written.

Whitehall, July 24th, 1775

Sir,

I have already, in my letter to you of the 5th Instant, hinted that the time might possibly come when the King, relying upon the attachment of his faithful allies, the Six Nations of Indians, might be under the necessity of calling upon them for their aid and assistance in the present state in America.

The unnatural rebellion now raging there calls for every effort to suppress it, and the intelligence His Majesty has received of the Rebels having excited the Indians to take part, and of their having actually engaged a body of them in arms to support their rebellion,[69] *justifies the resolution His Majesty has taken of requiring the assistance of his faithful adherents, the Six Nations.*

It is, therefore, His Majesty's pleasure that you do lose no time in taking such steps as may induce them to take up the hatchet against His Majesty's rebellious subjects in America, and engage them in His Majesty's service, upon such plan as shall be suggested to you by General Gage, to whom this letter is sent, accompanied with a large assortment of goods for presents to them upon this important occasion.[70]

Whether the engaging of the Six Nations to take up arms in defence of His Majesty's government is most likely to be effected by separate negotiations with the chiefs, or in a general council assembled for the purpose, must be left to your judgment; but in all events, as it is a service of very great importance, you will not fail to exert every effort that may tend to accomplish it and to use the utmost diligence and activity in the execution of the views I have now the honor to transmit to you.   I am, &c.,

DARTMOUTH

The Minister of Colonial Affairs nodded in approval of his own work, folded the letter and placed it into a packet addressed to General Thomas Gage, supreme commander of His Majesty's forces in North America. Then he sealed the packet with a great glob of scarlet wax into which he impressed the Royal Seal.

"By the grace of God," he murmured. "Amen."

[*October 18, 1775 — Wednesday*]

While the Americans may have made the first definite move toward obtaining an Indian alliance by their application to the Stockbridge Indians and the Oneidas, their successes were piddling in comparison to those of Colonel Johnson.

Having at last received the direction he needed from Lord Dartmouth, along with supplemental and more specific direction from Supreme Commander General Gage, he had made great strides toward effecting what the Lord of

Trade had ordered. The fact that Guy Johnson suddenly had a large supply of excellent presents for the Indians, plus promises of much more to come, was no small inducement to offer.

The death of his wife had taken all levity out of the manner of Guy Johnson and left only a cold, implacable will to destroy those whom he blamed for it — the rebellious inhabitants of Tryon County in particular. To this end he had, since the Indian council held in Oswego the day after Polly's death, in essence been creating an army. Into the hands of John Butler, and to a lesser degree his son Walter, he had put the responsibility of recruiting and arming, in addition to the Senecas, other Indians of the lower Great Lakes region and assembling them at Fort Niagara to receive their presents and instructions. At the same time the Butlers were to welcome into their rather loose little army of Rangers and Tory militia any other Loyalists who were voluntarily coming to help or who were being driven out tarred and feathered and with the cries of "Damned Tory!" ringing in their ears. Colonel Butler was to be commander of this group and his son its lieutenant.

Immediately following this, Johnson, still accompanied by two hundred and twenty of the whites who had left the Mohawk Valley with him, had headed for Montreal to further his gathering of a force. Brant, who went with him partway, along with forty of the Iroquois, was dispatched en route to gather whatever Indians he could and bring them to a rendezvous at Montreal or, if that could not easily be effected, getting them to a state of readiness to join any sort of onslaught that might be launched into the Mohawk Valley.

With or without having Indians to come along with him to Montreal, Brant was to arrive there no later than the latter part of October, prepared for an absence of some months, as Johnson said he had something very special in mind for him.

Arrived at Montreal himself, Johnson placed his two young daughters with friends and then enlisted the aid of a very influential Frenchman by the name of Louis St. Luc de La Corne. A dark-haired, angular man whose features seemed more Indian than European, de La Corne had been Superintendent of Canadian Indians under the French regime. For several years after the French and Indian War his very name had been anathema to the colonists. It was he who was believed to have been responsible for the terrible massacre of troops that had occurred with the surrender of Fort William Henry at the head of Lake George in 1757.[71] After the capitulation of the French and their relinquishing Canada to the British, because of de La Corne's influence with the Canadian tribes, Sir William Johnson had, in the face of considerable opposition, enlisted him to work in his Indian department with Daniel Claus. It had proven a good arrangement and de La Corne, whose own roots were now deeply established in Canadian soil, had worked for the British ever since. Louis St. Luc de La Corne, aided by his son-in-law, Major William Campbell,

was now to gather and organize the northern Indians as a force for the King.
He, too, was to have them rendezvous at Montreal. Daniel Claus, who was
part of the retinue that left the Mohawk Valley with Johnson, at this time left
his family with Guy, detached from the party and went with de La Corne to aid
him.

Now, in writing to Lord Dartmouth about the situation at hand, Guy Johnson, who had not yet submitted the lengthy report he had begun writing at Fort
Oswego, recapitulated in abbreviated form the many difficulties and embarrass-
ments experienced in the Mohawk Valley prior to his departure under a false
premise, then continued:

. . . and having then received secret instructions from General Gage respecting
the measures I had to take, I left home the last of that month and, by the help of
a body of white men and Indians, arrived with great difficulty at Ontario [72]
where, in a little time, I assembled 1,455 Indians and adjusted matters with
them in such a manner that they agreed to defend the communication and assist
His Majesty's troops in their operations.

The beginning of July, I set out for this place, [73] with a chosen band of them,
and Rangers to the number of 220 (not being able to get any craft or even
provisions for more) and arrived here the 17th of July, and soon after convened a
body of the northern confederacy, to the amount of 1,700 and upwards, who entered into the same arrangement, notwithstanding they had declined coming in
some time before on Governor Guy Carleton's requisition, their minds having
been corrupted by New England emissaries. . . .

Johnson stopped and looked at the figures, nodding in mute approval. His
Lordship would be impressed. With the additional warriors pledged from the
Iroquois League when Brant's appeared at Montreal three days ago, this was
now a total of 3,280 Indians committed to assist the King. [74]

Guy Johnson chuckled as he bent back to the letter and began to explain to
the secretary what he had in mind now for Joseph Brant, the new Iroquois
League war chief.

[October 20, 1775 — Friday]

While on the surface of things professing to be making no effort to recruit Indians in the cause against the King, the American colonists were still trying to
winnow alliance and not having a great deal of success except where the
Oneidas were concerned. Because of the ramifications involved, that was a
momentous exception.

Only a few weeks after Guy Johnson's departure from the Mohawk Valley,
delegates of the German Flats District of Tryon County, along with some from

Albany County, held a council with the Oneidas and Tuscaroras. Even a few of the Mohawks remaining at Canajoharie were there.

The speech by the delegates was begun with the usual protocol of expressing delight in the opportunity to communicate sentiments in friendship and to once more renew the covenant chain of peace and brotherly love. Then they expressed dismay that Colonel Guy Johnson had departed, for who then was there to protect the rights of the Indians?

"We did him no harm," they told the assemblage, "and you well know that none of us ever did and, you may depend on it, there was no such thing meant against him. He told our people he was going up to Cosby's Manor to hold a council fire with our brothers, the Six Nations, there. We gave him provisions to give to you there, everything he wanted that we had. But now he is gone away from among us and he has told some of our people that he will come back with company which will not please us. If true, his intentions are very bad, but he should know that we don't care what kind of force he may bring against us."

The voices droned on and at the end of the day presents were distributed to the Indians and they were invited, as friends, to attend a larger and more important council to be held at Albany with the commissioners on August 23. If they came, they would receive gifts and they would not be asked to fight against the King.

In addition to agreeing to come, the Oneidas promised they would communicate to the other tribes of the Iroquois League what a great mistake they were making and encourage them to turn their backs on those who were advocating that they raise their hatchets in behalf of a King on the other side of an ocean who cared nothing about his subjects except for what tribute could be exacted from them.

In the interval between this council and the one in August, Colonel Ethan Allen was busy moving through the New York wilderness and wherever he was encountering Indians — and he was encountering many of them — offering money, blankets, tomahawks, scalping knives, paints and anything else there was in the army "to help me fight the King's troops." Mostly they refused, professing a desire to remain neutral. Some agreed to fight for him but took his presents and disappeared. None went with him.

It was Major General Philip Schuyler, commander of the Northern Department of the Continental Army, who held the Indian council at Albany in August. He was largely disappointed with the turnout. Seven hundred Indians showed up, including about thirty Mohawks from Canajoharie led by old Steyawa, but mostly they were only the Oneidas and Tuscaroras again, plus a contingent who said they represented the Seven Nations of Canada. There was also a handful of Caughnawagas.

In addition to General Schuyler, representing the Congress was Colonel Oliver Wolcott, Colonel Turbott Francis, Commissioner Volkert P. Douw and the missionaries James Dean and Samuel Kirkland. For seven days the talks continued but what it all boiled down to was "A Speech to the Six Confederate Nations," as formulated in July by the Continental Congress. It tended to ramble a great deal and much of it was phrased in the sort of symbolism the Congress felt would make greater sense to the audience, but what it said in essence was that the King was oppressing the Colonies, that there was now a contest being waged to relieve this oppression and that the Indians should not be concerned in it.

"This is a family quarrel between us and Old England," the speech said, reiterating a line that was becoming stale with its familiarity. "You Indians are not concerned in it. We don't wish you to take up the hatchet against the King's troops. We desire you to remain at home and not join either side, but keep the hatchet buried deep."

For three days following the speech the Indians digested and discussed what was said and at the end of that time, the unanimous reply was given that they would not support the King, nor would they raise their hatchets against the colonists or the King's soldiers.

Then, astoundingly, the aged Steyawa — Little Abraham — to whom the commissioners had accorded the respect due his station as principal chief of the Mohawks, made a statement that was greeted with great excitement and pleasure by the whites but that he had no right to make.

"Attend to what I say," he told them, "and let your ears listen closely to our words. We have fully considered this matter and this then is the determination of the Six Nations: The Iroquois League will not take any part in the struggle. As it is a family affair between you and your father across the great sea, we will sit still and see you fight it out."

Perhaps Steyawa, remembering the greatness of his brother Tiyanoga, hoped to become as great. Perhaps he felt that as one of the more venerable old chiefs of the Iroquois League his commitment on behalf of the League would be carried. Whatever the case, it was a serious error.

After the council had broken up, Steyawa and his small band of Mohawk followers joined with the principal chief of the Oneidas, Skenando,[75] and his three hundred and sixty Oneida warriors, and Sequatto, chief of the Tuscaroras, and his one hundred and twenty warriors, and they all went directly to the annual Grand Council being held, as always, in Onondaga at the time of the Council Fire of the Harvest Moon.

There, though many of the chiefs were missing from this council, having gone with Thayendanegea to Montreal, the Iroquois League learned the enormity of what Steyawa had done. They were stunned and, one by one as their turns came to speak, the chiefs unanimously denounced Steyawa for his action as well as the Oneidas and their wards, the Tuscaroras, for acting in a manner affecting the League as a whole without League vote or sanction. The denunciations were bitter, scathing, and ranged from the eloquent and powerful remarks of the youngest of the chiefs, the Seneca Red Jacket, to the stuttering Araghi, subchief of the Onondagas, who was speaking on behalf of the absent Rozino-ghyata.

The words had struck Steyawa as if they were clubs and when the castigation of him was all finished, he stepped forward slowly to the council fire and stared deeply into the coals. This was the great council fire ignited over two hundred and fifty years ago through the efforts of Hiawatha and the ruddy glow of it etched even deeper the lines of his face. He raised both bony hands high over his head and shouted:

"There is no more Iroquois League!"

With that he kicked the fire apart before their amazed eyes and, though his legs and feet were severely burned, did not stop until all the coals were scattered and the living fire was out. Then, even the coals were extinguished as a sudden heavy rain began falling.

It was the worst omen in Iroquois history.

[*November 11, 1775 — Saturday*]

The surprise Colonel Guy Johnson had in store for Joseph Brant was a large one indeed — he was taking the Iroquois war chief to England. Thirty of Johnson's white followers from the Mohawk Valley were also going, some of them planning not to return. Brant was the only Indian.

This morning the entire party, well bundled up against the bitterness of a raw wind, moved in haste down the steep incline from the fortifications of Quebec's upper town to the wharves of the lower town. They were four days ahead of schedule in boarding the ship *Adamant*, which lay faintly creaking and groaning with the relentless tugging of a powerful river that had been whipped into a heavy chop by the wind. The morning was bleak, dark gray. Occasional little particles of snow stung their faces. There was no levity in the party, only furtive and apprehensive glances cast toward the distant south shore of the St. Lawrence where, incredibly, the Rebel army under General Benedict Arnold was poised to attack.

The events of the preceding weeks had an unreal quality to them so far as Johnson was concerned and now all he wished for was the casting off of the lines and unfurling of sails to let this beastly wind thrust them away. While the others, including Daniel Claus along with his family and Gilbert Tice, disappeared below to their quarters, Johnson and Brant lingered at the quarterdeck rail, listening to the harsh commands being called by the *Adamant's* captain,

Brook Watson, and the activities of the crew as they obeyed, preparing for departure. The situation here at Quebec looked as bleak as the weather and the two men at the rail reflected in their own minds on how it had all come about.

Immediately after concluding the council with the Indians at Albany, Major General Philip Schuyler had set out for Ticonderoga and arrived there on August 30, very ill with terrible rheumatic pains and accompanying fever and nausea. There he'd found that Brigadier General Richard Montgomery had already gone, heading north to strike Montreal. Miserable though he was feeling, Schuyler nevertheless followed the next morning, overtook Montgomery on the morning of September 4 and assumed command.

From intelligence he'd received, Schuyler was convinced the Canadian residents were smarting every bit as much as the American colonists under the yoke of the British and that, with encouragement, they would defect. He drafted a message to the populace, addressing them sympathetically, telling them that under orders from General Washington and the Continental Congress, he was en route to expel the British who wished to enslave their countrymen. The Continental Congress, he wrote them, could not conceive "that anything but the force of necessity could induce you tamely to bear the insult and ignominy that is daily imposed on you, or that you could calmly sit by and see those chains forging which are intended to bind you, your posterity and ours, in one common and eternal slavery." He concluded by saying he would cherish the Canadians and sacredly guard their property, then placed the message in the hands of Ethan Allen and John Brown to take it to Chambly and deliver it to a merchant named James Livingston, who was a friend and who would see that its contents were broadcast.

The following morning, September 5, the army embarked down the swift Richelieu River and by three in the afternoon the fortifications of St. Johns became visible. They beached their boats two miles away and began an advance by land through a tangled swamp, gloating among themselves about how easy this was all going to be.

They had reckoned without the new Iroquois war chief.

Brant, leading a hundred shrieking Indians, their faces bedaubed in frightening patterns with war paint and moving in conjunction with a small body of whites under Captain Gilbert Tice, abruptly attacked the advancing army. Almost immediately the Americans had eight men killed and another eight wounded. Tice was wounded too, though not badly. The Rebels entrenched themselves and withstood an irregular bushfire until the fort's artillery began pounding them, when they withdrew a mile. The next morning, being finally apprised of the enemy's strength, Schuyler groaned and retreated toward Île aux Noix.

Brant and Tice carried the good news to Montreal, but the story became somewhat enlarged and what was little more than a skirmish became a major affair; the story told the grand tidings of how sixty Indians, fighting for the King, had beaten fifteen hundred Americans, killing forty and wounding thirty and then, without a single casualty of their own, putting the rest to flight. In celebration of the great victory, a grand mass with a Te Deum was sung and those Canadians who had contemplated joining Schuyler now abstained. And there was jubilation among the Iroquois for having so wisely named Thayendanegea their war chief.

By September 15, Schuyler's illness had become so bad that he was forced to put Montgomery back in command and himself head for home. Montgomery, swift to seize opportunity, at once turned right around and the next day laid siege to St. Johns, now much less well defended by a relatively small garrison under British Major William Preston. Montgomery also ordered Ethan Allen to move ahead and recruit Canadians.

Allen was a gigantic man and much more the backwoods frontiersman than the military strategist he pictured himself as being.[76] Broad-shouldered and tall, quite lean and straight and extremely powerful, he was reputed to be "the best goddamned cusser this side of Hell!"

When he had helped to take Ticonderoga last May 10, pitiable structure that it was at the time, it was the high point of his career and added enormously to an already insufferable egotism. Now, having collected a large number of Canadians, he was at Longueuil, across the river from Montreal, and suddenly struck with the thought of the glory that would be his if he were to take the town.

Allen's plans were dampened somewhat by the almost immediate desertion of eighty of the Canadians he'd gathered, but abruptly he encountered John Brown, who had been sent on a mission similar to his own and who had two hundred men. Allen laid out his idea and Brown fell in with it. They divided their force with the idea of having Brown's detachment cross the St. Lawrence above Montreal and Allen's below. At a signal from Brown, they were simultaneously to attack the poorly guarded Montreal from both sides. On the night of October 24 they crossed over, but Allen had so few canoes that it took three trips to get his men across. They went into hiding on the north shore and, with the dawn, waited for Brown's signal. It never came.

Before sunrise the news had hit Montreal with thunderbolt force that the "New Hampshire Horror," Colonel Ethan Allen, was just outside the walls with a small army. Instantly Governor-General Guy Carleton ordered the drums beaten and a party of less than forty soldiers, supported by about two hundred Canadian volunteers and Indians under Brant, poured out of Montreal's Quebec gate.

To his credit, Allen was prepared to make a stand of it and fight, but his flankers abandoned him and he had no recourse except an attempt at retreat. He had insufficient canoes to retreat across the river and, to his abject mortification, he was caught by an eighteen-year-old halfbreed Mohawk named Peter Warren Johnson — the son of Sir William Johnson and Molly Brant.[77]

With the siege of the fort at St. Johns well entrenched and the threat of its possible success overhanging Montreal, Guy Johnson and his party moved on, accompanied by Brant alone of the Indians, to Quebec. Ethan Allen and his fellow captives went with them under the rough treatment of the impeccably clad Brigadier General Richard Prescott, who looked with revulsion upon this unkempt colonial dressed in a dirty deerskin double-breasted jacket and undervest, rough sagathy breeches, shoes of hobnailed cowhide and a hat of red wool.

Prescott had been in a fury with Allen after the capture. Brandishing his cane, he called him some hard names for his having participated in the capture of Ticonderoga last May, but Allen didn't flinch. Instead, he growled, "Hit me with that cane and this" — he shook his balled fist — "will be mortality for you!" At this, some other officers interceded and Prescott spun around and ordered that a few Canadians among those captured with Allen be bayoneted. Instantly Allen leaped between them and the soldiers, offering himself as a target and shouting, "I'm to blame, not them!"

General Prescott had momentarily been taken aback, but he had the last word. "I'll not execute you now," he said, "but, goddamn you, you'll swing from a gallows at Tyburn!"

He meant it, and there was no way he was going to permit any possibility of escape. He had Allen handcuffed and then shackled at his legs to an eight-foot metal bar to which thirty-pound weights were attached. It was in this condition that Ethan Allen, along with the others, had arrived in Quebec.

The departure of Guy Johnson's party for England had been scheduled for November 15, but the war situation had become worse. On November 2, after a siege that had lasted fifty-five days, Major Preston at St. Johns capitulated to General Montgomery and three days later Montgomery marched his force to take Montreal. Even more frightful for those at Quebec, the army of General Benedict Arnold, having moved up the Kennebec River from the Atlantic, had appeared on the south shore of the St. Lawrence, across from Quebec and just upstream from Point Levis. Last night Arnold had planned to cross the river in the morning and attack,[78] but the assault had to be postponed because the weather had changed to this stormy, whipping wind that presently tore at the two men standing at the quarterdeck rail of the *Adamant*, watching the gap of water widen between themselves and Quebec.

"It's cold, Joseph," Johnson said at last, breaking the reverie of both. "Let's go below."

They went to their quarters, paying little attention to a hatchway they passed that led to the bowels of the ship. That passage led to an enclosed area of white oak planking about twenty feet long and two feet wide. Inside were thirty-four handcuffed prisoners, including Colonel Ethan Allen, still wearing his frontier garb. He'd be wearing it for a long time to come. The journey to Falmouth would take forty-six days.

In their cabins, Brant and Johnson settled in for the long, cold Atlantic crossing. They, of course, had no way of knowing that at this precise moment Governor-General Guy Carleton, under fire from the American shore batteries, was in the process of abandoning Montreal.[79]

[December 9, 1775 — Saturday]

In the Mohawk Valley, the only really bright spot of this entire year for Sir John Johnson had been the birth of his son, named William after his illustrious grandfather. That event took place when Mary Watts Johnson went into a slightly premature labor shortly after the departure of Guy Johnson.

Guy had conferred with John and urged him to come along with him but, with Mary in her advanced state of pregnancy, she could not go and John refused to leave her, even in the knowledge that she was probably in no danger. So, with Guy's reluctant acceptance of his decision, he had stayed on at Johnson Hall and watched fearfully the rising militancy of his former neighbors against him.

It was not terribly unexpected when the colonists deposed the Tryon County sheriff, Alexander White, and sent "that damned Tory sympathizer" to prison in Albany and installed in his stead an ardent Whig, Colonel John Frey. But after news arrived of the June 17 battle at Bunker Hill in Boston, the abusiveness of the neighbors became more pronounced and Sir John, as Guy had done at Guy Park Manor, fortified Johnson Hall and surrounded it with a couple of hundred well-armed Scottish Highlanders. There was continuous friction between them and the Mohawk Valley residents during the remainder of the summer.

A chain of events was begun as a result of that friction during the first week of September. The Tryon County Committee of Safety penned a letter to the New York Provincial Congress, complaining:

There is a great number of proved enemies against our association and the regulations thereof, who are proceeding in and about Johnstown at Kingsborough under the direction and order of Sir John Johnson, being Highlanders, amounting to 200 men, according to intelligence. We are daily scandalized by them, provoked and threatened, and we must surely expect a havoc of them upon our families if we should be required and called elsewhere for the defence of our coun-

try's cause. The people on our side are not willing that the Committee should proceed so indulgently any longer. We have great suspicions, and are almost assured, that Sir John has a continual correspondence with Colonel Guy Johnson and his party.

As a matter of fact, the Committee of Safety was exactly right. A steady flow of Indians came to Johnson Hall to "pay respects" to the family of the great Warraghiyagey, with messages hidden in the hollow handles of their tomahawks or sometimes in the ornamental shells they wore about their necks or dangling from their ears. They came from Montreal and the concealed messages were from Guy Johnson and Daniel Claus and John Butler.

The situation further degenerated when, seven weeks later, the committee wrote to Johnson himself, sending a copy to the Provincial Congress:

Tryon County Committee Chamber
October 26th, 1775

Honourable Sir.

As we find particular reason to be convinced of your opinion in the questions hereafter expressed, we request that you'll oblige us with your sentiments thereupon in a few lines by our messengers, the bearers hereof, Messrs. Ebenezer Cox, James M'Master, and John J. Klock, members of our Committee.

We wish to know whether you will allow the inhabitants of Johnstown and Kingsborough to form themselves into companies, according to the regulations of the Continental Congress, for the defense of our country's cause; and whether your Honour would be ready himself to give his personal assistance to the same purpose; also whether you pretend a prerogative to our county courthouse and jail, and would hinder or interrupt the Committee making use of the same to our want and service in the common cause.

We do not doubt you will comply with our reasonable request, and thereby oblige. . . .

The fury of Sir John upon reading the letter was prodigious. Those damned Rebels were going too far, even to the point of seeking his approval for jailing — *in his jail* — loyal friends of the King!

His reply, written early in November, showed remarkable restraint under the circumstances:

As to embodying my tenants, I never did or would forbid them, but you may save yourselves further trouble on that head, as I know my tenants will not consent.

Concerning myself, sooner than lift my hand against my King, or sign any association with those who would, I should suffer my own head to be cut off.

As to the court-house and jail, I would not deny the use of it for the purpose for which it was built, but they are my property until I shall be refunded £700.

I have further heard that two-thirds of the people of Canajoharie and German Flats have been forced to sign the association or else bear unspoken consequences. . . .

The committee pounced with glee on the last remark and replied by messenger that Sir John's source for the information had obviously spared the truth, since it was of itself ridiculous that one-third could have forced two-thirds to sign. Nevertheless, there was a faint bit of wrist-slapping — as well as approval — of the committee by the Provincial Congress in the letter they wrote to the committee today:

Albany, Dec. 9th, 1775

Sirs:

The Congress have this day entered into the consideration of your letter of the 26th of October, and are of the opinion that your application to Sir John Johnson, requesting an answer from him whether he would allow his tenants to form themselves into companies and associate with their brethren of your county according to the resolves of the Continental Congress for the defence of our liberties, was improper with respect to him, and too condescending on your part, as it was a matter that came properly within your province; and to which we doubt not but you are competent, as you have a line of conduct prescribed to you by Congress.

With respect to your second question, whether he would take any active part in the controversy at present existing between Great Britain and her colonies, we conceive it to be very proper and thank you for your information on that head.

As to the third question, we conceive that he has no claim or title to the court-house and jail in your county, as we are credibly told that his father, Sir William Johnson, did in his lifetime convey the same to two gentlemen, in trust for the use of your county. However, as an attempt to use the same for the purpose of confining persons inimical to our country may be productive of bad consequences, we beg leave to recommend to you to procure some other place which may answer the end of a jail; and we give you our advice not to molest Sir John as long as he shall continue inactive and not impede the measures necessary to be carried into execution from being completed.

Accepting the "advice," the Tryon County committee secured a private house to serve as a place of confinement for those whose fervor for the King became too strongly expressed and in some cases prisoners were sent to Albany and Hartford.

The Province of New York had so long been under the strong influence of the Johnson family that it could not now seem to raise its hand against Sir John and was content to leave him alone, an openly averred advocate of the enemy, as long as he behaved himself.

The commanding officer of the Northern Department of the Continental Army was not so magnanimous. On learning the contents of the letter by Congress today, he slammed his hand down on his desk with such force that it was like a gunshot and startled his aide so badly he accidentally pinched his fingers in a desk drawer.

"Damn them!" Philip Schuyler raged. "There is nothing in this world so blind as a politician! John Johnson is the most dangerous man in this country right now — and I don't mean just to New York. That makes him the concern of the Continental Army." He shot a look at the aide, who was wincing quietly with the pain in his fingers. "Write a letter to Colonel Herkimer at German Flats. Tell him I'll be coming for a confrontation with Johnson the first week of January and I want him on hand with his militia — in force. We're going to pluck Mr. Johnson's feathers."

[*December 27, 1775 — Wednesday*]

The arrival of the *Adamant* at Falmouth, England, this morning created a considerable stir. Crowds gathered quickly to see the notables who were disembarking. There was Colonel Guy Johnson, successor to Sir William Johnson in America and, with him in his quaint native clothing, an Indian. And there, too, was a ferocious-looking giant of a man in filthy bizarre garb, unshaven and smelly and wild-looking, chained at the head of over thirty other men, and almost instantly the word spread that this was the notorious Ethan Allen and his henchmen!

For their part, those who disembarked on this surprisingly beautiful sunshiny day — a rarity at this time of year — paid little heed to the crowd and entered the carriages that were provided for them. They were tired of the voyage and glad to be on land again. Many of them had been violently ill on the crossing and it would be some days before the sense of sea motion dissipated. But the journey ahead on land was also long and hard — over two hundred and fifty miles before London would be reached.

And now, for the first time, Joseph Brant began to understand fully the might of the British Empire.

[*January 7, 1776 — Sunday*]

The deposing of Sir John Johnson of all but his title had been swiftly and methodically completed. So little warning of its impending occurrence had come to Sir John that he was wholly unprepared. The first he knew of the approach of anyone was when some of his Highlanders reported to him in Johnson Hall that a couple of companies of Continental troops under command of General Schuyler had arrived in the area. [80] On the ice of the Mohawk River just south of Johnson Hall, the small force had been joined by three thousand militiamen under Colonel Nicholas Herkimer. This was particularly galling, since Sir John was nominally brigadier general of the militia and had not been informed of any activity occurring.

The force headquartered itself at Major Douw Fonda's place [81] not far from Johnson Hall and from here, with Fonda himself becoming the go-between, a series of spirited messages passed between Schuyler and Sir John. Schuyler was in no way polite. He stated flatly that Sir John's fortifications and preparations indicated "designs of the most dangerous tendency to the rights, liberties, property and even lives" of the patriots of the Mohawk Valley. He further wrote:

I call upon you, Sir, to surrender yourself, your guard, all weapons and military stores at once. You have my word that neither you nor Lady Johnson shall be molested in any manner if you comply at once.

Johnson protested vehemently, at the same time hurriedly burying in the garden Johnson Hall's store of sterling silver dinnerware, candelabra and other precious items along with his own personal papers, many of which were undoubtedly incriminating. [82] He had no choice but to surrender and he, along with his retainers at Fort Johnson, ceded, blustering about the indignity. Schuyler was unmoved. He ordered Lady Johnson taken into protective custody in Albany and housed in a private home under unostentatious guard. Sir John he ordered to be escorted to the Continental Army depot far down the Hudson River at Fishkill for confinement. In addition, all known or suspected Tories of the Mohawk Valley were now rounded up and confined, their property confiscated.

There was no longer any doubt that the entire Mohawk Valley was in support of the rebellion and now voices suddenly became stronger that the aim of the rebellion should not merely be, as it had been until now, for the gaining of certain rights and freedoms, but continuing as colonies under the aegis of England. [83] Rather, that it should be for the establishment of an entirely *independent* country comprised of united states.

It was a breathtaking concept.

[*March 20, 1776 — Wednesday*]

Joseph Brant created a sensation in London.

There was no doubt that the Mohawk chief was virtually as much on everyone's tongue as the King himself. Hardly an issue of any London newspaper appeared without a few interesting stories about him. He was in tremendous demand for parties and was afforded an enormous amount of respect. It was as if the entire city were bending over backward in an effort to make amends for the insult that had been given him on his arrival, even though Brant himself had not accepted it in that light.

On their arrival in London, Guy Johnson, Daniel Claus, Gilbert Tice and others of the party had been given posh accommodations close to Whitehall. The "Indian with Colonel Johnson," whose identity was not immediately known, was lodged at an out-of-the-way inn called The Swan with Two Necks, located in Lad Lane. When the realization dawned that this rather ordinary-looking Indian was, in fact, the war chief of the Six Nations, whose alliance with England in the present war of rebellion could be of paramount importance in winning that conflict, there was momentary horror at the faux pas that had been committed in putting him up at what might generously be called less than mediocre lodgings.

Immediately apologies were made to Brant and he was offered a choice of very fine lodgings. He refused them in a pleasant manner, saying that the proprietor of The Swan with Two Necks and his wife had been so kind to him that he wouldn't think of staying anywhere else. Overnight the inn became a landmark and was very soon catering to the elite of the social set.

While Guy Johnson was busy conferring with the British Secretary of State, Lord George Germain, who was also Lord Dartmouth's successor, Brant was being kept well entertained. He was, for several days, the guest of James Boswell and London's finest portraitist stunned everyone by putting in abeyance the projects upon which he was working — something he had never been known to do before — and he quickly completed a fine portrait of Brant.

Everything Brant did or said was of interest and his steps were dogged — discreetly, of course — by a corps of reporters from both magazines and newspapers. Their stories were less than literarily memorable: The Indian chief Brant speaks English very well and even writes in a tolerable hand; Brant wears mostly ordinary English clothing and he is really in no way outstanding in either looks or bearing; Brant, asked what musical instrument he likes, replies, "I like the harpsichord well, the organ better, but the drum and trumpet best of all, for they make my heart beat quick."

The article that appeared in *London Magazine*, accompanied by an engraving of Brant, was typical of the pieces appearing about him:

This chief has not the ferocious dignity of a savage leader, nor does he discern any extraordinary force of mind or body. . . . His manners are gentle and quiet, and to those who study human nature he affords a very convincing proof of the tameness which education can produce on the wildest race. . . . He is struck by the appearance of London in general, but he says he chiefly admires the women and the horses.

That he was thinking about what lay ahead when he would return to America was evident in his purchase of a heavy gold ring, upon which he had his own name deeply engraved. "Should I fall in battle," he told a London reporter, "then this ring will prove my identity. I have put it on now and I will not take it off hereafter." [84]

A number of important meetings were attended by Brant while in London, but the most important one was with Lord George Germain. It was held today, just after the departure for America of Major General John Burgoyne with a large reinforcement, whose immediate objective was to put an end to the ongoing siege of Quebec and win back Montreal. [85]

The Secretary of State was extremely pleased that the Six Nations — except for a few dissenting Oneidas and Tuscaroras — were throwing their might to the Crown. His Majesty, Germain assured Brant, would never be ungrateful for this. And, while Lord Germain may not have explicitly said the words, Brant left the meeting with the strong understanding in his own mind to pass on to his people on his return that the Iroquois alliance with the British meant, ultimately, the assurance of British rule in North America. Further, the assurance was implicit that after such a British victory, the Empire would help see to it that all Indian tribes in North America not then subjugated to the Iroquois would become so. With the great power of the Iroquois League having been on the wane for so many years, that was a tremendous carrot to dangle before the eyes of its war chief.

[*October 1, 1776 — Tuesday*]

The fortunes of war that had been going so relatively well for the Northern Department of the Continental Army took an abrupt about-face with the arrival of Burgoyne and his reinforcements at Quebec. Almost immediately the Americans lifted their siege of Quebec and withdrew, but not before General Montgomery was killed by a bullet through his head.

Montreal was quickly reoccupied by the British and once again Governor-General Guy Carleton made it his headquarters. Carleton sent Burgoyne to recapture Fort Chambly and Fort St. John, but the Americans evacuated both without resistance. A small battle took place at the Cedars, a point of land extending far out into the St. Lawrence River about thirty miles upstream from Montreal, where the Americans had a fortified post with Major Isaac Butterfield commanding. The British had about one hundred and fifty men, Canadian and English, under Captain Thomas Forster, plus five hundred Indians, mainly of northern tribes. It was an intimidating force and Butterfield was definitely intimidated. He surrendered without much of a fight. An American reinforcement under Major Henry Sherburne put up a strong resistance when ambushed, but they were overrun and taken. [86]

The Americans, driven out of Quebec and Montreal, the Cedars and Chambly and St. Johns, retreated to Ticonderoga, followed by the British as far as Crown Point. Burgoyne and Major General William Phillips both wanted to attack Ticonderoga but Carleton refused to let them do so, aware that the once paltry defenses there had recently been greatly strengthened by the famed Polish engineer Colonel Thaddeus Kosciuszko.

While all this was occurring, Sir John Johnson was finding himself in a very ticklish situation. Though under the orders of General Schuyler he had been taken to Fishkill and detained there a short time, he was quickly paroled on his own recognizance and advised to return home and remain removed from any further activities supportive of the King. As a measure to insure this, Lady Mary Johnson was also released from confinement in Albany to be with her husband at Johnson Hall.

Sick inside with frustration and a deep-rooted anger at his Mohawk Valley neighbors who had done this to him, Sir John for the first time in his thirty-two years had a goal upon which he fully intended to concentrate all his energies: He mentally vowed a great vengeance upon them. Returned to Johnson Hall, he knew he was under constant surveillance and so he left alone those things that had been buried in the garden and at once began as surreptitiously as possible attempting to find and gather around him again a body of men loyal to the King. There were not many left, but he did manage to collect about thirty. He was also able to convince about half of the remaining fifty or sixty Mohawks at Canajoharie to pledge themselves to him. By this time word of his activities had reached General Schuyler, who shook his head in exasperation and dispatched Colonel Elias Dayton to "go arrest that damned fool again!"

It wasn't to be. Friends of Johnson's in Albany sent a warning and as Colonel Dayton's detachment arrived via the King's Highway on the eastern edge of Johnstown, Sir John and his collection of tenants, retainers and Indians fled north. Once again Johnson left something of importance behind — his wife. Taken suddenly ill, she was unable to travel, and since Johnson was very poorly equipped for what lay ahead, chances were she couldn't survive the trip. When Colonel Dayton arrived at Johnson Hall, he found only Mary Watts Johnson and her infant son, William, in the care of a few slaves. Once again she was taken to Albany for confinement as a hostage to encourage Sir John not to do anything drastic.

Whatever drastics Sir John had in mind would have to wait a little while. With the Mohawks leading the way and living the best they could on extremely meager rations, Sir John and his party moved overland northward and slightly eastward to Great Scanandaga Lake and then through the wilderness until they encountered Lake Champlain below Crown Point. By the time they had traveled down the lake to Richelieu and at last reached Montreal, they had traveled for nearly three weeks and were in deplorable condition. But more than ever, Sir John Johnson knew he was going to make them pay.[87]

Far to the south at Albany, the New York Provincial Congress sent a report of Sir John's violation of his parole to General George Washington, began considering who should be named commanding general of the Tryon County Militia and then confiscated Johnson Hall and sold it at auction.

[*September* 5, 1776 — *Thursday*]

There was a sense of impending disaster throughout all of the frontier areas — Virginia, Pennsylvania and New York in particular. It was as if great forces were testing their muscles and baring their teeth to spring ripping and tearing at unprotected undersides. They were.

Along with this chilling sensation there was equally a feeling of great joy in the same areas — a joy inspired by a momentous declaration made on the fourth day of July: a declaration that, come what might, finally severed the long, convoluted umbilical cord that had bound the American colonies to Great Britain; a declaration hailed with uncontained enthusiasm and an unmitigated willingness to maintain it with lives and fortunes; a declaration that proudly bespoke the formation of a brand-new country calling itself the United States of America.

A declaration of independence.

The sobering knowledge was there, however, that though some of the Iroquois had professed a willingness to remain neutral in the war and some had even offered to help the new country, the majority of the Six Nations had taken up the hatchet in behalf of the King. Any doubt of it had been put to rest at the Battle of the Cedars. Here and there on the frontier, people were beginning to disappear, occasional scalped bodies were found, now and then an outlying house was burned. But these were only portents, mere samplings of what was to come, and everybody knew it. No one felt prepared.

In the Wyoming Valley of the Susquehanna River in northern Pennsylvania, a committee of inspection was established throughout the whole area for the protection of the inhabitants, but it didn't do much to settle the growing fears. The area was dangerously exposed to attack. The Indians were known to be a little farther upriver at Tioga and in their swift canoes they could descend to Wyoming in less than twenty-four hours if they chose to.

Now it was resolved by the Continental Congress that two companies of Continental troops be raised in Wyoming "and stationed in proper places for the defense of the inhabitants of said town and parts adjacent, till further orders of Congress." The Wyoming inhabitants were jubilant, but they should have paid more attention to that final clause. As prescribed by the congressional resolution, Wyoming immediately set about raising the two companies of eighty-two men each for their own defense but then were aghast when those companies, as soon as they were formed, were marched away to aid in the war effort elsewhere. Wyoming was left more vulnerable than ever now, with the cream of its manhood taken away. The cries of protest were loud; it was inconceivable and unconscionable that this, one of the most exposed areas on the entire frontier, should have from five to seven per cent more of its natural protectors taken away than were removed from the population of any other part of the state or nation. The complaint went unheeded.

Fears in New York's Cherry Valley, a dozen miles south of the Mohawk River, were also growing. Not quite so remote a settlement as Pennsylvania's Wyoming, Cherry Valley was nevertheless in a dangerous situation. A principal Indian trail ran directly through it, from the Indian villages of the upper Susquehanna in the southwest — especially the large village of Oquaga [88] — to the Mohawk village of Canajoharie, on the Mohawk just to the northeast. The few Mohawks remaining at Canajoharie under Chief Steyawa were keeping strictly to themselves and had promised neutrality, but the Indians of the villages southward had not.

One of the residents of Cherry Valley, Captain Robert McKean, raised a company of Rangers, but it was the story of Wyoming all over. No sooner were they raised than orders came directing them to go somewhere else and Cherry Valley was more vulnerable than ever. A strong petition was drafted and signed by all the residents of Cherry Valley and sent to the New York authorities, asking protection. It was granted and a company of Rangers under Captain William Winne arrived. The house of Samuel Campbell occupied a rather commanding position on elevated ground and so it was fortified with an encircling embankment of logs and earth. It wasn't much, but it was something. The fears of the residents were not greatly relieved.

During this transitional summer of evolving from a colony to an independent state, the same sense of unrest was evident elsewhere in New York, but especially in Tryon County. Numerous parties of scouts and militia were sent out to patrol the borders and they, with some help from Continental troops, managed to keep the occasional lurking parties of Indians and Tories at a distance. It was quite obvious that better fortification had to be made before the expected trouble arrived.

At Albany, General Schuyler detached Colonel Goose Van Schaick to Johnstown and Colonel Elias Dayton farther up the Mohawk. The militia was called out to help and Dayton, with a notable lack of modesty, built a small fort adjacent to the mouth of West Canada Creek at German Flats, which he named Fort Dayton. [89] He then pushed on to the great carrying place on the Mohawk where the old Fort Stanwix was more or less moldering away and here did a halfhearted job of restoring the place. As if in atonement for his earlier immodesty and no doubt to please his commander, he renamed the place Fort Schuyler, but mostly people still called it Fort Stanwix. [90]

Little by little, Tryon County was girding itself for what might lie ahead. A new Committee of Safety was elected in May and Sheriff John Frey became its chairman. He was also made colonel of the militia. One of the first acts of the new Tryon County Committee of Safety was to instruct all its county delegates to the Provincial Congress to vote for the entire independence of the colonies and this was one of the reasons the news of the Declaration of Independence had created such joy in this area.

By all these preparations, which were occurring here and there, it was almost as if a huge stage were being prepared for a great play and actors being cast for the principal roles. One more preliminary and one more casting were required before the drama could begin and that was taken care of in its session today by the New York Congress:

September 5th, 1776

RESOLVED: That the Militia of Tryon County be formed into a brigade separated from the Militia of Albany; and whereas Nicholas Herkimer, Esq., [91] *is justly entitled to be appointed to Brigadier of the brigade of Militia of Tryon County, as well as from his military rank in that county, as from his great merit and many exertions in the present glorious struggle for liberty, THEREFORE,*

RESOLVED, unanimously, that Nicholas Herkimer, Esq., be appointed Brigadier General of the Militia of Tryon County, and that a commission issue to him accordingly for that purpose.

[*September 23, 1776 — Monday*]

Sir John Johnson had acquired a new strength and purpose. It was as if the rigors of his nineteen-day trek through the wilderness from Johnson Hall to Montreal had hardened him into a better man. His eyes seemed brighter, his chin stronger, his movements surer. He had lost a good bit of weight and it had done him no harm, for there was no longer any flabbiness about him. The crucible of hardship that will often make or break a man had made of Sir John Johnson more of a man than he had ever been before.

As soon as he reached Montreal he had reported to Governor-General Carleton and was commissioned a colonel in the British service. Immediately he was placed in command of two battalions of men, at first called the Royal Regiment of New York and comprised mostly of Presbyterian Scots who had lived near Johnstown and who had preceded Johnson to Canada, accompanied him there or followed shortly afterward. There were also a number of Lutheran Germans among his eight hundred men. This force of Johnson's was provided with green uniforms and immediately the name Royal Regiment of New York was lost and they became known as Johnson's Royal Greens.

Closely associated with Sir John was a tough company of men gathered up under the command of Colonel John Butler who were poorly uniformed, if at all. They were being called Butler's Rangers. Loosely — but not officially — associating themselves with either Johnson or Butler were a large number of disaffected people, driven out of New York, Pennsylvania and New England by the Americans, who had more or less become refugees around the British camps and garrisons. These were the vengeful and undisciplined ones who refused to be placed under the strictures of military discipline. Already they had begun disguising themselves as Indians and, sometimes in company with real Indians or sometimes by themselves, were beginning to attack outlying settlements with increasing degrees of inhumanity. They contended that this was only the bare beginning and that the "damned rebels" would soon be squealing for mercy . . . and finding none.

The preparations being made were not wholly secret to the Americans. A number of proficient spies had infiltrated and were gathering bits and pieces of intelligence to forward to General Schuyler at Albany. Sometimes the best information came from deserters, of which there seemed to be a growing number among the British in Canada, information that usually filtered through Fort Ticonderoga. That was the object of the letter being written to Schuyler this evening in the yellow glow of light from three candles on his desk at that Lake Champlain fort by Lieutenant Colonel Jeduthan Baldwin:

Ticonderoga — 23rd Sept.

Sir.

A sergeant, who deserted from the British army at Point Aux Trembles, between Montreal and Lores the 31st of August last, says that Col. McLane's Regiment was quartered at Point Aux Trembles, 1,200 foreigners are at Quebec and all the 34th Regiment at Montreal except two companies with Colonel Johnson and his Indians at Lachine.

This sergeant contends that he heard the officers compute their army at 7,000, in which were the combined regiments of the 9th, 20th, 21st, 24th, 29th, 31st, 34th and 49th, and also the Germans.

There are none of the Canadians in the King of England's service, but they are in a worse situation than the Children of Israel in Egypt, for the regulars have robbed them of every necessary of late and now compel them to work without any prospect of reward. These Canadians universally wish we were in possession of their country again, declaring that their eyes are now fully opened.

He says also that Burgoyne had a few gondolas, two sloops, and a few floating battery buildings at St. Johns. He added that he frequently heard it said that they would cross the lake to Crown Point as soon as their naval preparations were perfected.

The sergeant said that the troops in general were very sickly, the foreigners in particular being afflicted with the fever and flux.[92] And that 50 of the soldiers had signed an agreement to desert together but, betrayed, were condemned to Senegal for life. . . .

[*December* 30, 1776 — *Monday*]

Joseph Brant stood at his window and gazed out at the town. Though it was not snowing, the late afternoon wind was picking up snow crystals from the ground and they rattled cheerlessly against the glass panes and he pulled the blanket more snugly around himself.

Brant did not like the village of Oquaga as much as he liked his own home at Canajoharie, but he was much happier here than he had been in London. Oquaga was no insignificant village. It had always been rather substantial and, since the outbreak of the Revolution, it had grown quite a bit. Not only were there about three hundred Indians here — mostly Senecas and Cayugas, but with a lesser number of Mohawks and a scattering of Onondagas, Oneidas, Tuscaroras and a few Delawares — there were also about a dozen families of the so-called Tories, mostly from the Mohawk Valley or from the area near Wyoming, who had been driven out by their neighbors. The town now held thirty or forty well-built homes of hewn planks or logs and around eighty large wigwams. One of the better houses was Brant's. He had moved into it only a few months ago and now, established in Oquaga on the right bank of the Susquehanna, he was preparing himself and the Iroquois for what he felt would be one of the most eventful years in their history. During those last few months he had been in London, the time had passed with incredible slowness, largely because he was anxious about his people and longing to be back here, helping them.

He was very glad the waiting to return was over and now the only waiting left was the wait for spring and better weather when raids could be commenced against their enemies. From Oquaga, parties would be able to move out and quickly be back in the midst of the Mohawk Valley to harass the neighbors who had driven them away, then melt into the forests and return to the safety of this place. And, though it was unlikely to occur, if any sort of attack were mounted against Oquaga, a swift downstream journey on the Susquehanna would take them to the mouth of the Chemung River where Tioga was located — an Iroquois stronghold that was considered to be the "south door" of the Iroquois longhouse.

For this winter at hand, the majority of the Iroquois were in their own towns — except for the Mohawks — or else gathering under Colonel John Butler at Fort Niagara.[93] It was over a year since Brant had seen Butler and he had been glad to learn of the safety of this powerful man and his son Walter at Niagara. Probably just about as well as any other white man on the frontier now, since the death of Sir William, John Butler understood the Iroquois and knew how to work with them well. Brant was looking forward to spring when he'd be seeing him again.

The thought of not having seen Butler for so long made Joseph reflect further on his long absence from this country he loved. The prolonged stay in London had lasted until June. Along with Guy Johnson and Captain Gilbert Tice, he had finally returned to Falmouth and boarded the packet ship *Lord Hyde*. The ship was bound for New York City and it cast off on the morning of June 3. With the weather so accommodating, the voyage was a far more pleasant one than had been the case aboard the *Adamant*.

The *Lord Hyde* was not properly a warship but rather a swift, relatively light craft especially well suited for carrying messages, mail and some passengers. Not being a warship, she was not prepared to stand and fight if enemy ships appeared, but rather to flee at a pace faster than the more cumbersome vessels of war could achieve. Several times during the passage they were briefly pursued by Rebel vessels but always outdistanced such pursuit until, emerging from a fog near Bermuda, they found themselves virtually face to face with the American privateer *Warren*, commanded by Captain Richard Cochrane of Boston.

The *Warren* was about the same size as the *Lord Hyde*, but not as swift because it was more heavily armed, having a crew double the size of the *Lord Hyde*'s and carrying fourteen six-pounders and swivels to the packet ship's twelve three-pounders. Before the *Lord Hyde* could swing around and flee, the *Warren* opened fire. For an hour and a half the fight raged, with all the passengers of the *Lord Hyde*, including Brant, helping in the defense, even if it meant no more than shooting small arms. Though the *Lord Hyde* suffered some pretty severe damages, including the loss of a mast and much rigging, plus the surgeon being shot through the leg and five crewmen slightly wounded, it was the *Warren* that finally retreated, utilizing the freshening breeze to outdistance her damaged pursuer. Having thus become the first Iroquois chief in history to participate in a naval engagement at sea, Brant had quickly admitted to Guy Johnson that he much preferred forest warfare.

Guy Johnson was carrying special dispatches for the new supreme commander of His Majesty's forces in North America, General Sir William Howe, and so he stayed aboard ship to await a messenger from the general. Brant and Tice, however, went ashore in a small boat under cover of darkness when the *Lord Hyde* landed at Staten Island on July 29. Brant was dressed in English clothing and looked the part of an ordinary gentleman. Tice was disguised against possible recognition by many who knew him here. Until they reached their separate destinations, Johnson had cautioned them, it was important they not be recognized.

The danger was minimal at first, but shortly after leaving the city and starting the overland trek it became acute and they traveled with great care, moving through the most dense cover, using little-known trails and avoiding cities and towns. Tice's goal was Niagara, to carry messages to John Butler and the Indians there, encouraging them with news of full support of the Crown for their attacks to come against the settlements.

Brant's job was to return to the Mohawk Valley, enlist all the Indians he could who were still maintaining their neutrality and keep them prepared for what was to come. Brant told Johnson he would make his own headquarters at Oquaga and Johnson approved of the choice.

"We'll meet again in spring, Joseph," Johnson said, shaking his hand as the Mohawk and Tice were preparing to leave the *Lord Hyde*.

"In Montreal?" Joseph asked.

"Possibly. Perhaps in Niagara or Oswego. You'll get my message."

Both men got through all right and both accomplished their missions. Tice remained at Niagara for the winter, where Butler was amply providing the Senecas with gunpowder for their winter hunting, and Joseph, after getting promises from at least one hundred more heretofore uncommitted Indians to support the King, had retired with numerous others to his place here at Oquaga.

It hadn't taken long for the word to spread that Joseph Brant was back and once again, as the settlers put it, "the blood-lust was rising in the savages." Although the Indians of Oquaga still moved about easily through the countryside, professing peace, bothering no one and ignoring the malevolent glances sent their way whenever they encountered the American residents, everyone knew that time was running out. True, they had expected 1776 to be a pretty bad year but, under the circumstances, it hadn't been too bad after all. Nonetheless, there was still not a whisper of optimism for "the year of the three sevens," now at hand.

Twilight had begun to fall and Joseph turned away from the window. At the table, where she was making him a pair of calf-high, fur-lined moccasin boots, Wonagh looked up at him and smiled.

"Are you cold, Thayendanegea? I can put more wood on the fire."

He shook his head wordlessly, squeezed her shoulder and then sat down across from her and, for the third time since its arrival this afternoon, read again the letter he'd received from the Reverend Eleazar Wheelock in Connecticut. As soon as it had become known that Brant had returned and was recruiting even more Indians for the King's service, Wheelock had been contacted by a delegation from Tryon County. They requested that he, having once been very close to Brant and understanding him, write to him and attempt to persuade him to support the Americans or, failing that, to at least remain neutral. Wheelock had agreed to try and wrote the letter, asking Brant to remember their friendship and most of all to remember his training at the school, to be guided in his decisions now by what Wheelock himself had taught him. He did not reckon on the photographic clarity with which Brant remembered so many things.

Now Brant dipped his quill pen and in a slow but clear hand wrote his reply:

Oquaga, December 30th, 1776
To My Old Friend and Teacher, Rev. Dr. E. Wheelock — Honoured Sir. Your letter has flown to my hand and I am sorry you have become concerned in this matter. You have asked me to be guided now in what I do by the training I received at the Indian School and especially by what you yourself taught me. I remember well all those things. I recall to mind the happy hours I spent under your roof and especially the prayers and family devotions to which I listened. One passage was so often repeated at that time that I could never scratch it from my memory — "That we might be able to live as good subjects, to fear God and to Honour the King!"

Brant smiled as he boldly underlined the last four words and then concluded:

If this is not what you said, then perhaps you would write to me again and tell me what it was you did say.

Jos. Brant

He was still smiling as he folded the letter. He didn't really expect he'd hear from Wheelock again.

[*February 27, 1777 — Thursday*]

Arriving in Montreal and finding Colonel Guy Johnson so disgustingly drunk that he could not even stand up and so ugly-tempered that he could not speak without invective had filled Brant with anger. This was the man to whom was entrusted the future of the Iroquois League? This was the man to represent to the King and his ministers the true needs and demands of the Indians? This was the man who was to protect and preserve for the Indians the lands upon which they lived and in which their ancestors were buried?

For the most part, Brant kept his temper, but it was difficult. Throughout the entire territory, the Indians were in need. The usual degree of winter hunting had not been possible because normal gunpowder rations had not been available. When it did become available in meager amounts, it had to be hoarded for the expected troubles to come. There was a need for that and for blankets and food and other items for which the Indians had long depended upon the British, and the man who was supposed to see that they received them was so staggeringly drunk he could not see anything.

"You have encouraged us to uphold the King," Brant said tightly, "and to do so we must have the things which have been promised to us."

Blearily, Johnson had nodded, promising that he would get them and even more than he expected. He explained that he had been having difficulties with Sir John, who seemed determined to take over the duties of providing for the Indians when it wasn't his responsibility to do so.

"It's *my* job, Joseph," he said, his voice a near-whine, "an' Johnny's got no 'thority to step in."

Brant shook his head. "Do your job so we may do ours. Send on to us what we need without delay. That is all I have to say."

He turned and left, but before he departed from the Montreal area he saw Sir John and was impressed with the change in him. He was more sure of himself and obviously on top of the situation. He commiserated with Brant and promised to do what he could to help. Great quantities of supplies had been forwarded to Colonel Butler at Niagara for distribution to the tribes and it would be a good idea for Brant to go there. Butler, he said, had already been instructed to provide Brant with whatever he needed, and Joseph was to be guided in what he was doing and planning to coordinate his movements with Butler.

"I have heard, Joseph," he said softly, framing his words carefully, "that an evil thing occurred at Onondaga and that the Iroquois League is broken. I'm sorry. I'm glad my father couldn't know."

Brant looked at him sharply. This was something the whites did not know about and he was surprised that indication of it had reached Sir John. He paused a long while and then nodded.

"As far as our enemies — or any outsiders — know now, we have had only a disagreement among ourselves which time and need will cure."

"But it won't, will it?"

Brant shook his head and was surprised and ashamed of the tears that abruptly burned in his eyes and he turned away from Sir John so this weakness could not be seen. "No," he replied levelly, "it will never be the same. Our common need now keeps us together as we are, but it is not the bond of the League. It never will be again. Onondaga is no longer the heart of the Six Nations. The council fire has been extinguished and it never can be rekindled. Once the need is past which now keeps us together, we are individual tribes without common bond. You shouldn't speak of it."

"I won't." He reached out and placed his hand on Brant's shoulder. "But I'm sorry and my heart breaks for you and them. I will do what I can to help."

At that moment Joseph Brant liked John Johnson better than at any time in the association that spanned their lives. He also felt that Sir John could be relied upon and so together they discussed what lay ahead. Brant would go from here to Niagara to see Butler and get what supplies he could. He should then send out parties all over the frontier to get intelligence and to harass and disrupt and create diversion wherever possible. If the food and supplies to be obtained through Butler at Niagara were not enough — and here Sir John paused and wrote out further authorization for Butler to provide Brant with whatever it was in his power to provide — then he was to take it from the settlers.

"You may have lost your League, Joseph," Sir John said quietly, "but the Mohawk lands are still there. You are not on them now, but they are still your lands and you will have them again. I promise it."

Brant believed him.

[*March 26, 1777 — Wednesday*]

Major General John Burgoyne's grand plan, which he had entitled *Thoughts for Conducting the War from the Side of Canada*, was boldly conceived and beautifully presented to George III. One of the things the King liked about it was the manner in which it involved the Iroquois and other Indians and took fullest advantage for the Crown of their particular skills. His Majesty was so intrigued with *Thoughts for Conducting the War from the Side of Canada* that he gave it his full approval, confident that in Burgoyne he had one of England's finest military minds.

Ever since that cold, windy day last autumn, when Governor-General Guy Carleton had ordered the retreat from Crown Point on Lake Champlain when Fort Ticonderoga was all but in the palm of their hands, the plan had been formulating in Burgoyne's mind. During his early November trip down the St. Lawrence, before it could be closed by ice, and during the journey back across the Atlantic to England, he continued to develop the plan.

Arriving in England, Burgoyne's reception by Secretary of State George Germain was icy at best because Germain at this stage was linking Burgoyne with what he considered to be the incompetency of Carleton to handle affairs in Canada, culminating in the withdrawal from Lake Champlain. Germain's dislike of Guy Carleton was little short of vitriolic.[94] Burgoyne was suave and unruffled, well deserving of the nicknames he had worn throughout much of his career as "Gentleman Johnny" and "Handsome Jack." With tremendous finesse, involving no overt criticism of Guy Carleton, he put across the point that he concurred with Lord George's estimate of the character and worth of the man and equally deplored, without really putting it into words, the withdrawal when Ticonderoga had been within their grasp. So won over by Burgoyne's charm was Germain that within mere days of the general's return from America the secretary had provided him open access to the King and Burgoyne was enjoying brisk morning rides with His Majesty in Hyde Park. That's when he broached to the King the idea he had for crushing the revolt in America.

The King digested what Burgoyne had said and as they parted company one morning late in December he said, "It's an intriguing plan, John. Why don't you put it into writing for me?"

The two months that ensued became two of the most intense months in the life of Burgoyne. Pressed by his physicians to see to his health, he secluded himself for two months at Bath on the beautiful Avon River. Here, while the healthful waters worked wonders on him physically and the gentle babbling of which he was so fond worked wonders for his spirits, his keen mind refined the plan. Toward the end of February he returned to his fine home on Hertford Street in London and wrote the final polished form of his *Thoughts for Conducting the War from the Side of Canada*. This he submitted to Lord George Germain who, in turn, passed it on to His Majesty.

In essence, the plan amounted to splitting in half the Rebel forces in America, thus rendering each half less than effective because of an inability to depend upon or be supported by the other half. To effect this split, Burgoyne was to assemble his army at Montreal, march up the Richelieu and Lake Champlain, taking Crown Point, Ticonderoga and Skenesborough and reaching the navigable waters of the Hudson at Fort Edward. From there he would sweep down the Hudson, engaging and destroying the Northern Department of the Rebel army under General Philip Schuyler as he progressed, shoving it before him until Albany was taken. Meanwhile, the supreme commander of His Majesty's North American Military Forces, General Sir William Howe, moving from the south, would sweep *up* the Hudson and Schuyler's army, bottled up in Albany and inescapably caught in the pincers, would be annihilated.[95]

To guarantee further the effectiveness of the plan, Burgoyne outlined, it would be necessary to negate whatever possible strength Generals Washington or Schuyler might be able to draw from the Mohawk Valley. To effect this, a third force, in addition to his own army and Howe's, diversionary in objective, should move from Montreal at the same time as Burgoyne, but this force to go up the St. Lawrence and into Lake Ontario to Fort Oswego, then drive directly up the Oswego River to the headwaters of the Mohawk and, as Burgoyne would be doing on the Hudson, sweep down the Mohawk River destroying all forts and resistance in its path and forming a timely junction with Burgoyne at the mouth of the Mohawk for the great assault upon Albany.

Obviously, Burgoyne suggested smoothly, knowing that what followed would delight Germain, it would be necessary for someone to remain in Canada and protect the King's interests there while the campaign was under way and this could "most reasonably" be the governor-general of Canada, Sir Guy Carleton, who could protect that front with three thousand troops left with him for that purpose.

The invading force from the north, Burgoyne went on, should be of approximately eight thousand seasoned regulars, sufficient artillery for effective bombardment of installations, and bateaux and their crews sufficient enough for transportation of the whole, including the portage from the headwaters of Lake Champlain to the navigable tributary headwaters of the Hudson. Additional support should come from two thousand Canadians drafted for the project and one thousand Indians already committed to the Crown to disrupt the frontier so that it would be so busy protecting itself it could not lend support to the American army.

As a final note — and as a precaution against being thwarted by restrictions possibly being placed on him by Carleton — Burgoyne suggested that the general in charge of the operation, meaning himself, be given full latitude to act as he might think fit in view of unforeseen contingencies of the time and stress of circumstance.

One question remained: Who was to have command of the diversionary third wing that would sweep through the Mohawk Valley and form a junction with Burgoyne at Albany? There were a number of possibilities but Burgoyne's recommendation was accepted. His choice was Lieutenant Colonel Barry St. Leger, who had impressed him considerably this past summer at Lake Champlain.

St. Leger, who had become an ensign in His Majesty's service in 1756, had served in America beginning the following year and had been very active during the remainder of the French and Indian War. By 1760, when the war ended, he had acquired a wide knowledge of the habits of the Indians and their methods of border warfare. St. Leger was at present a brevet colonel, but for this operation he should have the temporary rank of brigadier general. Approval was given by the King himself.

So, having equally received the approval of George III for the plan, Burgoyne began preparing his force for as early a departure from England as possible. Germain, for his part, was to send instructions regarding the plan to both General Carleton and General Howe by the first packet ship.

Germain knew he should write and send his dispatches to the supreme commander first, but so anxious was he at this opportunity of slapping General Carleton that, in a letter from Whitehall, he wrote first to the Canadian governor. To him he briefly outlined the plan and, in respect to Burgoyne and St. Leger, adding:

With a view of quelling the rebellion as quickly as possible, it is become highly necessary that the most speedy junction of the two armies should be effected, and therefore, as the security and good government of Canada absolutely require your presence there, it is the King's determination to leave about three thousand men under your command and to employ the remainder of your army upon two expeditions, the one under command of General Burgoyne, who is to force his way to Albany, and the other under command of Lieutenant Colonel St. Leger, who is to make a diversion on the Mohawk River.

As this plan cannot be advantageously executed without the assistance of Canadians and Indians, His Majesty strongly recommends it to your care to furnish both expeditions with good and sufficient bodies of those men; and I am happy in knowing your influence among them is so great that there can be no room to apprehend that you will find it difficult to fulfill His Majesty's expectations.

It is the King's further pleasure that you put under command of Lieutenant Colonel St. Leger:

Detachment from the Eighth Regiment	100
Detachment from the Thirty-fourth Regiment	100
Sir John Johnson's Regiment of New York	133
The Hanan Chasseurs	342
	675

together with a sufficient number of Indians and Canadians as may be thought necessary for the service. After having furnished him with proper artillery, stores, provisions and every other necessary article for his expedition, and secured to him every other assistance in your power to afford and procure, you are to give him orders to proceed forthwith to and down the Mohawk River at Albany and put himself under the command of Sir William Howe. I shall write to Sir William Howe from hence by the first packet. . . .

The biggest matter sticking in Germain's craw in regard to Carleton had still not been mentioned, but toward the end of his communiqué he let his anger get the best of reason and added an inflammatory paragraph suggesting cowardice and stupidity on the part of Carleton last summer in not taking Ticonderoga when it had been possible for him to do so. He wasn't content with just this. To an able commander who had just been passed over for command of what might well be the most significant campaign of the entire war, the words Germain now wrote were veritable hammer blows:

I have had the mortification to learn that upon your repassing Lake Champlain, a very considerable number of the insurgents in those parts immediately marched from thence and joined the Rebel forces in the Provinces of New York and New Jersey and thereupon set about worrying the army of Sir William Howe. It appears that the unfortunate circumstance in New Jersey was the result, which has brought a new encouragement to the Rebel forces which at

Christmas were at the lowest ebb of morale and who, without such inspiration having been given to them at this crucial time, might have soon withdrawn from their foolish pursuit and begged the King for his mercy.

Although Germain followed his letter to Carleton with dispatches to Sir William Howe outlining Burgoyne's entire plan and Howe's own key role in it as supreme commander, his mind was still on Carleton and he was very anxious that the Carleton dispatches be readied without delay. Leaving his originals at the office in Whitehall, with instructions that all were to be fair-copied for his signature and then dispatched, he hastened home to prepare for a long-anticipated jaunt through the lovely countryside of Sussex.

"I'll stop by on my way to the country to sign the dispatches," he told his secretary. "Have them ready then." He paused and then added as an afterthought just before the door shut behind him, "Begin with those to General Carleton."

A few hours later, his carriage waiting in front, Lord Germain walked swiftly back into his Whitehall office. The dispatches to Carleton were all completed and he signed them with an almost malicious thrusting of his pen. Those to the supreme commander of the British forces in America had not yet been fully fair-copied and so he told his secretary to send out the dispatches to Carleton at once, that he would sign General Howe's dispatches and get them off to him when he returned to town.

An hour or so after his departure, the fair-copied dispatches for Sir William Howe were pigeonholed for the return of Germain. But Germain, when he returned, had forgotten all about not having signed or dispatched them.

No one thought to mention it to him.[96]

[*March 28, 1777 — Friday*]

Major General Philip Schuyler, commander of the northern district of the American forces and presently headquartered at Fort Edward, high on the Hudson, was not at all a popular man. His poorly clothed, fed and munitioned army of a thousand men, including even a large proportion of the officers, was made up largely of somewhat less than the gentry. His aristocratic airs — his mother was a Van Cortlandt, his wife a Van Rensselaer — grated upon those with whom he was in contact and there were few who shared any degree of compatibility with him. He was also a little too much the disciplinarian. Nevertheless he was, in his own way, a reasonably astute commander, despite the constant little subtle intrigues instituted against him by his next-in-command, Major General Horatio Gates.

An example of that innate sagacity came to the fore now as he considered the fundamental defensive capability of his territory and grunted sourly. The fact that Burgoyne and Carleton had moved up Lake Champlain as far as Crown Point last season and had then abruptly turned and abandoned their advances had been little short of perplexing. However, there was the possibility that they might be back and it would be wise to be a little better prepared.

Fort Ticonderoga, obviously, needed major repairs and he was simply not in the position materially at this point to order that such repairs be carried out. To the west, however, far up the Mohawk at the great carrying place from that river to Wood Creek, a bit more work might be done to strengthen Fort Stanwix. That was New York's most exposed frontier post and it was always possible that some sort of attack might be launched at it from out of the wilderness in that direction.

General Elias Dayton had done "some repairs" to the place not long ago, but Dayton himself simply shook his head and rolled his eyes when the general asked him if the place were really defensible. If not, Schuyler reasoned, then it should be made so. Who could know what sort of trouble might be coming this summer?

The square enclosure with four bastions that was the fort built in 1758 by Colonel John Stanwix under orders of General Abercromby was only barely adequate for its time and certainly not serviceable now, according to Dayton, and so this morning Schuyler had summoned to headquarters one of his more enterprising officers, Colonel Peter Gansevoort.

At twenty-seven, Gansevoort was a self-confident man of very erect stature with a certain vague resemblance to George Washington. His was one of the oldest Knickerbocker families of Albany and his great-grandfather Harmen Gansevoort had settled there in 1660. Peter had already well established his leadership qualities in the military. Two years ago [97] Congress had appointed him a major in the 2nd New York Regiment and he served under Montgomery during the siege of Montreal/Quebec. Just a year and a month ago [98] he was promoted to lieutenant colonel and last November 21 he became colonel of the 3rd Regiment. It was whispered about that he was attracting favorable attention in high places and chances were good for his becoming one of the new nation's youngest brigadier generals. He also had a quality that Schuyler secretly envied — the ability to evoke the unqualified respect and devotion of the men who served under him.

"I want you," he told Gansevoort now, "to take your Third Regiment and whatever detachment you need of the Massachusetts line to fill your ranks to seven hundred and fifty, and march to Fort Stanwix on the Mohawk. Take along a company of artillery as well, within that total strength of seven fifty."

"Yes, sir," Gansevoort said. "What is the general's pleasure when we arrive there?"

"From what I can gather, Colonel, the works are greatly dilapidated. Make a fort of it. A strong one. Rebuild it from the ground up. Your force will be the garrison."

"Yes, sir."

Gansevoort left General Schuyler and went immediately to his own second-in-command, Lieutenant Colonel Marinus Willett. He explained their orders and said they would leave in the morning. Willett nodded and grinned.

"We'll be ready, Colonel," he said.

[*May 20, 1777 — Tuesday*]

Sir Guy Carleton could remember no time in his entire career as an officer in His Majesty's service when he was more infuriated. It was not so much that Burgoyne had returned from England in command of a large force of men, to lead an expedition which by all that was just and proper should have been his own; it was more the humiliation suffered at Secretary Germain's treatment of him and the imaginings of what more this unspeakable ass might be doing right at this very moment to undermine him in the eyes of the King.

It was only with enormous effort and self-control that he was able to keep his hand from trembling with rage as he penned his reply. Speaking of himself, he wrote:

. . . any officer entrusted with supreme command ought upon the spot to see what is most expedient to be done, better than a great general at three thousand miles distance. It would be difficult for anyone who is warm and secure in the offices at Whitehall to know anything whatever about the rigors of the winter in Canada. As far as the charge goes that my failure to attack Ticonderoga set free troops to annoy Lord Howe, that is incomprehensible. If, by "that unfortunate circumstance in New Jersey" your Lordship means the affair at Trenton, a little military reasoning might prove the rebels required no reinforcement from any part to cut off that corps, it being unconnected and alone. The force they employed upon that occasion clearly demonstrated this.

Without my troubling your Lordship with any reasoning upon the matter, a little attention to the strength of General Howe's Army will, I hope, convince you that, connected and in a situation to support each other, they might have defended themselves even though all the rebels from Ticonderoga had reinforced Mr. Washington's army.

Concerning the operation last autumn on Lake Champlain, in spite of every obstruction a greater marine force was built and equipped and a greater marine force was defeated than had ever appeared on that lake before. Two brigades were taken across and remained at Crown Point till the second of November for the sole purpose of drawing off the attention of the rebels from Mr. Howe and to facilitate his victories during the remainder of the campaign. Nature had then

*put an end to ours. His winter quarters, I confess, I had never thought of cover-
ing. It is supposed, it's true, that his was the army favored by your Lordship,
and in which you put your trust, yet I could never imagine why, while an army
to the southward found it necessary to finish their campaign and go into winter
quarters, Your Lordship could possibly expect troops so far north should continue
their operations, lest Mr. Howe should be disturbed during the winter. If that
great army of Lord Howe's near the sea-coast had their quarters assaulted, what
could your Lordship expect would be the fate of a small corps detached into the
heart of rebel country in that season?*

*For these things I am so severely censured by your Lordship. I cannot under-
stand the why of it. I can only reiterate what should to all be a fact apparent
that my one wish is for the prosperity of the King's arms.*

*I regret that because of some private enmity of yours against me, Your Lord-
ship has seen free to treat me with slight, disregard and censure. . . .*[99]

[May 21, 1777 — Wednesday]

The leak in British security was incomprehensible.

In mere days after the arrival of the reinforcements under Burgoyne in
Canada, everyone seemed to know the full details of his great three-pronged
war plan.

Everyone included the force that Burgoyne brought with him but that was
uninformed of the plan before their arrival. *Everyone* included Sir John's regiment of Royal Greens and the Indians collected under Daniel Claus and the
disaffected irregulars collected under Colonel Guy Johnson and Colonel John
Butler. *Everyone* included Joseph Brant and his combined Indian forces. *Everyone* included, as well, General George Washington, General Philip Schuyler,
General Horatio Gates and Colonel Peter Gansevoort. *Everyone* included all
who had ears with which to hear in the Mohawk Valley. *Everyone* included everyone except the one with the greatest right and need to know.

Totally in the dark about Burgoyne's plan was General William Howe,
supreme commander of the British military forces in North America.[100]

[May 29, 1777 — Thursday]

In his quarters at Montreal, Major General John Burgoyne felt the first stirrings
of apprehension that the campaign he had taken such pains to develop might
have a minor flaw or two. On his desk was a letter bearing the seal of the Canadian governor that had just come by express from Quebec. He wondered if
perhaps it might not contain yet another distasteful or disruptive surprise. He
had been here less than a month and had already had more than his fill of such
surprises.

The first one had been the worst. Burgoyne had reached Quebec from England on June 6. Within days his new force of eight thousand men was at ready and, following conferences with General Carleton, he moved on to Montreal.[101] That was when he discovered that his entire war plan was known. At first he'd been furious but then, pragmatist that he was, he accepted the reality of it more with curiosity than anything else. As he wrote in a letter on May 12 to General Harvey:

One thing more occurs. I had the surprise and mortification to find a paper handed about at Montreal publishing the whole design of the campaign, almost as accurately as if it had been copied from the Secretary of State's letter. My own caution has been such that not a man in my own family[102] has been let into the secret. Sir Guy Carleton, I am confident, has been equal. I am therefore led to doubt whether imprudence has not been committed from private letters from England, and wish you would ask my friend D'Oyley,[103] to whom my very affectionate compliments, whether there is any person within the line of ministerial communication that he can suspect to be so unguarded? It is not of great consequence here, except as far as regards St. Leger's expedition, but such a trick may be of most prejudicial consequence in other cases, and should be guarded against.[104]

One of the immediate results of the exposure of his war plans became rather ironically amusing to Burgoyne. When the news of it flashed through the Mohawk Valley, it was as if it touched off a migration that had been awaiting just such a stimulus. Almost at once scores of residents who had vacillated in their loyalties now slipped away to join the British in Montreal or Quebec. There was also issued by Tryon County an order for the apprehension of Joseph Brant, John Butler, Walter Butler, Guy Johnson and John Johnson.

The second of the discomfiting surprises for Burgoyne was how impracticable he had been in his plan in counting upon the Canadians themselves to provide a valuable force for him. As he wrote with some disgust to Germain on May 14:

I cannot speak with much confidence of the military assistance I am to look for from the Canadians. The only corps yet instituted, or that I am informed at present can be instituted, are three independent companies of 100 men each, officered by Seigneurs of the country who are well-chosen; but they have not been able to engage many volunteers. Then men are chiefly drafted from the militia, according to a late regulation of the Legislative Council. Those I have yet seen afford no promise of arms — awkward, ignorant, disinclined to the service, and spiritless. Various reasons are assigned for this change in the natives since the time of the French government. It may partly be owing to a disuse of arms, but I believe principally to the unpopularity of their Seigneurs, and to the poison which the emissaries of the rebels have thrown into their minds.

In a letter he had written to Sir Guy Carleton three days ago, Burgoyne complained bitterly about the fact that already, before any action was seen, his force was being weakened by desertion of the Canadian troops. Even without desertion they were not the force he had, in his war plan, depended upon their being. As he had explained it to Carleton:

When the plan of my expedition was framed, the ideas of government respecting armed Canadians went to six times the number. Without that dependence I have reason to believe the proportion of regulars would have been larger. To remedy in some measure this deficiency, I have to propose to your Excellency a Corvée of a thousand men to attend the expedition for a limited time for the purpose of labour and transport.

Now Burgoyne broke the seal on the letter just received from Carleton and, while it carried no further unpleasant surprises, as he had anticipated it might, it underlined his own growing disappointment in the Canadian troops. With customary directness, Carleton had written:

The desertion you gave me notice of in your letter does not surprise me. It has been the same here, and was no more than what I expected. If Government laid any great stress upon assistance from the Canadians for carrying on the present war, it surely was not upon any information proceeding from me. Experience might have taught them (and it did not require that to convince me) these people have been governed with too loose a rein for many years and had imbibed too much of the American spirit of licentiousness and independence, administered by a numerous and turbulent faction here, to be suddenly restored to a proper and desirable subordination. . . .

[June 1, 1777 — Sunday]

As always occurred to him at the start of a major campaign, there was a surge of pride and martial fervor in the heart and mind of Major General John Burgoyne as he watched on this bright sabbath morning the real beginning of the movement that he was sure would change his own destiny as well as that of his country.

Led by an advance corps of fifteen hundred, his ten thousand fighting men were this moment taking their first steps on the move southward to the rendezvous point called Cumberland Head on Lake Champlain. Heading up the St. Lawrence at the same time in the flotilla of bateaux was the substantial force of six hundred and seventy-five regulars under Brigadier General Barry St. Leger, accompanied by somewhere between seven hundred and nine hundred Indians under Sir John Johnson. Burgoyne was quite sure that William Howe, at British headquarters in New York City, was certainly already beginning to move his force of from seventeen thousand to twenty thousand soldiers and sailors up the Hudson River for the ultimate junction at Albany with his own army.

Burgoyne estimated that as success followed success in the march, increasingly more vacillators and neutrals would throw their support to the British forces and increase the total strength of the anti-American forces substantially. Within Burgoyne's mind was a picture of the glorious sight it would be when the St. Leger force reunited with his own on the Hudson River just north of Albany, while just south of that city Howe's powerful force stood poised. Then the combined British force of perhaps as many as thirty thousand men would surround the American forces for a great victory. Such a vision was indeed enough to stir one's blood!

Unfortunately, there was one whose blood was stirring very little just now. Remaining behind in his basically crude Montreal quarters until he could get himself together enough to move into more elegant accommodations in Quebec was Colonel Guy Johnson, whose vow for vengeance for his wife's death seemed to have been forgotten. He was, at the moment, monumentally drunk.

[June 2, 1777 — Monday]

Joseph Brant watched the British flag rise to the top of the makeshift flagpole in Unadilla[105] but experienced no great satisfaction at the sight. A deep-seated anger still smoldered within him at what had occurred during his absence from Oquaga.

Only a short time after he had left that Susquehanna River village to go first to Montreal and then Niagara, an incident had transpired that he knew would not have been possible had he been on hand. It was almost as if his movements had been watched and action taken as soon as he had moved safely out of the way.

The incident involved a militia officer of Harpersfield with whom Brant had long been familiar — Colonel John Harper. Alarmed at the substantial increase of Indians under Brant at Oquaga, the New York Congress directed Harper, who commanded the fort at Schoharie, to go to Oquaga to determine whether or not these Indians could really be considered a threat to the frontier, as the frightened residents at Cherry Valley and Unadilla were contending. He was also to determine if these Indians were in the process of mounting an invasion to come against the settlements.

Wisely, Harper had instructed his militia captains to hold their companies in readiness to attack should he run into trouble, and then he alone, with just one Indian as a guide and another white as a companion, moved boldly into

Oquaga. This was in late February, less than a fortnight after Brant's departure. Arriving in the village, Harper listened to denials by the Indians that any invasion was being planned, which he believed, and the assurance that the Oquaga Indians wanted nothing more than peace, which he didn't believe. He provided a steer for them to roast, complimented them on their good sense in maintaining the peace and then withdrew, confident that while no immediate major invasion of the frontier was being mounted, they were not only capable of it, they very probably had a few minor raiding parties out at that moment. His questions concerning the whereabouts of Brant had gone unanswered. Harper considered the situation at Oquaga as being volatile and the threat of substantial attack from that quarter to be real enough for Tryon County authorities to be actively concerned.

While returning to Schoharie and not far from Harpersfield, Colonel Harper encountered a party of fifteen warriors from Oquaga going back to their town. They claimed they had been attending a congress at Onondaga, but because of the direction from which they were coming, Harper was sure they were one of the raiding parties that were currently harassing the frontier. He also decided they were actually en route right then to attack the Johnstone settlement near Unadilla. He immediately moved on swiftly into Harpersfield, collected fourteen men who were in the process of tapping sugar maples, and recruited them into a small force to help him.

Under cover of darkness they had crept up on the camp of the fifteen Indians near the mouth of Schenevus Creek. The Indians were all asleep, lying in a circle around the campfire, their feet toward the coals for warmth. The surprise was complete. The Indians were disarmed and bound and then marched to Albany and imprisoned.

This, then, was the news that had greeted Brant on his return and why he was furious. It was why now he had led his party of eighty warriors into Unadilla. The settlement was not large — perhaps twenty or thirty houses — and located about five miles below the junction of Unadilla Creek with the Susquehanna, roughly twenty miles upstream from Oquaga.[106]

An hour ago Brant had confronted the Reverend George Johnstone, whom he knew vaguely, and the two nondescript white men who claimed they were officers of the Unadilla militia company, though Brant knew no such company existed. They had listened sullenly to the Mohawk's demands.

"My people at Oquaga are in need of provisions," he told them. "Because of the rebellion against the King by your people, we are forced to move away from our Mohawk villages and the fields and gardens we had. The provisions which should have come to us have been confiscated by you Rebels. Now it is up to you to repay them."

"By God," one of the alleged officers said darkly, "we didn't take no supplies of yours an' we —"

He was interrupted by Brant's abruptly upraised hand. "If," the Mohawk continued, "you will not consent to give us what we need without difficulty, then we will have to take them by force. And we *will* take them. Your people are raising their hands against us everywhere. Without cause, Colonel Harper has imprisoned fifteen of my warriors and we will not sit quietly and continue to bear the threats being made against us by General Schuyler. Our agreement with King George is very strong. It would be unpleasant for you if you force us to take from you the things we need."

There had been no need for force.

Expressionless now, Brant watched as the British flag just raised hung limply at the top of the pole in the windless air. His Indians were just finishing their loading of the Unadilla packhorses with the newly butchered sheep and cattle from the village, along with a dozen loads of miscellaneous supplies. At his signal, they began moving off down the trail along the river. Brant kneed his horse to a stop close to where the group of about thirty of the settlement's whites were watching.

"For any of you here who do not support the King," he said flatly, "this has become a dangerous place. My advice to you is to leave. Our next visit may not be as friendly as this."

He reined his horse around and without a backward glance trotted off. The men looked at one another, both angry and fearful. As unprotected as Unadilla was, there was no doubt now what they would do. Within two hours of Brant's departure for Oquaga, over two-thirds of Unadilla's population was heading for the greater safety of the Mohawk Valley, already framing in their minds the official complaint they would register with the commander of the Tryon County Militia, General Nicholas Herkimer.

[*June 18, 1777 — Wednesday*]

Colonel Daniel Claus squatted before the small campfire, staring unseeingly at the licking flames. A dozen Iroquois, mostly Cayugas, sat or crouched around the fire close to him. Their leaders were two large, bare-chested, well-muscled warriors whose heads were shaved clean except for a strip of hair an inch or so wide, cut short and brushlike, running from above the brow to the nape. One, a Mohawk, wore a string of black bear claws around his neck and the other, a Cayuga, wore a gorget of silver and wide bands of the same material around his upper arms. Both were wearing loincloths and moccasins. They were named, respectively, Odiseruney and Hare. Both had been dubbed with the name John by the English. Claus did not refer to them by that name.

The Indian agent lifted his eyes from the fire and let them pass slowly over the ten warriors and then come to rest on their two leaders. He nodded.

"These men should be enough. You'll be moving swiftly and quietly. You have horses?" At their nods he said, "Good. When you've finished, rejoin us. By then we'll be at Oswego."

"How many prisoners do you want?" Odiseruney asked.

"Not many." Claus shrugged. "Four. Maybe five."

"How many scalps?" Hare asked, and they all joined him in the laughter.

"As many as you can take without losing your own. Not that you have much to lose," he pointed out. They laughed again.

"These prisoners," Odiseruney went on, "you want them only from the fort they call Stanwix?"

Claus nodded. "Only from Stanwix. General Carleton said he had late intelligence that the fort is not going to be any real obstacle to General St. Leger. He said he is told it is only a poor picketed defense works with no more than sixty men. Maybe he is right. Maybe not. I want to be sure. That's your job. Scout it out and see what you think. More important, capture some of the garrison and bring them to me. They'll tell us what we need to know."

There was no more conversation. In less than a minute the dozen Iroquois had melted into the darkness and Claus was alone at the fire, staring into the coals. He thought they would probably do a good job, but he wasn't accustomed to working with them so he couldn't be sure. He wished he were with the Indians he knew better and wondered again why he was not.

For fifteen years, mostly under Sir William Johnson, Daniel Claus had seen to the control and care of the Indian tribes of Canada. He knew them well, understood their needs and knew how to handle them. They liked and respected him. Yet, the hundreds he had collected for the campaign were now with Burgoyne, moving up Lake Champlain, while he was here with St. Leger and Johnson, with one hundred and fifty less familiar Iroquois and Mississaugas under his direct control.

Claus broke a small stick in half and tossed it onto the coals. Smoke began rising from it and in a moment it burst into a small flame and was quickly consumed.

"It doesn't make much sense," he said aloud.

No one heard him.

[June 21, 1777 — Saturday]

Clad in the full splendor of his regimentals, with his officers attending him and an honor guard spread out on either side, Major General John Burgoyne looked out over the sea of over four hundred Indian faces watching him and cleared his throat. He was sure this would probably be the only chance he would have of addressing his red allies together in one group and he had been rehearsing mentally what he would say.

All had gone well thus far on the march southward from Montreal. His completed forces, stores and ammunition had all arrived at the Cumberland Head rendezvous on Lake Champlain as planned, without incident. From there he had traveled with a smaller contingent up the Bouquet River to this place at the falls, which, he had been informed, was a place considered very good by the Indians for talking plans and for starting great things. Realizing the importance of playing to the superstitions and beliefs of the Indians, Burgoyne had taken the trouble to come to this point to address them. The more auspicious the beginning of a campaign as important as this one, the better.

Now he held up his arms, greeted the assemblage with the standard cry of "My brothers!" and then began to speak. His words were loud and forceful and rather stilted. He stopped at the end of each phrase and each sentence to allow the interpreters time to finish repeating in the several Indian dialects what he had just said.

"I welcome you from my heart," he said loudly. "I am flattered by your being here, but I know that you are too sagacious and too faithful to the King to be deluded or corrupted — except for the refuse of a small tribe which has been led astray from their brothers by the perfidious promises of the Rebels.

"We go from here into battle with those Rebels, but before we do there are certain laws and customs of war to which you must agree to conform."

He paused and faintly cleared his throat, looking back and forth across the crowd while the translators caught up. Then he outlined the restrictions:

"I positively forbid bloodshed when you are not opposed in arms.

"Women, children and old men, as well as those of our enemies who become our prisoners, must be held sacred from the knife or hatchet, even during the time of actual conflict.

"You will be paid for the prisoners you take and turn over to us, and so, also, will you be paid for each scalp you have taken of the dead killed by your fire in fair opposition.[107] But you are not to scalp the wounded or dying on any account or pretense."

As the interpreted versions reached them, it was obvious that the Indians were in part pleased and in part not. They did not at any time appreciate having restrictions placed upon them in the matter of warfare. Obviously, though, they were excited at the prospect of this campaign and what its results might be, and so whatever objections they felt were held in check. Who could tell what would occur in the heat of battle? Also, who could tell from a scalp itself whether or not it had been lifted from an enemy killed "in fair opposition"?

Burgoyne was reaching the conclusion of his address and he became more expansive, more exhortative.

"Chiefs and warriors! The great King, our common father, has been greatly satisfied with the way you have acted since the beginning of the troubles in America. You have restrained yourselves while waiting the King's call to arms, and that is the hardest proof to which your affection could be put. The King

would feel guilty were he to make you wait any longer. It is therefore my responsibility, as general of one of His Majesty's armies, to release you from the
bonds which your obedience to him imposed. Warriors, you are free! Go out
now and strike for your cause and for ours; strike at the enemies of Great Britain; strike at the disturbers of public order, peace and happiness, destroyers of
commerce, the would-be destroyers of their own King! You see around you the
chiefs of His Majesty's European forces. His princes and his generals esteem
you as brothers in the war and so, too, do his allies."

It was Kisensik, principal chief of the Nipissings of Canada, who responded
for the assembled tribes. He spoke loudly so all could hear, but addressed his
remarks to Burgoyne.

"We receive you," he said solemnly, "as our father. We love the King and
our hatchets have been sharpened by that affection, and so now we have all
come on his behalf to make war against his enemies and ours. All the men who
are able to make war have come forth, leaving behind at our villages only the
old and lame with our infants and wives. With one common assent we promise
a steady obedience to your orders and we wish that the Great Spirit will give you
many successes."

The roar of approval when he finished was signal enough of the full accord
of the Indians gathered here at the falls of the Bouquet River to support the
British. For whatever the result, a commitment was made by both sides, one to
another.

Later, in a somewhat pompous effort to absolve himself of the horror he may
have unleashed, Burgoyne issued a lengthy proclamation to the Americans in
which he said, in part:

*Let not people consider their distance from my camp provides them safety. I have
but to give stretch to the Indian forces under my directions — and they amount
to thousands! — to overtake the hardened enemies of Great Britain. If the
frenzy of hostility should remain, I trust I shall stand acquitted in the eyes of
God and man, in executing the vengeance of the British government against the
willful outcasts.*

[*June 25, 1777 — Wednesday*]

The men in his command had worked extremely hard and Colonel Peter Gansevoort was very proud of them. Considering what it had looked like two
months ago, Fort Stanwix didn't look too bad at all right now, even though
there was still a lot to be done to make it properly defensible. The situation
here had been far worse than Gansevoort had anticipated. He had understood
from General Schuyler that Colonel Elias Dayton had refurbished the place
and made it at least to some degree defensible, but when he arrived late in

April that was not what he found. The entire place, except for a small, better-fortified cabinlike structure in the middle, was almost wholly indefensible. In fact, it was even untenable.

He had called a meeting of his principal officers, including his second- and third-in-command, Lieutenant Colonels Marinus Willett of the New York Line and Robert Mellon of the Massachusetts Line. Also on hand was the Reverend Samuel Kirkland.

"Gentlemen," Gansevoort had said, "we have a huge job to do. It won't be easy, but we're going to do it. I don't know how much time we have before the enemy strikes, but we must assume there will not be time enough. We have a garrison of seven hundred and fifty good men and everyone, without exception, is going to work as if his life depended upon it. There's an excellent chance it may."

They had indeed worked. New log pickets had been cut and sharpened and raised, embrasures had been fashioned for the limited artillery, bastions were rebuilt, crude quarters had been erected and defenses of every nature were strengthened. The men were in a state of almost perpetual exhaustion and yet somehow morale remained high. Perhaps it was because there was a purpose behind the work — the salvation of their own lives. It was known that a large force under St. Leger would be coming against them. It was just not known exactly when. Such a threat overhanging kept them very busy.

News had come just recently that Congress had adopted the Stars and Stripes as the American flag and someone pointed out that however much the overall shortness of supplies was affecting them here, they ought to be able to make their own United States flag to hoist on a staff. At once Gansevoort ordered that one be made, contributing his own rich blue camlet cloak to the cause.[108] A woman's petticoat of scarlet supplied the red and some linen soldiers' shirts, the white. They made thirteen stripes of alternating red and white, which they knew the flag was supposed to have, but they were not sure what was supposed to be in the blue field, so there they fashioned the cross of St. George superimposed over the cross of St. Andrew. That didn't make any difference. It was, to everyone at Fort Stanwix, the flag of the United States of America, and when it was finally raised, it was to a burst of artillery and a cheering of the men.[109] Patriotic fervor was very high.

No one had yet seen any Indians or enemy troops, but that some form of the enemy was hovering nearby was becoming ever more apparent. Now and then parties detached to leave the fort for one reason or another would be fired upon, but those who fired — more likely Tories than Indians — always fired and fled and so none had yet been caught or killed. A few of Gansevoort's men had been slightly injured, but the situation remained more annoying than serious.

Some of the detachments sent out were tree-cutting parties. They included one hundred and fifty men dispatched to move up Wood Creek, which was heavily canopied by overhanging branches, and cut down trees so they would fall into the water and block the passage of St. Leger's boats when they came. Other groups were sent downstream to cut sod squares along the riverbank to be brought back to the fort and used to cover the roofs of the quarters to make them less flammable should the enemy try to burn them out.

One of those parties, sent out this morning by Lieutenant Colonel Willett, was composed of fifteen men under command of Captain Laurence Gregg. It included Lieutenant David Casper, Corporal Asmon Ball and a dozen privates. They moved downstream a few miles on the Mohawk and immediately set to work. After an hour or so, with the cutting progressing nicely, Captain Gregg beckoned Corporal Ball to his side and then walked over to the other officer.

"Lieutenant Casper," Gregg said, "the corporal and I are going to see if we can find a few pigeons to shoot. Keep things going here."

The captain and the corporal, both with their guns and with Gregg's little black dog named Cricket bouncing at their heels, walked off. Unfortunately, the birds were not cooperating at first. Several scattered individuals passed over in swift flight but none seemed to be landing. They walked a little farther and then a small flock of the big passenger pigeons alighted on a dead branch near the top of a beech tree. Immediately the birds began billing one another and preening their own plumage.

Both men raised their guns and two shots rang out almost simultaneously, but neither shot came from their weapons. Grunting and half-turning at the sudden pain in his side, Gregg saw Corporal Ball fall without a word. He stepped toward him but his own legs gave way and he fell. Everything suddenly had a dreamlike quality and through the glaze of pain clouding his vision he saw a huge Indian, shirtless and wearing only moccasins and a loincloth, running toward him with a tomahawk in his hand. Another was close behind him. Then there were others, behind them.

Gregg tried to move, but his limbs wouldn't function. He tried to cry out, but even his mouth wouldn't open, and the bad dream became a hideous nightmare as the first Indian reached the scene and plunged his tomahawk into the back of Corporal Ball's head, yanked it out with some difficulty, then swung the reddened weapon at Gregg. The captain saw it coming, felt it strike and then there was darkness.

Odiseruney's second tomahawk blow had not been as hard or as well placed as the first. It glanced off the side of the officer's head just over the ear, opening the flesh in a wide gash but not breaking the skull. The captain went limp and immediately Odiseruney dropped the tomahawk, jerked the sharp knife out of his waistband and cut a deep circle in the scalp from the hairline of the forehead to the crown. With a tremendous jerk on the hair, he pulled the scalp off and then turned to the other man.

Hare was already there, kneeling on the dead man's back and cutting his scalp free. Odiseruney frowned and picked up his tomahawk.

"That scalp is mine, Hare," he said, holding up his tomahawk. "I killed him with this."

Hare completed removing Corporal Ball's scalp and shoved it into the stained pouch attached to his waistband. He shook his head and his voice was tight.

"My bullet killed him, not your tomahawk. The scalp is mine. You have yours."

For an instant they stared at one another, angry. Scalps were money now. Big money, not just war trophies. Each one meant payment from the King. It was already creating jealousies. After a moment more, Odiseruney shrugged and shoved the scalp of Captain Gregg into his own belt pouch. "It is yours," he said.

They took the guns belonging to the men, rifled their pockets for anything of value and then started away. From some brushy cover there was a sudden sharp yelp. A little black dog stood there. The Mohawk Odiseruney raised his tomahawk as if to throw it and the dog yelped again and fled, tail between its legs.

All of the Indians laughed and the tension between them was gone. Odiseruney clapped Hare on the shoulder and shoved his tomahawk back into his belt. There would be other scalps to take very soon.[110]

Some distance away, at the area where the little detachment was still cutting sod, the sound of the two shots in the distance had been heard. One of the soldiers had straightened and grinned toward the officer.

"Sounds like the cap'n and Ball got 'em some birds, Lieutenant."

Lieutenant Casper had nodded. He liked hunting and wished the captain had taken him along instead of Corporal Ball. He had returned his attention to the job at hand and supervised the loading of the remaining stacked squares of sod onto the flat cart. The job was nearly finished when Casper heard a faint sound in the woods behind him. He smiled and turned, thinking it would be Captain Gregg returning. Instead, he was roughly grabbed and a knife held against his throat. At the same instant a ragged volley of shots rang out.

Every man who was holding or near a gun at that moment, with the exception of Casper, was killed. Five others, frozen in the act of walking with or loading squares of sod, were captured and bound in moments. The scalps of the eight dead were taken and all weapons gathered up. The whole attack had taken no more than three minutes.

Half a mile away, where the forms of Captain Gregg and Corporal Ball lay still upon the ground, one of them moved. A deep groan rose in the throat of Captain Gregg as he raised his head and then vomited. The effort nearly made him collapse again, but somehow he got to his hands and knees and crawled to where Ball was lying a dozen feet away. There was no life left in him and Gregg sank down again, his head cushioned on the small of Ball's back.

That was when Cricket returned. Frightened, the skinny little dog crept forward on its stomach, whining. When it reached the two men it nuzzled Gregg's hand and Gregg responded, touching Cricket. The dog went wild with joy. It leaped about yipping and crying, licked Gregg's hands and his face and then even raced around and licked the bare bloody area of skull and tissue where the scalp had been.

"Stop it," Gregg muttered. "Cricket, stop! My God, if you want to do something, go get help!"

Incredibly, Cricket leaped up and stood still, looking at him with head cocked. Then he raced off up the shore of the Mohawk. In about two miles, still more than a mile below the fort, he came to three off-duty soldiers who were fishing. The dog pranced around in a frantic circle, barking, racing away, coming back and repeating the whole action until at last they realized the animal wanted to be followed.

In less than an hour they were returning to Fort Stanwix, carrying the wounded Captain Gregg on a makeshift litter.[111]

[*June 27, 1777 — Friday*]

Fundamentally an honest and forthright man, General Nicholas Herkimer greatly disliked what he was doing now. It was not only underhanded and against all his precepts of integrity, it was also murder. He stepped back after shaking Brant's hand in the open square of Unadilla and looked at the Indian he had known in passing for many years.

This was the man he was going to assassinate.

Back at German Flats it had all seemed such a good idea. Everyone agreed that Brant was dangerous and that his avowal of allegiance to the King on the second day of June, when he plundered the residents of Unadilla of supplies and food, justified the plan. If Brant were not stopped now, the consensus went, the entire Mohawk Valley would flow red with the blood he would let.

It was easy to believe that, but assassination was another matter. To deliberately take a man's life in cold blood was not the sort of thing Herkimer imagined he could ever do. Yet, here he was, prepared to do just that. He licked his lips, hoping everything would go as planned, glancing at Joseph Waggoner and his three friends standing slightly to the right. They would be the men to draw their hidden guns and fire at Brant when the signal was given.

To Herkimer's left was Colonel Ebenezer Cox of Canajoharie District and a member of the Tryon County Committee of Safety. Beside him was Captain Henry Eckler and behind them were two militia lieutenants. Eckler knew Brant best, having attended school with him at Wheelock's in Connecticut, but it was

Colonel Cox who passionately hated Brant and was to give the signal for the assassination. That signal would be when he said the words: "The matter is
ended!"

They had marched down from German Flats, this force of three hundred
and eighty men under Herkimer. All had backpacks with provisions enough for
the march here to Unadilla and the return, plus one day extra. All had rifles
and ammunition enough to fight, if necessary, a considerable battle. The
march south had been swift and uneventful and with runners moving between
Herkimer and Brant in irregular procession. It had been agreed upon by both
sides to leave their forces outside the village and meet in the open square of
Unadilla. Brant was to have no more than ten men with him for the talks,
including himself, all unarmed. The same restriction was to be on Herkimer.

The army was allowed to sit and rest in a meadow adjacent to the town, in
full view of the village square. They were instructed to give the illusion of
being carelessly at ease but ready to snatch up their weapons and fight at a
moment's notice.

On the other side of the town, Brant had one hundred and thirty men standing loosely in a clearing, mostly armed only with tomahawks. Brant had only
four warriors with him for the meeting and they did not have blankets wrapped
about them. They wore leggings or loincloths and were barechested and there
was no place for them to hide a weapon. They stood behind Brant.

"Well, Joseph," Herkimer said after stepping back from their handshake,
"we've been hearing some rather surprising things about you. Things which,
since I know you, I am not inclined to believe unless I hear them from you."

Brant said nothing and so he went on. "We have been told that you com-
mandeered supplies and food from this village."

"I did."

"By what right?"

"By the right of need. By the right of it being Tryon County's responsibility
that my people are in need because supplies and ammunition have been withheld from them. By the right that they have been forced out of their homes and
away from their crops in the Mohawk Valley. By the fact that our lives are in
danger if we are seen there."

"Joseph, you have friends here. I have known you for years. Captain Eckler
here was your friend in school. Colonel Cox was your neighbor in Canajoharie, as was Joe Waggoner. We have not come here in the cause of creating
trouble; we have come here in the cause of peace. There is no strife between us
yet and there need not be."

"You have brought nearly four hundred soldiers with you," Brant pointed
out.

"And you have one hundred and thirty."

"As usual," Brant said, the trace of a smile turning up his mouth corners, "we Indians have the odds on our side, since to make it an even contest the difference should be four to one in your favor."

"Why, damn you, Brant!" It was Colonel Cox interrupting and he was furious. "I've never heard such an arrogant —"

Herkimer cut him off with a gesture of his hand and he, too, was smiling faintly. "Any time such odds are available to us against an enemy, regardless of whom, I will gladly accept them," he said quietly. "But, as I have said, there is no strife between us and we are not here as enemies. Our purpose is to settle what may be differences. Let me ask you this: If your grievances are rectified, will you remain at peace?"

With his usual directness, Herkimer had come to the crux of the matter in one simple sentence and Brant's respect for him increased. His own answer was equally direct.

"No," he said, shaking his head. "Just as our grandfathers and fathers were in agreement with the King, so too are we. We have made a strong alliance with the King and we will honor it. You, General Herkimer, and the rest of you here and in the Mohawk Valley — you people have joined the Boston people against the King. The Boston people are strong and stubborn, but the King will humble them. And we will support him. Mr. Schuyler or General Schuyler or whatever you want to call him is not very smart in his dealings with the Indians. He says kind words to us and makes big promises, but in truth he has never provided us with even the smallest item of clothing or cared if we were in need."

"Our government is just forming, Joseph," Herkimer put in. "We are barely able to sustain ourselves. But we are very strong and it would not be wise to oppose us, as the King himself is learning."

Again Joseph shook his head and there was a distinct edge to his voice now. "If you think to bring fear to our hearts with such talk, you have underestimated us and your memory is short. The Indians made war against you white people when you were all united. Can you possibly think, now that you are divided among yourselves, that we are frightened of you? There is no purpose in our talking further."

"By God, then," Cox spoke up, "if that's his resolution, then the matter is ended!"

Though all four of the would-be assassins — Waggoner and his three friends — were to have drawn their weapons and killed Brant at this signal, only Waggoner made any real effort to bring out his hidden pistol. It caught in the folds of cloth and in that moment Brant raised his right hand high.

Immediately a loud, keening signal cry came from the clustered Indians in the clearing. Before the call had even died away, over five hundred musket-armed Indians leaped into view from where they were hidden, completely circling Herkimer's force and their weapons pointed. The one hundred and thirty had also sprung into action and their weapons were aimed at the ten whites standing before Brant. A fierce war whoop was rising from practically every Indian throat, creating a frightful din and instilling a monumental fear in the white men. Joe Waggoner's weapon never came into view. Sheepishly, very slowly and carefully, he withdrew his empty hand and let it fall away.

"I did not come here to fight, Joseph," Herkimer said, a faint lacing of fear in his voice.

Brant turned and spoke in an undertone to the men behind him and at once one of them gave a signal for the Indians to remain still and hold their fire. Brant then returned his attention to Herkimer.

"It would be easy to mistake your intentions, General," he said. "If you want war, now or later, we are ready for you."

There was a little more talk after that, but it was awkward, strained and accomplished nothing. Herkimer demanded that all the deserters and Tories who might have joined Brant be turned over to him but Brant refused.

"It would seem, Joseph," Herkimer murmured, "that the next time we meet, which could be very soon, it may be as enemies."

"It will certainly be as enemies," Brant replied, "but perhaps more honorably than today."

And Nicholas Herkimer, for the first time in many years, was deeply ashamed.

[June 28, 1777 — Saturday]

Colonel Peter Gansevoort had known the Oneida Indian standing before him for many years and had great faith in him. His Indian name was Ahnyero, but he was far more familiar to his many white friends in the Mohawk Valley as the blacksmith called Thomas Spencer.

"You realize," Gansevoort said, "they'll kill you if they catch you spying on them up there at Oswego."

"First," Ahnyero replied, smiling, "they have to catch me. I don't intend to let them do that. St. Leger does not know how to catch an Indian who does not wish to be caught."

"Brant does."

Ahnyero nodded. "Yes, Thayendanegea is a danger to be watched. I don't intend to let him catch me. I'll send back reports regularly by runners. Treat them well. When you see me again, it will be because I am bringing the last report and attack will be close." With that he was gone.

[June 29, 1777 — Sunday]

Barry St. Leger walked around the American soldier standing in his tent and studied him closely. He was an American lieutenant but there was little left of his garb to show any rank or even military connection. His body was bruised and gave evidence of other mistreatment. One eye was swollen shut and the fingers of his left hand were severely burned.

St. Leger stopped circling the man and stood in front of him, his hands on his hips. "Mr. Claus said in his report that you are a lieutenant and that your name is Casper. David Casper. Is that correct?"

Casper, staring at St. Leger with his unimpaired eye, nodded but did not speak.

"And that you are of the garrison under Colonel Gansevoort at Fort Stanwix?" At Casper's nod he continued: "He also says that you told him, under questioning, that the fort is being repaired and is now in relatively good shape, fortified into a regular square with four bastions and garrisoned by seven hundred and fifty regulars, is that true?"

"It is."

"You lie!" St. Leger's voice was a whiplash. "Do you think we are stupid to believe such as that? We know the place is falling apart and we know it has perhaps sixty men."

"You go right on believing that, General," Casper said softly. "Right up until the time you get there and we knock the hell out of you."

St. Leger's nostrils flared. "You also told Mr. Claus that Colonel Gansevoort not only knows we are coming, but our strength and by what route. From whom did he learn this?"

"I don't know."

"Does he know *when* we're coming?"

"I don't know."

"You have already undergone some suffering, Lieutenant. Maybe if you suffered more your answers would carry more truth."

Casper shifted uneasily, remembering the pain. He shook his head. "I've told the truth. I can't answer what I don't know."

St. Leger grunted and then called for the guard to come take the prisoner away and bring in the next one. Successively he questioned the other five. Their answers corresponded, with no major discrepancies. Once again St. Leger looked at Claus's letter written yesterday from his camp, fifteen miles ahead. Claus had said his party of Indians had captured the six men and killed ten others a few miles from Fort Stanwix but they had not themselves seen the fort, deciding it was too risky to approach any closer. But, Claus had added, the men were questioned separately and their stories coincided: Fort Stanwix was a lot stronger than previously imagined and St. Leger's plans were known.

St. Leger was still more or less inclined to dismiss it as untrue, but deep inside a little tendril of worry had begun taking root.

[*July 25, 1775 — Friday*]

Almost a thousand Indians had assembled at Oswego for the council and there, for the first time, Joseph Brant met Brigadier General Barry St. Leger.

Brant had arrived with several hundred of his warriors only a few days ago, having encountered no difficulty with the Americans en route. At Oswego he met the forces under John Butler and Walter Butler, which had arrived from Niagara with a few hundred Indians more. He also met Colonel Claus and learned that Guy Johnson had decided not to accompany the expedition but rather to remain in Montreal for "reasons of his health."

Brant had been extremely disappointed in the lack of supplies provided for the Indians. Promises made in Montreal and Niagara simply had not been kept. The Indians were to have been given all they would need for joining the expedition against the Mohawk Valley, yet there wasn't near enough for them and it took the combined soothing and additional promises by Claus, Butler and Brant to get them to remain at Oswego until St. Leger arrived. Then Claus had received orders from St. Leger a couple of days ago to meet him at the mouth of the Salmon River, with instructions that they would proceed overland from there to Fort Stanwix.[112]

There were two reasons for this. St. Leger originally had visions of piercing swiftly through the wilderness with experienced light infantry, hitting Fort Stanwix hard with small-arms fire and quickly taking it. That was before the intelligence had been obtained from the prisoners of the strength and refurbishing of Fort Stanwix and its increase in garrison strength, which St. Leger was still not wholly believing. The second reason was because St. Leger only had a few score Indians with him at Salmon River; he'd made the mistake of trying to mollify them by giving them each a quart of rum. Too late he learned that this was no way to quiet the Indians. They had, of course, become beastly drunk and to keep them under control was the primary reason St. Leger had sent Captain Gilbert Tice to Oswego to get Colonel Claus and bring him back.

Reluctant to disobey the orders of his commander, Claus was seriously considering leaving with Tice and it was at this point that Brant put his foot down. He told Claus that he must not join St. Leger at Salmon River because if he left here the assembled Indians, already ill provided for, would feel abandoned and they would certainly begin to disperse. The only way to hold them, he advised, was to remain here and let St. Leger come the remaining few miles from Salmon River so that all the Indians here could receive more of what they needed from St. Leger's stores as well as being able to see the size of the force St. Leger had, which would encourage them.

St. Leger was at first furious that his plans had been changed "at the whim of a savage," and he came on with his force to Oswego fully intending to reprimand Claus for not following orders. However, when the situation was explained to him, not only by Claus but by the Butlers too, he realized the folly of what he had been planning and accepted the change with rare grace.

At forty, Barry St. Leger was no fool. On the plus side, he was considered tenacious, prompt, scholarly, intelligent and attentive to detail. For twenty years he had been in the King's service and he knew military operations well. Still, he was neither an expert strategist nor a daring and imaginative commander, which was why his permanent rank was still only lieutenant commander of the 34th Foot. Usually he could be counted upon in a subordinate position. He was well aware that it was a mark of distinction to have been chosen to lead an independent corps on an important campaign. This being his first major offensive command, he was extremely anxious to do well and he was being very cautious. Wisely, his first move was to accept the recommendations of Claus, the Butlers and Sir John in respect to what needed to be done to satisfy the Indians and keep them as a viable force.

St. Leger was sensible enough to recognize his own limitations in dealing with the Indians. With Guy Johnson having abdicated his responsibilities in respect to them, St. Leger now officially named Colonel Claus to act as superintendent of the Indians of this expedition, empowering him to act with his best judgment for His Majesty's service in regard to distribution of equipment, presents and other goods.

Immediately Claus distributed as lavishly as possible all the supplies brought for the Indians. This was the type of thing they expected and understood and they were greatly heartened. They were also very much impressed by the strength of the force St. Leger commanded. Assembled as it was now at Oswego, it was an army bristling with firepower and in excellent shape. The journey here from La Chine near Montreal had toughened it more than sapped its strength and somehow it imparted the impression of a powerful leashed dog awaiting only the slipping of a catch to hurl itself with great savagery at the enemy.

St. Leger's force included one hundred seasoned regulars each from the 8th and 34th regiments, the one-hundred-thirty-three-man Tory Regiment of Sir John's Royal Greens, a company of Tory Rangers under Colonel John Butler out of Niagara, and three hundred and fifty Hanau jaegers, or chasseurs — meaning hunters — these being special light German infantry troops especially trained for rapid maneuvering. In addition, there were forty experienced artillerists equipped with a pair of six-pounder cannon, two three-pounders and four cohorns, or royals.[113] Finally, there were about fifty Canadian irregulars and nearly two hundred axmen, boatmen and other noncombatants. With the thousand Indians assembled under the principal command of Joseph Brant and subcommand of Cornplanter of the Onondagas and Gu-cinge of the Senecas, St. Leger had a combined force of approximately two thousand men.[114]

In addition to being heartened by the size and seeming competence of St. Leger's force, word had spread rapidly among the Indians about the confrontation Brant had had with General Herkimer at Unadilla, how he had thwarted the assassination attempt and how he had forced Herkimer to back away. It was a very good omen.

As the council continued, it was obvious to the Indians that this army was not merely to be one force against another in a matter of ordinary warfare where personalities are not involved. Sir John and his party of Royal Greens, along with the Tory company under Colonel Butler, involved men with close ties to the country they were headed for; bitter men who would be facing opponents they knew personally — sometimes even sons or brothers — who had driven them out and confiscated all they owned. There was a great, abiding need for revenge for such wrongs among these men led by Johnson and Butler. It was something the Indians could understand, relate to and be encouraged by.

Finally, the greatest inspiration of the council came when Colonel Butler addressed them. Fluent in their dialects and long a favorite white man with many of them, Butler was shrewd, daring and extremely resourceful. His greatest weakness seemed to be his son Walter, who continued to ride everywhere on his father's coattails without ever contributing much, yet always resentful of the strength and prestige of his father. One day, Walter knew, his chance would come and when that occurred he intended to make the most of it.

"You need have no fear of what lies ahead of us," John Butler told them. "Our army marches tomorrow morning at dawn, but we do not expect you to attack Fort Stanwix. That will be this army's business. All you will have to do is look on and watch Fort Stanwix fall and take courage in the ease with which it happens. When that is done, then the whole of the Mohawk Valley is open to you and there will be no hindrance to you on the warpath. You may enter into battle with no limitation set on your style of warfare, and for every scalp you lift from the Mohawk Valley farmers who have taken your lands, you will receive twenty pounds' worth of presents from the King. You need have no fear of those you will face in the Mohawk Valley. They are like General Herkimer and you all know what happened with him at Unadilla a short while ago. Those Dutch Yankees are puddingfaces who will let themselves be robbed and scalped practically without resistance because they are stupid farmers, not fighting men. They have no chance against real warriors!"

The howl of approval this brought from a thousand Indian throats echoed for long minutes over the placid waters of Lake Ontario. With the exception of the Oneidas and some of their wards, the Tuscaroras, the Iroquois were still bound in common cause and fully committed to the British.

The exception was important. Even while the shrieks were still resounding, one of the Indians ceased his own howling and stamping and slipped off unseen into the darkened woods. In ten minutes he was back at his hidden camp talking to one of his warriors, explaining to him in detail what the Oswego council had entailed and that the whole force would begin its move in the morning to come against Fort Stanwix.

Cohdah — better known among the whites as Captain Louis [115] — listened to Ahnyero closely and nodded. He would carry the information to Colonel

Gansevoort immediately. Ahnyero watched him go and smiled. Then, with the others of his party following his lead, he sat on the ground and dipped his fingers into the paint pots and began drawing the designs of war upon his face. The Indians back at Oswego would be doing this now, too, and he was glad to apply it to himself. The war paint would greatly help disguise him and there would be much less chance than earlier this evening that he would be recognized by anyone as Thomas Spencer.

[*July 28, 1777 — Monday*]

Word of how General Herkimer had been faced down at Unadilla by Joseph Brant and his Indians swept the Mohawk Valley. No one really blamed Herkimer for backing off. Under the circumstances it was all he could do. Yet, there was a lessening of confidence in him because of it and a few murmurings that perhaps such a man should not be commanding general of the Tryon County Militia.

During the early part of this month Herkimer continued on the move with his force, investigating the fearful complaints of residents at Cherry Valley and Cobleskill and other settlements but finding always that any enemies had melted away before his arrival. As the month progressed his circle of coverage had dwindled and he remained closer to German Flats with his force.

His letters to the Continental Congress, along with those of the Committees of Safety of Tryon and Albany counties, requesting regular army detachments to help protect this frontier came to nothing. The Continental Congress, more intent on hotter revolutionary problems elsewhere, continued manifesting an almost complete indifference to the Mohawk Valley's need for defense.

Then Colonel Gansevoort, from some secret source of his own — Ahnyero's messengers, of course — had received the sure intelligence of the massing of St. Leger's force at Oswego and the ill-contained fear on the New York frontier bloomed into near panic overnight. To his credit, General Nicholas Herkimer was not slow in rising to the emergency. At once he issued Tryon County's first militia draft proclamation:

TO ALL CITIZENS OF TRYON COUNTY, NEW YORK
Whereas it appears certain that the enemy of about two thousand strong, Christians and savages, have arrived at Oswego with the intention to invade our frontiers, I think it proper and most necessary for the defense of our country — and it shall be ordered by me as soon as the enemy approaches — that every male person being in health, from 16 to 60 years of age in this our country, shall, as in duty bound, repair immediately with arms and accoutrements to the place to be appointed in my orders, and will then march to oppose the enemy with vigor as true patriots, for the just defense of their country.

And those that are above 60 years, or really unwell and incapable to march,

*shall assemble there also, at the respective places, when women and children will
be gathered together, in order for defense against the enemy if attacked, as much
as lies in their power.*

*But concerning the disaffected and those who will not directly obey such or-
ders, they shall be taken, along with their arms secured under guard, to join the
main body.*

*And as such, an invasion regards every friend to the country in general, but of
this county in particular, to show his zeal and well-affected spirit in actual
defense of the same.*

*All the members of the Committee as well as those who, by former commis-
sions or otherwise, have been exempted from any other military duty, are
requested to repair also, when called, to such place as shall be appointed, and
join to repulse our foes.*

*Not doubting that the Almighty Power, upon our humble prayer and sincere
trust in Him, will graciously succour our arms in battle for our just cause and
victory cannot fail to our side.*

> NICHOLAS HERKIMER, Brig. Gen.
> *Commanding*
> *Tryon County Militia*

There was a certain satisfaction in seeing how quickly Herkimer had risen to
the occasion. Such response was not any too visible elsewhere. As much as the
populace had not cared personally for Major General Philip Schuyler, they had
depended upon him and his army to protect the frontier. Instead, he was in
flight.

Schuyler, whose posts at Fort Ticonderoga and Skenesborough[116] had already fallen to the powerful advance of Burgoyne's army, had now abandoned
Fort Edward and continued his precipitate retreat down the Hudson. What
little faith the people had in him previously was now all but eliminated and
many were openly accusing him of treachery. John Adams very soberly declared, "We will never be able to defend a post until we shoot a general," and
George Washington was so upset by the retreating, especially from Ticonderoga,[117] that he wrote to Schuyler:

*It is an event of chagrin and surprise, not apprehended nor within the compass
of my reasoning: this stroke is severe indeed and has distressed us much. . . .*

Thus, the letter received this morning by the Tryon County Committee of
Safety from Schuyler did nothing to encourage the residents. Schuyler had
written:

*If Burgoyne can penetrate to Albany, the force which is certainly coming by way
of Oswego will find no difficulty in reaching the Mohawk River and, being ar-*

rived there, they will be joined not only by Tories but by every person that finds himself capable of removing and wishes to make his peace with the enemy, and by the whole body of the Six Nations. . . .

By late afternoon a copy of the Schuyler letter had found its way to the settlement of Deerfield, the most remote settlement on the Mohawk River. Located on the north bank of the river, it was exactly halfway between German Flats and Fort Stanwix — fourteen miles from each.[118]

By nightfall, Deerfield had been abandoned.

[July 31, 1777 — Thursday]

This was the evening of the sixth day since they had left Oswego and, on the whole, St. Leger was pleased with their progress. Not one untoward incident had occurred thus far and of the whole army, not a man was incapacitated by sickness or injury. Morale was high and there was a sense of mounting excitement among the men. If things continued as they were going, it would mean they could arrive at Fort Stanwix by the evening of the day after tomorrow. With the weather cooperating, an attack could be launched the next morning.

Of course, there was the pleasant possibility that there would be no need for an attack. Fort Stanwix might be so weak that its commander could be induced to surrender without a fight. That, in fact, was precisely what Colonel Claus had already been promising the Indians.

The only disturbing news had come just a few hours ago when an Indian employed by Molly Brant had brought the news to Joseph that two large bateaux well filled with supplies — food, clothing and ammunition — was en route up the Mohawk from Albany, accompanied by an escort of two hundred men who would stay at Fort Stanwix as a reinforcement. This party was under command of Lieutenant Colonel Robert Mellon, whom Colonel Gansevoort had sent down the Mohawk as soon as he had received word of St. Leger's army arriving at Oswego.

Even though St. Leger's army was moving along extremely well, it was unlikely they'd be in time to cut off that supply train. What it was bringing to Fort Stanwix could be crucial to what was to follow. That was when St. Leger chose twenty-four-year-old Lieutenant Herleigh Bird to push ahead rapidly with an advance detachment and try to take the Lower Landing at Fort Stanwix, thus preventing the supplies getting through.

Bird was bright, ambitious, courageous and cool-headed and he had accepted the command with obvious pleasure. With St. Leger's approval he hand-picked thirty skilled riflemen from Major Stephen Watts's battalion and, joined by the Cayuga Indian named Hare and about two hundred of the Iroquois, surged ahead for Fort Stanwix. With luck, even though St. Leger's force would be pushing up close behind, the detachment would probably get there half a day or more ahead of St. Leger.

It would be a race to see who reached the Lower Landing first, Bird or Mellon.

[*August 2, 1777 — Saturday Dawn*]

The lieutenant led the tall Indian to the door of Colonel Gansevoort's quarters inside Fort Stanwix and knocked gently. After a moment, when there was no response, he knocked again, somewhat louder, and the sleepy voice of the commanding officer bade him enter. Motioning the Indian to wait, he went inside, closing the door behind him. The wait was not long. When the door reopened, Gansevoort himself was there, stuffing his blouse into his trousers, his hair tousled but his manner alert. He nodded when he saw who was waiting and said, "All right, Lieutenant, thanks. You can leave now."

As the lieutenant strode away, Gansevoort stepped aside and tilted his head toward the interior.

"Come on in, Thomas."

Thomas Spencer — Ahnyero — moved inside, his lips a thin straight line. That was unusual because he was nearly always smiling. Gansevoort noticed the lack and commented on it. Spencer shook his head.

"There is no basis for smiling today, Colonel. I told you the next time you saw me would be my last report to you because the enemy would be near."

"How near?" Gansevoort asked quietly.

"They will be here tomorrow, perhaps even late today. They have artillery and they are very strong. You won't have an easy time."

Gansevoort smiled without warmth. "No, I suppose not. Are you staying?"

"No. I'm going on to see Herkimer at German Flats. They have to know what's coming."

The colonel nodded. "Yes, they have to know. Thank you, Thomas. I hope we'll see one another again soon."

Ahnyero shook his head. "No," he said, his voice dead level, "I have looked ahead. You and I will never see one another again. Good-bye."

He turned and left. Gansevoort, pondering that final remark, realized that it undoubtedly meant one of them was going to die.

The question was . . . who?

[*August 2, 1777 — Saturday Sunrise*]

"Oh, damn!" muttered Lieutenant Bird.

From cover he watched, dismayed, what was occurring at the Lower Landing, several hundred yards away. Without even knowing he was a contestant in a race, Lieutenant Colonel Robert Mellon had won. The two huge bateaux had already been beached at the landing and were in the process of being

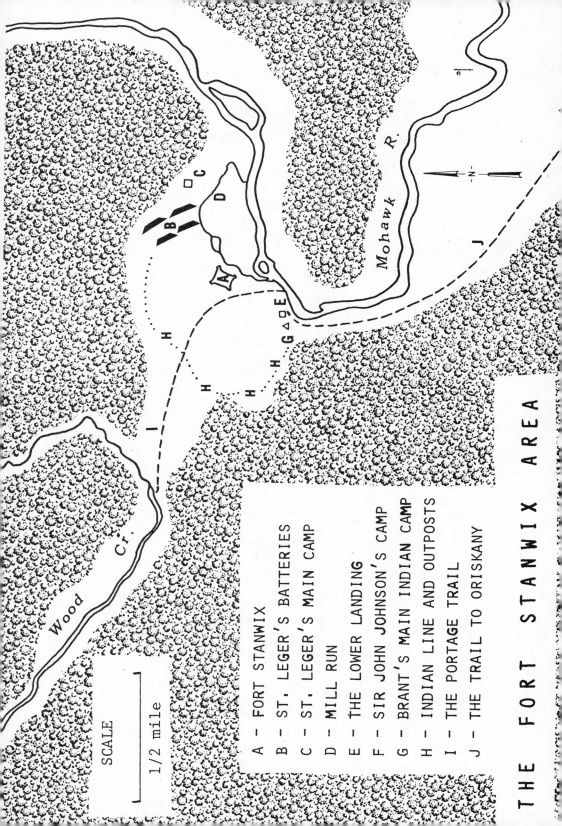

SCALE

1/2 mile

A – FORT STANWIX
B – ST. LEGER'S BATTERIES
C – ST. LEGER'S MAIN CAMP
D – MILL RUN
E – THE LOWER LANDING
F – SIR JOHN JOHNSON'S CAMP
G – BRANT'S MAIN INDIAN CAMP
H – INDIAN LINE AND OUTPOSTS
I – THE PORTAGE TRAIL
J – THE TRAIL TO ORISKANY

Wood Cr.

Mohawk R.

-N-

THE FORT STANWIX AREA

unloaded. The whole contingent of escort soldiers, plus a hundred or more that had been sent out of the fort by Colonel Gansevoort, were bringing in the supplies.

Shielding his eyes against the brightness of the newly risen sun and almost aching with the desire to attack, Bird held himself and his men still. Obviously they were outnumbered now, even with Brant's Indians to back them up, and there was nothing that could be done except grit one's teeth in frustration and try to ascertain as best as possible the fort's strength.

From the reports of spies, he had expected Fort Stanwix to be larger and stronger than it appeared to be. The fortifications were very crude and in his judgment the place could be carried by one well-concentrated rush. He didn't make the rush but he did send this view, along with a report of what had happened, to St. Leger by messenger.

Just as the last of the supplies disappeared into the fort, Hare and his Indians, having crept up on the two bateaux, attacked. It was a shallow victory. Only five men still remained with the boats — the two bateau captains and three crewmen. In the brief skirmish, one of the bateaumen was killed and the other four were captured.

A quarter mile away there was a heavy thudding sound as the heavy, reinforced gate of Fort Stanwix closed and the cross-timbers were dropped in place.

[August 3, 1777 — Sunday]

The last miles to reach the portage that spanned the short distance from the headwaters of Wood Creek to the upper Mohawk River were very difficult for St. Leger's army. For mile after mile, trees had been felled across Wood Creek, slowing their progress tremendously. St. Leger ordered cleared only enough to allow passage through, deciding to dispatch a detachment later to clear away the remainder. The important thing was to get to Fort Stanwix.

The portage itself, though lined with trees on either side of the portage trail, was a wide open plain over basically stony ground that gradually inclined from west to east. Near the central portion of it a sort of elevated plateau formed, which continued to the bank of the Mohawk. It was on this plateau that Fort Stanwix was located.

St. Leger had received notification of the fort's supposed weakness from Lieutenant Bird and, while he'd sent an express back cautioning Bird against making any movements himself against the fortification, he was sure it could be taken without any great difficulty. The thing he felt to be very important was to impress the Fort Stanwix garrison immediately with the strength and grandeur of his army, to strike terror in their hearts and encourage them to a swift surrender.

Arriving on this beautiful, calm and clear morning at last at the portage that the Iroquois called Deowainsta, he assembled his entire force and gave his instructions for the two-mile march from this point to Fort Stanwix. They were to uncase their standards, change into their finest wear and march with military bearing and pomp under banners unfurled at their head.

Within the hour the whole of St. Leger's army marched toward Fort Stanwix in precise ranks and files, the regulars clad in scarlet, Johnson's Royals in green and the Germans in blue, with the early sunlight glittering off the swords and unblackened gun barrels, and all the while, moving from cover to cover on each flank, the nearly one thousand war-painted Indians with tomahawks, knives, war clubs and muskets. From the ranks came the spirited notes of bugles and fifes and the stirring, cadenced rattling of the marching drums and the piercing squeal of bagpipes; all of this accompanied by the unnerving cries erupting from the Indians.

As St. Leger had intended, it was very impressive.

Within the fort the situation was tense. Fear was there, certainly, but not panic. The work done over these past weeks to make Fort Stanwix defensible had helped, but everyone was only too aware of the intrinsic weaknesses of the place. Whether or not it could stand against the pounding of artillery, no one knew. But even if it did, how *long* could they hold out? The nick-of-time safe arrival yesterday of the supplies and reinforcements had been a blessing, but ammunition was still scarce and, since much of their beef had gone bad, the food supply, even with the strictest of rationing, could not last more than six weeks.

Before the St. Leger force had shown up, Colonel Gansevoort had called a full assembly of his nine hundred and fifty troops to explain their situation fully and to get the tenor of their minds. To a man they had affirmed their resolve not to give in, no matter what.

"We have," Gansevoort told them, "fourteen pieces of artillery here in the fort. They are small and without the range or effectiveness of the artillery which our intelligence indicates St. Leger is bringing with him. Ours will not be able to reach them in their positions, but if the enemy try to carry us by storm, they will be of great benefit.

"Our gunpowder supply is good, thanks to the arrival yesterday of Colonel Mellon's detachment. Unfortunately, much of the ball we received is too large and will have to be remade. Worse, our supply of lead is very low. So low, in fact, that I am ordering a positive ban on random shooting from the fort. Shoot only when a sure target is in sight and shoot to kill. For now I am limiting the riflemen to nine shots each per day. Captains of the rifle squads are to name squads detailed to recover any enemy lead that is shot into this place and melt it down into new balls for us. All right, let's man the parapets. By the grace of God, we are going to defend this place!"

There was a rousing cheer and within minutes the entire banquette[119] was lined shoulder to shoulder with defenders. Now they gazed in silence over the ramparts at the glittering, awesome array of power moving their way from the westward. Not a shot was fired on either side.

St. Leger very wisely kept his forces well out of effective rifle range. He established his own command position within six hundred yards of the fort, northeast of it, effectively placed his batteries there and then ordered them covered by three redoubts.[120] The Indians were pretty much scattered in a broad encirclement of the fort.

Sir John Johnson established his Royal Greens, Canadians and Loyalist refugees from the Mohawk Valley to the south, out of cannon range of the fort, with the Mohawk River and its Lower Landing immediately to his right and Brant's principal encampment of Indians in the woods to his left. Finally, a smaller detachment of Loyalists was guarding the position on Wood Creek west of the fort.

Getting into position, setting up the batteries and constructing the redoubts took up much of the day, but this work was fairly well completed before sunset. Still no shots had been fired by anyone and the whole situation was taking on an unreal character.

Gansevoort was at this time in his quarters writing a report of the situation to General Schuyler when Lieutenant Colonel Marinus Willett approached him with a piece of paper in his hand.

"St. Leger has asked for our surrender."

The colonel leaned back and rubbed his eyes. "As expected. And if we refuse? Suppose we march out against them?"

"In that case," Willett glanced at the paper and read, "he says, '. . . the messengers of justice and of wrath await you in the field, and devastation, famine and every concomitant horror that a reluctant but indispensable prosecution of military duty must occasion will bar the way to their return.' "

"Rather lofty, wouldn't you say?" Gansevoort murmured, expecting no answer and getting none. He leaned forward and began reading over what he had written to General Schuyler. "I suppose I'll have to include it in the report," he added. "Leave it here."

"What about the message, sir? St. Leger's man is waiting outside the gate."

"Ignore it. And ignore him. He'll get tired of waiting. That's all the answer they need."

"Yes, sir!" Willett replied. He was grinning broadly.

[*August 3, 1777 — Sunday Afternoon*]

At almost the same time, some thirty miles down the Mohawk, eight hundred men were to rendezvous at Fort Dayton in German Flats in response to the emergency order issued by General Nicholas Herkimer. Poorly armed and largely without any real discipline or order, they were formed into four regiments of two hundred each. The Canajoharie District Regiment was placed under command of Colonel Ebenezer Cox, the Palatine District under Colonel Jacob Klock, the Mohawk District under Colonel Frederick Visscher and the Kingston–German Flats District under Colonel Peter Bellinger.

With numbers had come a peculiar and self-deceiving sense of invulnerability and invincibility. The men were in a carnival mood, with laughter and repartee almost constant and swept by a tremendous desire to move out without any delay whatever to destroy the force that had come to lay siege to Fort Stanwix. It would still be well into tomorrow, the officers were sure, before all the militia troops were assembled. So, despite their impatience, they would have to wait that long. Tomorrow, though, they would march up the Mohawk with all possible speed.

In an effort to tone down their enthusiasm and make them realize — and, in turn, pass this realization on to their men — the very great seriousness of the situation facing them at this time, General Herkimer called a meeting of all the officers.

"Our warning of what is happening at Fort Stanwix has come from Thomas Spencer, whom most of you know. He's an Oneida and he understands the Indian method of warfare better than any of us. He has given some warnings which we must not fail to heed."

"We don't need an Indian to tell us how to fight, General," Colonel Klock said brusquely.

"As a matter of fact," Herkimer contradicted him, "we do. Thomas says they'll be expecting us to come to Fort Stanwix's relief and there is no doubt whatever in his mind that in such knowledge they will lay an ambush for us."

"Is Spencer going to fight with us?" asked Colonel Cox.

"He is."

Cox nodded. "Then obviously there's not the danger he warns of. If there were, he wouldn't be walking into it with us. Just remember, General, he's an Indian, not a white man. We can't be all that sure whose side he's on."

Herkimer bristled. "There is no question of his loyalty. He is on my side."

An unidentified voice rose from the crowd. "Maybe. But whose side are *you* on, Herkimer?"

[August 3, 1777 — Sunday Night]

Molly Brant, in a little house on the edge of German Flats, paid no attention to the faint din of noise that filtered through the blanketed windows from the assembled troops in the darkness outside. She was speaking in her own language to a young Mohawk of about twenty.

"With all haste, go to my brother. Tell him that General Herkimer has assembled his army here. Tell him there are eight hundred men and that they are going to march against St. Leger's army tomorrow. Most of all, be sure to

tell him that instead of continuing to come up the north bank of the river until
they reach Fort Stanwix, the army plans to cross over the river at Deerfield and
camp at old Fort Schuyler [121] and then continue up the south bank along the
trail to Oriskany."

When she was finished, the youth slipped off into the night without a word.

[*August 5, 1777 — Tuesday*]

On the whole, Barry St. Leger was pleased with the way matters had gone in
the opening of the siege against Fort Stanwix. It would have simplified matters,
of course, had Colonel Gansevoort been one of those timid field commanders
who sometimes come along and run away if a fist is shaken in their direction,
but he hadn't really planned on that. As St. Leger had been quite sure would
happen, Gansevoort had ignored the first surrender demand. When the time
came for the second, the American colonel might be more inclined to give it
his attention. First he had to be softened up some.

Throughout most of the night of August 3, construction had continued on
the redoubts, from which riflemen could protect the batteries from being attacked, and with this completed, all but about two hundred and fifty of his men
had been detailed to help with the work at Wood Creek. Rather than try to
clear the waterway of the numerous trees that had been felled into it by Gansevoort's men, St. Leger was hastily clearing a road for sixteen miles through
the woods from some pine ridges on Fish Creek, which was as far as the
heavier supplies could be brought by water. This was with the assistance of
Captain Johannes Yost Herkimer, who was not only St. Leger's quartermaster
general but the brother of Nicholas Herkimer. [122] As soon as that road was
cleared, the material could be transported here. [123]

At nine o'clock yesterday morning, General St. Leger had given the order
and the light field pieces of the artillery opened up against the fort. Almost immediately sporadic rifle fire also commenced, especially directed from the Indians against anything they could see moving on the fort's ramparts. Before
very long, St. Leger realized the light field pieces were having very little effect
and so he switched to bombardment by his heavier cannon and supported this
with cohorns lobbing occasional fragmentary shells directly into the fort. These
caused a few deaths and some injuries at first, but then sentinels were stationed
to watch every match being applied to the artillery and to shout out the warning "Shot!" or "Shell!" at which everyone inside would immediately prostrate
himself until after the small impact explosion.

As much harassment as the artillery fire was, the rifle fire by the Indians was
worse. They had settled down to do some sniping at soldiers who were still
working to cover the fort's interior roofs and parapets with sod. One of the best
of these snipers was Ki, a Mohawk who had been a friend of Joseph Brant since
they were raised together at Canajoharie.

Brant had sent Ki up to the top of a dense pine tree, where he took a comfortable position well screened from the fort. He took his time in shooting, but whenever he shot he hit his mark. Immediately following the shot he would lower his rifle by the cord attached to it and draw up another from below, all primed and ready to shoot. Within a couple of hours Ki managed to kill three American soldiers and wound seven others. Finally the Americans saw a telltale puff of smoke from the top of the pine not much more than a couple hundred yards distant. At once they moved one of the cannon into position, loaded it with grapeshot, aimed and fired. It was the first American cannon shot of the siege and a very good one. Along with a rain of branches cut off by the grape, Ki fell to the ground, dead. A shout of triumph rose from the soldiers in the fort. After that, the Indian rifle firing came from considerably farther away and was much less effective.

The artillery bombardment continued with scarcely a pause throughout the day and only ceased when there was no longer light enough to aim. At dawn today the barrage had been resumed and it continued until sunset.

That was when Daniel Claus, Sir John Johnson and Joseph Brant all came in a group to see General St. Leger.

The British commander listened carefully but without comment as Claus and Johnson told of the intelligence that had just been received by Brant from his sister, Molly. He then questioned the Mohawk war chief carefully:

"From what your sister says in regard to the route being used by General Herkimer to come against us, is there any place in that direction where an ambush could be laid with any reasonable hope of success?"

Brant nodded. "Yes. They are coming by the trail which goes through Oriskany on the south bank of the Mohawk. There are many defiles there where ambush could be made, but one I know in particular which would be ideal."

St. Leger chewed his upper lip a moment and then came to a decision. "Chief Brant, how many men would you need to ambush them?"

Brant considered. "At least four hundred. Better to have more."

"Take twice that. Hit them hard. Sir John"—he turned his attention to Johnson — "you said a few minutes ago you wanted to be in on this. You're sure?"

Johnson's eyes glittered with anticipation and he nodded. "Yes, I'm sure."

"All right. You command our people. Take all your Royal Greens. Colonel Claus wants to go too. Take him. Captain McDonald also." He turned back to Brant. "You're in top command, Joseph, since you know the ground. How long will it take to get there?"

Brant glanced at the dusk settling over the area. "An hour to prepare, maybe more. Oriskany, assuming we can engage them there, which we don't know for certain yet, is three hours' fast march by daylight, but we'll be moving after dark. Say four, five hours at best. Spreading out, taking position, getting hidden, another hour or so." He shrugged lightly. "Dawn comes early. We'll be in position and waiting before daybreak."

St. Leger smiled tightly. He liked Brant's quickness. "Excellent. I wish you success."

Now, late in the evening, even though there still came the occasional cracking of a rifle or muffled call, there was an unnatural stillness around Fort Stanwix. Though the garrison behind those walls had no way of knowing it, St. Leger had virtually split his force in two. For a little while it would be a dangerous situation.

General St. Leger sat in his tent at a little makeshift desk, a small lantern shedding light enough to write by. He began his report of this date to General Burgoyne with a sentence he knew would make his commander very happy:

Sir. The fort will be mine directly, and we will speedily meet as victors in Albany.

[*August 5, 1777 — Tuesday, Midnight*]

Herkimer studied the four men before him in his tent at the ruins of old Fort Schuyler across the river from abandoned Deerfield. He'd known Adam Helmer for many years and if any man from this region could get through, it ought to be Adam. And Adam had chosen his companions well. One of them *should* make it. The general took the pipe from his mouth and pointed the stem at Helmer.

"Repeat the instructions."

Helmer nodded. "We move to Stanwix as rapidly as possible and tell Colonel Gansevoort you're on your way. He's to hold fast in the fort but to fire three consecutive cannon shots so you'll know the message is received. He is then to send out a sortie as a diversion to keep the enemy occupied as you approach the fort to attack them. At your attack, Colonel Gansevoort is to rally his entire force remaining inside the fort and emerge to support your attack, striking the enemy from the other side and cutting off retreat."

"Good. Excellent. God bless all four of you. We'll be listening for the cannon."

CHAPTER III

[*August 6, 1777 — Wednesday*]

THE mood of General Nicholas Herkimer was every bit as dark as the heavy clouds that filled the sky this morning. He was angry at his officers for their accusations and insinuations, but even more than that he was angry at himself for the stubborn Dutch pride that was forcing him to go on despite his own better judgment.

He turned in his saddle and looked back at the double column of men behind him and his expression was grim. Though the men maintained the double line, it was ragged at best, without any real sense of precision or discipline. The men talked loudly, laughed, complained, held their rifles by the barrel and over the shoulder as if they were clubs or sometimes even used them as canes to help in walking over the rougher terrain. Eight hundred men were in this formation, stretching back for well over half a mile, with the final two hundred bringing up the rear behind the supply wagons, but having fallen behind somewhat.

Since the march began this morning almost three hours ago, they had covered less than five miles, but there seemed to be no way to speed things up. The sense of apprehension in Herkimer's mind would have been much worse if it hadn't been for the Oneidas joining them last night. Now, with about a third of them fanned out on the narrow road ahead of him, he felt a little more secure in their progress. If there was going to be any sort of attack made against them, as Thomas Spencer had warned at Fort Dayton and again last night, the Oneidas leading the way would undoubtedly sense it and give warning.

Herkimer turned and faced the front again, looking at the way the twenty Indians ahead moved along and wishing his own men were even half as alert. The Oneidas, sixty of them, had joined Herkimer's force last night.[124] Incredibly, instead of being grateful, some of the officers — Colonels Cox and Paris especially — were suspicious of them.

"We can fight our own wars," Ebenezer Cox had declared, "without having to side with the likes of them!"

The Oneidas were unruffled. "We promised long ago," Chief Coh-ega told Herkimer, "that we would help when the time came. That time has come and we are here."

It was about half an hour or more after Herkimer had dispatched Adam Helmer and his three companions with the message for Gansevoort that Coh-ega and his men had arrived. Since then the friction between Herkimer and his officers had become all but unbearable. Though the men were weary, for some reason they demanded to push on another mile or so before camping. The whole army crossed over Sauquoit Creek and camped on the relatively level meadow to the west of it. [125]

The disagreement between Herkimer and his officers had finally flared into the open first thing this morning during a conference Herkimer called. Of the five colonels — Cox, Paris, Klock, Campbell and Visscher — both Cox and Paris were contemptuous of any danger ahead and railed at what they considered to be Herkimer's overcautiousness. Klock and Visscher were less vocal, but they tended to support the stance of Cox and Paris. Only Samuel Campbell, third in command after Herkimer and Cox, seemed supportive of the general's position. The officers and men were for pushing on toward Fort Stanwix at once and their arguments in favor of doing so indeed had some sense to them. What if St. Leger's force overran Fort Stanwix? Where then would there be any protection for the Mohawk Valley? Every instant lost in haggling could work toward the enemy's advantage.

Herkimer was at first unbudging. He had argued that in size St. Leger's force was well over twice their own strength and prudence demanded that they wait for the three-gun signal from the fort. Suppose, he had further argued, that the enemy force divided and half of them attacked this militia force while the other half moved down the Mohawk and ravaged the homes and farms? He pointed out that Brant, as they all knew, had recently been at Unadilla with many warriors and he might attack from that direction. Finally, seeing he was getting nowhere with them, he told them disgustedly that those who were demanding so loudly to move on would be the first to panic and run if they smelled burnt powder. He had then appealed to Thomas Spencer for support and the Oneida spoke to them.

"You must believe," he had said, "that I know how Joseph Brant will act in a situation like this. If he doesn't attack us along the way to Fort Stanwix, he'll attack us when we're weakened from fighting St. Leger and he'll wipe us out. There is a great need for the caution and discipline General Herkimer advises."

The officers had refused to listen to the arguments and began accusing Herkimer of cowardice and, even worse, of complicity with the enemy. It was well known that Nicholas Herkimer's brother, Johannes Yost Herkimer, was St.

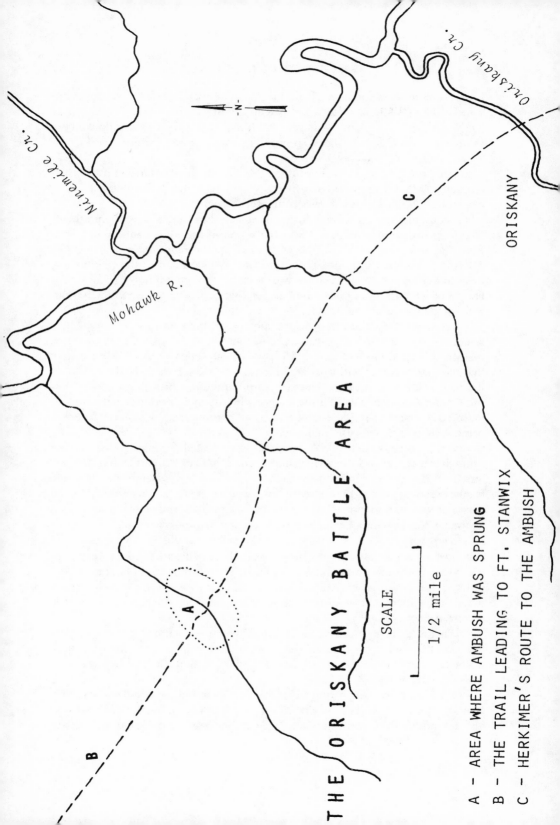

THE ORISKANY BATTLE AREA

SCALE

1/2 mile

A — AREA WHERE AMBUSH WAS SPRUNG
B — THE TRAIL LEADING TO FT. STANWIX
C — HERKIMER'S ROUTE TO THE AMBUSH

Mohawk R.

Ninemile Cr.

Oriskany Cr.

ORISKANY

A

B

C

Leger's quartermaster general. Didn't this suggest there was some sort of collusion occurring? The fact that a fair percentage of the men in Herkimer's army had friends or relatives in St. Leger's or Burgoyne's army was of little concern to them. It was Colonel Paris who put the consensus into words.

"Either lead us on now or step down!"

So Herkimer, enraged, had shouted, "March on, then!" and, against his better judgment, had mounted his fine white mare and led them, the familiar black pipe clamped grimly between his teeth.

Every moment of the march during these first three hours now behind them, Herkimer had been straining to hear the sound of the triple cannonburst from Fort Stanwix. Not yet having heard it, his apprehension continued to grow. The march this morning had proceeded in the flood plain of the river valley, westward along the narrow two-rut wagon trail rather grandiosely called the Albany Road,[126] running along the base of the steep wooded slope to the left, which towered about one hundred feet over the road most of the way.

Three and a half miles from where they began their morning's march, they waded across the ford of Oriskany Creek and passed through the place where many years ago there had been a Mohawk village called Oriska.[127] It was here that the march began getting more difficult. The steep hills pressed in closer to the Mohawk River and now the road ran up and down hills that were increasingly difficult to negotiate. This was where the supply train of ox-drawn wagons followed by the two-hundred-man rear guard commanded by Colonel Visscher began falling back from the main body.

Almost a mile west of Oriskany Creek they passed through a steep ravine through which ran a little rivulet and then, less than a quarter mile farther, they passed another. Half a mile later they crossed a third and now they had begun entering the fourth one, which was the worst yet. So steep that at some places it was almost precipitous, the narrow road moved down into a deep ravine at the bottom of which was a substantial brook without any official name,[128] spanned by a causeway of logs. As steeply as the road went down the east side, so too it rose sharply on the west and the distance from one side of the ravine to the other was about half a mile. Even on days with bright sunlight the road here was deeply shaded by the overhanging trees. On a cloudy day, as today, even though it was now just about 10:00 A.M., there was almost the gloom of deep twilight in the area.

It was just as Herkimer and the twenty Oneidas preceding him were nearing the top of the western slope, with the whole force behind them stretched back through the ravine to the top of the eastern slope, that the perfectly executed ambush was sprung.

The brilliance of Joseph Brant in selecting the ambush site and planning his strategy attested to the faith placed in him by the Iroquois League. His force of about a thousand Indians and whites had arrived here about three or four in the morning and, at Brant's direction, had taken their places. Care was observed that no footprints showed on the dirt of the road, that no plants were broken down to indicate anyone had passed, that no down-hanging tree branches were broken to get them out of the way. The force simply flowed into the area and then melted out of sight of the road. The whole eastern side of the ravine and part of the slope on the west were under the hidden guns of the Indians. The rest of the western slope was under the hidden guns of Johnson's Royal Greens and the Rangers under his second-in-command, Major Stephen Watts.

It was incredible; a thousand or more men hidden mere yards from the road, hidden so well that not a man of Herkimer's army, not even his Oneida allies leading the way, had any idea of the trap they had entered. Brant had planned to box the entire Herkimer army in this ravine and his instructions had been for no shot to be fired until this was accomplished. But because the two-hundred-man rear guard supply wagons had now fallen several hundred yards behind, it wasn't entirely possible. If they waited, the front of the army would be passing out of the trap. The time to strike was now. Brant cupped his mouth.

"Sa-sa-kwon! Sa-sa-kwon!"

In a ragged, rumbling, thundering chorus beginning at the west end of the line but almost instantly taking in the whole of it, a thousand or more rifles fired. Instantly the ambushing Indians at the eastern slope moved together from both sides of the road, closing off escape. Farther east, Colonel Visscher's rear guard pulled up short and in that instant they panicked, turned and fled, Colonel Visscher himself in the lead, pursued by a howling body of attackers who quickly caught up and engaged them.

The first volley was devastating. In those initial seconds of the firing, about two hundred Americans were shot. Immediately Herkimer wheeled about on his horse and bellowed an order to close up. On the very heels of his words, a bullet smashed into his leg just below the knee, shattering the bone. Simultaneously another ball struck his large white mare, killing her. Herkimer was catapulted out of the saddle but immediately sat up, shook his head to clear it and continued calling out orders for his troops to close up toward the center to make a stand. In other areas of the line, Major John Eisenlord, Major Dennis Klepsattle and Major Harmanus Van Slyck were killed in the first few seconds.

Colonel Isaac Paris of the Palatine Committee of Safety was shot through the fleshy part of his lower arm and captured almost immediately. He begged for mercy and wept and was led away.[129]

Colonel Ebenezer Cox rushed up to Herkimer, shouting, "I'm taking command, sir! You're out of commission. I am taking command!" It may have been one of the shortest-lived commands in history. As the words were uttered, a rifle ball passed through his head, killing him. Immediately Colonel Samuel Campbell of Cherry Valley took command, though still allowing himself to be guided by the comments of the original commander. Herkimer was quickly carried to a slightly safer place by Captain Christian House, who seated the wounded general on his saddle at the base of a huge beech tree, against which he propped him for support. His men began forming a circle around him and here, ignoring the pain of his shattered leg, he calmly loaded his pipe and continued to direct activities as best he could.[130]

At the head of the line practically all the Oneidas were killed by the murderously accurate fire from Johnson's Royal Greens and the Rangers. One of those killed was Chief Coh-ega. Another was Ahnyero — the blacksmith Thomas Spencer[131] — who indeed would never see Gansevoort again.

Adding a hideous cacophony to the rattling of gunfire were the shrieks of the Indians, who, having fired their guns, were now charging to the attack with tomahawks and war clubs. To this were added the screams of men dying or wounded or those simply filled with panic. The din was frightful and the hand-to-hand combat fierce beyond belief.

At the rear, all the supply wagons were already in control of the Indians and some were being plundered or burned. The large segment of Indians that had given chase to Colonel Visscher's panic-stricken rear guard caught up with them, cut their lines apart and killed or captured the greater percentage, along with whatever supplies, firearms and ammunition they had.

In the early part of the fighting, the prior instructions of Brant to his warriors now paid dividends. "Keep under cover until you see a gun fired your way from behind a tree," he had told them, "and then run as swiftly as you can to that place and tomahawk your enemy before he can reload." It was good strategy that worked well until at last what was happening began to dawn on the Americans. Then two men would hide behind the same tree but only one would fire. When the Indian would then rush up, the second man could shoot him dead.

In the general fighting now, the forces of Brant and Johnson were taking severe punishment too. Hare fell dead in midrun, hit virtually simultaneously by three different bullets. Chief Gisu-gwatoh of the Senecas was all but beheaded by the slashing of Colonel Campbell's sword. A lead ball passed through the upper chest of the Cayuga chief Ghalto, miraculously missing any vital organs but putting him out of commission and causing him to be one of the few Indians captured alive. Here and there other chiefs and a great many warriors were falling. Fair numbers of the British Rangers under Major Watts and the Greens under Johnson were being hit, many of them fatally. Watts was badly wounded in the leg but continued to fight.[132] Lieutenant Singleton of his command was wounded by a bullet that had first passed through the heart of Lieutenant McDonald.

Private William Merckley of Palatine, moving to join a large circle of defenders around General Herkimer, took two bullets almost simultaneously through the legs. One, in his lower right leg, was not too bad. The other, high in the left leg, severed the femoral artery. As he lay there watching the blood spurting in great gouts, a neighbor from Palatine, Adam Thumb, stopped to help him. Merckley shoved him away savagely.

"Take care of yourself," he rasped. "Can't you see I'm dead?"

Thumb hesitated, then ran on to the line. Coming on similarly toward the circle from the other direction, Major Samuel Clyde of Cherry Valley ran as he had never run before, leaping over logs, dodging around trees and plunging through brush. He had lost his rifle, and so headlong was his run for safety that before he could check himself, he ran into one of Johnson's Rangers, who knocked him down with his rifle butt. The Ranger was just on the verge of bayoneting Clyde when John Flock of Johnstown shot him dead. Clyde scooped up the fine Queen Anne's musket his assailant had used and raced on beside Flock to the circle of defenders.

For two hours the battle had been raging and then an even greater sound overwhelmed them. The dense clouds overhead suddenly burst in a great storm of rain and lightning and thunder. It was the most vicious thunderstorm of the entire year thus far in the Mohawk Valley and it made all the flintlocks inoperative. Immediately the battle virtually ceased as men lay on their arms to protect them.

To the white attackers it was a respite.

To the Indian attackers it was a very bad omen.

To the defenders it was an incredibly providential reprieve.

The battle was by no means over, but something very important was happening. The longer it rained, the gloomier became the outlook of the Indians. Brant had been outstanding in the battle, leading his warriors with harsh cries, striking left and right with great courage and strength and deadliness, a constant inspiration to them. Now he tried to encourage them, telling them it was just a storm and they should take advantage of it and rush in for hand-to-hand combat, at which they so excelled, while the Americans could not fire their guns. The Iroquois refused. The omen was bad enough as it was without tempting the total wrath of the Great Spirit by ignoring it or by continuing to do what quite obviously the omen had been sent to stop.

For nearly an hour the rain fell in torrential downpour while the eyes of the combatants were dazzled by the brilliance of the blue-white flashes of lightning and the ear-splitting crescendo of the thunder made the ground tremble beneath them.

Herkimer used the temporary lull in the battle to discuss the situation with Colonel Campbell and got him to strengthen the circle of his men. Before the rain it was a large circle, actually an elongated oval in shape, perhaps two hundred yards long by fifty or sixty wide. With the tightening, it was pulled in on itself so that by the time the rain stopped it was no more than forty yards wide and eighty yards long.

On the British side, Colonel John Butler was devising a stratagem of his own. To about thirty volunteers of the Royal Greens he proposed a bold ruse to try breaking the strengthened American circle of defenders. The hats the Greens were wearing were very similar to those worn by the American soldiers. And the green jackets, when turned inside out, looked remarkably like those of the Americans. Now, as the storm was ending, he had them invert their coats, wear their hats, form themselves into a platoon and march boldly toward the Herkimer lines. He was sure they would be mistaken as a reinforcement sent from Fort Stanwix. He was right.

The first man in the American line to see them coming was Private Sampson Sammons of Fonda, a member of the Committee of Safety. He let out a great whoop of joy and ran to tell his officer, Captain Jacob Gardinier of the Mohawk District, the good news. Gardinier came to the line, took a look and was equally deceived. Gardinier had only seven men holding this position of the circle but, as luck would have it, one of the privates abruptly recognized an old acquaintance in the approaching platoon and ran with outstretched arms to greet him. At once his arms were grabbed and he was dragged near some bushes as a prisoner. Witnessing part of this, Captain Gardinier ran from the line and hit one of the private's captors with his fist, leveling him and setting the private free.

As he turned to rush back to the line, Gardinier was mobbed by others of the Greens. One of them he killed with his gun and the second he wounded with his sword, but three more of the Greens attacked him together. Two of the men knocked him to the ground and impaled him there with their bayonets through his thighs. The third Green thrust his bayonet at Gardinier's chest, but the captain grabbed the blade in his left hand, jerked so that his attacker fell on top of him and then held him there as a shield atop himself.

Private Adam Miller saw what was happening and plunged to the rescue, bowling over the two upright Greens with his rush. With the bayonets pulled free of his legs, Gardinier thrust away the enemy still on his chest and then ran him through with his sword. It was just at this moment that a group of twenty or thirty Americans burst onto the scene, led by Captain Andrew Dillenback of Palatine.

"For God's sake, Captain," one of the soldiers yelled, "you're killing your own men!"

"Goddammit!" Gardinier shouted. "They're *not* our men. They're Tories! Shoot!"

They did. The ruse was ruined and the firing was virtually a signal for the renewal of the battle on all fronts. Dillenback rushed into the midst of the Greens to give the wounded Gardinier a chance to get back to the circle. As he did so, Dillenback was himself attacked. One of the Greens grabbed his rifle, but he jerked it back and brained the man with it, killing him. Another rushed up and Dillenback shot him through the throat. A third came on and the Palatine captain bayoneted him through the chest. As the man fell and Dillenback tried to pull his weapon free, a bullet from the Greens caught him in the spine and killed him.

The resumed battle continued strong on all fronts for perhaps another hour. A great mutual hatred existed between Herkimer's militiamen and Sir John's Greens, who were mostly Mohawk Valley refugees. Now, with their ammunition expended, hand-to-hand combat became severe. Then, even the impetus of that wore off. The eagerness for the battle had all but fled from the Indians and now they began to grow afraid. How could this force of Americans, attacked so savagely and suffering so great a loss of men, continue to defend itself so determinedly? Wasn't the rainstorm a warning from the Great Spirit to withdraw themselves from this sort of white man's battle? It was not the Indian way to stand and hold ground and battle. It was the Indian way to strike and run and strike again. This time, because of the encouragement of Sir John Johnson and Colonel Daniel Claus and Colonel John Butler, they had not done so and look at what had happened: already the losses it had cost them in chiefs and warriors was near the greatest in their history, and so the fear grew greater.[133]

To most of the combatants down in the ravine with the battle sounds a continuing din swirling all around, the significant sound went unheard. But to Sir John, who was near the western top of the ravine, it came clearly enough. It was three successive heavy thumps of cannon fire from a great distance. Fort Stanwix!

Sir John quickly began giving his officers orders to pull their men back and reform. Within moments, Brant was aware of what was happening, and immediately he cupped his mouth and four or five times repeated the cry that only he, as war chief, had the authority to initiate.

"*Oooo-nah! Oooo-nah! Oooo-nah! Oooo-nah!*"

It was the cry to retreat, and immediately upon its being sounded, it was relayed by chiefs and subchiefs. They began to leave at once, picking up their dead and wounded and whatever plunder and weapons they could find. Within ten minutes no more shots were being fired.

The Battle of Oriskany was over.

Of the eight hundred Americans involved, less than three hundred survived. Some two hundred and fifty were killed at the battle scene and another two hundred and fifty were mortally wounded and died on the way back to Fort Dayton or after reaching there. About fifty were captured.

On the other side the totals were smaller but no less grim. The Indians suffered most, having lost twenty-three of their chiefs and sixty-eight warriors. As many more were wounded and a handful, including Chief Ghalto, were captured. Johnson's white forces had thirty-three men killed and forty-one wounded.

War had come to the Mohawk Valley.

[*August 6,* 1777 — *Wednesday Afternoon*]

Adam Helmer was a man who rarely took chances of any kind. He was also a considerable egotist — enough so that he never questioned his own belief that however long it took him to get safely through to Colonel Gansevoort at Fort Stanwix, everything would hang fire until he did.

When he and his three companions left General Herkimer about midnight, they began following the path toward Fort Stanwix. Hardly an hour later, just a little distance west of Oriskany, they had been forced to take refuge in some heavy underbrush to avoid being detected by a large number of Indians and some whites passing them in a double file, going in the opposite direction.

"You reckon they're gonna hit Gen'ral Herkimer an' our boys, Adam?" whispered one of the men.

"Hard sayin'," Helmer whispered back.

"Don't you reckon we oughta circle 'round an' go back an' tell the gen'ral 'bout this?"

Helmer shook his head. "We got our orders. Don't talk. I don't fancy gettin' caught by 'em."

After the main body of the party passed them, smaller groups kept coming along and sometimes even individuals, hurrying to catch up. For over an hour they continued to pass and Helmer, exercising complete caution, remained hidden with his companions for another couple of hours beyond that. At last, moving with extreme caution and silence, they slipped out of hiding and once again moved toward the fort. Now, fearful of moving along the path, they kept to the woods parallel to the path, but the going was so difficult in the darkness that their progress was very slow.

Daylight had come when they were still about two miles from the fort and, becoming now very visible, the four kept even more out of sight, slipping from cover to cover. The last mile took them longest of all. As they began seeing little individual Indian camps in a perimeter running from the Mohawk River in a semicircle westward toward the big cedar swamp southwest of the fort, they lay in hiding again for a long while, trying to determine how to get past.

There was no artillery firing this morning, but scattered rifle shots were heard. The enemy seemed to have the fort surrounded and it looked to Helmer as if there were no way to get in safely. Herkimer had told him about the little sally port located on the east side of the fort and he knew that was where they would have to enter. There would be no opening of the main gate on the south side for them.

By 11:00 A.M. the sky had darkened appreciably with storm clouds and Helmer decided on his plan. As the rain began to fall heavily, he led his companions unseen to the river's edge and entered the water. There, close to shore and with only their heads exposed, the three moved slowly upstream. Twice they had to stop and wait long periods for enemy scouts to pass before continuing. The most difficult passage was at the Lower Landing, where there was a sizable Indian and Ranger camp. Most of the enemy were absent from it, but their effects were there, along with a guard of about a hundred men. Fortunately, after a considerable wait, the skies literally burst and under cover of the extremely hard rain, which drove the attackers into shelter, the four moved along in the water fifty yards or so past the landing to where a small muddy brook entered the river on their side. This they followed upstream and it took them to within a stone's throw of the southeast bastion of the fort.

Just as the storm was lettng up, the four left the rivulet and hastened to the sally port. The enemy spied them at this point and a few shots were directed their way from a distance, but none of the four was hit. Lookouts on the ramparts saw them coming and an alert was called. A platoon, bristling with weapons, was waiting just inside when the sally port was opened a body's width for their entry.

The Helmer party was taken immediately to Colonel Gansevoort and he listened carefully to what they had to say. A few minutes afterward he held a council with his officers and then sounded full assembly of all the men inside the fort not on rampart guard duty and addressed them, informing them that help was near, that General Herkimer's relief column was on the way, comprised of all the effective militia of the Mohawk Valley. There was understandable excitement and cheering at this news. It was tempered, however, with the report that a large force of Indians with some whites had been heading that way last night and may have gone to cut them off. There was a considerable murmuring of voices after that.

Abruptly Lieutenant Colonel Marinus Willett held up his hands until the men had quieted and then he addressed them loudly: "Men, you've heard that General Herkimer's force is on the march to our relief. We wish him success in his encounter today with the enemy from here who went to cut him off. We think he will have just such success. In the meanwhile, it seems that now Sir John's camp is very much weakened. I am planning on making a sortie against that camp while the enemy force is split. As many of you as feel willing to go with me and attack it, and aren't afraid to possibly die for liberty in the process, shoulder your arms and step out one pace in front."

Willett grinned as practically two hundred men stepped out simultaneously. By the time they had been formed up and instructions given, another fifty had joined them, and Colonel Gansevoort authorized Willett's taking along one of the fort's wheeled three-pounder cannons.

Acting on General Herkimer's message, Colonel Gansevoort had three cannon prepared and then fired in rapid succession, all three shots within fifteen seconds. Immediately the sally port was opened and Willett charged out with his force, heading for the camp of Sir John, which was commanded in his absence by Lieutenant Herleigh Bird.

At his position in the other direction near the British artillery, Brigadier General Barry St. Leger saw what was happening and formed up a detachment of his own men under Captain Eugene Hoyes to cut in on the rear of Willett's force while they were attacking Sir John's camp and Lieutenant Bird was keeping them occupied in front.

It didn't work out that way. The attack was swift and unexpected. Bird, not prepared for the rush of Americans coming his way, tumbled out of his tent in shirtsleeves,[134] saw what was happening and, in the face of the bayoneted rifles charging them, immediately fell back with his men, hardly engaging Willett's force at all. The cards all seemed stacked in favor of the Americans at this point. Captain Hoyes attacked Willett's rear but was driven back after a brief, hot fight and forced to keep a distance away, leaving six of his men dead on the field and four captured. Willett had a couple of men slightly injured and none of his officers were harmed.[135]

Willett pressed his advantage. Sir John's camp was pillaged and everything that could be taken was gathered in piles. A small detachment was sent back to the fort for wagons, of which the quartermaster had seven he could send out. Three times, under fire, all seven wagons were loaded and brought into the fort with all the confiscated goods, including camp equipage, clothing, cooking utensils, food, blankets, stores and a small number of weapons and some ammunition. The booty also included an unexpected prize — all of Sir John's personal equipment, including his papers and maps, correspondence, journals — even his hat and five British flags. Two injured men, unable to flee, were captured in the camp and taken prisoner. They were Lieutenant Warren Singleton and Captain Geoffrey Watts.

Brant's Indians had traveled lightly to go to the attack against General Herkimer's army, clad mostly in just loincloths or leggings, without shirts and without any weapons beyond what they needed for the fight. All the rest of their supplies and equipment — shirts, trousers, blankets, wampum, food, silver ornaments, paints and weapons — had been left at the camp and now Willett confiscated them and had them taken into the fort. Twenty-one full wagonloads were taken in before Willett decided they had pushed their luck far enough and ordered his detachment back to the fort.

St. Leger wasn't holding still. Beside himself with anger at the poor showing his detachments had made, he took two light brass cannon with him and directed his men to follow him and try to cut off Willett's retreat. For a few fearful minutes it looked as if he'd succeed, but a concentrated support fire from the fort drove St. Leger's detachment back and Willett's detachment made it back inside the fort without the loss of a man. The excitement and enthusiasm inside Fort Stanwix was unparalleled and immediately the captured British flags were run up the flagpole to hang limply beneath the makeshift American flag.

[*August 6, 1777 — Wednesday Evening*]

"Damn it, sir, we have *got* to follow up with an attack down the Mohawk Valley!"

John Johnson's eyes flashed angrily as he spoke to General St. Leger and his voice shook. It had been a hard day. He'd lost more of his force — especially among the Indians — than he'd anticipated and, that not being bad enough, had returned to find his camp attacked and plundered and hardly anything left, all that apparently occurring in plain sight of St. Leger. Everything Johnson had was gone and his fury was scarcely containable.

"We will continue the siege here, Sir John," St. Leger replied icily. He didn't elaborate. He didn't have to, knowing Sir John was well aware that since Willett's successful sortie this afternoon, he'd taken steps to prevent anything similar from occurring. He had given orders to complete a two-gun battery and mortar beds in their rear. This would enable him, in case of another sortie from the fort, to counter with a larger body of the King's troops. He'd also sent Captain Henry Lernoult with one hundred and ten men and a three-pounder to the Lower Landing to hold and protect that area and help prevent any further sallies from the fort. Obviously, now that the horse was gone, St. Leger was strongly barring the barn doors.

Johnson closed his eyes momentarily and took a deep breath. He was a little more under control when he opened them and spoke again.

"You don't know these Mohawk Valley people as I do, General," he said. "You don't understand the impact of what happened to them at the battle today. They've been all but crushed. Somewhere between a quarter and a half of their entire force has been killed and most of the rest are wounded. They're disheartened. They're out of ammunition and they're not professional soldiers. They're not conditioned to stand and fight in such circumstances. They'll run. I *know* they'll run. Leave a detachment here, if necessary, to keep Gansevoort bottled up in the fort so he can't attack our rear, but right now we *must* sweep down the Mohawk. Everything in front of us will fall if we do, and we'll have no trouble forming the junction with General Burgoyne on the Hudson."

St. Leger was shaking his head all the while Sir John had been speaking. "You have," he told Sir John imperiously, "no concept of military strategy, sir. Routing a ragtag army of militia will not have the effect on the country that destroying a well-garrisoned fort of regular soldiers will. We'll continue here until we take the fort."

Sir John shook his head, almost beside himself with frustration. "Listen to me! My Indians are barely containable now. Don't you realize what a blow it is to them first to lose so many of their chiefs and warriors in the battle and then to return here and find everything they owned gone? Don't you realize that right now they're eager to take revenge on the Americans, but if you hold them here, eventually they're going to turn that anger against you. They'll begin to hold you responsible for their losses, both here and at Oriskany."

"We'll continue here, Sir John," St. Leger repeated flatly. "I am in command by order of the King and I will not kowtow to the whims of a group of savages. This campaign has thus far been conducted in a military manner and it will continue that way. Now, bring the two American officers to me."

John Johnson continued staring at him a moment, unwilling to believe any human being could be so shortsighted and ego-driven. Then, without a word, he wheeled and left the tent. He felt that if he stayed a moment longer, he might strangle the commander. Five minutes later he returned with the American prisoners.

"This," he said, pointing to one who was wounded with a bullet hole through the left upper arm, "is Major John Frey, sheriff of Tryon County.[136] The other is Colonel Peter Bellinger."

St. Leger looked at the two sullen officers, somewhat battered and disheveled, and spoke to them harshly.

"You two will write and sign a note to be sent in to Colonel Gansevoort. You will beg him to surrender. You will —" He broke off as both men began objecting and cut off their comments with a shaking of his balled fist toward them. "You *will* do it. I am not asking it, I am ordering it. If you do not do it immediately, I will turn you over to the Mohawks and let them do whatever they wish to you."

There was no doubt that St. Leger meant it and the two American militia officers acquiesced. At the direction of St. Leger, Colonel Bellinger sat at the small table and wrote the note, which both he and Frey signed. They were then led away by their guard. St. Leger picked up the letter and read it:

> 9 o'clock P.M. — *Camp before Fort Stanwix*
> *6th August,* 1777
>
> Sir,
> *It is with concern we are to acquaint you that this was the fatal day in which the succours, which were intended for your relief, have been attacked and defeated with great loss of numbers killed, wounded and taken prisoners. Our regard for your safety and lives, and our sincere advice to you is, if you will avoid inevitable ruin and destruction, to surrender the fort you pretend to defend against a formidable body of troops and a good train of artillery, which we are witness of: when at the same time you have no farther support or relief to expect. We are sorry to inform you that most of the principal officers are killed, to wit — Gen. Herkimer, Cols. Cox, Seeber, Isaac Paris, Captain Graves, and*

many others too tedious to mention. The British army from Canada being now perhaps before Albany, the possesson of which place of course includes the conquest of the Mohawk River and this fort.

> Peter Bellinger, Colonel
> Major John Frey, Tryon County

Brigadier General St. Leger called for his adjutant general, Major Wesley Ancron, and directed him, in company with Colonel John Butler, to take the message to the fort under a flag of truce and deliver it to Colonel Gansevoort and at the same time demand the surrender of the installation.

The pair were gone for more than an hour and returned with the same message in hand. St. Leger, his expression hard, listened to their report, then excused them. On the back of the note written by Bellinger he now scribbled a few hasty words of his own:

Gen. St. Leger, on the day of the date of this letter, made a verbal summons of the fort by his Adjutant General and Colonel Butler, and who then handed this letter; when Colonel Gansevoort refused any answer to a verbal summons, unless made by Gen. St. Leger himself, but at the mouth of his cannon.

St. Leger blotted the writing, folded the paper and placed it inside his dispatch case. He sighed deeply. Somehow, things just weren't going so smoothly as he'd anticipated. But he knew they would . . . as soon as Fort Stanwix capitulated.

[*August 6, 1777 — Wednesday Night*]

The shattered remains of the Tryon County Militia sank to the ground near the ruins of old Fort Schuyler, where they had stopped on their march toward Fort Stanwix. Nearly fifty hastily constructed litters had been made for carrying the wounded, including General Herkimer. That wasn't enough and many other wounded were being carried on the backs of friends or in their arms. Most of these men, the wounded ones, with the initial shock of their wounds wearing off, were in intense pain and the sounds of their agony were a continuous din in the camp.

There was some agitation among the unharmed survivors to kill the wounded Chief Ghalto and the other Indians who had been captured, but Colonel Samuel Campbell wouldn't allow it. Haggard and disheartened, he remained in command of the militia army, wishing desperately that there were something he could do to help the wounded beyond this effort to get them back to Fort Dayton and then on to their own homes where their wounds could be treated. So *many* were dead! How could there possibly be any protection for the army in case of a follow-up attack by the enemy? In his despair, he knew now beyond any doubt that if the Indians and British should attack again, it would result in total annihilation for the militia if they did not immediately surrender unconditionally. There was simply no ability or resource left for defense.

But the feared attack did not occur.

[*August 9, 1777 — Saturday*]

The two British officers who approached the main gate of Fort Stanwix under the flag of truce walked with a sprightly step and showed no trace of the apprehension that filled them. One was a regular major, dressed in scarlet jacket and immaculate white breeches, the other was a colonel of the Rangers in soiled green coat and dark trousers.

The pair began slowing as they came up to the gate. At this time it opened only enough for four Continental officers in their blue coats and white trousers to emerge. The two parties stopped an arm's length apart and it was the red-coated major who spoke, addressing his comments to the tall lieutenant colonel who was the ranking Rebel officer.

"I am Major Wesley Ancron. I take it from your rank, sir, that you are Lieutenant Colonel Marinus Willett?" At that officer's nod, he continued: "This is Colonel John Butler, in command of the King's Rangers with this army. We have come with a proposal for your commander from General St. Leger. Would you be so kind as to take us to Colonel Gansevoort?"

Willett nodded. "If you have no objection to being blindfolded until you can be led to a room where any discussion can be held."

At their affirmative, Ancron and Butler were blindfolded to prevent their observing the state of the works within the fort and led inside to a room. They blinked as their blindfolds were removed and looked about themselves with mild curiosity. The windows of the room were tightly shuttered and three pairs of candles were burning on the table. The American officers also took seats at the table and light refreshments were served, during which the men toasted one another's health. When these civilities were completed, Major Ancron dabbed lightly at his mouth corners with a napkin and then stood.

"Sir," he said, directing his remarks to Willett, "I am directed by General St. Leger to inform the commandant of this fort that the relief force that had been en route to you has suffered a most terrible defeat. Since then it is with the utmost difficulty that the general has prevailed on the Indians to agree that if the garrison will, without further resistance, deliver up themselves and their public stores, the officers and soldiers shall have all their baggage and private property secured to them. And in order that the garrison may have a sufficient pledge, Colonel Butler accompanies me to assure them that neither soldiers nor Indians will harm a hair of their heads. Colonel Butler?"

Butler nodded slowly. "Some of you know me. All of you know that my word is my bond. I give my word to it in this matter before us."

"I am likewise to remind the commandant," Ancron went on, "that the defeat of General Herkimer must deprive the garrison of all hopes of relief, especially as General Burgoyne is now in Albany; sooner or later this fort must fall into our hands. General St. Leger, for an earnest desire to prevent further bloodshed, hopes these terms will not be refused, as in this case it will be out of his power to make them again. It was with great difficulty that the Indians consented to the present arrangement, as it will deprive them of the plunder they always calculate on receiving, as they have on similar occasions."

Ancron paused and licked his lips, wishing his forehead was not beading with perspiration as he knew it was at this moment. None of the officers said anything and so, after a moment more, he went on.

"If the terms are rejected, the Indians, who are numerous and much exasperated and mortified from their losses in the action against General Herkimer, cannot be restrained from plundering property and probably destroying the lives of the greater part of the garrison. Such indeed is their ire at the loss of several of their chiefs who were killed," he added earnestly, "that unless the surrender is agreed to, they threaten to march down this country on both sides of the Mohawk River, destroying the settlements and not sparing even the women and children."

Willett waited a moment and then pretended to be confused as he replied. "Do I understand you, sir, that you come from the British commander who invests this fort? By your uniform you appear yourself to be in the regular British service, yet if I comprehend your address, its purpose is to tell the commander of this garrison that if he doesn't surrender it into the hands of the British commandant, this officer will send his Indians to murder our women and children." His tone became hard. "Please reflect, sir, that their blood, if this occurs, will be upon your head, not ours. We are doing our duty. This garrison is committed to our charge and we will take care of it. After you get out of it, you may turn and survey the walls. But never, sir, expect to come within them again unless you come a prisoner."

Butler had come to his feet as Willett's words became more harsh and Major Ancron was frowning. Willett, however, went on without pause. "I consider the message you have brought to be degrading for a civilized enemy to send and by no means reputable for a British officer to carry. For my part, I declare that before I would consent to deliver this garrison to such a murderous force as — by your own account, sir! — your army consists of, I would suffer my body to be filled with splinters and set afire at every pore."[137]

"I would point out to you, sir," Ancron replied stiffly, "that I am merely relaying the orders of my superior officer. I would also like to point out that the demand for surrender requires a reply from *your* superior officer."

There followed a lengthy period of reducing the demand to writing and then presenting it to Colonel Gansevoort in his quarters. The commander did not need to study it long to pen his reply. It was delivered by an orderly, who handed it to Willett. The lieutenant colonel glanced at it, smiled tightly and handed it to Ancron.

"Major, you and Colonel Butler may leave now with Colonel Gansevoort's reply. I don't believe there is any way in which it can be misinterpreted."

Before being blindfolded again to be led from the fort, both Ancron and Butler read the note. As Willett had indicated, it was quite clear. Gansevoort had written:

Having been entrusted by the United American States with the command of the fort, it is my determined resolution to defend it to the last extremity against all their enemies.

There was nothing further for the British representatives to say, and even as they were being led back to the fort's gate to return to their commander, General St. Leger was in his tent writing a letter to General Burgoyne:

The completest victory was obtained at Oriskany; above four hundred lay dead on the field, amongst the number of whom were almost all the principal movers of the rebellion in that country. There are six or seven hundred men in the fort. The militia will never rally; all that I apprehend, therefore, that will retard my progress in joining you is a reinforcement of what they call their regular troops by the way of Half Moon, up the Mohawk River. A diversion, therefore, from your army by that quarter will greatly expedite my junction with either of the grand armies.

[August 15, 1777 — Friday]

On the Hudson River, things had not been going well at all for General Philip Schuyler. His retreat down the Hudson Valley from Fort Edward by stages to Stillwater had gone far in making the officers and men under his command lose faith in him as a leader. Everything he did now was suspect and even though entrenchments were being built at Stillwater, many voiced the opinion that it was only something to do while waiting for the next order to retreat.

The pall of gloom that overhung the northern army grew even worse as word came of the Battle of Oriskany and the siege at Fort Stanwix. It appeared that the Mohawk Valley, as well as the Hudson, was on the point of being lost. Confirmation of the devastating battle at Oriskany had come from no less than the officer second in command at Fort Stanwix, Lieutenant Colonel Marinus Willett.

Willett, along with Major George Stockwell, had slipped out of Fort Stanwix from the sally port at night and crept through enemy lines at great personal risk during a storm and armed only with their swords. They had made it to Fort Dayton first, where the full impact of the Oriskany disaster was still so evident. Then Willett alone, after conferring with the wounded General Herkimer at his home, borrowed a horse and continued eastward to Schuyler's shifting headquarters.

General Schuyler had called a council of his officers, let Willett explain the situation again and then listened with growing anger as his subordinates argued strongly against Schuyler's proposal to send a relief column immediately to Fort Stanwix. If, they argued, St. Leger's army could so devastate Herkimer's force of eight hundred, what chance would a relief column have? Sending one from here would only weaken the army at a moment when Burgoyne was all but panting at their heels. The possibility of Albany being taken would be greatly increased. If, they continued, General Schuyler felt he could not stand against Burgoyne at any number of places along the way from Fort Ticonderoga to here at Stillwater, then how could he even begin to consider weakening his army's strength more by sending help — which would probably be insufficient to begin with — to Fort Stanwix? Insinuations about Schuyler's own loyalty began being muttered and the commander, pacing back and forth as his officers argued, finally became so angry that he bit the stem off the clay pipe gripped in his teeth. He tossed the pieces into a corner and whirled on them, demanding silence.

"I have heard more than enough!" he fumed. "Gentlemen, I remove the matter from debate and take the responsibility upon myself. Fort Stanwix and the Mohawk Valley will be saved. All I need to know is, where is the brigadier who will command the relief?"

It was a major general, not a brigadier, who volunteered — Schuyler's second-in-command, Benedict Arnold. Schuyler immediately put him in charge of a relief column of eight hundred men and dispatched him up the Mohawk, followed by a smaller column under another volunteer, Brigadier General Ebenezer Learned.

Though they still didn't like it much, there was now a grudging respect among the officers for Schuyler's decision. For the first time since Ticonderoga, he was at least doing *something* besides running.

[*August 17, 1777 — Sunday*]

The thirteen men gathered at the home of Hector Shoemaker in German Flats, just two miles north of Fort Dayton, lounged indolently in the large parlor of the house, some sitting in chairs, others on the floor with their backs against the wall. The windows had been heavily draped for security. They were a nondescript lot of Mohawk Valley Tories bound together by a common intensity immediately apparent. All were at this moment listening closely to what one of their number was saying. The speaker was an officer who, accompanied by ten soldiers of the 8th Regiment and three of Brant's Mohawks, had come from St. Leger's army to inspire them and enlist their aid.

Walter N. Butler at twenty-five had hawkish features and eyes that burned with zealot fire. He smiled as he spoke to these men he knew so well and who knew him as the son of John Butler, confident that they would aid him in executing General St. Leger's plan. With them, along with others he might enlist farther downstream, especially in the area of Johnstown, their object would be to contact other settlers in the valley and plant seeds of fear and unrest in respect to what would happen to them and their property when St. Leger took, as he would, the entire Mohawk Valley. The way to avoid possible loss or worse, of course, would be to commit themselves secretly to rise upon St. Leger's approach and support him against the existing authority in the valley.

Among Butler's listeners was a slack-jawed, loutish young man of about twenty named Hon Yost Schuyler.[138] Although generally considered to be at best simple-minded, Hon Yost, who lived with his mother and brother at nearby Little Falls, oddly enough was respected by the Indians. They were superstitious about him, believing that in his simplicity he had the gift of vision, and however wild his prattlings might be, they always listened carefully to what he had to say. That was the reason for his being here. There were still some Mohawks under Chief Steyawa at the Upper Mohawk Castle of Canajoharie and a few others at the Lower Mohawk Castle of Teantontalago who needed to be convinced to abandon their stance of neutrality and to join Brant. With Hon Yost instructing them to do so, they probably would.

That matter was not to be put to the test. A clumping of footsteps on the veranda made Walter Butler pause and look toward the door. The others followed his gaze as it was opened and two of Butler's soldiers entered, looking very glum. It was Butler who realized immediately and with a jolt that their rifles and swords were gone and he opened his mouth to shout an alarm, but it was too late.

The two soldiers were roughly thrust aside and a dozen American soldiers poured into the house, their rifles leveled. Others could be heard outside. In a moment an officer entered and the German Flats residents recognized him as the commanding officer at Fort Dayton, Lieutenant Colonel James Wesson.

"This house," he said quietly, "is surrounded and all of you are under arrest as spies and enemies of the United States of America."

[*August 19, 1777 — Tuesday*]

It had been one retreat too many.

Since August 3 Schuyler's men had been working on the entrenchments and fortifications at Stillwater, then suddenly, incomprehensibly, General Schuyler gave the order to retreat again — this time to a place just above Albany called the Sprouts of the Mohawk.

The Sprouts, at the mouth of the Mohawk River, was a fordable area formed by three islands — Green, Van Schaik's and Haver. It was on Van Schaik's Island that Schuyler gave the orders to halt and once again began the erection of fortifications. And it was here, today, that he was met by Major General Horatio Gates, who had come directly from General George Washington with orders.

Schuyler read the papers Gates handed to him and then, though it was the most distressing moment of his entire military career, accepted the decision without protest. He would continue his efforts on behalf of the United States but, from this moment on, he was no longer in charge of the Northern Department of the army.

Major General Horatio Gates was the new commander.

[*August 20, 1777 — Wednesday*]

The march of Major General Benedict Arnold to Fort Dayton had been uneventful except for the lack of support he found among the Mohawk Valley residents. Since the shattering of the militia, which had touched practically every household with death or injury, both fear and apathy had become rampant. Under Arnold's orders to reform as militia and join him, the men of the Mohawk Valley who were still able-bodied at first refused. It took a very stern message from Governor George Clinton, headquartered at Half Moon, to the several district colonels of Tryon County to reinstate some degree of obedience. Clinton wrote:

Sirs — While I have the highest sense of the loyalty, valor and bravery of the militia of Tryon County, manifested in the victory gained by them under the command of their worthy General Herkimer, [139] *for which, as the chief magistrate of the free and independent State of New York, they have my most hearty thanks, it gives me the greatest pain to be informed that any difficulty should arise in their joining the army under General Arnold, and thereby enabling him to finish the war in that quarter by raising the siege at Fort Stanwix and destroying the enemy's army in that quarter, and restoring peace and safety to the inhabitants of Tryon County. Their noble exertions against the common enemy have already gained them the greatest honor; their perseverance will secure them peace and safety. In both I am greatly interested and it is my duty, and I hereby positively order that you immediately join General Arnold with one-half of your regiments, completely armed, equipt and accoutred, and march under his command to the relief of Fort Stanwix. As soon as the service will admit, General*

Arnold will dismiss you. If any are hardy enough to refuse to obey your orders given in consequence of this, you are immediately to report the names of the same to me, that they may be dealt with, with the utmost rigor of the law.

                              I am your obedient servant,
                                   GEORGE CLINTON

Fortunately, that did the trick and while much of Tryon County's militia was incapacitated from wounds, Arnold was nevertheless joined by just over a hundred militiamen at Fort Dayton. Immediately upon his arrival there, Arnold sent an express to Gansevoort with word that he would be with him in a few days. Then he issued a brief proclamation in which he grandiosely gave himself the title of commander-in-chief of the Army of the United States of America on the Mohawk River and soundly denounced General Barry St. Leger as "a leader of a banditti of robbers, murderers and traitors, composed of savages of America and more savage Britons." Somewhat surprisingly, this proclamation resulted in more militiamen coming to help him, including even some of the wounded from the Battle of Oriskany.

One of the wounded who could not come to Arnold's assistance, though he would have liked doing so, was Brigadier General Nicholas Herkimer. At his beautiful home nearby, called Danube, Herkimer was in very bad shape. Since being carried the thirty-five miles back to his home in a litter following the battle, his shattered leg had been tended almost constantly and bathed several times each day. Despite this care, gangrene had set in and there was no longer any doubt that the leg would have to come off. There was not a doctor in the vicinity, however, until Arnold's detachment arrived. A Frenchman, Louis Chambreau, on his own recommendation, had been assigned to Arnold's force as a surgeon.

Dr. Chambreau, unskilled in amputation, badly bungled the job, cutting the leg off squarely without taking up the artery to be properly tied off. Unable to stop the bleeding but leaving behind assurances it would soon cease, Chambreau hastened away muttering to himself. As the bleeding continued, Herkimer weakened. Abruptly the militia general called for his Bible and assembled his family around him. He opened to the Thirty-eighth Psalm and read aloud in a clear voice:

"O Lord, rebuke me not in Thy wrath; neither chasten me in Thy hot displeasure. . . . There is no soundness in my flesh because of Thine anger . . . my wounds stink and are corrupt because of my foolishness. . . ."

His voice faded remarkably as he read and the great scarlet stain from the bandaged stump of his leg spread widely. The Bible fell closed from his hands and he turned his eyes to his family and smiled. He opened his mouth to speak, but there was no sound. Then he closed his eyes and immediately lapsed into a coma.

In less than half an hour, Nicholas Herkimer was dead.

At almost this same moment, a few miles away at Fort Dayton, Major General Benedict Arnold, as president of a board of court-martial, was sentencing the Tories and soldiers caught three nights before at the home of Hector Shoemaker. Walter Butler's ten soldiers and three Mohawk warriors were all sentenced to "an indefinite term of imprisonment" in the jail at Albany. Butler, along with Shoemaker and the other eleven Tories, was also sentenced to be taken to Albany, but there to be executed by a firing squad. One of these men was, of course, Hon Yost Schuyler.

Instantly after the sentencing, the young man's brother and tearful mother sought audience with General Arnold and, when it was given, pleaded with him to have mercy on Hon Yost, saying that he was too simple-minded even to realize that what he had done was wrong. There followed a conference with some of the area residents and gradually, at the suggestion of Lieutenant Colonel John Brooks, who understood both Hon Yost and the superstitious aura he held among the Indians, a plan developed. At length Arnold, with several of his officers and Chief Hanyerry and a few other Oneidas who had survived the Oriskany battle, met with the Schuyler family. Slowly and patiently, making sure it was clearly understood what was expected of him if he was to be spared, Arnold told Hon Yost Schuyler what he had to do. Hon Yost, his lips upturned in the almost constant idiotic smile he wore, nodded all the while the general spoke.

"I am told," Arnold concluded, his eyes boring into those of the young man, "that in all this world, Hon Yost, there is only one thing that really means anything to you — and that is your mother and your brother. Listen then: in your place, we are taking your brother into custody. When we learn that you have been successful in your mission, we will release him. If, however, you are not successful, regardless of the reason, your brother will hang. Do you fully understand?"

Hon Yost was still nodding but he was no longer smiling.

[*August 22, 1777 — Friday*]

There was a deep ache between his shoulder blades and Brigadier General Barry St. Leger groaned as he straightened somewhat, then slouched again as he returned to his writing. The irregular reverberation of his artillery was a background noise he was almost accustomed to, but it brought little comfort. His whole manner exuded dejection, and for the third time this morning since beginning the report to Burgoyne about the continued siege here at Fort Stanwix, he crumpled the paper into a wad and threw it aside.

Though he would never admit it, he realized now that Sir John's recommendation for a sweep down the Mohawk Valley immediately following the Oriskany battle had been the thing to do. How could he now tell his commander that with nearly two thousand men and far superior artillery, he was not able to reduce Fort Stanwix to a state of surrender? How could he explain his inability to take the initiative and follow up the Oriskany battle with a crushing defeat of the survivors, which, he realized now, would have been so simple a matter? How could he explain the lethargy that still gripped him and kept him pinned here under the excuse of maintaining the siege when everything dictated that he marshal his forces and, as originally planned, march down the Mohawk at once to join Burgoyne?

Nothing had gone right since Oriskany. To Burgoyne he had claimed victory there and he supposed it was a victory, since the enemy lost so many, even though it was the British and Indian force that left the field of battle first. But was it really a victory after all? No, deep inside he knew it was not; not for himself and not for the Rebels. It was simply an indecisive engagement that had left the militia greatly weakened and the Mohawk Valley vulnerable, but that at the same time had shaken the confidence of his own troops and had almost caused the en masse desertion of his Indian forces due to the great losses they had suffered. Since then there had come word from Brant's sister, Molly, that an army of American regulars was en route up the river and now it was taking all his energies just to hold the Indians and keep their support in maintaining the siege. Why didn't that blasted Gansevoort give in? Despite the supplies he got right at the beginning of the siege nearly three weeks ago, he *had* to be very nearly out of food and ammunition. Why didn't he surrender?

Now, at the sound of a great many voices coming closer, he frowned and stood up, then shouldered his way past the tent flap and went outside. At least two hundred Indians and a number of Sir John's Royal Greens were approaching and it was obvious from their attitude and tone that something was terribly wrong. Brant was not with the Indians and for an instant St. Leger wondered where he was. Then he remembered that Brant, with about fifty of his men, had gone to destroy the Oneida village a few miles south of Oriskany in retaliation for the Oneidas' having helped the Americans. But even with Brant gone, it didn't take long to learn the source of this present trouble.

In the van of the Indians was a retarded-looking white individual who was grinning insipidly and absently shoving his finger through a hole in his coat. There were a number of such small round holes. They were, the young man told him, bullet holes from shots that had been fired at him when he escaped from the Rebels. It was very fortunate he got away, because there was terrible news that General St. Leger must know: Walter Butler and his men had been captured and were sentenced to be executed; Burgoyne had been defeated and was in full retreat toward Montreal with the army of General Schuyler hot on his heels; worse, a major military force of regulars under Major General Benedict Arnold was coming up the Mohawk. They were right behind him, only hours away. They had tremendous artillery and great numbers of men and new weapons and they were taking no prisoners. All Indians, Tories and soldiers caught alive were being summarily executed. It was terrible . . . just terrible! Hon Yost had worked himself into a state and had tears streaming down his cheeks as he finished. It was obvious the Indians believed him. The British commander was not sure what to believe.

"How many men does Arnold have?" he asked brusquely.

Hon Yost rolled his eyes and then pointed at the trees. "Like the leaves," he murmured mysteriously. "Like the leaves. Two thousand, three thousand . . . five thousand . . ." He shrugged. "Who knows? Maybe more. They are like the leaves. Like a flood. They will be here by sunset. You must prepare to fight them!"

"No! We will fight this way no more!" It was Gu-cinge, the Seneca. "It is not our way to shoot bullets at log walls. Even your big guns can do nothing against them, as you have seen. We must go. We *will* go, far into our own country."

"You can't go!" St. Leger thundered. "Fort Stanwix is on the verge of surrender. You can't leave now. You promised to support us."

Gu-cinge cut him off with a wave of his arm. "No! I have said it. No! When we marched down, you told us there would be no fighting for us Indians. You told us that we would come here and smoke our pipes and watch as the fort surrendered to you. Yet now almost a moon has passed and many of our chiefs and warriors are dead and still the fort stands. And now you mean to sacrifice us as more of the enemy come" — he pointed at the trees as Hon Yost had done — "and they are like the leaves. We will not stay!"

They didn't. Within an hour most of them were ready to leave and equally ready to take with them a large quantity of the St. Leger stores. Ammunition, clothing, food and other necessaries were taken as they left, not in theft but as their due. Their own goods had been confiscated during Willett's sally from the fort while they were off fighting the Oriskany battle, so it was St. Leger's fault. It was up to him to replace what they had lost. Further, they were being cheated out of the plunder they had expected from Fort Stanwix. That, too, was St. Leger's fault, because they had been told the fort would fall easily. It was up to him to make up for that. If St. Leger wished to leave with them, he was welcome to do so, but in whatever case, they were leaving now. There was really no choice.

St. Leger's shoulders slumped as he gave the orders.

[*August 22, 1777 — Friday*]

"Sir! *Colonel!*" The orderly raced into the room where Colonel Peter Gansevoort sat behind a desk, talking with several officers, assessing their desperate situation here in Fort Stanwix and wondering if Willett and Stockwell had managed to slip undetected through the enemy lines. The men all turned to look at the orderly. "Sir," he went on, coming to a halt, "excuse me, sir, but they're leaving. The enemy, sir. They're raising the siege. We've won!"

There was instant excitement and Gansevoort, followed by the officers and orderly, left the room at once and walked quickly to the ramparts, noting the conditions as if in a dream. The interior of the fort was in deplorable shape. There was practically no ammunition left. No one had had decent food in days. Clothing was in tatters. Though many of the forty-six bodies of his dead, including four officers, had been buried, some still lay under blankets. Most of them had been killed by the punishing mortar fire St. Leger had lobbed over the walls for so many days. Was it all really ending now? He suddenly felt weak with the sense of relief that filled him, yet resolved not to become buoyed up too quickly. He noted the colors still flying, even though bullet-tattered, and a surge of pride flooded him. Every day the flag had been raised and lowered to the accompaniment of music and artillery, even though they could ill afford the expenditure of the gunpowder, and he wondered if that had had a demoralizing effect upon the enemy, as he had meant it to have, just as it had had an inspiring effect upon the garrison.

He climbed the ladders to the parapets and peered over the tops of the upright pickets. Westward in the distance could be seen the long line of St. Leger's army moving away. They were taking their artillery with them and from their attitude and the precipitousness of their flight, it became immediately obvious that this was no ruse.

The siege of Fort Stanwix was ended.

[*December 31, 1777 — Wednesday*]

There were not many matters in which Joseph Brant saw eye to eye with Gucinge, but one thing in which they were now in total accord was that never again would the Iroquois help lay siege to a fort in the white man's manner of fighting. Exposing oneself to the fire of an enemy, laying siege to fortified positions, attacking disciplined troops on their own ground and in their own way — all these were ridiculous.

Oriskany had been a hard lesson, but one well learned. The alliance of the League with the British remained strong, but henceforth whatever fighting the Indians would engage in would be done in the Indian way and on their terms unless it was their own choice to do it differently. One great truth about the difference between white warfare and Indian warfare was now clearly apparent. To the whites, men — and sometimes very good ones — had to be sacrificed to gain ascendency over enemies. To the Indians, no warrior was expendable, *ever*. For every white who fell, on whichever side, others came to fill the gap. For the Indians, the place of a fallen warrior remained vacant.

The remainder of the year following Oriskany and Stanwix had been disastrous for the British and the Indians. Following his precipitate retreat from Fort Stanwix to Fort Oswego, as if hellhounds were breathing down his neck, St. Leger had experienced the utter mortification of learning he had neatly been duped. Burgoyne had not been defeated. Arnold had not been approaching with a gigantic military force. To the contrary, Burgoyne until then was practically calling the shots and on the Mohawk River, except for the bottled-up garrison in Fort Stanwix, there hadn't been an enemy soldier within forty miles of St. Leger. His haste to leave, his leaving behind tents and equipment and even some broken-wheeled artillery, had been a total fiasco. General Arnold had not arrived at Fort Stanwix until August 24 and the force he brought was still considerably inferior to St. Leger's. Arnold's most difficult task had been burying the dead that still lay on the Oriskany battlefield. After that, he simply returned to the Hudson.

St. Leger's inglorious retreat was devastating to the officers involved and Colonel Daniel Claus seemed to sum up the general feelings when he wrote in his report to Secretary of War Henry Knox in London:

Thus has an expedition miscarried merely for want of timely and good intelligence. . . . All the good done by the expedition was that the ringleaders and principal men of the rebels of Tryon County were put out of the way; but had we succeeded, it must have been of vast good effect to the Northern operations; and its miscarrying, I apprehend to my deep concern, to be the reverse. . . .

The retreat had another effect that was very serious. Residents of the Mohawk Valley who had been vacillating in their loyalties, afraid to support one side or the other openly, now supported the Americans. Even the Oneidas, though badly chastised by Brant and uprooted from one of their principal villages after the Battle of Oriskany, came to the Americans at Albany and, three hundred strong under the leadership of Chief Hanyerry, offered their services. To prove their worth, they helped to defeat Burgoyne at Saratoga and returned to the headquarters of the Northern Department of the army with one hundred and fifty British scalps and thirty prisoners.

Burgoyne's promotion to lieutenant general late in August brought him no pleasure. Too many misfortunes were then occurring on all sides. St. Leger started it with his wild retreat and his failure to form a junction with Burgoyne on the Hudson as he might have been able to do. Burgoyne then made his own tactical error by launching a spearhead campaign against Bennington, only to find his troops beaten back with sharp losses by Brigadier General John Stark of the New Hampshire Militia. The most stunning blow to come his way, however, was when General Howe failed to come up the Hudson to form the junc-

tion with Burgoyne, or at least send General Sir Henry Clinton to do so, as everyone believed he would.[140] Without the support — and St. Leger's
diversion — Burgoyne's great plan collapsed.

The first Battle of Saratoga at Bemis Heights was a tremendous setback for
Burgoyne; the second, a disaster, resulting in his surrender. The might of the
British in the north had been pricked as if it were an overblown balloon and the
position in which this left the Indian allies of the Crown was not an enviable
one.

Obviously, the war was far from over and there was every reason to believe it
would ultimately be won by the King, but now it would simply take longer and
be more difficult. For the Indians, a lot of ground had to be won back, and as
soon as winter's grip on the country relaxed, this was what Joseph was planning. Until then, along with many of his Mohawks, he remained in winter
quarters at Fort Niagara, drifting farther away from both of the ineffectual
Johnsons, Guy and Sir John, and drawing closer to the man who had a much
greater understanding of the ways of Indians and their warfare, Colonel John
Butler.

[*February 13, 1778 — Friday*]

Even after Pickering's screams had finally stopped, John Jenkins continued
hearing them in his own mind. How long had they been going on? Two hours?
Three?

"Goddle-mighty, John, they've et 'im!" The declaration changed to a question. "You reckon they've really et 'im?"

Jenkins shook his head, wishing York would just once stop talking so much.
For almost three months now he'd had to listen to them — York and Fitch
both — and that was almost as bad as being a captive of the Indians. He rolled
over and his back inadvertently touched the stone wall of the cell they were in
and he recoiled. Though an inside wall, the stones were covered with a heavy
frosting of ice crystals. He wondered if he'd ever feel warm again.

"I don't know, Amos. Guess maybe they did. I don't know." He shook his
head again, opening his eyes to look at Amos York, who sat crouched in his
own little pile of straw several feet away. Beyond him, on a similar bedraggled
strawpile, Lemuel Fitch sat wordlessly, his eyes haunted.

Jenkins sighed. Of all people to have been captured with, he could hardly
have chosen worse than these two. Both men were essentially stupid, decidedly
cowardly and basically churlish in nature. Jenkins was sure the three of them
might have escaped a long while ago had any sort of cooperation been possible
among them, but it never was.

"They *said* they was gonna eat 'im, John," York persisted. "You heard 'em.
That's what they said when they took 'im out. Didn't they, Lem?"

York turned to the other man, but Fitch made no reply. York inclined his head toward the older man and spoke to Jenkins. "Ol' Lem jus' ain't hardly fit company no more, John. Right?"

Jenkins looked at York and then shook his head and turned his back to the man, pulling up the ragged shred of blanket around him in the perpetual endeavor to get warm. It didn't help much and the shivering continued. Would he ever feel warm again? "I don't want to talk, Amos. About anything right now."

Jenkins heard York snort in disgust but paid no attention. He had, in recent weeks, begun to feel that he would never again see Bethiah Harris and a welling of almost physical pain rose in his breast. She was so beautiful and he loved her so much. Being separated from her was so hard to bear, and for her it must be even worse because she had no idea whether he was alive or not. He looked at the icy rock walls and wondered in his mind why he was here and if he would ever get out. For the second question he had no answer, but the first he knew: they'd been captured, the three of them, along with Old Man Fitzgerald, late last November. November 27, in fact. It was a date Jenkins couldn't well forget — his twenty-sixth birthday. The thought of Old Fitz brought the ghost of a smile to Jenkins's lips. Richard Fitzgerald. Fine old man. He went out the way a man ought to — sticking up for what he believed in.

The four of them had traveled together from Wyoming on the Susquehanna upstream to Standing Stone. It was a nice area for settling, with occasional homes along the river where pioneers had been established for varying periods. Jenkins had pointed out to them — though they didn't seem to mind — that the farther upstream they went, the more the sympathies of the residents remained with the King. This was his first trip upstream since the Oriskany battle and he thought there was a possibility of problems with them. Enmities had flared considerably. From Tunkhannock northward, Jenkins told them, it was mostly Indians and Tories, living mainly at Tioga and Newtown and Chemung on the Chemung River. The men hadn't seemed to care much.

"Live an' let live," York had laughed. "Goddle-mighty, I got me a wife an' kids, so I ain't 'bout t' make trouble. I'll leave them alone an' they'll leave me alone."

York and Fitch had been bearable then, Jenkins remembered. Not the sort he'd have picked for company if he'd had the choice, but bearable. Anyway, he'd had no choice. The three others were on their way upstream to see lands they'd bought from the Susquehanna Land Company and as agent, surveyor, conveyancer and tax collector for the company, it was part of his job to get them there. He was also, at times, a schoolteacher, constable, farmer, merchant and ironmonger, as well as a lieutenant in the Wyoming Militia.

"Was you born in Pennsylvania, John?" Fitch had asked while they were paddling upstream.

"Nope. New London, Connecticut — at Gardner's Lake. In fifty-one. My father — he was John Senior — was a judge at East Greenwich in Rhode Island, originally. Anyway, we came here from New London in sixty-nine."

They'd been pulling to shore as he said that, just above Tunkhannock, and looked up to find themselves in the midst of a party of Tories and Indians. There was not the remotest opportunity for flight or struggle, so they'd simply given up. At first they hadn't been treated too badly, except for Fitz.

They'd killed him.

Again the memory of Richard Fitzgerald made Jenkins pause in his thoughts. The Tories had started badgering him that evening, at first in a joking sort of way, to make him cringe and beg. They didn't know Old Fitz very well. When one of them made a rude remark and tweaked his nose rather harshly, Fitz promptly spat in his face.

That was when they'd bound his wrists and ankles and lay him on his back on the ground and kicked his sides and groin until he was gasping. Then they'd told him if he didn't renounce his Rebel ideas and declare allegiance to the King they would kill him. One of them — a brutish man named Gilbert Newbury — held a huge boulder above the old man's head to add emphasis to the words. Fitzgerald had merely glared up at him.

"I'm an old man," he said, "and I can't live but a few years at best. I'd a whole hell of a lot rather die now, a friend to my country, than live a few years as a Tory!"

Newbury dropped the rock.

The Indians had laughed as Newbury cut off the scalp from the crushed head. After that they'd carried him over to the riverbank and pitched him out into the current. Fitz sank right away and they never saw him again. Next morning York, Fitch and Jenkins were started on their march north toward Fort Niagara and this was where they'd been ever since.

There had been other prisoners here too, such as the little fat man David Pickering, whose screams they'd just been listening to. Plus maybe a dozen others. It was hard to keep track. They came and went and no one seemed to know from where or to where. Except in the case of Pickering. Somehow, while everyone else suffered from the cold, from lack of clothing and blankets and became skeletal from the maggoty, moldy food provided at irregular intervals, Pickering managed to retain his plumpness. He used to giggle nervously when the Indians would occasionally enter with drawn knives and one by one feel the arms or legs of the prisoners to determine who was the fattest. Pickering always won that contest and they would laugh and joke and say in broken English that soon he would be in a pot and they would eat him. Pickering would giggle nervously again, going along with the joke.

Until today. Today there had been no levity in their manner. They came in, complaining about their hunger and saying it was time for good meat. They marched directly to Pickering and dragged him screaming and struggling from the rock-walled room, dropping the great beam back in place on the outside of the door as they left.

Pickering's screams had lasted for five or six minutes and then ceased for about half an hour. Then abruptly they started up again and this time they lasted for a long while before dwindling away.[141]

Now, once again John Jenkins shivered. This time it wasn't just from the cold.

[*February 28, 1777 — Saturday*]

Throughout the frontiers of New York and Pennsylvania, bloodletting was becoming more frequent. Outlying homes of settlers were being burned, horses and livestock stolen, families slain or taken into captivity. Time and again small parties of men — from vigilante groups to ill-organized militia to companies of seasoned regulars — were moving to retaliate for such outrages. That was no deterrent. The incidents increased sharply and, though mostly they were the work of small raiding parties of Indians, as pressure grew stronger and stronger against the Tories, the more those frontier Loyalists supported the Indians, helped them, supplied them and even joined in their raids.

The abduction of the John Jenkins party was only one of half a hundred similar or worse incidents and the fear they caused became a palpable thing in every frontier community. Before long, so many Tories were raiding with the Indians that strong steps were taken to put a stop to it.

Colonel Nathan Denison, commander of the Connecticut Regiment of militia in the Wyoming Valley, was furious at the disappearance of Lieutenant Jenkins, who was not only a fellow militia officer but a close friend. Denison was advised of the capture by a British deserter, Malcolm Boyd, who had been living in the Wyalusing area since his defection but who now moved to Wyoming. Though not sure whether or not Jenkins was still alive, Denison nevertheless determined to retaliate. Calling his militia together and guided by Malcolm Boyd, he marched them eighty miles up the Susquehanna, captured thirty whites thought to be Tories and brought them back to Wyoming. Ten were kept in jail there, the other twenty sent to Connecticut to be placed on trial for their lives.

The Tories upstream who were not caught considered this a terrible effrontery and they in turn retaliated by totally destroying Wyalusing, the largest white settlement in the Susquehanna Valley of Pennsylvania above Wyoming.[142] This was only the beginning.

The vicious circle was becoming daily more vicious.

[*March 16, 1778 — Monday*]

Although he had been relieved of his command of the Northern Department of the United States Army, Major General Philip Schuyler continued other military duties in the Hudson River Valley, complaining not at all and doing quietly and methodically all that was required of him and more. Because he had for so long been in contact with the Iroquois and could read their intentions just about as well as, if not better than, any high-ranked military man in the service of the United States, he was concerned with what he envisioned would soon occur. Over five weeks ago he had written from here in Albany to Congress about it, saying:

There is too much reason to believe that an expedition will be formed by the Indians against the western frontiers of this state, Virginia and Pennsylvania. . . .

There had been no response at all. Schuyler knew there were still many people about who hated and distrusted him, who hadn't understood his strategy in retreating before Burgoyne and thus, in effect, giving Burgoyne enough rope to hang himself, which had occurred. That the credit for Burgoyne's defeat had gone elsewhere was galling; it still did not sour him and he remained very concerned about the welfare of the United States.

Now, on this blustery day with menacing gray clouds scudding across the sky and spitting stinging snow crystals now and then, he penned more words to the Congress, which he hoped to God *someone* would pay some attention to:

A number of the Mohawks and many of the Onondagas, Cayugas and Senecas will commence hostilities against us as soon as they can; it would be prudent, therefore, early to take measures to carry the war into their country; it would require no greater body of troops to destroy their towns than to protect the frontier inhabitants. . . .[143]

The Congress *was*, vocally, a little concerned with the Indian problem but the steps they took at this time to combat it were incredibly lax. At the very moment Schuyler was composing his latest warning and advice to that body, they in turn were reacting to entreaties for help that had been received from the Wyoming settlement. With great gravity they made an official resolution today:

March 16, 1778. RESOLVED: That one full company of foot be raised in the town of Wyoming, on the east bank of the Susquehanna, for the defense of the said town and the settlements on the frontier in the neighborhood thereof against the Indians and the enemies of these States; the said company to be

enlisted to serve one year from the time of their enlisting, unless sooner dis-
charged by Congress; and that the said company find their own arms, accou-
trements and blankets.

If the situation had not been so serious, this effort would have been laughable. The essence of the resolution was to give the Wyoming Valley settlers
permission to defend themselves without the government committing itself to
provide any tangible aid whatever.

[*April 11, 1778 — Saturday*]

Joseph Brant was back at Oquaga again and glad to return to the valley of the
upper Susquehanna. The events of the past year had tempered him, endowed
him with a greater sense of destiny and increased his influence and stature
among his people. Even his physical aspect had changed somewhat for the better. Always before he had been a rather chunky man physically but now, at
thirty-seven, he had reached the peak of his physical maturity. He was considerably more spare than previously and this made him appear taller and somehow stronger.

He stood now with Wonagh beside him, he surveying Oquaga and she looking at him admiringly, impressed with this man who was her husband. He
wore proudly the fine doeskin blouse and breeches and calf-high moccasins she
had made him and the glitter of the silver armbands and necklace and brooches
he wore complemented his garb. The broadcloth blanket he wore over his
shoulders was of the finest weave and was distinctive with its deep red borders.
Wonagh was glad his black hair was still shoulder length and that he had not
adopted the style of so many of his Mohawk warriors of shaving his head except
for a brushlike tuft of hair from pate to nape.

"It is good to be home again, Wonagh," Brant said. "I've missed it."

A few houses had been built since he'd left Oquaga late last fall for Niagara,
but it was essentially the same. His own comfortable home had been cared for
well by Wonagh and it *was* good to be back again. He missed the Mohawk
Valley, of course. That had been his childhood home, at Canajoharie. He
loved it and the belief was strong in him that one day he would again live there
with his people, at peace with the whites, the Rebels having been defeated and
the King abiding by the promises made to the Iroquois to live in respectful
coexistence. That, he knew, was yet a long way off, but it was what he and all
the others here were working toward. Deep in his heart he was convinced that
one day it would be reality.

Nevertheless, not having the Mohawk Valley, the upper Susquehanna Valley in general and the village of Oquaga in particular were a close second
choice as a place to live. There was a slight difference of terrain — it was
hillier here and travel was more difficult and there were fewer beautiful little

gem-blue lakes — but it was still very pleasant. Part of the beauty of it was, of course, its remoteness from the whites. True, there were white men's cabins here and there along the rivers and even here at Oquaga a few whites lived with their families, but they were mostly those who were loyal to the King and, just as had occurred with Brant, had been driven from their homes in the Mohawk Valley or from farther down the Susquehanna in the Wyoming region. The few who were not loyal to the King lived quietly, if fearfully, minding their own business, taking no part in actions against the Indians and trying to retain a peaceful neutrality. Theirs was a difficult position to occupy, a position that Brant knew had to become untenable. He intended to pursue border warfare with increased fervor this coming season and he knew that then people such as these on the Pennsylvania and New York frontiers would have to make a choice of sides, whether they liked it or not.

Brant was weary. The long journey from Niagara had been by an entirely different route now that there was such danger in traveling through the Mohawk Valley. From Niagara, Brant had led his eighty warriors by boat to the mouth of the Genesee River at Irondequoit Bay, then up the Genesee into Seneca country to the largest of the Seneca towns, Chenussio. The route then went overland to the headwaters of the stream the Senecas called Cohocton. Traveling downstream on the Cohocton they had passed the village of Teaoga, where the Cohocton and Tioga rivers merged. At this point the stream down which they had been traveling was known to some as the Cayuga River but was more commonly called the Chemung River. On this stream they passed the substantial villages of Skwe-do-wah and Newtown and Chemung and finally, at the river's mouth where it emptied into the Susquehanna, the important village of Tioga. From there the journey had moved upstream on the Susquehanna essentially eastward past the villages of Ahwaga and Oochenang until, in about seventy miles, the great bend of the Susquehanna turned southward into Pennsylvania, then northward back into New York again. Fifteen miles upstream from the great bend of the river was Oquaga.[144]

Weary though he was, Brant knew that with only a few days of rest he would be ready to lead the warriors who had come with him from Niagara against the outlying settlements. In these days ahead he would have them see to their equipment and weapons. They would hold their war councils and decide where to strike, not only with the greatest likelihood of success but with the least chance of themselves being harmed. He already had a good idea of what those targets would be — Cobleskill on Schoharie Creek, Andrustown above the head of Otsego Lake and Cherry Valley on the creek of that name. Assuming success in such raids, perhaps they would even hit more substantial and better defended Rebel centers in the upper Mohawk Valley, such as German Flats and Stone Arabia.

As he walked now to his house, his arm about Wonagh's shoulders and hers

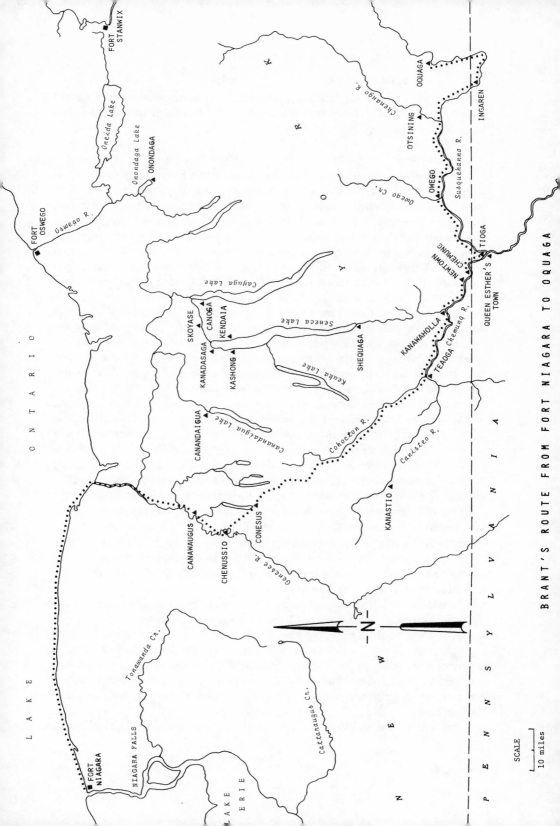

BRANT'S ROUTE FROM FORT NIAGARA TO OQUAGA

about his waist, Brant was already considering the strategy for moving against these settlements. The New York frontier was about to learn what border warfare really meant.

[*April 21, 1778 — Tuesday*]

From scouting patrols sent out from the various little forts of the area — Fort Plank at Canajoharie, Fort Dayton at German Flats, Schoharie Fort at Schoharie — the intelligence gradually filtered in of the buildup of Tory and Indian forces on the upper Susquehanna, especially at Unadilla and Oquaga. It was also known that those forces were preparing to move against the outlying settlements, most of which were wholly without defense.

Cherry Valley felt itself a prime target and fear rode heavily on the minds of the residents. Cobleskill and Andrustown and Schoharie felt the same. Appeals to authorities for help were thus far receiving little attention.

Cherry Valley residents appealed to Brigadier General Edward Hand, now at Albany, saying they must have troops to protect them or they would abandon the town and seek safety elsewhere. Hand was sympathetic but replied that the latest army intelligence reports indicated there was no real need for alarm and that it would be foolish of Cherry Valley residents to leave their town, since that would only encourage the enemy to take possession of it in an effort to become established even closer than they were now. Cherry Valley, he said, would be well protected by the garrison at Fort Plank under Colonel Klock. They were only thirteen miles distant and could come quickly if trouble loomed. The residents digested this in a disgruntled manner and then voted to remain. However, they also voted this day to convert the house of their leading citizen, Colonel Samuel Campbell, into a fort of sorts and store there for safekeeping in event of attack their valuables, their finer furnishings and their art.

Cobleskill, too, was without defense and the local militia commander, Captain Christian Brown, applied to the Middleburg Fort, six miles above Schoharie, for assistance. They received none and so the twenty families there made an effort to increase their own militia strength, inducting new members from among those males previously considered too young or too old. Jacob Borst was named as lieutenant under Brown.

The ten-family village of Andrustown had grown hardly at all during its fifty-five-year history. [145] It had begun in 1723 with the settlement of six families — the Bells, Osterhouts, Crims, Starings, Leppers, Hoyers and one other. After the close of the French and Indian War in 1760, the town had its biggest population increase in its history: three more families moved in — Reese, Shepperman and Powers. Except for one family, the entire population had become rabidly revolutionary. The single exception was Powers, an irascible, outspoken Tory.

Now, fearful of their safety, the nine families today paid a group visit to Mr.

Powers and invited him to leave . . . permanently. When Powers did not accept this suggestion with alacrity, he was provided with encouragement. A sticky concoction of pine pitch was smeared on his arms, legs and chest, then he was liberally bedaubed with chicken feathers. After that he had a change of heart, arriving at the conclusion that, yes, it might be wise for him to leave. The residents had suspected him of being close friends with Indians. They had no conception of how close or they might have been a little more genteel in their persuading Powers to leave.

The self-avowed Tory had among his small circle of Indian friends a well-known Mohawk, to whom he now directed his steps to complain of the ill treatment he'd had at the hands of his neighbors.

That Mohawk was Joseph Brant.

Even the residents of Albany no longer felt any too secure. Rumors were rife that parties of Tories and Indians were planning to slip in and fire the town and, while Brigadier General Abraham Ten Broeck did not really believe it, he nevertheless increased the number of sentries and night patrols at the city's fringes. He also held in readiness for instant use the regiment under command of Colonel Ichabod Alden.

Security was tightened even more when only a day or two later confirmed word came from Fort Stanwix that two soldiers of the garrison, who had been bathing in the Mohawk River, had been very silently killed and scalped. That was about the time that another small community asked for help — the village of Schoharie and Schoharie Creek, about thirty-five miles due west of Albany. Because a reasonably substantial fort was already there, General Ten Broeck now detached a company of thirty-seven soldiers of Alden's regiment under Captain William Patrick of Stoughton, Massachusetts, to Schoharie with orders to "keep the country from the ravages of Tories and Indians," including not only Schoharie itself, but Cobleskill, Andrustown and Cherry Valley as well.

It was a lot of territory for thirty-eight soldiers to protect.

[May 14, 1778 — Thursday]

What had a few months ago appeared to General George Washington to be the most wonderful thing that could have happened to the United States in regard to winning the war was now causing some second thoughts. The United States badly needed allies in the war against the British, but other nations had been holding back to evaluate how things were going. It became quite obvious how they were going when Burgoyne surrendered at Saratoga.

Throughout history, France had never had any great love for England. Only two days after he received news of Burgoyne's surrender, the King of France extended recognition to the United States as an independent country. It was more than recognition, it was an alliance and all that was needed to consummate it was the signing of a formal treaty in this respect. That had taken place on February 6. When it was published in March, the British ambassador left Paris for London, and France and England were abruptly at war.

The eagerness with which France leaped to help was at first a blessing to Washington. The American commander in chief desperately needed the help of seasoned regular soldiers and officers, so initially everything looked rosy. What couldn't an army do with the likes of the great Marquis de Lafayette on its side? Unfortunately, the Gallic officers who now swarmed to America to help were not all so skilled nor so valuable as Lafayette. Some, in fact, caused disruption far out of proportion to their value. George Washington found his already busy days made much busier by having to attend to an abundance of petitions from French officers who wished impressive commands to be bestowed upon them because of their alleged glorious battlefield records in Europe. Some, such as the Count Philippe du Coudray, held Washington accountable for fulfilling promises made by others in his name.

The Count du Coudray arrived in America not only with eighteen subordinate officers and ten sergeants in tow, he also presented an official paper he had received in Paris from the American representative there, Silas Deane. This paper, incredibly, placed the Count du Coudray in command of American artillery forces with the rank of major general. Washington objected: Deane had no authorization to issue such an offer. Congress shook its collective head regretfully and put George Washington down, saying that because of the Deane authorization it had to be done. Then du Coudray caused an even greater problem. He demanded that he not only be commander in chief of the artillery — a post already occupied by General Henry Knox — but that his commission be retroactive to such date as would give him seniority over such American major generals as Knox, John Sullivan and Nathanael Green. There was one more bit of icing for his cake: the demand included his becoming second-in-command to Washington himself of the whole United States Army.

Incredibly, Congress acquiesced!

Almost instantly Sullivan, Knox and Green threatened to resign if this occurred. It was a very touchy situation. For its part, Congress was infuriated with what it considered the temerity of the American generals in interfering with the prerogatives of Congress. These were already being fiercely guarded as being synonymous with the liberties of the people, and John Adams opined that the threatened resignations must be considered a perfectly marvelous idea. He wrote:

I wish they would all resign. For my part, I will vote upon the general principles of a republic for a new election of officers annually. . . .

With a great number of frazzled tempers in the process, the whole matter was settled in a sort of compromise. The American generals did not resign and the count received his commission as a major general, though not backdated.

Nor did du Coudray become Washington's second-in-command or commander in chief of the artillery. It was just as well because he didn't last very
long. With his overblown flair for the dramatic and to the rousing cheers of his
officers and sergeants, he galloped his fine large stallion onto the Schuylkill
Ferry at such speed that he could not stop the animal in time and it plunged off
the far side of the boat. Always having avoided anything he considered com-
monplace or vulgar and therefore beneath the dignity of a French gentleman,
du Coudray had never learned the art of swimming.

He drowned.

Lafayette, on the other hand, was a great asset to George Washington and
the American cause. Commissioned a major general by Congress, with this
time the full concurrence of Washington, he was sent to observe the frontier
settlements, especially in New York, and make recommendations in regard to
defense in that quarter.

Only a short time later, resplendent in his fine uniform and boots, General
Lafayette strode through Cherry Valley and shook his head disbelievingly when
he saw the makeshift fortification that had been made of Colonel Campbell's
residence.

"This," he declared, "will never do! In relation to Albany and the intermedi-
ate posts at Schoharie and Canajoharie, Cherry Valley is an extremely important outpost. I will recommend at once that a more suitable fortification be
erected here."

He did so, to the well-contained annoyance of the military authorities in Albany, who considered this an invasion of *their* prerogatives. They could not
reject his recommendation out of hand, but what they authorized was hardly
what Lafayette had envisioned.

The new fortification at Cherry Valley was now being constructed by regular
troops detached from Colonel Ichabod Alden's Massachusetts Regiment but it
left much to be desired. Instead of a real fort with bastions and abatis, traverses
and counterscarps, it was no more than a simple heavy stockade of upright logs
enclosing the village meetinghouse, church and graveyard.

It was one of the residents, Hugh Mitchell, who hesitantly murmured as the
fortification was nearing completion, "Aren't there supposed to be holes for the
defenders to fire guns through if we're attacked?"

Captain Aaron Hickling of Boston, chief engineer of the construction,
blushed deeply. He had forgotten the embrasures.[146]

[May 21, 1774 — Thursday]

Although he had left Fort Niagara with four hundred white men, principally
his own Rangers and Tories, plus about two hundred Indians, Colonel John
Butler continued gathering warriors as he progressed southeastward. At the
great Seneca village of Chenussio others joined him, and so did more as he

passed through Kanandaigua.[147] Second only to Chenussio in size, but more important because of its position as the capital of the Seneca tribe, was Kanada-saga,[148] and here, as the force paused to rest for a day, nearly a hundred more warriors joined them, mainly Senecas and Cayugas. Here too he was joined by nineteen more Tories under Lieutenant Adam Chrysler. They had come from Unadilla. As they continued their march and moved southward up the thirty-five-mile length of Seneca Lake to Shequaga[149] at its head, other warriors joined them and a few more attached themselves to his force both at Kanawa-holla[150] and Newtown and Chemung.[151] By the time they reached the point from which he planned to launch his attack — Tioga[152] — Colonel Butler's force was a very significant one of nearly nine hundred Indians in addition to the four hundred whites.

Here at Tioga, John Butler planned his strategy carefully, including the two renowned Seneca chiefs with him, Gu-cinge,[153] the Seneca war chief, and Kayingwaurto. Obviously, they were going to need boats to move swiftly down the Susquehanna for their surprise attack. Some boats had become available to them at Kanawaholla, Newtown and Chemung, as well as here at Tioga, but they were only a small part of what would be needed for such a force. Kaying-waurto agreed to have about five hundred of the warriors help the whites con-struct whatever boats would be needed, while Gu-cinge would lead the remain-ing four hundred on the southwestern Indian trail from here to go against the small white settlements and isolated cabins on the West Branch of the Susque-hanna.[154]

After Gu-cinge and his warriors left Tioga this morning, those who were left behind, whites and Indians alike, set to work building the canoes and flatboats for the downstream invasion. Butler and Kayingwaurto discussed whether or not they should send for Brant, still at Oquaga with four hundred and fifty war-riors of his own, but decided against it. Instead, Butler sent runners to Brant asking him to gather up his warriors and whatever whites were at Oquaga and Unadilla and concentrate on striking the outlying settlements northeast of him while Gu-cinge was hitting the West Branch settlements.

John Butler was in charge, but there was no doubt that this was a different sort of campaign than those at Fort Stanwix and Oriskany. This was the sort of campaign Brant had insisted it would have to be if the Iroquois were to partici-pate. It was Indian war . . . and at this point, except for vague apprehensions that it might sometime occur, the Americans did not even know it was about to be launched.

[*May 21, 1778 — Thursday*]

To Lieutenant John Jenkins, it seemed that he had been in a state of constant motion for weeks. Now, because of what had just this moment been done by

Sagoyewatha — Red Jacket — the swiftest and most desperate motion was at hand.

The Indian guard sitting at the fire and casting occasional glances at them had no idea of what had just occurred. He had, in fact, grinned and then chuckled aloud as he had watched Sagoyewatha slap Jenkins's face three times in succession. They were sharply cracking, stinging blows that the young white man could not avoid because of the rope around his throat binding him to the tree.

Still in the seated position with his ankles and wrists bound before him and his back and head held firmly against the coarse bark by the rawhide ropes around his waist, chest and neck, Jenkins blinked to clear his eyes of the tears that had come into them from the viciousness of the slapping. He glanced downward and saw on the ground between his legs the knife that Sagoyewatha had dropped. The young Seneca's final whispered words to him still rang in his ears.

"Tomorrow morning we will reach Kanadasaga. There you will be tortured to death because of Ghalto's death. I have come to like you and I would oppose it, but my words would not be enough. Your death would do nothing. It is pointless. I leave you with the way to escape, but wait until we sleep."

It was then that he had dropped the knife between Jenkins's legs and slapped him so harshly before returning to the fire and rolling up in his blanket with his feet toward the coals, as the others already were except for the guard. Jenkins's heart was beating with such thuds that he felt sure the guard must hear it. He wished the Indian would doze but the man still seemed wide awake. To compose himself, Jenkins deliberately calmed himself and then briefly let his mind relive the things that had occurred since he and York and Fitch had left Fort Niagara.

It was about five or six weeks ago when the three prisoners had been taken from their clammy stone cell at Fort Niagara and, under heavy guard, taken by boat to Montreal. Temporarily in British hands there, Amos York and Lemuel Fitch had been lucky. Jenkins had watched enviously as the pair were turned over to the authorities and placed in a British transport to be sailed to some undisclosed port in New England, there to be exchanged for British prisoners of war in American hands. [155]

Jenkins was scheduled for exchange too, but in a different way. Because, unlike York and Fitch, he was a soldier, even if only a militia lieutenant, he was to be taken by a deputation led by Red Jacket — Sagoyewatha — under a flag of truce to Albany, to be exchanged for the Cayuga chief Ghalto, who had been in prison there since being wounded and captured at the Oriskany battle.

They had arrived at Albany just five days ago, on May 16, and learned to Jenkins's horror that only two days before that Ghalto had died of smallpox. The exchange no longer possible, the Indians had refused to release Jenkins.

When they left Albany the next morning, they took him with them to be disposed of with finality.

Throughout their journey from Montreal, Jenkins had become familiar with Red Jacket and had grown to like him. The young Seneca chief was bright and engaging and obviously genuinely sorry for Jenkins having become a victim of circumstance. In the four days since leaving Albany they had encountered three separate small parties of Indians — one Onondaga and two Cayuga — heading rapidly southward. During the day today, as their own party had continued toward Kanadasaga, Red Jacket told him of the massive preparations being made for war and that Colonel John Butler was by now at Tioga on the Susquehanna with perhaps twelve hundred men or more, both Indians and whites.

With a sense of dread, Jenkins had asked what their objective was, somehow knowing even before Red Jacket replied what the answer would be.

Wyoming! His home was there, his friends. More than that, Bethiah Harris was there! The fear that rose in him at that thought was worse than any he had experienced for himself.

It was at that point, while they were still moving toward Kanadasaga, that Jenkins, in undertones unheard by anyone except Red Jacket, begged the young chief to help him escape. Red Jacket suddenly became Sagoyewatha again, the Seneca, who recoiled at the idea and moved away from Jenkins, not coming close to him again during the remainder of the day's march, his expression dour and deeply troubled. Jenkins was sure he had ruined his chances, however slight they might have been. Now it was obvious that he had not; instead, he had planted in Sagoyewatha's mind a seed that had required some germination time to sprout in the mind of Red Jacket.

Jenkins, who had been sitting with his eyes closed as he reminisced, opened them in mere slits and saw that the guard at the fire was still sitting up, but the manner in which his head was forward with chin nearly on chest convinced Jenkins he was asleep. Slowly, with great care, he moved his bound hands and picked up the knife by the blade, wedging it between his heels, cutting edge up. Then, also slowly, he began rubbing the rawhide tugs that bound him across the edge. The knife was sharp and in moments he had cut through. Still taking his time and working by feel, his eyes locked on the guard, he freed his hands and then cut the tugs binding his ankles. The cords around waist, chest and neck were next and abruptly he was completely free. Carefully, still moving very slowly and utterly without sound, he came to his feet, gathered up the cut cords and stuffed them inside his shirt, kept the knife ready for use in his hand if necessary, and melted into the darkness.

Only one Indian in camp stirred. At the fire, still wrapped in his blanket, Red Jacket abruptly raised his head and looked in the direction where Jenkins had been but was no more. He grinned briefly and then lay back down, murmuring a little prayer to the Great Spirit for understanding what he had done.

Lieutenant John Jenkins was fully three hundred yards away before he broke into an easy trot that he knew he could maintain for hours. Come daylight, he would wade streams lengthwise and take other precautions for throwing off pursuit. Until then, he would put as many miles as possible between him and them.

Ahead of him stretched nearly two hundred miles of wilderness he had never traversed, a wilderness filled with hostile Indians and Tories who would undoubtedly kill him on sight. Yet John Jenkins had always been a very resourceful young man and he had supreme confidence in himself. He had no intention of being caught. The news he was carrying was far too important to be lost.

He was on his way to the Wyoming Valley . . . and Beth.

[*May 29, 1778 — Friday Morning*]

From the top of Lady Hill, just a mile east of Cherry Valley, Joseph Brant studied the village carefully and frowned. It had been his plan to attack the town with the four hundred and fifty Indians and Tories who had accompanied him here from Oquaga and Unadilla, but now he didn't like what he saw. Cherry Valley had changed some.

Below in the town there was a new fortification, upon which work was still being done. It didn't look particularly strong and was obviously more a stockade to be used as a place of refuge than a fort from which to fight. There were also crude fortifications of a sort at Colonel Campbell's house, with which Brant was already familiar. What he didn't like were the twenty or thirty individuals in ranks on the green in front of Colonel Campbell's place. They all wore the same sort of pointed hats; they all had swords at their belts and rifles over their shoulders.

For a few minutes Brant watched their drilling and concluded that the troops were very green and did not yet know well how to follow the commands of the one who was marching them, but the very fact of their presence suggested the possibility of more out of sight in the colonel's house or inside the meetinghouse within the stockade.

Even as he was watching, Brant saw something that particularly interested him. Two mounted men cantered into town from the north along the wagon road that led to tiny Tekaharawa Falls,[156] and then turned eastward toward Canajoharie. One of these men was wearing a fine uniform and he snapped a salute toward the drilling company as he and his companion pulled up, dismounted and entered Colonel Campbell's house. There was a good chance that these were messengers carrying expresses from Fort Plank at Canajoharie or even from Albany. Very likely they would return by the same route and if they could be captured, perhaps the real strength of Cherry Valley could be ascertained. If the town had no more military strength than the company he had been watching as they drilled, then they could easily sweep into the town and overrun it. Without definitely knowing the strength, however, Brant was not going to lead his men against Cherry Valley. That was the white man's way of fighting, and he had expendable men. Brant did not.

The Mohawk chief pulled back from his vantage point and murmured a few words to his chiefs and to Captain Ian McDonald, a Scot in charge of the fifty Tories with this party. In a few moments the whole force was on its way to Tekaharawa Falls.

[*May 29, 1778 — Friday Afternoon*]

In Cherry Valley, Lieutenant Frederick Wormwood and dispatch carrier Peter Sitz were preparing to depart. The last few hours had been taken up with waiting for Colonel Campbell to finish writing the four sets of messages he was preparing for Colonel Jacob Klock at Fort Plank in Canajoharie and Colonel Ichabod Alden in Albany. The first pair of messages once again complained to Colonel Alden of the almost total defenselessness of Cherry Valley and its increased need for a strong military force to be stationed here in view of increased attacks by Indian parties against outlying homes and settlements. The messages also acknowledged receipt of the news that Wormwood and Sitz had brought, that Colonel Klock would be sending a squad of a dozen militia soldiers to Cherry Valley tomorrow under Lieutenant Wormwood. This was an appreciated gesture, he said, but it really did not do much to alleviate Cherry Valley's vulnerability to attack. What was needed, he wrote, was a full company or more of regular troops permanently assigned here.

The second pair of messages were very brief. They were also bogus. One, addressed to Klock, thanked him for the company of experienced soldiers now lodged at Cherry Valley and especially for the three pieces of artillery that would be of such value in helping protect the village from attack. The other, addressed to a wholly fictitious Colonel Cord at Albany, said they were looking forward to his arrival soon with his entire regiment and added that "a perfect site has been selected for construction of the new fort you have been authorized to construct here."

While these messages were being prepared, Lieutenant Wormwood and Peter Sitz, who were both from the Palatine District, sat in a couple of chairs on the front porch, enjoying the balmy day and chuckling as they watched the little company drilling on the green close by. The "company" was made up of twenty-six boys who had armed themselves with wooden swords and make-believe rifles also made of wood and whose uniforms consisted of pointed hats made of folded paper. These were the "soldiers" whom Wormwood had saluted when he rode into town.

Now, walking out with the lieutenant and the dispatch carrier to where their horses were tied, Colonel Campbell handed the messages to Sitz. The bogus set, folded and wax-sealed, Sitz placed in his saddlebag. The other set he rolled and placed in a wooden tube with a waterproof cap, which he shoved inside his blouse. It was a customary procedure with him. While he was doing this, Wormwood was untying the portmanteau from his own saddle.

"No sense in me taking this back," he said, setting it on the Campbell house porch, "when I'll be coming back here with my platoon tomorrow." He saluted Campbell. "See you then, sir."

The pair went northward out of town, riding abreast on the wagon-rut road that would take them to Fort Plank. Two miles from Cherry Valley they were just passing Tekaharawa Falls on their left when, from behind an outcropping of rocks, stepped a half-dozen war-painted warriors led by a Mohawk whom Wormwood recognized. The Indians signaled them to halt.

"It's Brant!" Wormwood shouted. "Let's go!"

Both men immediately spurred their horses into a gallop in the direction they were heading and within instants there were rifle shots. One ball buzzed past Sitz's ear and another plucked at his sleeve but did not hit him. Wormwood wasn't as lucky. A ball entered his back and exited from his chest, leaving a gaping hole from which a great gout of blood spurted, splashing over the saddle and his horse's mane and neck. He somehow managed to stay in the saddle for a dozen yards or more but then fell to the ground. He tried to rise, tried to draw his sword from its scabbard; his movements were sluggish, uncoordinated, as if in a nightmare. But this was no dream. Before he could even get fully to his knees, a warrior raced up and buried his tomahawk in the man's temple.[157]

Sitz had continued to gallop forward, beginning to descend the steep wooded slope down which Tekaharawa Creek tumbled to make the falls. The moment he was screened by the trees and rocks and out of sight of the Indians behind him, he jerked the dispatch tube from inside his shirt and flung it from him.[158] In another moment he rounded a bend in the road and then jerked to a halt as he found some disreputable-looking whites and half a hundred Indians barring his path. There was nothing to do but surrender.

Lieutenant Wormwood's horse, unharmed but blood-streaked, which had been following Sitz's, reared and snorted at the sight of the Indians and then turned and galloped back the way it had come. Eyes rolling in terror, it streaked past the place where its owner lay dead, his scalp being removed by the warrior who had killed him, and thundered back toward Cherry Valley.

Within a few minutes, Peter Sitz and his horse had been returned to where Brant was and it was the Mohawk chief who opened the saddlebags and found the false dispatches. He scowled as he read them. They tended to confirm what he had witnessed from atop Lady Hill. Cherry Valley was too strong to risk attacking it now.

"We will strike Cobleskill instead," he said.

[*May 30, 1778 — Saturday*]

The forty soldiers under command of Captain William Patrick of Stoughton, Massachusetts, were all part of Colonel Ichabod Alden's regiment. They were just now approaching Cobleskill,[159] forty-five miles from Albany. They had been detached from the rest of the regiment at Albany and sent to the stone fort at Schoharie just in time to meet Captain Jonathan Miller, back from a reconnaissance of the Cobleskill area. There was plenty of evidence of a fair number of Indians and perhaps some Tories skulking about in the area and so Patrick and his men were ordered to get the help of the Cobleskill Militia and disperse any of the enemy they could discover.

Cobleskill was much smaller than Cherry Valley, having only twenty homes, a church and meeting hall and a collection of outbuildings. Now, as the little detachment reached the home of Captain Christian Brown, commander of the Cobleskill Militia, Patrick's force was increased by Brown and twenty of his men. It was Brown who said that reports had come in of some Indians having been spotted near the residence of Lawrence Lawyer, about a half mile north of town.[160] Lawyer wasn't there when they arrived, but his wife, obviously very frightened, said the Indians that had been hovering around had moved off southwest toward George Warner's house on Cobleskill creek.[161] Warner was an influential committeeman of the region and so Patrick immediately marched his combined force of sixty men in that direction.

The most Indians anyone had yet reported seeing in the area was about ten or twelve in a cluster and so there was no great fear that they would encounter any sort of large force. Nevertheless, when they reached Warner's place, he was just leaving with his family for the greater protection of the stone fort at Schoharie, ten miles east of Cobleskill. Assurances by Captain Patrick that they really needn't panic this way did nothing to assure the Warners. They reported that they, too, had seen Indians — about twenty of them — along with a few Tories in their midst and they didn't like what was shaping up. Earlier this morning, Warner told Patrick, Lieutenant Jacob Borst of the militia, along with his younger brother Joseph and a neighbor, John Freemire, passed on their way a little farther up the Cobuskill to go fishing and they hadn't been seen since. To Warner this boded no good and he didn't mean to stay around with his family in jeopardy.

Standing about leisurely in front of the Warner house, Captain Patrick's company watched the Warners leave. The troops rested awhile. The house was on a commanding piece of ground and it was as good a place as any to catch their breath.

A quarter mile upstream, where long ago a tree had fallen into Cobleskill Creek, causing the current to dig a deep hole that had become a haven for bass and other fish, the Borst brothers and John Freemire had been having good luck. As a matter of fact, Freemire had just hooked a large bass on the hook and line attached to the long limber willow pole he'd cut and was having a good bit of sport trying to bring it in while Jacob and Joseph cheered him on. They had no idea anyone was even near until suddenly rifles crashed. Freemire was shot through the heart and fell into the creek. Jacob took a bullet through the fleshy part of his left upper arm. It knocked him down but he rose with his rifle swiftly enough to kill the Indian who was rushing upon him with raised tomahawk. Another Indian was already grappling with Joseph but when he saw his companion shot, he broke free and raced off into the woods shouting.

The sound of the shots reached Captain Patrick at Warner's house and he immediately alerted his troops and sent a sergeant and five privates to investigate. Within minutes they came running back and with them was the wounded Lieutenant Jacob Borst, bleeding badly from his arm, and his brother Joseph. The voice of the sergeant carried to Patrick easily.

"Captain Patrick! Lieutenant Maynard! Indians coming!"

Patrick instantly ordered his company and the Cobleskill Militia to follow him. His company did, but thirteen of the militia failed to do so. The soldiers had advanced a few hundred yards when from the woods emerged twenty-five Indians and a few Tories and momentarily the fire became extremely fierce. Abruptly the party of Indians began to flee and Captain Patrick's force was in immediate pursuit. For nearly a mile they chased them. For a good many that pursuit, ending in a small swamp, was their last mile.

Brant's trap was sprung.

Suddenly, hundreds of Indians leaped up from hiding on both sides and now it was the Americans who took a heavy fire and began falling back. Three times they held, fired and then retreated in orderly manner, but when Captain Patrick was downed by a shot in his groin, his remaining unharmed men turned and fled. As they passed the Warner house, Captain Patrick's second-in-command, Lieutenant Jonathan Maynard of Framingham, managed to stop some of them. The militiamen who had stayed behind at the house were gone. As the majority of the soldiers continued their retreat toward Cobleskill, Maynard and his handful of men took refuge inside the house and, firing from the windows, held the attackers at bay long enough for the others to get away and warn the Cobleskill residents to flee if they could.

Maynard, taking a position at the front door of the Warner house, coolly loaded and fired several times, bringing down two Indians and a Tory named Christopher Service before himself taking a ball through the throat, which killed him. [162]

As Maynard fell in the doorway, Private Jonathan Young tried to help him and in the process was shot through the side. Kneeling, he still tried to defend himself with a large knife as an Indian raced up and pierced him through with a lance. The Indian dragged him a short distance from the house, jerked the lance out and then ran him through with it again, killing him. Young was then scalped and his body cavity ripped open with a knife. His heart was cut free and thrown to one side and his entrails were jerked out and stretched around a tree and then back to him and wrapped around his left arm.

While this was occurring, Captain Ian McDonald, in charge of the Tories, set the house afire at several places. Six soldiers inside the place burned to death. After committing a few more atrocities on the dying or dead, the attackers moved together the remaining half mile into Cobleskill and found it all but abandoned.[163] The homes and outbuildings were all plundered of anything valuable or useful and then burned.

A few Indians had been killed, but only a few, and one Tory soldier. For the Americans, it was a different story. Thirty-one were killed and six wounded.[164]

Cobleskill was destroyed.

For the Iroquois, this was only a beginning.

[*June 2, 1778 — Monday*]

The area called Wyoming was a beautiful place. It had been settled primarily by settlers from Connecticut, rather than from Pennsylvania or New York. The Connecticut settlers claimed it as being included in the original Connecticut grant by King Charles II. It consisted of eight townships, each five miles square, placed on each side of the Susquehanna in an area of that stream that could only be described as lovely.

In the years since its settlement began, Wyoming had grown and prospered and was now the largest isolated settlement on the frontiers of New York, Pennsylvania, Maryland or Virginia. It was fiercely patriotic to the American cause and had already sent 'over a thousand men to serve in the Continental Army. That was the problem. So many had been sent that the four principal forts in the area were practically empty and therefore unable to suitably defend themselves or their surroundings.

That was the situation when, at ten o'clock this morning, Lieutenant John Jenkins stumbled into Wyoming. Twelve days in the wilderness, mostly without food, fire or shelter, skirting Indian villages and small war parties and Tory settlements and, finally, the massive gathering of the enemy at Tioga had rendered him almost totally exhausted. His clothing was tattered beyond belief, his hair was disheveled and, for the first time in his life, he had a substantial growth of beard.

Much as he wanted to be with Beth, other things took precedence. He paused at his own fortified place in Exeter — Jenkins Fort[165] — long enough for their deliriously happy reunion; long enough to tell her again how much he loved her and to hastily set the date for their wedding for three weeks from today; long enough to shed his shredded clothes and don something serviceable;

long enough to grab a hasty bite to eat. Then, without further pause, he reported to Colonel Nathan Denison.

The Wyoming Valley Militia commander was just then talking with Colonel
Zebulon Butler, an officer of the Continental Army who was on leave and who
had just arrived. What began as a meeting between these three grew steadily as
word spread and more officers and responsible citizens of the Wyoming Valley
came to hear what he was saying. They all paled at his words and, though fear
had never been very far from them in these past couple of years, now it blossomed in every breast.

What Jenkins had heard while with the party led by Red Jacket was wholly
corroborated by what he himself had witnessed as he made his tortuous way
overland back to this valley. The culmination had been when, unseen, he
slipped past Tioga and there, at that village and at the sister village of Queen
Esther's Town across the mouth of the Chemung, witnessed the incredible
preparations that were under way for an invasion. Many hundreds of men were
there, white and Indian alike, and they were building a whole armada of canoes and flatboats for their downstream invasion against the Wyoming Valley.

As if to underline the peril, Jenkins related how only the day before yesterday, as he passed the area of Tunkhannock where he had been captured with
Amos York and Lemuel Fitch and where old Fitzgerald had been killed by the
Tory named Newbury, he had watched from hiding as a pair of Wyoming men
he had known — Bill Crooks and Asa Budd — were attacked by a party of Indians. Crooks was dead for certain; he had watched the Indians scalp him and
toss the body into brush onshore. However, Budd had escaped from them.
Whether he got away or was caught later Jenkins didn't know.

"He got away, John," Colonel Denison said softly. "He got back here last
night in the boat he and Crooks had gone up in. What he told us coincides
with what you've said."

"He's all right?" Jenkins asked.

Denison nodded grimly. "All right, yes, but gone. He packed up and left
early this morning. Heading for Easton. He said he'd never come back. I don't
imagine he will." He shook his head. "Bad things happening all over. Sebastian Strope, up at Wysockton,[166] came to get a detachment to escort his family
down because an Indian they had befriended once came and warned him of an
attack coming. The escort went up with him. All they found was ashes. His
family was gone — wife, mother, father, children, and his wife's three sisters — nine in all."

"That and the Brooks and Budd incidents were bad enough," Zebulon
Butler put in, "but we had no idea it was presaging a full-scale invasion. That'll
make more people leave when the word gets around."

"But there'll be plenty who'll stay," Denison put in. "By God, we don't intend to give up what we've poured our sweat and life blood into." He looked at

Jenkins sharply. "*You're* going to stay on, aren't you?" At Jenkins's nod, he went on: "Good. Thought you would. We need manpower badly. Every male from young boys to old men are all in the militia now. We're low on gunpowder, so the women are pulling up the floors of their houses and digging up the earth beneath, leaching it and collecting the saltpeter. They mix it with charcoal and sulfur and it makes a passable gunpowder, but we need a lot more than that."

When he paused, Jenkins smiled wryly and finished for him: "But you need something I can do?"

Denison nodded. "You've been through a lot and I hate to ask it, but no one else can make the report you can make — about what you've seen at Niagara and Montreal as well as up at Tioga. I'd like you to get a few hours' rest and then be ready to move again. We have a couple good horses you can use. By the time you're refreshed, we'll have the dispatches ready for you to carry. I want you to take 'em to General Washington personally. Tell him everything. Tell Congress, too, if necessary. Stress the immediate peril and ask — no, demand! — no, I guess you'd better ask . . . but strongly! — ask that the two full companies that were taken away from us, which were originally formed for our protection — Captain Durkee's and Captain Ransom's — be sent back to us right away. And any additional men and supplies they can send. Will you do that?"

The lieutenant was quiet for a long moment. He'd been held captive by the Indians for half a year, marched across the wilderness, finally escaped and fled through more wilderness in a grueling journey and now, without his yet having had rest or sufficient time with Bethiah, he was being asked to do even more.

Jenkins smiled wearily. "I will."

[*June 10, 1778 — Wednesday*]

The boat-building at Tioga was completed and Colonel John Butler, with Captain James Caldwell of the Royal Greens beside him, looked over the veritable armada drawn up onshore. Side by side, there were over two hundred canoes — poorly constructed, to be sure, but serviceable for the need they had to fill — and another thirty or forty larger boats for cargo. The canoes would each be capable of carrying six men and some baggage. The larger boats, even with cargo, could hold a dozen men.

On a sort of tripod affair in the middle of camp, a small white dog was hanging by one hind leg, kicking and yelping in fear. It had just been hung there and now a roar went up from the five hundred Indians gathered around. Chief Kayingwaurto of the Senecas approached and a hush fell over the assemblage. As if realizing what was in store, the terrified dog snarled and snapped at him as he reached for it, but Kayingwaurto easily avoided being bitten. His hand shot

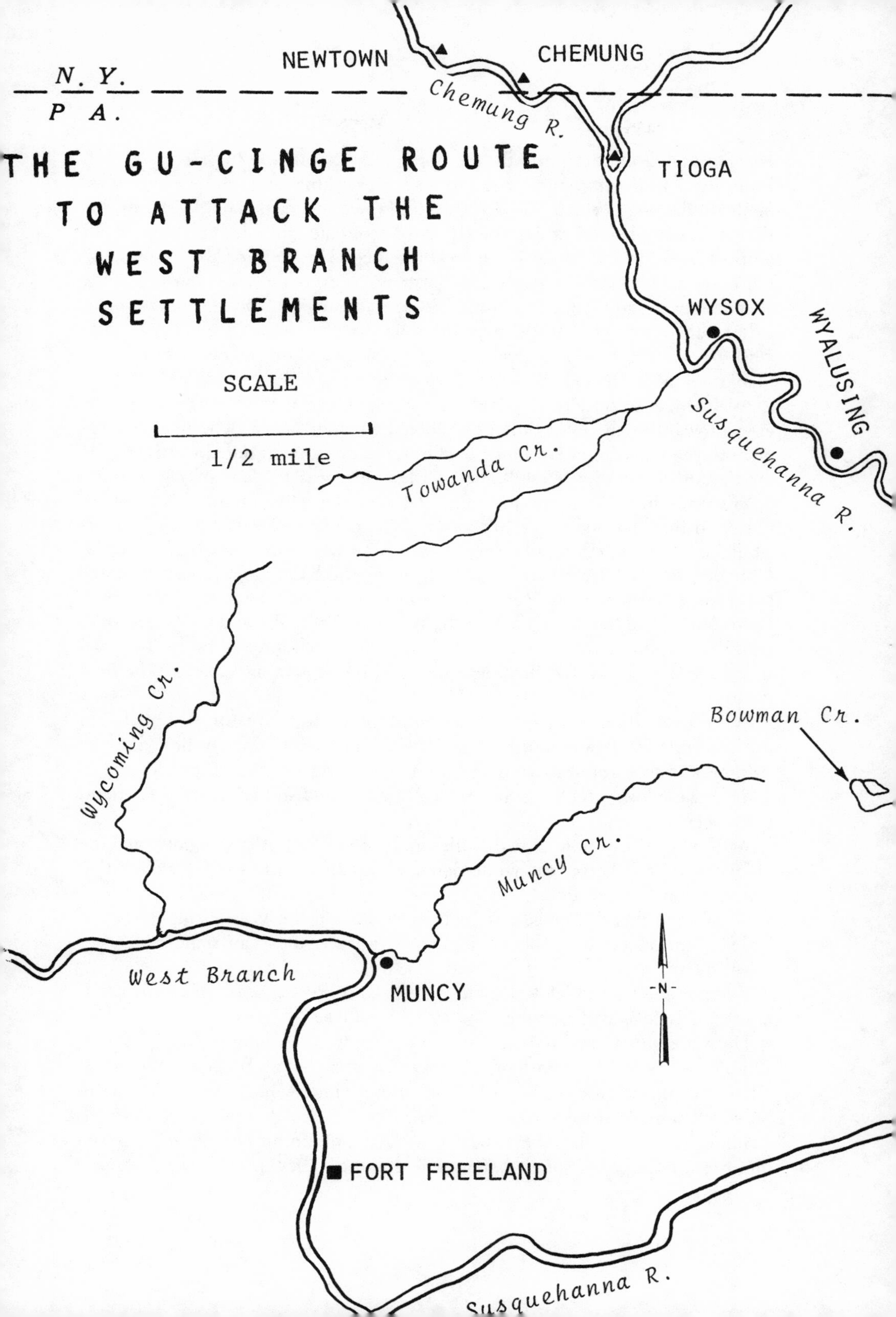

THE GU-CINGE ROUTE
TO ATTACK THE
WEST BRANCH
SETTLEMENTS

N.Y.
P A.

NEWTOWN

CHEMUNG

Chemung R.

TIOGA

WYSOX

WYALUSING

Susquehanna R.

SCALE

1/2 mile

Towanda Cr.

Wycoming Cr.

Bowman Cr.

Muncy Cr.

West Branch

MUNCY

-N-

FORT FREELAND

Susquehanna R.

out and took a powerful grip on the dog's muzzle, holding the mouth closed. From his belt, Kayingwaurto took out his scalping knife and in one fluid movement slit the dog's throat. Blood gushed and the dog jerked about. Very quickly its movements slowed, then ceased. An incredible din of shrieks and yells erupted from the Indians. It was a good sacrifice. The dog would remain hanging there as a tribute to the Great Spirit, who, everyone knew, would come after they were gone and take the dog's skin and make a tobacco pouch of it. When they returned from the expedition against the Wyoming Valley — successfully, of course, as this good sacrifice betokened — an identical sacrifice of thanks would be made.

As Kayingwaurto resheathed his knife and then threaded his way through the crowd toward them, John Butler considered what lay ahead. The plan now, as prearranged with Chief Gu-cinge before he led his four hundred warriors away for the attacks on the West Branch settlements, was to float sixty-four miles downstream from Tioga to the large flat just above the mouth of Bowman Creek on the west side of the Susquehanna across from Tunkhannock.[167] This would serve as something of a staging area from which the campaign could be launched. It was also where they would wait until Gu-cinge's party rejoined them from the west. Whatever plunder Gu-cinge brought back with him would be loaded aboard the larger boats at the Bowman Creek flat and left there under guard of a hundred or more men, while the combined force of twelve hundred Indians and whites would then descend upon the Wyoming Valley in the light boats.

So far everything had gone perfectly and there was no reason why it should not continue so. It was possible that they could take the Wyoming Valley by surprise and this would make easier what lay ahead, but even if the element of surprise were lost, which was most likely, they would still certainly overwhelm the place.

As Kayingwaurto now joined Butler and Caldwell, Butler congratulated the chief on the sacrifice of the white dog as a supplication to the Great Spirit. It was an augury of success.

"Assuming that Gu-cinge has been successful on the West Branch," Butler added, "and meets us as planned, there is no way they can stand against us downstream."

Kayingwaurto and Caldwell both nodded and the Seneca spoke with assurance. "Gu-cinge will be where he said he will be."

He was right. On a straight line some seventy miles almost directly south, Gu-cinge was in the midst of ravaging the small West Branch settlements. They had no defense against him and those whites who did not flee at his approach were destroyed, along with their homes. Already it was becoming difficult for his force to travel because of the large amount of plunder it had taken and the number of prisoners being herded along. A few more days, perhaps a

week, Gu-cinge reckoned, and he would move back up the West Branch of the
Susquehanna to Muncy Creek and then up to its headwaters and eastward to
join Butler and Kayingwaurto on schedule. And then would come what this
present little expedition was only a practice run for — the attack on the Wyoming Valley.

Gu-cinge fingered the fresh scalps hanging at his belt and grinned wolfishly.

[*June 18, 1778 — Thursday Evening*]

In his headquarters at Valley Forge, General George Washington talked quietly
with the old Seneca chief whose Indian name he could not pronounce but
whom he had known for years as Big Tree, chief of the village of Conesus.[168]
Although, in view of what had occurred today, there were scores of things to be
done before moving out, Washington had taken time to see the chief on his arrival and greeted him with genuine warmth.

"This has been an important day for you," Big Tree said. "Will you now
move back to Philadelphia?"

He was referring to the fact that at 11:30 A.M. today the British had abandoned Philadelphia and were now on the march in New Jersey. The American
commander-in-chief nodded, then qualified it by saying that he personally
would not be returning to Philadelphia, although he would send a detachment
to occupy it. For his own part, he would be leading his force farther north and
make an effort to engage the British somewhere in New Jersey.

"There are troubles everywhere," Big Tree murmured. "Some of the worst
are on the frontiers. My people are very restless."

Washington looked up sharply, wondering if somehow Big Tree knew what
he and the young lieutenant from the Wyoming Valley had discussed this afternoon and then decided he did not. Big Tree's influence among the Senecas
was legendary. For years he had been a leading adviser in all treaties and councils of the Senecas. He was, as such, an important ally and the only prominent
Seneca who was a friend of the Americans. He also knew a great deal that people often did not even suspect he knew. But, Washington was sure, he did *not*
know about Jenkins's visit this afternoon.

Washington had spent nearly an hour with Jenkins, listening with interest to
his report on Niagara and Montreal, on his escape from the Indians with Red
Jacket's help, and his rigorous journey back to Wyoming to warn them of impending attack and even of having witnessed some of the preparations at Tioga
for that attack.

The commanding general had sympathized deeply with the young lieutenant, stating that he wished he could take some instant action to help alleviate their problems and reduce the jeopardy they were currently experiencing.
He would, in fact, send in some regular companies very soon, but he could not
send them immediately. In view of the pending action against the British in

New Jersey, he would have to wait a little while to see how best to deploy his strength. Colonel Zebulon Butler was on leave in the Wyoming Valley now. Washington could authorize Butler's help in leadership while he was on leave there if Butler himself were agreeable. If, as appeared likely, within the next week or so it seemed that he could safely do so, he would send the requested companies under Captains Durkee and Ransom, and possibly those of Captains Clingman and Franklin as well. But right now, regretfully, he could not. Jenkins had left immediately.

Now Washington looked at Big Tree and smiled wryly. "Yes, there are troubles everywhere, my friend. I'm sorry your people are restless. I wish they were not, because if they should cause trouble to our people, it might mean that we would have to raise our hands against you and that would be painful to us both. I would hope that you could stay with me for a while and observe how this army operates. Then, perhaps, you might go back to your people and tell them how foolish it is for them to support the King against us."

Big Tree considered this and then nodded. "I am already convinced of the foolishness of opposing the United States, but what convinces me may not convince them. I will stay with you awhile, as you ask, and learn more things to take back to my people in order to convince them."

[*June 18, 1778 — Thursday Night*]

"You're sure this is what you want to do?" John Jenkins asked. He looked earnestly at the men in the tent.

"What else *can* we do, for God's sake?" It was Captain Samuel Ransom who answered him. "We may not have our companies, but there is no way we're going to stay here while a thousand of our people — our *families!* — are in danger of being destroyed."

Captain Robert Durkee backed him up completely, as did Lieutenants James Welles and Perrin Ross. Lieutenant Simon Spalding, of Durkee's company, shook his head.

"I don't see that it'll accomplish a thing," he argued. "Hell, Wyoming's my home too, and I want to protect it just as much as the rest of you, but we need manpower to do that. Individually we're not much good, but in company strength we can fight. Doesn't that make sense?"

"Maybe," Durkee said, then added flatly, "but I'm still going to see the regimental commander right now. I just don't want to stay here. Anyone coming with me?"

There was a little more discussion and then they all went. It didn't take long. Sympathy was there, certainly, but orders were orders. The Wyoming companies would be sent, of course, but not until it was authorized from above and that was final. With anger and disgust, Durkee, Ransom, Ross and Welles all resigned their commissions on the spot.

Spalding remained and, elevated to the rank of captain and placed in command of the two Wyoming companies that had become leaderless at the resignations of Durkee and Ransom, he went with them to the edge of the camp and shook hands warmly with each.

"I'll come with the troops just as soon as I possibly can," he said earnestly. "I won't let up on it. We'll be there. I promise."

"Just get there soon," Durkee said.

"And fast," Ransom added.

"And in time," Jenkins put in. "For God's sake — and ours! — get there in time. There's *no* possibility of our standing them off if you don't."

[June 23, 1778 — Tuesday]

The situation at Wyoming was growing daily more tense. A score of times or more each day the individual residents would pause in whatever they were doing and gaze in the direction from which would come the expected help that Lieutenant John Jenkins had been sent to get. When three weeks had passed and it still hadn't arrived, the pressure had become all but unbearable.

There was no longer any doubt that an attack was coming. They'd had no cause at all to doubt him, but nevertheless everything Jenkins had told them had been corroborated. An enormous force of the enemy was upriver preparing to come against them. Two of the four small spying parties that had been sent out returned with full verification of it. The other two hadn't returned at all, which was even more frightening than an affirmative report. One of the parties that did return had reported that it appeared the enemy at Tioga was on the verge of floating down the Susquehanna by boat to the Wyoming Valley.

Everyone in the valley who could stand and walk was working to help with the fortifications, but the defenses were still pitiable. Long ago the cream of Wyoming's young men had been formed into the two strong companies that had then been withdrawn from the valley for use elsewhere in the war effort. Now, although there were still a number of able-bodied men here, there were mostly women and little children and old men who were working as much as twenty hours a day to strengthen defenses.

In addition to about a dozen halfheartedly fortified houses in the various Wyoming Valley districts, there were seven forts. Of these, only two really deserved to be called forts — the one at Wilkes-Barre on the east side of the river, and the one called Forty Fort, which was across the river and slightly upstream from Wilkes-Barre Fort.[169] The others were simply reinforced public gathering houses or private homes that had been slightly stockaded. These included, beginning with the farthest downstream in the area, the public fort at Plymouth District, which was located on the west shore and hardly could be called a fort at all, and one very similar to it on the east shore of the river about a half mile southwest of Wilkes-Barre Fort, called Wyoming Fort.[170]

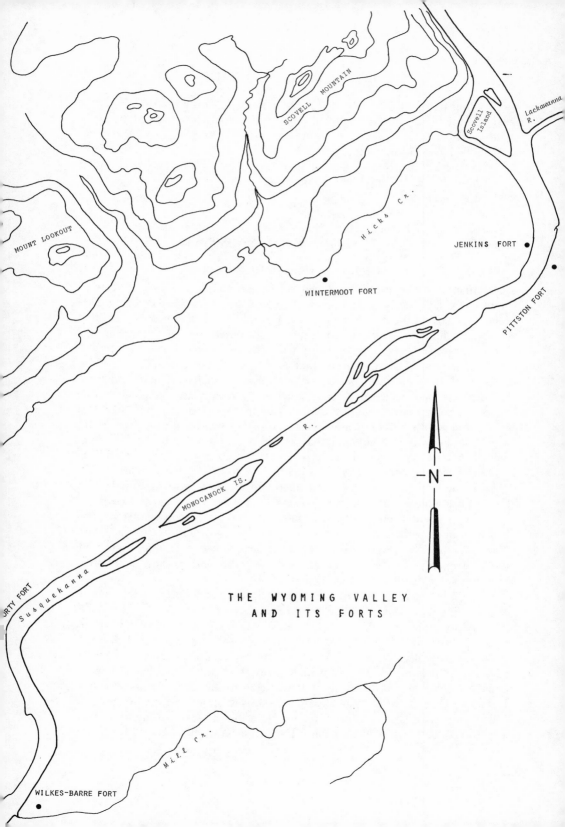

THE WYOMING VALLEY
AND ITS FORTS

Wintermoot Fort, on the west side of the river, was simply the fortified residence of the Wintermoot family, who were suspected of being Tories or at least of having Tory sympathies.[171] This fort was located about a mile and a half downstream from Jenkins Fort, which itself was the farthest upstream in the valley and the most vulnerable to attack. As with Wintermoot Fort, it was a reinforced house, belonging to Lieutenant John Jenkins, which had been fortified with a stockade of sharpened logs. On the west bank, it was just slightly upstream from Pittston Fort, located on the east side.[172]

Meetings of the militia officers were being held daily, presided over by Denison at Forty Fort, usually with his second-in-command, Lieutenant Colonel George Torrence, sitting in. Also quietly on hand was Colonel Zebulon Butler, still on leave, who thus far had declined to act in more than an advisory capacity unless his doing so could be authorized by higher authority. The officers discussed what to do about protecting the inhabitants and what course of action should be followed when the enemy did show up.

As the meeting was being held yesterday, two demoralizing events occurred. The first was the return of a party that had gone out from Fort Jenkins a few days previously to reconnoiter upstream. That party, led by Stephen Jenkins, John's younger brother, had set out in two canoes. They had gone some twenty miles upstream and late the day before yesterday, just as they were approaching Tunkhannock, they ran into trouble. As they rounded a bend two miles above a place called Cowyards Riff, they spied an enormous camp of the enemy. Not having expected to find any such encampment before reaching the Tioga area, they immediately stopped paddling and drifted backward until they were out of sight and hoped they hadn't been seen. They paddled back to Cowyards Riff and pulled their canoes up on the west bank opposite the upstream end of a half-mile-long island just below the riffle.[173]

They left the canoes and climbed up the forty-foot bank to the plateau above, only to see a large party of Indians and Tory Rangers running toward them. In the lead of the Rangers, only thirty yards distant, was Elijah Phelps. He was immediately recognized by his brother Joel, who was one of the Jenkins party.

The Wyoming men spun about and raced back down the embankment to their canoes and, with three men in each, shoved off. They were hardly in midstream before shots were fired at them and they paddled furiously in an effort to get the island between them and their attackers. One of the canoes made it all right. Jenkins's canoe, however, was not fast enough. At almost the same instant three rifle balls struck them — one cutting off Jenkins's paddle right between his hands, one striking Joel Phelps in the shoulder, a third striking Phelps's brother-in-law, Miner Robbins, in the middle of the back. For a few moments they drifted aimlessly, then Phelps managed to toss his paddle back to Jenkins and, as the other canoe had, they slipped behind the safety of the

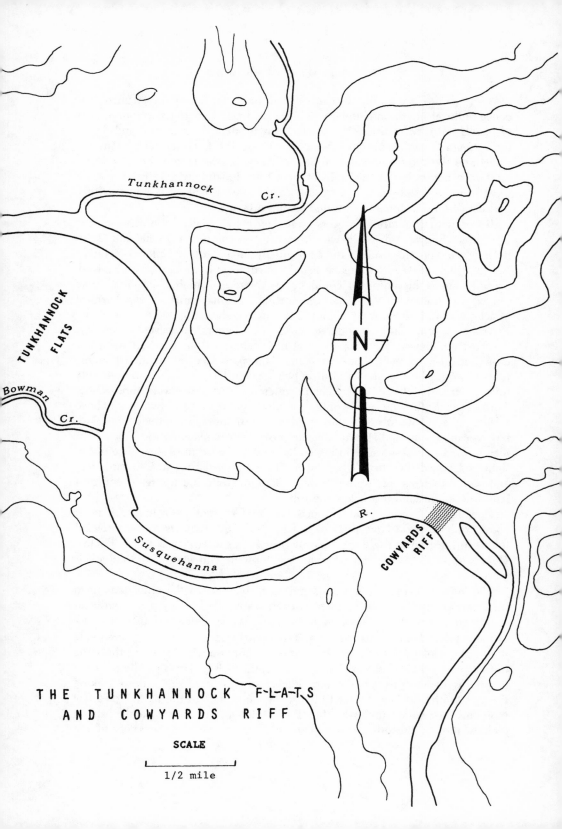

Tunkhannock Cr.

TUNKHANNOCK FLATS

Bowman Cr.

N

Susquehanna R.

COWYARDS RIFF

THE TUNKHANNOCK FLATS
AND COWYARDS RIFF

SCALE

1/2 mile

island. By the time the two canoes rejoined the main channel of the river again below the island's lowest point, they were out of range of the enemy.

Darkness overtook them before they traveled half the distance back to Jenkins Fort and they had pulled up onshore, made a fireless camp and treated the wounds of Phelps and Robbins as best they could. Phelps was in a great deal of pain, but his wound did not appear to be dangerous. Robbins, however, was in shock and in bad condition. At dawn yesterday morning they had resumed their downstream passage.

Before noon, Miner Robbins had died.

The second demoralizing event of the day was the return, just a few hours later, of Lieutenant John Jenkins from General Washington's headquarters. Although he reported that help was promised, he could not say when it would come. Colonel Zebulon Butler had been authorized to stay and help if he cared to, but that was not an order. Jenkins had also brought back with him the four Wyoming Valley officers, Captains Durkee and Ransom and Lieutenants Welles and Ross — without their companies. Only five men instead of the minimum of five hundred that they so desperately needed.

With dusk approaching last evening, John Jenkins and Bethiah Harris, reunited after much too long a time, had strolled hand in hand along the riverbank close to Jenkins Fort. For a while they said nothing, content at merely being close. Beth had soft, light brown hair and large, warm brown eyes. There were those who said her smile could melt an iceberg. Two years younger than John, at twenty-four she was by far the most beautiful woman in the Wyoming Valley. She had come here well over a year ago from Colchester, Connecticut, with her father, Jonathan Harris. She and the rather dashing young lieutenant had been engaged for almost a year now, although for more than half that time Jenkins had been in captivity. Finally together again, the future was not very promising.

"What's ahead, John?" she had asked abruptly, her eyes searching his face. "Are we going to make it?"

They stopped, facing one another, and he took both her hands in his and shook his head. "I don't know, Beth. It doesn't look good. I wish you'd leave while you can."

"Would you come with me?"

"I can't. You know that. I'm needed here."

"Then I won't go either," she said firmly. "My place is with you, regardless of what's happening. I won't leave you. I want us to go ahead with our plans tomorrow. If we're going to die, then I want to be your wife when it happens."

They had kissed then and briefly had been able to shut away the pall of gloom that overhung the valley. And now, today, they were being married, with twenty-two people to witness the brief ceremony.[174]

The same thought was in everyone's mind when the Reverend James Whit-

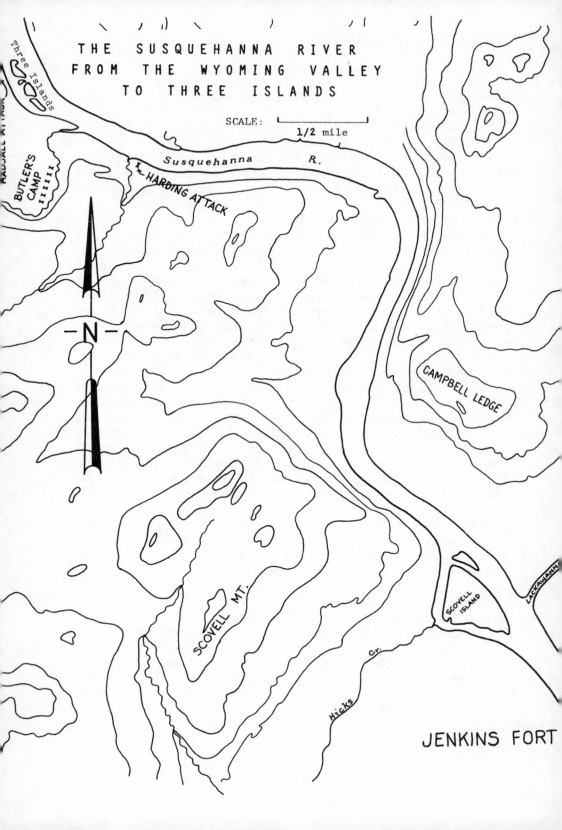

THE SUSQUEHANNA RIVER
FROM THE WYOMING VALLEY
TO THREE ISLANDS

SCALE:

1/2 mile

Three Islands

RANDALL ATTACK

BUTLER'S CAMP

Susquehanna R.

HARDING ATTACK

- N -

CAMPBELL LEDGE

SCOVELL MT.

SCOVELL ISLAND

LACKAWANN

Hicks Cr.

JENKINS FORT

tlesey intoned the words that joined John and Beth as man and wife and concluded with "till death do you part."

That might be very soon.

[June 30, 1778 — Tuesday Afternoon]

There was great excitement in Colonel John Butler's huge encampment across the river from Tunkhannock when, late yesterday, the four-hundred-warrior detachment under Chief Gu-cinge came into view at the mouth of Bowman Creek. Their onslaught against the isolated settlements on the West Branch of the Susquehanna had been entirely successful. They had taken some thirty scalps and fifteen prisoners, yet not one of their own had suffered even the slightest injury. With their plunder they had followed Gu-cinge up Muncy Creek to its source.[175] From there they had gone overland for ten miles. They had crossed a mountain and found the headwaters of Bowman Creek.[176] From there it was an easy trail along the north bank of the creek to its mouth.

By late morning, with all the plunder they had brought back with them restowed aboard the larger flatboats and left in the care of a detachment of nearly a hundred Indians and a small number of Butler's Tories, the remainder of the force, about twelve hundred strong, set off downstream in the canoes.[177] The four hundred Rangers had painted their faces with war paint much in the manner that the eight hundred Indians had and the whole body of invaders was rather frightening to behold, especially as they traveled almost entirely without sound, their passage swift and menacing.

In less than four hours, having passed a few abandoned houses and fields of young corn, they reached a place about fourteen miles downstream from Tunkhannock where the main channel flowed east of three islands, each about two hundred yards in length and separated by narrow channels. Three Islands was only six miles upstream from the closest of the Wyoming Valley forts, Jenkins Fort. The water on the west side of the islands had little current and formed a gentle eddy and it was there, on the west shore below the southernmost island, that they put ashore.[178] They had come as far as they would by water.

Even now they continued to work silently, each knowing what was expected of him. All the canoes, as was customary in such situations, were carried well up onto the shore and hidden from passing view by a tall growth of weeds. Then the entire force moved about a quarter mile inland and a half mile south and set up a camp on the bank of a substantial little creek.[179]

In the morning, Butler planned, screened by the low mountains here, they would move westward a little and then almost directly southward to the Wyoming Valley. And now, as usual, leaving nothing to chance, Butler sent out several scouting parties to check out the area, both upstream and down.

[*June 30, 1778 — Tuesday Evening*]

In view of the reports that there was a large force of Indians and Tories about twenty miles upriver, it was with no little nervousness on their parts that the party of twelve had left Jenkins Fort just shortly after dawn today, despite the suggestion of Lieutenant Jenkins that they remain close to the fort.

It was forty-six-year-old James Hadsall who made the decision to go anyway. His young cornfields and those of the Hardings in the vicinity of Upper Exeter had been too much neglected recently and needed care now. If they weren't seen to, the crop would be lost. Everyone knew how serious the food shortage had been here last winter and how hundred-pound sacks of flour carried on men's backs all the way from Stroudsburg had been their only salvation, although it nearly killed the men to accomplish it. If this year's crop didn't pull through, how could they possibly make it through another winter? Benjamin Harding nodded and he and his thirty-year-old nephew supported Hadsall's contention.

Hadsall agreed with Jenkins that it might be risky, but three or four of them would be reasonably well armed and they should be able to hold their own if anything threatened. Still, even though admittedly a dangerous undertaking, the work had to be done. Hadsall gave the order and his party formed up and set off. In addition to himself and his twenty-year-old son, Jim, and twelve-year-old son, John, an eleven-year-old companion of John's, Peter Rogers, came along. The Hardings included the elder Ben and his son Stukeley, who was twenty, and the nephew Stephen Harding, Jr. John Gardner was along too, as were Hadsall's sons-in-law, Ebenezer Reynolds and Daniel Carr. The final two in the party were William Martin's black slave, Quocko Martin, and Daniel Wallen.

By eight o'clock this morning the party had reached the first of several cornfields — those belonging to Stephen Harding, Jr. — about five miles above Jenkins Fort in a fertile little river bottom area only a few hundred yards below the mouth of a creek.[180] Here the party split. Stephen, Stukeley, Ben, John Gardner and young Peter Rogers stopped to work here, planning to remain until the others, going farther upstream, returned on their way home.

A half mile upstream the other seven passed another creek mouth.[181] Half a mile beyond that, just opposite the uppermost of Three Islands, they halted. Here Jim Hadsall and his younger brother John along with his brother-in-law Ebenezer Reynolds and Daniel Wallen all began to work in a cornfield belonging to the elder Hadsall on the northernmost island. The final three — James Hadsall, Sr., his son-in-law Daniel Carr and the slave, Quocko Martin — were in another of Hadsall's cornfields adjacent to a cleared area that he had often used as a tannery yard for leather-making. This area was on the plateau about twenty feet above the river, about three or four hundred feet west of the shore and screened from the river by weed growth.

The work in the fields was difficult. Weeds were not only around the corn-fields, they had sprung up abundantly between the rows and had to be chopped out with hoes. The workers in each of the fields were pretty much isolated in their own little spheres. Neither of the two Hadsall parties was aware of it when some two hundred canoes filled with twelve hundred war-painted men slid silently past in the eddy and landed about three-quarters of a mile above the Harding party.

Now, just after sunset as the workers were preparing to quit and return to Jenkins Fort, the scouting parties sent out by Colonel Butler struck. At the Harding field, only minutes before the Indians showed up, Stephen Harding and the Rogers boy left the three men and went to the creek a few hundred yards away to wash up and refresh themselves. The bank was harder there than at the river and the water clearer. The two had no guns. They were out of sight of the others, screened by creek brush, when the attack came.

Rifles barked and the shrieks of Indians could be heard. Immediately, Ste-phen told Peter to keep down and stay where he was and then raced back a short distance to where he might get a glimpse of what was happening. Still un-seen, he pulled up short when he found a dozen or more Indians between him and the Harding cornfield, their attention centered on the white men there. Stephen melted back into heavier cover and returned to Peter Rogers.

"They're under attack," he whispered. "I don't know if they can hold out, but we've got to get back to the fort and try to get help up to them. Come on!"

They started away, forced to move in a northerly direction first to skirt the at-tackers, who had seemed to be approaching from the west. They would then cut westward themselves after a while and attempt to circle past the attackers unseen.

Back at the cornfield, Stukeley and Ben had both been hit in the first firing from the Indians, but they were only superficially wounded. John Gardner had not been hit at all. The three had taken refuge in a nearby rocky area and Gardner, having no weapon, merely dropped flat and moaned softly in his fear. Both Ben and his son leveled their rifles and fired at the Indians running toward them. They couldn't see whether or not they'd hit anyone because im-mediately after they fired, and before they could reload, the Indians rushed upon them, shrieking wildly and brandishing tomahawks. Both men gripped their rifles by the barrels and swung them viciously. They had no chance. Overwhelmed by sheer numbers, they were hacked to death with tomahawks.

Gardner, groveling on the ground between the rocks nearby, pleaded for mercy and surrendered without resistance. Even after Ben and Stukeley were dead, the attackers continued to stab and slash at them, slitting their throats and abdomens with knives, chopping at their arms and legs with tomahawks and finally taking their scalps. By this time, already almost a quarter mile away, Stephen Harding, Jr., was racing through the darkening woods, dragging Peter Rogers behind him by the wrist.

At the two Hadsall work areas above, things were no better. Unaware of the party working on the island, the Indians attacked the three men working in the cornfield adjacent to the tanning area and, though guns were fired, no one was shot. The elder Hadsall, Quocko and Carr were captured. However, the party working on the island under Hadsall's son-in-law Ebenezer Reynolds heard the shooting and immediately dropped their hoes, ran to the canoe and paddled across. The three men had their guns ready when they reached shore and leaped from the canoe, leaving it in charge of twelve-year-old John Hadsall, and raced up the bank. The instant they reached the top more shots were fired and Jim Hadsall was killed. A ball went through Reynolds's lower arm, but he and Wallen made it safely into the woods. Because they still had rifles and it was growing dark, they were not pursued.

Young John Hadsall, at the canoe, saw what was happening and realized he was trapped. If he tried to reach the woods he'd be caught and if he tried to flee in the canoe they would certainly shoot him out of it. Instantly, he slipped into the water, swam to a heavy thicket of willows that had become a trap for floating driftwood and debris and then surfaced with just his head exposed to the nostrils so he could breathe. A cluster of moss and leaves in the drift pile clung to him, cloaking him, and by remaining motionless he was well-nigh invisible.

Moments later an Indian plunged down the embankment and looked inside the canoe, which John had grounded just enough to keep it from drifting away. Seeing nothing there, he carefully peered all around for anyone who might be hidden. He searched for five or ten minutes and at one point even walked out on the pile of debris where it was strengthened by a log. He stopped within two feet of John, but the boy remained frozen and the Indian turned and left. There was nothing of any value inside the canoe so he disregarded it and went back up the embankment to where Jim Hadsall had been scalped and the elder Hadsall, Carr and Martin were being led away in the deep twilight toward the main camp.

At the river shore, young Hadsall remained in the drifted debris, totally motionless. A greater fear was in him than he had ever known and in one small corner of his mind he was amazed his whole body was not trembling so violently that it would have given his position away to anyone who looked. Not until full darkness had fallen did the twelve-year-old ease his way back to the canoe. Without getting out of the water he pulled it free from where it was grounded, took the cord attached to the bow and pulled the light craft after him out into the river. At any moment he expected to hear shouts and then shots and he knew if he weren't hit he would surely die of fright. But no shots came. He didn't make it across to the islands until the lower edge of the second island. There he eased into the narrow channel separating the second and third islands and quietly got into the canoe. A few moments later he sped out of the channel on the east side of the islands and into the main current. Staying as close as practicable to the east shore, he began paddling steadily for home.

For the first time since all this began, John Hadsall was crying.

In the woods, Stephen Harding and Peter Rogers, moving more slowly now, abruptly saw the twinkle of firelight northward in the woods ahead and they turned directly west. In a little while, due to a curve in the creek along which the Indians were camped, they saw more firelight and turned farther southwest. It would undoubtedly be a long, difficult passage back to the Wyoming Valley, but for the first time they began to feel a bit more confident that they might make it.

Much the same was happening with Reynolds and Wallen. The former was in a good bit of pain from his arm wound, but he complained little. They too saw the glow of firelight in the woods ahead of them as they moved south and so they made a wide detour to the west for a couple of miles before turning south again. For them it would also be a hard night's hike back to Wyoming, but with luck they'd get there.

Luck was a commodity that had pretty well run out for Quocko Martin, James Hadsall, Sr., Daniel Carr and John Gardner. In the Indian camp they were questioned briefly by Colonel John Butler, but none would give any information except John Gardner. Then, because the Indians captured them and they were, according to their customs, the property of the Indians to do with as they wished — and Butler was not fool enough to attempt to deny them this claim — he turned the three uncooperative captives back over to the red men. When Gardner saw what happened to the first two — Hadsall and Martin — he talked even more volubly and in much greater detail. There was hardly any aspect of the Wyoming Valley defense he did not reveal, even to the intelligence that they had only one piece of artillery but no cannonballs. They used it only for morning and evening salute.

Carr and Gardner, prisoners of the Indians, were permitted to stay alive for now, but the deaths of Martin and Hadsall were very slow and very painful.[182]

[July 1, 1778 — Wednesday, 1:00 A.M.]

It was one o'clock in the morning before the canoe scraped ashore at the Jenkins Fort landing and the Hadsall boy ran toward the fortification with his urgent news. He ran swiftly and silently and very nearly had his head blown off by Lieutenant John Jenkins, who happened to be on guard duty at the time. Only the fact that the Hadsall party had not returned when due made Jenkins pause long enough to see that the one approaching was only a boy. He thought he recognized him in the darkness.

"Johnny?" he called softly. "John Hadsall? Over here!"

John Hadsall was sobbing aloud as he veered in his course and literally threw himself into Jenkins's arms. It took several minutes for him to get control of himself again.

And then John told him everything.

[*July* 1, *1778* — *Wednesday,* 2:00 P.M.]

The three officers astride their horses, with two companies of mounted men behind them, stared wordlessly down at the badly mutilated remains of Benjamin Harding and his twenty-year-old son, Stukeley. It seemed pointless now to search any farther for the others. More than ever the vulnerability of the Wyoming Valley was apparent to them. Not a man among them did not feel the overpowering need to turn at once and get back there as swiftly as possible to make whatever final preparations they could for what was so inevitably coming.

"Damn those God-rotting savages!" Colonel Nathan Denison shook his head disgustedly. "Isn't it enough just to kill them?"

Colonel Zebulon Butler, beside him, nodded in agreement but said nothing. Denison faced the third officer.

"Get a detail to tie the bodies to horses, George," he directed. "We'll bury them at Wyoming."

Lieutenant Colonel Dorrance nodded and wheeled his horse around in a choppy, nervous prancing to the company behind and gave the order. Six soldiers, at the direction of their captain, dismounted and moved toward the dead men, who were lying near a large boulder and pile of rocks. Denison watched, expressionless, anger and sadness welling up strongly within him. Ben Harding had been a close personal friend. His hopes had been strong that the Hardings might have survived since, from the story told this morning at the fort by Stephen Harding, Jr., it had seemed a remote possibility.

It had been a long and fearful morning. Before five o'clock all of the principal officers had been summoned to a meeting at Forty Fort to listen to the report of little John Hadsall, who'd made it back to Jenkins Fort alone after escaping from the Indians. From what he said, it appeared he might be the only survivor from the two parties that had been on the upper island and at his father's tannery field. However, he knew nothing at all about the five of the Harding party, who had been farther downstream.

Even while they were trying to decide what to do, Stephen Harding, Jr., had shown up in the first light of dawn, Peter Rogers riding on his back. They had traveled all night through the woods to get here. Their story was also sobering, but it still didn't shed any light on the fate of Ben and Stukeley Harding, Daniel Carr and John Gardner.

Half an hour later, equally exhausted from traveling all night, Dan Wallen and Ebenezer Reynolds arrived, the latter faint from the pain of his wounded arm. From what they said, there was evidently no hope for the remainder of their party, but they had no definite word on the Hardings. From all of the stories, there was no indication that at any time there had been more than twenty or thirty Indians involved, despite the fact that the glow of campfires suggested there might have been a larger party camped in the woods. That was when Denison had issued the order for two companies to mount up as a rescue mission. It was also then that he formally requested Colonel Zebulon Butler to accept co-command of the Wyoming Militia with him and Butler had agreed.[183] They had forthwith led the mounted companies up the west bank of the Susquehanna to this area. No, there was no longer any doubt of what had happened and not much point in searching further for survivors.

As the six soldiers moved on foot into the rocky area where the two Hardings had obviously taken refuge before being killed, two Indians suddenly sprang from hiding, fired their guns at the soldiers and then sprinted toward the river. It was clear they had hidden at the site in an attempt to ambush anyone who might come to help the fallen men, but they had not expected so large a rescue party. They had been cut off and remained hidden until exposure was imminent.

One of the Indians' shots had missed entirely. The other had just grazed the neck of a horse, sending it into a panicky rearing. At least a dozen rifles barked simultaneously and one of the Indians was killed. The other, wounded, staggered the remaining distance to the river and plunged in, with a fusillade of shots causing little gouts of water to spurt up all around him. He submerged and swam downstream as far as he could with one breath, but it wasn't far enough. Zebulon Marcy followed along the riverbank on foot and, the instant the Indian surfaced for air, shot him through the head. The current swept his body away so they could not scalp him, but they more than made up for it with the one who had been downed onshore. First he was scalped and his beaten silver arm bracelets and necklace were taken, along with his gun, knife, tomahawk and moccasins. Then his body was struck numerous times in a very vicious manner with a tomahawk. Similar blows were struck to his head and arms. His genitals were severed and placed in his hand, which was stretched above his head. Deep gashes were slashed across his chest, face, arms and legs. It was at this point that Colonel Denison, sickened by the barbarity of his own men, stopped it.

The detail swiftly tied the remains of the Harding father and son behind the saddles of two horses. No comments were made as this took place, only a respectful silence. Within twenty minutes the entire force was on its way back to Wyoming, leaving behind where he fell the mutilated warrior.

[*July 1, 1778 — Wednesday, 2:30* P.M.]

The Seneca woman known by the name of Queen Esther was extremely influential in her tribe and not much less so throughout the entire Iroquois League.
For generations, the women in her family had been very powerful, in charge of
their own villages, their opinions sought and carrying great weight at the
League councils.

Although she had traveled widely, all her life except for a few extended absences had been spent in the valley of the Susquehanna River. Though not certain of her age, she was about forty-five and, unlike many of the tribe's women
her age, she was still tall and handsome and clear of eye. She had never
chewed rawhide to make leather and so her teeth were not worn down. Her
breasts were still firm and full and her figure was good.

Queen Esther was really named Esther Montour. She was the granddaughter
of the powerful Seneca chieftainess Kithinay, who had married a Frenchman
named Montour and who ever afterward was herself known as Madame Montour, a name in which she delighted. They had had two sons and a daughter.
That daughter was named Margaret Montour, but she was better known by the
name of French Margaret and it was she who had established a village at the
mouth of the Chemung River, directly across from Tioga. French Margaret
had married a Seneca subchief and, at her insistence, their two daughters had
been named Catherine Montour and Esther Montour.

Catherine, the elder, had eventually established her own village near the
head of Seneca Lake. Its name was Shequaga but as often it was called Catherine's Town or French Catherine's Town. Catherine had a son named Roland
Montour, who had eagerly joined Colonel John Butler's force as it had passed
through en route to attacking Wyoming.

The other daughter of French Margaret, Esther, at her mother's death from
smallpox, took over leadership of the town, and because of her regal bearing
she was dubbed by some traders Queen Esther. She liked the sound of it and
adopted it permanently. She further developed the village until it was very substantial and had become known as Queen Esther's Town.

Queen Esther was quite well known to the whites. She was not illiterate, as
her sister Catherine had remained, but instead had been reasonably well educated, was schooled in the amenities and had acquired many of the behavioral
patterns of civilized life. In her earlier years she had spent much time in Philadelphia and had always been quick to voice her opposition there or in the great
councils at Onondaga to hostilities between her people and the whites. Only a
few months ago she had saved the lives of some Wyoming people who had
been brought to her town after having fallen into the hands of the Indians.

About a quarter of a century ago, Queen Esther had married a Seneca named Eghobund, who later was chief of the village of Sheshaquin, a few miles down the Susquehanna from Queen Esther's Town.[184] Queen Esther and Eghobund had only one child, a son whom they named Gencho. From the day of his birth, Gencho was the brightest ray of light in Queen Esther's life. He was just about the same age as his cousin Roland Montour. Like Roland, he eagerly joined Butler's expedition against Wyoming. Queen Esther went along too, not to fight but to watch Gencho fight, since this would be his first time in battle and she was certain she would become even more proud of him.

That was what she had thought.

Ten minutes after the mounted soldiers had disappeared down the shoreline, Queen Esther and a small group of her warriors came out of the woods on-shore. Now she stared mutely down at the mutilated body of Gencho and wept with the most terrible grief she had ever known. For long minutes she stood over him and at last, when she raised her face skyward, there were no more tears. There was only a coldness and hardness, an implacable hatred.

When she spoke, her voice was strange. It was so unlike her normal voice, so cold and harsh and guttural in its quality, that her nephew Roland Montour, along with the other warriors with her, stepped away slightly, frightened and awed by it, certain that she was under possession of a spirit. This was some-thing that all of them knew could occur, but it was seldom witnessed and cer-tainly none of them here had ever seen it before. They would tell others of her being possessed in this way and by the end of this day all of the Indians con-nected to this expedition would know of it. But that would come later. Now they simply listened to what she had to say and they were themselves chilled by it.

"They have taken my Gencho," she said. "They have taken from me the only thing that was dear. They have taken my warmth and my mercy. They have taken my heart. They have taken my life. As they have taken mine, I will take theirs, and they will never be able to forget what they have done to me, because they will never be able to forget what I will do to *them!*"

[*July 1, 1778 — Wednesday Evening*]

Colonel John Butler stood in a small opening in the forest on the southwestern slope of Scovell's Mountain, where his Indians and Rangers were making their fireless camp, and in the fading light of day looked southward out across the Wyoming Valley.[185]

There, to his right, stood the strongest fortification in the valley, Forty Fort. Close across the river from it was the second most substantial fort, Wilkes-Barre Fort. To his left was the tiny stockaded house called Jenkins Fort and, close across the river from that, the little Pittston Fort. And there, directly below where he now stood, just as the directions had said it would be, was Wintermoot Fort.

Butler smiled. He would lead a fair-sized detachment of his men down there as soon as it was full dark and walk into Wintermoot's as if a welcome mat were out for him. That was the way it had been planned and agreed to earlier. Wintermoot's would become their own little bastion of safety while they wiped out this enemy territory. Butler was glad the Wintermoot family, along with the Van Alstynes and Elisha Scovell and others, had remained loyal to the Crown and had notified Butler that the gates to their fort would be thrown open to him on his arrival.

It was a tribute to the planning that went into this advance that even though the Wyoming Valley was strongly on the alert that an invasion was coming, Butler's force had managed to reach this point without anyone being aware that he was at this moment above them and poised to strike. That the Americans were fully aware of the attack to come had been quite evident from the information he was able to glean in questioning yesterday's prisoner, John Gardner.

It was to be regretted, of course, that they had missed an encounter with the militia commander's two companies of men on the Susquehanna shore where those prisoners had been taken. Butler reflected on the vagaries of luck in situations such as this. Had he postponed by just half a day moving out of his camp on the creek near where the Americans had been taken in their cornfields, the whole of the American force could easily have been surrounded and wiped out. With the river at their backs they would have had no place to go and there was no way they could have stood against Butler's force. But, as luck would have it, just as the Americans were moving northward along the riverbank this morning at the eastern foot of Scovell's Mountain, Butler was moving his force southward along its western slope. Butler smiled, detached enough to enjoy the humor such a picture presented.

Following the directions given to him both by the Wintermoots and the captured John Gardner, their route had taken them upstream on the little creek on which they had been camped the night before. About a mile and a quarter west of the Susquehanna, they had turned south, away from the creek.[186] Along a small hunting trail they moved south up a moderate slope and forded another creek, which flowed out of a large marshy area.[187] Continuing south, they passed the marsh and just beyond it turned slightly southeast until they crossed yet another creek, which was running southwardly off Scovell's Mountain.[188] Here the trail led them up over the west hump of the mountain about three hundred feet below the crest. And that was the trail that had brought them to the rather broad plateau on which they were now encamped overlooking the Wyoming Valley, reasonably well screened by trees.[189]

Noting how the positions of Pittston Fort and Jenkins Fort placed them almost opposite one another guarding the river entry into the Wyoming Valley from the north, Butler experienced reinforced pleasure that they had not moved in by canoe on their invasion as he had initially planned until warned against it by the Wintermoots and Gardner. To have done so would have been to make themselves vulnerable to a deadly crossfire between the two forts and, though by sheer numbers Butler's force would have taken them, they would undoubtedly have suffered considerable losses in the process. Their infiltration now would practically preclude such potential losses.

Pittston Fort, Butler realized, could be a problem if, during the midst of operations west of the river, Captain Jeremiah Blanchard, its commander, suddenly brought across his company as a reinforcement to the Americans under attack. Though he was sure such an eventuality could be handled in stride by his own force, it was not John Butler's way to leave things to chance. He made a mental note to endeavor somehow to negate such a potential.

As Butler stood looking out over the scene, Helmut Wintermoot appeared and came directly to where the commander was standing. They shook hands warmly and Wintermoot reconfirmed that his family's little fort was ready for them, that the gate was unlocked and they could enter without problem. He warned that a few of the fort's inhabitants were Rebels — and they thought the rest were, too — and they might cause some minor problems. This included such men as David Ingersoll, who was rabid in his hatred of Indians and British. At any rate, Wintermoot went on, it was being seen to that the guard patrol tonight was being made up only of those who were sympathetic to Butler's force. As such, they should not be harmed. Once inside the fort, the relatively small numbers of Rebels could easily be forced to surrender.

As far as the fighting strength of the Wyoming Valley was concerned, it was really nothing to fear. Of enrolled militiamen, there were only three hundred and thirty, and the absolute maximum number in the valley tonight who could oppose Butler's force, if they were foolish enough to try, was between four hundred and four-fifty, which included some seventy old men plus some boys. They were gathered mainly in Forty Fort under command of Colonel Denison.

Most of the residents on the other side of the river, on the return of the detachment with the bodies of Ben Harding and his son, had spent the remainder of the afternoon moving into Wilkes-Barre Fort, where Captain James Bidlack was in command, on the "safe" side of the river. Bidlack, however, had a garrison of only thirty-eight men. At the moment, the Continental Army officer Colonel Zebulon Butler was there, but he'd been moving around a lot lately and that could change. Pittston Fort, Wintermoot said, was small but it could pose a problem.

"I'll take care of Pittston," Butler told him. "What about on this side of the river other than Forty Fort?"

Wintermoot told him then that the public fort at Plymouth had already been abandoned and only a few settlers were left inside Wyoming Fort. Jenkins Fort was tonight being defended by only three able-bodied men. That's all who were left in fit condition of the garrison of nineteen just a few days ago.[190]

Butler listened to it all with approving murmurs and, when Wintermoot was finished, he clapped the little man warmly on the shoulder.

"Fine job," he said. "It's almost dark now. Suppose I get back to my men and after a bit we'll come down and take possession of your place. Then, first thing in the morning, we'll take a look at Jenkins Fort."

Wintermoot bobbed his head and set off downslope through the darkening woods.

Butler, steeped in thought, moved slowly back toward his Ranger detachment. As defenseless as the Americans below appeared to be, they did have a couple of reasonably strong fortifications in Forty Fort and Wilkes-Barre Fort. If they were smart enough to keep themselves secured in those forts, man their walls well and make their shots count, there was no way Butler's Indians and Rangers could take them. The Indians would want immediate scalps and plunder and there was no doubt they'd scatter throughout the Wyoming Valley as soon as the force entered and start their depredations. They would burn and loot, but that would be all, and he knew what the end would be. Little by little they'd be picked off by riflemen from the fort and as soon as the first great enthusiasm for burning and plundering was over, they'd begin to assess their losses, lose interest and leave. It was the Indian way and he knew it would occur.

Having come to this realization, he changed direction slightly and moved to where the Seneca chiefs Kayingwaurto and Gu-cinge were resting with their men. With them were some of the other Iroquois chiefs — Stuttering John of the Tuscaroras, Blue Throat of the Onondagas and the powerful Little Beard, chief of the largest of all the Seneca villages, Chenussio. It was up to Butler to convince them to hold their forces together.

For over an hour he talked with them earnestly, explaining the situation, planning what they could do. Without artillery, there was no possible way they could take the principal forts by storm, so they'd have to plan on something else. There was an off-chance that if he sent a small party in under a flag of truce, demanding surrender, the Americans might give in. If so, the entire valley would belong to Butler's force. If it failed, then they could attempt the old ruse of luring them out of the security of the fort to attack a smaller force — a stratagem that worked remarkably well considering how many times in the past Americans had fallen for it. Would the chiefs hold their men in check until then?

Gu-cinge and Kayingwaurto said it would be difficult, yes, but they would hold them in readiness as a group at least until these plans by Colonel Butler had been tried.

[*July 2, 1778 — Thursday*]

When word spread throughout the Wyoming Valley this morning that not only had at least part of Colonel John Butler's force arrived but that during the night they had taken possession of Wintermoot Fort, the fear that had prevailed earlier turned into a very real panic. It was only with the greatest of difficulty that Colonel Denison kept the lid on the situation.

His greatest problem was tempering the feelings of those officers and men within Forty Fort who were so hot to throw open the gates and charge out after the invaders. As so often occurred in these situations where general councils were held among the officers and passions rose while, in direct proportion, common sense diminished and was looked upon as cowardice, charges and countercharges were hurled back and forth.

The Americans had no good estimate of the enemy's strength. Some of the officers contended that Butler probably had no more than a few hundred Indians and maybe fifty or sixty Tories with him. Others thought the figure might be somewhat higher, in view of the inclusive reports turned in by their own scouting parties. But no one really appreciated the size of Butler's force, which, as yet, had not shown itself except for the moderate number who had taken Wintermoot Fort last night.

Early in the morning Colonel Denison sent expresses out ordering such captains of outlying posts as John Franklin with his thirty-five men, William McKarrachen with his thirty, and Stoddart Bowen and John Clingman, each with their thirty, to leave their positions and hurry to Forty Fort with their companies. He also sent an express in the direction from which the most important help was expected — the regulars under Captain Simon Spalding — with the urgent plea that Spalding come at once by forced march to help relieve this critical situation.

Then Jenkins Fort was taken. Quietly and without any violence. Colonel John Butler simply sent Captain James Caldwell with a small party under a flag of truce to Jenkins Fort to demand its surrender, not really believing he would get it. He did. Lieutenant Jenkins was conferring with Captain Stephen Harding, Sr., who had come from Forty Fort early in the morning to discuss the situation and suggest that Jenkins and the people within his fort abandon their position and fall back to Forty Fort, when the British Rangers showed up under Caldwell.

Jenkins and Harding met them and listened to the surrender demand and then, knowing that with a garrison of only three effective men there was no possible way to defend the place, attempted to get the best possible terms. Not really believing he'd even be listened to, Jenkins agreed they would surrender the fort to Caldwell on the condition that nothing should be taken from the inhabitants of the fort except for such items as could be used against an enemy, and even those items taken to be paid for. Further, the Wyoming Valley residents who had taken refuge in Jenkins Fort were to have the liberty to return to their farms in peace and not take up arms in the war. It was almost ridiculous to consider that Captain Caldwell would agree to such terms when he didn't have to, but he did.

Everyone left in Jenkins Fort surrendered his arms and then, with personal possessions, crossed the river by boat to Pittston Fort. Incredibly, even Jenkins was permitted to go with them. At Pittston Fort, leaving Beth and the other Jenkins Fort people in care of Captain Blanchard, Jenkins immediately broke his agreement and went to Wilkes-Barre Fort and then crossed back over the Susquehanna to Forty Fort. He knew there could be no further terms where he was concerned. If caught again, he would be executed immediately.

Back at Wintermoot Fort, Colonel John Butler contained his delight admirably. Without any sort of struggle he was in possession of both Wintermoot and Jenkins forts, while both Plymouth Fort and Wyoming Fort had been abandoned. On the other side of the river, everyone not in Wilkes-Barre Fort under Captain Bidlack and his thirty-eight men was at Pittston Fort under Captain Jeremiah Blanchard and his forty men. It meant that the only position still held on this side of the river by the Americans was Forty Fort.

Tomorrow he would turn his full attention in that direction. Between now and then, he would devise some sort of plan to lure the Americans away from the safety of that fortification.

CHAPTER IV

[*July 3, 1778 — Friday,* 10:00 A.M.]

S IR! Three men approaching under a white flag."

Colonel Nathan Denison acknowledged the guard's report and followed him to see. John Jenkins and George Dorrance went with him up to the ramparts of Forty Fort and peered through an embrasure. The three men approaching were still fifty yards away but one was easily recognizable — David Ingersoll of Wintermoot Fort. The other white man had streaks of paint on his cheeks and forehead. The third man was an Indian.

"Well, let's go down and see what they have to say," Denison said.

They placed the gate under a strong guard detail and stepped out a dozen feet or so to meet the trio. It was Ingersoll who spoke, rolling his eyes and shaking his head.

"I am being compelled to bring this message to you, Colonel," he told Denison, "with Lieutenant Chrysler here" — he indicated the Ranger — " as my guard, along with this Indian, whose name is Blue Throat. Colonel Butler — *their* Colonel Butler, that is, John Butler — is headquartered at Wintermoot's." He frowned. "Our fort was turned over to them without defense by the Wintermoots and Scovells and Van Al——"

"That's enough, Ingersoll," Chrysler interrupted sharply. "Just the message Colonel Butler told you to give."

Ingersoll looked at him with contempt, but then went on with the message. "Colonel Butler's headquartered there now. From what I could see, he doesn't seem to have as many as you and he's —"

He broke off as Lieutenant Adam Chrysler gripped his upper arm roughly. "If you make any further attempt to give intelligence about Colonel Butler's force," he grated, "you will be shot when we return. Understood?"

Ingersoll's frown deepened, but he nodded. He looked at Jenkins. "John, they demolished your fort this morning."

The Ranger officer glanced sharply at the lieutenant whom Ingersoll had just addressed. Now it was he who was frowning. "You're Jenkins," he said accusingly. "You have broken the terms. You were released because you gave your word not to lift arms again in this war."

Jenkins smiled faintly. "I lied."

Chrysler stabbed a finger in the air in his direction. "There will be no further clemency for you." He glanced at Ingersoll. "Continue. Include Jenkins with the other three."

Ingersoll rolled his eyes again and then shrugged and returned his attention to Denison. "Sir, except for this fort, Colonel John Butler is in control of the west side of the river. In the name of the King, he demands that you surrender this fort and its stores. There is no room for negotiation but he feels that his terms are generous. If you surrender without further resistance, all noncombatants will be allowed to leave in safety with their possessions. All military — regular and militia — will turn over their weapons to us and be required to swear that they will not again during the course of this war raise their arms against the King's men. If this is done, they will be released also, but without personal possessions. Colonel Butler specifically demands the surrender of three men" — he glanced at Jenkins and amended his remark — "*four* men. Lieutenant Jenkins here, for disobeying the terms under which he was released, the two Continental officers presently in this valley — Captain Dethick Hewitt and Colonel Zebulon Butler — and the deserter from the King's service who has taken refuge with you, Malcolm Boyd. If these terms are not immediately complied with, there can be no alternative but the destruction of this fort and all who are in it. He is aware that all residents on the west side of the river have now taken refuge in this fort and noncompliance will mean their destruction as well, since once Colonel Butler releases the Indians who are with him to begin the destruction, there will be no way to stop them."

Denison looked at Blue Throat, who had said nothing during all of this but who appeared to have understood the intent if not the words. Lieutenant Chrysler stood waiting for the reply and Denison addressed him directly.

"I presume Dan Ingersoll was chosen to deliver the message so we would believe what he said." He pursed his lips and nodded. "We believe him, but we would have believed you as well. It makes no difference. Tell your Colonel Butler that so far as I am concerned, the only way he is going to get this installation is through force. Tell him I don't think he has a strong enough force to do it. Tell him we are determined to fight to the last extremity if necessary.

"However," he added, "although I command the militia here, the ranking officer is Colonel Zebulon Butler. My own personal decision is as I have stated it, but officially I will follow the dictates of that officer and the other officers in this fort. I therefore send you back to Colonel John Butler with the request that he give us a reasonable amount of time to discuss the terms and reach an official decision. That is all we have to say now."

"Colonel Butler wanted your decision immediately," Chrysler said.

"I have given you *my* decision, sir," Denison said shortly. "For an official decision, your commander will have to wait."

Denison turned his back on them and reentered the fort, followed by Lieutenant Colonel Dorrance and Jenkins. Dorrance addressed Denison as soon as the gates were shut behind them.

"What's your estimate as to what'll happen now, sir? I know you wanted to buy some time if you could. Do you think they'll hold off?"

"No, I don't." Denison shook his head, then shrugged. "It was worth the try. I think they'll move on us right away, just as they said. But Wintermoot's is four miles away and it'll take them time to get back there and then come back here. Ingersoll managed to let us know they don't have any more men than we have. That changes the complexion of things some. If they don't have artillery, we should be able to hold them off. Right now, send a message across to Wilkes-Barre. We're going to need Zebulon Butler's help. Ask him if he'll come over here with the two Wilkes-Barre companies and the Hanover company. Then we'll decide what to do."

[*July 3, 1778 — Friday, 2:45* P.M.]

The meeting of the officers in Forty Fort had turned into a heated, highly emotional affair. For over an hour the council of officers had been talking and on the basis of what Dan Ingersoll had said to Denison outside the fort gates, the consensus was that at best the enemy force was no larger than their own. To even consider surrendering Forty Fort to them was ludicrous, but the matter in question was what they should do at this point.

"We should," Denison cautioned, "treat Daniel Ingersoll's remarks with question. We feel strongly that he is loyal to us, but who's to know for sure. There are others who were at Wintermoot's whom we also felt were loyal and who evidently were not. Even if Ingersoll were telling the truth, he may not have had all the facts. Suppose he saw only a small portion of the enemy force?"

There was an immediate murmur of negation at this. The consensus was that if there were more of them, they would have surrounded Forty Fort before the demand was made, to add emphasis to the demand and to prove they had the requisite strength to take the fort. An even more telling point was the Indians: everyone here knew how the Indians were in such a situation and what they did. Certainly, if there were more Indians, the scattered instances of burning and plundering that had occurred so far — which were very limited — would have been greatly increased. Indians could be contained in such a situation. They all knew that. It just wasn't possible, unless they were in a force much smaller than their enemy's.

Zebulon Butler, who had conferred with Denison and Dorrance immediately upon his arrival here with the Wilkes-Barre companies under Captain James Bidlack and the Hanover company under Captain William McKarrachen an hour ago, rose to speak and the officers quieted to hear what he had to say.

"It seems to me," the colonel said, "that our wisest course is simply to remain here, within Forty Fort, and let the enemy make his move, whatever it will be. Some of you have already suggested we form up and move out against them. I believe this would be a grave error. We do expect the reinforcements of the companies of Captains Franklin, Clingman and Spalding before too long and common sense dictates we wait for them."

Almost immediately there were charges of cowardice and countercharges of foolhardiness and the debate grew even more heated. Those reinforcements, it was argued, might not get here for days, perhaps weeks. Indian Butler, as they had begun calling John Butler now, had not immediately sent a force to destroy the fort, as he had threatened to do, so didn't this tend to confirm that he didn't have the necessary strength and was just bluffing? If they remained bottled up here in Forty Fort, afraid of their own shadows, then certainly the Indians and Tories would grow bolder and, with no opposition to stay them, would begin plundering and burning the homes of all those who were taking refuge here in the fort. Wasn't this military force here specifically to prevent such an occurrence? Were they simply going to stand by behind the fort walls and watch this happen?

Those were telling arguments, with a strong underlying sense of manhood impugned of those leaning toward remaining in the fort. Most of the men and by far the greater majority of officers were strongly in favor of carrying the battle to the enemy at once instead of waiting for the enemy to choose time and place. The upshot of the situation was that passions prevailed and the decision was made to leave a small force — primarily old men and boys — in the fort under command of Lieutenant Jenkins and the rest to march out in strength and attack.

And so now, at close to 3:00 P.M., the general call to arms was sounded and the militia companies hastily formed up. At the same time, scouts that Denison had sent out earlier came back in a rush saying they had been fired upon and that the enemy force, fairly small, was presently on the march against them. At this there was a great deal of excitement.

Denison sent the patrol back to scout some more in the vicinity of Wintermoot's. Then he gave the official order to march and there was a rousing cheer as the gates of Forty Fort were thrown open. Even the several hundred women, children and elderly spectators inside the fort were caught up in the martial fervor and cheered and applauded as the Stars and Stripes were raised at the head of the column and the small group of fifers and drummers struck up a stirring rendition of "St. Patrick's Day in the Morning."

At the gate of the fort, Lieutenant John Jenkins watched them go, the great crowd of civilians peering past him, a certain amount of fear descending on them now that things were actually in motion, but obviously very proud of their men. While he stood there, a lad of fourteen moved up beside him. He was Jabez Elliott, who had moved to the Wyoming Valley with his family two years ago, and Jenkins knew him well.

"I wish I were going with them," Jabez said, bitterly disappointed at being left behind.

Jenkins smiled and put an arm around the boy's shoulders. "Henry's with them," he said, referring to Jabez's father, "and your brother Joe, too. That's enough from one family. Anyway, we might need you here to help us if anything goes wrong."

Young Elliott shook his head and kicked angrily at the earth. "What can go wrong? They're going off into probably the best battle we'll ever have a chance to see here, and I'm going to miss it! I wish," he repeated wistfully, "I were going with them."

"You know what, Jabez?" Jenkins said, squeezing his shoulders. "I wish I were going with them too."

Jabez stared at Jenkins, abruptly grinned and jerked a rifle away from the lieutenant and began running after the column. "I've *got* to go with them," he called back to Jenkins. "I've just *got* to!"

The four hundred men were by this time far down the road that led toward Wintermoot Fort, but the sound of fifes and drums could still faintly be heard. The running boy soon caught up with them, ran alongside the ranks for a while until he evidently located his brother and father and then joined them. The soldiers all marched with a sprightliness and jauntiness that attested to their supreme confidence in their own invulnerability and their certainty that the enemy force was no larger than their own and probably much smaller.

They had not the faintest inkling that they might be outnumbered by more than three to one.

[*July* 3, 1778 — *Friday*, 3:15 P.M.]

In his headquarters at Wintermoot Fort, Colonel John Butler watched the final preparations being made to burn down the place. He sympathized with Helmut Wintermoot, who had been angrily denouncing the preparations, demanding they be stopped and reminding Butler of his promise to protect Wintermoot's property as a repayment for his assistance. The protests, however, were ignored.

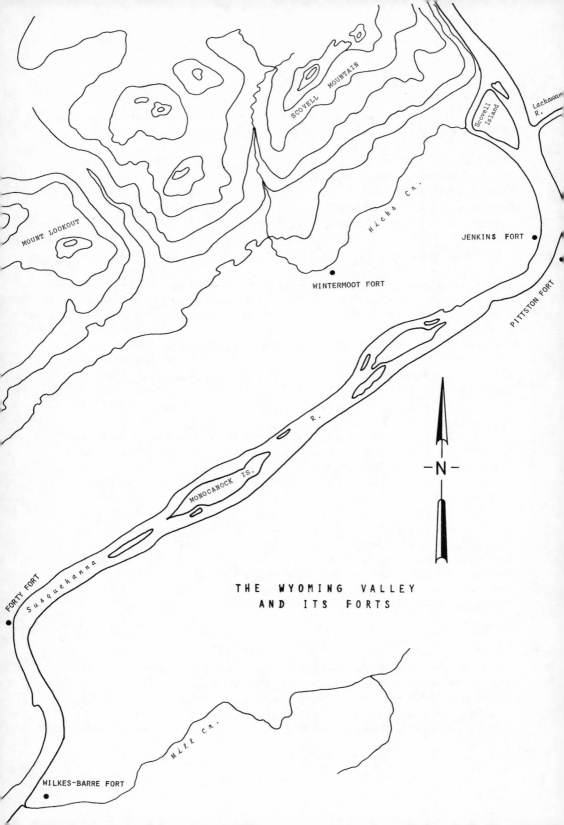

The burning of Wintermoot's would be the final touch to lure the Americans into the trap he had prepared for them.

Another minor coup that would contribute to that end had been pulled off after midnight last night by his Rangers. Thought of it brought the flickering of a smile to Butler's face. It was so simple, so effective. The Rangers, their faces blackened with charcoal, had slipped across the river from Jenkins Fort and, under the very noses of the Americans, stole all the boats at the Pittston Fort landing. Now, when the Americans on this side of the river expected reinforcements to come under Captain Jeremiah Blanchard from Pittston, there would be no way for them to cross the Susquehanna.

Now, well hidden in a horseshoe configuration behind fencerows, in ditches, in deep grasses, woods and elsewhere, at least seven hundred of the eight hundred Indians and two hundred of the four hundred Rangers at this very moment waited for the exposed force of two hundred Rangers and one hundred Indians to lure the Americans into their grip.

The exposed force of Rangers and Indians had left this headquarters almost an hour ago, advancing as if they were the attacking army, marching boldly along the road from Wintermoot Fort to Forty Fort. Their own spies brought word the Americans were marching, too. Butler's men had spotted a small patrol of Americans coming and fired on them, killing one and wounding a couple of others. Taking their wounded with them, the patrol had fled back in the direction of Forty Fort.

Soon, Butler knew, his decoy force would engage the Americans and, after a convincing show, begin falling back gradually, though continuing to defend themselves well all the while. The burning of Wintermoot's would give credence to the belief they were pulling out of the valley and destroying as they left. Obviously, the Americans would follow.

Obviously, that would be the beginning of the end.

[July 3, 1778 — Friday, 3:30 P.M.]

The march of the Wyoming Militia from Forty Fort continued in its sprightly manner to the lilt of fife and drum until it reached the narrow stone bridge that crossed Abraham's Creek about a mile northeast of the fort.[191] Here on a hill just five hundred feet below the bridge, where the creek formed a sort of elbow as it flowed past, Denison and Zebulon Butler stopped their men and deployed them in a position to resist an attack if it occurred. Thus far there had been no sign whatever that the enemy was anywhere nearby. It had been when they were halfway to this position that Denison had sent another scouting patrol ahead to see what they could discover.

They had only been here ten or fifteen minutes when several men who had been part of the scouting party returned at the run. Others were coming behind them, they reported, helping the wounded. They'd been fired upon and one of the privates was dead.[192] The news flashed through the lines and now everyone was confused. What did it all mean? Since Indian Butler's threatened march upon Forty Fort had not transpired this morning, did this mean the threat was mere braggadocio? It seemed very likely and the more the conjectures flew back and forth, the more the rank and file were eager to be up and after the enemy. Why, they asked, sit here on a hill waiting to be attacked? Didn't it stand to reason that if Butler had the force he was alleged by some to have, he would have attacked by now?

At this critical juncture a scout returned who had been separated from the others. He had hidden for a while and now was bringing back some startling intelligence. Some of the enemy, he was sure, were pulling back. He pointed toward a faint dark smudge in the sky eastward of them.

"Not only that," he panted, "they're burning places. Houses, barns!"

That was the clincher. It was apparent the enemy was beginning to pull out. Supposing, while the army sat here waiting to be attacked, the enemy burned all the houses and everything else and then spilled across the river to take Pittston Fort, plundering and massacring as they went? The discussion was now becoming very heated and once again charges of timidity and cowardice were being voiced.

Colonel Zebulon Butler held up both arms for silence and then asked the men to be patient. "Our futures," he said, "and those of our families depend on the steps we take at this time. We can't afford to go off on mistaken tracks. I recommend most strongly that we wait here at least awhile longer to see what develops."

Grudgingly the troops and their captains agreed. Now, at 3:30 P.M., another messenger had just arrived, but this time from the direction of Forty Fort. It was Lieutenant Timothy Pierce, who, four or five days ago, had been sent to discover, if he could, where Captain Spalding was with his company of regulars and how soon they would arrive. Pierce brought the heartening news that Spalding was definitely on the way with two full companies but that there was no way he would arrive before Sunday.

"Then the very smartest thing we could do at this time," Zebulon Butler announced, "is get back to Forty Fort and stay there until Spalding's reinforcement arrives."

There were howls of protest at once. Private Lazarus Stewart, who was forty-four years old and a renowned hothead and who had occasionally run afoul of vested authority in the past, now strode forward and pointed a shaking finger at the American colonel.

"You're a damned coward!" he shouted. "By God, I've a mind to report you to headquarters as being unfit to hold the rank you've got!"

Colonel Denison stepped forward immediately. Lazarus Stewart was an old friend and a good one — so good that Denison had named his own son after him — but there was no way he could tolerate a militia private being insubordinate to a regular army colonel.

"Lazarus Stewart," he said, "you're under arrest as of now."

"The hell with that!" This was the voice of Stewart's commanding officer of the Hanover company, Captain William McKarrachen. "If Lazarus Stewart is put under arrest, then as of this moment I resign as commanding officer of this company."

The dark-haired officer was young and very angry. There was no doubt, however, that he had the support of his company because all of the men were now on their feet, encouraging him and adding their own derogatory remarks about the stupidity of returning to the fort and just staying there. They also made it clear that they so thoroughly supported Stewart that now, in a quick voice vote in which there were unanimous "Ayes!" they elected Stewart their company commander in McKarrachen's place.

Colonel Denison, noted for always being a calm and collected man, now made an effort to reason with them. "It is only good common sense, in a situation such as this," he said, "to consider carefully all alternatives, to move with care in whatever we're going to do and to realize the danger that lies in acting hastily. I strongly suggest that it would be much better to wait till we know more of the enemy's strength and position. The way it looks now, it's hardly possible the enemy's going to try to overrun the valley. If we delay, it can only provide us with more information that will be of value to us so we can act more intelligently. Besides, by that time there is a chance that Captain Spalding's companies — and perhaps Franklin and Clingman's — will be here to support us."

His final sentence was a bad choice for argument. The men, who had begun being swayed by what he was saying, were jerked back to their former stance by his reference to reinforcements. It was Stewart who put their thoughts into words.

"If we remain here or, worse yet, go running back to Forty Fort with our tails between our legs, it'll be a disgrace that will never be forgotten . . . nor forgiven! If we continue to wait here at this bridge, without an enemy in sight, or go back to stand shaking in our shoes at the fort while the enemy is devastating our valley, burning our homes and making off with our wives and children and parents unhindered by a military force that is too cowardly to offer the least resistance, then by God, we will deserve whatever scorn and disgust we are subject to thereafter. I, for one, will not hold still for that. Who feels as I do? Who will go with me where our officers are too frightened to lead us?"

He had raised his voice toward the end so he was clearly heard by all the men assembled and there was an eruption of cheers and support for what he said. It was quite clear they had no intention of withdrawing back to the fort. If there were any men on hand who recognized a similarity between what was happening now and what had occurred immediately prior to the Oriskany battle eleven months ago, when similar charges of cowardice or worse were hurled at General Nicholas Herkimer, no one voiced the thought.

With a glançe at Colonel Denison, who faintly shrugged and nodded, Colonel Zebulon Butler raised his hands and waited patiently until the hubbub died away. "I hereby discharge Captain Stewart from any arrest charges, but I have to add to you that Colonel Denison and I cannot agree with the wisdom of your views. Nevertheless, we will continue to lead you against the enemy, if he is to be found. I will show the men here that I will dare to lead wherever they will dare to follow. To the very hinges of hell, if need be!"

The die was cast. It was now four in the afternoon.

[July 3, 1778 — Friday, 4:20 P.M.]

If there were lingering doubts in the minds of the American commanders about pressing against the enemy, they disappeared with the arrival of another set of scouts from the vicinity of the enemy. They raced up to the two commanding officers, pointed excitedly to the larger column of smoke rising from far ahead and reported that Wintermoot Fort was on fire.

Wintermoot's! The enemy had possession of that one; it was their bastion, their headquarters, their toehold in the valley. Its being burned could mean only one thing — the enemy was leaving the valley. Therefore, their total strength must be much less than anticipated. For the first time, the two American colonels felt better about going against their own better judgement to strike the enemy.

Since leaving the stone bridge they had moved another half mile toward Wintermoot's and now a halt was called and the entire force, which till now had been marching in column, was ordered into battle formation.[193] Since Captains Robert Durkee and Samuel Ransom, along with Lieutenants James Welles and Perrin Ross, had no immediate commands of their own, they were now detailed to mark off the ground and form up the line of battle. This deploying movement was made to the column's left.

The battle line was in two wings, with Colonel Nathan Denison and Lieutenant Colonel George Dorrance commanding the left. The right wing was under command of Colonel Zebulon Butler, with Major Jonathan Waite Garrett as his second-in-command, assisted by Anderson Dana as adjutant.[194] From left to right in the line there were six companies, respectively commanded by Captains Dethick Hewitt, James Bidlack, Jr., Rezin Geer, Asaph Whittlesey, Lazarus Stewart and Aholiab Buck. Then, arriving at double time from the direction of Forty Fort, amid the cheers of the men, Captain Stoddart Bowen's thirty-five-man Salem and Huntington Company arrived and was put into the line to the left of Captain Whittlesey's company. The unassigned officers — Captains Durkee and Ransom and Lieutenants Ross, Welles and

Pierce — were now assigned to positions on the field as aides. The only Wyoming Valley company not represented on the field now was Captain Jeremiah Blanchard's from Pittston Fort. They decided to wait no longer for it.

The march, in battle-line formation, was resumed. It was 4:40 P.M.

[*July 3, 1778 — Friday, 4:45 P.M.*]

Colonel John Butler had hoped his ruse might work, but he was all but flabbergasted at how well everything was turning out. A number of his scouts began returning at intervals of about two or three minutes with reports of what the Americans were doing. Thus far, they had done just as he had hoped they would do but which he had not really expected. Now they were moving right into the very midst of the trap he had prepared, using the burning Wintermoot Fort as bait.

Butler had, by this time, called in all the scattered forces that were still out and had them join the majority who were already hidden and waiting for the American advance. From their position before Wintermoot Fort, a rather extended marsh stretched to the west, formed by a small creek running through the valley flats here.[195] Butler's Rangers and other white troops were on the right, from the base of the mountain to the marsh in an arced line, under himself, Captains George Benjamin, William Pawling, Francis Hopkins and James Caldwell, and Lieutenant William Turney. The Indians were also in an arced line to the left under Chiefs Gu-cinge and Kayingwaurto, stretching beyond the marsh. Chief Little Beard was there as well as Blue Throat, Stuttering John, Old Smoke and Roland.

Much of the line was along a fence row overlooking a meadow in which there were only a few scattered trees and rocks and no real cover of significance. The line itself formed a deep crescent, almost a horseshoe shape, but it was wholly out of sight, hidden in deep grasses, behind fences and a low wall, behind trees and bushes and whatever other cover was available. With luck, the Americans might be lured directly into the open mouth of the crescent and not realize their peril until too late.

As the bait, there was the smaller party of Indians and Rangers that had been sent ahead, in view, to encounter the Americans, fight them briefly and then fall back, luring them into the ambush. They were led by the tall, bare-chested Seneca chief, Tawannears.[196]

[*July 3, 1778 — Friday, 5:00 P.M.*]

From the point where Colonels Nathan Denison and Zebulon Butler had halted to form the American battle line, the advance had been slow but steady. Only one soldier was missing from the lines — a private from the Hanover company under Lazarus Stewart. His name was Richard Inman. Along with his six brothers, Isaac, David, Elijah, Moses, Edward and Israel, Inman had sat down along the fence to rest as the battle line was being formed. Unlike his brothers, Richard had had no sleep the previous night, having been on guard duty. Almost immediately on taking this rest, he had fallen asleep with his rifle in his arms. When the march order was given, Captain Stewart looked at the sleeping man and grinned, shaking his head at the other Inman brothers.

"Let him sleep," he said. "He can catch up to us later. He's deserved a little rest."

They had moved out without him and now, only a quarter mile from Wintermoot Fort, the Americans could see the burning remains clearly. Far in the distance, a few of the enemy could be seen running from cover to cover, out of rifle range. At this point Denison called a halt and sent forward a small patrol to reconnoiter. The patrol had not marched more than fifty yards when a group of about forty Indians, under an especially tall, bare-chested leader, sprang up from hiding in the meadow grasses, fired a volley at the patrol that wounded a couple of men, then immediately fell back themselves as a scattered mass without grouping, in retreat toward the burning fort.

At once the chase was on. That portion of Colonel Denison's line closest to the retreating Indians fired at them and set off in pursuit, with the whole line moving forward as prearranged when formed. More scattered groups of Indians along with some Rangers popped up in a similar manner, fired and fled, but little damage was done. Earlier, the line of about four hundred and fifty Americans had been counted off from right to left in odds and evens and now, as advance was made in pursuit, commands were given and the odds moved forward five paces, stopped and fired, then knelt to reload while the evens stepped up, passed them by five paces, stopped and fired. Alternately in this manner the lines moved forward abreast, ten paces at a time and in a relatively smoothly flowing manner.

Astride his horse, the American co-commander, Colonel Zebulon Butler, rode back and forth immediately behind the advancing lines of soldiers, shouting encouragement. "Be careful," he warned. "They may be stronger in force ahead of us somewhere. If so, it'll be hot work, so be prepared. Remember your homes, your women and children! You must save them from the scalping knife and tomahawk. Remember what happened to the Hardings. Victory means safety; defeat means death! If every man does his duty, we'll win!"

The Americans continued pushing ahead but their firing had little effect, as it was generally unaimed and only shot in the direction of the enemy, which was retreating in such a scattered manner that only one Indian was seen to fall. After advancing a score of yards in this manner, another small group of the enemy leaped up before them — all Rangers this time — and they also fired their guns haphazardly before retreating in a preplanned scattered manner to catch up with the fleeing Indians. At this the Americans became jubilant.

"See!" Zebulon Butler shouted, standing high in his stirrups and pointing toward the enemy. "They're retreating — Indians *and* British! We have them on the run, men. Be firm and the day will be ours!"

He was more than a bit precipitate in his evaluation of the situation. They were now opposite Wintermoot Fort and in the midst of the only cleared area on this plain — an area of about three or four acres of ankle-deep grass without a speck of cover. Ahead, the small force of Indians and Rangers had more or less consolidated and was still fleeing with occasionally some of them pausing to turn and fire toward the Americans, though without much effect. As the retreaters approached the heavy log fence, some of them leaped over it without even touching it. Others jumped to the top of it and then to the ground on the other side. Still others hurriedly clambered over and dropped out of sight behind. Here the retreat of the British and Indians stopped and suddenly a warmer fire was being directed at the Americans from the fence row and with greater effect. The American advance slowed but did not stop until it was about fifty yards from the fence. That was when the whole affair suddenly reversed itself in deadly fashion.

It was now 5:30 P.M.

At the bellowed commands of Colonel John Butler, relayed instantly in English and in the Indian tongue, the whole force of the ambushing party rose from behind the log fence and fired a deadly rain of bullets into the American line. A staggering number of Americans fell in that first volley and immediately the flanking Indians on the American right, hidden in marsh grasses, leaped in and began to close off the rear to prevent a retreat, howling in exultation as they did so.

Still in their marching formation, the Americans — often whole families of them — were mowed down by the continuing fire. Of the six Inman brothers on hand, from fourteen-year-old Edward to thirty-year-old Moses, only sixteen-year-old David and twenty-year-old Isaac were not killed in the first firing. [197]

The Weeks brothers, Philip, Jr., Jonathan and Bartholomew, along with their uncle Jabez Beers, their cousin Josiah Carmen, their brother-in-law Silas Benedict, and a boarder, Robert Bates, were all killed within thirty seconds of the outbreak of the battle.

The Shafford brothers, Darius and Phineas, were side by side as they had been all their lives when, at the onset, Darius took a bullet through the chest. Phineas caught him as he fell and lowered him to the ground. With dimming vision Darius gasped, "I'm done, Phin. Take care of Lavinia." Then he died. Darius Shafford had married Lavinia Blackman only three weeks ago. [198]

Seventeen-year-old William Ross was in the American line directly between his two brothers, Perrin and Jeremiah. Lieutenant Perrin Ross, the father of five children, would have celebrated his thirtieth birthday tomorrow. He didn't make it. Neither did nineteen-year-old Jeremiah, a private. Both of them took bullets through the head almost simultaneously. William was unscathed.

The five Gore brothers — Daniel, Samuel, Asa, George and Silas — sons of Obediah Gore, Sr., and their brothers-in-law, Lieutenant Timothy Pierce and Private John Murphy, were close together and in the first firing five of them were killed.[199] Only Samuel and Daniel were not, but Daniel, a lieutenant, had his arm shattered by a bullet.

It was instantly apparent to the American commander, Colonel Denison, that they had fallen into a trap and that the odds against them were heavily in favor of the enemy — perhaps as much as three to one. Throughout the entire American lines, tremendous casualties were occurring. The greatest danger, Denison knew, was the Indians converging on their rear, turning the crescent shape of the trap into an encirclement. There were still some gaps through which the army might escape the trap, but they were closing quickly and there was no time to lose in grasping whatever chance remained. Denison realized the first thing he had to do was order his men on the left to fall back slightly and form an oblique position to the right. This would bring them into position to face the enemy. At once he cupped his mouth and shouted.

"Fall back and oblique! Fall back and oblique!"

The order was misunderstood and abruptly it was being repeated down the line by subordinate officers as: "Fall back and retreat!"

The line was not formed and in moments there was utter confusion and a veritable rout began. Efforts by Denison and Lieutenant Colonel George Dorrance to check it failed and the retreat picked up momentum, pouring through the gaps that the Indians had not yet closed in the rear. While in the midst of giving an order for the troops to halt and hold their position, Lieutenant Colonel Dorrance took a bullet through his side that knocked him from his horse.

Everywhere now, Colonel John Butler's Indians and Rangers were pouring in a terrible fire and pressing ahead in their front. The original crescent shape of their ambush lines became an elongated U, with the Americans fleeing, still with some degree of control, out the open end and back toward Forty Fort. The control was quickly degenerating. Confusion increased among the Americans, leading to disorder and to broken lines and mass flight. Those who fell wounded were slaughtered by the swiftly following enemy and their scalps were taken, both by the Indians and by the Indian-painted Tories and Rangers. Dorrance was one of the exceptions. Recognized as he lay on the ground as one of the principal American officers, he was taken alive. Other officers were not so fortunate. Every one of the company commanders, now or during the retreat, was killed — Captains Lazarus Stewart, Dethick Hewitt, James Bidlack, Jr., Rezin Geer, Asaph Whittlesey and Aholiab Buck. So were Durkee and Ransom and Lieutenants Welles, Ross and Pierce.

Dozens, scores, of individual dramas were occurring in the midst of the great all-encompassing drama of the battle. A squad of fourteen more Americans were standing their ground, unaware that a rout was occurring. Among them was Henry Elliott and his sons, eighteen-year-old Joseph and fourteen-year-old Jabez, who, having caught up, now fought determinedly beside them. They stood in a small group, protecting one of their men who had fallen severely wounded, John Caldwell, their courage incredible under the circumstances. Not until the enemy actually rushed past them in pursuit of the retreating Americans did they realize they were cut off. Caldwell was dying, so they left him and began moving off together across the field, heading for the river. Two more men were wounded and now the remainder scattered, trying to reach the dubious safety of some bushes. Henry Elliott fell with a bullet in his back. Joseph yelled at Jabez to run on and stopped to help his father. It was too late. Henry Elliott was already dead. The pause proved disastrous for Joseph, too. He was captured, along with nine others of the group. Only Pherfen Grates and young Jabez Elliott escaped. Jabez made it to the river and plunged in, swimming across with strong, sure strokes. Grates, less skilled a swimmer and weighted by heavy shoes and clothing, made it to just beyond midstream and then sank.

Many of those in retreat were heading for the Susquehanna, the river seeming to be an avenue of escape. For some, such as young Elliott, it was. For others it was not. Lieutenant Elijah Shoemaker, his rifle lost, fled toward the river and plunged in. Some Indians and Tories who had been pursuing him stopped on the shoreline. Shoemaker could not swim well and knew he probably couldn't make it across. He stopped in water chest deep, afraid to go farther, yet determined to try if pursuit continued. Then he was amazed to hear someone on shore calling his name. He looked more closely and saw that one of the men who had been following him, even though hard to recognize because of the war paint on his face, was Henry Windecker. The Tory had previously worked for Shoemaker here in the Wyoming Valley and Shoemaker had done many favors for him.

"Come on back to shore, Elijah," Windecker said. "You know you can't make it across. You'll drown. You'll be safe with me. Come on."

Shoemaker hesitated and Windecker grinned. "Come on, man, you don't have a lot of choice. You've helped me a lot in the past. Now it's my turn to help you. Don't worry about these others." He dipped his head toward his companions close by. "I'll protect you. Come on." He held out his hand.

Shoemaker still hesitated, considering this, but the fear of drowning was strong and so finally he waded back and accepted Windecker's outstretched hand. Windecker began pulling him and then, with his free hand, suddenly jerked a tomahawk from his belt and drove it deep into the back of Shoemaker's head, killing him. He scalped the lieutenant and then shoved the body out into the current.[200] Still grinning, he waded ashore with the scalp in one hand and knife in the other.

Two boys who had been in the battle line together were now fleeing together, with Indians in close pursuit. The younger of the two boys, fourteen-year-old William Buck, was nearing exhaustion and unable to keep up with seventeen-year-old Roger Searle. One of the war-painted Tories pursuing them shouted, "Stop! Give up and we won't hurt you. If we have to run you down, we'll kill you."

Buck, hearing this, stopped and held up his hands. Searle, still running, turned in time to see the pursuers rush up to the youth and one of them bury a tomahawk in his head. If possible, Searle ran even faster after that, and he escaped.

Privates George Cooper and Abraham Westbrook had been fighting side by side on the left wing near the marsh where the retreat began. Both men had just fired their rifles and Cooper was reloading. Westbrook looked around and his eyes widened.

"George! Our men are retreating!"

"I'll have one more shot," Cooper replied. He finished ramming the charge home and jerked out the ramrod, dropped it, leveled the rifle and sent a ball through the head of an uncommonly tall onrushing Indian no more than thirty feet away. It was the Seneca chief Tawannears.

The fall of their leader caused the Indians coming up behind him to hesitate and Cooper and Westbrook sprinted off toward the river. The Indians were in pursuit again and Westbrook didn't make it. A thrown tomahawk severed his spine. Cooper cleared the log fence at a bound, but the pursuers leaped upon it and it collapsed beneath them, tumbling four or five of them into a grunting tangle of arms and legs. Cooper reached the river at a flat-out run and plunged into the water. He swam across the northwest channel of the river to the large Monocanock Island, which lay in the Susquehanna at this point.[201] On this low, siltage island he came ashore and immediately plunged into the riverine growth, which acted as a shield to hide him from the Indians who had by this time regained their feet and pursued him to the Susquehanna shore. Reaching firmer ground, he ran across the island and entered the water again to cross over the main channel to the southeast bank. Standing in the shallows on the east side of the river he encountered John Abbott, who was shaking and moaning and who told Cooper he couldn't swim. Cooper didn't point out that he *had* to have been able to swim in order to get to the island. Instead, he simply told Abbott to hang onto his shoulders and he pulled the frightened man the rest of the way across the river to safety. As they stood up in the shallows and waded ashore, Cooper was in the lead. He suddenly became aware that Abbott was no longer wading behind him. Turning, he saw the man face down in the ankle-deep water and raced back to him. He raised Abbott's head and a gush of blood spurted from the man's throat. A stray bullet from across the river had struck him in the back of the neck and severed the jugular. Cooper recoiled, dropped the body and continued ashore.

Still on Monocanock Island was Private Giles Slocum, who had been one of the first to get there. Exhausted by the brief swim just to reach the island, he knew he'd never be able to swim the remainder of the swift Susquehanna. Fearful that the enemy would come to the island, he found a secluded sandy spot in some bushes and buried himself except for his head. Soon he heard Indians nearby and then a voice begging for mercy, but the plea ending in a scream of finality. Slocum was not discovered.[202]

In the principal part of the retreat, two distinct bodies of men had formed, both heading as swiftly as possible òver the path they had come, returning now to Forty Fort. One of these parties surrounded Colonel Zebulon Butler, still on his horse; the other surrounded the similarly mounted Colonel Denison. The latter abruptly broke away, ordered his men to continue toward the fort and put his horse into a canter back toward the enemy to make sure all his men who could retreat had done so. Bodies were everywhere and as his horse moved among them, one of them stirred, raised to its knees and then came to his feet. This was seventeen-year-old Rufus Bennett, whose temple had been creased by a bullet, which had knocked him senseless for a while. He was still a bit dazed.

Colonel Denison ordered the youth to grip the horse's tail and run with him if he could. He then turned back toward the fort, pulling the raggedly running, frequently stumbling Rufus along. The boy was being dragged almost as much as he was running, but he clung grimly. Indians had begun pursuing them and were coming up rapidly. As the colonel and the private reached the place where the army had first stopped to form its battle lines, Denison saw an outstretched form along the fence sit up. It was Richard Inman, who had earlier gone to sleep there and was just now awakening. He rubbed his eyes unbelievingly with one hand, still holding his rifle with the other.

"Is that gun loaded, Inman?" Denison asked.

"Yes it is."

"Then shoot that Indian!" He pointed at the foremost of the pursuers, just then coming through the fence a short distance away.

Inman threw his rifle to his shoulder, took careful aim and shot the Indian through the heart. Immediately those with him fell back and took refuge behind the fence. Now, with Bennett still hanging onto the horse's tail and Inman running alongside, the three set out again for Forty Fort.[203] They were the last to reach it safely. Immediately upon entering, Denison resumed sole command, relieving Colonel Zebulon Butler, who had already relieved Lieutenant John Jenkins of his temporary command.

Outside the walls of the fort the Indians were now taking scalps from the dead and killing all the wounded. Holding his side to staunch the flow of blood as he lay upon the ground, Lieutenant Colonel George Dorrance raised himself to an elbow and gazed expressionlessly at the Indians coming toward him now. In their van was none other than Gu-cinge, who demanded Dorrance's sword, still in its scabbard. Dorrance refused.

Gu-cinge said something guttural to his companions and one of the warriors stepped forward and grasped the scabbard, trying to rip it off Dorrance's belt. Dorrance grasped the hilt of the sword and began drawing it from the scabbard and, on seeing this, the warrior hurriedly switched his grip from scabbard to blade. Still pulling, Dorrance sliced the warrior's hands severely and the man leaped away and then stared at his bleeding palms.

At this, Gu-cinge spoke sharply, stepped forward himself and twisted the sword out of Dorrance's weakening grip. In almost the same motion he swept it through the air in a vicious arc and cut off Dorrance's head. He then held the severed head to the ground with his foot while he removed the scalp and stuffed it into his already bulging belt pouch. Then he calmly removed the scabbard from the headless body, attached it to his own waistband and thrust the sword into it without even cleaning the blade.

Elsewhere nearby and along the shattered army's path as it had made its way back to Forty Fort the atrocities continued. The body of Captain Samuel Ransom lay where it fell not far from Forty Fort, the clothing gone and one thigh split to the bone with a knife, all the way around and from hip to knee. Beside him lay the decapitated body of Captain Aholiab Buck, the head nowhere to be seen. Closer to where the battle had broken out, Captain James Bidlack, Jr., one knee shattered, was dragged screaming to the ruins of Wintermoot Fort and bodily thrown upon the still-burning timbers. Twice he managed to crawl off the logs but he was thrown back on and the third time he died and his body drew up in the characteristically pugilistic attitude of death by fire.

Joseph Elliott and the nine who had been captured with him were tied together in an area where a post had been erected and surrounded by a ring of brush and wood. One by one the captives were being tied so that they could run around the post but not get away from it. Then the ring of flammable material would be ignited. The screams and howls of the men trying to get away from the living fire licking at them was terrible and could be heard clearly by those inside Forty Fort and even across the river at Wilkes-Barre Fort. As one by one the prisoners expired, the coals would be scraped away, fresh brush piled up and another victim selected. When Joseph Elliott's turn came and the bonds about his wrists were cut away so he could be tied to the post, he abruptly kneed one of his captors in the groin, butted another in the stomach and raced for the river. He was pursued but outran them and plunged in, swimming as far as he could under water before surfacing for air. Twice he broke surface briefly to breathe and heard bullets smack into the water close to him. The third time one of the bullets went through his right shoulder, but he kept on and the current swept him out of range. Eventually he staggered into the shallows on the far shore and made it safely to Wilkes-Barre Fort.[204]

Daniel Gore, in severe pain with his shattered arm, was hidden in some dense brush waiting for nightfall so he could escape. He was trembling violently, but he became rigidly still when he heard some men approaching. As they passed, one of them was saying, "It has been a sore day for the Yankees." The other replied, "It has indeed. Enough blood has been shed." The second speaker was the enemy commander, Colonel John Butler. However, despite the comment, there was still blood to be shed.

With the residue of the American defenders safely bottled up in Forty Fort, the victorious Indians and Rangers moved swiftly throughout the valley on the west side of the river, burning every house and fort, looting, killing the wounded and otherwise causing havoc. With this, the panic expanded on the east side of the river by those who had taken refuge in Pittston and Wilkes-Barre forts. Each report of what was occurring on the west side of the river was worse than the last. The horrifying knowledge was there: the greater part of the Wyoming Militia had been wiped out and those left, temporarily within the haven of Forty Fort, would be unable to hold out for long. Apparently all was lost and for those women and children and survivors on the east side of the river, it was a night of terror beyond description, underlined by the eerie glow of the homes and barns still burning in the growing darkness and punctuated by the screams of those being tortured to death.

Before full darkness came, however, John Butler led some of his Indians and Tories across the river and surrounded Pittston Fort. Captain Blanchard was still in charge, with a handful of men and a host of refugees. Fortunately for him and his garrison, he had not been able to join the American force late in the afternoon due to the theft the night before of all his boats. Now, in the face of the enemy confronting him, there was nothing left to do but capitulate and beg that the women and children be spared.

Butler took possession and, retaining the military as prisoners, released all the others. The women and children immediately fled into the wilderness, although Butler assured them they would not be harmed. No one believed it and facing the wilderness without food or proper clothing was preferable to facing the whim of the attackers.

News of Pittston's fall reached Wilkes-Barre Fort and those who had taken refuge there fled also, striking out into the darkness of the wilderness without anything except the clothing they wore. Mostly these refugees scattered eastward or southward, but some made a wide circle and came to the river again downstream from the forts and headed for help by following the river.[205]

Those still inside Forty Fort, as darkness came on, grew increasingly fearful about what would happen on the morrow. Certain that Colonel Zebulon Butler, being a Continental officer, would be summarily executed if captured,

Colonel Denison ordered him to leave, along with his wife, who was also in the fort. They were to cross the river and get whatever help they could find. The one hundred and eighty women and children in Forty Fort were, at the same time, transported across the river under a guard of thirteen men for refuge in Wilkes-Barre Fort, which would be safer. Colonel Denison said the remaining men in Forty Fort would do their best to hold out for as long as possible to give reinforcements a chance to get here. Failing that, they would hold out long enough for the women and children to escape.

Arriving on the other side of the river, however, the refugees from Forty Fort found Wilkes-Barre Fort abandoned except for three wounded men too badly hurt to be moved. They told of the fall of Pittston Fort and so now all hope was gone. The refugees, no longer wishing to stay together for fear that the attackers would follow a large group, family groups seeing only to their own set off into the darkness, leaving the glow of the fires and screams of the tortured behind. In the darkness, many wandered into a great swamp east of the Wyoming Valley and perished there. [206]

It was a terrible night for everyone, but the horror of it was not yet completed. The worst of the cold-bloodedness, in fact, was just now beginning — manifesting itself in the shape of the demonic woman called Queen Esther.

In the direction of Jenkins Fort, just a half mile from where the battle had originally broken out, a huge flat rock four or five feet square protruded above the ground two feet at its highest point and disappeared into the ground at the rear. The sixteen American soldiers who had been captured were arranged in a ring at this rock, surrounded by some two hundred Indians. A large fire sent weird shadows flickering among the rocks and trees and there was an unreal, almost supernatural quality to the whole scene.

At the midpoint of this rock stood Queen Esther, clad only in a loincloth. In her hands she held a huge war club shaped like a bird's beak at the outermost end, with a rock firmly embedded in this opening. That rock was about the size of a grapefruit. Her face and bare upper body were garishly painted with fearsome-looking sworls and lines of alternating black and white. Large, dead-white circles had been painted around her eyes and the eyes themselves were like black holes in a sort of living skull. She was a terrifying apparition.

For nearly an hour Queen Esther had murmured and wailed and implored, jerking her body spastically atop the rock and reaching her hands upward in the darkness, beseeching powerful spirits to be with her, imploring them to make what was to come now a fitting retribution for the death of her only son, Gencho. Abruptly she signaled toward the warriors and several moved to the circle of captives and brought one of them to the front center of the rock and made him sit with his back against it. Then Queen Esther stepped forward and gripped the prisoner by the hair, jerked his head until the back of it was against the rock surface and the terrified eyes were staring straight upward into the night. Then, with a scream of the word "Gencho!" she brought the war club down on the forehead with all her strength, crushing the skull as if it were no more than an eggshell.[207]

Among the prisoners was Lebens Hammond and, with his companions, he watched aghast as one by one the captives were led to the rock and murdered to the harsh cry of "Gencho!" The surface of the rock was slippery with blood and tissue, yet the executions continued. Hammond had no idea what the word she was shrieking meant, nor did he care. One thought was paramount in his mind. There was absolutely no way he was going to allow himself to be led steerlike to the slaughter as his companions were doing. They all seemed to be in a state of shock.

Not Lebens Hammond.

Eleven of the sixteen had been executed when it came his turn. Just as, unbeknownst to him, Joseph Elliott had earlier escaped from his captors, now Hammond kicked and struck and broke free of those holding him. He dashed through the ring of Indians before they could spring into action and stop him. Never in his life had he run more swiftly than he did now, heading for the deep woods northward on Scovell's Mountain. But the furious cries of the Indians alerted others ahead of him and he was cut off. Immediately he doubled back in the darkness toward the river but again he was cut off and he sped for the rank darkness of the marsh. He plunged into it, easing swiftly yet quietly through the thickest portions and then finding a hollow in which he could hide perfectly, screened by overhanging brush. For two hours he remained here until the searching for him ended and the large fire near the sacrificial rock had dimmed. At last, making no more sound than the deeper shadow he was in this night, he made his way to the river and swam down it in midstream to Forty Fort.

The Battle of Wyoming Valley — which survivors were already calling the Wyoming Massacre — had grim statistics. Of the twelve hundred Indians and British under Colonel John Butler, only eleven lives were lost. Of the four hundred and fifty American soldiers who had marched out of Forty Fort under Colonels Nathan Denison and Zebulon Butler, at least three hundred had been killed and many others wounded.

As it had in New York at Oriskany, the Revolutionary War had come — with a vengeance! — to the Pennsylvania frontier.[208]

[July 6, 1778 — Monday]

Colonel John Butler took one last look at the Wyoming Valley behind him and was flooded with a sense of grim satisfaction. Perhaps what he had accomplished here would serve to give warning to other frontier areas of the strength of the Crown and of the foolhardiness of rising against the King and his allies.

In the distance, half a hundred columns of dark smoke continued to rise from the ruins of homes, forts, barns and outbuildings that had been fired after being pillaged of their valuables. Nothing was left now and, to Butler's way of thinking, the only course remaining to those Americans left alive in the valley was to leave it and try to reconstruct their lives elsewhere.

For the most part, Butler was pleased with his own planning and accomplishments here and with how he had been able to handle the Indians. Everyone knew that the Indians became very unmanageable after a victory and that they looted, burned and killed indiscriminately. True, Butler had not been able to prevent their looting and burning — nor had he really tried to — but he had been able to prevent their committing any further atrocities after that first night that culminated in the executions of the Americans by Queen Esther.

It could have been much worse. The women and children and elderly who were refugees from the valley were everywhere in the woods and along the trails and there had been some talk by the Indians of following them and destroying them for their scalps, but Butler had dissuaded them, saying that the King would not pay for scalps taken in such a manner.

Then, too, after the capitulation of Forty Fort the next morning, he had again been able, with some difficulty, to keep atrocities from occurring to the remaining soldiers under Colonel Denison, who had surrendered to him.[209] Indignities occurred, it was true, even to the point where the very clothing Colonel Denison was wearing was stripped off his body and taken, but the survivors were not physically harmed and that was saying a lot.[210]

Gu-cinge was strong for wanting to kill all the prisoners after their surrender. Kayingwaurto was inclined in that direction, also, but once more John Butler had prevailed against such an idea and warned that if they did what they were suggesting, he would wipe his hands of them and advise the King to do the same, and then the Iroquois would be defenseless in the face of the wrath of the Americans. The argument made enough sense that they grudgingly followed his directions.

Everything of value was of course taken and the Indians and Rangers and Tories with him were heavily laden with their plunder now as they retraced their steps toward where they had hidden their flotilla of boats. Only one deliberate killing had occurred following the surrender of Forty Fort and Butler knew that no one, considering the facts of the matter, could fault him for it. That exception was made when, after the surrender, Butler recognized one of his men who had deserted from the British and gone to the enemy. That man was the twenty-five-year-old private named Malcolm Boyd.

Butler's eyes had widened when he saw the man and Boyd had blanched when he realized he had been recognized. Immediately Butler had pointed to a nearby tree outside the gates of Forty Fort.

"Go to that tree, Boyd," he ordered brusquely.

"I would hope," Boyd replied, not moving, "that Your Honor would allow me the rights of a prisoner of war."

"You have no rights as a prisoner of war," Butler said coldly. "You betrayed your own people, deserted your own fellows and joined the enemy against us. You are a traitor. Go to that tree instantly."

Boyd did so, and as he reached the tree and turned around, Butler gave a signal and half a dozen rifles barked, ending Boyd's life. It was execution, not murder. The man was a traitor and traitors and deserters are summarily shot in time of war. Butler knew there would be no criticism for his action in this instance.

The principal regret he harbored was that the few Continental troops who had fought here, aiding the militia in its defense, had escaped his grasp. That such men as Colonel Zebulon Butler and Lieutenant John Jenkins had escaped across the river during the night was a great disappointment to him.[211] At that point there had been nothing to do but order the destruction of what remained of the settlements in the Wyoming Valley. That in itself had been a big job and had taken all of yesterday, the day before and part of today.

Now, completing his last long look at the destruction he was leaving behind, Butler nodded and turned away. The Battle of Wyoming Valley had been a great success for the King's forces and it would indeed prove to be an object lesson to those who thought they would consider revolution.[212]

[*July 10, 1778 — Friday*]

The size of the party traveling with Captain Simon Spalding's company had grown considerably as it moved through the wilderness and now, to the immense relief of all, they were approaching the first town of any size east of the Wyoming Valley — Stroudsburg, Pennsylvania, across the Delaware River from New Jersey.

John Jenkins, moving along with the party, craned his neck to see ahead and searched the faces of the group of people coming out from Stroudsburg to meet them. None was familiar and his heart fell.

Following the orders of Colonel Denison to escape from Forty Fort during the night of July 4 while the capitulation terms were being considered, Jenkins had stopped briefly at Wilkes-Barre Fort on the other side of the river, found it deserted by all but the few ailing refugees unable to travel and at once moved out on the southeast trail by which it was expected the relief column under Captain Spalding was coming. Jenkins traveled on foot all day on the fifth and part of that night. Early in the morning of the sixth he encountered Spalding's mounted company and immediately joined it, reporting to Spalding all that had transpired.

The pace was quickened and by midafternoon the company had stopped on the top of the mountains overlooking the Wyoming Valley. Below a scene of devastation was still occurring. Indians were racing about gathering plunder, homes and barns were being burned and Forty Fort itself was in flames. Well over a thousand of the enemy were still down there and Captain Spalding shook his head.

"It would be suicide for us to move in and try to be of any help to our people," he said grimly. He indicated his column with an offhand gesture. "What could a hundred do against so many?"

Jenkins nodded glumly, knowing he was right, but sick inside. He wondered where Bethiah was now and if he would ever see her again. He knew that the women who had been in his fort had been released, but of their fate when they were at Pittston Fort as it capitulated, he had no idea. It was possible they were all dead.

As Spalding's company had approached the Wyoming Valley, ever-increasing numbers of refugees met him and he cared for them as best he could, wherever possible sending them farther east toward safety. Still there were many who attached themselves to his company and stayed with him and they were a problem for him, slowing him down and increasing his responsibility. There were also arguments. Some of the men who had escaped and reached him — Matthias Hollenback, for example — were very vociferous in their demands that he march into the Wyoming Valley and attack Butler's force. Others, Hollenback included, demanded that, failing the first, he should at least immediately send out rescue detachments to round up those refugees who had become lost and who would die in the woods without help. For both, the answer had to be no. As Spalding had pointed out, it would be suicidal to attempt any attack against Butler's Ranger and Indian force, and there was no way patrols of his men could adequately cover the vast wilderness to look for lost refugees. The only compromise he could make was to move eastward along the central trail toward Wind Gap and Stroudsburg, since this was the most likely route that the refugees would have followed, and help those along the way who could be found. This is what was done and many refugees were picked up. The pace of the company slowed with the difficulty of moving women and children, the ill and lame and elderly, toward safety. A few had died. Many were suffering from exposure. But a great many were saved.

Now, as a large number of people from Stroudsburg surged to meet them, there were cries of joy at reunions, tears and gloom at not finding those whom it was hoped would be found. They moved farther into the town, Jenkins greatly downcast and more fearful than ever. But, as they entered the town proper and passed an inn, a door abruptly flew open and a woman cried, "John! *John!*"

Jenkins spun around to look and then Beth was in his arms and for the moment nothing else mattered to either.[213]

[July 14, 1778 — Tuesday]

Because of the great burden of plunder they were carrying upriver with them, the force under Colonel John Butler in its flotilla of boats did not reach Tioga again until July 10. Since that time little had been done except to inspect and divide the plunder and pack it away for traveling. Just as a white dog had been sacrificed before the expedition as an appeal to the Great Spirit for good luck, now another was killed and hung in the same way as a sacrifice of thanksgiving for a highly successful enterprise.

Now, on the verge of departing for Niagara, Colonel Butler received a message from Joseph Brant at Oquaga, advising him of Brant's plans to engage in striking white settlements on the New York frontier and asking for whatever reinforcements Butler could send. To this end, Butler dispatched a company of Rangers under command of Captain James Caldwell, along with a number of Indians to assist Brant in his operations. However, before their march had even begun, some petty jealousies and animosities broke out among the Senecas and now they refused to go along with Caldwell to help Brant. The Indians dispersed, heading back toward their villages. Butler, irked at the unpredictability of the Indians and yet in a way glad to be finished for a while with any operation involving them, sent Caldwell on his way to help Brant. Now, with his second-in-command gone, he set out himself with the remainder of the Rangers for Niagara.

He was sure that at Fort Niagara there would be dispatches awaiting him from Montreal and Quebec and he could then plan the future operations to be launched against the Americans the remainder of this year. At that time he would also have the opportunity to consider the problem of getting his son Walter free of his present imprisonment-awaiting-execution in Albany.

[July 18, 1778 — Saturday]

Joseph Brant's destruction of Andrustown was, because of the community's small size, anticlimactic after the massive destruction in the Wyoming Valley by Colonel John Butler and the Senecas, but it was no less indicative of how well the fortunes of war were going for the enemies of the rebellious Americans at this time.

A pleasant little community of twelve families totaling forty-five people, Andrustown was located near the head of Otsego Lake.[214] It was just over seven miles west of Cherry Valley and six miles southeast of Fort Herkimer, close to the now nearly useless Fort Dayton in German Flats.[215]

At Andrustown, this was baking day, and early this beautiful sunshiny morning most of the women and many of the men were at the town's only oven baking their week's bread and wholly unaware that any danger was near.

Abruptly, Brant and his party of about fifty Indians and a couple of Tories burst from cover and a frightful few minutes ensued.[216] The closest house to the ovens was that of the Frederick Bell family. Bell himself, along with his sixteen-year-old son, James, was out in the field hoeing and closest to where the Indians emerged. Immediately he shouted a warning and he and James started to run toward the house. A bullet struck the elder Bell and brought him down, and before young James had even reached the house his father's scalp had been taken. The boy, screeching a warning with every step, threw open the door of the house and was reaching for the gun hanging above the door when he was shot and killed. His mother screamed and snatched up her two-year-old son, Tom, from the floor where he was playing, but there was no place for them to go and they were captured.

At the ovens, as the attack took place, the residents scattered as if they were startled quail, each heading for his own house or the nearest possible cover. Henry Passage was shot dead at the ovens and his wife, two small daughters and infant son were taken prisoner. Both Frederick Lepper and his wife, Mary, were killed just as they reached their house.

George Staring's wife, mother, sister, son and daughter were all taken captive near the ovens, but Staring himself was in the house at the time and, seeing from an upper window what was occurring, he ran downstairs and hid himself in a small fruit cellar under the floor. He died there when the house was set afire.

George Hoyer and his wife and daughter were captured alive, but his slave, a young black woman named Emma, was killed at the ovens after she tried to club one of the Indians with a heavy iron poker.

Frederic Bulsome and his wife, Sarah, had run toward some rocks for protection when the attack began. Sarah didn't make it. A rifle ball passed through her heart. Bulsom made it to the rocks and then fled from there in a wide circle toward Fort Herkimer to try to get help. In a swamp a short distance away he met the fleeing family of Stephen Frank, including Stephen, his wife, three daughters and two sons. They all moved together toward the fort.

The Paul Crim family, which included his wife, three sons and a daughter, concealed themselves beneath a large storm-toppled maple tree near their house and remained there watching the destruction until the attention of the Indians was elsewhere, at which time they slipped away toward the fort and reached it safely.

The newlyweds Adam and Mary Reese, at the ovens together, joined hands and ran as fast as they could toward the woods. They didn't quite make it. Mary was hit by a bullet and fell. Adam sat on the ground with her in his arms and wept as she died a moment later. He was still holding her and rocking back and forth in his grief when the Indians came up to them. As one raised his tomahawk to kill the young man, Brant intervened, shaking his head and telling them to take him prisoner instead, which they did.[217]

John Osterhout, along with his wife, son and daughter, were at their house, farthest from the ovens, when the attack broke out. They managed to slip into the woods unseen and got away, heading toward Fort Herkimer. Their neighbors Andrew and Esther Sheapperman were not so lucky.[218] Both were wounded by gunfire as they fled from the ovens and both were tomahawked and scalped as soon as the Indians reached them.

One final life was taken. The warrior who had shot Frederick Bell where he was hoeing and took his scalp abruptly noted that his body was not out in the field where it had fallen. Curious, he walked out there and found that the man had not been killed. Bell, though scalped, had dragged himself off toward the woods. The bullet wound had partially paralyzed him and, though he reached the trees, there was no way he could hide his trail. The Indian followed it easily and caught up to Bell in the woods as he was still crawling away. The warrior picked up a large rock nearby and slammed it down on the back of Bell's head, crushing his skull and killing him. He then returned to the area of the ovens.

Within fifteen minutes it was all over. Eleven had been killed.[219] Of the remaining thirty-four, fourteen had been captured, including two men, six women and six children. Miraculously, eighteen had escaped and no pursuit of them was made. The remaining two were the Tory John Powers and his wife, Evelyn, who were unharmed and left with the Brant party.

Before leaving the area, Brant's warriors plundered the houses of anything valuable, killed what livestock they did not want and then methodically set fire to every house except that of John Powers. Into this house the twelve women and children were placed and allowed to remain behind, unharmed, as Brant and his men left with their plunder and the two men prisoners, Adam Reese and George Hoyer.

Less than an hour after the attack was begun, Andrustown was no more than a memory and once again the fear reached a high pitch on the New York frontier.

[August 1, 1778 — Saturday]

Only a few days away from his thirty-ninth birthday, Colonel Ichabod Alden was a plodding, unimaginative man who had risen as far in the military service as he was capable of rising. Of medium height and having sparse, dark sandy hair, he was inclined toward being overweight. His superiors thought him to be a good soldier because he always followed orders to the letter and left improvisation or daring measures above and beyond the call of duty to other officers. He was perfectly content to do exactly what his rank required him to do but very little beyond that.

Alden, who was inordinately proud of the fact that he was a direct-line descendant of John Alden of *Mayflower* fame, had been born in Duxbury, Mas-

sachusetts, on August 11, 1739. A few years ago he had married Mary Wake-
field and since then they had had two children: a son, John, born November
25, 1774, and a daughter, Rebecca, who would be a year old next Friday, on
August 7.

That he had been promoted to lieutenant colonel in 1775 was attributed by
his superiors to his being "a good soldier" at a time when the young nation desperately needed almost any kind of military leadership. His subordinates were
not quite so convinced of the validity of these good leadership qualities he was
supposedly endowed with so well. When he was promoted to full colonel in the
Continental Army and placed in command of the 7th Massachusetts Regiment
stationed in Albany, even his superiors raised their brows and the general assumption was that the promotion had come because of "connections" in high
places.

Above all else, Ichabod Alden was a very pompous individual who rarely listened to reason from those who were — or whom he considered to be — his
subordinates, in either rank or social station. This pomposity was not long in
making itself known to the residents of Cherry Valley, whom he had been
sent to protect with his regiment.

Oddly enough, while the Wyoming battle had taken far more lives and was
being decried as a "monstrous massacre" by practically all Americans, it was
the fall of tiny Andrustown, just over seven miles distant from Cherry Valley,
that most upset the residents here. They felt naked, defenseless, isolated, vulnerable. Ever since last spring the residents had been begging for protection,
and even when General Lafayette had been here in May he had strongly recommended that a proper fort be built to replace the clumsy and flimsy fortifications that had been thrown up around the house of Colonel Campbell's residence.

The fort had gone up, though it was scarcely deserving of the name. A
stockaded wall surrounding the village meetinghouse, church and graveyard
was all it amounted to and even the embrasures had been forgotten and had to
be cut into the walls later as an afterthought. The unnamed stockade was not
much, but it certainly was *something* and, after its construction, the Cherry
Valley residents had little by little been moving their better pieces of furniture,
art and other valuables inside the walls to protect them in case of unexpected
attack. At the news of the destruction of Andrustown, so close by, a near panic
welled in the people and there was a much more pronounced movement to
place valuables and fine things inside the walls for protection. At the same
time, new and more urgent pleas had been made for a strong garrison to be assigned.

A small detachment of Alden's men had been at Cherry Valley ever since
the stockade had been constructed, but they were very few and hardly a defense
for any determined enemy to take seriously. At last, however, the military com-

mand in Albany, itself alarmed by the brazen attack on Andrustown by Brant and his warriors, decided that greater protection was justified. At once Colonel Peter Gansevoort, who had so well protected Fort Stanwix against Barry St. Leger, asked to be given command of the force to be sent. The request was denied and in its infinite wisdom, the Northern Department commander had ordered Colonel Ichabod Alden to repair at once with his regiment of two hundred and fifty men to Cherry Valley and establish a strong military garrison there. The fact that neither Alden nor his Massachusetts regulars had had any experience in Indian warfare seemed not to make a difference.

Today, therefore, was the day Colonel Alden, riding a fine chestnut gelding and followed by his second-in-command, Lieutenant Colonel William Stacy, led his regiment into Cherry Valley under gaily fluttering colors, smiling broadly and with practically messianic self-importance at the cheers of the residents, who felt that now their worries were over. That glow of reassurance, however, began to fade almost at once. Alden made an immediate tour of the village, nodding appreciatively at the quality of some of the finer homes, such as that of Robert Wells. Following that, Alden and Stacy inspected the so-called fort. Alden wore a dour expression as he walked through it and viewed the quantity of furniture and valuables the residents had stacked up inside.

"This will never do," he said stiffly, pointing to the goods. "This installation is not a supply depot. Nor is it a compound for the protection of personal items belonging to civilians. It is a fort. I repeat, a fort! As such, it is for the use of the military for, in accordance with orders, defense of the inhabitants. Not the household furnishings of the inhabitants. All this material will have to be removed at once."

Noting the dismay in their expressions, he tempered his speech a bit. "You must realize," he said, "that with a garrison of so many soldiers to be quartered in here, there would be very great temptation to plunder and I cannot take the responsibility of placing the military in that sort of a position."

The protests of the Cherry Valley residents were to no avail, even when they expressed the far greater fear of their possessions being taken by the Indians. Alden simply met their remarks blandly and with a reassuring smile.

"Have no fear," he told them. "Your goods will not be plundered nor even damaged. My men will quarter themselves within these walls and they will be on hand to protect you and your possessions should the savages be foolish enough to threaten. I must say that I find it inconceivable Brant would even consider attacking us. This is not a unit of green militia such as tried so ineffectively to protect the Wyoming Valley. These are regular soldiers of the Continental Army!"

The residents were no little angry about it, but they glumly removed their goods from within the walled fortification and returned them to their homes. Then Alden had another surprise for them.

"To prove my confidence in the strength of our position here and the unlikelihood of any sort of attack occurring, even though my men will arrange quarters for themselves within the stockade, my officers and I will take up lodging in the homes of the citizens. Lieutenant Colonel Stacy and I, for example, will lodge with Mr. Wells."

Robert Wells had not been consulted about this, but he was embarrassed at the thought of objecting and also a bit thankful that he'd have the extra protection under his own roof, so he only nodded in agreement.

One final thing occurred this day that was somewhat indicative of the character of Colonel Ichabod Alden. Still, with many residents of Cherry Valley clustered about him, he swept his arm out toward the stockaded walls.

"This fortification," he said grandly, "has had the misfortune of being without a name since its construction. We will rectify that immediately. Henceforth it will be known as Fort Alden."

[August 15, 1778 — Saturday]

Having spent nearly a month in Stroudsburg with Captain Simon Spalding's company, chafing at the delays that kept them there, Lieutenant John Jenkins had been more than pleased when Spalding had finally given the order for the company to move out with the object being to return to the Wyoming Valley and reclaim it, whether or not the enemy was still there.

Today they had reached Wyoming.

Seven miles from Wilkes-Barre Fort, Captain Spalding sent two detachments ahead to reconnoiter the situation. One of these was under Ensign Matthias Hollenback. The other was under Jenkins. Cautiously leading his twenty-two men back into the valley, Jenkins struck the Susquehanna at the mouth of the Lackawanna, where Pittston Fort had been but which was now a pile of ashes. Until now they had encountered no one, but as they moved downstream toward the agreed-upon rendezvous at Wilkes-Barre Fort, they encountered two Indians who fired upon them. No soldiers were hit and the detachment fired back, but the Indians escaped and no pursuit was mounted, Jenkins being only too familiar with the Indian ruse of seeming weakness to lead an enemy into ambush. Faintly downstream they heard the sound of gunfire and suspected it might be the Hollenback detachment.

They were correct. When they reached the place Wilkes-Barre Fort had been and which was now also only a jumble of charred and fire-blackened timbers, they were met by the ensign's detachment marching toward them from downstream. Hollenback told Jenkins that he and his men had gone down the mountain from the point where they had split off from Spalding and struck the Susquehanna at the line of Hanover and Newport. There they had sighted a small party of Indians who immediately fled. They had fired upon them and wounded one, but all had escaped to the opposite side of the river in a canoe and then disappeared into the woods on the other side. One of Hollenback's men swam across the river and brought the canoe back. Then they marched up to meet Jenkins here.

Even as they talked, Captain Spalding and the remainder of the company came into view and soon joined the two detachments. There was nothing but devastation as far as they could see except for a few homes of men who, prior to the Wyoming battle, had been thought to have Tory leanings. These would temporarily provide shelter for the men until a new fort could be erected.

The greatest horror, they knew, lay on the other side of the river, where the battle had occurred. Sooner or later it would come time to send a party across the river to bury the remains of the dead and assess the situation, but that time was not yet. Although it no longer seemed likely, a large Indian force could still be hidden over there. Spalding knew his force was too weak even to consider becoming vulnerable to attack with only a river at their backs.

"If they mean to attack us," he said, "it'll have to be on this side of the river. However, I really believe they've gone. We'll check things out for a few days and if, in fact, they are gone, we can then send word back to the settlements for any of the residents who may wish to do so to return. I think it is important, as much from a morale sense as anything else, to have this place resettled and rebuilt so the enemy comes to the realization that we can't be permanently driven away even when we've been badly beaten."

Both Hollenback and Jenkins nodded, but it was the latter who replied. "I think we're back to stay," he said slowly. "For my part, I know I am. I've planted my roots here and if necessary my bones can be planted here as well. I won't be driven off again."

[*August 17, 1778 — Monday*]

In the grim jail cell in Albany, Walter N. Butler was not aware that it was just a year ago today that he had been captured by the Rebels near Fort Dayton, court-martialed and then incarcerated here. The sentence of death for treason still hung over him and yet, though his public hanging had three times been scheduled, for one reason or another it had been postponed.

In the dim light filtering into his cell, he once again read the note that had been slipped to him earlier in the day by a visitor to another prisoner. It told him to pretend, immediately after eating his meager dinner, to be gravely ill, as if suffering from food poisoning. Everything else would be prepared.

Young Butler had no idea what "everything else" meant or even who the note was from, but his spirits leaped at the thought that escape might be pending. He wondered if his father had somehow arranged it. He felt fairly sure that was the case. Now he rolled the note into a small ball and buried it in the small mound of lumpy mashed potatoes in his food bowl. Then, half tipping the bowl over on the floor, he abruptly let out a shriek and doubled over, gripping his stomach. He was still rolling over on the floor and gasping when the doctor, summoned by the guard, entered the cell and examined him.

The head jailer was there too, showing no concern for Butler and only a faint irritation at having had his evening disrupted. He seemed in no way suspicious and only nodded impatiently when the doctor said that Butler was very ill, possibly dying, and should be moved to where he could receive constant attention. The hospital, such as it was, was already overflowing with war-wounded patients and there was no room for him there, so the head jailer acquiesced to the doctor's insistence that Butler be taken to a private residence not far away and put to bed for treatment — with a full-time guard, of course.

Within an hour, as dusk was gathering, Butler was in the small back room of a house a few blocks from the jail, still moaning and thrashing with his "illness" but becoming slightly subdued as the medicine the doctor allegedly gave him took effect. The guard at the door, obviously very bored, sat watching him without curiosity until Butler seemed to fall deeply asleep. He was Sergeant Adam Hunter of Colonel Alden's regiment and on occasion had guarded this notorious prisoner before. The present duty was no less boring for him than those in the past had been until unexpectedly a pretty young lady of about eighteen showed up with a tankard of ale for him.

Sergeant Hunter perked up considerably.

Her name was Lily and she was cheerful and engaging and uncommonly buxom. Several times she left briefly to refill the tankard and had little difficulty moving just far enough to avoid the hungry hands of Hunter as they sought her bosom. Quite soon Hunter had drunk himself into a stupor and passed out. When he would not rouse to the girl's shaking of his shoulder, she whispered to Butler to follow her and he sprang from the bed and did so. She took him to another room in the house where an older couple, secretly Tories, wrung his hand warmly, gave him a pouchful of supplies, told him where the horse was located outside that had been readied for him and instructed him to head immediately for Fort Niagara, where his father would be waiting for him. Until he got clear of the Mohawk Valley, he was to travel only at night and to avoid all contact with people.

Nothing had ever tasted sweeter to Walter Butler than those first few lungsful of free air he drew as he rode quietly through the darkness. The air was cool, even though it was late summer, but he didn't notice it. Within him burned a fire of hatred that made the physical chill insignificant, a hatred that long ago had inspired a desire for revenge that was so consuming that it occupied his thoughts almost constantly. A full year of his life had been wasted behind bars in the Albany jail and for that, he promised himself, the Americans would pay dearly. Very dearly.

[*September 10, 1778 — Thursday*]

In his rather lavish quarters in New York, where reports from the frontier had filtered to him in an irregular manner, Colonel Guy Johnson refilled his glass with Madeira, quaffed it without pause and then bent again to the long letter he was writing to Lord George Germain. He had already written of the recent escape of Colonel John Butler's son from custody in Albany and that Walter had successfully reached Niagara and been reunited with his father. He also mentioned that it appeared young Butler was uncommonly envious of the great victory his father had had in the Wyoming Valley and was very desirous of leading a major foray of his own against the settlements. It seemed unlikely that he would be able to do so any longer this year, however, since the season was too far advanced to launch any major expedition. Johnson continued:

Your Lordship will have learned, before this can reach you, of the successful incursions of the Indians and Loyalists from the northward. In conformity to the instructions I conveyed to my officers, they assembled their forces early in May and one division, under Mr. Butler, proceeded with great success down the Susquehanna, destroying the posts and settlements at Wyoming, augmenting their numbers with many Loyalists, and alarming all the country; whilst another division, under Mr. Brant, the Indian chief, cut off 294 men near Schoharie and destroyed the adjacent settlements with several magazines, from when the Rebels had derived great resources, thereby affording encouragement and opportunity to many friends of government to join them. . . .[220]

[*September 12, 1778 — Saturday*]

Throughout the summer and into the budding autumn, Joseph Brant had ranged far from his headquarters at Oquaga. Often he showed up in Unadilla and he was reportedly seen in Montreal, Quebec and Oswego. Occasionally he was glimpsed in scattered areas of the New York frontier. He had been in Niagara at least three times since April and there were reports that he had been seen as far west as Fort Pitt. There he was reputed to have ignited strong fires of hostility against the Americans among the Delawares and some of the Shawnees, among the Wyandots — those offshoot members of the Huron tribe — and among those of the loose confederation still calling itself the Mingo, in the very area of the Ohio River below Fort Pitt where Brant had been born thirty-eight years before.

The fact was, Brant was moving almost constantly, and when not actually leading forays against the settlements, he was active in inciting others to do so. He traveled swiftly on horseback, accompanied by only a few trusted men. He had a compelling nature about him, an ability to make the imaginations of his listeners soar, to make them have a towering confidence in their own abilities and a strong awareness of their responsibilities to prevent the Americans from encroaching farther into Indian country even in the midst of their war with the British.

An example of this American audacity was the arrival, only yesterday, on the west bank of the Tuscarora River in the Ohio territory of a force of fifteen hundred men from Fort Pitt under Colonel John Gibson. Their orders from General Lachlan McIntosh were to build a strong fort in the wilderness that would serve as a "reminder to the savages of the strength of the United States and a deterrent against their taking up the hatchet against us in support of their Iroquois brethren in New York and Pennsylvania. It will intimidate and serve to bring to terms the Indians in this quarter."

Unaware that it would have almost precisely the opposite effect and greatly antagonize and stir up the Indians there, Gibson's men fell to the job of construction at once and, though very early for the place to be given a name, Colonel Gibson immediately dubbed it Fort Laurens, after Henry Laurens, the president of Congress. It was a constant reminder to the Indians who viewed it from hiding with mounting anger that what Joseph Brant had told them was true; even fighting a devastating war in the East was not preventing the insidious tendrils of encroachment of these whites who continued moving westward and rooting themselves. The answer was simple. Fort Laurens would have to be destroyed.[221]

Much as Brant was moving with great rapidity throughout the frontier, he was not omnipresent. He would have to have been in order to have been responsible for all the attacks taking place. Just as he had been blamed and was universally hated and feared for the Wyoming Valley destruction, in which he had taken no part, so too he was held responsible for the ravages being committed in the valleys of the Hudson, the Mohawk, the Schoharie and the Delaware.

On August 24, a party of Indians and Tories swept into the Susquehanna River settlement of Nanticoke,[222] half a dozen miles below the Wyoming Valley, and destroyed it. Luke Swetland and Joseph Blanchard, two prominent settlers, were taken into captivity, with Joseph Brant named as the Indian who personally took these two — yet Brant was at this time two hundred miles away. In this way, Brant was being named the perpetrator of every act of aggression against the Americans on a considerable frontier. The antipathy held toward him by the Americans was tremendous, as was the fear they harbored for him. In point of fact, there were numerous parties of British regulars, Tories and Indians with whom Brant had no contact but who were also actively striking various parts of the frontier with varying degrees of success.

The principal identifying factor of an actual Brant-led attack was that life-taking was held to a minimum, especially among noncombatants, with a greater concentration on destroying homes, barns, magazines and storage buildings and the confiscation of livestock. These, Brant knew, were the things that would most discourage the settlers from very quickly coming back.

That very line of reasoning was especially apparent today when Brant, commanding a large party of Indians and Tories — the latter under subcommand of Captain Gilbert Tice and Lieutenant Adam Chrysler — fell upon German Flats and utterly destroyed it. Enough of a warning had preceded Brant's attack that virtually the entire population had taken refuge in three strongholds — Fort Dayton, Fort Herkimer and the church. That was precisely as Brant had planned it. Instead of attacking these strongholds, Brant had turned the energies of his force to the burning of the town. In a very short time, German Flats had ceased to exist as a settlement and all its sheep, horses and cattle had disappeared. The Brant trademark was very evident — not one of Brant's own party was injured and only two residents of the populous settlement were killed.

The attack upon German Flats and its destruction, however, had an effect that Brant had not foreseen. The New York authorities now determined to punish both the Onondagas and Mohawks severely for what they had done by carrying the war to *their* villages for a change. They also decided to enlist the aid of the Oneidas in doing so.

Far to the south, a military commander was being kept apprised of what was being planned and he was determined to keep closely attuned to what would happen. He was a very important commander who was decidedly intrigued by the possibilities this engendered. His name was George Washington.

[*September 28, 1778 — Sunday*]

The Oneidas under Chief Hanyerry were determined to prove to their American allies that they in no way supported Joseph Brant and that their sympathies did not lie with the British, as was the case with the other tribes of the Iroquois League.

Immediately after the destruction of German Flats, on being told that the New York Militia was going to mount an invasion against Brant and his Mohawks in late October and that the Oneidas should become part of it, Hanyerry demurred.

"That may be too late," he told the New York authorities. "It is *now* that Brant is gone. He never sits still but is always in motion. Now he is southward, on the Delaware, making mischief on the settlements there. The cattle and goods he took from German Flats he has stored at Unadilla. Only a few Tories remain there to guard it and they can easily be taken, but it must be now. Late October will be *too* late. Hit now, hit hard, before he returns."

The New York authorities shook their heads and said the expedition they were planning could not be launched any sooner and they implied that Hanyerry was using his argument as a device to get out of a ticklish situation, that his sympathies were really with the Mohawks after all.

"That is not true!" Hanyerry grated. "You will see."

He proved his point. Early this morning, wholly without warning, Hanyerry and his mounted Oneidas swept into Unadilla and surprised the Tories and the few Mohawks still there. They took ten Tory prisoners and burned four of the largest houses, from which they first removed the plunder that had been taken at German Flats. Then they recovered a substantial number of the cattle and sheep Brant's force had taken and brought them back to the Mohawk Valley.

There was no longer any doubt about the loyalty of the Oneidas to the Americans. Thus far, in what had been a very grim year, it was the first encouraging ray of light.

[*October 16, 1778 — Friday*]

The right hand of the Americans seemed to have no idea what the left hand was doing. In part, the reason was still a jealousy and vague hostility existing between New York and Pennsylvania that was a carry-over from land disputes over royal grants, charter boundaries and Indian treaties. Pennsylvania had never quite gotten over the fact that while it always seemed to suffer the worst of the Indian depredations, as both a colony and a state, yet the Supervisor of Indian Affairs post had been given to the Johnsons, who were New Yorkers, and the Johnsons had ever since meddled in Pennsylvania affairs. The New Yorkers, on the other hand, considered the Pennsylvanians to be brash, hot-headed and incapable of handling Indian affairs with anything less than sledge-hammer diplomacy. It also rankled the New Yorkers considerably that the seat of American government was now at Philadelphia instead of at Albany.

At any rate, the two states rarely confided in one another in respect to what they planned to do concerning the Indians or anything else. Thus, just at the time New York was planning a major onslaught against Brant's dominions from the north in retaliation for the destruction of German Flats, Pennsylvania was planning a major onslaught against Brant's dominions from the south in retaliation for the destruction of the Wyoming Valley settlements.

It was strictly accidental that both expeditions were successful. It happened that way only because of the coincidental extended absence of Brant as he, with nearly six hundred warriors, attacked a number of settlements including Pine Bush and Peenpack in the valleys of the Neversink and Mamakating, both tributaries of the Delaware. Brant was virtually unopposed and therefore took more time than he'd anticipated in destroying settlements and individual homes and barns and generally terrorizing the Delaware Valley in the region where New York, New Jersey and Pennsylvania all met. Had he swept in and out on rapid hit-and-run attacks as he had initially planned, returning to his Oquaga headquarters by mid-October, his force undoubtedly would have destroyed both the expedition led by New York's Colonel William Butler and that led by Pennsylvania's Colonel Thomas Hartley.

That didn't happen. Both expeditions, coincidentally, took exactly fourteen days, though Hartley's began on September 21 and William Butler's on October 2. Both expeditions were remarkably successful.

With two hundred and seventeen men — and joined by Colonel Zebulon Butler when they reached the Wyoming Valley — Hartley moved up the Susquehanna and wholly destroyed three principal Indian towns. These were Sheshaquin, the village of Chief Eghobund, Queen Esther's Town, at the mouth of the Chemung River, which, with Tioga, exactly opposite, was the so-called southern door of the Iroquois League. There was a special satisfaction in destroying them because Queen Esther's Town and Tioga were the staging areas that had served Colonel John Butler in his invasion against the Wyoming Valley settlements. Hartley's force had continued up the Chemung a little way above the Susquehanna, but upon meeting some unexpectedly heavy resistance near the village of Chemung, they had wisely turned about and returned to Wyoming. There they dropped off Colonel Zebulon Butler and continued downstream on the Susquehanna to the fort at Sunbury, where the West Branch splits off from the main stream. They reached Sunbury on October 5. In the course of those fourteen days of the expedition, Hartley's force had marched three hundred miles, recovered fifty head of cattle, confiscated twenty-eight canoes and many other items of property, destroyed three important Indian towns, killed eleven Indians and taken fifteen prisoners. Of Hartley's force, only two men were killed and two wounded.

The expedition from the north under the American colonel William Butler began when the colonel left Fort Defiance at Schoharie with two hundred and sixty men. They followed the Schoharie River upstream to its headwaters, then the west branch of the Delaware to Will's Mills. They marched overland from there to Aleout Creek, which they followed downstream to the Susquehanna, which in turn they followed downstream as far as just a little below Oquaga. They destroyed not only about forty good frame houses in Brant's headquarters town of Oquaga, and the small villages of Tuscarora Town and Lae-nee just below it, but also three other Indian villages, a Scots Tory village they called the Scotch Settlement, and a larger Indian village named Conihunto. Very importantly, they also burned the entire town of Unadilla, including both its sawmill and gristmill. In the process of all this they had one man wounded. Today, after a march of three hundred miles, they reached Fort Defiance again.

Now it was the turn of the Iroquois — especially those now moving about the country with Brant — to view with gloom the wreckage of their homes and loss of their possessions. The desire for retaliation filled them.

[*October 22, 1778 — Thursday*]

Lieutenant John Jenkins thought he would never in his life again be able to smile or feel any semblance of the happiness he had once known here in the Wyoming Valley. It was still home, but forever it would be clouded by the memories of what had happened, culminating in today's activities. Today, for the first time in many years, he had wept unashamedly. So had many of his men.

He looked at them now and knew by the grimness of their expressions that they were experiencing the same feelings affecting him. He nodded at them.

"Let's go home now," he said.

They moved back toward the boats that had brought them across the river and Jenkins looked over at where the Wilkes-Barre Fort was being rebuilt and where a number of houses had already sprung up to replace those that had been destroyed. Once again, as he so often had been during these days, he was struck with the resiliency of the human spirit. The place was now temporarily being called Camp Westmoreland, after the name of the county.

Within a couple of weeks of his return to the Wyoming Valley with Captain Simon Spalding's company, Jenkins was pleased to see the trickle of returning settlers become a wave of them and then the wave become a flood. It was incredible, almost beyond comprehension, that after such horror as they had lived through here any would want to return at all. Yet they came back, hundreds of them, and the Wyoming Valley — at least on the east side of the Susquehanna — was being rebuilt.

Three weeks ago, on October 1, Colonels Hartley and Butler had returned from destroying the Indian villages upriver and this helped raise a great burden of fear that had been pressing down on the returned settlers. With those villages gone, the likelihood of an attack being launched from upstream was markedly diminished. The expedition had returned laden with much recovered plunder belonging to the Wyoming inhabitants, which was redistributed to them wherever possible. Zebulon Butler remained to command here as Hartley continued downstream to Sunbury at the mouth of the West Branch. Just in the past few days there was an even greater influx of returning settlers in the wake of the rapidly spreading news of the successful Hartley expedition and the destruction of Sheshaquin, Tioga and Queen Esther's Town. Some of the former residents would never return, but it was gratifying to see so many coming back to pick up the shattered pieces of their lives and rebuild. It was good, Jenkins thought, to have Beth back again. She had arrived here almost a fortnight ago and ever since seemed to be in perpetual motion with her work. She made no secret of the fact that she was deliriously happy to be back with her husband again and vowed she would never undergo another period of separation from him.

It was yesterday that the commanding officer had posted the order on the side of the building being used as headquarters at Wilkes-Barre.

Camp Westmoreland, Oct. 21, 1778

ORDERED:

That there be a party, consisting of Lieutenant John Jenkins, two sergeants, two corporals and twenty-five men, to parade tomorrow morning, with arms, as a guard to those who will go bury the remains of the men who were killed at the late battle, at and near the place called Wintermoot Fort.

In addition to his own men for this duty, Jenkins escorted thirty returned settlers across the river to perform the melancholy chore of finding, gathering up and burying the remains of friends and brothers, neighbors and fathers and sons, who had been killed four months ago and whose remains had lain exposed to the elements ever since. They took across the river with them some shovels and two-tined wooden hayforks in two carts.

This was the first time any of them had been on the west side of the Susquehanna since their return. The frequency with which skulking Indians had been seen across the river and the possibility of renewed attack from that direction had early on caused the issuance of a general order that no one was to cross to the west side of the river for any purpose whatever without written approval of the commander. Understandably, no one had applied for such permission.

What they found this morning after crossing over had appalled and disheartened them. The weather had been so hot and dry for so long that many of the corpses had shriveled rather than rotted, but in most cases there was no way of identifying the individuals except by their clothing. Drying out as they had, the remains had become so light that it was easy for two men, one at the shoulders and the other at the knees, to lift a body on the forks and place it in the cart.

Passing along the line of retreat toward Wintermoot Fort from where Forty Fort had stood, they found corpses scattered everywhere. They were not halfway to the battlefield before both carts were filled and a halt had to be called to dig a hole as a common grave and consign into it what they had so far recovered. Then they found that they had dug a hole large enough for many more than they'd collected, so they continued to the battlefield and picked up all they could find there and brought them back to the common grave.

There were shocking sights everywhere, but no one commented much about them. Thirty-six bodies were found on the line of retreat and sixty at the battlefield proper. As soon as all these were deposited in the hole, the grave was closed up. Of them all, certain identification had been made on only two individuals; Darius Shafford was still recognizable and Captain Robert Durkee was identified because it was known that he had lost the first joint of one finger many years before.

Not until the grave had been closed were another twenty-three bodies discovered. These were in two circular situations, the first being the ring from which Joseph Elliott had escaped where the men had been burned to death at the fire post. The remains of nine men were here. The other, with the remains of fourteen, was at the huge emergent rock where the victims had had their skulls crushed with the war club wielded by Queen Esther — the ring from which Lebens Hammond had so miraculously escaped. All of these remains were buried where found. [223]

The grisly job had taken all day, and as Lieutenant John Jenkins said, "Let's go home now," there was a collective sigh of relief. It was a day none of them would ever forget and one that would, for many of them, inspire nightmares for years to come.

[*October 28, 1778— Wednesday*]

A great anger had filled Brant's mind and a coldness had gripped his heart when he returned to Oquaga after the series of raids he had just completed with his warriors in the Delaware Valley. His home was no more — a pile of blackened ashes. His village was demolished. He had made a tactical blunder and he knew it. Angry as he was at the Rebels for what they had done here, he was angrier with himself for having let it occur. With forethought, he would have left word for runners to gallop to him immediately at the first indication of trouble. He would have led his warriors back apace and, even if not in time to prevent the destruction of Oquaga, at least in time to cut off the enemy before they escaped back to their own territory.

Also, word had come of the destruction of Unadilla, the Scotch Settlement, Conihunto and the other smaller villages upstream, and then the equally devastating word of the destruction of Sheshaquin, Queen Esther's Town and Tioga by another force of Rebels. Such losses, Brant knew, were the wages of war, but it was never easy to bear, even when one realized they must inevitably occur.

What it occasioned now was a whole change of plans. Brant had thought to spend his winter at Oquaga, planning his strategy for onslaughts into the Mohawk Valley next spring. Now, with the destruction of homes and food supplies, clothing and possessions, it would no longer be possible to winter here. He would have to lead his followers to Fort Niagara and winter there. It would be a difficult winter at best.

Not all of his warriors were going with him. Some decided to go to villages on the West Branch of the Susquehanna and others to a variety of villages throughout the League in the central and western parts of New York. But now, as he mounted and rode out of what had been Oquaga, following the autumn leaf-covered trail that eventually would lead to Niagara, some two hundred and fifty of his warriors fell in behind him.

Thayendanegea was their leader, their war chief. They would follow wherever he went so long as he would lead them, and they knew that one day Brant would lead them to an appropriate satisfaction for what had been done to them here.

[*November 1, 1778 — Sunday*]

The three Tryon County officials and Colonel Ichabod Alden sat before the blazing hearth in the fortified home of Colonel Samuel Campbell at Cherry Valley and held up their glasses in a toast. The wine was deep red and the glow of the fire reflected off the glasses.

"To the continued safety of Cherry Valley, gentlemen," said Alden.

There were murmurs of "Hear! Hear!" and they drank the toast with pleasure. Alden set the glass down on the end table and delicately brushed at his lips with the knuckle of his index finger.

"I know," he said, "when I first came here with the regiment you felt that I was somewhat overbearing, but I hope you now see that I was quite right in my assessment of the situation. There has been no attack by Brant's people and there will be none. He is obviously cowed by the military strength we have on tap here."

The two members of the Tryon County Committee of Safety — Colonel Campbell and Major Samuel Clyde — nodded, but it was John Moore, delegate from Tryon County to the Provincial Congress, who replied.

"Evidently that's correct, but you must admit, sir, that there was every justification for Cherry Valley residents to be fearful of an attack. Look what has happened this year around us — destruction at Cobleskill, Wyoming, Andrustown, Schoharie, even German Flats. I feel quite sure that had not our pleas for troops been granted, Cherry Valley would have fallen as well."

"Quite!" seconded Clyde. "But the danger's not past."

Campbell pulled at an earlobe and shook his head. "Well now, I wouldn't quite say that. Perhaps the danger's not past permanently, but certainly it should be over for this year, don't you agree, Colonel?" He looked at the Fort Alden commander.

"Of course, of course! I assure you, gentlemen, Cherry Valley can breathe freely again. The season is much too advanced now for any sort of attack to be launched against us. This is especially true since Brant's bases of operations at Oquaga and Unadilla have been destroyed. As for the next spring" — he shrugged — "that's another matter." He chuckled lightly and added, "Perhaps Brant will die of pneumonia during the winter, now that we've burned his wigwam."

They all laughed and Moore raised his glass again. "I'll drink to that!"
"Hear, hear!" said the others and they drank too.

[*November 2, 1778 — Monday*]

Joseph Brant did not like the evil-tempered, fiery-eyed Walter N. Butler, nor
did he especially care for Chief Little Beard, yet here he was, riding with them
as a part of their expedition. Brant was silent as he rode beside Butler, vaguely
regretting that he'd let himself be talked into joining this enterprise, especially
since he was not to be in command of the Indians who were participating. It
could never have happened if young Butler had not caught him just when he
was so dispirited at what had happened to Oquaga and at a time when his
followers so much wanted to take revenge. Yes, he too had wanted vengeance
and so here he was, part of an army of over six hundred Indians — mostly
Senecas — and two hundred English, determinedly moving northeastward
through the wilderness toward their target.

That target was Cherry Valley.[224]

Gu-cinge was part of the force, as was Kayingwaurto, and Brant talked with
them as they rode, as well as to the chief of Chenussio, Sakayengwaraghdon,
whom the whites knew as Little Beard.[225] Often his town of Chenussio on the
Genesee River was called Little Beard's Town and it vied with Kanadasaga as
being the most important of the Seneca towns. Although Kanadasaga was the
capital of the Seneca nation, Chenussio was larger and more impressive and it
was also considered as being the western door of the Iroquois longhouse.

Notwithstanding the fact that Gu-cinge was war chief of the Senecas, Little
Beard was in charge of the Indians of this expedition. He had assumed this
command before Gu-cinge had joined the expedition and therefore, because of
his station and importance, he could not be removed from command except at
his own desire, and that was not the case.

The force had begun collecting at Niagara very early in October and Colonel
John Butler, well aware of the need within his son to lead a successful expedition, put the white forces who would accompany it under Walter's command.
Actually, the elder Butler had wanted to lead the expedition himself but he also
well understood the obsessive need his son was experiencing: a need not only
for revenge for being imprisoned and under the shadow of death for a year, but
equally a need to salve his jealousy of his father and do something that would be
of the same sort of significance as the elder Butler's destruction of Wyoming.

"We, His Majesty's officers, are instigating this expedition," he told his son,
"and the Indians will be coming along to help. Ostensibly, that places you in
command of all, but bear in mind that the Indians are hard to control in such
situations. Little Beard is strong-willed and he will attempt to override your authority. Be firm. Don't antagonize or insult him, but be firm. Gather whatever
extra warriors you can at Kanadasaga, Newtown and elsewhere, but they must

understand that while Little Beard commands the Indians, you are in overall command."

"What if we meet Brant?" Walter Butler asked. "After all, he's war chief for the whole League."

"I hope you do meet him. I was going to tell you to plan your advance so you will pass through Oquaga and there can enlist him and his men. Tell him the same. Even though he is war chief, he will respect the fact that Little Beard was named in command of the Indians as the expedition was formed and he will not try to usurp that position. That is not the Iroquois way. If he objects to Little Beard being in command, he will simply not join the expedition, but I don't think that will be the case. If he goes along with you, he does it in the knowledge that he is not in charge." Butler looked at his son narrowly. "And you curb your temper. You need him. Do all you can to enlist him."

Captain Walter Butler, with Captains William MacDonald and James Caldwell and Lieutenant Adam Chrysler beside him on his left, had ridden away from Niagara at the head of the two hundred and fifty Rangers and Tories. To Butler's right was Chief Little Beard on a dark gray stallion and scattered to his right and behind in no formation at all were about one hundred Iroquois Indians, chiefly Senecas.

At each village through which they passed, more Indians joined them. Nearly threescore attached themselves to the party at Little Beard's own town of Chenussio, almost ninety more — including many Onondagas and Cayugas — at Kanadasaga and an additional thirty at Newtown. A slight disruption occurred at Kanadasaga, where the chief of the Seneca village of Conesus, Big Tree, had just returned from his summerlong stay with General Washington, watching the progress of the war and viewing the growing strength and ability of the Americans. Big Tree strongly advised against the expedition, declaring that it would bring destruction down upon their heads. Red Jacket — Sagoyewatha — seconded him, urging that the whole plan be scrapped and that now, in this eleventh hour, the Iroquois as a League make every effort to establish peace with the Americans lest the League be destroyed. Neither chief was heeded and neither joined the expedition.

It was at Newtown, upriver from where Tioga had been, that the war party under Captain Butler and Little Beard learned of the destruction of the Indian strongholds in that quarter, including the loss of Tioga, Oquaga and Unadilla. And it was between Oquaga and Newtown, on the Warrior's Trail, that the large war party had intercepted Brant's party of two hundred and fifty, mostly Mohawks, en route to take up winter quarters at Niagara.

They stopped and held a long council and the upshot was that Brant, after considerable persuasion, finally agreed to add his force to the war party under Little Beard and relinquish the office of war chief to him for this one attack. The party now totaled about eight hundred men.

Much as he gave an outward show of grace in accepting a subordinate position in this expedition, Joseph Brant grew increasingly regretful that he was not acting as war chief — and increasingly regretful that he had agreed at all to participate in the attack on Cherry Valley.

[*November 9, 1778 — Monday*]

With unexpected suddenness, the aura of fear returned to Cherry Valley more strongly than ever. Not even the presence of Brigadier General Edward Hand, who was visiting Cherry Valley at the moment, did much to dispel the apprehension.

The sense of relief that had flooded the town since the beginning of the month was dashed on the receipt by Fort Alden's commander of a warning letter from the commander of Fort Stanwix, who had just completed an urgent meeting with the Oneida chief, Hanyerry. The letter, carried personally by Captains James Parr and Michael Burd, was brief in the extreme.

Fort Stanwix, Nov. 6th, 1778

Sir,
We were just now informed by an Oneida Indian that yesterday an Onondaga Indian arrived at their castle from one of the branches of the Susquehanna, called the Tioga. [226] *That he was present at a great meeting of Indians and Tories at that place and their result was to attack Cherry Valley, and that young Butler was to head the Tories. I send you this information that you may be on your guard.*
        I am, Sir, yours, &c.
        ROBERT COCHRANE, *Major, Commanding*
Colonel Ichabod Alden
Fort Alden — Cherry Valley

It was unsettling, to say the least. Alden, who received the letter at the home of Robert Wells, where he was residing, dictated an answer immediately:

Maj. Robt Cochrane, Cmdr, Ft. Stanwix
Sir, Received yours of the 6th Inst by express, informing me of the intelligence you obtained by one of the Oneida Indians of a large body of the enemy, who were collected on the Susquehanna and were destined to attack this place. I am much obliged to you for your information and am, Sir,
        Your very Humble Servant,
        ICHABOD ALDEN, *Col., Cmmdg.*
P.S. General Hand is now here, arrived at this place the day before yesterday, will soon return to Albany.

Having sent the message off by express, Alden then grew angry with himself for having let Wells read Cochrane's letter and hear his own response because his host became very nearly panicky and immediately leaked the news to a few others. Within an hour there was not an adult in Cherry Valley who had not heard about it and consternation reigned.

Once again a deputation of the residents came to Alden and requested permission to place their valuables inside the stockade. When Alden seemed disinclined, they carried their petition at once to General Hand, appealing to him to revoke Alden's order, asking that, if nothing else, at least they be allowed to have a secure chest placed inside the Fort Alden stockade for their important papers, jewelry, letters and the like.

"After all," said their spokesman, John Moore, reasonably, "we ourselves had the fort built for our protection to begin with and Colonel Alden merely took it over and made some improvements to it. Surely we have a right to use it to our best advantage."

The brigadier, who was just then in the process of departing for Fort Defiance at Schoharie, en route to Albany, considered the request not to be unreasonable. To Alden he said, "I don't see that there would be anything wrong with letting them store whatever they want inside the fort."

Hand's response left itself open to individual interpretation and Alden preferred to interpret it as merely an opinion, not an order. When Hand was gone he continued to refuse the Cherry Valley residents the use of the fort for any purpose except to take refuge in themselves, should the need arise.

"I'm very confident," he told them, "that such a need will not arise. Look about you. The fort here has two cannon. In addition, with the detachment General Hand left here, we now have fully three hundred soldiers — regulars at that! — to protect us. I am, right at this moment, sending out two good scouting parties to watch for any sign of approach by the enemy. If and when they should appear, which I doubt very much will occur, those scouts will give us timely warning, rest assured. There is no way that an undisciplined clutter of savages can harm us."

The scouting parties he was talking of consisted of one of a corporal and five men, which he now sent westward on the road that led toward the ruins of Andrustown. The second party — ten men, including their leader, Sergeant Adam Hunter — he sent southwest on the road toward Beaver Dam.[227] Both of these patrols were to maintain their scout along their respective roads for five days. These were the only two roads leading into Cherry Valley from the direction the enemy logically would come and with these approaches well covered, Colonel Alden was confident no enemy force could reach the town undetected.

Unfortunately, Ichabod Alden had wholly overlooked an old Indian path long fallen into disuse and barely discernible any longer. That path came up

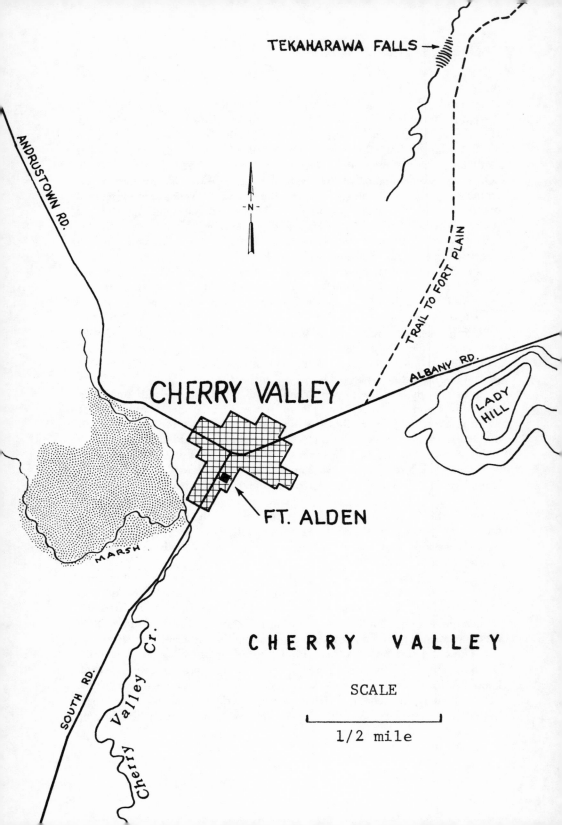

TEKAHARAWA FALLS →

ANDRUSTOWN RD.

-N-

TRAIL TO FORT PLAIN

ALBANY RD.

LADY HILL

CHERRY VALLEY

FT. ALDEN

MARSH

SOUTH RD.

Cherry Valley Cr.

CHERRY VALLEY

SCALE

1/2 mile

from the southwest somewhat to the west of the road to Beaver Dam and paralleled that road for the last couple of miles into town, with only ten to twenty yards separating the two on that final stretch. [228]

So confident was Colonel Alden in the strength of his position and his precautions that he sent word on to Colonel William Butler about it via Captains Parr and Burd, who had brought him the message from Cochrane. In the manner of many regular officers, Alden was more than a little contemptuous of militia and he knew that William Butler's garrisons at the upper and lower Schoharie forts were largely comprised of militia. He therefore, in his letter, offered to aid Butler if he should require it.

Now, toward sunset, with heavy clouds beginning to gather, a reply came from Fort Defiance.

Sir,

General Hand has been here and gone on to Albany. He advised me of your preparations at Fort Alden. I have also received your letter, brought by Captains Parr and Burd and concur with you in respect to the militia. I have sent off six small scouting parties by different routes and am convinced the enemy cannot approach undiscovered. Your proposal of joining me in case of need makes me happy. I removed the rifle corps to the upper fort immediately, and brought the militia here, 23 of whom ran away the same night. I have also the mortification to inform you that the greater part of the militia at the Lower Town have also deserted.

I am, Sir, with respect,
Yr. most humbl. svt., Wm. Butler, Col.

Col. Alden
Ft. Alden, Cherry Valley

[*November 10, 1778 — Tuesday, Before Dawn*]

Sergeant Adam Hunter was no less skeptical of a concerted Indian effort against Cherry Valley occurring at this time of year than his commander. Winter was very definitely on the way and the bite in the air for the past couple of days underlined his skepticism. He was sure that the Indians didn't like the cold any more than he and his men did and that they'd much rather be sitting around warm fires in their wigwams than forming up to initiate a major onslaught.

It just didn't make any sense that there would be an attack now and Hunter couldn't blame his men for grumbling about having to take part in this pointless patrol. Last night had been their third night out and, disgusted with having to huddle half-frozen in their blankets in a fireless camp, Hunter had told his men they could have a fire. He was glad he did; their morale had improved

considerably during the evening as they sat around the blaze toasting themselves to at least some degree of comfort.

The men had rolled up in their blankets, feet toward the fire and rifles beside
them, and all of them went to sleep. Sergeant Hunter did not think it important or necessary to post a night guard. He had no inkling that the glow of the
fire had been seen from a considerable distance and even as they rolled up to
go to sleep they were being observed by half a dozen of Joseph Brant's warriors
while several others raced back to the main camp of the war party to alert
them.

Adam Hunter and his men slept on and now, dawn was approaching and the
fire only a bed of coals. They did not hear a sound as the main war party came
up and twenty Indians slipped stealthily among them and collected every one of
their weapons. The first indication Hunter had, in fact, that there was any
trouble afoot was when someone tapped his shoulder in the gray light of dawn
and he opened his eyes to find himself looking at Captain Walter N. Butler
squatting beside him and a solid ring of Indians and Tory Rangers encircling
him and his men.

"Good morning, Sergeant Hunter," Butler said pleasantly, a thin smile on
his lips. "I presume you remember me?"

Adam Hunter, eyes widened with fright, nodded. He most definitely remembered Walter Butler. He had come within a hair's breadth of being demoted
because of Butler's escape from Albany when he was guarding him. Only by
claiming he had been drugged by the young woman, who then had vanished,
had he been able to escape demotion, but not without a severe reprimand.
Since then he had been tabbed for every unpleasant duty that came up, such as
this scouting patrol sent out from Fort Alden. Now, as the others of his patrol
were awakened and immediately bound, Hunter was questioned closely about
the present situation in Cherry Valley. His captors left no doubt that if he did
not talk he would die in the most painful manner.

Sergeant Hunter took one good long look at the force of eight hundred men
and then talked volubly.

Within an hour Walter Butler and his subordinate officers, both Tories and
Indians, had a spectacularly clear picture of the existing situation at Cherry
Valley. The nearly three-hundred-man garrison was the 6th Massachusetts
Regiment under command of Colonel Ichabod Alden. Most of the rank and
file were quartered within Fort Alden proper, but the works and accommodations there were not yet completed and so almost all the officers were lodged
in private residences. Principal among these was that of Robert Wells, located
about four hundred yards from the fort. This was where Colonel Alden was
quartered, along with his second- and third-in-command, Lieutenant Colonel
William Stacy and Major Daniel Whiting. The adjutant, Captain Aaron Hickling, was there too. He was also chief engineer. A few other officers were

quartered there as well as a rotating guard of forty privates outside the residence.

The captive sergeant also very explicitly described each of the private houses that, as in the case of the Wells mansion, was presently lodging any of the officers. He also told them the houses of the three men in particular whom Butler wanted to take — three who were soundly hated because of their great zeal in the Rebel cause — Major Samuel Clyde and Colonel Samuel Campbell, both of the Tryon County Committee of Safety, and the delegate to the Provincial Congress, John Moore.

As for the fort, Sergeant Hunter went on earnestly, its stockaded perimeter was strong enough but it was far from finished inside and, though there were two small cannon under the direction of Captain Hickling, there were no raised embrasures through which to fire them at an enemy. Neither were there any banquettes, the raised step upon which soldiers could stand to fire over the parapets at the enemy. There were at present, Hunter went on, about three hundred civilian residents in the town but they were ill prepared to defend themselves and were almost wholly dependent upon the military for that service. There was suspicion that an attack was to be made, but the commander did not really believe it. General Hand had been at the fort a few days ago, but he had gone back to Albany and there were no reinforcements requested or anticipated.

Sergeant Adam Hunter was being extremely cooperative. When he was finished telling all he knew, Walter Butler had him taken back to where his platoon was being held and tied up with them. He then called a meeting of all his officers and the principal Indians, along with certain noncommissioned officers and subchiefs. The attack was planned carefully and fully calculated to catch the entire community by surprise.

Some of Butler's Rangers had "friends" living in the town and they asked permission to slip into Cherry Valley before the attack to warn them so they could escape. The request was vehemently refused. No warning of any kind was to be given to anyone. Butler exacted promises from Chiefs Little Beard, Gu-cinge and Brant that they would control their Indians and not let them engage in excessive barbarity. Brant immediately agreed. Gu-cinge agreed too, but there was a strong sense that he didn't care and didn't really mean it. Little Beard, whose response in the matter was the most important, couched his reply, saying he would be guided "by what the Great Spirit indicates to me he wants."

At that, a Tory lieutenant, Rolf Hare, exploded in a great guffaw and was immediately silenced by a stern look from Butler. Hare had fallen under disapproval in the past for his own thinly masked acts of cruelty.

When the planning was all completed, Walter Butler looked across the faces of the men before him and asked if there were any questions. There were none.

Butler nodded and told them to prepare to move toward Cherry Valley immediately along the old Indian trail, which Brant had strongly suggested they use.

"We attack at midnight," he told them.

[*November 10, 1778 — Tuesday Afternoon*]

The residence of Robert Wells in Cherry Valley could indeed be called a mansion without the stretch of imagination. Though it was only a two-story frame house, it was very expansive and certainly the largest building in town. A gracious, rather stately and imposing structure of more than a dozen rooms, it was encircled by a wide veranda and six stark white pillars holding up the upper porch imparted a baronial aspect to the place. The beautiful furnishings inside were· of well-polished mahogany and maple, oak and walnut. Fine framed paintings graced the walls and a gorgeous tapestry covered the wall overlooking the broad staircase leading to the spacious, nicely appointed upstairs.

It was very large, but then, Wells needed a large house. Thirteen people lived in it, exclusive of the temporary residence there of Colonel Alden and his officers. Wells's family consisted of his wife, Mary, his mother, Martha, his brother John, sister Jane, his four sons, Robert, Jr., Samuel, William and John, and his daughter, Eleanor. In addition, for the past week there had been a couple of house guests from Schenectady, the sister and brother-in-law of Wells, Eleanor and Andrew Wilson. Also, Wells had three resident slaves.

Robert Wells was a very generous man and had a wide range of friends and acquaintances. Two governors had stayed in this house and many generals. Joseph Brant was one of the many important Indian leaders who had stayed here on occasion and with whom Wells had maintained friendship. His generosity made it difficult for him to turn people away and ever since his impulsive offer to let Colonel Alden and his principal officers stay here until Fort Alden was completed, the mansion had become rather crowded. Still, he retained his geniality, knowing it was only a matter of time until things returned to normal. At any rate, the departure of three people from the house today would help a little in easing the cramped conditions.

Eleanor and Andrew Wilson were returning to their home in Schenectady and they were taking· with them, to enter school again there, their nephew John, Robert Wells's youngest child, who was only eight. The preceding summer he had visited Schenectady and liked it very much. When his aunt asked if he'd like to come back again in the fall and enter school there, he had agreed. In September he returned there, but found he didn't like the school so much as he thought he would and he also missed his family and friends in Cherry Valley. When he came back home for this visit, along with his aunt and uncle, he declared he wanted to stay. Robert Wells shook his head.

"You made a decision, son," he said, "one which involved getting you entered into another school and established in another home. It is too soon for

you to change your mind. Finish out this school year and then, if you still
want to come back here, of course we would want you to do so. Agreed?"

Reluctantly, John Wells agreed. Now, having a little difficulty holding back
some unexpected tears, the eight-year-old climbed into the neat black carriage
with his aunt and uncle and they pulled away to a chorus of good-byes. Pulling
out of Cherry Valley on the Sharon-Albany Road, they had not the slightest
suspicion that more than a hundred Indians and Tory Rangers were watching
them from hiding. No attempt was made to stop them, even after they were out
of sight of the town.

[November 10, 1778 — Tuesday Midnight]

Throughout the evening hours the weather had progressively degenerated. The
overcast sky became heavier, the clouds lowered and there was a persistent
damp chill to the light breeze. A promise of snow was in the air and, as the
brother-in-law of Robert Wells, the Reverend Samuel Dunlop, had remarked
to his wife after briefly sticking his head outside his own house at about nine
o'clock this evening, "It's a night not fit for man nor beast."

A dismal misty rain had begun falling by that time and in another hour it
had become a steadily drumming rain. Crouched in a dismal, fireless camp on
the side of a densely wooded hill only a hundred yards or so from Cherry
Valley Creek and a mile southwest of Fort Alden, Captain Walter N. Butler
cursed the misfortune of it in a low hissing voice. Less than a quarter hour ago
he had passed the word to his lieutenants — and they to the rest of the force,
Indians and Rangers alike — that the planned midnight attack was being postponed till near dawn. It would undoubtedly take a fair amount of time to get
into position without being seen and so the actual attack might not occur until
midmorning or even later. However, they would definitely begin moving out
then to get into position to start the attack, irrespective of whether or not this
frigid rain had ceased. In the meanwhile, they were to remain in place here on
the hill, take cover as best they could wherever they were, doze lightly if possible and keep their weapons and powder dry — by covering them with their
own bodies if necessary.

A few minutes ago, just before midnight, it had stopped raining.

Now it had begun to snow.

[November 11, 1778 — Wednesday]

The snowfall continued sporadically throughout the night, accumulating to a
depth of two or three inches. Then, just before dawn, the wind began picking
up and the precipitation changed to a stinging sleet that carried with it the miserable chill of the snowfall as well as the extreme discomfort of the rain. The
paint with which the Indians and so many of the Tory Rangers and even a few
of the British regulars had decorated their faces in hideous sworls and lines had

smeared and run until the effect had become ghastly to observe and certainly distinctly capable of striking terror into any who saw such a visage bearing down on them.

With the onset of the sleet the misery of the Butler force increased and the Indians and soldiers, huddled in blankets in an effort to keep warm, became sodden and even colder with a chill that seemed to penetrate to the bone. Soon they were moving, many of them simply stamping in place and flapping their arms in order to get circulation going better, others walking in small circles, their breaths being expulsed in fragile white puffs that were instantly shredded by the wind.

Then came the word from Captain Butler and Chief Little Beard: move out, but move deeper into the woods to the west to avoid detection; do not cross openings visible for long distances; do not make any sound; keep weapons at ready; once deeper in the woods, move northward again until opposite the town and then gradually move eastward again to where the woods give way to the little marsh; in all instances, keep to cover and don't be observed. Once in position, study the town, memorize the positions of buildings, the layout of streets, the placement of barns and other outbuildings, the location of Fort Alden. The inclination would be to move rapidly, to get warm and get matters moving as soon as possible, but this was not good; move slowly; they were strong men and strong men could bear a little cold. Move slowly.

Although all belonged to the same force, the line of demarcation was clear between the groups as they seemed almost to flow through the dimness of the forest — Captain Caldwell in the van, leading his fifty regulars; Chief Little Beard's Senecas next, except for those still maintaining their all-night vigil in strategic positions around the town, clustered and grouped, moving with utter silence in the muffling snow; Walter Butler then, with about two-thirds of the Tory Rangers, the other third still on the northeast of the town to prevent the enemy's retreat; then Brant and half of his force of mainly Mohawks, moving as silently as the Senecas, the other half of Brant's men having moved to the woods on the east of the village the evening before. Cold as was the air, grim as was the sky, there was something about this force that was much colder and grimmer than the elements could match — an implacable deadliness, atavistically menacing.

Dawn came as they were moving and it was a deep gray, heavy dawn, filled with hostile promise. Halfway to their positions, the sleet stopped falling and the wind dropped. The clouds lowered and the tops of the trees disappeared into them and then they lowered even more and became a thin, enshrouding fog, unpleasant and clammy and yet an ally to those moving through it, masking their movements, muffling their sounds, hiding their sinister purpose.

It was about 5:45 A.M. as dawn came, but almost three hours beyond that before the entire force had stealthily and wholly unobserved by anyone in

Cherry Valley moved into their well-hidden positions to await the prearranged signal by Butler — three shots in rapid succession.

Part of the reason they were not observed was that at first not too many residents were up and about. Gray, grim, cold mornings are always conducive to snuggling deeply under warm covers, wallowing in a delicious disinclination to move out of the practically womblike comfort. Nevertheless, a few people in Cherry Valley were awake and busy.

A few officers strode here or there in solitary manner or in quietly talking pairs. Foursomes of morning guards strode briskly from the fort and out of the village on the road to Albany, the road to Andrustown, the road to Fort Plains, marching a prescribed one thousand paces each way and then methodically wheeling and turning back to retrace their steps, supremely confident that no one was about and no danger lurking since the only fresh tracks in the new snow on the road were their own and those of a wandering deer or two. Soon all sixteen men had vanished within the fort again.

Near the edge of the town at the Shankland house, Henry Shankland and his eighteen-year-old son, Andrew, had been up since five o'clock, seeing to the livestock, feeding and then harnessing the team to the flatbed wagon, then loading four large sacks of grain to take to Robert Wells's mill for grinding into flour this morning, as previously scheduled.

The elder Shankland murmured that he hoped they could be all finished before noon today, as he had some important things to do here at the house. He was glad the snow had been relatively light but gloomily forecast that one of these mornings they'd wake up with a foot or more of it on the ground. When the wagon was loaded, both father and son went back inside for a quick breakfast that Shankland's wife, Katy, had fixed for them. After that they would head for the mill near the Wells house at the confluence of the two small streams that merged to form Cherry Valley Creek. Just on the other side of the creek was the small marsh where many of the enemy were presently hiding.

Just behind that marsh, in the woods, Brant and two of his lieutenants had come up from the rear and joined Butler and Little Beard. Brant's expression was frozen in dour lines. He had known the Wells family since he was a boy and liked them immensely. Many times he had eaten under the roof of this huge house before them now and a real closeness had developed between them. He regretted deeply that this was where the officers were quartered and resolved to try, if at all possible, to save Robert Wells and his family. Even as he was considering this, more of their force was still easing into position. Little Beard agreed to hit the soldiers first — the headquarters guard who were up and about, casually moving in and out of the back door of the house. Mostly the soldiers were staying on the porch in an effort to keep dry, as the sleet had once more turned to rain.

All around the perimeter of the town, especially congregating in those areas where there were houses worthy of special attention — Moore's, Campbell's and Clyde's, for example — the attackers were settling into position, awaiting the signal to attack. As it turned out, the signal did not originate from Walter Butler.

It was close to 10:30 A.M. when, nearly a half mile down the road, heading toward the Wells place, Timothy Hamlin came riding along, having earlier left his own house several miles down the valley. [229] Without warning, two Indians leaped from the woodland near him and shot. One bullet missed; the other went through Hamlin's arm, nearly jolting him off his horse. Instantly he put the animal into a gallop.

Along the whole front of the attackers there was confusion. Was that the signal? Weren't there supposed to be three shots? They hesitated, unsure of what to do. At the Wells place, which was on a slight but imposing rise of ground, the quarters guards on the porch craned their necks, looking in the direction from whence the shots had faintly been heard. Incredibly, not a man among them moved to pick up his own weapon in case it was an emergency. In just a few moments hoofbeats were heard and then Hamlin came into view crouched low over his animal's back, his left arm dangling from the elbow and stained with blood.

Galloping up the hill on the private road leading to Wells's mansion, Hamlin entered the immediate yard and jumped from the saddle. He fell when he hit the ground, rolled over and then scrambled back to his feet. Then he ran up onto the porch and into the house, shouting "Indians! Indians!" at every step.

That was when, in a ragged manner at best, the real attack began. Rifles that had been carefully kept dry all night and during these morning hours spoke harshly now as Little Beard's Seneca warriors charged from the marsh toward the house. A half-dozen soldiers on or near the porch fell at the first firing and the others began running around confusedly, not unlike ants in a disturbed anthill. Brant, realizing that the officers inside would probably leave by the front door and head for the fort, ran at a tangent to the others to get around the house. At his heels pounded two of his most trusted Mohawks, Captain David — also known as David Hill — and his brother Aaron Hill, called Little Aaron, whose Mohawk name was Kanonaron. [230] Behind them were a dozen or more other Mohawks. Elsewhere throughout the community other groups of Indians and Rangers were taking position swiftly now, concentrating on their own little spheres of activity.

Inside the Wells house as the attack began, Colonel Ichabod Alden, still in shirtsleeves and slippers, had been having an ordinary morning meeting with some of his principal officers, including Lieutenant Colonel Stacy, Major Whiting, Captain Hickling and Ensigns Abraham Engle and David Williams.[231] When the wounded Hamlin came stumbling in, his shattered arm flopping and spattering blood all over the furnishings and fine carpets, they listened incredulously to him. Here inside the house they had not heard the shots when he was wounded. However, a few more shots came from closer at hand while he was talking. When he finished gasping out his story, Colonel Alden shook his head. The shots outside seemed to have made no impression upon him.

"It can't be a major attack," he said firmly. "Otherwise he'd've been killed and the whole town would be under fire now. Evidently it's just a small party, but let's take some action against them, gentlemen. Get to the fort at once," he told his officers, "and sound the alarm. Call in the guard and mount patrols and let's get these rascals. Go now. I'll be along directly."

As they raced from the room, Alden put on his jacket and then kicked off his slippers and began putting on his boots. The four officers running from the front door of the house saw a small group of Indians racing around the house to cut them off and they split — Dan Whiting and Aaron Hickling ran off together, plunging pell-mell down the road toward the fort, while Stacy, Engle and Williams ran toward a sparse stand of trees between the Wells house and the fort.

The major and captain reached the stockade unhurt amid a rain of bullets and got safely inside. The others were not so fortunate. Brant and his warriors pursued them across the field. Brant himself overtook Stacy and, brandishing his tomahawk threateningly, ordered Stacy to concede or he was dead. Stacy nodded and dropped the unused flintlock pistol he was holding in one hand.[232] In a similar manner, David and Aaron Hill overtook and captured Ensign Engle. Ensign Williams was the least fortunate. Fleeter of foot than Stacy and Engle, he was maintaining his distance ahead of the pursuing Mohawks when one of them threw a spear that penetrated his left buttock and tumbled him in the sloppy snow. Instantly they were upon him and, even before he had a chance to rise, a knife had been plunged into his heart. His was the first scalp taken of the day.

Back at the Wells house, the attack on the quarters guard by Little Beard's Senecas had increased in intensity and, amidst the shrieks and cries and gunfire, twenty-six of the forty soldiers were killed. The panic of these soldiers was evident for not one of the Senecas was even injured in this particular action. Just as those Indians began pouring into the house through the back door, Colonel Alden, finally realizing that this was indeed a major attack, sped out the front door with his pistol in his hand, his tunic not yet buttoned and flapping wildly. He followed the Wells's private road to the main road and there struck out in a straight line northward toward the fort — the same route Major Whiting and Captain Hickling had used.

As for the Wells family, an enormous terror had engulfed them. Looking out of their upstairs windows, they witnessed the carnage occurring below and Wells seemed to realize at once that there was no hope of escape. Among them they had only two rifles. These were loaded guns that the older Wells boys had snatched up at the first alarm, but they had no other powder or lead. The boys shot from the upper windows into the milling mass of Little Beard's Senecas below. One shot wounded a soldier in the side. The other passed through a second soldier's wrist and into the foot of a third. As marksmen, the boys were sadly lacking. Their shooting had been done from the window of the large upper parlor where, except for two members, all of the Wells family and domestics had quickly gathered. There were nine of them, including Wells and his wife, his brother John, three of his four sons and the three blacks. The only ones missing were Wells's spinster sister Jane and his attractive sixteen-year-old daughter, Eleanor. He was briefly thankful that his fourth son, John, had departed for Schenectady yesterday.

"Our only hope now," Wells said, "lies in God. Kneel — all of you. We'll pray."

They dropped to their knees, some of them with eyes closed and heads bent, with foreheads pressed against hands folded in prayer. Two of the domestics were having difficulty stifling their crying and Wells's wife moved to them and touched the head of one and the shoulder of the other to bring them comfort.

"Heavenly Father," Wells said, "in this hour of desperate need, we pray that you will have mercy upon us and spare —"

The door burst open and both Indians and Rangers, led by Walter Butler himself, poured into the room with tomahawks and knives in hand. It was Butler himself who now tomahawked and scalped Robert Wells. In less than a minute these six of the Wells family and the three domestics were hacked and stabbed to death and scalped.

Downstairs, Jane Wells and young Eleanor, thus far undetected by the attackers, had taken refuge in a pantry. Eleanor tried to get the window open but it was stuck and her aunt came to help her. It slid open abruptly with a loud bang and both of them crawled through and dropped outside. Jane had gasped for them to head for the mill but they saw their way was cut off so they separated. Eleanor raced toward the woodpile and hid behind it, but Little Beard himself, who had been scalping dead soldiers in the yard, saw her and ran in that direction, followed closely by a young Ranger. As they came up to the cowering girl, Little Beard wiped off his blade, sheathed the knife and pulled out his tomahawk. He gripped her by the arm and pulled her to her feet. Eleanor knew a few words in the Iroquois tongue and now she begged for her life. Abruptly her eyes widened as she recognized the young Ranger as Peter Smith, who had been a servant in her father's employ until the war broke out, when he had run off.

"Peter!" she cried, stretching out her arms to him. "Help me! Oh, please, help me!"

Smith nodded and spoke to Little Beard in the Seneca dialect, claiming the girl was his sister, not one of the Wells family, and should be spared. Little Beard's lips curled in a sneer and with one hand he thrust Smith backward out of the way and with the other buried his tomahawk in Eleanor's temple.

Jane alone of the Wells family remained alive. Having separated from Eleanor, she ran on, not knowing where she was going, only trying to get away. She ran into the orchard, perhaps because this is where she had spent much of her time. The orchard had always been her joy and she guarded the apples there each year from the depredations of little boys who tried to steal them when they were green and bigger boys who often tried to sneak a few when they were ripe. Not infrequently, of late, she had used a large straight stick as a club to chase away soldiers from Fort Alden who had come into the orchard to help themselves. Now she snatched up this club and turned to face her pursuers. She managed to stun one of them momentarily with a powerful swing of the club, but before she could recover for another swing, she was knocked to the ground and killed by tomahawk blows. The soldier she ·had stunned was the burly, black-haired lieutenant named Rolf Hare. He had re-covered his senses, but blood was flowing freely from the split in his brow caused by the club. Now he picked up his tomahawk from where he had dropped it and approached her body. She had already been scalped and so he methodically chopped off one of her arms, swung it in a circle over his head and tossed it up into one of the largest of the apple trees. Ironically, it lodged in the branches in such a manner that it seemed to be reaching for an old withered apple hanging only inches from the outstretched fingers.[233]

As the incident in the Wells house started to occur, Colonel Ichabod Alden had run out of the front door, heading toward the main road and fort. All the attackers were pretty much occupied and, incredibly, at first no one saw the commander escaping. He was halfway down to the road before one of the Mohawks with Brant suddenly shouted, "There goes the colonel!" In-stantly he and several others raced after him, but by now Alden had a great head start. Seeing what was happening, Brant, still gripping Stacy, thrust the officer from him into the arms of Aaron Hill.

"Hold him, Kanonaron," he rasped, and then, tomahawk still in hand, he was off, running with the speed and agility of a deer, angling diagonally through the woods in an effort to cut off Alden before he could reach the fort, dodging past trees, ducking under branches, clearing windfalls in great bounds. He reached the main road seventy or eighty yards from the fort only an instant after Alden had raced past. At the fort the log gate was still being held open a man's width to allow him entry.

Alden might have made it had he continued running without breaking stride. However, hearing the sound of pursuit and looking over his shoulder, he observed Brant chasing him and at this he committed his final act of stupidity. He abruptly stopped and leveled his flintlock pistol toward the Mohawk war chief.

In that same instant Brant, still thirty feet distant, threw his tomahawk. Before the trigger could be squeezed, the blade caught Alden in the center of his forehead and killed him. Those in the fort could see what was happening, but due to its poor and unfinished construction, they were unable to shoot well without badly exposing themselves.

Ignoring the scattered bullets now kicking up clots of slush in the road around him, Brant ran up to Alden, jerked the tomahawk out of the officer's head and scalped him. By this time a covering fire from some Rangers was protecting him and the fort's gate had closed. Then, with hardly a backward glance, Brant trotted back toward the Wells house.[234]

Henry Shankland and his son Andrew had carted their coarse grain to Wells Mill on Cherry Valley Creek before the trouble began. The bags had been carried into the mill and the two of them worked at feeding the whole kernels onto the mill wheel to be ground into flour. The slapping of the paddlewheel in the water, the creaking and groaning of the heavy timbers and the deep rumbling of the millstone made an all-pervasive din and they heard nothing from outside. It was not until the first bag had been filled with milled flour and Andrew hoisted it to his shoulder to carry it outside to the wagon that they became aware of anything amiss.

Andrew was a husky youth, but the sack was very heavy, and to help prevent its splitting or tearing Shankland followed his son out the door to help him place it in the wagon. That was when they heard some scattered shooting from the direction of the Wells house and, as they stopped in their tracks to look, a group of about twenty Tories and Indians took them prisoners. Henry Shankland's irate demands to see Joseph Brant, whom he claimed as a friend, were ignored.

Brant by this time had returned to the Wells house, still intent on possibly helping Robert Wells and his family if he could. What he found did not greatly surprise him, but it sickened him and he was regretful that he had arrived too late. Still, there was another family he might help if he hastened — the Shanklands. He remembered with fondness the times when, as youths, he and Henry had hunted together. It was Henry, in fact, who had first taught him how to reload a flintlock rifle while running — a feat few could perform well if at all. Henry had eventually married a young widow named Katy McCulloch, whom Brant had never met, who had already had a two-year-old son named William. Afterward Henry and Katy had had children of their own, the eldest of whom was Andrew. William McCulloch and Andrew Shankland had fought side by side in the Battle of Oriskany, and it was Andrew who had returned home to Cherry Valley with the sad news that William had been killed.

Now, hoping to spare the family further tragedy, Brant left the Wells house and headed for Shankland's. Immediately Kanonaron fell in beside him.

"The others are taking care of the officer we caught," he said, and Brant nodded.

As they neared the Shankland house on the edge of town, which had been bypassed by the attackers because they had earlier seen Henry and Andrew drive off toward the mill, Brant directed Kanonaron to head for the home of the Reverend Samuel Dunlop, a half mile northwest of Fort Alden.

"You know him, don't you?" Brant asked.

"I know him."

Brant nodded. "He's a fine old man. His younger sister Mary was Robert Wells's wife. Go there now and see if you can protect him and his wife. They're apt to be killed."

Kanonaron nodded and left. Brant continued to the Shankland house, which he was relieved to see still seemed untouched. He entered without knocking and was surprised to find a woman calmly working at her spinning wheel in a corner of the large front room. Five young children, the eldest only nine, all of them very frightened, clustered behind her facing the door.

"Are you Katy Shankland?" he asked her.

"I am."

"Why are you sitting here spinning when all around you your neighbors are being killed? Why haven't you fled or hidden? Haven't you heard what is happening outside?"

"I've heard," she replied. "We have nothing to fear. I am a loyal subject of King George. My husband is a friend of Joseph Brant, and if Brant is with the Indians, he will save us."

"I am Joseph Brant," he replied, "and your loyalty to the King isn't going to matter to those out there when they come in here. They will treat you as merely another Cherry Valley resident."

Her composure was fast fading and her lip trembled but she looked directly at him and her voice was level. "If in fact you are Joseph Brant, then you will save us. Henry told me that if ever there was trouble with the Indians, you would save us. Just," she added somewhat triumphantly, "as you will undoubtedly save the Wells family, who are also your friends."

Brant shook his head. "I am not in command today and I have no control over what happens." His voice softened. "The Wells family is dead already. They were very dear to me, but I was too late to help them. Perhaps I can help you. I'm not sure, but I'll do my best."

He told her to get into bed immediately and pretend she was sick and that the same should be done with the children. At this she crowded the two youngest children, Margaret and Robert, aged two and three respectively, into the large cradle together, covered them to their necks and rubbed some flour on their faces to make them look wan. The three older children, Nancy, four, Jane, seven, and Gilbert, nine, she took into bed with her.

Brant wet his finger and stuck it into a pouch at his belt. Powdered red ocher was clinging to it when he withdrew it and on the forehead of each of them, Katy included, he made his mark.

"Now," he said, nodding, "maybe you will be safe.[235] But do not object to anything anyone does here as long as you are not hurt."

Just at that moment he saw, through the window, the approach of some Senecas and he ran to the door. "There is only a sick woman here with her children," he told them. "They are sick too. I have not seen such an illness before, but it looks very bad."

Very fearful of white man's diseases, the Senecas were only too glad to go about their business. Brant waited a short while and then gave a short war whoop when he saw some of his Mohawks. Immediately they came to the house, nine of them, and Brant instructed them to stay here and protect the family until the next morning and that he would return then. She called after him, asking worriedly if he knew where Henry and Andrew were and if they were all right. He didn't reply. At the moment he didn't know, but he suspected the worst.

At the home of John Moore, delegate to the Provincial Congress, Moore himself was not at home, having two days previously gone to Albany. However, his wife and daughter were at home and on hand to lunch with them today were two young officers from the fort, Lieutenant Roland Beebe and Captain Jonas Parker, both of whom were interested beyond mere courtesy in the attractive nineteen-year-old Priscilla Moore. The officers were enjoying the warmth of the fire in the hearth and the singing of Miss Moore as her mother played the piano in accompaniment. Inside the closed cheeriness of the house, the distant outside sounds were so muffled that they had not penetrated the consciousness of the little group. Not until just about the time they were ready to stop the entertainment and sit down to lunch did a heavy booming reach them, and the officers stared at one another.

"That's a cannon!" Parker exclaimed. He and Beebe raced to the front window and looked out and then were appalled. Indians and Rangers in war paint were moving about everywhere and far in the distance the mansion of Robert Wells, high on its rise of ground, was belching a great cloud of dark smoke, at the base of which flames were beginning to show.

"Oh, my God," Beebe murmured. "Brant's attacking!"

The officers called to the women to get ready to move out, that they'd be right back. Then they ran outside. They had to go a considerable distance before the fort came into view, but they saw at once that it was surrounded and under fire. Very little firing was being returned to the enemy, but again a cannon sounded and they saw by the puff of smoke that it was shooting straight upward, meaning that the gun was being fired as a signal rather than as a weapon.

"Hell of a lot of good it's going to do to shoot up into the air," Parker growled, but both he and Beebe knew the reason; it couldn't be shot as a weapon if there were no properly placed embrasures from which to shoot at an attacking enemy. That was precisely the case at Fort Alden. Parker shook his head. "Let's get the women out of here."

They turned back but then jolted to a stop. Just in this brief time at least a score of green-coated soldiers and painted Indians had intervened between them and the Moore house. Not yet seen themselves, the two officers ducked behind a large tree and watched as the enemy ran up on the porch and burst into the house. There was nothing the pair could do and they knew it.

Parker gripped Beebe's shoulder. "You get to Van Alstine's place at Canajoharie if you can. I'll head for Schoharie. We have to spread the alarm and get some reinforcements here."

Beebe started to reply and then merely shook his head, gripped Parker's hand for a moment and then ran off to the north, dodging from cover to cover in an effort to keep from being observed. Parker did the same. Both men were able to reach the surrounding woodland unobserved.

Back at the Moore residence, both Priscilla and her mother surrendered without resistance and were taken prisoner.[236] A slightly different situation was occurring at the home of one of the other two principal Rebels the attackers were seeking. Colonel Samuel Campbell's house was north of Fort Alden on the same road, but Campbell, like Moore, was away. Yesterday he had gone to one of his distant fields to do some farmwork there and since he'd been unable to complete it, he had stayed the night in a small tenant cabin there and resumed the work today. At the Campbell residence were his wife and four children, including an infant, and Mrs. Campbell's father, Matthew Cannon, a crusty old former sea captain from the north of Ireland who was now living at Middlefield and, along with his wife, Eleanor, was merely visiting his daughter for a few days.

The only other males on hand to help in any kind of defense were some black servants. At the outbreak of the trouble, grumbling that "no damned crazy painted Injin" was going to make him give up without a fight — and against the vehement protests of Eleanor — Cannon sallied out of the house with a stock of muskets and a young black named Daniel to load for him. He fired numerous times at the approaching Indians, cackling with laughter each time he shot, but he was eventually downed with a bullet through the leg. Young Daniel was tomahawked, but Cannon's life was spared because he'd put up such a courageous defense.

While the fighting had been going on, Mrs. Campbell and her mother got to their knees inside the house and prayed for deliverance. Another of the slaves, a huge black woman called Mozzie, who was nursemaid to the children, shook her head, declaring that "the Lord God All-Mighty, he don't he'p no one what don't he'p theyselves."

With this she scooped up a Bible and thrust it into the hands of Mrs. Campbell's oldest boy, a seven-year-old. She also snatched up a blanket and then hustled the youngster out of the back door and ran with him to a fence row. Helping him to the other side, she hollowed out a little nest in the heavy brush, wrapped him in the blanket, still with the Bible in his hands, and sat him down in the hollow. Tucking the blanket around him snugly, she patted his head.

"You set still now, Georgie," she warned. "Jus' don't you move roun' for nothin', else them painted devils'll surely git you!"

Then she turned and waddled back to the house, returning to the front room just in time to look out the window and see Mr. Cannon get shot through the leg and the black youth, Daniel, tomahawked. Daniel was her son.

Another slave, William, was shot dead when he ran outside to attack the Indians, his only weapon a poker from the fireplace. However, when the Indians entered the house, no one else was harmed. Mrs. Campbell and her other four children were simply taken prisoner along with her mother and Mozzie. The house was put to the torch as soon as it was plundered.

Colonel Campbell, far distant in the field and continuing his work, paused as he heard the cannon fire and then stared aghast at the columns of dark smoke rising from the direction of town. His first impulse was to get to his home and help defend it, but when he came within sight of it and saw it engulfed in flames and surrounded by Indians, he turned and hastened toward Fort Herkimer.

As coincidence would have it, the third principal Cherry Valley resident the attackers had wanted to capture was also away when his residence was stormed. As a result of a premonition that had come to her during the night that a devastating Indian attack was imminent, forty-one-year-old Catherine Wasson Clyde had gotten little sleep and was a nervous wreck by morning.[237] The Clydes had ten children, mostly girls, and she was greatly fearful for them. As soon as her husband, Samuel, had awakened this morning, she had begged him to go to the fort and get permission for them to move in there for a little while, even into the enclosed church if necessary, as long as they were within the protection of the fort's walls. Major Clyde had never seen her so worked up and so he agreed to do what she asked and went to the fort. The officers had not yet arrived when the attack broke out and he was inside the fort when Major Whiting and Captain Hickling managed to get into the fort from their hairbreadth escape. By then, so many of the enemy were scattered throughout the town that it would have been all but suicide to go outside and move around. The Indians were so bold, in fact, that even as Clyde watched through a chink in the stockade wall, he saw one pursue Colonel Alden himself to within a short distance of the fort's gate and kill him with a tomahawk.

Back at the Clyde house, due west of the fort, a lad of twelve who had been living with the Clydes, Charles Scott, had gone outside at the first sound of trouble and moved close enough to the fort to watch what was happening. He saw the chase and death of Colonel Alden. Immediately he raced back to the house and reported what had transpired and suggested that he harness the horse to a wagon and transport Mrs. Clyde and all the children to safety. Abruptly they realized there was no time for that because far to the northeast, in the direction of the Campbell house, an ominous billow of smoke was rising.

"To the woods!" Mrs. Clyde ordered. "Follow me!"

She led them out at a run, their little white dog, Spook, following with happy yappings as if enjoying this new game. In moments the family was in concealment in the woods behind the house. Coming to one of the brooks that formed Cherry Valley Creek, Catherine waded in it so as not to leave any more footprints in the slush, carrying the two smallest children and the older children behind her carrying others and wading also. Spook trotted alongside the brook until one of the children snatched him up. He was no longer yapping. When they came to an area barren of snow, they left the water and moved to a large outcropping of rock beneath which was a sizable hollow. Within it they hid, huddling together for warmth, Mrs. Clyde and Charles Scott and nine Clyde children. *Nine!* Abruptly Mrs. Clyde realized that Abigail was not with them. No one remembered seeing her since they had left the house.

"Abbie's a big girl. She's sixteen. She can look out for herself very well," Mrs. Clyde assured the others. But inside she was sick with worry and not at all sure of her own words.

Abigail Clyde had always had a burning curiosity and it was working very actively at this time. When her mother had suggested they get to the woods immediately, she had raced upstairs to get her most prized possession, a beautiful gold pin her father had given to her on her sixteenth birthday a few months ago. While upstairs she glanced out of the window and that had been her undoing. Held by a morbid fascination, she remained rooted in place watching the destruction of Cherry Valley — the attack against the fort, the fine homes going up in flames, the killing of people she had known all her life. Not until the blast of a cannon from the fort was she jarred into the realization that she had been watching a long while. She ran downstairs only to discover everyone was gone.

Retaining her presence of mind, she ran to the barn. No one was there except Grey Tark, her father's gentle mare, in her stall. There was no time to saddle her, so Abbie simply opened the stall gate, patted Tark's neck and then climbed on the gate in order to get onto the mare's back. Using her knees and hands to guide the animal, she sent Tark into a canter into the woods at an angle from the direction her mother had taken with the others. Less than ten minutes after her departure, the house was ransacked and burned. She traveled over a mile into the woods before stopping and then, terrified at her aloneness, she tied up Tark with a long strip torn from her skirt and curled up in the hollow base of a tree for some degree of protection. Then Abbie Clyde wept.

Throughout Cherry Valley now the destruction was widespread and the horror grew. Most of the Senecas and some of the Mohawks had become steadily wilder, more destructive and crueler as the day progressed. They were virtually unopposed and became even bolder. Their finding occasional stores of liquor did little to calm them. Atrocities became more frequent and the pillaging of the town was general. After the initial attack was under way, Walter Butler directed that a continuous musket firing be maintained against Fort Alden to keep the garrison bottled up and prevent a sally being made from within, but there was nothing he could do to harm the fort without artillery. At the same time, more attention was being paid to plundering the town of any valuables. Now there was some regret among the attackers that a number of the finer homes, such as those belonging to Wells, Clyde and Campbell, had only been very haphazardly searched for loot before being burned, for much that was very valuable had been lost in these conflagrations. Now the torch was not applied until a thorough search had been made and anything worthwhile taken.

The barbarous nature of many of the attackers was only thinly disguised at best under normal circumstances and now, without restraint, it burst forth in a horrifying show of bestiality. At the Reverend Samuel Dunlop's residence a half mile northwest of Fort Alden, Kanonaron, the Mohawk, had arrived in time to preserve the lives of the aged minister and his daughter, Elizabeth, but not that of his wife. Sarah Dunlop had sealed her own fate by hitting an Indian on the head with a heavy iron frying pan and splitting his scalp so that he was stunned and bleeding profusely. Aided and abetted by a Tory officer, Lieutenant Rolf Hare, a halfbreed named William of Canajoharie, the nephew of Joseph Brant and the son of Sir William Johnson and Molly Brant, had simply run amok. He tore Sarah out of the protective arms of her husband, threw her to the ground and, as other Indians crowded around to watch, caught by the spell of his incredible barbarity, hooting in approval, he ripped and cut her clothing from her, stabbed her to death and then cut a chunk of flesh from her body and crammed it into his mouth. Becoming as frenzied, another Indian joined him and did the same and then another, and a fourth and a fifth in a weird and frightening contagion. More might have been done but it was then that Kanonaron had run up and viciously kicked William of Canajoharie away from the body and fiercely denounced the others as animals. In retaliation, Lieutenant Hare hit Kanonaron a blow that staggered him, knocking him several feet away. In a half-crouch, Kanonaron whipped out his knife. It was a dangerous moment, with William of Canajoharie and Lieutenant Hare and the blood-lusting Indians teetering on the very brink of killing Kanonaron as well. Then Captain William MacDonald strode up to them at the head of a squad of soldiers and, appalled at what had been done, denounced them even more harshly than Kanonaron had. The fury of the moment passed and the Indians, except for William of Canajoharie, backed off. His face, hands and clothing were streaked with blood not his own and his eyes held the wild, insane, ravening look of a rabid dog. His voice was a guttural croak.

"I'll have her scalp."

It was the final stroke. Elizabeth Dunlop, the dead woman's daughter, screamed, pulled away from her father and threw herself atop the mangled body of her mother, covering the head with her breast so the old woman could not be scalped. She stared up defiantly at William of Canajoharie.

The halfbreed Mohawk took a single step toward her and then found himself staring into the muzzle of Captain MacDonald's fine, long-barreled flintlock pistol at a distance of no more than six feet.

"One more step . . . one more *motion* . . . in this direction," he said softly, "and I will put this ball into your brain." He paused a moment and then, without taking his eyes from the halfbreed, added to Hare, "That goes for you, too, Lieutenant."

A pregnant hush had fallen upon those at hand and the moment of indecision stretched out interminably. Then the wildness abruptly left the eyes of the halfbreed and he stepped back a pace and resheathed his knife. His half-smile was mirthless.

"One day I will kill you, Captain."

MacDonald stared at him with cold contempt. "Only if you come at my back, like the coward you are," he said, "because if you come at me from the front, as a man would, it is you who will die."

Still with the ugly half-smile on his face, William of Canajoharie looked at the captain a long moment more and then turned and shouldered his way through the ring of spectators and, at that, the gathering broke up and the generally destructive activities resumed.

Everywhere in Cherry Valley carnage was occurring and there were scenes enough to supply a lifetime of nightmares. One of them occurred almost a mile east of the fort at the home of Hugh Mitchell, a big, bluff man long noted for his good nature. He had been working in the field, chopping out some old stumps, and was unaware of anything occurring until the dull boom of the cannon made him look around. Smoke was rising from the direction of town but, worse yet, from the direction of his own home as well. Immediately he sprinted into the woods close by and made a half circle toward the house. He was aghast when he peered out from cover and saw his place on fire and a horde of Indians and Tory Rangers just finishing looting his possessions. Of his wife and four children he could see nothing and he prayed they had been taken prisoners and not harmed.

Mitchell's prayers were not answered. As soon as the attackers moved away, he raced to the door and entered, then jolted to a halt, sickened. His wife and four children lay scattered about where they had fallen upon being tomahawked. The fire inside had not caught hold well and, though smoke still filled the place and poured out of the door and windows, there was little fire. Mitchell moved swiftly from victim to victim, hoping to find sparks of life. In only one was he rewarded. His twelve-year-old daughter, bleeding profusely from a wound on the side of her head and from being scalped, was still alive. He pulled her away from the small fire still smoldering, doused the embers with water from a half barrel and then checked the others again to make sure they were dead. He returned to his daughter and got down on his knees beside her, trying to help her. It was too dark and smoky inside and so he carried her to the doorway and propped her up with her back against the jamb. He had not had time to do anything, however, when he heard voices.

Mitchell ran to an opposite window and was shocked when he saw, less than fifty yards away, another group of Tories and Indians coming. He ran to the doorway again but knew he could never carry his daughter away fast enough to avoid detection. Hoping they would merely go past, he sped from the door, raced across the wide back lot, keeping the house between himself and the enemy, and leaped over the log fence. He dropped flat behind it just as the attackers came around the house.

The small group was led by a Tory noncommissioned officer whom Mitchell recognized — an ugly-tempered man named Gilbert Newbury[238] who was now a Ranger sergeant. The man shouted an oath and pointed when he saw the semiconscious girl propped in the doorway. When she moved an arm in a helpless manner, he ran up to her, jerking out his stained tomahawk. He swung the weapon savagely and buried it in her head, then cursed as he had a difficult time pulling it free.

With tears streaming from his eyes, Hugh Mitchell crawled on his stomach behind the fence until reaching the wood and then he ran far into it, heading for an immense hollow log he knew where he could hide and perhaps escape. But even when he got there and lay shaking inside, the vision of what he had witnessed all but deranged him. Only one thing was important anymore — a burning desire for vengeance against Sergeant Gilbert Newbury.

By two in the afternoon, Cherry Valley was a scene of almost total destruction. Every building except those within the stockaded walls of the fort was on fire and now the crackling of blazes and popping of burning wood had largely replaced the gunfire, although here and there shots were still being fired against the fort. Soldiers inside the fort were also still shooting sporadically whenever an enemy showed himself within range, but this was only infrequently at best and the shooting was largely ineffective.

Taking advantage of a lull that he thought might be preliminary to an all-out attack on Fort Alden, Major Daniel Whiting, having now taken command, hurriedly wrote two similar messages. The first was addressed to the nearest possible help, Colonel William Butler at Schoharie:

Cherry Valley, Novr 11th, 1778

Dear Col: —
This day at 11 o'clock I was attacked by a large body of Indians, who still keep up a steady fire. I would, therefore, have you do what you can for our assistance.

I am your humble servant,
D. Whiting, Major
P.S. Col. Alden is dead.

His second letter, to General Hand in Albany, was essentially the same and asked for a reinforcement. He apologized for not being able to take time to give particulars. Whiting had no idea how he was going to get the messages through, but as soon as any sort of opportunity occurred he would dispatch them.

Outside, the Indians were gradually bringing together into one central area south of the fort, but out of range of the soldiers' musket fire, all the plunder they had gathered up in the various houses before setting them afire. In this same area were herded the sixty prisoners under a strong guard.[239] Most of them were in shock at the barbarities they had witnessed and petrified with fear in the belief that any wrong move might be cause enough for a tomahawk to strike or a sword to slash.

The day had remained blustery and cold, the sun hidden behind the heavy mantle of leaden clouds as, off and on during the day, a dismal rain had fallen. Now, at the orders of Walter Butler, all of the men who were prisoners were forced to remove their clothing and stand naked and shivering in a group. The women, ill clothed for the weather, were permitted to remain clad. It was now about 3:30 P.M. and even though sunset was yet an hour away, the day was growing darker and a certain nervousness had begun manifesting itself among the Indians.

In another half hour, fearful that word might somehow have gotten out to surrounding areas and an attack might be mounted against them, the whole force, Rangers, Indians and captives — with the latter forced to carry the plunder — began a nightmarish exodus southward down the valley. Fortunately, the evening's march was not long. It also did not involve all the Indians. A certain segment of them remained behind and continued sporadically firing at the fort and destroying what buildings remained.

The only house still untouched was the Shankland place, where Brant's nine Mohawks were still in possession and where Katy Shankland and her children still lay in their beds shuddering with fear. They had not been harmed and Brant had said he would be back to help them, but he had not reappeared. The Mohawks had left the woman and her children alone, but they'd made the inside of the house a shambles. They had split open featherbedding and, laughing uproariously, scattered the contents everywhere. When they became hungry, they went out in back and brought in a pig and butchered it on the floor, then dressed it out and half-roasted chunks of it in the fireplace. They also went into the cellar and got all the winter butter and finished up all the bread in the house, but gave a few pieces to Mrs. Shankland and her children. Numerous times Little Beard's Senecas came to destroy the house but passed it by when the Mohawks claimed it and said they would take care of it when they were finished with it. Now it was the last house remaining.

In the meanwhile, the prisoners only moved two miles down the valley before camping for the night, with the captives huddled together, wet, cold and utterly terrified. Groups of Indians kept passing back and forth between the camp and the burning town, each group that came to the camp carrying more of the plunder still being found.

Major Samuel Clyde's wife, Catherine, still hidden in a dense clump of brush with nine of her children plus the twelve-year-old boy, Charles Scott, and the little dog named Spook, tried to calm her little ones, telling them that although it would be a long, cold night, at least they were safe here, but that they would have to remain still until at least the next morning because if they were discovered they probably would be killed. Her words and seeming calmness were reassuring to them, but she wished someone could reassure her. Inwardly she was teetering on the brink of panic and she had grave doubts that any of them would get out of this alive. All it would take to bring the Indians down upon them was one of Spook's yapping spells. She loved the dog but now kept him close beside her with her hand on his collar, for if he began barking, she was fully prepared to strangle him to death. More than anything else, she feared what might have happened to Abbie and prayed for her daughter's safety. Throughout the evening the glow of Cherry Valley burning was reflected from the low clouds and frequently they heard Indians passing and repassing nearby, but they remained undetected.

By seven o'clock, some time after full darkness had descended, no more gunfire could be heard. There were still survivors in the fort and hidden in the surrounding woods, but Cherry Valley was utterly silent and no one moved about within it. At just about this same time, a letter was being written in haste at his Mohawk River headquarters by Colonel Fred K. Fisher to General Hand at Albany.

> *7 o'clock at night, Tryon City, Novr 11th, 1778*
>
> *Honoured Sir:*
>
> *This minute I received intelligence from Cherry Valley by Martin G. van Alstyne at Canajoharie, that Lieut. Beebe came from that place, and gave the following account: that Lieut. Beebe went to one Mr. Moore's to dine, nigh upon twelve o'clock this day. When he was in the house, said Beebe heard a cannon shoot, and looked out and saw Mr. Wells' house in a blazing fire, and the enemy all around the fort; that the aforesaid Beebe could not get into the fort. Captain Parker was in company with him. Parker went to Schoharie, and Beebe to van Alstyne's. Said Beebe thinks that all the field officers are taken prisoner at the house of Wells; and after Beebe left Cherry Valley, they kept a constant firing.*
>
> *I am, Sir, your humble serv^t.*
> *FRED K. FISHER, Col.*

Hardly before an express messenger had galloped off toward Albany with the letter, Fisher was putting the wheels into motion to get reinforcements to Cherry Valley, but it was much too late now. The destruction there was all but complete. Seventy-four people had been killed — forty-two of them military, mostly at or near the Wells residence, and thirty-two civilians. Thirty-two out of thirty-three houses had been burned, along with thirty-one barns, two mills and a blacksmith's shop.

Even though Cherry Valley's Fort Alden garrison numbered some three hundred regular soldiers, none of the attackers was killed and the only one even injured was the Indian who had been hit on the head with a frying pan by Sarah Dunlop. Due to the culpability of one man, Cherry Valley had paid a very dear price. That man was Colonel Ichabod Alden.[240]

[*November 12, 1778 — Thursday*]

When relief in the form of a military reinforcement did not appear in Cherry Valley in the early morning hours, an uneasy silence overhung the smoldering ruins of the town. The single boom of the cannon within the walls of Fort Alden was the only sound for a long while to break the unnatural stillness.

More than a mile distant from the fort, Catherine Wasson Clyde heard the report of the gun and tears filled her eyes. She stood up stiffly, her whole body aching from the cold of the long night and the hunched position in an attempt to keep warm. Around her the ten children looked up at her hopefully, shivering, saying nothing. She thought the gun meant that the garrison — possibly including her own husband — was still in possession of the fort. If so, then perhaps the big gun was a signal that it was all clear and safe to come in. If not . . . She felt a shiver run down her back and knew it was not from the cold alone. She knew she couldn't survive another night similar to last night.

"Charlie," she said, addressing the only one of the children who was not her own, "we're going to start moving toward the fort now. I would like you to move ahead of us, as fast as you can, to sort of see what's happening. If our people are in the fort, bring help. If not, try to get back to warn us."

Shivering badly and with teeth chattering, twelve-year-old Charles Scott nodded and came to his feet. He walked slowly at first, stiffly, but then faster and finally broke into a trot. It was good to be moving again. Anything was better than crouching as they had all night.

Catherine and the others, with the older children helping the younger, moved toward the fort now, too, but at a much slower pace. By the time they came to the edge of the woods, they saw a detachment of a dozen men coming their way and abruptly Catherine Clyde felt a wash of emotion such as she'd never before experienced. Not only was help coming, the leader of the group was Major Samuel Clyde.

Moving faster, she led the children to the creek bank and then to a place where a tree had long ago fallen across the water, forming a sort of natural bridge. One by one the children crossed, the two youngest being carried over by the eldest. But when it came Catherine's turn, she was shaking so badly she couldn't do it.

"Come on, Cath," Clyde was coaxing, holding out a hand imploringly toward her. "Come on."

She tried, but she just couldn't cope with the slickness of the log. The first time she slipped off standing up, but the second time she fell heavily and hurt her hip. The third time she managed to get on the log but then could only stand there, shaking and crying. It was the first time she had cried since all this began and she just couldn't help herself now. Clyde started to kick off his shoes but one of his privates suddenly said, "I'll get her, Major," and he plunged into the bitterly cold water, which was waist deep here. The current tugged at him but he pulled himself across by holding onto the log and then he took the major's wife by the hand.

"Trust me, Mrs. Clyde," he murmured. "Just take a good grip on my hand and let me lead you across. We'll make it just fine." He tried not to stammer but the cold was affecting him badly and his lips had become bluish, his actions stiff and not well coordinated.

She took his hand and, with him in the water and she on the log, he began leading her across. With painstaking slowness they inched their way and then, just as they got near the middle, there was the sound of rifle fire and several bullets plowed into the water close to them, sending up little geysers, and others struck the log right at her feet. The difficult passage suddenly became much easier and without knowing how she did it, Catherine was abruptly moving swiftly and with sureness on the log, pulling the young soldier along behind her in the water. They made it ashore and she all but fell into Clyde's arms, crying his name over and over.

Soldiers snatched up the younger of the children and carried them while others took the hands of the older ones and everyone ran toward the fort. There was more gunfire, but somehow they got there safely. Just as they were approaching the gate, they heard the drumming of hooves and turned to look. Approaching them as fast as Grey Tark could gallop, sixteen-year-old Abigail was guiding the mare with a twig in one hand, hanging on to the mane for dear life with the other. She was no more than a hundred yards away, but then some Indians charged out of the woods, cutting her off, and she wheeled Tark around and galloped back toward the woods again. In a moment she was gone from sight, but the sound of her mournful, wailing cry still hung in the air. The Clydes hastened inside the fort and the large gate was closed and barred behind them. With one of Major Whiting's shirts on, which the commander gave her, Catherine Clyde stayed outside and kept watch for Abbie's return. Abbie did not come back. [241]

The Indians had returned in reasonably large numbers now to complete any destruction they had neglected the evening before and to gather up what livestock could still be taken. The horses, cattle and sheep that could be herded they took with them back down the valley toward the camp of the previous night. Those that refused to be herded or would not move along well enough were killed in their tracks.

At the Shankland house, Joseph Brant had just returned, his features grim and his carriage weary, as if he had not slept at all the previous night. After shaking his head at the mess his warriors had made of the house and murmuring a few words to them in the Mohawk tongue, he turned to Katy Shankland and told her to get up and dressed hurriedly. He and Kanonaron, who had returned with him, helped get the children dressed in all the clothing they had.

He then murmured instructions to Kanonaron and put the four-year-old Nancy on his shoulders and lifted young Robert up in his arms.

"Trust me and follow me," he told Katy. "Bring the other children."

They left the house through the back door and, with Kanonaron and his nine warriors in a cluster behind them so they couldn't be seen, walked directly to the edge of the woods. There the warriors, except for Brant, broke away and returned to the house. Brant and the family continued into the woods about half a mile. In a secluded hollow they stopped and he gave them a parcel of Indian bread from his pouch.

"This will hold you," he said. "Stay here and keep hidden. The others may search for you and if they find you, I will not be able to save you any further." For the first time a faint smile touched his lips. "I have some good news. I found Henry and Andrew. They have not been hurt, but they're captives. I will try to set them free. Do as I say and stay here, well hidden. I'll tell them where you are so they can come and find you."

Katy Shankland reached out and put her hand on Brant's upper arm. "You're a good man, Joseph Brant," she said. "Just as Henry always maintained. I don't know how we can repay you."

Brant shook his head. "There is no need for repayment. War should be a thing men fight between them. It should not be visited upon women and children. Keep well. Keep hidden. Good-bye."

He left them then and by the time he returned to the house it had already been plundered by the Mohawks and was now afire — the last standing structure outside the walls of Fort Alden. At a motion from Brant, the Mohawks fell in behind him and they skirted Fort Alden out of effective rifle range and headed toward where the captives were being held. They were out of sight and hearing of Cherry Valley when a detachment of three hundred militia from the Mohawk Valley, under Colonel Jacob Klock, arrived within four miles northwest of Cherry Valley and were spotted by some parties of Tory Rangers that had been sent out by Captain Walter Butler.[242] The Rangers hied back to Cherry Valley and then to where the prisoners were being held and, even though it was now fairly late in the day, a rapid withdrawal was begun lest the militia approaching was only the vanguard of a strong retaliatory force.

All of the prisoners, especially the naked men, had suffered severely from the cold the preceding night and during this sudden enforced march it was very difficult for them to move well. Little sympathy was shown for infirmity, difficulty or weakness and they were hurried along at the points of jabbing knives and spears.

Toward the middle of the line, somewhat apart from the Rangers in the lead and the Senecas bringing up the rear, Brant and his Mohawks moved along with the rest. Brant had gradually brought himself close to that portion of the straggling line of prisoners where Henry Shankland and eighteen-year-old Andrew, naked and suffering from the cold along with the rest, stumbled on almost automatically in a haze of personal agony.

At one point, sixty-one-year-old Eleanor McKinery Cannon stumbled and fell. Two men close by, long past any sense of embarrassment at their nudity, helped her to her feet and she moved on. By this time the only Indians nearby were Brant and some of his warriors. Abruptly he reached out and cut away the thong that bound Shankland and his son neck to neck.

"Listen to me!" he said. He told them where Katy and the children were hidden in the woods and then ended with: "Now, slip into the woods and hide till the line is past. Be sure the rear guard, five minutes behind the rest, passes you before you move."

Without another word, Brant moved off. Shankland and his son, revitalized beyond anything they had thought possible, walked a little farther and then abruptly sprinted to one side, leaped over a large log and then squirmed down into a small space on the other side, flattening themselves as much as possible. For a long while more captives, soldiers and Indians passed within mere yards of them on the other side. Then all was quiet. They remained still and after another five or six minutes a group of twenty more Senecas passed, occasionally talking quietly among themselves. Again there was quiet and after another five minutes the two came to their feet and, avoiding the trail they had just come along, circled widely back toward Cherry Valley.[243]

By now the rapid march had carried the other captives quite far and patience with those who had begun faltering wore thin. Soon the prisoners learned the hazard of not being able to keep up. Once again Eleanor Cannon stumbled and fell. She got to her feet slowly, this time with no one nearby to help her. Fifty feet ahead, her daughter, Mrs. Campbell, turned to come back to help her but it was too late. A warrior whipped out his tomahawk and chopped the elderly woman across the back of the neck, severing her spine. He scalped her and left her lying where she had fallen. Mrs. Campbell was given no opportunity to grieve. There were other problems besetting her, not the least of which was that her youngest child had also begun to falter. When warriors glowered at the child and began fingering their tomahawks, she picked up the little one and carried him. He was heavy and, feeling her own strength failing, she wondered in an abstract manner how long she could last.

Back at Cherry Valley the militia, realizing the enemy was gone, emerged and began the job of looking for survivors and collecting the remains of mutilated and burned bodies and returning them to the fort. Hugh Mitchell, having emerged from hiding in the woods, hitched himself to a sled and pulled the bodies of his wife and four children to the fort, all but blinded by his own tears. Those bodies, along with all the others that could be found, were buried in a common grave dug in the old graveyard behind the church inside the fort.

Late in the evening, having covered far fewer miles than he had anticipated due to the increasing inability of the captives to travel any faster, Captain Walter N. Butler at last called a halt. He ordered that all the prisoners be brought together in one tight group. While this was being done — to the great fear of the prisoners that these were their last moments and that they were being brought together to be butchered — Butler sat on a log and wrote a letter. Afflicted with a growing apprehension that his force might be pursued and captured, he was now taking steps to portray himself as a humane person and to shift most of the blame for the atrocities to Brant and the Mohawks. At the same time, he also hoped to secure the release of his mother and younger brothers from imprisonment in Albany.

Butler ordered that clothing be returned to the naked male prisoners now and as soon as all of the Cherry Valley captives were in a group before him, he addressed them, telling them that all of the women and children — with the exception of the families of John Moore and Samuel Campbell — were now going to be released and they could return to Cherry Valley themselves.[244] There was great joy among them but also great sadness because the captive men were not being released and there was a dread foreboding that many of these husbands and fathers would never be reunited with their families.

The only man released with the women and children was the aged Reverend Samuel Dunlop. Into his care was entrusted the letter that Butler had just composed, which included a listing of the names of the prisoners he was releasing. It was addressed to General Philip Schuyler at Albany.

near Cherry Valley, Nov. 12th, 1778

Sir,

I am induced by humanity to permit the prisoners, whose names I send you herewith, to remain, lest the inclemency of the season, and their naked and helpless situation, might prove fatal to them; and expect that you will release an equal number of our people in your hands, amongst whom I expect you will permit Mrs. Butler and family to come to Canada. But if you insist upon it, I do engage to send you, moreover, an equal number of yours taken either by Rangers or Indians, and will leave it to you to name the persons.

I have done everything in my power to restrain the fury of the Indians from hurting women and children, or killing the prisoners who fell into our hands; and would have more effectually have prevented them, but they were so much enraged by the late destruction of their village Oquaga, by your people.[245] I shall always continue to act in the same manner. I look upon it as beneath the character of a soldier to wage war with women and children. I am sure that you are conscious that Colonel Butler or myself have no desire that your women or children shall be hurt. But be assured that if you persevere in detaining my fa-

ther's family with you, that we shall no longer take the same pains in restraining the Indians from making prisoners of women and children, as we have heretofore done.

I am, Sir, your humble servant,
WALTER N. BUTLER
Captain of the Rangers

TO: Gen¹ Schuyler

Despite what he had written, no one was fooled by Butler's release of the prisoners into thinking him to be a great humanitarian. The horror of what he and the Iroquois had done to Cherry Valley had burned itself deeply into a multitude of American minds and a great vengeance would have to be exacted before the matter would be shelved.

CHAPTER V

[*January 1, 1779 — Friday*]

AFTER reading the letter, General George Washington looked for a long quiet moment at the man seated across the desk from him. The New York governor, George Clinton, returned the gaze soberly and then made a slight motion toward the letter, which Washington had dropped to the desktop.

"It speaks for itself, General," Clinton said, "but maybe I should stress the fact that the help requested is only food and clothing, not troops. Obviously, troops can't do much to help Cherry Valley now."

"Except," Washington replied, "insofar as they may prevent a recurrence of such a situation."

"The Indians and Tories don't hit where there are sufficient troops to retaliate. They pick their target long in advance and take advantage of weaknesses. There is no way that we in New York, or those in Pennsylvania, can substantially enough fortify every frontier town in order to prevent attack. Which brings us back to the problems underlined by Clyde's letter there. What do we do to help such people? How do we prevent its happening again?"

"I think," said Washington slowly, "there is a way." He picked up the letter and once again read the bitterly eloquent words that had been penned by Major Samuel Clyde at Canajoharie on the Mohawk:

To His Excellency, George Clinton, Esq.,
Governor of the State of New York, at Poughkeepsie.
Sir: —
The unhappy circumstances that we are reduced to, by the late massacre and destruction by Butler and Brant at Cherry Valley, I cannot help acquainting

you of, and of the hard struggle and difficulty we have had these two years past to maintain our settlement. Being a frontier, with the disaffected amongst us doing their endeavors to disappoint all our measures by giving the enemy intelligence and robbing us of our horses and cattle, we could scarce lay down one night in fear of our lives.

This last spring when we found that the enemy were collecting at Unadilla, and that they intended to cut off the frontier settlements, we immediately informed our generals at Albany that we must either quit the settlement or they must send us some troops to help us; which, if they could not do so, to give us notice, that we might move away. But they seemed to make light of our intelligence and sent us word that we must by no means quit the post, that they intended to protect it; but that they did not think we should be disturbed either by Indians or Tories that summer. This was about twelve days before Cobleskill was burnt.

Then we assembled together and fortified our meeting house, brought in our provisions and effects and, with the assistance of the militia, maintained the post until Colonel Alden arrived with the Continental troops. He immediately ordered us out of the garrison which we had made ourselves. He would not allow us the liberty to keep one chest in it — that he would protect us. Few of us having wagons to ride our effects away, we were obliged to carry them back to our houses again and so continued there, in fear, till we were drove out by the enemy.

General Hand being in Cherry Valley a few days before the attack, recommended us to move our effects into the fort but, when he was gone, Colonel Alden would not allow it, saying that he had out good scouts and that he would give us timely notice when to move in. It was not in our power to convince him that the enemy would attempt to come there; which has occasioned us the loss of our all. The greater part of us have neither provisions, body clothes nor bed clothes to cover us in this cold season of the year. If we cannot get some relief to help us through the winter, we must suffer either by cold or hunger. We cannot get either clothing or grain to buy for money if we had it.

We are mostly moved out to the River, but we can get no farther. The inhabitants here are in general riding down their grain and effects and storing them. They hold themselves in readiness to move as soon as they hear of the approach of the enemy, and those that can't help themselves must fall a sacrifice to the enemy.

This, Sir, is real fact.

From your Most Obedient and
Most Humble Servant,
SAM CLYDE.

The American commander in chief sighed and shook his head. "We can't permit such a thing to happen again. It should not have happened to begin with."

Clinton stiffened, taking the remark as an effront. He was frowning as he spoke. "Sir, that is precisely why I am here. I agree that it should not have happened to begin with, but the problem is in properly defending the frontier. How do we send each community the protection it needs when the cream of the men of every community are already in the military service and ordinarily serving elsewhere, as on your fronts. This is not," he added hastily, "to say your actions are not of the utmost importance, but what do we do on the New York frontier? What do they do on the Pennsylvania frontier? How do we combat an enemy that can materialize out of the wilderness, strike and destroy and disappear again?"

George Washington stood with his hands clasped behind his back, staring into the fireplace. He was thinking of the remarkable degree of success of the two minor expeditions against the Indians last fall before Cherry Valley — the one led by Colonel Hartley northward from the Wyoming Valley of Pennsylvania and the one led by Colonel William Butler southward out of Schoharie against Oquaga and the other Indian strongholds in New York.

George Washington now knew what must be done.

So long as there were Indians in western New York and Pennsylvania who were lending their support to the British, such attacks as those that had occurred at Wyoming and Cherry Valley, Cobleskill and German Flats and Andrustown would continue. To prevent further such outrages, the perpetrators would have to be rendered incapable of mounting attacks. In essence, the Iroquois League would have to be destroyed. Washington turned his gaze from the fire to Clinton and answered the New York governor's questions in a single sentence:

"The only certain way of preventing Indian ravages is to carry the war vigorously into their own country."

[January 21, 1779 — Thursday]

The seventeen warriors of the Mingo Confederation experienced an increased respect for the British liaison officer to the Indians, Simon Girty, as a result of what had occurred. Just as Girty had predicted, the gate of Fort Laurens in the eastern Ohio country opened and the wagon detachment rode out directly toward their place of concealment.

This fort on Indian soil was a hateful thing to the Mingoes and when one of their scouts had ridden up with word of a full wagonload of supplies having just entered the installation from the east, they wanted to attack immediately. Girty, who had been counciling with the chiefs of the tribes making up this loose confederacy, discouraged this. They could do nothing against the fort with only the few men in this party but, if they waited, the wagon and detachment would come out again soon and could be taken in ambush.

So now, coming toward them on his return trip to Fort McIntosh in Pennsylvania, was Captain John Clark, his sergeant and fourteen men of the 8th Pennsylvania Regiment, wholly unsuspecting of danger. As they drew close to the place selected for the ambush, the men could be heard laughing and talking and one of the Mingo warriors grew too eager to be the first to draw blood. He rose and shot the sergeant through the chest. In the turmoil that resulted, the voice of Captain Clark could be heard above the fusillade of shots shouting, "To the fort! To the fort!" and the company wheeled about in a frenzied dash for safety.

Girty's party followed, keeping mostly to cover so their scant numbers would not be determined. One of the soldiers was captured when his horse stumbled in a hole and threw him; another who wheeled back to his defense was shot dead. Four more of the soldiers were wounded before making it back to the fort, where the huge gate in the east wall was slammed and then locked behind them.

The Mingoes still kept to cover, taking occasional long shots at imprudent heads that showed momentarily above the walls. The captured soldier, breaking free of the Mingo who was holding him, ran into the open. Before he could shout to his comrades that the Mingoes were only a small party, an arrow buried itself in his back and he staggered. He took two more steps, holding a hand out toward the fort as if begging aid, and then another arrow caught him in the back of the head with an ugly sound.

Now Girty turned to Chief Hailstone, who was in charge of the warrior party, and told him to keep firing upon the fort at intervals from all sides. He would go immediately to his headquarters at Detroit and return as soon as possible with men and ammunition. Until then, they should maintain a siege. Hailstone nodded and Girty spurred off.

Less than an hour later, just after the Mingoes had split their small force, with five each going to the north and south sides and seven remaining at the point of ambush, the gate of Fort Laurens opened briefly and a rider galloped off to the south, hoping to outrun the savages and reach Fort McIntosh for help. He was still fifty feet or more from the protective cover of the woods when three shots rang out and he slumped in the saddle, then fell. A trio of Mingoes rode out and as one caught the loose horse, another triumphantly scalped the soldier and then shook the hairpiece tauntingly at the little fort. A volley of shots sent him hopping back onto his horse and into the woods.

The garrison in Fort Laurens was now convinced it was surrounded.

[*February 10, 1779 — Wednesday*]

Throughout January and into this month of February, a whole series of councils of the Iroquois had taken place at Fort Niagara. The British installation was having one of the busiest winters in its career, for the influx of Indians who had taken up camp under the shelter of its walls was substantial. Foremost among them were the displaced Mohawks under Brant. Now they had become nearly nomadic, since their villages on the Mohawk and Susquehanna had been taken over or destroyed.

The Senecas, to their credit, had offered the Mohawks land along the Genesee upon which to settle, but that was Seneca land and the Mohawks were too proud to accept, too proud to allow themselves to become, in substance if not in fact, the wards of a brother tribe of the Iroquois League. And so, unlike the Senecas also gathered here at Fort Niagara in great numbers for the winter, the Mohawks came and went with greater frequency than normally occurred among the Indians during the winter months. Raid after raid was led by Joseph Brant against the weaker and more isolated stations and homes, usually with considerable success, but no one knew better than Brant himself that these were hardly more than token forays and that more concentrated efforts had to be made, such as those already achieved at Wyoming and Cherry Valley.

It was significant that while the Mohawks, Cayugas and Senecas were at Fort Niagara in numbers, there was only half of the warrior force that might have been expected from the Onondagas. The Tuscaroras were represented only by a small handful of men and the Oneidas were wholly absent. It was indicative of the severe rupture within the League and a fact that some of the prominent Indians present took to be an omen of grave consequence. One of the most outspoken of these was young Sagoyewatha — Red Jacket — of the Senecas.

"Hear what I have to say and be guided by my words," he told them at one of the grand councils. "The ice this winter is thin and where once we walked upon it boldly, we must now feel our way with care, lest it collapse beneath us. We have walked into the lair of the great panther and we have slapped him in the face with our hard hand and we have brought tears to his eyes with the blow, *but we have not killed him!* His claws are still long and his teeth are still strong. And now, for what has been done to him, he must be very angry and we must tremble as he growls with his rage.

"Hear me, brothers! Believe me! I see what lies ahead for us and it is bad. *Very bad!* Behold my vision: I see many of our villages destroyed — forty of them or even more reduced to ashes. I see hunger pinching the bellies of our people. I hear the crying of our women and children. I see diseases touching us and I see us losing the wisdom of our elders because the old will not be able to

withstand such diseases and they will die. I see bad times ahead unless now —
now, before it is too late! — we beg the Americans for peace."

Violence very nearly broke out at his words and there were few who supported him. He was jeeringly called "cow-killer" by those who opposed him
because of his alleged fear of killing anything more dangerous than that. They
labeled him a coward, afraid to fight, and they were scornful of all he had to
say. And they berated him soundly for such advocacy at the very time when
Brant was striking the enemy again and again in the name of the League.

"Destruction of villages? Hunger? Diseases? Bad times? Sagoyewatha," they
told him, "look around you. Do we not have good food here in abundance,
provided by our friends the British? Does not our Father the King continue to
give us weapons and men to support us? Are we and our families not protected
here? Are we not provided with good liquor to drink before and after our con-
tests with the Americans? Have we not shared in the bounty of plunder that has
been taken, and in the prisoners?[246] Have we not been paid well for scalps? In
the face of all this, why then should we even think of begging the Americans
for peace?"

As if to underline the validity of their arguments, they pointed to how everywhere on the frontier the Americans were feeling the power of the Indians —
not only in the Mohawk Valley where Brant was centering his activities, but
on the Susquehanna, where Gu-cinge was presently active, on the Allegheny
and throughout western Pennsylvania, where the Delawares were attacking, in
eastern Ohio country and on the upper Ohio River, where the Mingoes were
disrupting them, supported by the British at Detroit, and even at the budding
American settlements in the Kan-tuc-kee country, where the Shawnees were
attacking.

"No, Sagoyewatha," they reiterated, "you are wrong! Go back to your cow-
killing and let warriors do their work. Things have never looked so good for us.
Last year we crippled the Americans. This year we will destroy them!"

But there were those in a position to know who did not sneer at what
Sagoyewatha had to say. One of these was Big Tree, chief of the village of
Conesus. Having spent such a long time with General Washington the preceding year, watching how Americans fought, he strongly felt that what Sagoyewatha said was true and that very bad times were ahead for the Iroquois.

[*February 15, 1779 — Monday*]

Colonel John Gibson, commander of Fort Laurens in the eastern Ohio country, blew on his hands to take the chill off them, but the stiffness of his fingers
made the writing jerky and childlike in execution. Gibson had always been
proud of his ordinarily neat and flowing handwriting and so he now looked
with distaste at what he had written:

Midnight, 15th Inst.

Gen¹ McIntosh, Cdg.

Sir: We are under siege. Four dead, four wounded. Food and powder low. Burning furnishings for warmth. Size of enemy unknown, but not likely over fifty. Help needed with all dispatch.

Yr. Obt. Svt.
J. GIBSON, Col.

He blew on the ink to dry it, folded the paper and slid it into a leather pouch. This he handed to the private who had been standing close by. Nodding, the soldier opened his greatcoat and thrust the pouch deep inside his blouse, then buttoned up again. The two men shook hands.

"Luck and godspeed," Gibson murmured.

Again the private nodded and a few minutes later he eased himself up and over the pickets from the ramparts and felt the rope snug up tight under his armpits.

"See you soon," he whispered to the pair holding the rope.

There was a faint scraping sound as the line snaked through the grip of the two and over the stockade wall. The messenger must have been nearly to the ground when there came two heavy thunking sounds and a muffled cry. One of the men lowering the private stuck his head past the picket points to look down and in the dim glow of moonlight he saw, twenty feet below, with his feet just off the ground, the private hanging limply with two arrows projecting from his back. Then came the crash of a rifle and splinters flew from the top of one picket beside the observer's face. The two men released the rope and scrambled for cover.

[*February 23, 1779 — Tuesday*]

Only a day earlier or later would have spelled the difference, but of course Colonel Gibson couldn't know. Fort Laurens needed wood desperately or the men would freeze. Daily, as the siege continued, he became ever more convinced that only a handful of Indians was around the fort. And so this morning he had made a decision. He called his garrison to assembly and expressed his belief about the lack of Indians, then asked for eighteen volunteers to take a wagon out of the fort to gather firewood. He got them, plus Captain John Clark to lead them.

At precisely this same moment, the Indians who had been besieging the fort met a force of well-armed Sandusky Wyandots and Mingoes at a rendezvous point out of sight but within a mile of the fort. At their head rode two British officers — Simon Girty and Captain Henry Byrd. The total Indian party had now been increased to one hundred and forty.

The wagon came out of the fort with eight men fanned out on each side, walking, their rifles ready. Even the wagoner held the reins in his left hand and a rifle in his right. Captain Clark moved along briskly in the lead, also on foot, thirty yards ahead of the team of horses, his head moving back and forth ceaselessly and his eyes taking in every detail of the surrounding cover.

They reached the edge of the woods unscathed and then Clark disappeared for several minutes. He returned smiling and with the welcome assurance that evidently the Indians were gone. Greatly relieved, the men relaxed a little and moved with the wagon into the woods.

The attack, when it came, was impressive, even to Captain Byrd, who sat on his horse beside Girty a quarter of a mile away to watch. The Indians had split their force in half and now, at a signal from Hailstone, seventy warriors galloped from the woods on the north and south, closed the gap in the center and then turned to swoop down upon the wagon and its escort. At the same time, anticipating that a covering fire would come from the fort, the remaining seventy Indians, thirty-five on each side, poured a hot fire at the blockhouse posts and embrasures. Those inside were scarcely able to show themselves enough to fire back.

The massacre was swift and complete. Within five minutes all eighteen soldiers and Captain Clark were dead and in the process of being scalped. Three men inside the fort were wounded and the total Indian losses were two men wounded, only one of them seriously.

Captain Byrd reached out a hand to squeeze Girty's arm. He was very impressed. "Your Indians, sir," he said, "are fighting devils. Thank God they are on our side!"

[*March 14, 1779 — Sunday*]

Unlike most winters during the times of Indian troubles, when the severity of the season caused a sharp cutback or even absence of frontier attacks, this year of 1779 was different. Everywhere throughout the frontier of New York and Pennsylvania, settlements were being hit and destroyed. In the Mohawk Valley and the valley of the Schoharie, southward from there in the area of Susquehanna at settlements downriver from Wyoming all the way to Sunbury, and in the area of Fort Pitt and the rivers above it — the Monongahela Valley southward and the Allegheny northward — destruction was rampant, though everywhere on a relatively small scale. Isolated homes, barns and mills were being burned and individuals were being shot from ambush or their families attacked in their homes. It was a time of terror unparalleled on a frontier where terror had always been known. The names of Joseph Brant and Gu-cinge, Hailstone and Black Fish, She-me-ne-to and Little Beard were spoken in fearful whispers. Was there no surcease? Was it always to be this way? Was there never to be relief from the horror?

Eleven days ago — on the third day of March — the situation had become critical. The daily food ration had been reduced to half a cup of parched corn and a sliver of jerked beef per man. Every burnable stick of wood within Fort Laurens had been consumed by the dwindling fire. Two of the injured had died and others might if they did not get adequate attention soon.

Private Jacob Lynch, an eighteen-year-old New Yorker, insisted he could get through if given the opportunity. Colonel John Gibson did not believe any man could get through, but he nodded with what he hoped would appear to be assurance and granted the youth permission to try.

For three hours that afternoon, with the help of his comrades, Lynch had blackened his clothing with bits of charcoal. He was given two cups of parched corn and a half-pound of jerky to put into his pouch. He wanted no gun, knowing its weight would slow him, but in his belt he carried knife and tomahawk.

As darkness fell they had blackened his face and hands with charcoal as well. It was a very dark night and in the midst of it, slowly and very quietly, the gate was opened just enough for him to slide through and immediately drop to a prone position, in which he squirmed soundlessly to the nearest section of woods, about a hundred yards distant. He was exultant as he gained his objective. There he had moved into a crouch and slunk farther and farther from the fort. Not until he was three miles distant was he sure that he had gotten away and his young heart nearly burst within him in triumph.

He had no way of knowing that at the very moment he had been blackening his clothing, the Wyandots and Mingoes had decided to end the forty-one-day siege. Quietly and unseen, they had stolen away and were gone long before dark. When Private Lynch left the fort, the entire garrison could have ridden out weaponless with impunity.

Now, at the beginning of this third week of March, the garrison at Fort Laurens stood and shifted uneasily and stared at the ground as General McIntosh dressed them down with an anger he had rarely exhibited. He had never, he declared, witnessed supposedly civilized men — soldiers at that! — behave so much like animals. He pointed an accusing finger at the splintered and despoiled flour barrels and the scattered foodstuffs and clothing lying in the mud. Was this the way civilized, disciplined men greeted succor when it arrived? He was well aware of the ordeal they had undergone and sympathized with their desire to eat heartily once more and dress warmly, but for an entire company of soldiers to virtually mob a supply wagon bringing them what they needed was unheard of. Now, ruined in the mud, lay close to half the supplies that had been brought, cast aside and trampled underfoot as the men of the garrison had swarmed over the wagon, stuffing edibles into their mouths as if they were a group of maniacs. The packhorses, with other supplies, had bolted in white-eyed terror as the men rushed upon them, and of the fourteen laden

horses only four had been recovered. For this alone, General McIntosh contended, every soldier in this fort ought, by right, to be court-martialed and
flogged.

The emaciated men shuffled their feet guiltily, unable to express the incredible relief and wild abandon that had swept through them at the sight of the
approach of McIntosh and his supplies. What did he know of hunger? What
would he have done at the approach of fresh food after living for weeks on
nothing more than a handful of parched corn daily?

They waited expectantly now for his comments, knowing that he must certainly order the fort abandoned as too weak and too remote to be defended or
maintained adequately. When, instead, he ordered them to stay on and defend
this miserable outpost, a deep and very nearly rebellious gloom enshrouded
them.

[*April 15, 1779 — Thursday*]

With the arrival of the major general presently seated before him, George
Washington was ready to launch a campaign of genocide — a campaign carefully calculated to destroy the enemy Iroquois.

Once he had decided upon eliminating the Iroquois as a force to be considered, George Washington had moved ahead with his plans at great speed. Of
necessity, the first step had been to secure approval from the Continental
Congress for the proposed campaign. This was not difficult to come by, especially in view of the recent disasters suffered at both Wyoming and Cherry
Valley. On February 27, the Congress passed a resolution authorizing General
Washington to take the most efficacious measures for protecting the inhabitants
of the states and chastizing the Indians. Washington assured the Congress that
a more detailed report would be submitted as soon as a full plan of operation
had been outlined. It was to that task that he set his mind — and the minds of
qualified subordinates — during the first three months.

The first priority in the planning had been finding the proper general officer
to carry out the campaign as Washington wished it to be carried out. This was
not as easy as he had at first anticipated it would be. In rapid succession four of
the generals Washington would have liked for the task had been ruled out. The
man before him now was, at best, only an adequate fifth choice, but it was all
the commander in chief had left and Washington prayed he was not making a
serious error in putting such a responsibility into this man's hands.

In a very broad sense, the plan of the campaign was simple in design. At this
time the Iroquois League consisted of six tribes, at least five of which were fully
or in part hostile to Americans. The only exception was the Oneida tribe.
Their proven support of the Americans at Oriskany and afterward made them
candidates now for a responsible part of this campaign. The other five — the
Tuscaroras to only a slight degree, but the Onondagas, Cayugas, Mohawks and

Senecas almost completely — were definitely pro-British and avowed enemies of the Americans. They amounted to about twenty thousand individuals in the tribes, but this boiled down to an active total warrior strength of from twenty-five hundred to three thousand. Most of them were in middle and western New York, especially in the country of the Finger Lakes, where they had upward of fifty towns, ranging in size from tiny villages to rather substantial cities. Throughout their territory and especially in and around each of the towns, extensive areas were devoted to fruit orchards, grain fields and vegetable crops.

Very early in the planning, Washington had decided against a campaign whose objective was to meet the enemy in head-on battle. To the contrary, this present plan called for battle to be engaged in only if the enemy held his ground. Otherwise, if the Indians chose to abandon their villages in the face of the approaching army, they were welcome to do so. Destruction of human life was not the keystone to the campaign. Rather it was to be destruction of the towns and the crops. The genocide would be an insidious aftermath of that.

At first Washington had thought in terms of an army in three wings, each making its onslaught through the Indian country to a central rendezvous point, from whence the entire body would then continue its drive through the heart of the Indian country, destroying all in its path. The projected rendezvous was at the mouth of the Chemung River, where it flowed into the Susquehanna — the place called Tioga. One wing of the army would drive southward from the Mohawk to the headwaters of the Susquehanna and down it to the rendezvous point. The principal thrust would be the army moving first westward from Easton, Pennsylvania, to Wyoming, then northward up the Susquehanna to the rendezvous. The third wing would move from Fort Pitt up the Allegheny to its headwaters, then cross-country eastward to the rendezvous. With continued study, Washington realized the impracticality of the western wing making such a sustained unsupported drive across the wilderness and this portion of the plan was altered. Only the two eastern wings of the army would unite. The western wing, under command of Colonel Daniel Brodhead, a force of over six hundred men, would be moving north out of Fort Pitt. In regular messenger contact with the main army, it would merely move up the Allegheny, destroying the villages encountered, and then return to Fort Pitt. The central and eastern wings of the army, however, would unite. Theirs was to be no piddling little operation but a full-scale invasion. Once the east wing of the army met the main body at Tioga, they would merge and, in a combined force numbering fully five thousand seasoned Continental troops, they would drive into the very heart of the Iroquois territory all the way to the greatest Seneca stronghold and its "western door," Chenussio.

With the basic plan roughed out, chain of command became the most important factor. In the hands of an unimaginative, overly cautious — or, for that matter, overly brash — commander, a real tragedy might result and, from such a tragedy, the war itself might ultimately be lost. As Washington put it in his letter to the president of Congress,

The Council are fully sensible of the importance of success in the present ex-pedition, and the fatal mischiefs which would attend a defeat. We should per-haps lose an Army, and our frontiers would be deluged in blood.

George Washington's first thought of the individual to take command of the operation was Major General Charles Lee, but Lee was so important in the area in which he was presently engaged that use of him was impossible. Second choice — although Washington's personal preference as number one — was Major General Philip Schuyler, but Schuyler was still so irate at having been relieved by Congress of his command of the Northern Department of the army that he was still seriously considering resigning his commission. The next in line, by way of seniority was Major General Israel Putnam, but such an intense dislike for the man had grown in Washington that he passed him by without much concern, even though his qualifications were good. By this time it was becoming imperative to get the operation on the move and so once again Washington turned to lean on the heretofore highly dependable officer who had assumed command of the Northern Department of the army from Schuyler — Major General Horatio Gates.

Although General Washington in no way anticipated any problem with Gates's acceptance of the command, time was now so short that he could not rely on chance and so he enclosed with his March 6 letter to Gates a letter to another general, to be forwarded to him in the unlikely event that Gates should decline. Washington's letter told Gates, in regard to the campaign:

It is proposed to carry the war into the heart of the country of the Six Nations, to cut off their settlements, destroy their next years' crops, and do them every other mischief which time and circumstance will permit.

Washington felt strongly that any general officer would consider such a com-mand a real plum and an excellent steppingstone to military fame.[247] Ap-parently Gates did not share his commander in chief's feelings. Incredibly, and much to George Washington's consternation, Gates did decline, blaming his own health, although Washington felt sure it was because Gates could not en-vision that a campaign against the Indians would be the gateway to glory that fighting the British would be. Gates's rather brusque reply to Washington said:

Sir —
Last night I had the honor of Your Excellency's letter. The man who under-takes the Indian service should enjoy youth and strength requisites I do not pos-

sess. It therefore grieves me that Your Excellency should offer me the only com-
mand to which I am entirely unequal. In obedience to your command, I have
forwarded your letter to General Sullivan.

I am, Sir, your obedient Servant,

HORATIO GATES, *Major General*

His Excellency the Commander
General George Washington

So the contingency letter had indeed been forwarded at once to Major General John Sullivan — probably the least inspiring of any major general in the American army.

At this time, John Sullivan was thirty-nine and in physical aspect hardly inspired admiration. Inclined toward obesity, his complexion was swarthy and his long black hair, which fell in clustered locks to his shoulders, framed a somewhat weak-chinned, petulant face whose main saving grace was a pair of rather piercing gray eyes. He was a well-educated man, but such was not unexpected in the circumstances in which he was raised. His father, Owen Sullivan, had immigrated to America from Ireland in 1723 and settled in the area of Berwick, Maine, where he was a schoolteacher. It was directly across the Piscataqua River from Berwick, at Somerset, New Hampshire, that John had been born on February 18, 1740. Under the guidance of his father, he was groomed for a law practice, reading law under the Honorable Isaac Livermore of Portsmouth, New Hampshire. After being admitted to the bar, he set up his own practice in Durham, New Hampshire. That was where he'd been living when the war broke out.

It was in 1772 that he had accepted a commission as a major of the New Hampshire Regiment and in the spring of 1774 he became a member of the Provincial Assembly of New Hampshire. The following September he was named as delegate to the Continental Congress and in December of that year, along with John Langdon, he led a force against Fort William and Mary as the first act of armed hostilities in the Colonies and confiscated gunpowder, artillery and other supplies that were later used at the Battle of Bunker Hill.

With such a background, it was not unexpected that the Continental Congress appointed him brigadier general in June, 1775. Thirteen months later, in July of 1776, while serving under Washington at Philadelphia, Congress elevated him to his present rank of major general. The following month, on August 27, while serving under Major General Putnam at the Battle of Long Island, Sullivan was taken prisoner, but he was exchanged for the British general Richard Prescott and rejoined Washington at Westchester. On Christmas Day that year he led the left at the Battle of Trenton. He was also with Washington during the bitter winter at Valley Forge and at the Battle of Brandywine in 1777 he'd had a horse shot out from under him.

It all seemed to be a pretty good record, but George Washington was not all that enamored with either the man or his record. They had clashed a time or two in their meetings and Washington disliked the way Sullivan would stand and scribble notes to himself in the field like a madman during the heat of battle — notes he himself would later be unable to decipher. On the whole, Washington's evaluation of John Sullivan was quite a long way from inspiring. He considered him to be a too-impetuous man inclined to vain posturings, talkative to the point of being garrulous, much too quick-tempered for his own good and, along with a fundamental lack of knowledge of books and men, he had a decided inclination toward bad judgment. There were those who considered Sullivan as a weak, undignified and contentious backwoods lawyer who, given the option, would rather sue than compromise.

All these things considered, it was a wonder that Washington chose him to command the proposed expedition. As a matter of fact, it was seniority rather than ability that had been the determining factor. That and Washington's initial feeling that Gates would accept the command. Nevertheless, since Gates actually had refused the command and forwarded the letter for Sullivan on to him, Washington was glad that he had been rather explicit in it. He had written:

Head Quarters, Middle Brook, March 6th, 1779
Dear Sir —
Congress having determined upon an expedition of an extensive nature against the hostile tribes of the Indians of the Six Nations, the command is offered to Major General Gates as senior officer, but should he decline, it is my wish it should devolve upon you. That no time may be lost by Gen. Gates' non-acceptance, I have put this letter under cover to him and have desired him to forward it to you should that be his determination. Should it therefore be sent to you, I must request you to set out as speedily as possible after the receipt of it, to Head Quarters, as the season is already far advanced. Upon your arrival, the whole plan of the expedition shall be communicated to you and measures concerted for carrying it into execution.

Nothing will contribute more to our success in the quarters where we really intend to strike, than alarming the enemy in a contrary one, and drawing their attention that way. To do this you may drop hints of an expedition to Canada by way of Coos. This will be the more readily believed as a thing of that kind was really once in agitation, and some magazines formed in consequence, which the enemy are acquainted with.

You may also speak of the probability of a French fleet making its appearance in the spring, in the River St. Lawrence, to cooperate with us. It will be a great point gained if we can, by false claims, keep the force ready in Canada from affording any timely assistance to the Savages, Refugees and those people against whom the blow is leveled.

I would wish you to keep the motive of your journey to Head Quarters a secret, because if it is known that an officer of your rank is to take a command to the westward, it will be immediately concluded that the object must be considerable.

I am with great Regard,
Dear Sir,
Your Most Obedient Servant,
GEORGE WASHINGTON

Major General Sullivan

Now, as General Washington began to speak softly but with crisp authority and direction, Sullivan listened intently, his eyes never straying from the commander's face.

John Sullivan was not unaware of the disapproval, if not antipathy, others harbored against him, nor was he so much immersed in himself that he was oblivious to the fact that perhaps some of the criticism was justified. At the moment he did not care a great deal what any others might feel about him except for Washington, whose opinion he considered very important. He by this time knew he had been fifth choice and chosen even then only because of his seniority. If this dismayed him, he gave no outward sign of it, but he mentally vowed that by the time this campaign was over, George Washington would be far more than merely pleased with his choice for its commander.

For more than three hours now they sat together, with Washington doing most of the talking, going over the fine points of the projected campaign — the details of weaponry, subordinate command, supply, transportation, communication and similar matters.

"The immediate objects," the commander in chief said, "are the total destruction of the hostile tribes of the Six Nations, and the devastation of their settlements, and the capture of as many prisoners of every age and sex as possible.[248] You are to lay waste to all the settlements around, so that the country may not only be overrun, but destroyed."

Washington told how he had been having a series of conferences with individuals having incisive knowledge of the Indians, their towns, their trails, their customs, their manner of warfare. These men included Colonel Zebulon Butler, Captain John Franklin and Captain Simon Spalding, all of whom overwintered at Wyoming and all of whom possessed extensive knowledge of the Indian country. He said he was also receiving regular intelligence reports from Major General Philip Schuyler, who was himself gathering and transmitting to

Washington the most important information he could glean from those who were conversant with the movements of the enemy.

"As you are commander of the expedition, General Sullivan," Washington said, "it is for you to select those brigadiers whom you think are most fitting for subordinate command beneath you, including your second-in-command, although I trust you will take my strong recommendations along these lines into consideration."

Sullivan nodded and seemed about to say something, but Washington waved him off and went on. "That's something we'll get into in greater detail shortly. What I wanted to say now is that there are three men on tap whom we should probably utilize as guides for your army when you enter the Indian country. Two of them are Indians themselves and have proven themselves several times over in our behalf. If you have any reservations about including them, I assure you that it will be to the full benefit of your expedition to put such reservations in abeyance. These Indians are part of the wedge which is currently splitting apart the Iroquois League. Our use of them cannot help but hasten that rupture. One of the two is an Oneida chief named Hanyerry. The other is Jehoiakim, chief of the Stockbridge Indians. Both have already volunteered their services in this department.

"The third man," Washington went on, "is one of our own people — a lieutenant — who knows their country quite well and was held captive by them in Fort Niagara for quite some time. He escaped from them only a short while before the Wyoming affair. As a matter of fact, he was the one who brought the first warning of the attack to come. I've had a number of conferences with him over the past few weeks and I think you should employ him as chief guide of the expedition. He's presently in Wyoming and would be meeting you there. His name is Jenkins. John Jenkins." [249]

[*April 21, 1779 — Wednesday*]

For over two hundred and fifty years Onondaga had been the capital of the Onondaga tribe and the seat of government of the powerful Iroquois League. The town itself was not large, considering its importance, consisting of less than fifty rather well-built frame and log homes patterned after those built by whites. Here and there on the fringes were quonsets of a reasonably substantial nature and there were also a score or more large wigwams, with the skins of which they were constructed decorated with painted scenes of the hunt and warfare and great councils that had been held here and other events of importance.

The most important and imposing building in the town was the principal longhouse where, when the weather was inclement, the grand council could be moved indoors and continue with but little interruption. The council fire that burned there, as well as the one that burned outside, were not the fires of the League that had burned continuously for a quarter of a millennium. That was the fire that old Steyawa had kicked apart and it could never be built again. The fires now were new ones and they were of a token nature, welding together the League only temporarily, for as long as the present emergency should exist, but even then doing the welding rather imperfectly. The council longhouse faced eastward and was only a short distance from the shore of Onondaga Lake. [250]

The population of Onondaga had fluctuated considerably over the years, ranging anywhere from as few as two or three hundred to as many as two thousand. The wars of recent years, especially the French and Indian War, which had ended less than a score of years ago, had resulted in the deaths of many warriors from Onondaga and the town was no longer the populous place it had once been. Now it boasted less than three hundred and a great many of these were not present at the moment. The warriors, most often with their entire families, had not yet returned from their winter hunt and many others under Rozinoghyata, the principal chief, had attached themselves to the sizable band that had congregated at Fort Niagara far to the west to take part in whatever new stroke would be made against the Americans.

Although April was already more than half over, spring was late in coming this year and both yesterday and the day before there had been snow and bitter winds. The Onondaga residents had been staying indoors by their fires, longing for the break in the season that would quickly have them out planting their crops for the year.

The blow that struck them today was totally unexpected — more unexpected, in fact, than the blow that had been struck by the Indians against Cherry Valley last November. The force of five hundred and fifty-eight Americans, including officers, were under command of Colonel Goose Van Schaick. They had marched swiftly from Fort Stanwix to Onondaga and they struck with the fire of vengeance in their eyes. [251] Mostly these were men of the Mohawk Valley whose homes and towns had been assaulted by marauding Indians so frequently over the past two years. Mostly they were men who had lost friends and fathers, sons and brothers, in the Battle of Oriskany and at Cherry Valley and German Flats.

That the Americans would attack was, even though unexpected, thoroughly understandable, but what hit the Indians hardest was that leading the attack was the principal chief of the Oneidas, Hanyerry, with sixty of his best warriors behind him. Oneidas! Members of the Iroquois League! *Brothers!* The treachery was unparalleled in Iroquois history.

In their whirlwind attack, which involved a forced march of one hundred and eighty miles in six days, the Americans and their Oneida allies had no one killed or even injured, but although most of the Indians escaped, twelve Onondagas were killed and thirty-four captured and upward of fifty fine homes were burned after being plundered of anything valuable. All food supplies were destroyed and it was total ruin for the capital city of the Onondaga tribe. But it was far more than that. Chief Hanyerry, who had himself so often sat as one of the most important member chiefs in council here through the years, was the one who applied the torch that ignited and then consumed the longhouse in a roaring conflagration. Word of this spread with incredible speed throughout the land and now, though many of the warriors would not acknowledge what they felt, they knew beyond any doubt that it was a terrible milestone.

On this day sounded the death knell of the Iroquois League.

[*May 1, 1779 — Saturday*]

With inexorable purpose, the forces that George Washington was putting into motion against the hostile tribes of the Iroquois League were gradually amassing at their various centers. The principal orders had been written and delivered, the commanders and subcommanders and their subordinate officers had been named, and throughout the land there was a great drawing together of military power.

The army, under sole command of Major General John Sullivan, was composed of four brigades. The first three of these were to converge at the rendezvous of Easton, Pennsylvania, on the Delaware River, the last major town on the western border. The 1st Brigade, also known as the New Jersey Brigade, was under command of Sullivan's third-in-command, Brigadier General William Maxwell.[252] It moved into its march from headquarters at Elizabeth, New Jersey, heading for the Delaware River, and the same was true of the 3rd, or Pennsylvania Brigade, which was under command of the youngest brigadier in the American army, thirty-four-year-old Edward Hand.[253] The 2nd, or New Hampshire Brigade, under command of Brigadier General Enoch Poor,[254] struck its tents at Camp Putnam in Connecticut, crossed the Hudson River and marched through New York State, heading southeast to help build the corduroy road[255] over the Pocono Mountains of Pennsylvania to Wyoming.

The 4th Brigade — or New York Brigade — under command of Brigadier General James Clinton[256] had a large assignment of its own before it was to join Sullivan and the rest of the army. Assembling first at Schenectady, it was to move up the Mohawk River to Canajoharie, then southward to Otsego Lake, which was the source of the Susquehanna River. At the outlet of that lake, where the river formed, Clinton was to hold his force in readiness until receiving marching orders from Sullivan. When these came he was to move down the Susquehanna, destroying all Indian villages as he progressed, and join Sullivan at Tioga.

There was almost a sense of revelry in the air, a lightness and esprit de corps that manifested itself in many ways, one of which was carelessness. The results were sobering and fatal.

A detachment of two hundred men under Major John Powell was sent ahead from Easton to quarter themselves at Wyoming and prepare that area for the arrival of the army. Their initial alertness gradually dwindled as day after day on the difficult trail there was no sign that any enemy was nearby. By the time they reached Bear Creek, some fifty miles west of Easton, there was really no longer any concern about being surprised by Indians. Wyoming was now only ten miles ahead and the greatest concern now was for making a respectable appearance on entering that valley. Toward this end the officers and even some of the men donned their best ruffled uniforms, powdered their hair, burnished their swords and polished their guns, then struck out with sprightly pace for the last lap into the valley to the strains of lively music. As they crossed over the wooded crest of the twenty-one-hundred-foot-high Wyoming Mountain, an advance guard reported having seen some deer ahead and immediately a small party of men led by Captain Joseph Davis of Hubley's regiment, Lieutenant Jones of the German Regiment and Corporal Butler set out to try to get some venison to bring into Wyoming with them.

Hardly four miles from the fort they were ambushed by a party of fifteen to twenty Indians. Davis, Jones and Butler, along with three privates, were killed. Captain John Franklin was wounded but managed to lead the survivors back to the main detachment. When the military returned in force, they found the bodies. Their scalps had been taken, their bodies hacked by tomahawks and punctured by spears.

Shallow graves were dug and the men were buried, with their names fixed on boards and a determination made that later their remains could be disinterred and a more fitting burial made.

There was no more levity now and when the detachment filed silently into the Wyoming Valley they brought with them a renewal of the sickening fear that had rarely been a stranger here.

[*May 29, 1779 — Saturday*]

The apprehension prevailing among the Indians in the area of Fort Niagara was very strong and Colonel Butler was not quite sure how to handle it. If Sir William Johnson were still alive, he knew, he would quickly salve their fears and in no time have them eating out of his hand and ready to do his bidding in whatever endeavor he felt was proper. But John Butler knew he had neither the skill of Johnson nor the late supervisor's uncanny knowledge of the Iroquois temperament and how best to appeal to it.

The Iroquois were still a powerful force — upward of three thousand experienced warriors who were tremendous fighters and more than a match for twice or three times their own numbers of regular soldiers, provided the battles were fought on their own terms. Yet, if the battles were brought to them by the soldiers, the outcome would be doubtful at best, especially in view of the fear that possessed them now and that, though they denied it vocally, clearly controlled their actions.

When word had come of the destruction of Onondaga and the Iroquois League's council fire, it was as if a similar flickering flame in the breast of every warrior was also snuffed out. They seemed suddenly spiritless and constantly worried and they watched the weather and the birds and the forest animals for occurrences that they could interpret as signs sent by the Great Spirit to validate their fears.

True, there was a great anger in them too — especially at the Oneidas for having betrayed the League. That the Americans would attack Onondaga was not so terribly surprising; after all, this was a possibility of war. But that the Oneidas would support the Americans, turn their backs on their own people and help in killing and capturing fellow Iroquois and then aid in the destruction of the very heart of the League, *this* is what troubled them so greatly. Eventually the Oneidas would have to answer for what they had done — especially their chief, Hanyerry.

Trying to imagine what Sir William would have done in such a situation was frustrating for Colonel Butler. He very briefly considered asking the advice of either Sir John Johnson or Colonel Guy Johnson but then shelved such ideas; both men had proven only too well their own ineffectuality in handling the Indians or anticipating their needs. In the end, Butler felt the most direct approach would be the best and so he had gathered a force of two hundred men behind him, Rangers as well as a small detachment of the 8th Regiment and the officers of the Indian Department and they, along with a similar number of Senecas and Cayugas and Mohawks, moved swiftly to Onondaga.

The destruction they found there was complete and too late Butler realized he'd made a mistake. The cold ashes of the Iroquois League longhouse were mute but graphic testimony to the extinction of the League, and when he watched many of the Indians rubbing their faces and chests with those ashes and tears making little crooked channels down the stained cheeks of the bravest of them, he knew with a certainty that the Iroquois as a fighting force could never again be what it once was.

Now, having returned to Fort Niagara, Butler addressed the Indians, expressing to them his sorrow for their loss. They accepted it with gratitude but their spirits did not lighten at all. Butler quickly assessed the accumulation of intelligence reports about the activities of General John Sullivan's army and, though at first report the Indians here had laughed aloud at the notion that an American army might penetrate very deeply into their country in an attempt to destroy it, they were now no longer laughing. The force was shaping up to be enormous and spies reported that it was planning to rendezvous at Tioga and then move up the Chemung River, then into the beautiful lake country that was the heart of the Iroquois world.

"Are we going to meet them?" Butler asked during the council, trying to stir some fire into them, trying to make them angry, make them care enough to fight again for what was theirs. "Or are we going to stand by and watch them as, unhampered by warriors who now fear them, they march in and destroy your villages and people?"

There were loud cries of "No! No!" and a flaring of the old fierceness. Butler continued haranguing them and bit by bit he won them over to a plan of establishing a place to ambush the strong army and attempt to destroy it in one great fight, or at least cripple it so that it must limp away and lick its wounds. The place selected for such a confrontation would have to be close to where the army was planning on having its rendezvous at Tioga.

Sullivan's army, coming up the Chemung, would have to pass the substantial village of Newtown. The Indian trail they would be taking would lead them through a defile somewhat reminiscent of the one in which General Herkimer's army was destroyed. What better place to show them that the Iroquois were still a strong league of warriors? Would Joseph Brant lead them in such an attack as war chief? Would Colonel John Butler join them with his Rangers to help destroy the enemy?

Both answered yes immediately, but they also looked at one another, and in the glance that passed between them there was strong doubt, coupled with a growing belief that if the Sullivan army was not stopped and beaten back at Newtown, it might not be stopped at all.

[*June 16, 1779 — Wednesday*]

Slowly but steadily the Sullivan force collecting at Easton grew from scattered companies to full regiments, filled with a strong determination to end, once and for all, the Indian menace on the frontiers of Pennsylvania and New York. John Sullivan was himself, on May 7, one of the first to arrive, surrounded by his coterie of officers as well as civilian advisers. From the very beginning problems blossomed. The first, upon which the general acted without delay, was to send more help to the regiments of Colonel Van Cortlandt and Colonel Spencer, which had been ordered by him on April 5 to construct a good road from Easton to the Wyoming Valley. That was no small task. The regiments had worked unstintingly but progress was slow and the work backbreaking. Quite often less than a mile of road was built in a full day's work and the lack of essential supplies was a tremendous hindrance. Now, at last, word had come that only the day before yesterday the road had been completed to Wilkes-Barre.

That road was following two old Indian trails that had eventually become the

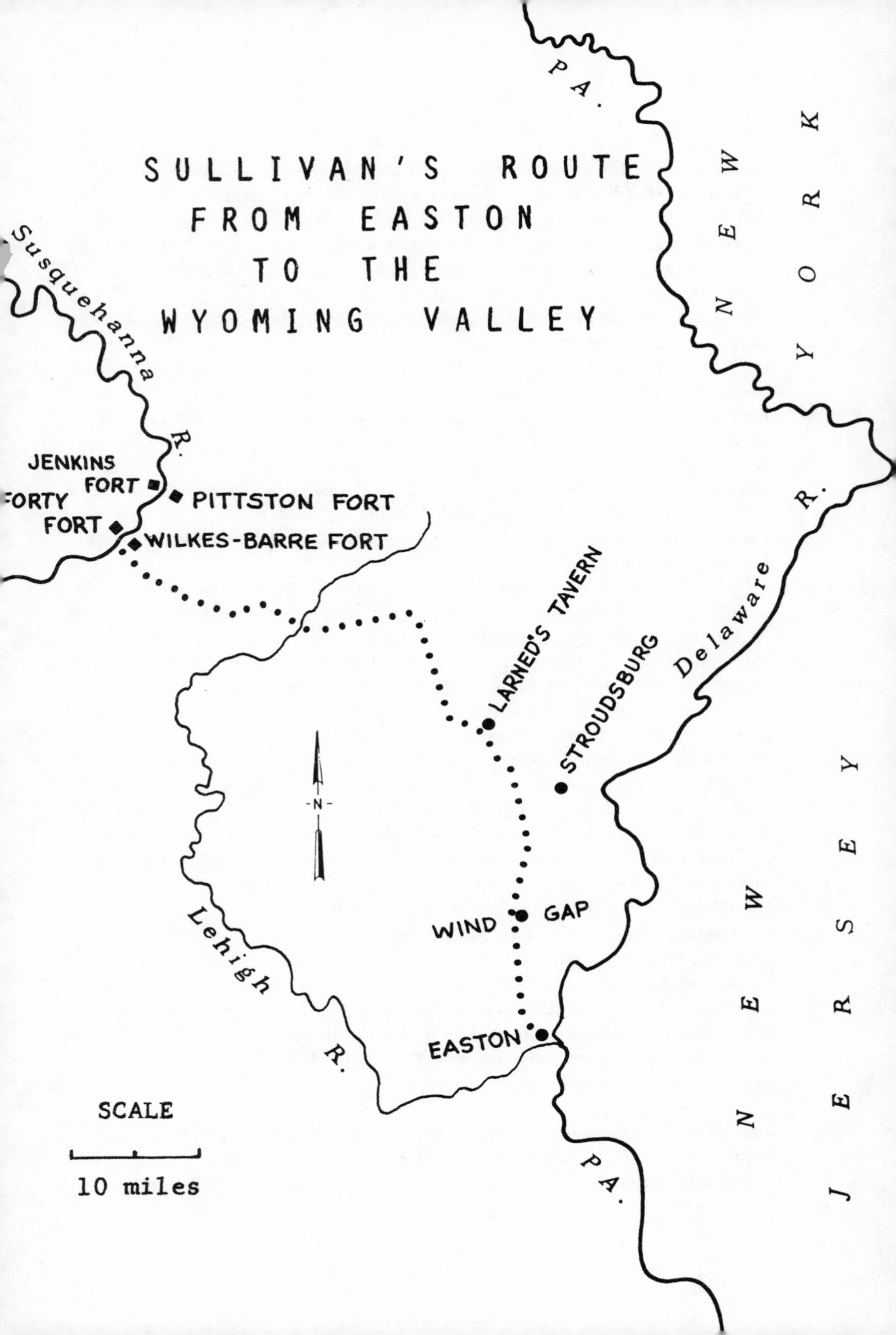

SULLIVAN'S ROUTE
FROM EASTON
TO THE
WYOMING VALLEY

Susquehanna R.

JENKINS FORT
FORTY FORT
PITTSTON FORT
WILKES-BARRE FORT

LARNED'S TAVERN

STROUDSBURG

Delaware R.

WIND GAP

Lehigh R.

EASTON

-N-

P. A.

N E W   Y O R K

N E W   J E R S E Y

P. A.

SCALE

10 miles

principal horse trails from Easton and Stroudsburg to Wyoming. These trails followed the easiest line of march; but in this country of steep, densely wooded hills and defiles, gouged by great ravines and blocked by windfallen timber, where they often led across streams that at times became torrential, even the "easiest line of march" was exceptionally difficult. This was particularly true where the road had to cross the now-infamous swamp called the Shades of Death, where so many of the previous July's refugees from the Wyoming battle were said to have perished.

The first Indian trail out of Easton to be converted into the army's road ran northward through that remarkable cut in the mountains called Wind Gap and then directly north along the highlands between the Delaware and Susquehanna rivers to the New York State line just southeast of Oquaga. The Sullivan Road, however, followed it only until about a point somewhat southwest of Stroudsburg.[257] There it was intersected by the second trail, which ran from Fort Penn at Stroudsburg westward through the wilderness, crossing Tunkhanna and Tobyhanna creeks and the Lehigh River and then on to Wilkes-Barre in the Wyoming Valley.[258]

Not only was the roadwork exceptionally difficult, it was done under a considerable strain. The Indian attack against the Major Powell party had occurred on this same route the road was following and the feeling was strong that it could happen again at any time. Scattered Indian attacks were still occurring all around and these were the types of attack at which they excelled — hit and run and hit again, never standing still long enough to be surprised, never striking where there was a strong defense force, never exposing themselves to danger if it could be prevented. Unexpectedly, Cobleskill had been attacked again and ten people were slain at Fantinekill and a settlement ravaged at Wawarsink. Indian tracks were being found constantly in the area of the road-building, yet the Indians themselves were never seen and this, too, caused fear and the prevailing sense that one was always under scrutiny from hidden eyes and that at any moment an arrow or bullet or tomahawk would find its mark.

On May 27, Colonel Cilly's regiment was sent to assist with the final leg of the road-building by Van Cortlandt and Spencer. That provided the needed impetus. When the regiments reached the place where Captain Davis and Lieutenant Jones of Powell's detachment had been slain, the bodies — along with that of Corporal Butler and the privates — were disinterred for reburial at Wilkes-Barre. A tribute of music was played — the tune of "Roslin Castle" — and the moment was so moving that Lieutenant John Hardenbergh became maudlin in his diary as he wrote:

The soft and moving notes, together with what so forcibly struck the eye, tended greatly to fill our breasts with pity and renew our grief for our worthy departed friends and brethren.

While the roadwork progressed, continually more troops assembled at Easton. The remainder of Colonel Spencer's regiment arrived on May 24 and both the 2nd and 3rd New Hampshire regiments two days later. On June 5 the 2nd and 5th New Jersey regiments arrived and, with that, troop strength was all but complete. Civil authorities were having a hard time coping with such an influx of men and there were nowhere near enough accomodations for them all. The result was that in a large clear area southeast of the town, where the Lehigh River emptied into the Delaware, a tent city was established. Almost immediately two soldiers were drowned. Private John Ten Eyck of Captain Abner French's company of light infantry of the 2nd New York accidentally slipped down a bank of the Lehigh and, unable to swim, sank. Friends recovered his body ten or fifteen minutes later but he could not be revived. Another private, Hector Swaeth of Colonel Elias Dayton's company of the 3rd New Jersey was drunk and bet his companions he could swim across the Delaware. They won.

Captain Daniel Livermore of the 3rd New Hampshire decided that he would maintain a graphic account of all that transpired on "this glorious campaign." On this day of his arrival, he wrote in his diary in a strong flowing hand:

The town of Easton is pleasantly situated on a level flat of ground, on a point made by the Delaware and Lehigh. The buildings in the place are plain and made of stone. Their State House is built in the center of the town, where four roads meet. It is built of stone and lime and makes an elegant appearance. They have one house of worship, near the State House. It is built of hewn stone; large and elegant, with a large organ. The inhabitants are chiefly low Dutch, and they worship wholly in that way. There are some few Jews living here, who are the principal merchants of the place.

Each company of men who came to Easton thought sure they would remain there only a few days. Those who had experienced similar stagings before and knew some of the problems of transportation, communication and supply opined that they might be at Easton a few weeks. No one, least of all John Sullivan, had any idea at the onset in early April that in mid-June they would still be in Easton.

The problem, more than anything else, was supply. The multitude of supplies the army needed and the means by which to convey such supplies had been worked out on paper very carefully long in advance, but in actuality it didn't occur that way. Pennsylvania simply was not supplying the independent companies and provisions that were promised.

In truth, the Pennamite Party of Pennsylvania was in no way eager to have Sullivan succeed in driving the Indians out of western Pennsylvania. The reason was that the Pennamite Party was composed almost entirely of men of great wealth and tremendous political influence, men who held title under

Pennsylvania law to considerable tracts of land located in the Wyoming Valley upon which Connecticut people had settled. The Connecticut people had proven their claim to it by the old grant and they had possession; they were not going to leave it simply because the Pennamites claimed it. The Pennamites considered them intruders and despite their loud commiseration for the suffering of the Wyoming settlers, there was a certain malicious glee resident in them at the thought that the Indians had driven them out and might yet prevent their permanent return . . . provided Sullivan did not open the doors again by driving out the Indians. If the Connecticut settlers could be kept out of that rich valley until the war was over, the Pennamites believed they could themselves take over the land to which they held title of sorts. Therefore, the opposition had begun showing itself in a pronounced lack of cooperation in furnishing both their quota of men and supplies for the army. About this Sullivan complained bitterly in a letter to George Washington and the commander in chief, himself well experienced in such difficulties, wrote back sympathetically:

I am very sorry you are like to be disappointed in the independent companies you expected from Pennsylvania, and that you have encountered greater difficulties than you looked for. I am satisfied that every exertion in your power will be made and I hope that your eventual operations will be attended with fewer obstacles.

At the same time, Washington and his aide Colonel Timothy Pickering were both writing to President of War Joseph Reed in Philadelphia, stressing the necessity for hastening forward the supplies for the army in the eighty to one hundred wagons that had been promised. Reed was president of the Supreme Executive Council of Pennsylvania. Pickering wrote:

We expected ere this time that all the stores would have been at least on their way to Easton but, for want of wagons, three fourths of them are in this city.

The complaints, even from George Washington, had little effect and the want of provisions in Sullivan's army worsened day by day. There could be no doubt, as many contended and as so often occurs during wartime, that the Commissary Department and Quartermaster Corps were being guided by people who were either incompetent or negligent. Or both. It was more than that. Apologists pointed out that considerable allowance had to be made for the fact that the country itself was greatly depressed, that the currency was essentially worthless and the people were poverty-stricken. To a certain extent this was perhaps true as well. But more than for any other single reason, Sullivan's army was being stymied by Pennsylvania state authorities who not only strongly disfavored the expedition to begin with, but who had no conception of the expedition's extent and requirements.

Troubles bombarded Sullivan from all sides. The Quakers now became vocal, raising their voices in righteous indignation at the prospect of an army of modernly equipped soldiers going out to butcher poor native inhabitants of the country who sought only to protect their lands and who were armed only with puny little knives and childish hatchets. Where, the Quakers asked, was the inherent decency of man, that such an expedition could even be considered, much less put into execution?

Spies and agitators were also no small problem. They were sowing seeds of discontent among the troops and often with great success. Already the New Jersey troops were approaching a state of mutiny because the New Jersey authorities had not only failed to take into consideration and provide for the depreciation of currency, but they had failed to pay the New Jersey troops even a nominal sum in the almost worthless Continental paper money. It took tremendous effort on the part of Sullivan and his officers to soothe the men with strong promises of eventual payment. And George Washington, learning of this, actually blanched.

"Nothing that has occurred during the war has so filled me with alarm as this," he said.

The spies and agitators creating this form of unrest went even further in their efforts to get men to desert the army and go to British authorities, telling them they would be well paid either in currency or in receiving high military commission for the intelligence they provided. Amazingly, some believed it and on May 16 seven of them did desert.

There was no longer any hope of hiding from the enemy the fact of the proposed invasion. Wrapping up his comments to Washington about both supplies and spies, Sullivan wrote:

I will do everything in my power to set the wheels in motion and make the necessary preparations for the army to move on. The expedition is no secret in this quarter. A sergeant of Spencer's, who was made prisoner at Mohacamoe and carried to Chemung, just returned. [259] *He says they know of the expedition and are taking every step to destroy the communications of the Susquehanna. I think the sooner we can get into the country, the better.* [260]

Discipline had to be maintained at all costs if the expedition were to succeed and the troops at Easton were quickly learning that half measures would not do. When three drunken privates of Colonel Adam Hubley's 11th Pennsylvania Regiment coldly killed an Easton tavernkeeper because he refused to sell them more liquor, they were quickly tried and found guilty of murder and highway robbery. The day before yesterday they were publicly hanged before a crowd of four thousand, including the whole of Sullivan's army on hand, which was ordered to witness the execution. As if this in itself were not enough a deterrent to others, the body of one of the men was exhumed and dissected by a doctor for "practice" and then reburied.

Even those guilty of lesser crimes were not treated any too gently. Two New Jersey privates, John Curry and Michael Sellers, were tried at the drumhead for stealing rum from the commissary and, when found guilty, their sentences were immediately carried into execution. Curry received seventy-five lashes and Sellers fifty. Again the troops were required to watch. Half measures were most certainly not to be this army's long suit.

The troops were chafing at the long delay, unable to understand why the days and weeks passed while they simply marked time in a town called Easton, which they neither cared for nor in which they wished to remain. Realizing that they had to have some liberties or morale would suffer, Sullivan instructed his commanders to become more liberal with the granting of passes to both officers and men. Some used the passes for such pastimes as hunting or fighting or visiting friends and relations within reasonable reach. Others took in what sights were available to view in neighboring communities.

Captain Daniel Livermore, faithfully continuing his practice of recording events and sights in his diary, was one of those who enjoyed seeing whatever of interest was available. This included his impressions of a little excursion he took on the last day of May to a town not too far away. He wrote:

Monday, May 31. This day I set out on a party of pleasure to Bethlehem in company with a number of gentlemen, officers of the Brigade. Had an elegant dinner, after which we walked out and took a survey of the town and its curiosities. The town of Bethlehem is a small, compact town, lying on the river Lehigh, about twelve miles from Easton. It lies on a small descent toward the south-east, and is pleasantly situated. The inhabitants are all Low Dutch and of that denomination called Moravians. They are much bigoted in their ways of worship, as also in their method of living. Their buildings are not elegant, though decent, and built wholly of stone and lime. They have but one place of public worship, and perform in the Dutch language; and one house of entertainment, which is supplied out of the public fund.

Just as the troops at Easton were chafing and wondering when the army would move, so too were those at Wyoming. For them there was little of a diversionary nature and a constant sense of apprehension plagued them. They were still slight in number here and only with the might of the whole army to bolster their strength would a sense of confidence return. Now, with the road having been completed into Wyoming and three full regiments of men suddenly filling the area, there was not room enough for them in the vicinity of

Wilkes-Barre and so, the day before yesterday, upon completing the road, they moved four miles above the garrison and set up camp on Jacob's Plains — a plateau on the east side of the river directly opposite the area called Abraham's Plains.

With the regiments was Dr. Jabez Campfield, the surgeon of Oliver Spencer's New Jersey Regiment. For many years he had regularly maintained a journal and his becoming attached to the army had not altered his daily habit of recording his impressions. On this day he wrote:

The Detachment rode into Wyoming, Col. Butler[261] *with a detachment from the garrison had opened the road. Wyoming is a beautiful place, through which runs the Susquehanna in a swift delightful course. Wyoming is distant from Easton 60 miles — and is capable of great improvement.*

This settlement consists of four different towns, before the cruel Butler[262] *destroyed them, being inhabited by upwards of one thousand families who, a few excepted, were entirely ruined, and such as he did not kill were left utterly destitute of every necessary of life, and obliged to fly for refuge into the lower settlements.*

The lands here are exceedingly good and fertile; the river abounds with various fish in the spring. It is full of the finest Shad. Trout and pickerel are also plenty here.

In passing the great swamp we cross several fine streams of water, which all abound with trout. The first is Tunkhanna, second is Tobehanna, the third is Lehigh. These are all branches of the same river and under the name of Lehigh fall into the Delaware at Easton.

In this way we passed a second swamp called Bear Swamp, through which runs a considerable stream of water, called the Ten-Mile Run, said to fall into the Schuylkill.

Four miles from Wyoming we cross a high mountain, which will render the land carriage always difficult from Easton to this place, could the other difficulties be removed.

The time of waiting — at least at Easton — abruptly ended today. General Sullivan was very pleased with the great efforts that had been made for such an extended period by those who had been preparing the road connecting Easton and the Wyoming Valley. The first of two General Orders he dictated today was an appreciation for that effort:

Head Quarters — Easton
The Commander-in-Chief returns his most sincere thanks to Colonels Cortlandt and Spence, and to the officers and soldiers under their command, for their un-

*paralleled exertions in clearing and repairing the road to Wyoming. He cannot
help promising himself success in an expedition in which he is to be honored with
the command of troops who give such pleasing evidence of their zeal for the service and manifest so strong a desire to advance against the inhuman murderers
of their friends and countrymen.*

The second General Order was for the entire army to march tomorrow for
Wyoming.

[*June 30, 1779 — Sunday*]

Never before in its history had the Mohawk Valley experienced such a sense of
organized activity in military operations. Accustomed to the laxity of militia assemblies and maneuvers that, at best, were ordinarily lackadaisical and fraught
with confusion, discord, disobedience and desertion when the going got rough,
Tryon County was now witnessing the smooth workings of a well-oiled military
machine.

The reason was the competence of the commander of the New York
Brigade, Brigadier General James Clinton. From the instant he had been
named to form this northern wing of the Sullivan expedition and to rendezvous
with Sullivan's force later at Tioga, he had been almost constantly in motion,
seeing to every detail with a practiced eye and running what an experienced sea
captain would approvingly have called a very tight ship.

As soon as the initial orders had come from Sullivan to get prepared to move
immediately on receiving word, Clinton began collecting his artillery, supplies
and boats and directing them to be taken to Fort Stanwix and held there in
readiness under a very heavy guard. By the third week of May, while Sullivan
was still having difficulty acquiring even the most basic of supplies for running
his operation on a day-to-day basis, Clinton had already stockpiled at Fort
Stanwix food stores sufficient to last his own force for three months, and with
over two hundred bateaux[263] in which to transport them.

Oddly, considering Sullivan's difficulties in getting anything, George Washington took a very dim view of such preparations and complained rather bitterly
to Sullivan about it, implying that Clinton's preparations were causing delay
and revealing the army's designs. In his communiqué to Sullivan, Washington
wrote:

*I am filled with inexpressible concern at the extent of General Clinton's prepara-
tions in provisions and batteaux. I had expected him to move rapidly and keep
his army quite light, with such provisions as necessary to serve only until reaching the rendezvous at Tioga. By his preparations, instead of having his design
concealed till the moment of execution, and forming his junction with you in a*

manner to surprise, the design is announced; the enemy watching him. And in place of moving light and rapidly and, as it were, undiscovered, he goes encumbered with useless supplies and has his defense weakened by the attention he must pay to his convoy.

Sullivan did not at all agree with his commander's appraisal and immediately rose to Clinton's defense. He praised his New York brigadier for his preparations, pointing out that it was not Clinton who was causing a delay, but Sullivan himself, because necessary supplies had not been acquired by the main army with the admirable facility with which Clinton was accumulating them. As for Clinton's preparations allegedly announcing the army's designs, Sullivan said that the enemy long ago was apprised of the army's preparations and intentions and secrecy of the basic objectives was no longer possible. And as for Washington's conception that Clinton should have only enough supplies to last him until he reached Tioga, Sullivan had a much different outlook. As he wrote to Washington:

I myself have not the most Distant prospect of keeping that part of the army that is with me from starving long enough to complete the expedition, so therefore it is essential that General Clinton bring with him full supplies for his own division for the whole period.

In a rather begrudging manner, Washington accepted the comments and explanations, refraining from further criticism of Clinton, but his reply to Sullivan was a bit edged as he rather curtly urged him to lighten his own troops to the greatest possible degree and hasten the operations.

In response to the orders received from John Sullivan, General Clinton had relayed his own orders to his commanders of the 2nd, 3rd, 4th and 5th New York regiments, directing them to prepare for the expedition and assemble their forces at Canajoharie immediately. From that point the difficult portage of bateaux and supplies would be undertaken along the twenty miles of road connecting the Mohawk River at Canajoharie with the Susquehanna River headwaters at Otsego Lake. Immediately the division was in movement and companies from Albany, Schenectady, Schoharie, Stone Arabia, Johnstown and Cherry Valley's Fort Alden began converging. At the same time, Clinton ordered the supply-filled bateaux to begin moving down from Fort Stanwix to Canajoharie.

By June 17, Clinton's full force of fifteen hundred men and some two hundred and twenty bateaux was assembled at Canajoharie and the portage begun. It was no easy job. Over five hundred wagons of all shapes and sizes had been acquired and brought to Canajoharie and now they formed a steady train all the way to the northeastern corner of Ostego Lake[264] and back. In addition, the large, heavy bateaux were each being pulled by four horses and they too became a part of the serpentine line of transport. It was an awe-inspiring spectacle to behold and there were more than just American eyes beholding it. The entire operation was under constant surveillance by Brant's Iroquois and Colonel John Butler's Tory Rangers. Mostly they observed unseen and sent runners with regular reports to Brant and Butler, but occasionally they grew careless.

Several times during early June the sentries detected and fired upon men spying on the American operations, but it wasn't until just after the midpoint of the month that a significant development came about. It was all due to the zeal of a twenty-two-year-old lieutenant named Thomas Boyd, at the head of one of Major James Parr's rifle companies.

Lieutenant Boyd had a great dream that he had cherished ever since he was a small boy: he wanted to become a national figure of heroic proportions. He pictured himself one day as a great general in a position perhaps not unlike General Sullivan's, leading his army into an unmapped wilderness after a fierce enemy and, by dint of his acuity, sagacity and strategic ability, defeating that enemy and returning home to the cheers of adoring throngs of his own people and eventually becoming honored as no general before him had ever been. Sometimes the dream became so real to him that he turned almost giddy at the prospect. To his credit, he knew that he had a long way to go, but he was always alert for ways that would increase his prospects. One had to be noticed to get anywhere, he knew, and to be noticed one had to do things that were rather spectacular and lifted the individual into prominence among his peers and to a position of favor among his superiors. To this end, Boyd was always applying himself.

A native of Derry, Pennsylvania, Thomas Boyd enlisted in the army there just prior to the Declaration of Independence in 1776 and, because of the manner in which he put himself across at the outset, he was given the rank of sergeant in Captain Stephen Bayard's company. This was the rank he held for a year and a half and during that interval he transferred to Captain Matthew Smith's company. He exhibited better than average leadership capabilities and so on January 14, 1778, he was promoted to the temporary rank of captain-lieutenant in the 1st Pennsylvania Regiment.

Because of his considerable skill as a rifleman, Boyd was given the permanent rank of lieutenant shortly after that and detached from his own regiment to become a company commander in Colonel William Butler's 4th New York Regiment, in General Hand's brigade. Here he became a member of one of the American army's most elite rifle corps, Morgan's Partisan Corps, and last July 1, just after the Battle of Monmouth, he became one of a three-company detachment of that corps, under Major James Parr, to be ordered to Schoharie, along with the 4th Pennsylvania Regiment, to help defend the borders of New York against Brant's Iroquois.[265]

Now, as part of General Clinton's brigade, young Boyd was one of those in command of troops disposed along the portage route to protect and assist the wagoners in their efforts. Almost ceaselessly he, along with others, rode back and forth on that road. Mostly it was dull duty, which generated carelessness among those engaged in it. Not so with Boyd. He was still constantly seeking ways by which to exhibit his courage and audacity and special talents. Perhaps that was why he saw something that no one else had detected — a faint bootprint on the road just southwest of Canajoharie.

There were, of course, multitudes of bootprints on the dusty road, but this one, just barely visible, was different. Instead of pointing down the road, it was leading off at a tangent. Numerous guards and wagons had already passed over it and mostly the track was obliterated when Boyd came along. However, there was just enough of the heel and toe impression that Boyd saw it. Very casually, without slowing pace, he raised his eyes and turned his head in the direction the print indicated and saw, in front of a little grove of trees a hundred yards off the road, a low jumble of rocks tossed there as the field had been cleared and cultivated.

He continued riding until hidden by a bend in the road, then tied his horse to a fencepost and began a stealthy, circuitous movement back toward the rocks. Coming up behind them, he found two men in civilian clothes crouched behind the rocks, carefully observing the convoy. Silently, Boyd drew his flintlock pistol and pointed it at them. The click as he cocked it made the two jerk around, startled, and Boyd smiled tightly at them.

"Gentlemen," he said, "you are under arrest."

The capture of the two had taken significant enterprise on Boyd's part. Not until later, though, did he and the whole army realize what a coup it had been. The two captured men were two of the most inhumane Tories known, a pair notorious throughout the frontier for their numerous barbarities, which had reached their most infamous peak during the destruction of Cherry Valley. One of them was Lieutenant Rolf Hare. The other was Sergeant Gilbert Newbury.

The two captives were taken into Canajoharie and jailed until, very quickly, a court-martial ordered by General Clinton was seated. On the testimony of the Reverend Samuel Dunlop that Lieutenant Hare was involved in the death of his wife, Sarah, at Cherry Valley, including the commission of atrocities upon her body, and the testimony of Hugh Mitchell, also of Cherry Valley, that he had actually witnessed Sergeant Newbury kill his twelve-year-old daughter with a tomahawk and scalp her, both men were sentenced to be hanged and were executed at Canajoharie on June 30.[266] The fame of Lieutenant

Thomas Boyd spread and the consensus was that here was a young officer who was truly going places.

The capture and execution of the two spies was a sort of commencement of a series of similar occurrences. On June 21, another Tory spy was captured and hanged at Canajoharie and three days later one of Clinton's own men, Private James Titus of the 5th New York Regiment, was caught after deserting, brought back to the camp and summarily shot. Spies were everywhere, watching the camp, observing the line of supplies and boats being transported to Otsego Lake and even infiltrating the ranks. Here and there men were wounded or killed who had only stepped off the road a short distance to relieve themselves. It was very dangerous to move about alone. One of the rifle officers sent his slave to a little brook about a mile from the camp to get some watercress for a salad and he was captured and taken away. On June 28, Colonel Peter Gansevoort hanged a spy in his camp.

Disruptive as these things were, progress was made every day. General Clinton's background as an engineer now became a decided asset. Early in the transport of goods and boats, he had sent Major Parr with a detachment of two hundred men on a three-day scout to check out the lower end of Otsego Lake [267] in order to see what the condition of the water was there as well as that a little farther downstream on the outlet, which was the Susquehanna River. Otsego Lake was eight miles long and two miles across and when Parr returned he reported that the water flow out the south end of the lake was still passable for bateaux but that it was apparent the water level was daily lowering and within another week or two the passage might become impossible for heavily loaded craft. However, Parr reported, at a point ten miles below the lake, after the river was fed by a number of tributaries and springs, it was quite definitely navigable. That was when Clinton immediately sent ahead two companies of Colonel Alden's 6th Massachusetts Regiment, still being commanded by Major Daniel Whiting, with orders to erect a dam across the outlet at the lower end of the lake. With the water impounded, when the time came for moving downstream, there would be a sufficiency to carry the heavy bateaux along on the crest caused when the dam was broken. It was a clever plan, but no one was quite sure it would work.

Today, thirteen days since the remarkable portaging of supplies and boats was begun from Canajoharie, the huge job was finished. So now, on this last day of June, Clinton wrote to Sullivan:

Everything is in readiness, Sir, for your order and embarkation will be immediately effected upon receipt of your order to that end. We have had some trouble with spies and deserters but swift action and harsh punishment, including the execution of a small number, have given both our enemies and those of our own ranks whose loyalties might be wavering, pause to reconsider and I think we will hereafter be little bothered by these two evils. I should mention, General, that we had with us for a fortnight some two hundred Oneida Indians under Chief Hanyerry. [268] *Only two days ago these Indians received a very threatening letter from the British commander, General Sir Frederick Haldimand, Governor of Quebec, which threatened the destruction of their towns if they joined our force. At this most of them deserted us and we are left now with only 25, but these include Hanyerry, who is angered at the threats and determined to continue with us and guide us into the Indian country after my junction with you at Tioga. Otherwise, Sir, it gives me the greatest pleasure to inform you that this division of the army is now entirely moved from Canajoharie and the entire complement of seventeen hundred men* [269] *has encamped at the outlet of the lake. The dam I mentioned has been built and is holding well and already the lake is backing up somewhat. Floating just above the dam are a total of 220 bateaux fully loaded with supplies and provisions enough to maintain this wing of the army for three months. Everything is in readiness and embarkation will begin downstream from this point as soon as your order in that respect is received.*

I am, Sir,
Your Most Humble Servant,
J. CLINTON

Maj. Genl Jⁿ Sullivan

[*July 3, 1779 — Saturday*]

The army of General John Sullivan most certainly did not provide, as Clinton's wing did, an expeditious movement of troops and gathering of supplies. Not until June 18 had they actually left Easton and started the trek northward and westward toward the Wyoming Valley. The road had been fairly easy as they at first moved north through the Wind Gap. [270] Through this unusual pass in the Blue Mountains, with the slopes rising steeply six hundred feet on either side of them, the more than three thousand men, along with their wagons and horses, filed through and continued north to Pocono Point. Concerning this passage, Major James Norris wrote in his journal:

We came through a narrow pass of the Blue Mountain, called the Wind-Gap, a passage apparently designed by nature for a communication; and according to the description given by Cornelius Nepos, pretty much resembles the Straits of Thermopylae where 300 Greeks under Leonida checked the progress of 80,000 Persians commanded by Xerxes. After having taken rest and refreshment, the troops marched nine miles farther to Learns's [271] *Tavern near Pocono Point and encamped. At this place a rattlesnake was killed having seven rattles on his tail, and a full-grown bird in his stomach, which would seem to confirm the notion of snakes having the power of fascinating or charming their prey. The land through this day's march is mountainous, barren and uninhabitable, but well watered and the streams abounding with trout.*

As the route of the army then turned essentially westward, the march became rough in the extreme. For all the work that had been done in carving out a road to the Wyoming Valley, it was still a tremendously rough passage. The road was rocky and narrow, the country barren and ugly. Wagons broke down with dismal frequency. Sometimes they could be repaired, but all too often they had to be abandoned and their loads distributed to other wagons and packhorses, making the burden on them even more difficult. Before they had even reached the twenty-mile-long Shades of Death swamp, horses had begun dying under their loads. Nearly half a hundred died before that difficult passage was completed and the way was littered with their carcasses. Food was so limited that many of the men took to killing and cooking as food the most abundant form of wildlife seen — rattlesnakes. Colonel Henry Dearborn, trying the meat for the first time, tried to be impartial in his judgment as he wrote in his journal:

I ate part of a fried rattle snake today, which would have tasted well, had it not been snake.

Throughout all the difficulty, General John Sullivan was grimly determined to have his army perform the job it was supposed to do. No one had ever intimated that an expedition setting out to effect the annihilation of practically a whole race of people was going to be a simple matter. But Sullivan had expected the difficulty to come from outside sources, not from within.

As it had been from the beginning for him, supply was the greatest problem. Everything was in short supply and all the complaints and demands had had little effect. The army arrived at Wyoming on June 23 after a rigorous five-day march, fully expecting to have a bounteous supply of food and clothing awaiting them there that was supposed to have been ferried upstream on the Susquehanna to Sunbury and then relayed from there to Wyoming. A small portion of what had been expected arrived, but all of the salted and brine-packed beef was spoiled and almost all of the remainder of the foodstuffs was so bad it had to be condemned. Sullivan let his bitterness show plainly in his letter to Congress about it:

My duty to the public and regard to my own reputation compel me to state the reasons why this army has been so long delayed without advancing into the enemy's country. The inspector is now on the ground, by order of the Board of War, inspecting the provisions, and his regard to the truth must oblige him on his return to report that, of the salted meat on hand, there is not a single pound fit to be eaten, even at this day, though every measure has been taken to preserve it that could possibly be devised. About one hundred and fifty cattle sent to Sunbury were left there, being too poor to walk, and many of them unable to stand.

A stupid blunder had caused the spoilage of the meat on which the army was to have depended. The salted meat was packed in brine in the customary manner for doing so, except that the casks had been newly made out of green lumber. This caused the brine to sour and the meat to spoil. The Pennsylvania War Office reply was an apology of sorts, but it didn't ease the difficulty of the situation. That office wrote:

Your remarks on the Staff Department have undoubtedly but too much foundation; at the same time we must observe that they are in many cases almost insuperable difficulties in the way; among these may be reckoned the want of men and proper materials. Of the former the country is much drained, and of the latter the old stocks are generally worked up or used and no provision made for future wants. Hence in particular they have sometimes been obliged to use green stuff for casks, which in summer is ruinous to whatever is put in them. To this cause may be imputed the badness of some of the salted provisions destined for your army; for we have upon inquiry received satisfactory evidence that no care was wanting in the salting and repacking of the greater part of them.

The excuses did little to mollify the seething anger that filled Sullivan and now he was more than just a little thankful that General Clinton, from whom he had just heard, had a full three months' worth of supplies and provisions on hand for his seventeen hundred men. That amount of supplies might have to be carefully hoarded and distributed in meager rations to the entire army of five thousand. It was a damnable way to start a campaign leading into enemy country. A few more supplies, it was hoped, would be brought up the Susquehanna from Sunbury before the army left here, and some other supplies beyond that were to be brought by Lieutenant Colonel James Pawling, who had been ordered to rendezvous with General Clinton at Oquaga.[272]

The men in Sullivan's army were becoming increasingly mutinous. On June 26 three men who had been found guilty of desertion had sentences meted out to them. Private Oliver Arnold was executed by a firing squad; Private Edward Tyler was forced to run through a gauntlet made up of the men of two regiments, and Private John Stevens was given one hundred lashes. These sentences were passed in a quiet way and made little impression on the troops. Within a few days two more privates, these from Colonel Spencer's regiment, were given harsh punishments for having dressed up as Indians and threatened the life of one of their officers — a practical joke no one appreciated. One of the men was forced to run a gauntlet through three regiments and was so severely beaten he could not walk for a week. The other was tied to a post and given one hundred lashes.

Still, the mutinous sense continued mounting throughout the whole army and Sullivan now determined to nip it thoroughly. When two more men, this time of the Jersey Brigade, were convicted of traitorous crimes, he had his opportunity to make an example of them. Privates Laurence Miller and Michael Rosebury, both of Sussex County, New Jersey, not far from Easton, were tried by court-martial and found guilty of enticing soldiers to desert. They were sentenced to be hanged at 4:00 P.M. on July 1 and this time Sullivan ordered that the execution be witnessed by everyone at Wyoming. The evening prior to the event, two of the chaplains attached to the army, the Reverends William Rogers and Samuel Kirkland, visited the condemned men to administer spiritual comfort in their last moments. As Rogers put it in his journal:

Mr. Kirkland accompanied me in paying these two unfortunate men a visit; found them ignorant and stupid. Our endeavors were, upon this occasion, to open unto them the nature of man's fall and the dreadful situation of those who died in a state of impenitency and unbelief. When we went to see the prisoners, Miller appeared much softened, distressed and anxious about his future state. Rosebury said but little. I enlarged particularly at this time on their awful condition by nature and practice, their amazing guilt in the sight of an Holy God; the spirituality of the Divine Law; the necessity of an interest in Jesus Christ; their own inability to obtain salvation, and the great importance of a due preparation for another world.

After their meeting with the condemned, both ministers conferred at length with one another and then in the morning met with General Sullivan and especially recommended that mercy be shown to Miller. Sullivan heard them out and then spoke to them at length. Saying little, the two ministers nodded gravely at intervals and then finally took their leave. That evening the Reverend William Rogers again wrote succinctly in his journal:

Thursday — July 1.
Before breakfast visited the convicts; spoke to them on the realities of heaven and hell, and the justice and mercy of God. Miller appeared still more penitent, and freely confessed the sentence of death passed over him to be just. The other excused himself and insisted much on the innocency of his life. Mr. Kirkland and myself waited on the commander-in-chief, in order to recommend Miller to mercy. His Excellency was so obliging as to inform us that it was his purpose, on account of Miller's wife and numerous family, his decent behavior on trial, the recommendation of the court and former good character, to pardon him under

the gallows fifteen minutes after the execution of Rosebury; and requested that it might remain a secret with us until it was publicly known. P.M. — *At the hour appointed the prisoners were taken under guard to the place of execution, attended by Messrs. Kirkland, Hunter and myself. In walking to the gallows we of course conversed with them on the most serious subjects. Upon arriving there, the military being under arms, and a number of inhabitants present, it fell to my lot to address the spectators, after which Mr. Kirkland prayed. Rosebury was then turned off; he died to all appearance the same stupid man he was at the first of our visiting him. Poor Miller was much agitated at the sight, expecting every moment the same punishment. He was employed in commending himself to God. Upon hearing his pardon from the commander-in-chief read, he was greatly affected. On recovering himself he expressed the utmost thankfulness for his great deliverance. The scene throughout was very affecting.*

When the pardon was read, it stated that this was the last instance of mercy that would be shown to any man in the army convicted of a similar offense. Though other men had been executed, this instance seemed to have quite a profound effect upon all who witnessed it, as Sullivan planned it should. Even more affecting than the execution was the release of Miller to return to his family near Easton. Every man of the army who was keeping a diary or journal — and there were many — wrote of the incident feelingly. One of the shortest of the journal entries concerning it was that written by Sergeant Thomas Roberts:

July 1st   There was two men condemned for to be hung that was drove to the gallows with their halters round their necks. One was hung and the other reprieved, which shocked him so he almost fainted away.

It was the last case of the campaign where men from Sullivan's own army were convicted of and executed for treason.

Now, with the army poised at Wyoming, General Sullivan found himself still unable to move because of the lack of supplies. Every day they waited, that much more of what was needed for the campaign — both by Sullivan's men and Clinton's — was being consumed. If it was not replaced soon and abundantly, the whole of the campaign could collapse. The delay was grating to everyone except the inhabitants of Wyoming, who were perfectly content to have the army remain here permanently. It was the first time in the history of the area that they'd ever really felt secure.

Today, July 3, was the first anniversary of the great tragedy that had taken place here at Wyoming and now, for the first time since their arrival, a group of officers including General Sullivan, General Poor, Colonel Dearborn, Major Norris and others crossed the river and toured the scenes of that terrible time of a year ago. They were led by the commander of Wilkes-Barre Fort, Colonel Zebulon Butler.

"This," said Butler soberly, as they paused at the scene of the principal battle, "is where they destroyed us. I pray, sir, that your supplies will come soon so that you can move into their country and similarly destroy them."

John Sullivan nodded slowly. "Whether or not our supplies come as anticipated, Colonel, I promise you that they will be ruined. That is what we are here to do. That is what will be done. When we have finished with this campaign, I promise you that the Iroquois will no longer exist as a force capable of inflicting such a tragedy."

[*July 5, 1779 — Monday*]

Since the third anniversary of the declared independence of the United States fell yesterday, on a Sunday, and Sundays were not days on which exuberant gaiety could be exhibited and alcoholic spirits consumed, festivities had been put off until today in both the main army under General Sullivan and the New York Brigade under General Clinton. The delay had in no way dampened the enthusiasm for it. Tomorrow morning at Wyoming a detachment under Colonel Adam Hubley was heading downriver to Fort Freeland at Sunbury where they would meet and escort upstream at least forty huge bateaux loaded with supplies. When they arrived, the army could be put into motion. At the moment, with celebration in the offing, no one was thinking much about the march being resumed.

Far to the northeast, at General Clinton's camp at the foot of Otsego Lake, a huge celebration was already in progress. There had been laughter and games, speeches and food and drinks. At three in the afternoon the troops paraded on the south bank of the lake and their assembly was punctuated by the firing of a thirteen-gun salute to honor the thirteen states. The reverberation of those cannon shots booming across the lake seemed to personify the indomitable spirit imbued in this army. Standing with his remaining two dozen warriors in a small cluster to one side, Chief Hanyerry spoke softly in the Oneida tongue.

"Listen, my children," he told them. "Those great thundering guns speak words that all the people of the Six Nations should listen to, but refuse. They speak words of death and destruction and an end to the way we and those before us have always lived. Our world is no more the world we once knew; we are no longer the way we were. Our world changes before our eyes and if we cannot change with it then we, like our brothers among the Mohawks and Senecas, Cayugas and Onondagas and Tuscaroras, will become no more than a memory."

Following the thirteen-gun salute, a bonfire called a *feu de joie* was fired and then the brigade chaplain, the Reverend John Gano, gave a divine service. The formal festivities were ended and the informal fun began, commencing with the drinking of thirteen toasts to the American cause, its friends, and the officers' wives and sweethearts at home.

At Wyoming a very similar situation was occurring, with General Enoch Poor undertaking to provide for the entertainment of all the officers, aided in some degree by General Edward Hand. At Poor's camp a huge booth of sorts had been set up, eighty feet long, in which were makeshift tables formed from planks on two-foot-high log sections covered by cloth. A large marquee was pitched at each end and, though rations had been poor for weeks, on this day the tables abounded with wild turkey, venison, trout, grouse and other fish and wild game. After all, this was the third anniversary of United States independence and, while everyone thought it, no one voiced the uncomfortable possibility that had similarly plagued them last year, that it might be the last. There was still no way to know how this war was going to end.

Before the meal was served to the eighty-seven officers attending, patriotic services were held for the different brigades by the Reverends Hunter, Kirkland and Rogers. Afterward thirteen cannon blasts rent the air and then gills of rum were distributed to the privates. Most of these soldiers were content to loll about watching, and occasionally tossing fresh wood on, the huge *feu de joie.* Some simply wrote letters or slept.

At General Poor's camp, the jollity went into high gear immediately after the religious services. The fine meal was devoured with great appreciation and enjoyment and then a whole series of favorite songs were sung, sometimes as solos by the more accomplished tenors and baritones among them, sometimes with everyone joining in. Then, as at Clinton's celebration, came the toasts — thirteen of them. The first was to the Fourth of July, '76 — the ever-memorable patriotic era of American independence. The second was to the United States itself and the air resounded with cries of "Hear! Hear!" A drink to the Grand Council of America was the fourth toast and the fifth was to General George Washington and the army. The King and Queen of France received, as allies, the sixth toast. Major General Benjamin Lincoln and his southern army, which had just won an important victory at Charleston, South Carolina, along with Major General John Sullivan and his western expedition, shared the seventh toast. By the eighth, the toasters were becoming a bit more loquacious and philosophic.

"May the counselors of America," the toaster intoned with exaggerated gravity, "be wise . . . and her soldiers invincible!"

"A ninth toast!" shouted a captain, standing on a log and teetering slightly as he held his drink high. "That we have a successful and decisive campaign!"

Casting an eye toward the area where Chief Jehoiakim and his small group of Stockbridge Indians were camped, the next officer shouted, "Civilization or death to all American savages!" There was no reaction from the Indians, who either did not hear or chose to ignore it.

The final three toasts were delivered in solemn stentorian tones and each brought a prolonged cheering.

"To the immortal memory of those heroes that have fallen in defense of American liberty!"

"Vigor and virtue to the sons and daughters of America and may this New World be the last asylum for freedom and the arts!"

"May the husbandman's cottage be blessed with peace and his fields with plenty!"

Thirteen toasts were not enough. A number of others were drunk after that — primarily to individuals and most specifically to certain ladies left behind — but after the thirteenth, no one was counting anymore.

[*July 30, 1779 — Friday*]

For five weeks, since arriving at Wyoming, Major General John Sullivan had been fuming at the delays caused by the lack of supplies. Now, at long last, it appeared that the time of waiting was over. The condition of the army, so far as provisions were concerned, was certainly not good but it was also certainly much better than it had been at any time since the army's arrival here on June 23. If there was to be a campaign against the Indians this summer, it had to be put into movement immediately.

Marking time in the Wyoming Valley had spread a pall of gloom over the entire army and morale was at a very low ebb. This did not surprise Sullivan. Any army keyed up to move on an expedition against a savage enemy and then forced to stand in place because of unconscionable problems in regard to supply was bound to lose a sense of forward momentum, a sense of spirit and enthusiasm. The whole general feeling prevailing throughout the army was epitomized in the entry that Dr. Ebenezer Elmer of the 2nd New Jersey Regiment wrote in his journal toward the middle of July after having been stalled at Wyoming for three weeks:

A kind of thoughtful melancholy possessed my mind this evening which prevented my taking any rest until the latter part of the night, constantly ruminating on the past transactions of my life and future prospects therein.

In essence, Dr. Elmer was asking himself the same question that, in one way or another, around five thousand men were asking themselves at about this time: what am I doing here, especially when it's obvious that nothing is going well? There was no answer, of course, only the necessity for continuing to do what was required — wait.

Small incidents became matters of tremendous importance. The entire army talked for a whole day or two about the incident that occurred on the morning of July 6. It was a muggy morning, with heavy and strange black clouds having a sort of boiling character to them rolling across the skies soon after daybreak. Most of the soldiers, realizing a storm was coming, stayed indoors. Outside chores were ordered postponed until the passage of the storm and most of the men were content to sit about and do nothing. In the 3rd New Hampshire Regiment, however, Private Luke Winslow decided he would take advantage of the unexpected free time to take a bath in the river. With a couple of friends he went there and lathered up in the refreshingly cool shallows at about eight in the morning.

When the storm hit, there was very little warning. One minute the air was totally devoid of breezes and leaves hung limply on the trees. The next minute a gust of wind of near-gale proportions swept across the countryside, snapping some trees, scattering limbs and leaves with a frenzy and picking up clouds of dust and debris. At the same time a horrendous crashing of thunder occurred.

Winslow's companions, close to the cover formed by an overhanging bank, took refuge there. Winslow was more than a hundred feet away from them in water to his waist. He laughed at the way his friends leaped for cover. The laughter was short-lived. Abruptly hail began to fall. The pellets were at first the size of peas, but in moments they had increased in dimension until they were the size of hen's eggs, though lumpy and rough rather than smooth and oval. These chunks of ice hurtled with great speed earthward and where they struck trees and plants they broke them off, smashed them, crushed them, beat them down and destroyed them. The effect was hardly less devastating on a human.

The huge icy lumps struck Winslow with no less force than those striking the vegetation. Immediately he let out a cry and flung up his arms to protect himself, but it was futile. Within a moment he was bleeding profusely on his head, shoulders and arms. He tried to take refuge under the surface of the water but the hailstones became even bigger while he was submerged and when he surfaced to breathe, they struck his head with the force of rocks, stunning him. He staggered, floundered and came momentarily erect, his face and body severely injured, and then he fell back into the water and was gone. Five minutes later the hailstorm ended. It took nearly three hours to recover Winslow's body.

Just as the whole army had talked in hushed tones about this weird death of Private Winslow, so they had chuckled together about the incident involving one of their principal officers — Lieutenant Colonel Henry Dearborn.[273] An especially eligible bachelor, Dearborn at twenty-eight was the youngest regimental commander in Sullivan's army. It was known that he was the target of many an amorous young lady but he had thus far been successful in avoiding matrimony. Now he had received a letter from his hometown that congratulated him upon his marriage and commented most favorably on the attributes of his wife without speaking of the woman in question by name. No little bemused by the circumstance, Dearborn wrote in his diary:

I received several letters from New Hampshire today, in one of which I am informed of being married, but have not learnt to whom.

Minor incidents with Indians were occurring every now and then, but little of significance. About one night in ten, army sentries would fire at Indians seen skulking nearby. None was hit, however, and none returned any fire; they were obviously merely spying out what was occurring in the Sullivan encampment, but the knowledge they were about caused an apprehension that lodged in every man's breast and made him nervous. That form of nervousness added its weight to the edginess experienced by most of the men at being away from women for so long. Sexual hungers, which could be put down well enough by most of them during an active campaign, were hard to live with when day after day the weeks passed without any real activity and without relief. As customary, a fair-sized number of camp followers had attached themselves to the army. Although a few were wives and sweethearts of specific men, the greater majority — perhaps a hundred or more — were loose women, as they were genteelly referred to. The biggest problem with them seemed to be, as one Jersey sergeant put it, "There just ain't enough of 'em to go around." In addition, there were a limited number of young ladies in Wyoming, some of whom were quite attractive. Their presence always caused a stir but usually they were very haughty, as if realizing only too well their position of being able to pick and choose practically anyone from a very large selection. Sometimes the officers were able to associate with them for brief periods, but the troops rarely, if ever, were so fortunate. Captain Daniel Livermore and Major James Norris were fortunate enough to spend half a day with some of the Wyoming ladies, but hardly in a manner that afforded any degree of privacy or lent itself to the relaxing of inhibitions or the release of tensions. They helped escort a party of young ladies who appeared with the Wyoming garrison's commander, Zebulon Butler. As Norris wrote of it:

We received a visit from Colonel Butler and his lady and a half dozen young ladies from Wyoming, with whom we passed an agreeable afternoon. Colonel Butler showed us a death mall, or war mallet, that the Indians had left by a man they had knocked on the head. The handle resembles that of a hatchet, with a string drawn through near the end to hold it by. It is made of the root of a tree with a large ball worked on the head of it and looks not unlike a four-pound shot in the bill of an eagle, with a tuft of feathers on the crown. The end of the handle shows the face of a wildcat.

For General Sullivan the problems were legion. The greatest one, and still the one that occupied him most pertinently, was the lack of supplies, but there were other matters that compounded his difficulties. Although since the execution of Rosebury and reprieve of Miller there were no more cases reported of men among the troops actively urging them to engage in treason, there was still much unrest bordering on rebelliousness. That was the case when, on an especially warm night in mid-July, thirty-three men of the German Regiment deserted en masse. Their excuse — and it was a reasonable one — was that their term of enlistment had expired, which it had, and they had no desire to remain at Wyoming for more endless weeks, pointlessly waiting and not even being paid for it. Utilizing the tracking ability of Chief Jehoiakim, Sullivan sent a detachment of mounted troops in pursuit and all but four were promptly caught and brought back. Immediately they were tried by court-martial with General Poor sitting as president of the court. The five German officers who were the leaders were each sentenced to death and two corporals were demoted. The latter two were sentenced, along with the twenty-two privates, to run a gauntlet through three regiments of men. Again General Sullivan was hoping that by making an example of them he would forestall any others who had similar notions. On petition from the entire group of convicted men, Sullivan issued the following order on July 27:

The Commander-in-Chief, having received a petition from the prisoners of the German battalion now under sentence, manifesting their consciousness of their crimes for which they have been condemned, and promising in case of pardon to distinguish themselves in the future as brave and obedient soldiers, which petition, being laid before a board of general officers in hopes that an act of lenity may have a proper effect on their future conduct as well as that of others, they have unanimously advised a pardon of all the offenders without discrimination. The General, wishing to extend mercy where it can be done without injury to the public service, has accordingly consented to pardon each and every one of the offenders tried and sentenced by general court martial, whereof General Poor was president, and directs that they be immediately released and restored to their duty. Lest this unparalleled act of lenity should be abused, and any soldier take the same unjustifiable measures hereafter, the Commander-in-Chief absolutely declares he will not in the future pardon a deserter, or one who, though his time be expired, shall quit the corps without a proper discharge from his commanding officer.

Now and again there would be instances of good news about the war being received and these would be met with considerable joy and often with numerous toasts being drunk to whatever occasioned it. One such instance was when, in what was to be called the most brilliant exploit of the Revolutionary War, Brigadier General Anthony Wayne stormed the so-called impenetrable fortress of Stony Point on the Hudson River, commanded by Lieutenant Colonel Henry Johnson, was shot in the head with a musketball during the fierce engagement, yet continued to lead his men forward to an unbelievable victory. The Americans had fifteen men killed and eighty wounded, but the British suffered the staggering loss of sixty-three men killed, over seventy wounded and five hundred and forty-three captured, along with fifteen pieces of artillery and a considerable quantity of military equipment and stores. Before the battle, only two men had believed such a victory was possible. One of these was General George Washington, to whom Wayne had said before the battle, "General, if *you* will only plan it, I will storm *Hell!*"

The other man who believed in the possibility of it was the man known ever afterward by the affectionate nickname his men had given him for accomplishing the feat, Mad Anthony — General Wayne himself.

Unfortunately, matters were not going so well on the western frontier. Harsh Indian attacks had abruptly broken out to both the east and west of Sullivan's position and the populace was up in arms, questioning why an army with the strength of Sullivan's was sitting "within striking distance of the savage enemy" and doing nothing about that enemy's attacks.

The attacks in question included one led by Joseph Brant in the valley of the Delaware River at a place called Minisink, and one led by Chief Gu-cinge and his party of two hundred warriors accompanied by one hundred of Colonel John Butler's Rangers under Captain Robert McDonald and Lieutenant Adam Chrysler.

In the Minisink battle, Brant and his force made an incursion into the Delaware Valley about twenty miles upstream from where New York, New Jersey and Pennsylvania joined.[274] Engaged in a series of hit-and-run attacks that resulted in the burning of ten houses, a dozen barns, a fort and two mills and the carrying off of a considerable amount of plunder and several prisoners, and appearing by design to be a weak force, Brant once again successfully used the tactic that somehow always seemed to work in decoying the white man's military forces. As soon as a substantial force of whites under Colonel John Hathorn and Lieutenant Colonel Benjamin Tusten had been mounted and was in pursuit, he led them into a brilliantly executed ambush. Brant lost three men. The Americans lost forty-four![275]

The attacks at Forts Freeland and Sunbury were hardly less disastrous. Without warning the three hundred Indians and Rangers led by Chief Gu-cinge and Captain Robert McDonald swept in. Fort Freeland was located on the West Branch of the Susquehanna fifteen miles above its junction with the main body of the Susquehanna at Sunbury. The fort was garrisoned at this time by thirty-two men who, wholly surprised and unprepared, surrendered after a brief fight on the promise that they would be sent as prisoners to Fort Niagara and that their women and children in the fort would be allowed to go free. This was agreed to. However, the firing of the guns had been heard. Colonel Thaddeus Cook at Fort Sunbury, alerted to the attack, sent out an eager young captain, Hawkins Boon, with eighty men to help the garrison. However, Boon's own force was surrounded and attacked with the loss of forty men killed, including Boon. Thirty miles of settlements were burned, as far distant as Shamokin. The only Indian killed was Roland Montour, the son of Catherine Montour, the Seneca, the nephew of Queen Esther.

While these deeply disturbing matters were happening on both sides of him, John Sullivan at Wyoming was still coping with the monumental problem of getting his army moving and, in order to do that, acquiring the desperately needed supplies. The condition of his army was deplorable. Numerous parties had been sent out by him in July to meet and escort back to Wyoming the expected supplies, but they were very slow in coming. On July 14, Colonel Adam Hubley wrote to President Joseph Reed of the Supreme Executive Council of Pennsylvania in an effort to add his voice and whatever weight it carried to the multitude of complaints being lodged in the matter. He was also strong in his support of General Sullivan, who was being sharply attacked from many quarters because of the army's inactivity in the face of so much Indian disturbance. Hubley wrote:

Our expedition, Honoured Sir, is carrying on rather slow, owing to the delay of our provisions, &c. I sincerely pity General Sullivan's situation. People who are not acquainted with the reasons of the delay, I'm informed, censure him, which is absolutely cruel and unjust. No man can be more assiduous than he is. Unless some steps are taken to find out and make an example of the delinquent (Quartermasters and Commissaries), I fear our expedition will be reduced to a much less compass than was intended.

At last, as July went into its third week, all the efforts at getting supplies to Wyoming began to bear fruit. On July 21, eight hundred head of cattle, five hundred horses and five hundred wagons arrived from Easton. On July 24, a fleet of one hundred and twelve heavily loaded bateaux, brought upriver a hundred and twenty miles from Middletown, arrived at Wyoming under command of General Hand, who had been sent by Sullivan to get them. Finally, on July 28 another eighty wagons filled with stores, along with one hundred and fifty more packhorses, arrived from Easton.

All these supplies were far from what Sullivan considered as being the requisite to launch his campaign, yet he knew it could no longer be delayed. He sent off an express to General Clinton at Otsego Lake, instructing him to start downstream at once for the rendezvous, destroying whatever Indian towns he encountered en route. He also mentioned that he hoped Clinton still had some good Indian guides with his force, as his own Stockbridge Indians, with the single exception of Chief Jehoiakim, had all deserted the army during the past few days. With that dispatch on its way to Clinton, he then issued the order for the main army to move upstream out of the Wyoming Valley and into Indian country beginning early on Saturday, July 31.

That was tomorrow.

Obviously, today had been an extremely busy day for everyone. Excitement was at a high pitch and the whole Wyoming Valley was abustle as everyone prepared for the march. Packhorses had to be loaded and put under the care of packhorsemen; bateaux had to be packed and their crews readied. From six o'clock this morning until nine this evening, Wyoming was the center of a great flurry of preparation as over six hundred men especially assigned to the task packed and stowed, cinched and tied and secured baggage aboard boats and on horses. While they were doing this, probably no less than half the army, having completed their personal packing, were writing letters to friends and relatives, abruptly fearful that these might be the last words they would ever write to their loved ones.

Colonel Hubley was writing too, and once again it was to President Reed. Despite the supplies that had arrived, it had to be stressed to the civil authorities that more were needed and must be forwarded to the army even while it was in motion. If this was not accomplished, Hubley warned, almost certainly the campaign could turn into a monumental disaster for America. He wrote:

Tomorrow we march and, I am sorry to say, exceedingly ill provided to carry through the extensive expedition. The same unparalleled conduct of those employed in supplying this army, seems still to exist. I hope to see the day when the delinquents will be brought to the proper punishment. My regiments, I fear, will be almost totally naked before we can possibly return. I have scarcely a coat or blanket for every seventh man. The State stores are issued and delivered up to the regiment.

Even General Sullivan himself was busy with final-moment correspondence. Bombarded from both east and west with reports of the Indian attacks that had occurred, he was certain that these were no more than diversionary attacks, well calculated to cause him to split his force to send out rescue or retaliatory detachments. In doing so he would weaken the army as a whole and defeat the purpose of the campaign. And now, more than at any time since the very beginning of it, Major General John Sullivan was determined that there was going to be a campaign and a very successful one at that. No one was more strongly convinced than he that the Indian threat had to be eliminated. That was the purpose of this campaign and that was what was going to be accomplished. It could not, he knew, be accomplished by reacting to the affairs at Minisink or Fort Freeland. Now, having already regretfully refused to send assistance to the Delaware Valley, he was writing a very similar refusal to the earnest appeal for help from Colonel Thaddeus Cook at Sunbury:

Nothing could afford me more pleasure than to relieve the distressed, or to have it in my power to add to the safety of your settlement, but should I comply with the requisition made by you, it would effectually answer the intention of the enemy and destroy the grand object of this expedition. Tomorrow the army moves from this place, and by carrying the war immediately into the Indians' country, it will most certainly draw them out of yours.

In General Sullivan, the British and Indians on the frontier had an adversary indeed worthy of note.

As he finished sealing the letter, a slight disturbance outside caused him to look up just as a youth of about fifteen burst into the room, followed by an agitated captain, the general's aide.

"I'm sorry, sir," said Captain Jonathan Dayton. "When I told the boy you were too busy to see him, he ran right past me."

Sullivan, studying the boy who stood in a slightly defensive stance a few feet to one side, smiled faintly and then nodded to his aide. "All right, Captain, thank you. You can leave us alone for a while."

Reluctantly, Captain Dayton left the room and, as the door shut behind him, the general turned back to the boy and raised an eyebrow questioningly.

"General Sullivan, sir, nobody'll let me help!" The words were blurted out and the boy went on: "I want to go on this expedition with you. I *have* to."

"You *have* to?" Sullivan murmured. He shook his head and spoke gently but firmly. "I think not. Warfare is a matter for grown men, son. It is not a lark. It is most especially not a lark when it involves fighting against Indians."

"I'm aware of that, sir," the boy said, his gaze direct. "I've already fought them."

Sullivan was surprised. "You have? Where? When?"

"Right here, sir. My name is Elliott. Jabez Elliott. I was in the battle here, at Wyoming, a year ago. I was younger then. Fourteen. My brother, Joe, he was in the battle, too. And my father, Henry. My father was killed. That's why I want to go with you."

The general nodded slowly. "I can see where you would. Still, you are too young to be inducted as a soldier in this army. I'm sorry."

Elliott shook his head. "No!" At the sudden frown on Sullivan's face he stammered slightly, but went on: "I . . . I mean, there is a way, sir, that I could go. I'm good with horses. Very good. You need drovers to herd the cattle. You need packhorsemen. I can do those things. Please. As a civilian employed by the army, just like the bateaumen and drovers and packhorsemen. *Please!"*

The frown remained on Sullivan's face a moment longer and then his expression softened. "Go home," he said. "Go to bed." As a crestfallen look came onto the boy's face, Sullivan continued. "I always insist that, if possible, my drovers have a good night's sleep prior to a long day's march. As I said, go home and go to bed . . . and be ready to move out with us tomorrow."

[*August 7, 1779 — Saturday*]

It was at exactly eight o'clock in the morning that General James Clinton raised his right arm high and the silence of the morning was shattered by the heavy boom of one of the two pieces of artillery the brigade had. It was the signal everyone had awaited since the end of June. The campaign was at last under way.

Preparations in the camp here at the south end of Otsego Lake had been feverish ever since early yesterday when the express from General Sullivan had arrived with orders for immediate march. Practically every man of the force grown now to eighteen hundred was put to work immediately in helping to move the two hundred and twenty bateaux. Because of the danger of upsetting the loaded boats if they were to try to navigate the break in the dam, Clinton ordered all the boats portaged from the lakeshore a few hundred yards to the river below the dam. Here they were positioned on the shore of the nearly dry riverbed of the Susquehanna and tied up, then each one fully loaded. Eighteen hundred pairs of hands assisted in the work but, even at that, the job was extremely difficult and took practically all day. Twelve boats were so damaged in the portage they were beyond use, but the rest were now positioned, loaded and ready to go.

There was a feeling of gaiety among the troops that had been growing by the hour. The long wait was at last over and they were actually *doing* something, actually engaging in a real forward progress again. Each of the boats was to be manned by three people and the remainder of the force was to march on either side of the river.

At six o'clock last evening General Clinton had given the signal for the dam to be broken. A few well-placed charges of gunpowder were exploded simultaneously and did the job admirably. Above the dam, in the more than a month that had passed since its construction, the level of Otsego Lake had risen over three feet.[276] When the holes were blown in the dam and the water gushed through it quickly carried away much of that area of the dam not already broken. The result was as General Clinton had anticipated. The first great wash of water spread down the nearly dry river valley in a turbulent froth and was littered with debris from the dam. By midnight, just about all of the dam that was going to be carried away by the waters was gone and the current was now a strong stream only slightly extending above and beyond the normal high water mark of the river. By six in the morning, when the first gun sounded, the river looked almost as it would during a normally strong spring flow.

Now, with the signal gun booming at 8:00 A.M., the army went into motion. On each side of the river nearly six hundred men began to march while two hundred and eight boats, well loaded and manned by three men each, cast loose from their moorings and were swept smoothly over shoals and bars and moved along neatly downstream on the liberated waters. It was an incredible sight to see and one that would never be repeated here — a large army on the move and a huge flotilla of bateaux riding grandly on the crest of a river that heretofore in this area had never known the passage of a craft larger than a frail bark canoe.

[*August 9, 1779 — Monday*]

The statistics at the end of the first ten days of the march of General Sullivan's army were not good. Three men and five horses were dead, one man had suffered a tomahawk wound, a large quantity of flour and an entire boatload of ammunition were lost, and the commanding general was confined to his bed. It was hardly an auspicious beginning, especially in view of the fact that there had as yet been no physical contact with the enemy.

Except for a little delay in beginning the march, things had certainly started out well enough. Instead of the march beginning early in the morning on the last day of July, the army did not go into motion until 3:00 P.M. at the booming signal from the cannon on board Colonel Thomas Proctor's flagboat, the *Adventure*. Nevertheless, everyone was in a festive frame of mind. Proctor's artillery regiment was in boats because of the great weight of the big guns and their ammunition, but the greater majority of the army was either afoot or on horseback.

It was practically a storybook start to the operation, for with the firing of the gun, the weighing of anchor and the whole army set in motion, suddenly flags were flying in the light breeze, drums were tapping and fifes were piping. There were a few bagpipes wailing out their wheezing melodies and the regimental band — also part of Proctor's force — played a bright and lively tune. From its head to its rear, the army spread out for over two miles.

The post of honor, the front command, had fallen to General Hand and his light troops. They moved a mile ahead of the main body of troops and formed themselves not only in an advance guard on the so-called Warrior Trail or Great Warrior Road they were following, which was really only an Indian footpath, but also by smaller flanking parties several hundred yards out on each side to prevent a surprise flank attack by the enemy. It was only one example of how not only the whole Brigade but the whole army was arranged so as to be instantly effective in case of attack. The packhorses for the march had been positioned so General Sullivan's immediate command party had twenty of them for their baggage and necessaries. Three hundred each had been allocated for the brigades of Brigadier Generals Maxwell and Poor, as well as the same number for the public stores, which were under supervision of Colonel William Bond. Two hundred packhorses were allocated to General Hand and one hundred for Colonel Proctor and all the others. More than a score of horses were being used as saddle mounts by the drovers, including young Jabez Elliott, who were keeping the seven hundred beef cattle tightly bunched between the main army and the rear guard.

After Hand's advance guard came General Maxwell's brigade, advancing by the column's right in files, sections or platoons, according to the topography of the country they were passing through. Exactly opposite Maxwell's brigade on the right was Poor's on the left in the same manner. For the duration of the march, regiments were to be taken alternately from Maxwell's and Poor's brigades for duty as the rear guard. Today's march began with Colonel Joseph Cilly's 1st New Hampshire Regiment of Poor's brigade pulling that duty. Captain William Gifford of the 3rd New Jersey was detailed with a detachment of sixty men to go up the west side of the river to prevent any surprise or interruption from that quarter, with four well-manned light boats to keep abreast of them to ferry them across the river to the main army immediately in the event they were attacked by a superior force. It was an excellent marching arrangement for moving through enemy country and one that Sullivan meant more or less to maintain during the entire campaign.

The fleet consisted of two hundred and fourteen large bateaux into which were loaded the artillery,[277] ammunition, salted provisions, flour, liquors and heavy baggage. These boats were manned by four hundred and fifty enlisted boatmen, with Colonel Proctor's regiment and two hundred and fifty men under his command.

The Wyoming Valley fort at Wilkes-Barre had been left in command of Colonel Zebulon Butler, who had two captains, six subalterns and a garrison of one hundred men. He was charged with forwarding any further supplies that might come. The army had been put into motion about two miles below Wilkes-Barre and, as the head of the fleet passed the fort, Colonel Butler gave an order and a thirteen-gun salute boomed out, which was then answered by the fleet, still with the music being played and the flags fluttering in the breeze. The fact that a light rain was falling did not dampen the prevailing festive sense.

The music did not last long. In a short while the fort was left behind and all energies were taken up with the march. It was much more difficult than had been anticipated. Unskilled loading of the packhorses and improper adjustment of slings was quickly causing many of the loads to shift and become so imbalanced that the horses were stumbling and falling. Also, some of the loads were

bursting the straps and falling off. The problems did not stop there. The boats
had similarly been misloaded, with the weight not properly balanced. In addition, a preponderance of the boatmen were unskilled in handling the bulky
craft and progress upstream was painstakingly slow. The result was that control
of one boat heavily loaded with ammunition was lost. It spun in the current,
smashed into a huge rock and immediately sank. Only the men aboard were
saved. Within an hour the same thing occurred with a boatload of flour but
this time, along with the crew, most of the kegs of flour were saved, even
though the boat itself was lost. The fleet was unable to keep up with the land
march and was soon very far behind. All festive feeling had long since departed.

By evening, the army onshore, having marched only ten miles, had reached
the mouth of the Lackawanna, crossed over it and encamped on the north
bank.[278] The day's march past the remains of Pittston Fort and scores of homes
that had been burned some thirteen months before also helped to diminish the
levity that had affected the troops on their departure from below Wilkes-Barre.

Sergeant Thomas Roberts[279] of Captain John Burrowes's company in Colonel Oliver Spencer's 5th New Jersey Regiment was neither as articulate nor as
grammatical in his writing as others who kept journals of the march, but having never seen this area before, his words written at the close of this day were
nevertheless rather succinct and colorful:

*31st. Marched from Wyoming 10 mils up the River and Incamped at Lacken-
wanney whear the Land is the Best that Ever I see   Timmothy as high as mu
head and the Bildngs ar Burnt by the Saviges   the Warter is but Poor   the
Wild turkes very plenty   the young ones yelping throug the Woods as if it Was
inhabbited Ever So thick.*

So far behind had the boats fallen in their clumsy efforts to move upstream
that hours after darkness had fallen and the army was mostly asleep they were
still far downstream. As a matter of fact they did not catch up to the main army
until one o'clock the next afternoon. Disgruntled at the delay and determined
that every day was not going to be so bad, General Sullivan permitted them
only an hour's rest before starting the army in motion again at 2:00 P.M.

The march on the first day of August was, if anything, even worse than the
march of the day before, although it commenced with a sight that, for its
beauty, raised the spirits of many a soldier and officer — a beautiful cascade
called Falling Springs, which gushed from a spring at the mountaintop almost
seven hundred feet above them and dropped in three successive falls before
flowing into the Susquehanna.[280] In describing the place in his journal, Colonel Adam Hubley wrote:

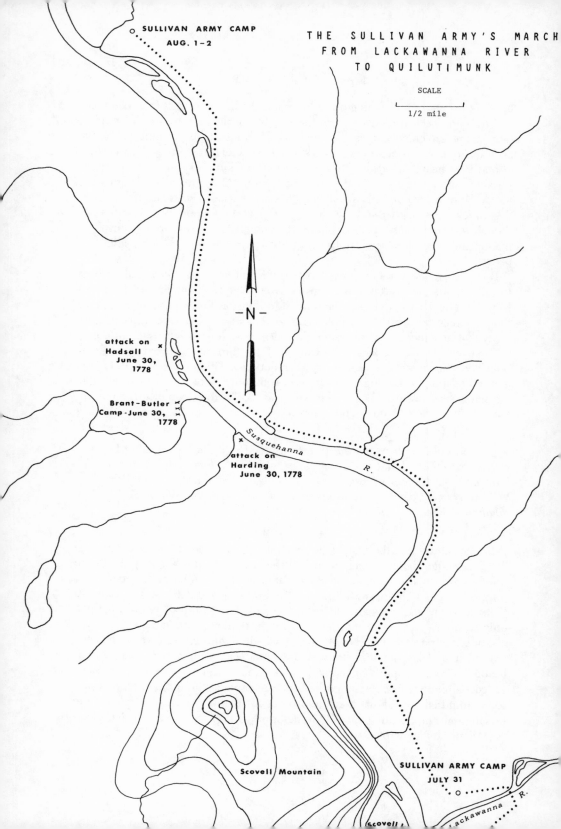

SULLIVAN ARMY CAMP
AUG. 1-2

THE SULLIVAN ARMY'S MARCH
FROM LACKAWANNA RIVER
TO QUILUTIMUNK

SCALE

1/2 mile

-N-

attack on
Hadsall
June 30,
1778

Brant-Butler
Camp-June 30,
1778

Susquehanna

R.

attack on
Harding
June 30, 1778

Scovell Mountain

SULLIVAN ARMY CAMP
JULY 31

Scovell

Lackawanna R.

To attempt description of it would be almost presumption. Let this short ac-
count thereof suffice. The first or upper fall thereof is nearly ninety feet perpen-
dicular, pouring from a solid rock, uttering forth a most beautiful echo, and is
received by a cleft of rocks considerably more projected than the former, from
whence it rolls gradually and empties into the Susquehanna.

Beautiful as the Falling Springs cascade was, both to see and hear, the defile
through which the army had to pass where the river lapped at the foot of the
mountain was extremely stony, narrow and difficult to traverse. It was a mile in
length and hardly allowed for more than a single-file passage, which consumed
a great deal of time. Then the Great Warrior Path moved into a three-mile-
long valley below the hills bisected by two small rills and a substantial creek
flowing into the Susquehanna. [281]
Another difficult defile faced them then, this time a mile and a half in
length but not quite so troublesome to traverse as the first. In the valley beyond
it, called Quilutimunk, [282] only seven miles from where the day's march began,
the army encamped at 6:00 P.M. This time, because the going had been so
much rougher onshore, the army had not pulled so far ahead of the boats, but
Sullivan knew that the boatmen would have to have a good rest this night. Besides, so much packhorse baggage had been lost en route this day, mainly
liquor, ammunition and kegs of flour, that it became necessary to send back a
special detachment with packhorses to recover the lost parcels. Almost the
whole next day was passed in this pursuit. Already some of the horses had gone
lame, including the mount of Lieutenant John Jenkins. Animals and men alike
were badly fatigued.
The two nights and a full day of rest the troops enjoyed at Quilutimunk were
greatly needed by them all. The only incident worthy of note for that whole
day was when Private David Brown of Captain Simon Spalding's company
tripped and fell on his own tomahawk, puncturing his side rather badly.
Fortunately, the army's pace picked up a little after this slow start. The lessons learned by both boatmen and packhorsemen during the first two days
began making the going much easier. Once again, on August 3, the march
along the Great Warrior Trail was resumed. Now, because the trail did not exactly follow the course of the river but shortened the distance by going over the
crests of some hills, the marching army far outdistanced the fleet. Almost immediately after leaving Quilutimunk and crossing just such a ridge, the army
encountered Buttermilk Creek, which was crossed about forty yards above the
falls. [283]. That falls was fifty feet in height and the water below was pounded
into a white froth that flecked the surface until it flowed into the Susquehanna,
hence the name Buttermilk, which it resembled. Pushing on after the falls, the
army followed the river again below the looming heights of four small moun-

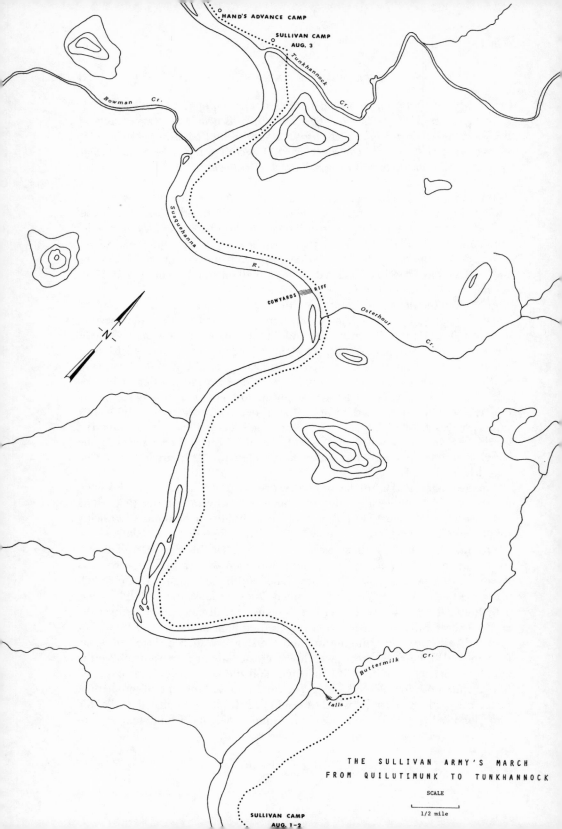

THE SULLIVAN ARMY'S MARCH
FROM QUILUTIMUNK TO TUNKHANNOCK

SCALE

1/2 mile

tains before reaching Tunkhannock Creek.[284] This creek, where the army crossed it, three-fourths of a mile above its mouth, was very swift and about one hundred and thirty feet wide. It was very beautiful there and the Reverend William Rogers was smitten by what they were seeing. When, only a half mile or so farther, the army camped close to where the creek emptied into the river, he immediately wrote in his journal:

The path along which we came and on each side of it as far as we could see, wild grass had grown in abundance. Some places, owing to the herbage, emitted a most fragrant smell, and we frequently had the pleasure of viewing flowers of various hues. Hazelnuts were ripening for a long tract of country in amazing quantities, and beyond a doubt nature has been equally kind in causing these wilds to abound with other things delicious to the taste. Several deer were seen, both by officers and men.[285]

Because of alarms caused by indiscriminate rifle fire, General Sullivan had issued an order prohibiting gunfire unless directed at the enemy, but game was so plentiful in the area that two deer and a turkey that were startled by the troops became so confused that they ran right into the arms of the men and wound up being served as dinner for some of the luckier ones.

For all its beauty and abundance, the area also provided a sinister note. For the first time since the march began, Indians were spotted. Two of them, believing themselves to be safe on the west side of the river, boldly stared at the army on the east side until they suddenly realized that a sixty-man detachment was bearing down on them on their own side. They dispersed so rapidly that they left behind their canoe and some equipment, which the army confiscated. But now General Sullivan ordered that the flanking guards be doubled, along with the sentries, and that the troops march as compactly as possible. He also established a system of signals for communicating information to all parts of the army very rapidly. John Sullivan vowed he was not going to be found unprepared.

August 4 found the army crossing hills again rather than going around them. It followed the river to the mouth of Teague's Creek and then, guided by Chief Jehoiakim, up that smaller creek and, still on the Great Warrior's path, over another high hill.[286]

In a few miles the trail had taken them across another creek, called Meshoppen. Despite the severity of the route traveled and the fact that a number of cattle and packhorses were killed as a result of tumbling off narrow cliff paths to the rocks as much as three hundred feet below, the army traveled fourteen miles and camped for the night near the mouth of Black Walnut Creek at an abandoned farm called Vanderlip's.[287]

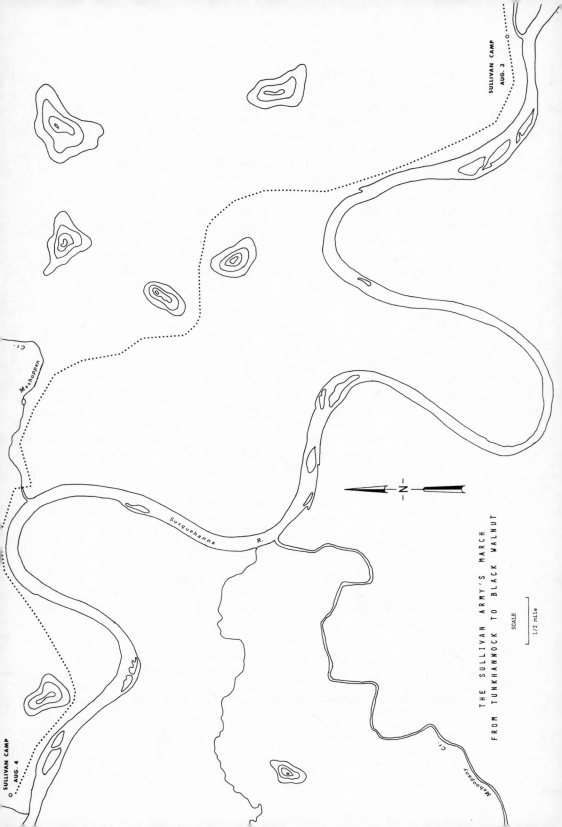

THE SULLIVAN ARMY'S MARCH
FROM TUNKHANNOCK TO BLACK WALNUT

SCALE

1/2 mile

SULLIVAN CAMP
AUG. 3

SULLIVAN CAMP
AUG. 4

Meshoppen Cr.

Susquehanna R.

Mehoopany Cr.

N

The daily marches were getting longer and the army was growing tougher and better able to withstand the rigors of such travel. But on the fifth day of August there was tragedy. The army that day marched to Wyalusing and three men died.[288] The first was a Private Samuel Totter, one of the drovers of Colonel Van Cortlandt's regiment, who fell ill in the morning and was unable to travel. The army went on, leaving him at Black Walnut with instructions to follow when he felt better. When he had not shown up after camp was established at Wyalusing, a guard was sent back to look for him and they found his body alongside the trail, where he had died.

Another soldier, a sergeant named Martin Johnson of the 2nd New Jersey Regiment, who was renowned for the amount of liquor he could drink, abruptly keeled over, dead of a massive heart attack just after the army stopped for the night. He and the drover, Private Totter, were buried side by side the next morning near what had once been the home of Nathan Kingsley, one of the area's earlier settlers.[289]

The final death was that of Private William Crestly, a boatman under Colonel Proctor. During a particularly difficult part of the water passage he fell overboard and, being unable to swim, drowned. His body was carried away by the current and never located. Reflecting on deaths such as these, Dr. Jabez Campfield sipped a glass of Madeira in his tent at the Wyalusing camp during the evening and morosely wrote a short entry in his journal:

How hard is the soldier's lot, whose least danger is in the field of action. Fighting happens seldom, but fatigue, hunger, cold and heat are constantly varying his distress.[290]

His writing may have been prophetic, for the next morning General Sullivan was himself suddenly so ill he could barely stand and so for two days the army stayed still until he felt well enough to travel, though not really very well at that.

During that interval while General Sullivan was too sick to travel, Brigadier General Hand came to him with a rather bold plan.

"I would like, sir," Hand said, "to take a strong party and march across country to surprise the Indians and Tories at Chemung. They'll be watching the main army here coming up the river by the common route and I'm sure we can hit them by surprise and capture a number of their important men — maybe even Brant and Butler."

Sullivan shook his head. "No," he said firmly, "I don't like the idea."

When Hand, extremely disappointed, persisted, Sullivan agreed to call a council of general officers and discuss it, but the result disappointed Hand even more and in his own tent he wrote bitterly in his journal:

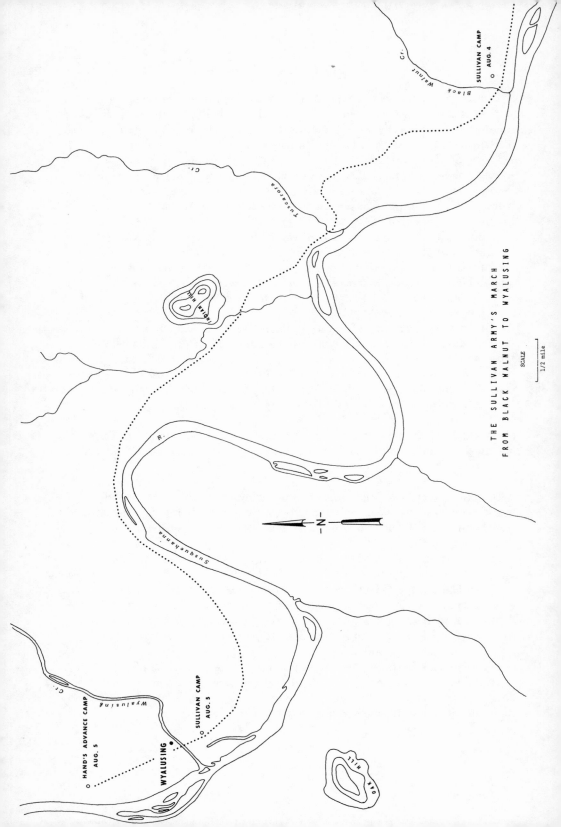

THE SULLIVAN ARMY'S MARCH
FROM BLACK WALNUT TO WYALUSING

SCALE
1/2 mile

SULLIVAN CAMP
AUG. 4

Black Walnut Cr.

Tuscarora Cr.

INDIAN HILL

Susquehanna R.

Wyalusing Cr.

HAND'S ADVANCE CAMP
AUG. 5

SULLIVAN CAMP
AUG. 5

WYALUSING

OAK HILL

N

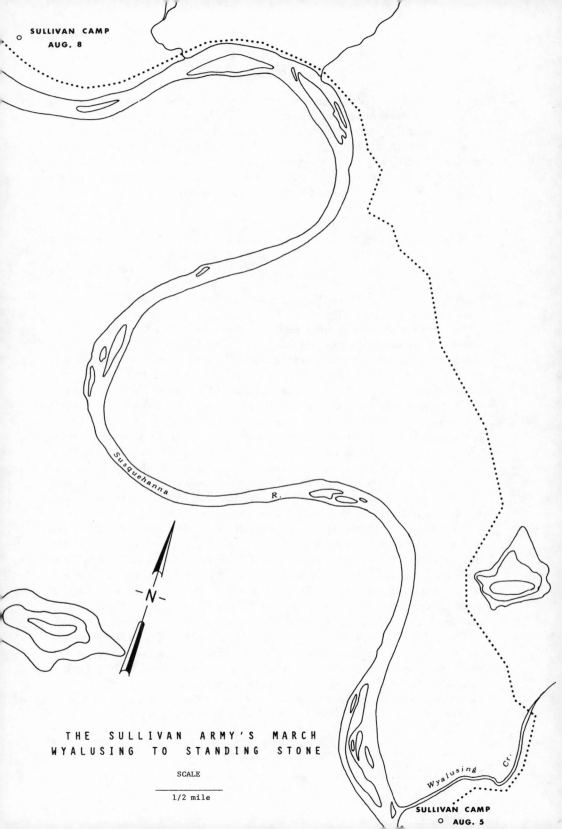

SULLIVAN CAMP
AUG. 8

Susquehanna

R.

-N-

Wyalusing Cr.

THE SULLIVAN ARMY'S MARCH
WYALUSING TO STANDING STONE

SCALE

1/2 mile

SULLIVAN CAMP
AUG. 5

A council of general officers indeed was called, but as the General's sentiments on the subject were previously known, it is no wonder my proposition was unanimously rejected. This was the first time I found that my having command of the advanced corps had given jealousy — or that it was possible that men engaged in their country's cause would oppose salutary measures because the honor of a brilliant action could not be immediately attributed to themselves, or to favorites who perhaps had no great desire to leave the beaten path.

Whether or not for the reasons to which he attributed it, General Hand was not permitted to carry out his plan and now his attitude became stiff and, if not uncooperative, at least not enthusiastic. He did not even take a great deal of interest in General Sullivan's sending out of several reconnoitering parties, including one under Sergeant Edgar Shoecraft of Colonel Van Cortlandt's regiment, guided by Chief Jehoiakim.

The army's march resumed yesterday morning. They forded Wyalusing Creek and continued marching until 3:00 P.M., when they encamped at Standing Stone. This place was so called because a large, long rock on the west side of the river, which had fallen from the mountain above, flattened all the trees in its path as it fell and then plummeted from a precipice and landed on end in the river near the shore, embedding itself in an upright position. The portion extending above the water was twenty feet high, fourteen feet wide and three feet thick. The main army camped directly opposite this on Standing Stone Flats and General Hand's advance corps directly opposite this on Standing Stone Creek. Standing Stone Flats was where Captain Simon Spalding's homestead had been before it was destroyed by the Indians and for nearly an hour after they stopped here he stood where his house had been and let his mind wander, flooded with memories of what had been but was no longer.

This was another case where the army did not follow the river exactly but took the overland trail, moving upstream on Wyalusing Creek about a mile and then crossing a hill directly north and not returning to the vicinity of the river until reaching the mouth of a small unnamed creek just a few miles downstream from Standing Stone.[291] Because of his continuing illness, General Sullivan was now being transported by boat, putting command of the army into the hands of Brigadier General William Maxwell.

The order for no rifles to be fired was still in effect, which rankled many of the men considerably because they were seeing a great deal of game that remained unavailable to them. It was difficult to understand what purpose it served not to be allowed to hunt for fresh meat for each night's camp, since they were obviously being continually watched by the Indians and their progress was no secret. As the Reverend William Rogers wrote about it:

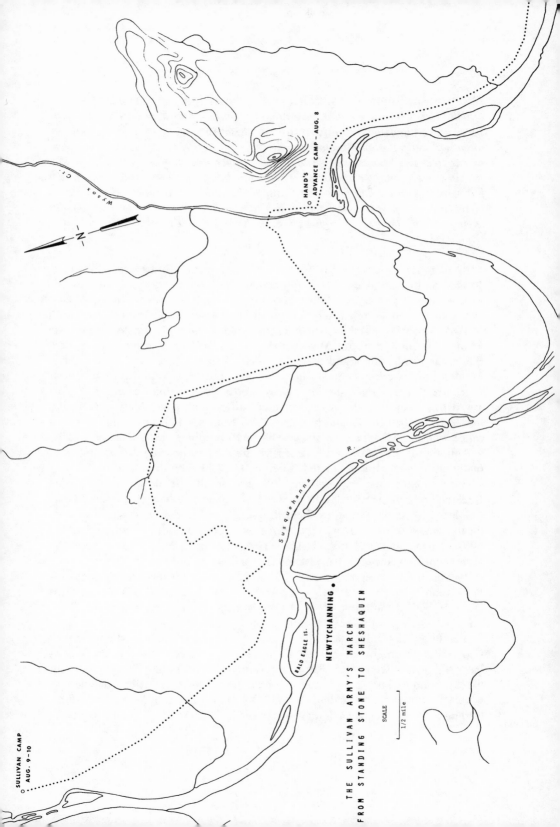

SULLIVAN CAMP
AUG. 9–10

WYSOX CT.

N

HAND'S
ADVANCE CAMP – AUG. 8

Susquehanna R.

NEWTYCHANNING.

BALD EAGLE IS.

THE SULLIVAN ARMY'S MARCH
FROM STANDING STONE TO SHESHAQUIN

SCALE
1/2 mile

*Across the river and upon an island we had the pleasure of viewing a large flock
of wild ducks; contrary to orders to fire, or we might have had an excellent supper. This country abounds also in turkeys which, in their flight near us, make us
often wish for repeal of the general orders. . . . On this day's march we saw one
or two places where the savages had lately encamped, also an Indian paddle
floating down the river and a canoe lying on the beach. A scouting party which
had gone forward many miles, returning, informed us that they had seen tracks
of Indians and a spot where they had lately sat down. They were undoubtedly
spying on our progress though as yet we have met with no impediment from
them.*

It was today, August 9, that positive action against the Indians was first inau-
gurated on this campaign. Feeling somewhat better, General Sullivan resumed
command and at 8:00 A.M. the main army broke camp and started upstream
again. In two hours they reached General Hand's advanced camp on the south
bank of Wysox Creek.[292] From here, to avoid a large impassable swamp, the
whole army moved up the Wysox about a half mile to a fording place where
they could wade across and then they filed along the base of a large, heavily
wooded hill towering some six hundred feet above them until, at its western
edge, the Warrior Trail abruptly veered north along a small creek. They followed this away from the river for three miles along a substantial creek that
flowed through the hills and that originated from a small lake. The creek was
called Franklin Creek after a settler who had lived there some years before.[293]

Although it was rainy and foggy, it was also a very hot and difficult day and
many of the men on foot faltered. Their course took them back toward the river
where they encountered a very steep hill just opposite the mouth of a very large
creek entering the river from the west.[294] They had to follow an extremely narrow ledge along a precipitous sheer drop of three hundred and sixty feet and,
during the course of their passage, three packhorses and three of the cattle fell
off the ledge and were killed.[295] Three and a half miles upriver from there, the
army camped again on a flat just south of a creek called Deer Lick.[296]

The boats following the river on a more circuitous journey were having a difficult time too. The river was treacherous in this area and in one place was
cluttered with a multitude of small islands with deceptive crosscurrents. Here,
one boat was lost with its entire cargo of about eight tons of flour.[297] They were
unable to get as far upstream as the point where the army camped and so they
stopped for the night just a short distance above a large island where several
bald eagles were seen. The island was promptly dubbed Bald Eagle Island. On
the west shore, just above the creek opposite where the cattle had fallen —
which was now being called Breakneck Hill — Captain William Gifford,
leading his sixty-man detachment, discovered a substantial Seneca village, the

first encountered. This was the town of Newtychanning.[298] It was devoid of people but it was obvious from the fresh tracks that the Indians had been gone only a short while. Here there were twenty-eight rather substantial homes, a few of frame construction, but mostly log houses. Although a few scalp boughs were found — special willow sticks bent and tied in a circle, on which to stretch and dry scalps — everything else of any value had been taken from the town when it was abandoned, except for three canoes on the creek shore. The town was now put to the torch by Gifford's men and cheers rose at this first burning of an enemy installation.

The army was at this time within about five miles of Tioga and despite the pleasure at the destruction of Newtychanning, there was a strong sense of tension in everyone, an apprehensiveness that could not be dispelled. Tioga was the point from which the attack against Wyoming had been launched and though it was supposedly defunct now, an entire army of Indians could well be just a short distance up the Chemung River from that point.

"Gentlemen," General Sullivan told his field officers at their meeting this evening, "tomorrow we reach Queen Esther's and perhaps Tioga. I think it is reasonable to assume that in that area or not far beyond it we can expect to meet the enemy in force. From this time forward and until further notice, the army shall lay upon its arms and remain at full alert."

[*August 9, 1779 — Monday*]

Tioga was not deserted.

On this long, narrow spit of ground formed by the junction of the Chemung River with the Susquehanna, at the very moment General Sullivan had placed his army on full alert five miles below, British Captain Robert McDonald and his second-in-command, Lieutenant Adam Chrysler, were having a meeting. A haphazard camp of a hundred Rangers and perhaps two dozen Indians stretched out on the point of land before them and McDonald shook his head in answer to a question that Chrysler had put to him.

"I wish you could. I'm sorry. There's nothing I'd like better than to have you go with me to Newtown to prepare for meeting Sullivan there, but Butler's orders are for me only to join Brant there. Sullivan's army will probably reach here tomorrow and look at what we have." His outstretched arm took in the piles of equipment and plunder that had been looted from the West Branch villages destroyed during the raid against Fort Freeland. "What would we do with all that? And what about them?" He pointed at the nearly forty prisoners tied together and sitting in a compact group surrounded by a strong guard. Again he shook his head. "No, we've got to get all your goods and prisoners up to Onondaga and then to Owego. That's your responsibility while I go on to Newtown. The Indians we have left here will go on with me. They've said they

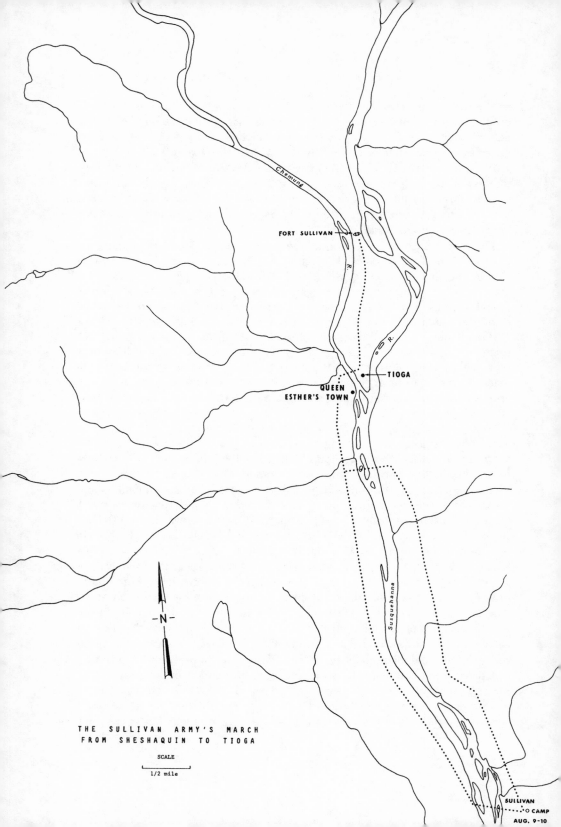

FORT SULLIVAN

Chemung

R.

R.

TIOGA

QUEEN
ESTHER'S TOWN

Susquehanna

-N-

THE SULLIVAN ARMY'S MARCH
FROM SHESHAQUIN TO TIOGA

SCALE

1/2 mile

SULLIVAN
O CAMP
AUG. 9-10

want to rejoin Chief Gu-cinge." McDonald nodded absently. Gu-cinge and almost all his two hundred warriors had left McDonald to join Brant's force to
help with the preparations for ambushing the American army. "It's a good
thing, too. We're going to need them there," he added.

"What about us?" Chrysler asked. "Those of us left and the prisoners. When
do you want us to leave?"

"Tomorrow morning. Alert the men. When I go up the Chemung with the
Indians, you move out upriver on the Susquehanna to Owego and then on the
Onondaga trail from there. We go our separate ways at dawn."

[August 11, 1779 — Wednesday]

Almost a mile and a half above the confluence of the two large rivers, at a
point where only two hundred yards separated the Chemung and Susquehanna
rivers, Major General John Sullivan ordered that the fort be built. It was not to
be a permanent fort because it was to be used only as a supply repository and
base of operations for the expedition while the army was in enemy territory, but
it was to be strong and defensible. The location here was only slightly over
three miles south of the New York border. With the very first stockade posthole
dug, the place was given a name — Fort Sullivan.

The general after whom it was named was worried, though he hid it well.
He was finding it hard to believe that the army had come this far wholly unopposed. Intelligence from scouting parties led by Chief Jehoiakim and Lieutenant John Jenkins indicated that the Indians and British were in force not far
ahead, but why the enemy would have allowed them to take such a strategic
piece of ground as Tioga without opposition amazed him.

The past two days had been a time of tightly strung nerves and numerous
false alarms, of moving over ground where footprints of the enemy were still
extremely fresh and the ashes of enemy fires still hot. Yesterday the main army
had lain still all day at the camp on Sheshaquin Flat just below Deer Lick
Creek, waiting for the fleet to catch up. When it arrived the boatmen rested
too, and this gave the army an opportunity to draw provisions, although now
the daily ration of each man was cut due to the supplies' dwindling rapidly.
During the day, detachments were sent out to try to locate a suitable fording
place and they had moved all the way up to Tioga and back.

Early this morning, Sullivan reinforced Captain Gifford's detachment on the
west bank with the regiments of Colonels Van Cortlandt and Cilly.[299] As the
west bank detachment made its way upstream on the Indian path that wound
along the precipitous slopes of the hills running directly to the river's edge, the
main army paced them on the east bank.[300]

The main army crossed Deer Lick Creek and followed the four-mile length
of the Sheshaquin Valley to a fording place the scouts had found a mile below
the confluence of the Susquehanna and Chemung. Here, just below the ruins

of Queen Esther's Town, which Colonel Hartley had burned last autumn, the main army crossed over and joined the west bank detachment.

Prior to the crossing, several six-pounder cannon shots were fired with grape-shot into the woods as a possible discouragement to Indians who might be lying in hiding to attack at this time. It was an extremely difficult river crossing and, if attack by the enemy had come then, it could indeed have been disastrous to the Americans. The water was at least waist deep and the current very swift. In order to keep their footing the men, burdened with their heavy packs, had to link themselves together by firmly holding hands. The men didn't like it much but the hazard and discomfort were considerably easier to bear when General Hand, who commanded the infantry, dismounted and waded across the river just as his men did. Several times during the crossing individual men were swept off their feet and, except for the grips of their companions, would have been swept downstream. At least three of them did get swept down some distance but were not drowned. One of these was saved by Lieutenant Colonel Francis Barber, adjutant general, at the risk of his own life. Nevertheless, the whole crossing was made entirely without interference from the enemy.

As soon as the crossing was completed, the army marched in battle order, with flags flying, drums beating and fifes playing another mile north through where Queen Esther's Town had been to where the Chemung flowed into the Susquehanna. This was where they crossed the Chemung at a relatively simple fording place much shallower and less than half as wide as the earlier one, and with that the army was there — at Tioga — spreading itself out over the ground on which one of the most important villages of the Iroquois League had been located until last fall. Here they camped on the large flat on the finger of ground between the two rivers, which itself was called Tioga.[301]

This was the rendezvous, the place where the army was to wait for the northern brigade under General Clinton, coming down the Susquehanna from Otsego Lake, to join them. During that interval of waiting, Sullivan decided, a strong supply depot should be made, to consist of four blockhouses and a central fortification for garrison and provisions. The result was, within hours of the army's arrival, they commenced to construct Fort Sullivan, which would stretch from river to river.

One of the first discoveries of note at Tioga was a longtime Indian graveyard. Almost immediately a number of men, to the disgust of some of their companions, began digging up the graves and taking whatever they could find of value. The ghoulish aspect of what they were doing did not at all seem to bother the perpetrators.

Only a bit over a dozen miles upriver on the Chemung, Chief Jehoiakim had reported, there was a sizable Seneca town itself called Chemung. As sunset was approaching today, Sullivan summoned his chief guide for the expedition, Lieutenant John Jenkins.

"Lieutenant," he directed, "I want you to pick seven other men and, as soon as it's dark, go up to Chemung. I don't want that town used as a rendezvous for enemy parties to make depredations against us while we're waiting here for General Clinton. Get whatever information you can that will allow me to surprise and destroy it."

"Yes, sir," Jenkins said, saluting. He started away, then stopped and turned around when Sullivan spoke his name.

"I am coming to depend upon you considerably, Lieutenant. Do try to keep from being killed."

Jenkins grinned. "I'll try, sir."

To this point the army had traveled about eighty miles since leaving Wyoming and they were extremely weary, yet still in very good spirits. That they had thus far met no resistance and the evidence that the enemy was fleeing before their advance had buoyed them up. That, along with the rumor that passed swiftly throughout the camp that they might remain here a week or longer, had everyone in excellent humor. It also gave a certain number of them more leisure in which to record their impressions, as the Reverend William Rogers did this evening:

I must doubt whether the army of Alexander the Great encountered as many difficulties with as much good humor as ours has evinced. . . . Surely a soil like this is worth contending for. . . . The land in general very fine. . . . Saw Captain Jehoiakim who, with four men, had come thus far forward the day before. He picked up one or two horses that had been left behind by the savages.

Twenty-three-year-old Ensign Daniel Gookin, a native of Northampton, New Hampshire, and an officer in the 2nd New Hampshire Regiment, was impressed with how the soldiers had withstood the march, writing:

To see with what patience the soldiers endured the fatigues of this march, wading rivers, climbing mountains and a number of other things too tedious to mention, affords a pleasant prospect that in time we shall have soldiers equal to any in the world.

The hardiness of the troops and their promise for the future was marred for many by the ghoulish grave-robbing that was continuing as the men settled in here at Tioga, although it didn't seem to bother some of the higher officers, such as Major James Norris, who simply commented:

Whether through avarice or curiosity, our soldiers dug up several of their graves and found a good many laughable relics, as a pipe, tomahawk and beads, &c. . . .

Lieutenant Erkuries Beatty, on the other hand, was considerably more clinical in his appraisal of the grave openings:

. . . went today to see an old burying-ground which lay just by our camp. There were about 100 graves, some of which our men had dug up. They bury their dead very curiously, after this manner: they dig a hole the length of the person they are to bury and about two feet deep. They lay him on his back in the grave with an old blanket or blanket coat around him and lay bark over the grave even with the surface of the earth, so as to prevent the earth from touching the body. Then they heap up the dirt on the top of the grave in a round heap which is from four to six feet high. The graves here are very old and many in number because this was a very capital town.

The desecration of the graves did, however, bother some of the men, Dr. Campfield among them. A shudder of revulsion at what man was capable of doing ran through him as he watched their activities and looked over the charred remains of what, as recently as last autumn, had been the important villages of Sheshaquin and Queen Esther's Town and Tioga. While others had cheered, he had deplored the sight of the columns of smoke that had blackened the sky as Newtychanning had been burned and he fervently wished that such further destruction would not be necessary. In the solitude of his own tent tonight, he wrote:

It is remarkable that we have come into this country by a long and difficult march, where there are but few miles in which a small party of our enemy could not, with ease, have much impeded our progress, and are now within twelve miles of one of their considerable settlements, and as yet we have neither seen or heard anything of them that we could, with certainty, depend upon. I very heartily wish these rustics may be reduced to reason by the approach of this army, without their suffering the extremes of war. There is something so cruel in destroying the habitations of any people (however mean they may be) that I might say the prospect hurts my feelings.

But war was war and there was not a man present who did not feel sure that the worst was yet to come.

[August 13, 1779 — Friday]

The longest day of the campaign thus far began yesterday at noon and was ending today at eight in the evening. The campaign was no longer merely a march, it was a war, a war that had brought casualties.

It began with the return to Tioga of the scouting party General Sullivan had sent up the Chemung yesterday under the guidance and leadership of Lieu-

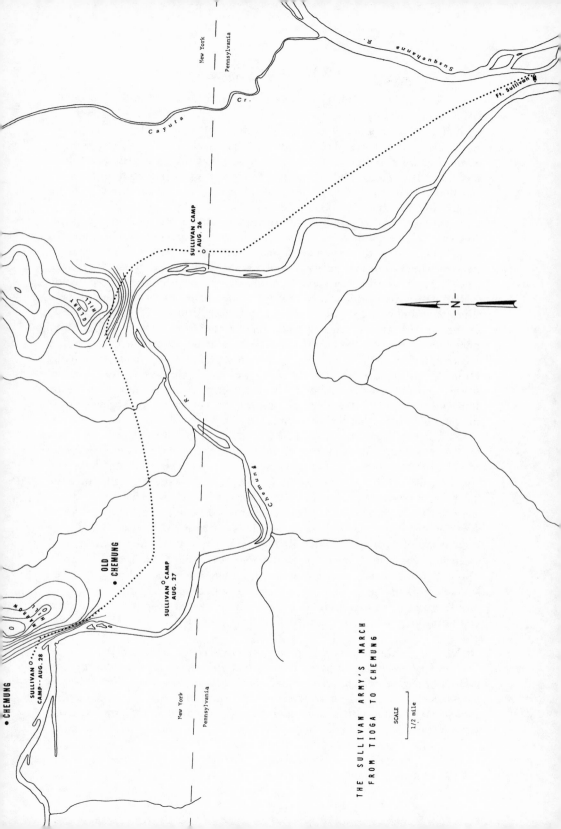

● CHEMUNG

SULLIVAN
CAMP - AUG. 28

OLD
● CHEMUNG

SULLIVAN CAMP
AUG. 27

New York
Pennsylvania

Chemung R.

GLORY HILL

SULLIVAN CAMP
AUG. 26

New York
Pennsylvania

Cayuta Cr.

Susquehanna R.

Ft. Sullivan

N

THE SULLIVAN ARMY'S MARCH
FROM TIOGA TO CHEMUNG

SCALE

1/2 mile

tenant John Jenkins. They returned bringing with them two fresh scalps lately taken by the Indians, on hoops, one of them judged by its thinness to be that of an infant. They reported immediately to the commander in chief. Skimming briefly over the details of the difficulty of their all-night hike up the Chemung River, they went into greater detail as they told how they had passed the site of a former village called Old Chemung, where the scalps had been found in an abandoned wigwam, and found themselves at dawn on the crest of a high hill overlooking the present Seneca village of Chemung.[302]

The village was spread out on the river plain some eight hundred feet below them and it was, as Jehoiakim had informed the general, a very substantial town. There were, they reported, at least fifty or sixty well-built houses in it, some of which were evidently still under construction. The strange thing was, however, that the village was in a fever of activity, with some of the population evidently preparing for attack and others in the process of moving the women, children and effects away on a major trail leading upstream. There seemed to be the greatest sense of urgency and no little confusion in their preparations. They had watched for the better part of an hour and were convinced when they left that no more than about fifty warriors and a few whites — evidently Tories — remained in the village. They were also positive that they had not themselves been seen and that the town could be surprised and taken easily. This and the fact that they had seen some large cornfields and vegetable plots convinced Sullivan that the place should be struck.

Immediately the commander had placed his entire army, much of which had been cutting timbers for the four blockhouses and stockade, on battle alert with the order to be prepared to march at a moment's notice, taking along only one day's rations. It was then the Sullivan camp that became a bustle of activity. Weapons were cleaned, equipment checked, everything placed at readiness and then the waiting began. Many of them had gone through this before — the urgent preparation and then the always interminable wait — and they knew it usually presaged a rough time. They were all the more convinced of it when the order came down that each soldier was to be given a gill of rum.[303] This ration of liquor was consumed with remarkable speed. Most of the men knew they should get some sleep if they could, but largely they were too keyed up. The official written preliminary orders were posted on a tree in late afternoon and for a long while they were a focal point for the troops. They said:

GENERAL ORDERS: *As the army will soon be called upon to march against an enemy whose savage barbarity to our fellow citizens has rendered them proper subjects of our resentment, the General assures them that though their numbers should not be equal, which he is sensible cannot be the case, yet it is his firm opinion they cannot withstand the bravery and discipline of the troops he has the honor to command. Nevertheless, it ought to be remembered they are a secret, desultory and rapid foe, seizing every advantage and availing themselves of every defeat on our part. Should we be so inattentive to our own safety as to give way before them, they become the most dangerous and most destructive enemy that can possibly be conceived. They follow the unhappy fugitives with all the cruel and unrelenting hate of prevailing cowards, and are not satisfied with slaughter until they have totally destroyed their opponents. It therefore becomes every officer and soldier to resolve never to fly before such an enemy, but determine either to conquer or perish, which will ever insure success. Should they thus determine and thus act, nothing but an uncommon frown of Providence can prevent us from obtaining that which will insure peace and security to our frontiers and afford lasting honor to all concerned.*

At eight o'clock in the evening, the orders came to march. Immediately the fifteen-year-old horse drover from Wyoming, Jabez Elliott, petitioned General Sullivan personally to be allowed to go along but, to his immense disappointment and irritation, his request was gently refused. He was not the only one to have his hopes dashed.

The Reverend William Rogers was also extremely anxious to go along and also bitterly disappointed — though he hid it well — when requested by his commanding officer to remain behind and care for his brigade's equipment. After the army had filed out, in fact, Rogers returned to his own tent amid the multitude of other empty tents and sat there morosely for a very long while and finally took solace in writing in his journal:

. . . between nine and ten o'clock at night the major part of the army marched with the utmost silence for the place with the Commander-in-chief, his family consisting of Generals Poor, Hand and others. General Maxwell, being unwell, tarried behind. To have been one of the party myself was my fervent desire, but I could not petition for it to be granted, after being requested by General Hand to stay and take charge of our family baggage and stores, which, among such domestics as we are blessed with, was the necessary duty of someone. . . . Tarried for my own part in my quarters and felt very lonesome.

As Rogers had said, the army moved out with utmost silence and the greatest possible speed, with the heaviest item carried along being the little portable cohorn. The silence lasted, but speed did not. In a very short while indeed, the Indian path going northward, following the bank of the Chemung upstream, narrowed to such extent that only four men were able to walk abreast on it. Then only three. Being heavily overcast, the night was extremely dark and, coupled with the unnatural silence of the march, there was an eerie quality about it. By the time they had marched four miles, to the point where the Chemung turned from its northerly direction to the west, the path had become only two men wide and very difficult. [304]

Within half a mile it was wide enough only for the passage of one man and extremely difficult in the darkness. [305] As usual, General Hand's advance corps led the way and General Poor's was second. General Maxwell's brigade, commanded now by Colonel Elias Dayton, head of the 3rd New Jersey Regiment, brought up the rear. Where the ground was low and level, it was swampy. Where it was dry, it was rocky and hard to walk upon and far from level. It was an extremely hot night and what with the muck, the rocks, the tangled thickets and bushes, the ledges and precipices and what seemed to be a million hungry mosquitoes buzzing about, it was a night of pure hell. In many areas the path was so narrow and the drops so steep that a single misstep might cause a man to fall a hundred feet or more to the rocks below. As a result, the march was very slow. Incredibly, in view of the hazards, only one man — Ensign Daniel Gookin — was hurt when he slipped and banged his knee on a rock.

At last the first defile was passed and the way became a little easier for them, although by no means simple. Here they had to wade through a rocky creek and then a mucky one. [306] Only three miles after passing the first defile, they came to a second that, although no higher, was even steeper and the path much worse. This was just after they had passed the site of Old Chemung. [307]

They were taking much longer to make the march than General Sullivan had anticipated, but then nature intervened with a sort of backhanded blessing. The darkness of the night was intensified by a smothering blanket of fog that enshrouded them. Although it made seeing more difficult, it also hid them from view of the enemy and muffled their sounds. Daylight came at 5:00 A.M., long before they reached Chemung, which they had hoped to surprise at dawn. But with the heavy fog still masking their approach, they came up on Chemung just as the fog was beginning to thin out a little, at 7:00 A.M.

As they neared the village, Sullivan ordered General Hand to circle around Chemung and close off the road at the other side to prevent any retreat of the enemy in that direction. General Poor was to wait only a short while and then drive right straight in. Very quickly both wings were ready, with fixed bayonets, and they surged inward.

Chemung was deserted.

In the poor light of the misty morning, only three or four Indians were seen momentarily, slipping away wraithlike in the dimness of the fog before rifles could be brought to bear on them. Those stragglers fled along the path General Hand was covering and the soldiers spotted them.

Immediately Hand, whose orders had been specifically to remain in the area of the town, sent a request to Sullivan, carried by Major Evan Edwards of the

3rd Brigade, that he be allowed to pursue. Permission was quickly granted, with the stipulation that Hand accept the support of Colonel Hubley's regiment and the Wyoming troops and that he promise to have the men under his command back to Tioga by the next morning.

Hand agreed. As soon as the other troops arrived, within only a few minutes, they set off again. Accomplished officer though Hand was and despite his knowledge of the Indians and their modes of warfare, he was decoyed with exactly the same sort of ruse that had so often before been the ruination of white troops in pursuit; that of using a small, apparently weak body of Indians in flight to lure on a larger body of whites until they fell into a preplanned ambush. Hand knew better, but the spell of the moment was upon him and the thought never struck him.

For a mile he followed their trail along a road now vastly improved — a road leading from Chemung to the four-mile-distant Newtown. In the van was Captain Andrew Walker and the rest of the 11th Pennsylvania, then the two Wyoming companies. The left was protected by the river and on the right Captain George Bush had out forty flankers, men of the 3rd Company, 11th Pennsylvania. It was as they were passing over a small, somewhat isolated hill about a mile upstream from Chemung[308] that the Indians struck.

The head of the column had pulled a bit too far ahead of the flankers at this time and as they came within about fifty yards of the summit, gunfire abruptly erupted from about fifty Indian rifles hidden in the bushes on top. If the Indians had been better shots and picked their targets, the effect could have been devastating. It was bad enough as it was. Six men — a sergeant, a drummer and four privates — were shot dead. Nine others were wounded, some of them very seriously. Those wounded included three officers and six rank and file.[309] Two of the worst injured, both of whom had taken rifleballs through their middles, were Captain John Franklin of the Wyoming Militia, who'd been acting as guide, and the very popular Captain Henry Carbury. Lieutenant William Huston, adjutant, was also wounded.[310]

Instantly, General Hand led a fierce, wildly shouting charge up the hill in which several Indians were hit and the Indians then retreated precipitately.

The firing of this skirmish was heard back at Chemung and a runner dispatched immediately by Sullivan to discover what had happened. As soon as the details were known to him, Sullivan countermanded his previous order and told Hand to abandon the pursuit and return to Chemung.

While the charge and skirmish had been going on, Chemung was surrounded by the remainder of Sullivan's army, but when they entered the village proper they found it wholly empty of people and with few valuables of any nature remaining. Obviously, despite the secrecy of Sullivan's march and the quiet it observed throughout the long night under such trying conditions, his approach was known before his arrival. It was greatly disappointing and it annoyed the commander tremendously because it foretokened a time ahead when the enemy would be met in force and most likely now without the element of surprise that had been planned here . . . or without troops so fresh.

First blood had been drawn in the campaign and it was apparent that the enemy had won all the points.[311]

The village of Chemung was sizable — about forty well-built log and hewn-timber homes and another fifty or more large wigwams in addition. Now, each building was carefully searched. After the pattern of wigwams, the houses were found to be floorless and without chimneys, with only a hole in the roof serving this latter function. As a result, the insides of the houses were sooty and filthy. The majority of goods of any value had been removed, but there were still some things to be collected, including between two and three hundred deer- and bearskins, baskets, knives, kettles, plates, buckets and ladles, as well as a few painted feathers and painted scalps. The only thing found of any real value turned out to be several colts running loose, which were captured.

There were also two longhouses that were not used for habitation but rather one for storage and the other for worship. In these Major James Norris later noted that they had found some extraordinary rude decorations and then went on to comment that in the longhouse,

which we supposed to be a chapel, was found indeed an Idol, which might well enough be worshipped without a breach of the second commandment, on account of its unlikeness to anything either in heaven or earth.[312]

The entire town was then burned and a great cloud of dense smoke rose over the Chemung Valley from the bonfire. At the same time, Sullivan dispatched General Poor to the other side of the river with five regiments to destroy the grain and vegetable fields that had been spotted over there, slightly upstream.

The vegetables, two hundred acres of them, included beans, cucumbers, squash, watermelons, pumpkins and potatoes, all of which were destroyed where they grew — the plants cut off at their bases, the vegetables, some of which were ready for harvest, crushed by stamping feet. The grain was corn. There were three or four fields of it, encompassing a total of one hundred acres. The ears were sizable and "just in milk" at this time. These stalks, too, were cut down with swords and tossed into heaps except for one forty-acre field that General Sullivan ordered be left standing for the troops to use when next they returned, which would be soon.

It was after the destruction of the vegetables and while the corn was in the process of being destroyed that the Indians struck again. Firing from the north side of the river, they leveled a volley into Colonel Cilly's New Hampshire

Regiment and abruptly another man was dead, another five wounded. Shots were returned by the troops, but seemingly to little effect.[313]

As soon as the destruction of Chemung and its crops was completed — by about two o'clock in the afternoon — the dead and wounded were loaded onto horses and the journey back to Tioga begun.[314] Without further attack from the Indians, they reached Tioga at eight in the evening. Totally exhausted, the men collapsed in their tents and even burial of the dead was put off until the morrow. No one was talking much about the statistics:

Loss for the Americans: seven dead, fourteen wounded.[315]

Loss for the Indians: a few wounded, a town burned and some crops destroyed.

No matter how one looked at it, there was difficulty in deeming it a victory for the army.

[*August 15, 1779 — Sunday*]

Far to the west of where the Sullivan army operations were occurring, the wing of the American army under command of Colonel Daniel Brodhead — in contact with but no longer a vital part of the Sullivan campaign — was just a tad more successful in its operations than Sullivan's had been thus far. The 8th Pennsylvania Regiment of Continentals under Brodhead, accompanied by some militia and volunteers — six hundred men in all — traveled up the Allegheny and struck the Indians hard. In a round-trip journey of some four hundred miles, they destroyed several Indian towns, amounting to two or three hundred Indian houses, destroyed five hundred acres of corn, engaged a war party of about forty Indians coming downriver, killing five and wounding numerous others, and did not have even one soldier in the least wounded. It was thus far the only really good news in an otherwise rather grim spring and summer.

[*August 15, 1779 — Sunday*]

Far to the north of where the Sullivan army operations were occurring, Colonel John Butler and his Rangers and a good number of Indians arrived late today at Kanadasaga, the capital of the Seneca tribe, and immediately a council was held to recruit all warriors not already committed to join them. There was still some opposition, some fading belief that no army of Americans would dare to penetrate into the heart of the Iroquois territory in an invasion. There was some innuendo that Butler merely wished to lead them on another expedition to harass the frontier. It was, they argued, a bad time to start such a thing. The season was too far advanced. Harvest time was already here for some crops and approaching rapidly for others. If they were not here to make that harvest, how would they and their families survive the coming winter? The taste of deprivation suffered this past winter had been bad enough. Anything worse would ruin them. No, they simply couldn't join Butler.

It was at about this point that a messenger arrived, having ridden two horses to death and the third one, beneath him, terribly jaded. He had been riding steadily since Friday afternoon, having come all the way from Chemung.

"Except," he told them urgently, "Chemung is no more! The Americans have destroyed it and all the crops there, too. Now they have pulled back to Tioga, but they wait only for another army coming down the Susquehanna to join them. Then it is their plan to attack us. Newtown is next. Thayendanegea is there, waiting for you. He says if we are strong and wise in our fighting we can hold them back, stop them before they can reach Newtown. There is a perfect place to ambush them there, but it will take all the warriors we have and all the soldiers you have." He pointed at Butler.

Butler nodded grimly and now he spoke to the assemblage with greater strength than before.

"Can you any longer doubt the necessity for you — *all of you!* — to help stop this American army? Does anyone here still think an invasion into this country, even as far as Kanadasaga here, is *not* coming and we can ignore what is happening?" He looked around fiercely and when no one answered he nodded. "Then it is settled. We will leave to join Thayendanegea at Newtown."

The war dance was held at Kanadasaga this evening.

[*August 15, 1779 — Sunday*]

Still slightly rankled that he had not been able to go on the operation against Chemung, Jabez Elliott complained to his fellow drovers about it and about having nothing to do or look forward to except the mundane care of cattle and horses. He received little sympathy. Most of the drovers were very well satisfied not to be included in operations involving extreme hazards and they did not, like Elliott, long to be in the front lines of anything.

The pique that the fifteen-year-old felt was not lessened any by the order that came late this morning for a corporal and four men, including himself, to cross to the other side of the Chemung from the Tioga encampment to collect the horses and cattle that had been allowed to graze in the pastures of Queen Esther's flat.

The five, astride their horses, crossed over the river at about noon and spread out, quickly rounding up most of the cattle and some of the horses. These were herded to the riverbank and, under direction of the corporal, were started across the Chemung to Tioga by two of the drovers. The other two — Samuel Weston and Jabez Elliott — were sent to look for the stragglers of the stock, which included a couple more steers and half a dozen more horses. Hoofprints indicated they'd wandered toward a large hill.

Ten minutes later Elliot and Weston, having already located one steer that they were driving ahead of them, were riding along casually chatting — Elliott doing most of the chatting and Weston most of the listening. They were perhaps a thousand feet from the others at about 2:00 P.M. when the shots came. One of the bullets caught Private Sam Weston in the shoulder and very nearly knocked him out of the saddle. Somehow he managed to stay on and, unbalanced, clung to the horse as it ran wildly back toward the river.

Elliott was not so lucky.

A bullet entered the youth's left side and exited from the right. In its passage, it destroyed his heart. For just a fraction of time he remained in the saddle with a shocked expression on his face and then he fell. He was dead before hitting the ground.

Almost in the same instant ten painted warriors burst from the bushes slightly above, shrieking wildly, and raced to the scene. The steer had also been killed in the firing and they caught the confused horse easily. In seconds Elliott's scalp had been cut off and the war whoop erupted from the throat of the warrior who held it aloft triumphantly.

The shots had been heard at the river, of course, as well as at the Fort Sullivan encampment on the other side. No one needed to be told what it betokened. A detachment of the 1st and 3rd regiments was mounted and, under Colonel Hubley, crossed the river. The injured Weston was brought to the fort, along with the corporal and the two uninjured privates. Shortly afterward they found young Elliott's body and brought that over, too. Even the dead steer was quartered and the meat brought back to the camp. But though the detachment scoured the hills and valleys there for over two hours and found plenty of footprints, they could not locate any of the Indians or the several steers and seven horses that had been stolen.[316]

This evening an order was posted — a General Order from General Sullivan, who was suddenly more anxious than ever to get his full army together and begin his drive through the enemy territory. Word had come to him that the Indians might be planning a major attack against General Clinton's army, still en route down the Susquehanna to join him, and that this suspected enemy force might well be augmented by the Indians who had fled Chemung before the army's arrival there. The Sullivan order issued now called for a detachment of over a thousand men under General Enoch Poor to set off on the morrow at 6:00 A.M. to go upstream on the Susquehanna to meet and escort Clinton's brigade the remainder of the way to Tioga.

There was one thing about the order that the men found most appealing. It was in one of the latter paragraphs:

One quart of whiskey to be issued this evening to each officer and a half-pint to

each non-commissioned officer and soldier of the detachment commanded by
General Poor. The officers are to see respectively that water be immediately
mixed with the soldiers' whiskey."

[August 18, 1779 — Wednesday]

The movement of General James Clinton's wing of the army downriver from
where it had encamped so long at the outlet of Otsego Lake was as rapid as possible under the circumstances and very eventful.

The raising of the lake level with the dam and then breaking that dam in
order to float down in bateaux had become far more important than anyone,
even General Clinton himself, had realized. Had not that excess water been set
free to help float the heavy bateaux over the shoals and bars, not only would
the first two days of travel downstream have been more difficult, there is every
possibility that it may have been impossible. Even with the water level raised,
many precious hours were used in forcing the boats over places still too shallow
for free floating. Everyone helped and by the time the brigade reached the
mouth of the creek that was the outlet for Canadaraga Lake,[317] where a more
substantial flow of water was coming in from the northwest, the men were
exhausted.

Once that confluence was passed, the normal flow of water was sufficiently
high to move the bateaux with ease over all but a very few bars. Just as the letting loose of the impounded Otsego Lake waters had helped, however, it had
also caused some unforeseen difficulties. One of these was that in flooding the
riverbed, it also flooded the low areas near the river — areas through which the
infantry was marching. The riflemen and light infantry were in the van on
shore, commanded by Colonel William Butler. General Clinton was with the
fleet. Opposite the over two hundred bateaux marched the flankers, who were
also helping herd the cattle. The whole was followed by a strong rear guard.
The unexpected problem caused by the raising of the waters and flooding of the
low areas was that this area was heavily populated with timber rattlesnakes,
many of which lived in rocky crevices and holes along the river. With their
dens inundated, they emerged, and literally hundreds of them were being encountered by the troops. Fortunately, no one was bitten, but they did present a
continual threat.

By the evening of August 11 — the third day of their march and float — they
had reached the mouth of Otego Creek and there they destroyed the small Indian village named Otego.[318] Though they saw no Indians, here they encountered fresh Indian tracks and the remains of several Indian campfires, alongside
one of which they found a knife that an Indian evidently had lost. They
camped for the night here two miles below the mouth of Otego Creek at the

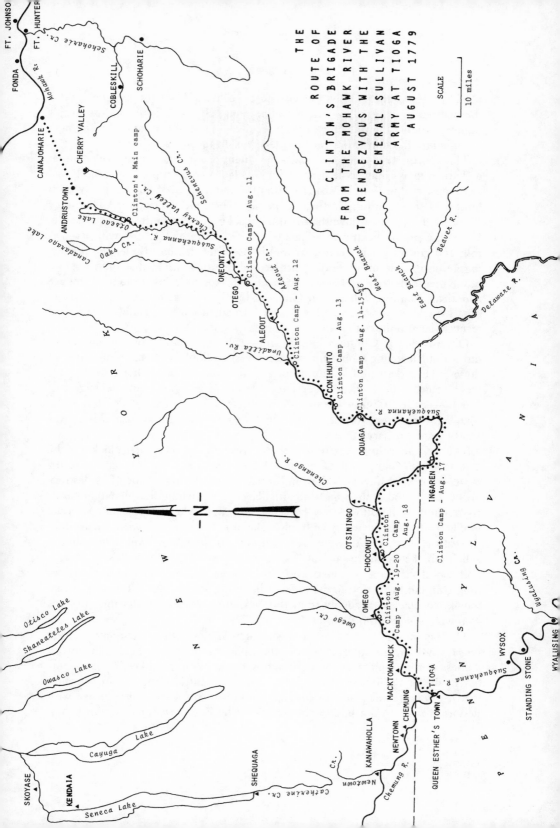

THE
ROUTE OF
CLINTON'S BRIGADE
FROM THE MOHAWK RIVER
TO RENDEZVOUS WITH THE
GENERAL SULLIVAN
ARMY AT TIOGA
AUGUST 1779

SCALE

10 miles

place where a settler named Ogden had once lived.[319] In his appreciation for the manner in which they were marching and behaving, General Clinton this evening ordered that his officers each receive a quart of rum and that the rank and file and the noncommissioned officers each receive a half pint.

The fourth day — August 12 — saw them move first some twelve miles downriver to a former settlement of Scots called Aleout on the east bank. It had some new buildings in it, abandoned at the moment, that had evidently been built by Tories returning to their properties. These were burned.[320] Then they resumed the journey downstream until reaching the mouth of the Unadilla River, the site of the Indian village of Unadilla[321] which, along with its sawmill and gristmill, had been destroyed by Colonel William Butler the preceding autumn. The only building Butler had left standing at that time was the house of a settler named Henry Gladford, who was believed at the time to have American leanings. Since then Gladford had gone over to the British and so now his house, on the east bank, was burned, along with another that had recently been built not far from it.

On August 13, Clinton's brigade moved down without stopping for twelve miles until reaching Conihunto, on the west bank of the river,[322] also one of those villages destroyed last autumn. A little over a mile farther downstream, the brigade came to five rather large islands in the river, on the largest of which — called Gunna Gunter — the Indians had cornfields.[323] On these islands the army encamped for the night after destroying the corn, which was nearly ready for harvest.

The next morning, August 14, the army marched at eight o'clock and by 2:00 P.M. they had reached Oquaga.[324] This had been Brant's village since his ouster from the Mohawk Valley and it had been, up to the time of its destruction last fall, one of the finest Indian villages in the whole Susquehanna basin. Its remains could still clearly be seen. This was where Lieutenant Colonel William Pawling, coming with his detachment of two hundred men from Wawasing, was to rendezvous with Clinton, but he was not yet here. Clinton called a halt to await his arrival.

It was at that time that General Clinton began the practice of firing an evening gun and the sound of the cannon booming this particular evening caused the sky to blacken suddenly from the density of a flock of passenger pigeons who were startled into flight by the noise.[325]

Throughout the next day there was no sign of Pawling's detachment, but the brigade was greatly appreciative of the opportunity to rest here. The pleasantness of the respite was marred only by the fact that a soldier, Private Murton Bealle of Levittown, Pennsylvania, died of "putrid fever" — an infection that his system, weakened by anemia, could not combat. He was buried with honors at noon and a brief service was read by Brigade Chaplain John Gano.

On the morning of August 16 there was still no sign of Lieutenant Colonel Pawling, so Clinton sent out a detachment under Major Thomas Church of the 4th Pennsylvania Regiment to meet him. Church moved out about six miles but, still not encountering any sign of Pawling, returned to Oquaga by evening. Clinton had had enough of waiting and gave the order to march the next morning.[326]

Yesterday, August 17, the army was on the move again and within three miles came to the Tuscarora town of Shawhiangto, where the Reverend Gideon Hawley had been a missionary many years before.[327] It contained ten or twelve empty houses, which they quickly burned before continuing on their way. Here the march, which had been almost due south, turned westward with the downstream course of the river. The river bottoms were wider here, more permissive of faster passage on land. They continued another ten miles to where the river turned back north again and here, at the Tuscarora village of Ingaren[328] they paused for the night, thoroughly weary. Ingaren had some fine orchards and the surrounding fields were burgeoning with crops of turnips, squash, parsnips, potatoes, beans and corn. The army ate well of whatever was harvestable, startled more of the wildlife with the evening gun and then slept well.

This morning of the eighteenth of August, after having destroyed the town of Ingaren and its crops, Clinton's brigade was on the move again and reached the mouth of the Chenango River, fourteen miles from Ingaren, by midafternoon.[329] While the main part of the force rested briefly here on the south bank, a detachment of one hundred of the best riflemen of Morgan's Partisan Corps was sent four miles up the Chenango to destroy the town of Otsiningo.[330] This elite corps moved out on its mission swiftly, led by Major James Parr. Riding beside Parr and still seeking the recognition he was sure would come his way in his climb to glory was Captain Thomas Boyd, newly promoted as a result of his capture recently of the notorious Tories, Rolf Hare and Gilbert Newbury.

Less than three hours from its departure, the detachment of Morgan's Partisan Corps returned to the brigade, which had established camp two miles downstream on the Susquehanna.[331] Major Parr reported to General Clinton that Otsiningo, consisting of twenty hewn-log houses and a few wigwams, had been destroyed.

Now they had hardly settled down when the sentries called out that someone was approaching. In a short while a pair of very tired men — Sergeant Asa Chapman and Private Justus Gaylord — were saluting General Clinton and reporting that they were advanced from the thousand-man detachment of General Enoch Poor, which was now less than ten miles downstream and which would escort Clinton's brigade the remainder of the way down to Tioga.

Brigadier General James Clinton grinned. "Fine," he said, "just fine! That being the case, this time our evening gun should be heard by more than just birds."

It was.

[*August 21, 1779 — Saturday*]

Practically torrential rains had delayed the junction of General Clinton's brigade with General Sullivan's army by at least a day and today, instead of the Clinton fleet rounding the final bend that would put them in sight of Tioga and Fort Sullivan, they were still about ten miles from there when they stopped for the night.

Matters had moved swiftly once Poor and Clinton joined forces. Together, as they had been doing individually, they destroyed whatever Indian towns and crops they encountered that were not already ruined. Some of these General Poor had deliberately left unharmed on his way upstream, realizing they might be of some benefit on the way down. As a matter of fact, the only destruction he'd engaged in had been two villages on the day of the junction. Both were known by the name of Choconut. [332] The one at the mouth of Choconut Creek had about twenty houses and a storage building. The one three miles farther upstream had fifty dwellings plus a longhouse and a chapel. All of the buildings had been burned by Poor's force on the morning of the nineteenth, just prior to the merging of the two forces. Then together, Clinton in the van, they moved downstream to the twenty-house village of Owego [333] and burned it in the evening. As at all these villages, the crops were destroyed.

At 11:00 P.M., Clinton sent an express message off to General Sullivan to advise him that the union of the two forces had occurred and that they were presently en route to Tioga. The express consisted of an officer and nine men and Clinton wanted a good, dependable, ambitious officer to head the group. It was no great surprise to anyone when he chose Captain Boyd.

On the twentieth, extremely heavy rains prevented the march of the combined forces and made them utterly miserable the whole day as they crouched together in sodden masses and thought of the twenty houses they had burned here yesterday, wishing they had their shelter.

Yesterday their prevailing mood was still down because of the previous day's drenching as well as because during this day two boatloads of ammunition capsized and though the cargoes were not lost, fourteen boxes containing twenty-seven thousand cartridges and three barrels of gunpowder were badly damaged.

The nearly three thousand men moved as far downstream as the place where Poor's detachment had stopped its first night out of Tioga — a place called Macktowanuck, but also known as Red Bank. [334] This was where Poor had destroyed a great many fruit trees and some vegetable crops and also the place from whence he had sent ahead the two Wyoming men — Chapman and Gaylord — as an advance to meet General Clinton.

Now, with the night's camp set up and the realization strong in everyone's mind that tomorrow would be the culmination of this fortnight of traveling through the wilderness toward a rendezvous few, if any, of Clinton's force had ever seen, the mood lightened and there was laughter and joking and a real anticipation of the morrow.

The union that had occurred a few days ago far upriver with General Poor's detachment had certainly been a joyous one, but it was low key compared to what was looming now. This was the moment that over five thousand men had been waiting for for so many weeks, the moment when the great Western Expedition united within itself and became a strong and bold entity, determined to destroy completely and forever that powerful League of Indians who called themselves the Iroquois.

[*August 22, 1779 — Sunday*]

It was at ten o'clock this morning that the whole of General John Sullivan's encampment at Tioga became electrified as, from only a mile upstream but still out of sight, came the deep, reverberating boomings of six regularly spaced cannon shots.

Clinton! And Poor! Immediately the Light Corps fired seven shots in return and then the whole place became a hubbub of activity as preparations were made for the actual arrival. Many of the men hurriedly dressed themselves in their best clothing and long before the Clinton force hove into view the Susquehanna shoreline of Tioga was crowded with men ready to burst into cheers at the first sight of the approach.

The six days that had passed since the departure of General Poor's detachment to meet and escort General Clinton's brigade had been reasonably quiet ones here at Tioga. One of the most important events was the completion, only yesterday, of the basic structure of Fort Sullivan. The fortification, built in a diamond shape, had a strong blockhouse on the water's edge at both the Chemung and the Susquehanna and two others, one north and one south, at the midpoint of the peninsula, the four being connected by a curtain of upright stockade poles. That curtain still needed some work but the place was, for the most part, completed and defensible.

In view of the death of Jabez Elliott, an order had been posted the next day forbidding soldiers to go beyond the lines of the camp on any pretext whatever. That same general order strongly covered other points as well. Troops were forbidden to imitate the Indian war whoop; a single gun fired was to be considered an alarm; an additional strong guard of a captain and fifty men was to be posted on Queen Esther's flats to guard cattle and horses. The men were morose over what had happened to young Elliott and even failed to have their spirits lifted much by news that came in an express from Philadelphia that Count d'Estaing had defeated the British fleet off St. Vincent's Island.

The following day, August 17, their spirits sank even lower. Six of the German troops — packhorsemen of General Hand's brigade — received permission to go beyond the sentry lines on Queen Esther's flats in search of hobbled horses that had strayed a little way. They were no more than three hundred yards past the lines when, in a situation much too similar to that of two days previously, they were fired upon. Four of the men fled back to safety unharmed and a strong guard was immediately mounted to go to the rescue of the other two. They encountered the fifth man staggering toward them in great pain, his right arm shattered just above the elbow. The last man, Private Philip Helter, who lived on Fifth Street near Market in Philadelphia and who was a biscuit baker by profession, had been shot three times, speared, tomahawked and scalped.

While no one was outwardly keeping score, the human statistics were nevertheless well known to all and the weight of them was pressing down relentlessly on the whole army. Thus far the army at Tioga had nine men dead and fifteen wounded and so far as was positively known, the enemy had suffered no more than a few wounds.

Once again, the day following Private Helter's death, the permanent guards outside the immediate encampment were increased by over threescore men — three different parties of a subaltern and twenty men each. However, it was not until the day before yesterday, in the midst of a tremendous rainstorm — the same one that held the Clinton force in place all day at Owego — that the spirits of the men of Sullivan's army began to rise. This was occasioned by the arrival of Lieutenant Thomas Boyd and his party of nine men with the message from Clinton.

When the Clinton force did not arrive yesterday as anticipated, a faint thread of apprehension became apparent in the encampment, but it was reasoned that they had probably been delayed because of the severe rain and would surely arrive tomorrow. They had been right. In the meanwhile, they were set to work cutting up a number of tents and sewing the canvas into sacks for carrying flour and ammunition. Commissary and hospital stores were being stored in kegs. Even though the army was going to move a long way into enemy territory, it was going to be moving as lightly and as rapidly as possible. All cumbersome baggage was going to be left behind.

The work of canvas sack-making continued early this morning, interrupted only by the meting out of a court-martial sentence. Three men of the 1st New Jersey Regiment in General Maxwell's brigade had been caught stealing rum from the brigade's supply. Lieutenant Colonel William D'Hart was president of the court-martial and when the three men — Sergeant Edward Olbe, Corporal Jonathan Wilson, who was the regimental drum major, and Private Thomas Perry — were found guilty, D'Hart sentenced them and the sentence was carried out immediately. Olbe and Wilson were both reduced to privates. Wilson was required to turn his coat and put it on backward, hang his canteen around his neck, be marched through the regiment in disgrace and then run a gauntlet. Perry was stripped naked and forced to run a longer gauntlet and for many days afterward bore the welts and bruises of the whipping he received. The men of the regiment did not take lightly to someone stealing their allotment of rum, which was considered meager to begin with.

The spirits of the men at Tioga rose even higher when, only half an hour before the booming cannon shots announced Clinton's approach, a detachment of General Hand's brigade brought in the body of an Indian they had killed and scalped about five miles upstream. The body was put on display for all to see. This was the first certain death of the enemy forces and morale suddenly soared. Therefore, when the guns boomed a short while later, the army was well primed for a celebration.

As the combined force of Clinton and Poor hove into view a few hundred yards upstream, a tremendous wild cheering erupted from the men. Immediately Colonel Proctor had his artillerists fire the six-pounder thirteen times in succession and as that thrilling, reverberating thunder of the guns finally died away, the army band broke into a stirring martial tune, then alternated other such pieces with the shrill, staccato playing of the fifes and drums.

Within an hour the entire army had united on the point called Tioga below the new Fort Sullivan and everyone seemed to be talking at once as news from both sides was exchanged and old friends were reunited.

The men newly arrived were really very fatigued — General Poor's detachment having marched eighty miles in the past six days and General Clinton's brigade having marched, since leaving Otsego Lake two weeks ago, one hundred and fifty-four miles. Yet, tired as they were, they were greatly buoyed up by today's events and not yet thinking very much about the rigors ahead.

A few of them were, though, and these few did not entirely share the levity. One of these was the Reverend William Rogers who, after a hearty reunion with his old friend and fellow man of the cloth from Clinton's force, the Reverend John Gano, retired to his own tent and wrote in his journal:

The provision brought by General Clinton did not, as to quantity, turn out so much as we expected, owing to their necessary consumption of same at Lake Otsego, where they were obliged to continue idle about a month as we were unprepared to meet them sooner at Tioga. The consequences which must result may be easily supposed. The first grand design of the expedition must in great measure fail.

Fortunately, this pessimistic appraisal was not shared by the leaders of the expedition. Major General John Sullivan and Brigadier General James Clinton greeted one another with a warm handshake and congratulations. Within an hour the commander in chief and his four brigadiers — Clinton, Poor, Hand and Maxwell — had gathered for a council. All preparations would be made with the greatest expedition beginning tomorrow and, leaving behind only a token force and the ill and unfit at Fort Sullivan, the invasion into the heart of the Iroquois country would, God willing, begin on Wednesday, August 6.

CHAPTER VI

[*August 26, 1779 — Thursday*]

ARE we going to be able to stop them, Joseph?"
John Butler looked at Brant soberly, but Brant did not return the British Ranger officer's gaze nor, for a long while, answer his comment. The two men were standing on the rise of ground overlooking the little stream called Baldwin Creek after the first white settler here, a Loyalist now a part of Colonel Butler's Rangers. In that little creek valley below them they could see the narrow road, hardly more than a path, that led from Chemung, east of them, to Newtown, only a bit more than a mile west, behind the hill upon which they stood.

Some distance ahead on that road a runner, clad in a loincloth, was coming on rapidly, his moccasins stirring up a trail of dust. Closer in, where the road crossed Baldwin Creek below them, it was very broadly marshy and a difficult passage under the best of circumstances. Anyone passing below could be attacked devastatingly from up here, as it was well within range of both arrows and bullets and there was nothing behind which the attacked could take cover. They would have to fall back and, before they could do so, perhaps a considerable number could be destroyed.

This forthcoming attack was to be under chief command of Brant, including even the British regulars, Tory militia and Royal Green Rangers. At Kanadasaga the command had become his when the Iroquois warriors announced they would join to help stop the Americans only if Brant were commanding and only if the plan of attack were his. Colonel Butler had grudgingly agreed, but now he was very impressed with the area in which Brant was setting up the ambush and how he was deploying his men. Butler did not believe, under the circumstances, that he could have done better.

Now, in answer to the question, Brant nodded slowly, his gaze still locked

on the approaching runner. "I think so, if we're fortunate. They will be following that road to get to Newtown. If they turn off before then, our men posted
on the other hills will know and alert us. It is reasonable to believe they will
not see our works here and will continue on the road. They not only have to
pass the marsh and ford the creek here, as they pass they have to go between
this hill and that one." He pointed to a long hogback ridge that jutted from the
river flats to their right between themselves and the Susquehanna.

"In the whole of that passage," he continued, "they will be vulnerable. A
strong simultaneous fire from us into their flanks could cripple them. If they try
to storm this hill when we attack, it will go even worse for them. The works
we're building will be strong enough to protect us from their fire and allow us
to fire at them without exposing ourselves."

He paused, on the verge of saying more, but then fell silent, still watching
the activity below. Over a thousand men, warriors and Rangers alike, were
working feverishly. The warriors were primarily working under direction of the
Seneca chiefs Gu-cinge and Kayingwaurto, Captain John of the Mohawks, and
Rozinoghyata and Araghi of the Onondagas. The Rangers were momentarily
being supervised by Captain Walter Butler. There were fifteen British regulars
under command of Captain Robert McDonald[335] and two full companies of
Royal Greens.

About two dozen fairly new storage buildings in the Baldwin Creek valley
were being dismantled and the pine timbers from them were, with considerable
difficulty, being brought up the hill and then laid as fortifications in a long line
going in a semicircle around the hill just at its first plateau crest below them.
The fortifications extended from the steep hill[336] far on their left up Baldwin
Creek a mile and a half to a point of the hill a half mile behind them on their
right. The portion of the fortification line where the timbers were already
laid — some of it chest high — was being covered over with earth. When the
Sullivan army came near it would detect nothing, because these fortifications
would be well camouflaged with newly cut saplings and scrub oak branches. In
addition, there were numerous one-man pits being dug that would provide protection. The work had been going on for three days and with there being no
time to hunt game, the only food eaten was corn and vegetables.

Butler studied Brant a long moment, then smiled and put a hand on his
arm. "My friend," he said, "I've known you long enough to know when you
are not saying all that you feel. Like now."

Brant smiled in return and looked at him. "You do know me." He stretched
out an arm. "We are how many? Twelve hundred? Thirteen? I have a thousand warriors. Your men make up the rest. We may get two or three hundred
more in a few days, if we're lucky, but we can't count on that. Say twelve
hundred.[337] The army from the Mohawk and the one from Wyoming have
united at Tioga. They are at least three times that many, maybe four. Those

are not good odds. Yet, with what we have here, we may turn them. There have been many times when powerful enemies have been stopped and turned back — even defeated! — by far less powerful or numerous forces. But the timing must be right and the follow-up to an initial success must be immediate and devastating. Remember what we lost by not following up swiftly with an attack down the Mohawk Valley after the battle at Oriskany. If we turn Sullivan's army here, we must be relentless. On that hill" — he pointed to a large hill northeast of them on the other side of Baldwin Creek — "we have almost half our force. As soon as the attack begins here, they must sweep in and attack the rear. That will throw the army into great confusion and thereby allow us to stampede their horses and cattle beyond recovery for a while. They must not be allowed to fall back only to regroup. When they fall back, we must press on them, destroy their baggage and supplies, push them, kill them. If we do so hard enough, with courage enough, with a strong enough show of power, we may convince them that we are many more than we actually are. If we do that, we may cause a rout and when and if they finally do regroup, it will not be to readvance into this country but to retreat to where they came from, because without their horses and cattle they cannot sustain themselves in our country. Destroying their cattle and horses is the most important thing of all. It will cripple them. It is the key! But though I would like —"

He broke off his monologue as the runner they had seen below came into sight now on the hill and ran up to them. It was Kanonaron, who had, at Brant's direction, established a relay system of runners all the way from Tioga to here. Kanonaron was himself the last relay in that line and he now stopped before Brant.

"Thayendanegea, they've started! The Americans. They've left Tioga, almost all of them, and they're headed this way."

Brant's nostrils flared and he nodded. "So now it comes. Tell the others, then come back here."

As Kanonaron raced off, Butler was looking at Brant searchingly, frowning. "You started saying something before," he prompted.

"I began to say I would like to believe we will do all this, but I don't know." Brant shrugged. "This is our last real chance, right here. Yet, they are very strong and we are very weak. Surprise may not be enough. If it is not, I will call the *Oonah* very quickly. I will not have my people stand and be killed pointlessly."

Butler nodded. "That makes sense and I know you won't call for that retreat unless that's all that remains. But why do you say that this, here, is our last real chance? There are other places for ambush — many of them — if this one fails."

Brant shook his head. "The places, yes, but not the heart. The heart of all of them" — he inclined his head toward the working Indians — "is here, in this attack. If it fails, the heart fails and there will be no heart for other attacks. We would not again be able to rally even a good part of what we now have here. It is why I have said that here is our last real chance. I do not wish to think of the alternative if we fail." He paused a long while and then his final words came almost as a whisper:

"We *must not fail.*"

[*August 26, 1779 — Thursday*]

Putting a large army into motion is never an easy task and is often fraught with unforeseen delays. Such was the case with General Sullivan's army today. It was finally on the move, but it had taken some doing to get it to that point.

Just as the people who make them up, armies have moods, and the lightness and ebullience that had prevailed for the remainder of the day Clinton's force arrived and into the next day, Monday, was abruptly changed that afternoon. As they have moods, so, too, armies preparing for campaigns look for signs or symbols, occurrences that may be translated into either auguries or omens for what lies ahead. Although it was an unfortunate accident, the shocking death of Captain Benjamin Kimball made itself felt as an omen of things to come and all levity was abruptly gone.

It was a stupid accident that should never have occurred, but did — which is, of course, the criteria for so many accidents. At 5:00 P.M. on August 23, a young private of Lieutenant Moody Dustin's company in the 1st New Hampshire Regiment, preparing to clean his rifle, snapped the trigger, believing the gun to be empty. It wasn't. It was, in fact, loaded with a ball and five buckshot. The deadly pieces of lead tore through three tents in succession. The first one — that of Quartermaster Sergeant David Gist — was empty and there was no damage done. In the second, a lieutenant in the New York Brigade stopped one of the buckshot in his leg. Between his tent and the next a soldier was just then marching and he was barely nicked on the forearm and the ball that touched him buried itself in the stock of his musket. The three buckshot and the ball still moving then entered the third tent. At that moment Kimball, of General Poor's brigade, was standing inside the tent near the entry, talking with several other officers. One ball hit him in the shoulder. Another hit him in the hip. The third one hit the tent pole. The rifle ball, however, smacked into his chest and passed through his heart. Oddly enough, Kimball, of the two men struck slightly and the three other officers in his tent, was the only one who was married. He also had five children. Kimball, who was paymaster of Colonel Cilly's regiment, had laughingly said upon getting that assignment, "I like it just fine; it's a lot less hazardous being in the pay line than it is in the firing line."

The mood of the army was decidedly sobered by the incident and the journal entry written that night by Major Jeremiah Fogg was reasonably representative of many:

23d. Unfortunate day — a hapless youth, as he was carelessly handling a musket charged with a ball and five buckshot, discharged it and the whole passed through a tent in which were several officers. Three of the shot struck Capt. Kimball, paymaster in the first Regiment, one passing through the center of his body immediately put an end to his life. He was possessed of every qualification to render him dear, useful and agreeable to his friends, and his integrity, capacity, good temper and strict attention to duty were such that all must mourn his loss. Man knoweth not his time. Capt. Kimball had served in five campaigns and though his duty seldom called him into danger, yet, at a time when there appeared the least danger, his life was required, while others exposed to ten thousand angry balls are spared.

Kimball was buried with full military honors the next morning at eleven o'clock. At noon, the official marching orders for the army were posted. A considerable amount of reorganization was done, but essentially thirty-five hundred men would march and the march order would have General Hand's brigade in the lead, Maxwell on the left, Poor on the right and Clinton in the rear. The nine pieces of artillery to be taken,[338] including the cohorn and three ammunition wagons, were in the center, preceded by the Wyoming Militia and followed by eight lines of packhorses led by two hundred and fifty essentially noncombatant packhorse drovers called pioneers by the army. Then followed the cattle.

Colonel Israel Shreve was being left to command Fort Sullivan with a nine-company garrison of two hundred and fifty men,[339] plus the sick and lame, numbering about fifty, plus almost a thousand others, especially boatmen and drovers, but including other nonmilitary personnel such as the several hundred wives, sweethearts and camp followers who were being allowed to trail the army no farther. Most of these nonmilitary people would soon be returning to Wyoming. The Reverend William Rogers was one of those who had expected to accompany the expedition but who now had been held back. He was ordered to stay behind and return to Wyoming as soon as convenient and take up duties there as chaplain. As he wrote in his journal:

This is in consequence of the dispersed state of the Third Pennsylvania brigade and the majority of those who are together, being attached to the light corps, whose duty, after they leave Tioga, will be such as to render my presence unnecessary, as no opportunity for preaching can possibly occur. These considerations caused me to comply without much hesitation.

With the march order well understood by all, a cannon was sounded at 5:00 P. M. for a practice loading of the packhorses and the army then to form itself in the proper order of march directly above the fort. This was done and it was at this time that it was discovered that even though many provision and ammunition bags had been made from cut-up tents, there still were not enough of them to carry the twenty-seven days' worth of provisions they had been ordered to take along, nor were there enough packhorses. The army was marched three hundred yards from the fort and then stopped.[340] They unloaded, pitched their tents and worked the rest of the evening and well into the night cutting up more tents to make additional bags for flour and ammunition. Orders from General Sullivan were that the march would begin in earnest the next morning.

It didn't.

A heavy rain fell almost all day on August 25 and the army remained encamped and quiet only that short distance above the fort, some still making bags, others writing letters or bringing their journals up to date, still others sleeping or merely resting. For most who wrote in their journals this evening, there was some question as to what the army could accomplish by beginning an invasion so poorly provided. Major John Burrowes wrote:

Wednesday — Tioga — Aug. 25th — Turn out again this morning and got things ready to depart from this. The morning looks like rain — at 8 o'clock it began to rain and continued the whole day, which puts a stop to our march this day. Hurrying our march is highly necessary and with all dispatch possible on several accounts. We have now but twenty-seven days provisions for the army and have to march one hundred and twenty miles farther in an enemy's country — horses growing poor, as there is nothing but Indian grass, and that very old. The season of the year is advancing when we should begin to think of winter quarters as the men are poorly clothed and not above one in twelve have a blanket, and nights are already very cool. . . .

With his usual pessimism, the Reverend William Rogers, in the reasonable comfort of the north blockhouse at Fort Sullivan, wrote in his journal by candlelight:

. . . they set out under great and diverse inconveniences. Their return must be so sudden as will in all probability prevent effecting much. Twenty-seven days provisions only. However ardent my wishes are, yet my fears more than counterbalance. Would to God they were better supplied.

Then, today, the fates seemed to smile upon the expedition and bestowed upon it some excellent weather — very dry and clear and bright and the temperature in the low seventies: ideal for marching.

Repacking of provisions into canvas bags and supplies and equipment onto packhorses took longer than anticipated and so the marching gun did not sound until 11:00 A.M. and the actual march did not begin until noon; but at least this time it really moved, paced in the river by four boats that it was felt might be of some benefit.

The army moved only four miles from the fort and encamped tonight almost exactly on the border of New York and Pennsylvania at river's edge.[341] As they stopped to set up their tents, a doe suddenly leaped from cover and ran through the camp to the accompaniment of a great hubbub, as men either dodged out of the way or tried to catch her. Major Jeremiah Fogg tried to grab her as she came by, but she leaped up and her head collided with his, knocking him down and stunning him. In the confusion that resulted she escaped.

But at last — at long last, and in however inauspicious a manner it might have been — the thirty-five-hundred-man army was on the move.

The Sullivan Indian Campaign had really begun.

[*August 28, 1779 — Saturday*]

"Colonel Gibson, sir, *look!*"

Gibson reined up at the sergeant's sharp cry and swung around. The noncommissioned officer was pointing back in the direction of Fort Laurens, some five miles behind them. A great cloud of smoke was rising in the still air and there could be no doubt what it was. The first fort in the Ohio country was obviously having its short life terminated.

"They didn't waste any time," he commented dryly. The line of mounted men stretched out behind him had their weapons in hand and were looking nervously from their commander to the smoke. Gibson shook his head and passed the order for the column to keep alert and ride on.

For his own part, Gibson smiled icily as they resumed the ride. It was just as well. Now there could be no countermanding of the order received this morning. It had read:

*Genl. McIntosh, Cdg., Western Army of the United States,
to Col. Gibson, Cdg., Ft. Laurens.
Colonel: It has been determined that due to its distance from the frontiers, Fort Laurens is untenable and the garrison should be recalled. Upon receipt of this message, abandon said post and return to this station at once.*

It was by far the most welcome military order John Gibson had ever received.

[*August 29, 1779 — Sunday*]

"I feel sure, gentlemen, that the enemy will engage us today."

Major General John Sullivan, hands clasped behind his back, abruptly stopped pacing in his tent — a habit for which he was noted during times of stress — and stared unseeingly at the ground, then nodded and lifted his gaze to the four brigadiers, letting it settle on General Hand.

"Edward," he said, "chances are your advance will be hit first. Still, it's possible they may hit the line anywhere. If we can avoid an attack on our flank, I want to do so. I want your men to be especially alert this morning. They're to keep a sharp lookout for anything suspicious. *Anything.* No rashness. If and when you are struck, take cover at once and get word back to me immediately. We'll reconnoiter then and I'll call you all in and we can decide on how we'll handle the situation. We're at a disadvantage not knowing the ground they'll choose, but we can bank on it that wherever it comes, the terrain will not be to our benefit. What we do have in our favor, I believe, is the fact that we outnumber them.

"Wherever we're struck," he went on, his gaze again moving from man to man as he spoke, "they're going to expect immediate retaliation in the form of a charge. Don't do it. Even if they try to force it. Dig in and hold. The best way to lose is to play on their terms. We're not going to do that. Questions?"

Hand, Poor, Maxwell and Clinton remained silent and Sullivan nodded again. "All right, let's get this army in motion again. Same order of march. Good luck, gentlemen."

As they filed out of his tent into the fresh, warm, morning air, Sullivan followed them to the doorway and then stood there at the flap, looking out over the huge encampment spread out in the early sunlight before the ruins of Chemung. It was a large and reasonably strong army, but their adversary was a tricky foe and it would not do to underestimate them. The Battle of Oriskany had been only too strong an example. Sullivan had no intention of allowing such a thing to occur to this army.

The major general let his gaze lift toward the hills and hoped they would not encounter a repetition of the type of terrain they'd had to pass through to get here. He could fully appreciate the resentment so manifest among the troops at the problems that had been caused by bringing artillery into such a country. That, more than anything else, had been the cause of their taking so long to get here. He had expected the first day's march from Tioga not to go very far, and it hadn't; the first day was always taken up with the problem of just getting the army into motion. So, having covered only four miles that day and stopping for the night on the New York border had not been a surprise.

The next day — August 27 — had been. By the time it was over, most of the men were in agreement that in the entire campaign thus far, no day's march had been more difficult. Even though a large team of the "pioneers" went forward to help clear the road for the wagons through that first tough defile, things had gone badly.[342] Having once already traversed that dreadful path en route to destroying Chemung on that muggy, foggy night of August 12, Sullivan was only too aware of its treacherous nature, but he had anticipated that even though still difficult, it would be a much simpler passage in the daytime. It was not.

The difficulties were enormous and the effort backbreaking. By the close of day, everyone hated the artillery. Two wagons had broken as they inched along the narrow path; one wagon had fallen off a ledge and crashed into hundreds of pieces on the rocky slope far below. Packhorses had lost their loads. Cattle had balked in fear and had to be whipped along by hand in small groups, sometimes even individually. One caisson had overturned and so did a portable forge. At one point a nearly perpendicular bank twenty feet in height, up which the ammunition wagons and caissons — and even the packhorses — had to be pulled, kept them stalled for seven hours. During the whole day the head of the army had moved only three miles, and for some the crossing of the first defile was not completed until the next morning.

The only bright spot had been the abundance of vegetables found growing on the flats on the other side of the hill. Major Jeremiah Fogg was one of the fortunate ones who completed the passage by 10:00 P.M. and still felt like making the effort to write about it in his journal:

27th. Marched about 8 o'clock and kept our order until arriving at a mountain, where we were obliged to deviate. The right column, commanded by General Poor, passing over it; from the top we had a most romantic prospect. Unfortunately, the river rose this day four feet and prevented our crossing it, so that the wagons were obliged to go through the narrows, where was a bank twenty feet high, almost perpendicular, the ascending of which delayed us until dark. After seven hours digging, with the assistance of a regiment with drag-ropes, the artillery and packhorses ascended the bank. The rear did not move from its yesterday's encampment. Several other defiles retarded the movement of the artillery, and we had not got three miles at 10 o'clock at night — the most disagreeable day's march since we left Wyoming. A universal cry against the artillery! Encamped in the most beautiful piece of land seen in this country, resembling the flats of the Raritan. Here was an immense quantity of corn, some of whose stalks measured fifteen feet. Beans and squashes were in abundance, and a greater quantity of which was never eaten in twenty-four hours by the same number of men.

Second Lieutenant Samuel Shute of the 2nd New Jersey Regiment underlined Fogg's final comment with his own succinct journal entry:

Friday, Aug. 27. Marched at 8 A.M. and encamped by a cornfield of about 100 acres which was destroyed that night. I myself ate 10 ears, one quart of beans & 7 squashes.

Because so many of the army did not make it across that first bad hill until at night or early the next morning, the result was a very late start the next day — yesterday — and it turned out to be a day hardly any better. Everyone knew there was a second defile between them and the Chemung village they had destroyed and that it was even more difficult than the first. The thought of it alone was staggering. Narrow Hill, as they were calling it now, was an absolutely impossible passage for wagons or carts and so Maxwell's brigade had forded the Chemung River with the heavy supplies just below the hill and then forded back to the north side of the river just above the hill. Neither fording had been a simple matter. The current was swift and the water deep. Several men and horses were swept downstream but fortunately no one was lost. Artillery, baggage, ammunition wagons and packhorses made the fordings and though no lives of horses or men were lost, a good bit of the lading was. At length Narrow Hill was behind them and late last night they had camped here at the site of the town they had previously burned.

Now, just before 10:00 A.M., General Hand's advance corps was already well on the move, heading for the major village of Newtown, which both Indian guides, Hanyerry and Jehoiakim, said was no more than another four or five miles upstream. That place, the Oneida and Stockbridge chiefs told Sullivan earnestly, with the Reverend Samuel Kirkland interpreting for them, was a very principal launching point for the Iroquois and British on their attacks against the New York and Pennsylvania frontiers. It was inconceivable they would allow it to be destroyed without a fight. General Sullivan was sure they were right and that today for sure the army would encounter resistance.

It did.

Hardly had General Hand begun to move his corps when it began being paced by an Indian party across the river. He moved his men steadily but not too swiftly and with great circumspection. He preceded the main body of the army by a mile and a half and sent a special detachment of Morgan's riflemen under Lieutenant Thomas Boyd a half mile ahead of his own advance corps. By about 10:30 A.M. the first two miles had been covered, and they were just a little farther advanced than the place where the Americans had been ambushed on August 13, when a party of ten Indians suddenly popped from hiding about two hundred yards ahead. One of them flung a hasty, poorly aimed shot in their direction, which struck no one, and then all ten ran off at full speed. Boyd kept his men from returning the fire and continued the advance.

The farther into enemy territory they went, the bolder and more numerous the enemy scouts became. Several more times other small groups of Indians popped up, fired hastily and ran off. The little detachment under Boyd still did not return the fire and began heading down a slight slope into a creek valley. The closer they came to Baldwin Creek, the more marshy the ground became. With the last small hill on their right now and the marsh and creek no more than three hundred yards ahead, they suddenly became very aware of the steep hill, heavily cloaked with pine and scrub oak, just on the far side of the creek. Lieutenant Boyd became very suspicious and called a halt.[343] It was 11:00 A.M. and all was suddenly very quiet. Boyd shook his head.

"Damn it," he muttered, "I don't like it. Something's not right. If I were going to ambush somebody, this is where I'd do it. Sam" — he motioned to Sergeant Sam Poleman — "take your glass and climb up a tree. See if you can spot anything on that hill ahead."

About this same moment, on that very hill beyond the creek and a hundred feet higher than the stream, Joseph Brant, face and bare chest bedecked in sworls and lines of vermilion and white, passed the word for his men and Butler's to remain down and out of sight behind the fortifications. Less than an hour before he had ordered all the women at the fortifications to Newtown. The only exception was Queen Esther, who declared imperiously that she intended to stay and fight. Because of her rank she had the right to such a decision and so Brant had merely nodded. Now she, like the others, ducked down behind the fortification line and remained still. Brant's words were passed along: an advance from the army was coming, moving along the road, heading toward Newtown. It wasn't to be touched. The important thing was that the men in that party did not see these fortifications, which extended for nearly two miles and behind which crouched some twelve hundred men and one woman. Only the few scouting parties that were out and the two reasonably sizable observation parties on the high hills flanking Baldwin's Creek were not behind the earthworks.[344] Brant had changed his mind about having a large force eastward of the creek, hidden and ready to attack the American rear. A small force — the observation force — could probably do as well by making a lot of noise and doing a hit-and-run attack.

The fortifications began at the point where the hill that towered six hundred feet over Newtown came closest to the river. Partway up the hill, perhaps a hundred and fifty feet above the Chemung River at this point but still far below the summit, the skillfully camouflaged fortifications wound southeastward directly over the road leading from Chemung to Newtown.[345] For the space of a mile and a quarter at least, the line of fortifications was directly over the road and in perfect rifle range, with a long hogback ridge on the other side of the

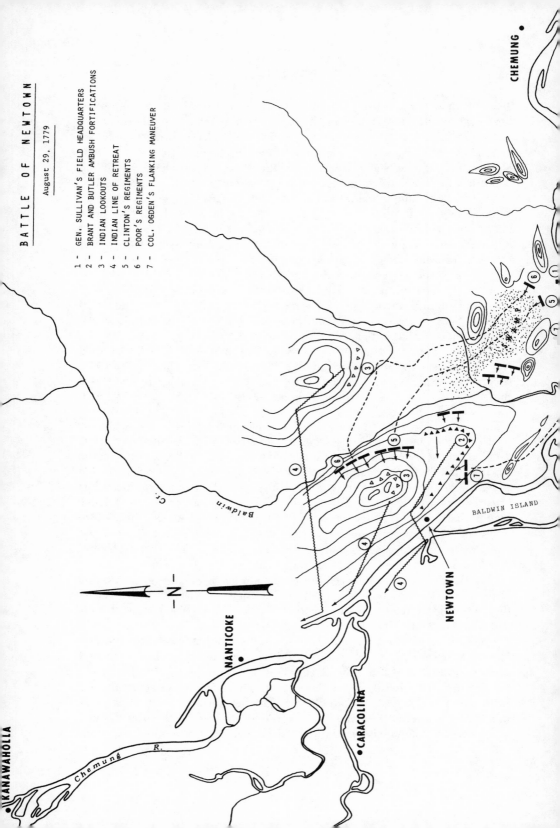

BATTLE OF NEWTOWN

August 29, 1779

1 - GEN. SULLIVAN'S FIELD HEADQUARTERS
2 - BRANT AND BUTLER AMBUSH FORTIFICATIONS
3 - INDIAN LOOKOUTS
4 - INDIAN LINE OF RETREAT
5 - CLINTON'S REGIMENTS
6 - POOR'S REGIMENTS
7 - COL. OGDEN'S FLANKING MANEUVER

CHEMUNG

SWAMP

BALDWIN ISLAND

NEWTOWN

Baldwin Cr.

N

NANTICOKE

CARACOLIRA

Chemung R.

KANAWAHOLIA

road to box them in and hold them in a sort of corridor. With proper timing and each man choosing his target, the Indians might, as the army passed below in its columns, kill hundreds upon hundreds of Americans in the very first volley at its right flank. The line of fortifications then swept around the southeastern slope of the hill and continued to follow the same elevation almost a mile more upstream above Baldwin Creek. This area was less heavily fortified and manned. It was a brilliantly positioned ambush and would undoubtedly work perfectly if not discovered.

Now, as the American advance patrol abruptly stopped some three hundred yards east of the creek, Brant felt a strong wave of premonition and was instantly concerned. He was quite sure the ambush had not been detected. This morning he himself had been down there looking up in an effort to spot it and, even knowing where it was, he had difficulty seeing it, so artfully had it been disguised behind freshly cut branches and saplings. Why, then, had the patrol stopped? He wasn't sure. Perhaps it was just for a rest, but once again he passed the order for his painted warriors and rangers to remain still.

Sergeant Sam Poleman of the 4th Pennsylvania Regiment remained a long while at the top of the tall pine he had climbed. The small brass telescope that he extended, then held to his eye and swept back and forth over the hill ahead, at first revealed nothing more than a verdant covering of bushes and trees with here and there some of the leaves already beginning to turn red as if in anticipation of autumn. Then he suddenly swore softly and held the glass steady on one small spot of such leaves and gradually an outline began forming. The red was not early-changed leaves. It was the vermilion paint on the chest of an Indian. The warrior was standing very still behind some brush, visible only from the chest up and even at that well hidden. Was he a lookout? Knowing what to look for now, Bolton moved the glass and his hand shook a little as he saw, not just a few or a dozen or a score, but *hundreds* of Indians, and then green-coated Rangers as well; and because of their positions he was then able to make out the long wavering line of the extensive and superbly camouflaged fortification.

By the time Poleman came down the tree, far more swiftly than he went up, it was 11:30 A.M. and General Hand, with the main body of troops of the advance corps, was just moving up behind them. Poleman reported to Lieutenant Boyd, who immediately rushed to Hand and told him of the discovery. Hand considered a moment, looking over the situation ahead, and then made a decision.

Rapping out orders swiftly, he moved his corps up to the advanced riflemen and then pushed the whole toward the creek, his stomach muscles tightening against the expected burst of gunfire meaning an ambush was being sprung. It didn't come and so, at Hand's command, relayed by subordinates, the advance corps, in battle lines, executed a quick movement and abruptly left the road, taking position directly beneath the steep west bank of Baldwin Creek. Here they would be protected from the downhill fire by the enemy force, now only one hundred and twenty yards distant. Then Hand ordered his riflemen to open fire.

Above, as the shots came, Brant's face set in angry lines. He knew what had happened and he also knew he now was left with one of two alternatives: either pin these men down with a continuing light fire and move a larger force around in a semicircle to attack and perhaps destroy one division before another could move up, or else send out a decoy force to attack the men below and then fall back in disorder to lure them into view for the ambush. The second alternative was by far the more favored idea and immediately Brant sent out a charge of four hundred warriors.

At exactly noon, amidst a bedlam of their own shrieking and scattered firing, the Indians plunged downhill from tree to tree, abruptly faltered as gunfire erupted from Hand's advance and then fell back. The temptation to leap up and charge after them was great, but Hand's orders had been emphatic: dig in and hold until the arrival of the main army or until further orders from himself.

Edward Hand, having placed Lieutenant Colonel Adam Hubley in charge of the advance force, was by this time already galloping eastward on the road back toward the main army. Within minutes he met them coming up, about a mile and a half to the rear.[346] Quickly but thoroughly he briefed General Sullivan on what had been discovered and into what disposition he had placed his troops to await further orders of the commander in chief. Sullivan was strongly approving of everything he had done thus far.

"It's exactly right," he said. "We don't know what the lay of the ground is here and we've got to find out. Let's get some patrols out right away and in the meantime have your men hold firm and continue their fire, but no advance under any circumstances. Alert Poor, Clinton and Maxwell. As soon as we have some solid intelligence, we'll hold a general council."

Getting intelligence was no simple matter. Eight different three-man patrols were sent out in varying directions to observe and make notes on topography. It was fully two hours before all the reconnoitering was done and Sullivan met with his four brigadiers. During that interval the Indians had repeatedly burst out from behind their hillside fortification only to falter and fall back at the firing of the Americans. The temptation to follow them, because of their seeming weakness, was very strong, but Colonel Hubley held them in place.

For half an hour the situation was discussed in detail, as sketchy maps were drawn and the position of the army and the enemy laid out as best as possible under the circumstances and then possible battle plans discussed. The final agreed-upon plan was almost entirely Sullivan's and it was brilliantly conceived.

"We are here," he said, pointing at the map, "about a mile or maybe a little more east of their main position, or what we at this time deduce to be their main position. We have to assume that their fortifications on the hill are forming a fairly extensive semicircle, commanding the road leading to Newtown and, for at least a little way upstream, the creek valley. Their heaviest strength would probably be here, where they've first been seen, overlooking the road where it crosses the creek, and then all along the road overlook, where they could strike a passing force in the right flank. From the reports we've gotten, those fortifications are strong and any attempt to take them with a single uphill direct frontal attack would be suicide — but that's exactly what they've been trying to entice us to do and that's what we have to make them believe we're finally going to do. In actuality, our main thrust will be in a flanking movement to turn their left."

Step by step the plan was laid out, modified here and there by suggestions of the brigadiers. In a remarkably short time, it was a very smooth, solid battle plan. First of all, Colonel Proctor's artillery, all of it, would be brought into position on the slight rise where Sergeant Poleman had climbed the tree and spotted the fortifications, three hundred yards distant. Those of General Hand's force not already occupied would support the artillery moving into position. This movement would be observed by the enemy and further strengthen the conviction that assault was to be made on the hill. At the same time, a detachment of two hundred and fifty men of Maxwell's brigade, the 1st New Jersey Regiment under Colonel Matthias Ogden, would leave the road ahead in a southwestward movement, following an Indian path that crossed Baldwin Creek near its mouth on the Chemung River, a bit over half a mile below the artillery. It would then move westward just south of the hogback ridge and rejoin the main road just before reaching Newtown. Ogden would ascend the hill there, hit the enemy's right flank and assist, if possible, in cutting off the enemy's retreat. If Ogden's progress was seen by the enemy, which was possible, this was all right, since it, too, would tend to confirm the idea that the Americans were concentrating their attention on the fortifications covering the main road.

While this was going on, the prime movement of about seventeen hundred Americans would take place. Well hidden from the enemy by small, intervening hills, General Poor's brigade would move northward from here, followed by General Clinton's brigade slightly to the right, to the base of a distinctively large hill about a mile and a half distant. There they would swing left, cross Baldwin Creek, ascend another large hill on the west side of the creek — the same hill the enemy was occupying at its southeastern point — and, on reaching the summit, the front to turn obliquely left to cut in behind the enemy lines. Poor and Clinton would be given an hour to effect this — one hour only. At the end of that time, the artillery facing the enemy would open up with a bombardment and Hand's advance troops would fein a frontal attack up the hill. This would be diversionary to keep the enemy occupied with what was ahead and below. But as soon as the artillery commenced firing, this was to be the signal for Poor and Clinton suddenly to swing inward with great force to hit the enemy's left flank and rear a crushing blow and at the same time attempt to cut off retreat toward Newtown. Ogden, on the enemy's right, who would then be coming up the hill near its closest approach to the river, would also swing in to cut off the enemy or, if necessary, join in pursuit. The remainder of Maxwell's New Jersey Brigade would be held as a *corps de reserve* to act as the occasion demanded and he would also back up General Hand's advance when he stormed the hill from the front in earnest upon hearing the Poor and Clinton brigades engaging the enemy left and rear. While this was going on, and for so long as it could be maintained without endangering American troops, Colonel Proctor would continue to enfilade the fortifications with sweeping artillery fire in an effort to keep the enemy pinned.

It was a complex but extremely well devised plan and, when all the aspects of it were laid out to them, the brigade commanders looked upon their commander in chief with a new respect, each of them wondering if he, in Sullivan's position, could have so quickly come up with such an excellent battle plan in so short a time.

By now it was three in the afternoon and immediately the 2nd Brigade under General Enoch Poor moved off the road in a northwesterly direction, with Clinton's 4th Brigade directly behind and slightly to Poor's right. Within only an eighth of a mile, a problem developed, and the farther the two brigades progressed the worse it became. The problem was a quarter-mile-wide swamp of dense alder and willow scrub, clustered at first but soon becoming so thick that it took incredible stamina to move ahead only a few feet at a time. The minutes ticked away swiftly and the quarter-mile stretch, instead of taking mere minutes, consumed nearly three-quarters of an hour.

The two brigades had by this time become slightly more separated and when Poor broke free of the swamp he bore sharply left at once toward Baldwin Creek while Clinton made a wider swing right and then swept back left across the foot of the big hill. Several things occurred at once about then. In the Baldwin Creek valley, which Poor was just then approaching, there were ten or fifteen new houses on both sides of the creek, but the ground was not cleared and the houses were not occupied. Except for having men glance inside for possible hidden enemies, he did not stop, but began wading the creek. That was when his column was spotted for the first time by the Indian detachment posted by Brant on the hill east of the creek. Instantly they cupped their mouths and shouted a complex series of halloos. These were echoed by the scattered Indians manning the slope of the hill west of the creek, directly above Poor, and in this way the signal was relayed to Brant's position. Simultaneously, hearing the cries coming from the hill above them, General Clinton's men fixed bayonets and the two farthest right regiments — Van Cortlandt's 2nd New York and Livingston's 4th New York — charged up the hill. The observation-post Indians, no match for such a force, immediately fled across the hill, down its north side and over Baldwin Creek much farther upstream, moving rapidly to ascend the west hill and join the observation-post Indians there. Van Cortlandt's and Livingston's regiments did not pursue but instead returned to the brigade, which fell in again behind and to the right of Poor's.

Now, just as Poor's brigade had finished wading across Baldwin Creek and began assuming battle lines with fixed bayonets, Proctor's artillery opened up with its deafening barrage. With shell and solid shot, grape and round shot, he pounded the enemy hillside severely. The screech of the cannon shot passing overhead, smashing through trees, tearing up great gouts of earth, smashing and exploding, accompanied by the yells of men and cracking of rifles, created an unbelievable din and, especially among the Indians, a great terror.

A huge black man, Colly Morse, clad in the garb of the Royal Greens, bellowed out, "Oh, my Lord, we are all killed sure!" Yet he, with the rest of the Queen's Rangers and Tory militia and Indians, continued to fight, which was little short of incredible. An artillery pounding is tough on seasoned troops. To Indians it is the most terrifying form of warfare; yet they rallied to the shouts of Brant and Gu-cinge and Rozinoghyata to fight on. Afraid they were; panicky they were not.

Brant seemed to be everywhere at once, racing back and forth, sometimes on foot, sometimes on horseback, loudly shouting encouragement and keeping his men in place despite the bombardment. Sometimes he was alone, sometimes with John Butler, sometimes with Walter Butler or Robert McDonald. Now and then Araghi or Kayingwaurto, Queen Esther or Gu-cinge or Kanonaron, would briefly stay beside him, but none could seem to keep up. He held in his hands a tomahawk, still unbloodied, and hardly knew it was there. He paused frequently to look northward, remembering the first calls that had come from that direction, oblivious of the cannon shells striking close. Gradually he began to realize what was happening. A runner raced up to tell him of a line of over two hundred men moving westward on the other side of the hogback ridge and he frowned, wondering how so small a detachment expected to accomplish anything there. Now the pieces began to fall together and the calls that had come from the east hill began to make sense; of course, the movement of the small detachment, the artillery bombardment, these were diversions! The real attack was coming up the hill to strike his weakest point, the left flank. Instantly he ran to the fortification line, shouting as he did so, gathering up men behind him as if he were a magnet and they only bits of metal drawn to the waves of power he emanated. Very quickly a great percentage of the Indians were behind him, running northward at a crouch behind the fortifications, leaving behind only one in ten to continue fighting beside the Rangers, moving out of the area being bombarded without the Americans even realizing it was happening.

Poor was advancing rapidly and was already well on his way up the hill west of the creek. He had sent Major James Parr with three companies of riflemen ahead as skirmishers while assembling his own regiments in battle lines. He placed Lieutenant Colonel George Reid with his 2nd New Hampshire Regiment on the left for the charge up the hill, with Lieutenant Colonel Henry Dearborn's 3rd New Hampshire Regiment to the right of Reid. Next right was Colonel Alden's 6th Massachusetts — the Cherry Valley Regiment — still under Major Daniel Whiting, and on the far right was Colonel Cilly's 1st New Hampshire Regiment, where Poor himself was located. As a right flanking unit, Poor had put out a detachment of two hundred and fifty men of the 5th New York.

General Clinton's left was directly behind Poor's right by a few hundred yards; his regiments in left-to-right succession being Colonel Peter Gansevoort's 3rd New York, Colonel Lewis Dubois's 5th New York, Colonel Livingston's 4th New York under Lieutenant Colonel Frederick Weissenfels and, finally, Colonel Philip Van Cortlandt's 2nd New York.

On the creek flat below them, smoke was already rising from the unfinished houses, as Clinton had detailed a few men to set them afire as his brigade passed.

Poor's line of advance was now about halfway up the steep hillside, sloping slightly downward from right to left. Above them on the slope a sharp but random fire was coming from the Indians who were dodging from tree to tree ahead, not being in sufficient force to check the advance of the Americans materially. Thus far none of their shots had hit anyone and Poor's brigade had not returned the fire, intent on closing the gap with the enemy. The hill was about a half mile from base to summit at this point and was considerably steeper on the left than on the right. As a result, Colonel George Reid's 2nd New Hampshire had fallen about three hundred yards behind the others. As the right-hand side of the line was about two-thirds of the way up the hill, Morgan's advanced riflemen began firing on the Indians without pausing in their climb. They were very close to the summit while Reid, on the far left, was just reaching the two-thirds point and badly out of breath when a howling mob of Indians led by Brant struck Reid's regiment heavily.

In the very first moments Reid's second-in-command, Major Benjamin Titcomb of Dover, New Hampshire, was hit by a rifleball that entered through his left arm, passed through his body and exited through his right arm, and that ended his activities for this campaign. A moment later, Private Joshua Miller fell dead with a bullet through his head.

For the first time, Reid's regiment began returning the fire. Though none of the Americans realized it immediately, the first Indian killed was Gu-cinge, war chief of the Senecas. Close to him a warrior fell also, wounded but not dead. Blood ran from his temple where a rifleball had creased him and, dazed, he was trying to get up but could not seem to coordinate his movements. Oddly, no one seemed to see him although many ran directly past.

The situation for Reid's regiment was worsening. Outnumbered by nearly three to one and suddenly finding himself within a semicircle of attacking Indians led by Brant, he was in real danger of having his regiment cut off entirely from the others. That was when the commander of the next regiment right, Lieutenant Colonel Henry Dearborn, looked back and saw what was happening. Instantly, he shouted a command for his regiment to halt, shouted an about-face and oblique right and charged his men into the affray.

At Dearborn's command a volley was fired that staggered the Indians and then a second one sent them into retreat. Clinton, far to the right and coming up fast, also saw what was happening and ordered his two left regiments, Gansevoort's and Dubois's, to assist Reid, himself continuing with the Livingston and Van Cortlandt regiments to follow Poor to the summit.

The help for Reid came none too soon. His regiment had suffered badly. Captain Elijah Clayes was shot through the body and blood was bubbling from his mouth in a froth. Sergeant Oliver Thurston was dead, a bullet through his heart and his scalp already missing. A sixteen-year-old nephew of Colonel Henry Dearborn, Abner Dearborn, was writhing in agony from a terrible wound in the genitals and another in his side. Sergeant William Lane was also shot in two places, but neither wound was very serious. Ensign Thomas Callis was dead, the side of his head caved in from a war club blow, but his scalp still intact. Lieutenant Nathaniel McCauley of Litchfield, New Hampshire, one of the best-liked young officers, was trying to help Captain Clayes when a rifleball passed through his shoulder and he stumbled against a tree and leaned there, moaning. A moment later another ball completely shattered his right knee and he fell to the ground with a scream. Captain John Combs, best friend of Major John Burrowes, was shot through the stomach and, in a state of shock, propped against a tree.

A score of others lay here and there, scattered on the ground, wounded in varying degrees, but now, with Dearborn's force united with Reid's, the Indians were being driven back. One of Dearborn's lieutenants, Jonathan Cass, stumbled over the dazed warrior who was still trying to regain his feet, and he paused only long enough to snatch the Indian's tomahawk from his belt and bury it in the man's head.

As badly as the Americans were taking casualties, the Indians were being hit worse. No less than a dozen had been killed already and among them, in addition to Gu-cinge, were some of the more prominent of the Iroquois —

Rozinoghyata of the Onondagas, Kayingwaurto of the Senecas, Captain John of the Mohawks, and the middle-aged Seneca woman Queen Esther.

By now Generals Poor and Clinton had reached the summit with their remaining regiments and were momentarily slowed by an exchange of shots with the observation guards posted there by Brant. Major Fogg had had the bad luck of his horse falling and breaking its neck, but he was safely reunited with his regiment later. Slightly below and southward, Joseph Brant had paused and looked about, sensing that something had changed but not knowing what. Then he realized that the artillery pounding had ceased and in the relative quiet could be heard the determined advance of more of the American army coming up the slope in front — the brigades of Hand and Maxwell — to attack Colonel Butler's Rangers and the Tory militia and the remainder of the Indians there. In that instant, Brant knew that not only was the battle lost, but that if retreat was not immediately sounded there was a good chance that they would be surrounded and annihilated. He cupped his mouth and shouted as loud as he could, over and over and in different directions:

"*Ooonah! OONAHHH! Ooooonahhh! OOONAH! . . .*"

They heard him and echoed his call and even the Rangers and Tories knew what it meant and fled at once. So close was the escape that Butler's force was nearly surrounded and all baggage and supplies were left behind in the pell-mell rush for safety. This included the loss to Butler of his own knapsack containing his commission, personal letters, money and some jewelry.

The entire force of Indians, British and Tories was now in full flight, only a hairbreadth from the pincer movement closing in on them. Colonel Ogden with his detachment was trying to cut off retreat from the base of the hill at the enemy's rear right and the four remaining regiments of Poor and Clinton were angling in on them from their flank left and moving southwest from the summit of the hill. All were pressing them very hard, including Hand and Maxwell surging up in front, but because of Brant's having shouted the retreat at the last possible moment, the enemy barely slipped out of the pincers and reached Newtown just in time to get away — some of them along the narrow defile pass on the northeast side of the river above Newtown,[347] others fording the river to the other side and fleeing into the woods there, and still others paddling frenziedly upriver in canoes, the women and children and others in the village having retreated ahead of them. Blood was found on the ground where the canoes had pushed off, but there were no bodies.[348]

A rousing three cheers suddenly indicated that it was all over. The Battle of Newtown had ended.

Incredibly, the whole action had taken less than two hours from the time the artillery signal had been given. Before six in the evening, the Americans had returned down the hill to the road and General Sullivan was rounding up his forces, taking accountings and ordering the destruction of Newtown, outlying cabins and the crops.

Only two prisoners had been taken — a Private Charles Hoghtailer of the British regulars and the huge black Ranger Colly Morse. Hoghtailer was found by Maxwell's men, lying on the ground by the fortification. They thought he was dead and were stripping him of his clothes when an officer came up, looked him over and could not find a wound.

"This man is not dead," he said. "By damn, this man is not even wounded!"

At that he slapped the British private hard on the face and told him to get up. Hoghtailer scrambled to his feet at once, begging for life. He was sent to General Sullivan for questioning. The black man, Morse, terrified, had become separated from the others at the beginning of the retreat and within a mile stumbled into the Americans and gave up. He too was questioned by Sullivan. Neither man was questioned in the presence of the other but their accounts were substantially the same, so Sullivan was fairly sure they were accurate. They told how the Indians had been losing heart for any more resistance and that the only reason they had agreed to fight was because Brant had been made their commander. They said that despite the abundance of crops in the area, they had been put on a strict diet — a ration of seven ears of corn per man per day for the past couple of weeks. The reason for this, they said, was that corn and vegetables were going to be vital to sustain the tribes over the forthcoming winter, especially since some of the sachems were predicting the worst winter anyone had ever seen.

The piece of news the prisoners passed on that General Sullivan found most interesting, however, was that the plan of the Rangers, Tories and Indians was, if they should be defeated here, to meet at Shequaga — Catherine's Town — a village at the head of Seneca Lake, twenty-five miles north of here. Coincidentally, Shequaga was listed on Sullivan's map as the next important place the army would head for.

More than anything else, John Sullivan was amazed at how few lives had been lost; a total of only twenty-seven. The Americans had eleven dead and thirty-two wounded.[349] The British had five killed — one regular private and four Tories — plus two taken prisoner and seven wounded. The Indians had twelve killed, of whom seven were scalped when killed, and an unknown number of wounded.[350]

Some of those American dead on the field were buried where they had fallen and then fires built over their graves to keep them from being unearthed and mutilated. Newtown was plundered before being destroyed but had little of any great value in it — a few guns and bows, mostly not in working condition, some broken tomahawks and knives, gun covers, blankets, a small amount of ammunition and a few arrows and spears. By 6:30 P.M., Newtown was rapidly becoming a pile of ashes.

Tomorrow the army would have a busy time destroying the crops here that the enemy itself had been too frugal to eat. Thinking again about what the prisoners had said about how these crops were to be so badly needed for the coming winter, Major General John Sullivan now realized to its fullest impact the long-range deadliness of George Washington's orders for all Indian crops to be destroyed and houses burned. It would have to be devastating — somewhat to the warriors, but mostly to the elderly and to the women and children. Realizing this, Sullivan was suddenly ashamed of himself and of the army and of this way of waging war.

The Battle of Newtown had certainly not been a bloody battle compared to others, but it was most certainly a significant one. This was the battle that broke the back of the Iroquois League . . . and the hearts of the people of the Six Nations.

[*August 29, 1779 — Sunday*]

The retreat of the Indians and Rangers up the Chemung River was a terrible journey. There was little speaking among them and the knowledge rode heavily upon them that if the attack of the Sullivan army had been just a little better timed — if the wing that was coming around their left flank had had more time to get into position before the artillery commenced firing — all would have been lost. Retreat would have been blocked and there would have been no options left except to fight to the death or surrender.

The retreat was without pause for five miles until they reached the point where the Chemung River turned sharply west. Here they paused to rest until the middle of the night at the little Cayuga village of Kanawaholla.[351] Here, some of the wounded were sent upriver on the Chemung to the town of Teaoga.[352] At Kanawaholla there was some dispirited talk by Butler about whether or not they should try to make another stand, but the suggestion was met with such horror and fear that it was immediately dropped. It was Brant who told John Butler that no more stands would be made against this enemy.

"We have done what we can against them and they have beaten us," he said simply. "Some of our greatest chiefs have been lost. Our hearts are filled with mourning and our minds are filled with fear. Their army is powerful and well equipped and disciplined and their commander understands us and how we fight and can anticipate our movements. Many are leaving now. They will not stop until they reach their own villages and they will carry with them the word of what has happened. After this we will be able to sit in our villages and wait and hope that the army cannot find them and will pass them by, but if this cannot be, then we will wait as long as we can and then pull away before the army comes, taking with us whatever we have of any value that we can carry away." He paused, then added grimly, "But how do we carry away cornfields and houses?"

John Butler was disgusted. He knew there were numerous passes where they could still stand and pick at the enemy, gradually wearing him down until he was infinitely weary and susceptible to being attacked more substantially, but he also knew he could not make the Indians see the value of this. Once they became afraid, once they set their minds to escape, once they determined to keep themselves out of reach of the enemy, nothing could change their minds. Yet Butler did try to change them and he knew he would continue to try as long as possible because he had faith they really could stop Sullivan's army.

As well as being disgusted, Butler was worried. About forty Rangers, including his son, had become separated during the headlong flight to escape. Whether they had gotten away cleanly or not, there was no way of knowing. They could only wait a while longer. The stop at Kanawaholla had been made primarily to give them a chance to rejoin the force if they were able to do so, but they would wait no longer than midnight.

Walter N. Butler showed up. Disheveled and wild-eyed and equally disgusted, he arrived leading the forty Rangers at about 11:00 P.M. and he wanted nothing more than to turn right around and hit Sullivan's army again, much in the manner his father advocated — by picking away at them from their perimeter until they were too weak to defend themselves well enough anymore, then sweeping in for the death blow.

Much talk went on but at last it was decided that, with the frame of mind the Indians were in, now was not the time to discuss it. Perhaps, when they settled down some, they could be convinced to become more aggressive again. They would push on to Shequaga and beyond and, by then, after the passage of several days, when the fears of the Indians had had a chance to dull, they could again be convinced to make a stand.

Brant listened to them and shrugged. It was, he said, possible but not likely. However, he and many of the warriors would accompany Butler as they moved toward Niagara and he would do what he could to reignite the fire for war in them. If nothing else, it was possible that with Fort Niagara to bolster them, he might be able to convince them to make a stand there.

With that they moved on, heading for Shequaga.

[*August 30, 1779 — Monday*]

Although the Sullivan army did not move from its encampment this day at Newtown, they hardly had what might have been called a day of rest. To the contrary, it was an exhausting day. From early morning until late evening the whole army was busy destroying crops and houses and yet another town.

The size of the crops was incredible and hardly a man in the army was not amazed at them. Ears of corn twenty inches long or more, growing on stalks as high as eighteen feet, were not uncommon. Pumpkins and squash grew to enormous sizes, some of them weighing as much as eighty pounds apiece. The potatoes were very large and firm and of excellent quality and the beans, turnips, cucumbers, watermelons, parsnips and other vegetable crops here were commensurately fine. The men ate all they could while engaged in the destruction, but the abundance was still staggering. By noon it was estimated that five thousand bushels of crops had been destroyed and there was still that much more in the ground. Part of the reason for the quality of the crops was the skill with which they had been planted and tended. The corn was in exact rows, well cultivated; the vegetables perfectly spaced and with no trace of a weed growing in any field. There was even evidence that water had been carried by hand to irrigate them. As agronomists, the Iroquois could obviously teach the whites a great deal.

Several detachments were sent across the river to destroy crops that could be seen growing there and one of these went upstream a couple of miles and then, finding a well-used Indian trail leading up a smaller creek that emptied into the river, followed it.[353] Within one mile they found a village of about half a dozen houses and burned it before returning to the main army.[354]

Another detachment, under Major Daniel Piatt of the 1st New Jersey, was sent out to the battle hill, which some of the soldiers were already calling Sullivan Hill, to search for any American bodies that might have been missed. None was found. They did, however, find the remaining five of the twelve dead Indians that had not yet been scalped. The scalping of these was not sufficient. Two of the dead Indians were skinned from the hips down to make two pairs of boots — one pair for Major Piatt, the other for Lieutenant William Barton. They also found and brought in some more plunder that had been hidden, including knapsacks with meager provisions and some blankets, along with several young horses.

Early in the morning, following the amputation of his shattered leg, Lieutenant McCauley of the 1st New Hampshire died and was buried. Late in the day all the wounded were loaded into the few boats that had come up from Tioga. Under the care of Dr. Kimball they would return — after dark, to lessen the chance of their being fired on from shore — to Fort Sullivan and then on to Wyoming where they could receive better attention. Captain George Tudor of the 4th Pennsylvania had become very sick with a fever and so he, too, was sent off with them.[355] Something else was loaded into the boats too, which gave a great lift to the army — all of the wagons and the heavier artillery, including the two six-pounder cannon and the two howitzers. The only artillery retained for further use by the army in its march were the four fairly light brass three-pounders and the cohorn. There was no doubt now that with the heavy artillery and wagons gone, the army could move along much faster.

During the day a General Order was posted for all to see. In it General Sullivan, who had himself been very busy all morning with his report to General Washington, gave his thanks to the army for a job well done and especially to General Poor's Brigade, which had borne the greatest onslaught.[356] At the same time an address from Sullivan was posted, asking, in carefully couched terms, that the army agree to go on the remainder of the campaign at half rations — a half pound of beef and a half pound of flour per man per day. Sullivan's skill with troop psychology was clearly apparent. Lieutenant Colonel Adam Hubley spelled out the details of it in his journal entry this evening after the troops had been polled.

Monday, August 30th — On account of the great quantities of corn, beans, potatoes, and other vegetables, in destroying of which the troops were employed, and the rain which set in after part of the day, obliged us to continue on the ground for this day and night. The troops were likewise employed in drawing eight days' provisions (commencing 1st day of September). The reason of drawing this great quantity at one time was, (however inconsistent with that economy which is absolutely necessary in our present situation, considering the extensive campaign before us, and the time of consequence it will require to complete it,) the want of packhorses for transporting the same, and in order to expedite this great point in view, are obliged to substitute our soldiery for carrying the same.

From the great and unparalleled neglect of those persons employed for the purpose of supplying the western army with everything necessary for them to carry through the important expedition required of them, General Sullivan was at this early period under the disagreeable necessity of issuing the following address to the army which was communicated by the commanding officers to their corps separately, viz:

THE COMMANDER-IN-CHIEF INFORMS THE TROOPS THAT HE USED EVERY EFFORT TO PROCURE PROPER SUPPLIES FOR THE ARMY, AND TO OBTAIN A SUFFICIENT NUMBER OF HORSES TO TRANSPORT THEM, BUT OWING TO THE INATTENTION OF THOSE WHOSE BUSINESS IT WAS TO MAKE THE NECESSARY PROVISION, HE FAILED OF OBTAINING SUCH AN AMPLE SUPPLY AS HE WISHED, AND GREATLY FEARS THAT THE SUPPLIES ON HAND WILL NOT, WITHOUT THE GREATEST PRUDENCE, ENABLE HIM TO COMPLETE THE BUSINESS OF THE EXPEDITION.

HE THEREFORE REQUESTS THE SEVERAL BRIGADIERS AND OFFICERS COMMANDING CORPS TO TAKE THE MIND OF THE TROOPS UNDER THEIR RESPECTIVE COMMANDS, WHETHER THEY WILL, WHILST IN THIS COUNTRY, WHICH ABOUNDS WITH CORN AND VEGETABLES OF EVERY KIND, BE CONTENT TO DRAW ONE-HALF OF FLOUR, ONE-HALF OF MEAT AND SALT A DAY. AND HE DESIRES THE TROOPS TO GIVE THEIR OPINIONS WITH FREEDOM AND AS SOON AS POSSIBLE.

SHOULD THEY GENERALLY FALL IN WITH THE PROPOSAL, HE PROMISES THEY SHALL BE PAID THAT PART OF THE RATIONS WHICH IS HELD BACK, AT THE FULL

VALUE IN MONEY. HE FLATTERS HIMSELF THAT THE TROOPS WHO HAVE DISCOV-
ERED SO MUCH BRAVERY AND FIRMNESS WILL READILY CONSENT TO FALL IN WITH
A MEASURE SO ESSENTIALLY NECESSARY TO ACCOMPLISH THE IMPORTANT PUR-
POSES OF THE EXPEDITION, TO ENABLE THEM TO ADD TO THE LAURELS THEY HAVE
ALREADY GAINED.

THE ENEMY HAVE SUBSISTED FOR A NUMBER OF DAYS ON CORN ONLY, WITHOUT
EITHER SALT, MEAT OR FLOUR, AND THE GENERAL CANNOT PERSUADE HIMSELF
THAT TROOPS, WHO SO FAR SURPASS THEM IN BRAVERY AND TRUE VALOUR, WILL
SUFFER THEMSELVES TO BE OUTDONE IN THAT FORTITUDE AND PERSEVERANCE,
WHICH NOT ONLY DISTINGUISHES BUT DIGNIFIES THE SOLDIER. HE DOES NOT
MEAN TO CONTINUE THIS THROUGH THE CAMPAIGN, BUT ONLY WISHES IT TO BE
ADOPTED IN THOSE PLACES WHERE VEGETABLES MAY SUPPLY THE PLACE OF A
PART OF THE COMMON RATION OF MEAT AND FLOUR, WHICH WILL BE MUCH BET-
TER THAN WITHOUT ANY.

THE TROOPS WILL PLEASE TO CONSIDER THE MATTER, AND GIVE THEIR OPINION
AS SOON AS POSSIBLE.

*Agreeable to the above address, the army was drawn up this evening in corps
separately and the same, through their commanding officers, made known to
them, and their opinions requested thereupon, when the whole, without a dissenting voice, cheerfully agreed to the request of the general, which they signified
by unanimously holding up their hands and giving three cheers.*

*This remarkable instance of fortitude and virtue cannot but endear those
brave troops to all ranks of people, more particularly as it was so generally and
cheerfully entered into without a single dissenting voice.*

Obviously the army was very high after its victory and not even the steady
dismal rain that began about noon and continued into the night could dampen
their feelings. Part of it was due to that victory, part to the fact that the majority
had had a good night's sleep, part to the fact that they hadn't spent the day in a
long, tiring march, and part to a significant fact that was noted only by
Lieutenant Jenkins, of all those who were writing accounts:

None of the Indians were seen today.

[*August 31, 1779 — Tuesday*]

The brief rest at the site of Newtown was brief indeed and it hadn't been much
of a rest. Early this bright, cool morning, the march was resumed with the
booming of a cannon. Word quickly spread that the cannon firing was now to
be a twice daily occurrence — morning and evening — at the order of General
Sullivan, who said he wanted the enemy to know the speed of his advance and
to keep alive in them the fear of the artillery and the knowledge that the army
still carried it, so they would not try another ambush as at Newtown. [357]

Within two miles of beginning the march upstream from the ruins of New-

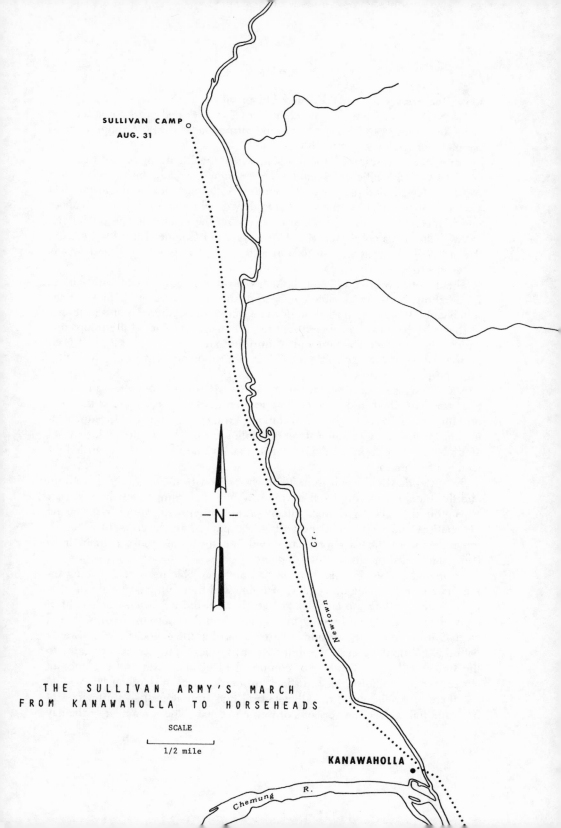

SULLIVAN CAMP
AUG. 31

-N-

THE SULLIVAN ARMY'S MARCH
FROM KANAWAHOLLA TO HORSEHEADS

SCALE

1/2 mile

Newtown Cr.

KANAWAHOLLA

Chemung R.

town, the army came to the small Indian village of Nanticoke, which they
called Middletown, having only eight houses and located on the east bank of
the Chemung.[358] It was immediately burned and the surrounding areas
searched for enemies, but none was found.

The march was resumed and at noon, where the Chemung turned west, the
army crossed the little creek called Tioga Branch, which the soldiers called
Newtown Creek, and just above its mouth were immediately in the abandoned
town of Kanawaholla. At the same time they caught a glimpse of some canoes
just disappearing around a bend far upstream on the Chemung and so General
Maxwell immediately detached forty-four-year-old Colonel Elias Dayton with
the 3rd New Jersey Regiment to pursue them.[359] He was also to destroy any
towns or crops encountered.

There were twenty quite well built hewn-timber houses faced with bark at
Kanawaholla and considerable evidence of the recent precipitate flight of the
inhabitants. In almost all the houses there were large featherbeds and in several
of them the bare earthen floors were recently disturbed and so the troops dug
and found a considerable amount of furniture and other goods that had been
buried. Some of this was taken as plunder, but most was left inside the buildings and put to the torch.

After the village was destroyed, the army was given an hour's rest and a notice posted in which the commanding general thanked the troops for their cooperation in agreeing to go on half rations. At 4:00 P.M. the army resumed its
march, leaving the Chemung River and following northward the path that ran
along Newtown Creek and that Chief Jehoiakim told General Sullivan led directly to Shequaga.[360]

By sunset they had reached the point where Newtown Creek veered eastward
and the Indian path continued north, and here they camped for the night on
good ground.[361] Though Indian attack was not anticipated, Sullivan was taking
no chances and he ordered the tents to be pitched in the form of a hollow
square, with all the packhorses and cattle on the inside to keep them from
being stampeded or killed by the Indians.

Meanwhile, Colonel Elias Dayton had not been able to overtake the escaping Indians on the Chemung River. He followed them upstream eight or nine
miles until reaching the area called Big Flats but did not again catch sight of
them. However, they did see a canoe beached on the shore by the mouth of a
creek coming from the east and so, after smashing the canoe, they followed a
path that led up the creek.[362] A little over two miles up this creek they came to
the Indian village of Runonvea, comprised of eight houses and evidence of
where several additional wigwams had until recently been standing.[363] No one
was there, but adjacent to the village was a fine crop of corn — thirty acres of
it — and half a dozen large stacks of well-cured hay. The remainder of the day

was spent in burning the hay and chopping down the corn. At nightfall they made their camp in the town.

The finding of such towns as Nanticoke and Kanawaholla and Runonvea abandoned and seeing only fleeting glimpses of wildly fleeing Indians underlined the fact that a great terror now filled the Iroquois and they wanted nothing more to do with this American army driving into their country. In fact, many were ready to sue for peace.

Brant and Butler forbade it.

[*September 1, 1779 — Wednesday*]

The commander of the British Royal Greens and the commander of the Iroquois warriors were only beginning to realize how strongly the Sullivan army would press them.

At close to noon today, Butler and Brant stood together in Shequaga and looked at the multitude of Indians before them. For over two hours they had listened to the frightened residents of Shequaga and they felt sorry for them, but they also knew that the decision they would give now would be final.

Since the arrival of the defeated Brant and Butler force, the fear here had been overwhelming. Some of the women had blackened their faces with ashes and charcoal and beat their breasts and sung the death song, because three of the warriors killed at Newtown had been from Shequaga and they had been the fathers or sons or brothers of these women. The whole village was in a state of shock at the deaths of the noted chiefs Gu-cinge and Kayingwaurto and Rozin-oghyata, but most of all at the death of Queen Esther, sister of the Catherine Montour who had established this town of Shequaga. The same shock was undoubtedly being felt over all the League, since runners had been dispatched with the evil tidings, but it was most prevalent here. How, asked the Shequaga villagers, could this have happened? What kind of devils were these Americans who could, with seeming impunity, come into the very villages of the Iroquois and destroy them and their chiefs, their homes and their crops? These were bad times indeed, the sort of bad times that the young sachem Red Jacket had warned were coming.

Not even the arrival yesterday morning of two hundred fresh young warriors from the north, warriors eager for battle, could ease the fear. And though these young warriors strongly demanded that another stand be made, perhaps best in the dense swamp just south of this very village, the warriors who had survived Newtown were vigorous in shouting down the proposal. No! Perhaps somewhere they would face these devils again, but not here and not yet.

Joseph Brant was reasonably sure, even with the addition of the two hundred warriors to their force, that they would not face them again anywhere. He hoped they would, as did Butler, but he simply didn't believe it. What bothered him most at the moment, however, was the strong desire of these Shequaga villagers right now to surrender themselves to the Americans, throw themselves upon the mercy of General Sullivan and sue for peace. They were ready to abandon their British allies and to promise to remain neutral for the remainder of the war. These were the words and thoughts that had filled the air here this morning.

For a short while after the Shequaga villagers had finished, Brant and Butler spoke quietly together and agreed upon what had to be said to them now. It was Brant who spoke and his deep voice was filled with sadness but laced with firmness.

"You say you wish to surrender yourselves to these Americans," he said, "trusting that they will accept your surrender and not harm you. Our friend here, Colonel Butler, warns of what would happen if you were to do this. He says you would be disarmed and then they would murder you and scalp you and throw your bodies into your houses here, which they would then burn over you to hide their deed. That is a possibility, but" — he shrugged and held out his arms and then let them drop to his sides — "I cannot say that is true. The fact that it is *possible*, however, should give you reason to think again before showing such willingness to such an action. Yet, I would not forbid your doing this on such grounds alone. But I *do* forbid this, as your war chief, on grounds that are much stronger!"

A strong murmur swept through the crowd and then died away as everyone listened closely so they would not miss what Thayendanegea would say next.

"I forbid this because even if you are treated well upon surrendering to the Americans, they will use you to bring us to our knees. They will hold you hostage and they will then make demands upon us, in exchange for your lives, which they could not make if they did not have you. And what then would we who remained do? Are we to turn our backs on the threats against you and let them do as they will — and believe me, *then* is when I think they would have no compunction against killing you! — or do we resign ourselves to their demands in order to save you?"

Brant shook his head. "You cannot put us into such a position, and you know it. Whatever happens, you cannot save Shequaga, so that is no consideration. What must be considered are your lives and those of your children and, equally, the lives of the rest of the Iroquois who would be affected by your actions here. There is only one course you can follow now: flee from here! Now! Take what you have of value that you can carry with you and leave here. Go over the hills there" — he pointed eastward — "and you will be safe, because it is we the army will be pursuing and we are going north, to Kendaia and Kanadasaga and Chenussio. Move out of the way of the army and away from our line of passage and you will be safe. Your village can be rebuilt at a later time. Your lives cannot be restored!"

They had gone. Within a couple of hours the thirty buildings of Shequaga were empty and the twenty large wigwams that had been scattered among them had been folded and taken away. All that remained were Butler and his troops and Brant and his warriors. Brant left behind a small rear guard with the village's horses. They were to stay here and watch for the advance of the Sullivan army, which might arrive as soon as tomorrow afternoon, but probably later. Whenever they appeared, the guard was not to fight them but rather to flee and ride at once for Kanadasaga and give the alarm.

The bateaux that Butler had used to come here in were still at the lakeshore of Seneca Lake, three miles distant, and so late this afternoon, having taken aboard some of Brant's wounded and afloat again, he and his Rangers headed northward down the lake toward its outlet, where the capital of the Seneca nation, Kanadasaga, was located. Brant and his warriors set out afoot for the same destination, along the east bank of the lake. They were all out of sight by six o'clock in the evening.

At 7:00 P.M., General Edward Hand's advance guard broke into view of Shequaga from the swamp to the south.

[*September 2, 1779 — Thursday*]

As much as he dared to do so, General John Sullivan was pushing his army forward. No one knew better than he the sad state his army was in with regard to supplies and necessaries. However much plunder had been taken from the villages they had burned, there was still an essential lack for the men. Fighting men, he strongly believed, needed a good regular diet of meat. They could fight neither well nor long as vegetarians. His men were not getting meat in sufficient quantity. Fighting men also needed proper clothing — warm coats, socks, shirts, trousers and sweaters, and they needed blankets — and mostly they were lacking these things. Those lacks had thus far caused minor discomfort, but soon it would be much worse than that. This was a fact that Brant and Butler had to realize and surely must be prepared to swing to their own advantage.

The whole matter of concern for provisions and clothing took on stronger meaning for Sullivan early yesterday. He had stepped out of his tent before sunup and there was a crackling under his feet. He looked down and saw that the grass was covered with frost. It was the first of the year, coming a bit early and bringing with it an omen. Sullivan knew if they didn't finish this mission quickly and get on the move homeward, his army might never return at all.

He ordered the morning gun fired and in a short while the army was on the move again in its usual order of march, Hand's brigade in front, Poor's and Maxwell's flanking the cattle and packhorses in the middle, Clinton's bringing up the rear.

Six miles west of the encampment the army just left was where Colonel Elias

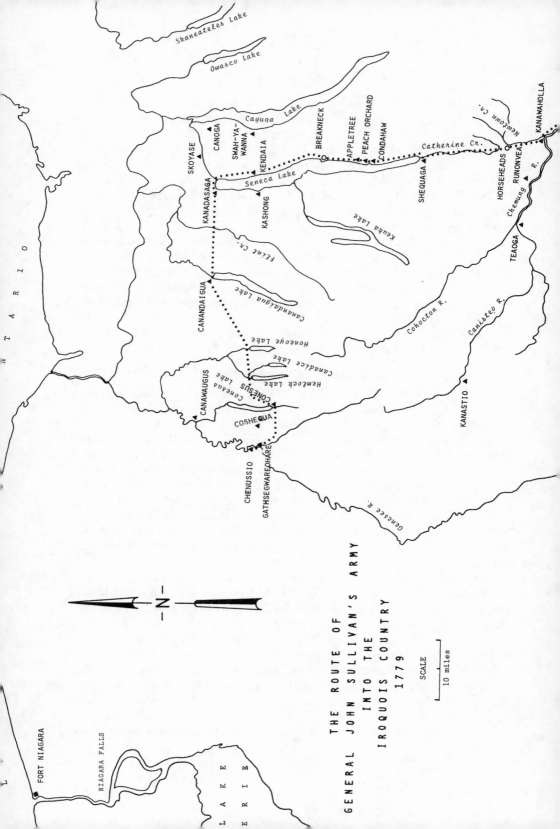

THE ROUTE OF
GENERAL JOHN SULLIVAN'S ARMY
INTO THE
IROQUOIS COUNTRY
1779

SCALE
10 miles

Dayton's detachment had destroyed Runonvea and its crops yesterday and were already well on their way to rejoin the main army. They had continued moving up the creek this morning, since a path was following it coming from the east. Within three miles the path left the creek, continuing east where the creek turned northward. Dayton and his men followed the path. Continuing eastward another three miles, Dayton's force came to the place where Sullivan's army had camped. It was just then 8:30 A.M. and they immediately moved northward on the army's trail at a faster pace. By 11:00 A.M. they had overtaken Clinton's rear guard.

The march north had started out well for Sullivan's army but quickly degenerated. After leaving Newtown Creek on the northward path, the army found itself crossing a significant flatland — a divide between the northward- and southward-flowing streams. Behind them, Newtown Creek flowed into the Chemung River, which in turn joined the Susquehanna, which then ran to the top of Chesapeake Bay and thence into the Atlantic. But the tiny rivulet they encountered next flowed northward into Seneca Lake, which in turn sent its waters into Lake Ontario and the St. Lawrence River and eventually to the sea.

They had no name for the creek and so, since it led to Shequaga, which they knew best by the name of Catherine's Town, they called it Catherine Creek.[364] For a mile or so it provided a pleasant walk. Then it became a mucky bottomland between steeply rising hills on both sides and the path crossed back and forth across the creek.

The path had been made for individuals or small groups, not for an army — especially not for an army driving along hundreds of cattle and packhorses. Soon the muckiness intensified, becoming so bad that the packhorses became stuck and had to be dragged out of the mud by groups of men pulling on ropes. The men cursed and wept and struggled and the situation became only worse. In the next eight or nine miles, at least twenty fordings of Catherine Creek had to be made, and the final three miles were the worst. More than one of Sullivan's men wrote journal entries claiming this to be by far the worst terrain encountered on the campaign. From rock-strewn areas through forests of incredibly thick pine, spruce and hemlock, it moved into an area of deep ravines across which bridges had to be built for cattle and horses. There were morasses, flooded areas where the water was knee deep but the muck below made them sink to their waists, areas where windfallen trees formed terrible barricades and areas of brush so intertangled that it was almost impossible to push through.

Two packhorses fell and broke their necks. Five packhorses died of exhaustion as they struggled to go on and could not. Half a hundred cattle refused to move and then broke and scattered away and were lost when the drovers beat them to make them move. Men carrying not only their normal packs but the additional weight of the extra rations for themselves that they had to shoulder fell fatigued and could not move. [365]

For General Hand's advance corps, leading the way, it was terribly difficult. For Clinton's corps bringing up the rear, following after an army of men and horses and cows that created a sea of muck with their feet and churning hooves, it was pure hell. It took nearly eight hours for Hand's advance to traverse the final three miles and dusk was falling before they finally broke free of it in a great meadow less than half a mile from Shequaga. It was just then 7:00 P.M.

Brant's rear guard and Hand's advance guard saw one another at the same time and instantly the Indians ran from their fires, leaped upon horses and thundered away, bearing northeastward. [366]

Shequaga was located on both sides of the creek and instantly Hubley sent in an elite advance of riflemen to reconnoiter. As soon as they moved out, he formed his regiment into two columns with bayonets fixed and orders to charge without firing if attack came. But, though dogs were howling ahead and fires were burning, over which food was being cooked, the town was empty by the time the riflemen reached it and Hubley's force marched in and took the sizable village unopposed.

The large but rather poorly built log houses were dominated by the much grander house that had belonged, so Hanyerry said, to Catherine Montour. It had a gambrel roof and was thirty feet in length and eighteen wide. A few horses were there, a few cows and calves and some pigs. There was abundant fruit in the large orchard — apples, peaches, plums — and there were large grainfields and extensive vegetable crops. But the Indians were gone.

By then it was becoming quite dark and Hubley's men, and then the rest of Hand's corps, could think of nothing else but resting and they fell exhausted. Their baggage had not come up so they had no blankets, but they were still the lucky ones of the army. Back in the swamp, Poor's and Maxwell's brigades still struggled to break free, but now it was so dark that the men had to hold on to the clothes of those in front of them in order not to lose their way. They didn't emerge from the swamp until after midnight, and still they were luckier than Clinton's brigade, three miles away at the rear, which didn't make it out until the following morning. As Major John Burrowes of Spencer's New Jersey Regiment wrote in a shaky hand in his journal this night:

French Catherines, Wed., Sepr. 1 — We reach this place at 11 o'clock at night, a march of 14 miles through roads that can't be described. Eight miles of the way was a most horrid swamp. The last four miles the army had to ford one creek 17 times. Mud holes were excessively bad. Our packhorses tired out; sticking fast in the swamps, the packs in the mud. The men giving out, they having

14 days provisions on their backs, exclusive of their baggage. We make up a fire and roast corn for our supper and layed down about one o'clock to sleep with the heaven covering us. We never had so bad a day's march since we set off, but what will not men go through who are determined to be free?

Clearly, there was no way the army could move farther for a while and so General Sullivan declared that it would remain at Catherine's Town at least until tomorrow morning.

During the course of last night, one of the houses was pulled down as firewood and burned, but it was the only one destroyed until this morning. Then, with at least Hand's and part of Maxwell's and Poor's brigades refreshed, the destruction of town and crops was undertaken at Sullivan's order. It was while this was occurring that an incredibly old Cayuga woman, unable to walk, was found nearby in the woods. Some of the men guessed her age at one hundred and twenty, but most said she was at least one hundred.[367] Very frightened, she was brought to General Sullivan's tent for questioning. When it seemed she could not understand him, both Hanyerry and Jehoiakim were summoned and they tried every Iroquois dialect without success.

Abruptly Sullivan nodded, convinced she was faking her incomprehension. "All right," he said to the guard. "Since she can't understand us and we can't get her to talk, she's of no value. Take her out and cut her throat."

Instantly the old woman shook her head and looked at the general. "Don't kill me," she said in halting English. "I am very old, but I still like living."

Sullivan's features softened. "If you cooperate and talk, you will not be harmed," he said. "When we leave here, we will leave you with food and shelter. The same may not be true if you don't cooperate."

She cooperated. Little by little, with help from Hanyerry and Jehoiakim Mothskin when words were not understood, she drew a picture of what had been happening here at Shequaga, as she called the village. Brant and Butler, she related, had arrived here with their men late in the morning on the day after the battle. Many of the warriors had been fearful and said they had been conquered and must fly or they would be killed. When it was learned who was killed in the battle, many women of the village lamented the deaths. The old men and women at Shequaga decided they wanted peace and told Brant and Butler this, but Butler had said the army would kill them if they surrendered and Brant had said they would be held hostage and as leverage against the League and that they would have to flee. That is what they did, she said. The old men and the women and children had gone eastward over the hills and Brant and Butler, joined by two hundred fresh warriors from the north, had gone back to Kanadasaga. Catherine Montour herself was in Canada this year.[368]

Sullivan dispatched Colonel William Butler with three hundred men and the cohort to search for the villagers and bring them back, but they were unsuccessful and returned in the evening empty-handed. In the meanwhile, all the crops at the village — except for a small amount the army planned to utilize on its return trip — were destroyed and the town itself burned. The men had an opportunity later in the day to rest and wash clothing in preparation for tomorrow.

Tomorrow, Sullivan said, the march would be resumed.

[*September 2, 1779 — Thursday*]

The American populace in the East, far from the frontiers and glutted with news of the war so close at hand, craved news of what was happening in the wilderness. A full-scale invasion was occurring against the mighty Iroquois and their British supporters in the West. How were they doing? Many friends and relatives of soldiers in Sullivan's army were concerned and uneasy. What was happening? Why weren't the people being told anything?

So, in the tradition of the best yellow journalism of the time, the *Continental Journal* published a story — a little of it based on fact, a fair amount based on rumor, and a very great deal of it pure fabrication:

POUGHKEEPSIE — August 23d

We stop the presses to give our readers a piece of intelligence just received, reported by credible authority.

That an advance party, about 60, of the division of General Sullivan's Army, under General Maxwell, had fallen in with and been killed or taken by a party of the Indians, regulars and Tories, some of whom had done the mischief at Minisink and were on their return. That during the action between the advanced party and the enemy, General Maxwell had surrounded the whole body, and killed and taken 700, among whom were prisoners they had made at Minisink, and in particular Col. Tuston, whose wife had been almost broken-hearted for his loss.[369]

This intelligence, we are informed, came to General Washington yesterday towards evening. Further, that our people had destroyed one of the Indian settlements and that Brant was dead of his wounds.

The circulation of the *Continental Journal* was particularly good in New Jersey and it just happened to be that General William Maxwell's brigade was made up of four regiments that included the 1st, 2nd and 3rd New Jersey regiments, as well as Spencer's regiment, also of New Jersey. In hundreds of New Jersey households this evening, families retired with a dreadful fear in their hearts that was not to be dispelled for a long while.

[*September 5, 1779 — Sunday*]

An anger such as he had seldom in his life known before was filling Joseph Brant at this moment. He stood in the huge longhouse council chambers at Kanadasaga and looked out over the sea of faces before him — over a thousand warriors — and many now averted their eyes from his accusing gaze.[370]

"What are we here?" he asked loudly. "A nation of mice? A league of rabbits? Where are the proud warriors of the Iroquois League who, in times past, would not quail at the advance of forces ten times as large as their own? If the shame in the mind of the Great Spirit at what is happening here comes anywhere near matching the shame filling my own heart now, then we deserve to have him turn his back on us."

Again he paused, as he had been pausing periodically during his harangue and, except for a faint shuffling of feet and muffled clearing of throats, there was no sound. His voice had carried well and outside very nearly as many women and children had gathered and stood silently, buffeted almost as much by the words of Thayendanegea as were the men inside. Never before had such demeaning words erupted in this great longhouse in the capital of the Seneca tribe, Kanadasaga.

This was the most important council ever held here in the tribe's history, a council presently deciding whether or not the Seneca capital — and, as a consequence, the Seneca territory — would be abandoned. And, incredibly, they were deciding that it should be.

The deaths of such powerful Iroquois chiefs at Newtown — especially that of the very chief of Kanadasaga itself, Kayingwaurto — to say nothing of the terrible defeat suffered and the manner in which total annihilation had been so narrowly avoided, had wrought a great change in these warriors.

Never before had the Senecas been so frightened and never before had they been so quick to quake and run and leave behind all that was meaningful to them — their homes, their crops, the graves of their ancestors, their lands. The few British regulars and Tories sat in an uneasy cluster a short distance away from the longhouse, wondering what was going on within, while their principal officers, Colonel John Butler, Captain Robert McDonald and Captain Walter Butler, sat inside close to Brant and watched the bellicose juices of the King's once-powerful ally draining away. For hours they had sat here as chief after chief had risen to speak, and it had become very obvious which way the ultimate decision would go.

Sagoyewatha — Red Jacket — youngest of all the Seneca chiefs, yet rapidly becoming one of the most influential, had spoken strongly against any further support of the British, urging an absolute neutrality for the Senecas and any others of the Iroquois League tribes who would join them. Obviously, he argued, they could no longer call themselves the Six Nations, since the Oneidas and their wards, the Tuscaroras, had largely defected, but they could still be a powerful league called the Four Nations. Could they not pull back, as a League, farther to the west — perhaps fully into the westernmost Seneca territory along the southeastern quadrant of Lake Erie, in the area from Niagara to Presque Isle — and there consolidate themselves, unallied to either the British or the Americans? He referred to General Washington as "The Great Town Destroyer" and warned darkly that unless they stopped fighting the Americans now and made peace with them, the Senecas as a nation would be wiped out. He also pointed out that already, in the short time since the Newtown battle, scores of Delawares and western Senecas had abandoned the upper Allegheny area to settle in greater safety farther westward in the northern Ohio country west of Presque Isle.

What had undoubtedly most influenced those in attendance, however, were the words of Grahta, who was not only the principal chief of the Senecas, but who was also one of the most influential and respected of chiefs in all the Iroquois League. His name meant "The Smoke Carrier" and he was called this because he alone, in all the League, had the right and honor to carry the smoking brand that each year had lighted the numerous council fires from the main, always-burning League fire at Onondaga. [371]

Grahta stood before them on this day with his hand upon the shoulder of his twelve-year-old grandson, Young King, and stunned the assemblage by stating in a soft and sorrowful voice that he was leaving Kanadasaga to resettle in the area of Niagara. He said that he was taking the women and children with him and recommended that the warriors here assembled come along, too.

"We all know the council fire of the League has gone out," he told them. "One day, those of our League who caused this to happen will be called to accounting. But because it has happened, we are driven back until we can retreat no farther. Our hatchets are broken, our bows are snapped, our fires are nearly extinguished. A little longer and the white man will cease to persecute us, for we shall have ceased to exist!"

Many chiefs had spoken since then and now Thayendanegea was the last of them.

"East of this great village of Kanadasaga," Brant continued, "is a place you all know as probably the best place for an ambush in this whole country. We *can* stop the Sullivan army there. We *must!* Will you take this last chance to be men again?"

His voice had risen to a stirring pitch, but now there were none who would support the Iroquois war chief. He expected no answer, having known in his heart before he began to speak that his words would be of little avail here.

"You have made a mockery," he said, his voice dropping and his shoulders now slumped, his whole aspect one of infinite weariness, "of the message I left on the trees for the Americans near Shequaga. It does not matter. Nothing matters now. We will go from here to Chenussio. It is the western door of our once-great League. Now it hangs open on broken hinges, unguarded, so we can slip through it and into the woods beyond with our heads bowed and our shame hung about us like a great cloak which we will never again be able to shed. You sit here and hope that General Sullivan will not come that far with his army, but I tell you that he will, and then where will you go?" There was no answer.

[*September 6, 1779 — Monday*]

The message on the trees of which Brant had spoken in council had been found by General Sullivan's men three days ago, just after they left the ruins of Shequaga.

On orders from Sullivan, the Oneida and Stockbridge guides, Hanyerry and Jehoiakim, had constructed a comfortable little lean-to for the ancient squaw he had questioned and that morning they left her there, supplied in reasonable comfort with a bearskin to cover her for warmth, a supply for firewood close at hand and at least a week's supply of food that could ill be spared, including even some meat.

"The Great Spirit," murmured the old woman, her eyes filled with tears, "has watched over me. I thank him. And I thank you."

A short time later the army moved out, the still-smoldering remains of every building of Shequaga causing a smog to hang low over the town in the quiet morning air. They marched eastward first for half a mile, crossing Catherine Creek one final time and having a bit of difficulty with the marshy ground for the first mile before finally moving partly up the rise of a hill and turning northward. In another couple of miles, following the Indian trail, they came to within sight of the southeast corner of Seneca Lake, where Catherine Creek emptied into it. Here there were a number of large old beech trees and it was here that they found the message left by the war chief of the Iroquois.

Carved on the smooth gray bark of the tree were twelve stick figures, each leaning forward and each with what appeared to be an arrow stuck through the body. There were some other lines, also leaning, leading away at an angle. Beside the big tree, a limber sapling had been bent down, twisted as if it were a rope and then tied to the ground with a stake.

Sullivan, summoned to the scene by his aide, Captain Jonathan Dayton, reined up at the tree and stared at it uncomprehendingly. A moment later Hanyerry ran up with another Oneida who had joined them at Shequaga, a minor chief named Blue Back. They stopped as they saw what was there and murmured together in the Oneida tongue. After a moment Hanyerry explained to Sullivan.

"It is a message to you from Chief Thayendanegea," he said, "he whom you know as Joseph Brant, the Mohawk. He says that in the battle at Newtown, twelve Indians were killed and that five of these were chiefs. Others who were wounded have been taken to safety. But in spite of that loss" — Hanyerry pointed now to the sapling — "he wishes you to know that however much you drive and distress them, you will not conquer them, and that your numbers do not make you safe in this country. He promises that more of your men will die if you continue to come farther into the country where you do not belong."

The commander in chief shook his head. "We'll see about that," he said. With his sword he struck the bent sapling, causing it to snap with a loud report. Then he rode on.

The march continued northward on the gently sloping hillside of the lake, mostly within view of the water. It was truly beautiful country, with the startling blue of the clear lake waters rimmed with verdant shores. The ground was firm here, with scattered trees and very little underbrush. It was by far the easiest marching thus far on the campaign. In all respects it was a good day. Only one hostile Indian was seen — far ahead, by the advance guard — and he disappeared almost immediately. At sight of him, however, General Sullivan sent ahead a small detachment of Jersey troops under Lieutenant Colonel William Smith of Spencer's regiment in the hope of taking a prisoner and then sending him back to his people with a message from the general: that women and children were urged to surrender and they would be well treated and in no way hurt. Smith caught one final glimpse of the Indian, along with four of his fellows now, far ahead. They raced off and after that no more Indians were seen during the day.

Three rather steep ravines had to be crossed, at the bottom of each of which a brook cascaded over rocks in a pleasant way and finally flowed into the lake. None was difficult or dangerous to cross, only time-consuming. It was at the second of these that they came to a small abandoned village on the lakeshore.[372] This, they learned from Jehoiakim, was the Cayuga village of Condahaw. It was comprised of one longhouse in which several firesites indicated it had been inhabited by three or four families, plus there were a few other individual houses that were much smaller. A couple of young horses were caught here and it could clearly be seen where Brant's force had butchered and devoured a steer, but there were no people. With hardly more than a pause, the buildings were set afire.

As had been the case ever since the campaign began, a considerable number of rattlesnakes were encountered. These were timber rattlers and, though a good many were killed, nobody was bitten and they were more of an annoyance than a real hazard. A much greater problem was that the packhorses were becoming extremely jaded under their heavy loads and from lack of decent food. Everyone hoped that wherever they stopped for the night there would be good pasturage. There wasn't. Not only was there not good pasturage, there was none at all. The horses were tied to trees over bare ground in the area where they stopped.

The halt was made late in the afternoon at the Indian village that the men called Peach Orchard. The place had only eight houses and they had not been empty for long, but no one was in sight. It was situated on a delta of land that had been built up by alluvial deposits from the stream that entered the lake here.[373] Despite the good marching conditions, only twelve miles had been covered due to the poor condition of the horses.

In the morning, Peach Orchard was burned, though it was at first difficult to get the fires going because of a rain that had begun falling during the night and continued into the morning. The march did not begin until 10:30 A.M. and within an hour the skies had cleared and it was another beautiful day. Four miles from Peach Orchard, with the smoke of the fires still visible in the sky behind, they came to the village of Appletree, which was discovered almost by accident. They had been marching about a half mile inland when they were suddenly confronted with a really severe ravine that would have been foolish to attempt crossing with the horses and cattle in such weakened condition. They promptly named the stream Breakneck Creek. Here they turned left and went back to the lake where the ravine smoothed out on the extensive point formed over the centuries by the creek deposits.[374] It was on this point that they discovered the six-house village of Appletree.

This was the narrowest part of the lake, being not more than a mile and a half straight across. From the point of land they were on there was a gorgeous view of the thirty-six-mile-long lake in both directions. Three more Indian horses discovered here were captured by driving them into the lake, but they did not make up for the six horses that had died during the day from exhaustion. Appletree village was burned and a small cornfield destroyed and they went on.

About twelve miles farther along the lakeshore they stopped for the night where there was an abundant growth of wild pea vines, which the horses devoured eagerly. Here a lovely meandering stream, weaving through fields of mandrake in fruit and hazel bushes laden with nuts, poured into the lake after emerging from a rather dense ravine.[375]

From this camp General Sullivan, with Hanyerry's agreement that it might prove worthwhile, dispatched the minor chief Blue Back to return to the tribe and rouse them to come and help the army, telling them to rendezvous at Kanadasaga at the north end of this lake. It was at this camp, too, that they discovered another message on a tree from Brant to Sullivan. Once again Hanyerry translated it:

"He says, 'The army may continue to pursue, but they will soon meet with trouble.' "

Sullivan snorted. "We'll believe that when it occurs."

It was yesterday that had turned out to be an unusually eventful day and a decided prelude for the events of today. Despite the wild pea vines the horses had eaten, the animals were still in very bad shape and it had been difficult to get them and the cattle moving. It had also been difficult to keep them moving. Only five miles had been covered before they were so played out that Sullivan was forced to call a halt for the rest of the day. However, that was not the only reason. At the end of those five miles, within a quarter mile of the lake, they had abruptly come to the oldest and most substantial village yet encountered on the expedition.

This was Kendaia.[376] Hanyerry said it had been named after Chief Kendaia of the Senecas who had fought bravely at the siege of Fort Niagara in 1759. The town had thirty houses and ten wigwams. Those houses were all of hewn timbers, half with bark facing, half with rough-finished wood that had been painted and looked quite civilized. One of them even had a chimney. Eleven of them stood prominently on a ridge overlooking the lake with a fine prospect. There was a large orchard of about two hundred and eighty very old fruit trees, mostly apple but also a number of peach and plum. Hardly had the army stopped before a detachment with axes was ordered out to girdle every tree and kill them. Scouts brought in word of a large cornfield a mile and a half distant, so Major John Burrowes was sent with a detachment to get some of the corn and destroy the rest.

Hardly had the advance guard entered the town when a barefooted, barechested man in ragged trousers ran toward them, calling for them not to shoot, that he was white — an escaped prisoner of the Indians. He was thin and in poor health and he nearly fainted in his excitement when, among men of the Wyoming Militia regiment, he began recognizing old neighbors and calling them by name. One of those whom he recognized and who was first to recognize him was Lieutenant John Jenkins.

The man was Luke Swetland, a settler of the Nanticoke area, not far downstream from Wyoming. It was there, a year and twelve days ago, on August 24, 1778, that he had been captured by the Indians. He explained that he had been brought here and adopted by a squaw to fill the place of her son, who had been killed. It was from Swetland that General Sullivan and the army learned for the first time that one of the Indians killed at Newtown had been one of the most prominent and well liked of the Iroquois chiefs, Kayingwaurto, chief of the capital town of Kanadasaga. Mourning throughout the Seneca tribe, Swetland said, had been great at his death — even more than the mourning at the death of their war chief, Gu-cinge, who also had been killed at Newtown, but who was not as beloved a man to his fellows as was Kayingwaurto. Swetland said the Tories he'd talked with were extremely dejected and felt their only hope now lay in flight, but that evidently Brant, at the head of a thousand warriors, was ready to fight Sullivan again and was trying to convince the other chiefs to back him up. Brant, he told them, had left Kendaia only two days before and had been talking about making a stand against Sullivan in a marsh at the foot of this lake, a marsh the army had to traverse in order to reach Kanadasaga.

Kendaia had something not seen in any of the other towns. Here there were three rather ornate and remarkable tombs over the bodies of venerable old chiefs. The bodies had been dressed in fine leathers and decorated with beads and feathers, accoutered with good knives and tomahawks and then wrapped in shrouding. Stretched out on a low platform, they had placed over each of them a sort of casement box through which the body could be seen. The box itself was painted in weird, brightly colored designs. The final work was four posts erected near the corners and then a heavy bark roof constructed over this to ward off the elements. They were, in their way, beautiful and touching monuments to greatly honored dead. They didn't stay that way for long. They were torn down, tipped over, broken apart, desecrated and plundered by the soldiers.

Certain that before very long they would be engaging the enemy again in battle, Sullivan gave an order as evening approached that resulted in unexpected and very disturbing consequences. He ordered that all the men fire their weapons to make sure the rifles were in good condition. The order was obeyed, but altogether too close to the cattle and packhorses, which, once again, had been picketed in an area where there was no food for them. They had rested some during the day, but now they were hungry and edgy. When abruptly something approaching three thousand rifles began firing almost simultaneously, they panicked and stampeded. Some were contained and held, but sixty or seventy of the cattle got away, along with twenty-seven horses. By then it was growing dark and there was no hope of capturing them until daylight.

Finally, as if to compound the problems, it was discovered that five packhorsemen — servants of Colonel Peter Gansevoort — had been missing all day and no one could remember having seen them or their horses since the afternoon of the day before.

Early in the morning today, numerous detachments were sent out to round up the scattered animals and a captain's guard was sent back to look for the missing packhorsemen. By noon a score of cattle and eighteen horses were still missing, nor were they ever found. It was a serious loss. The captain's guard, however, had better luck. At about the same time they returned with the missing men and their horses, plus one extra horse in excellent condition and a large quantity of apples and peaches.

The packhorsemen explained that late in the afternoon the day before yesterday they had become very weary and stopped to rest, allowing the column to go on. They tarried too long and, by the time they mounted up again and began trying to catch up with the army, it was growing dark. They followed what they thought was the army's trail well into the night and instead of going northward had gone eastward, practically to Cayuga Lake. There, coming to the small Cayuga town of Swah-ya-wanna,[377] they frightened off the inhabitants, who left the horse behind. Remaining there overnight, they burned the several buildings in the morning and, realizing their mistake, they loaded up with fruit from the trees there and retraced their yesterday's steps. Last night they had camped where the army had camped the night before and they were just on their way to catch up to the army this morning when the captain's guard found them and escorted them in. It was a pleasant surprise that they were safe, but also an object lesson; orders were immediately issued that no one was to leave the main army or fall behind unless acting on direct orders from his commander.

In the meanwhile, Kendaia had been undergoing the usual house and crop destruction by the army, but it was a very big job and not until three in the afternoon today did the army once again begin its northward move. In four miles they encamped again, at the mouth of another creek feeding into the lake, almost seven miles south of the northern end of the lake.

From this vantage point, a fairly good-sized Indian town could be seen two and a half miles away on the opposite side of the lake. Through a telescope, Indians could be seen driving horses there and Sullivan made a mental note to check it out at the first opportunity. Hanyerry told him it was the town of Kashong, one of the nicest of all Seneca villages.

A decided tension was rising in the army now, the closer they were coming to the northern end of the lake and Kanadasaga. All the signs indicated that a major battle might be shaping up ahead and John Sullivan found himself more watchful and careful. The size of the night guard was doubled tonight, but again there were no Indians seen or heard. It was eerie.

Just as darkness was falling an express arrived, mounted on a fine horse and trailing two others. He had come from Wyoming and Tioga. One piece of news he brought was greeted with great excitement. A general raise in pay had been ordered for all officers and soldiers in the Continental Army. But along with the good news there was some bad. Two more of the American soldiers who had been wounded at the Newtown battle had died. One was Private Abner Dearborn, the sixteen-year-old nephew of Lieutenant Colonel Henry Dearborn. The other was Captain John Combs, of Spencer's regiment. The latter news was particularly shattering for Major Burrowes, as Combs had been his very close friend. Tonight in his journal, Burrowes wrote:

An express arrived with letters from Gen'l Washington to Sullivan and a number of letters for the officers of this army. Among which I find the disagreeable news of the death of my dear friend. Captain Combs (when living) was possessed of everything that constituted a man. How did I feel? How was the countenances of all his acquaintances changed? It's beyond description. In the faces

of all his friends is seen nothing but sadness, and from the tongues of his ac-
quaintances only expressions of sorrow. . . .

[*September 8, 1779 — Wednesday*]

Kanadasaga, capital of the Seneca Nation, was destroyed.

The whole operation had gone with a smoothness that completely flabbergasted many of the officers of John Sullivan's army. The Senecas were a
powerful tribe, a tribe of warriors renowned for their ferocity. If anywhere attack were to be made against the army with any real hope of success, this was
the place. Even expecting it was not much help because the very approach to
the town made the army vulnerable.

Yesterday the march of the army had commenced at 7:00 A.M. and after
eight or nine miles they reached the outlet of the lake at its northeastern end.
The stream flowing out of the lake was the Seneca River, swift and clear, running eastward just a bit over ten miles before emptying into Cayuga Lake. Here
the army stopped and considered what lay ahead. For half an hour Sullivan
and his officers conferred with the Reverend Samuel Kirkland who, through his
previous missionary work here, knew Kanadasaga well. For two years — 1764
through 1766 — he had been a missionary and there was a certain sense of
nostalgia in him now as he spoke of the place.

"You know," he said, smiling, "Kanadasaga means 'Grand Village' and
that's just what it is. Beautiful place. More than a village, really. A city. Yes, a
beautiful city."

It was, he went on, only a few miles ahead, across the river and then past the
north lakeshore and a little way west of the northwestern corner of the lake.
The problem was, the only path from where the army was lay through a severe
marshy area. The trail itself, along the north beach, was firm but only wide
enough for two or three men and horses abreast. Even with flankers out to
plunge through the dense marsh grasses, the army would still be extremely vulnerable as it passed.

The officers learned that this was not the only hazard. Actually, the first
place the enemy would have a distinct advantage would be while the fording of
the lake outlet was made. The Seneca River here was only waist deep, but it
was twenty yards wide and very swift. Scouts were sent ahead to reconnoiter,
but they returned in half an hour, having found nothing. Nevertheless, as
much as possible, the crossing was made in battle order, but it was completed
without incident. What was happening? Where *was* the enemy? Surely he
wasn't going to let an army of whites enter his capital unopposed! Apprehension among the officers and men grew as they reformed on the west bank and
began moving westward in files along the north beach of the lake. Any semblance of battle formation here was lost. Two flanking divisions were sent out

into the marsh area and they had an extremely difficult passage through knee-deep water and cattails higher than their heads. If the enemy struck here, any sort of defense would be almost ludicrous.

No shots were fired, no one encountered.

As Major Fogg put it:

Nature could not have formed a better place for an ambuscade, as the lake was on our left and an impervious swamp on our right for half a mile.

The whole army breathed a universal sigh of relief when this bad traverse was completed without incident. After a couple of miles they came to where a tiny brook entered the lake and here was a tiny village of sorts called Nuguiage. It was only a few large, well-built houses on the bank. The little settlement was also called Butler's Buildings because one of the houses had belonged to a minor chief who called himself Butler, after Colonel John Butler. The larger of them, according to Hanyerry and Jehoiakim, was a summer house of the principal Seneca chief, Grahta. These buildings had a beautiful view down the length of the lake.[378]

These buildings were set afire and here, with better ground ahead, the marching order was rearranged to better advantage. Kanadasaga was only a little more than a mile ahead and so Maxwell's column was sent to encircle the town in that direction and Poor's was sent to the right for the same purpose. Their orders were to "surprise the Indians in their town, prevent any escape and capture them and their town."[379] The army was by this time becoming so certain that the enemy had abandoned the place that they were becoming very careless. As the detachments passed through the cornfields, the men pulled off ears of corn and stuffed them inside their shirts and they stuck pumpkins upon their bayonets to carry them. A festive mood was sweeping them now. However, because such activities delayed them, they arrived at the town very late and Sullivan's main army was already there; Sullivan himself was furious at the delay of the encircling troops.

In the last of the daylight, having emerged from the woods with Kanadasaga spread out before him; Sullivan was amazed to realize that this, the finest town yet encountered, one of such modern design and construction that it bore little resemblance to the usual Indian village, was indeed empty of Indians and to be taken uncontested. The principal buildings, especially those of the chiefs and the grand council longhouse, were extremely well constructed and looked much like the fine homes found in the towns of Americans in the East. Bisected by Kanadasaga Creek, the town was regularly laid out in a circle almost a third of a mile in diameter and was made up of about sixty very good houses, plus another forty less well built log houses, quonsets and wigwams. In the center of the village was a park of a few acres of quality English grass and here was visible the remains of the stockaded fort and blockhouses built in 1756 by Sir William Johnson. All around the town as well as here and there throughout it were excellent, neatly laid out gardens of peas, onions, squash, beans, carrots, parsnips, cabbage, cucumbers, watermelons and pumpkins, while farther out from town were extensive fields of corn bearing some of the best ears most of the men had ever seen. The town was also surrounded by numerous good fruit trees of considerable age, all of them bearing well, and including apples, peaches, plums and mulberries. As at Kendaia, there were a few sepulchers here in which the remains were evidently those of chiefs.

The Indians had not merely moved out, they had evidently abandoned the place in considerable haste, for there were many small items left behind that could have been carried easily enough had not a precipitate retreat been occurring. The army was relieved and yet there were those who were very confused by this rather incomprehensible Indian behavior. Dr. Campbell wrote in his diary:

The Indians had deserted the place some short time before our arrival. It seems that we are not to see any more of these people. It was expected they would have made a great stand at this place. It is difficult to account for the behavior of the Indians, who quit their towns and suffer us to destroy them, without offering to interrupt us. . . .

In addition to a confusion over why the Indians were not standing and fighting, there was a growing contempt for them, especially among the officers. Many referred to them as dogs running with their tails between their legs and to some the best answer to the problem they continued to present seemed to be extermination of them. Fogg wrote:

The land between the Seneca and Cayuga Lakes appears good, level and well-timbered; affording a sufficiency for twenty elegant townships which, in the process of time, will doubtless add to the importance of America. The communication of the Seneca with Cayuga is passable with boats and is about twenty miles. Whether the God of nature ever designed that so noble a part of His creation should remain uncultivated, in consequence of an unprincipled and brutal part of it, is one of those arcana yet hidden from human intelligence. However, had I any influence in the councils of America, I should not think it an affront to the Divine will, to lay some effectual plan, either to civilize or totally extirpate the race. Counting their friendship is not only a disagreeable task, but impracticable; and if obtained it is of no longer duration than while we are in prosperity and the impending rod threatens their destruction. To starve them is equally impracticable for they feed on air and drink the morning dew.

Kanadasaga was occupied by the army without the firing of a weapon. The only living human seen as the army approached was a small naked boy of about six years of age. He was frightened and emaciated and extremely hungry. He was also white.

It was obvious that the Iroquois dialects were familiar to him and that while he could reasonably well understand English, he could not speak it very well. When thirty-five-year-old artillery officer Captain Thomas Machin, himself ill and off duty, offered food to the boy, the child had to be restrained from making himself sick by devouring too much too soon. His pitiable condition, and the fact that there was no way of knowing who he was or when or where he had been captured, made Captain Machin's heart go out strongly to the boy. Machin petitioned to General Sullivan to have the child placed under his care and Sullivan agreed. Machin decided that if there was no way to locate the boy's family, he would adopt him as his own son. [380]

A strong guard was mounted for the night at General Sullivan's orders, but there were no hostile disturbances of any kind. The only noise, in fact, was the laughter of the men and the occasional breaking of wood as some of the less well built houses were pulled down for firewood.

Today had been a day of decision. Supplies for the army were critically low, yet it was known that some other important Seneca towns still lay to the west of here, not the least of which was the western door of the Iroquois League, the important town of Chenussio, home of the powerful Seneca chief Little Beard. Sullivan was for pushing on and destroying all towns up to and including Chenussio, along with their crops, before turning and heading for home, but he had to know the feelings of the army. Part of the problem was that the area they would head into now, if they went on, was unfamiliar to any of his guides.

A council was called, not only of the generals and field officers, but of all officers in the command. Opinions were asked in the matter and the situation weighed. This, Major Fogg thought, was a ridiculous way of doing things and he was not at all reluctant to write critically of it:

A council was held on the expediency of proceeding to the Genesee River — a march necessary but, to appearance, almost impracticable and by many thought to be imprudent. Pimps [381] *and tale bearers were brought from every brigade to ascertain the minds of the general officers and some attempted to argue them into the propriety of an immediate return. How incompetent are men of inferior stations to judge in matters of such a nature, especially when they are not availed of any of the principles on which to form their judgment. One instance of this kind happened in which the subject had well nigh been sent without sentries, with orders for them to fire in case of his return.*

As the conference was being held, other things were occurring, not the least of which was the dispatching of some detachments to destroy towns nearby whose locations were known. One of these was Kashong, the town on the west side of Seneca Lake, seven miles south of here, which the army had seen from across the lake on its way up. Major James Parr, Lieutenant Thomas Boyd and two hundred riflemen, carrying along the cohorn, were detached to destroy the town and they left about noon.

Another detachment was sent under Colonel John Harper to destroy Skoyase, an important Cayuga town seven or eight miles away on the Seneca River.[382] While the detachments were gone, Sullivan's main army busied itself with the destruction of Kanadasaga, cutting down the fruit trees and destroying crops as well as burning the majority of the buildings. All weapons were ordered to be fired and cleaned. All these matters, while important in their own right, took on lesser import in view of the council of officers being held. Throughout the day it continued. Men from the commissary department had been called upon to remark and they said that supplies were extremely low, but that with tight rationing of what they had and strong utilization of whatever crops they might find en route, they thought the army could go on the remaining eighty miles to Chenussio, but no farther. That was when agreement was reached to go on with the march and the army was immediately put on even more reduced rations than they had already been enduring — meat every three days, bread every five days and only a pinch of salt daily. Sullivan gave the marching orders for 6:00 A.M. tomorrow.

The detachments were still very busy. Harper's men arrived at Skoyase and found the town abandoned, so they destroyed its eighteen houses but left the crops for possible later use of the army on its return home. A most unusual find was a series of man-made ponds adjacent to the river, in which the Indians had been impounding fish alive for their own use.[383]

Parr's detachment found Kashong to be a fine new town and crops in such amazing abundance there that it was not possible for his detachment to destroy everything in the allotted time, so he sent Lieutenant Boyd back to request another detachment to help. Sullivan immediately dispatched another four hundred men to him, under Lieutenant Colonel William Smith. The destruction was completed by morning, but it was a huge job. The town itself had twenty well-built new homes and there were many hogs and chickens, stacks of hay and fields neatly fenced. There was a real beauty to the area that affected all the men.[384]

With the decision to continue the expedition as far as Chenussio, General Sullivan ordered the formation of another detachment to leave the army tomorrow morning. This detachment was to be under the command of Captain John Reed of the 6th Massachusetts Regiment. It was to include all the sick and lame, including Captain Machin and the emaciated little boy he had found, as well as all the horses that were no longer serviceable. Reed's small body of fifty able men would escort the detachment back to Fort Sullivan at Tioga. There,

Reed was to drop them off and return immediately to the site of Kanawaholla on the Chemung River, where he would build a supply depot and bring there from Tioga any supplies that may have come in for the army during its absence. In that way the army, on its return, would have relief well before having to go all the way back to Tioga, so that meant they could better utilize what supplies were on hand now for the days immediately ahead. The departure tomorrow of that detachment would also allow the remainder of Sullivan's army to move along speedily in wrapping up its expedition.

Sullivan was not entirely sure how to get where they were going, since his maps for the area from this point westward were poorly drawn and greatly based on hearsay and speculation, but Chenussio was definitely known to be west of here and the well-traveled principal road leading westward out of Kanadasaga would undoubtedly lead there. The army would follow it. Surprisingly, in the face of greater rationing and penetrating another eighty miles deeper into the Indian country, the morale of the army was rising rather than diminishing.

Even an extremely severe electrical storm that struck late in the day failed to dampen their spirits.

[September 9, 1779 — Thursday]

In his thirty-nine years, Joseph Brant had never seen his people so dispirited, so inclined to jump at shadows, so willing to give up without a fight everything that meant anything to them. After leaving Kanadasaga in the face of the advancing Sullivan army — a shame he still felt was unbearable — the Indians and British regulars and Tories had retreated here to Canawaugus, nine miles north of Chenussio.[385] Here the party remaining, now only about four hundred strong, including Indians and whites, had split up. Those that had split away after the departure from Kanadasaga had gone to Canada; now, with this split, those leaving were going on to the Niagara area. Some had gone on to Chenussio, not to attempt to make a stand there against the enemy, as Brant advocated, but only to gather up certain possessions to take with them to Niagara. Now Brant stood with Colonel John Butler and shook his head, his expression at once both hard and sorrowful.

"We are finished," he told Butler softly. "I have tried in every way I know how to try, ever since leaving Newtown, to breathe fire into them again, to make them care, to make them men again. It is no use. Something has gone out of my people and they will never be the same again."

Butler nodded sympathetically. "I've never seen anything like it. I wouldn't have believed it. It's as if a lampwick were turned down until it went out."

"That lamp," Brant nodded, "was the Iroquois League council fire at Onondaga. When that fire went out, the reflection of it went out in the breast of every warrior. There is no fire left."

"They won't fight again? At all?"

Brant shrugged. "Possibly. Perhaps when they realize that they have nothing left to lose, so it makes no difference, they will fight again. All they have left to lose now are their lives and lives without pride or self-respect are worth little." He paused, then nodded faintly. "Yes, they may yet do some fighting here and there. The younger ones. Those who joined us at Shequaga. Their blood is always hot. Some of them have talked of an ambush against the Americans before they reach Chenussio. Perhaps at Conesus."

Butler showed immediate interest. "How many warriors?"

"Interested? One hundred . . . two hundred. Maybe more. Maybe less." Brant shrugged again.

"That's not enough to attack the army," Butler pointed out, "even with my men in support."

"I know. They don't talk of ambushing the whole army. Just any kind of detachment that might be sent out. Anything to draw blood. Their pride, what little remains of it, requires that they draw *some* kind of enemy blood before leaving this country. It can do nothing much nor make any difference."

"Are you going along, Joseph?"

Brant looked at him in a speculative manner and then nodded. "Yes."

Butler smiled. "I'll go along, with my men. Maybe we, too, need to draw some blood, just to retain a little pride."

[*September 12, 1779 — Sunday*]

Lieutenant Thomas Boyd's eyes were sparkling with eagerness as he stood in the circle of lamplight before Major General John Sullivan in the commander in chief's tent and listened to the special orders he was being given. There was a glow of pride in him as he recalled the summons he had received from the general about half an hour ago. His own commander in Morgan's Riflemen Corps, Major Parr, had sought him out and told him that Sullivan wanted to see him immediately. Boyd had wasted no time getting there. Now, here he stood, still hardly daring to believe that John Sullivan himself had singled him out for this mission. He was certain that this was the great break he had been wanting, the matter that was going to catapult him to rank and fame.

The past four days since leaving Kanadasaga had been essentially uneventful so far as any contact with the enemy was concerned and Boyd had begun to think his time was running out on this campaign to prove himself against the enemy. Now it appeared that was changing. The army's march from Kanadasaga had been delayed until noon on September 9 because of rains. During that morning Captain Reed and his fifty men, escorting the sick men and jaded horses, moved off on the back trail toward Tioga. Colonel Smith and Major Parr had not yet returned from their mission to destroy Kashong, but Sullivan knew they would pick up the army's trail and follow it, so at noon he gave the orders to march. Much of this march was through a basically treeless area with head-high grass in some places, but in one area they were slowed for a while because of a four-mile-long swamp. The result was that the army put only eight miles behind them and camped for the night on the edge of a beautiful stream they had just crossed called Flint Creek.[386] It was here that the Smith and Parr detachment caught up, with the agreeable news that Kashong had been destroyed. However, there was a sad note as well; one of their soldiers had died of heart failure during the destruction.[387] They had buried him there.

The next morning, even though at Kanadasaga they had culled out all the packhorses they thought were unfit, another thirty were unable to walk and so they were left behind to graze at will in the lush meadows of the Flint Creek valley, with the hope that some of them might be rounded up on the return trip and be in better shape then to serve.

Eleven miles were marched this day and by 2:00 P.M. they reached the northern end of Canandaigua Lake, forded its knee-deep outlet and came to the Seneca town of Canandaigua a mile beyond.[388] Here there were twenty-three very fine homes, which some of the officers even referred to as elegant. Mostly they were frame homes or homes of hewn planks or logs and almost all of them had chimneys. The army paused only long enough to set them all afire and then continued the march another mile to some cornfields. Here they'd camped and destroyed fifty acres of corn before dark. In the town they'd found a white dog hung and disemboweled and decorated with strands of wampum and feathers.

The march yesterday — September 11 — was fairly difficult, the worst since the swamp before Shequaga. This was because of miry ground that was very tough on the packhorses. It was becoming obvious that these horses simply would not be able to continue much longer. By evening they had covered fourteen miles and reached the twenty-house Seneca town of Honeoye on the east side of the outlet of the lake of the same name.[389] It was here that Sullivan decided to split his forces again. Figuring that it was about twenty-five miles from here to Chenussio, which was no more than two days' easy march, he directed that the sturdiest house in town be fortified and the rest burned, so a detachment could be left here while the rest, traveling lightly and rapidly with a minimum of equipment and four days' rations, would head for Chenussio. Everything possible that could be left behind — supplies, ammunition, stores, baggage, jaded horses — would be left, along with the "L and Ls," the lame and lazy. These latter, two hundred and fifty of them, would be guarded by a force of fifty men left under command of Captain John N. Cummings of the 2nd New Jersey Regiment. Cummings was also left with the two three-pounder cannon. Immediately the captain had set his men to clearing away the other houses and cut loopholes into the walls of the strongest place, constructed an abattis around it of chopped-down fruit trees and strengthened its walls with kegs of flour and boxes of ammunition. Not unexpectedly, he named the place

Fort Cummings. The horses to remain here were turned loose to roam at will, grazing wherever they could, perhaps to be recaught for use on the way back.

Sullivan had planned an early march today, but rain again delayed departure until noon. Then only eleven miles were covered.[390] He had expected they would reach Conesus at the head of Conesus Lake, but instead was obliged to camp for this night in the woods a mile from the head of the lake and less than two miles north of that Seneca town.[391]

A strong reminder of the lateness of the season came this evening when it turned very cold and a heavy frost began appearing, settling over the grasses. The rimed grass had been crackly underfoot as Lieutenant Boyd strode to General Sullivan's quarters. Now he stood at casual attention listening to what his commander was saying.

"I've heard a number of good things about you, Lieutenant, and not merely your capture of Hare and Newbury near Otsego Lake. You seem to be enterprising and alert."

"Thank you, sir."

"Those are the qualities I need in the man I want to send on a special mission tonight. I think you can handle it."

"I'll do whatever you outline for me to do, General," Boyd replied. He was being straightforward, not boastful.

"Good. I want you to take five or six men, perhaps including Jehoiakim or Hanyerry, and make a scout toward Chenussio. Move fast and see if you can detect any sign of the enemy preparing for resistance or setting up a trap. I want you back here early in the morning; by sunrise, if possible. It may take you longer than that, but I hope not. It's eleven o'clock now and it shouldn't be more than ten miles from here to Chenussio. You should be able to get back here not long after dawn."

"We'll be back early in the morning, sir," Boyd promised.

Sullivan nodded, feeling good about his choice of Boyd for this assignment. "Excellent! We'll be busy here, clearing out Conesus, but we'll still want to get moving as early as possible. Clear?"

"Yes, sir!" Boyd saluted, spun about and left the tent.

[*September 13, 1779 — Monday Dawn*]

The character trait that was Lieutenant Thomas Boyd's greatest liability was his own ambition. He was willing to bend almost any rule a little to his uses if it helped promote his career and while, in the past, he had been fortunate in not letting ambition become a stumbling block, he was now tripping headlong over it. In the first light of morning he had already exceeded his authority in two different matters. The first occurred last night when he left General Sullivan's tent and, instead of selecting five or six men for an elite squad as the general had directed, he picked a light company of twenty-eight men, including Sergeant

Michael Parker of Captain Simpson's company, 1st Pennsylvania Regiment, and, as guides, *both* Hanyerry and Jehoiakim. Mounting them all on the best horses available, he had moved them out across the marshy inlet to Conesus Lake. Immediately on the west side of that stream, the trail diverged, part of it angling southward and then west, the other heading almost north and then northwest.

General Sullivan's rough map was quite old and it showed the location of Chenussio to be along an older trail — the one moving southward slightly and then west, running from Conesus through the village of Gothsegwarohare and then to Chenussio, whose location was shown to be where Canaseraga Creek met the Genesee River. Boyd was fully intending to go the way Sullivan's map indicated, but both Hanyerry and Jehoiakim insisted that way was longer. Chenussio was no longer where it had once been and the north and west trail was a shorter route. This trail followed the base of the hill west of the Conesus Lake inlet,[392] then cut over the hill and went directly northwest several miles[393] and then due west to Chenussio.[394] The guides had not been this way but had heard of it.

Trusting their judgment, Boyd led the party along the new trail and found they were right. They had first encountered a tiny deserted village of only three or four houses about four miles east of Chenussio, called Coshequa.[395] They passed it by with hardly a glance and, within a few hours of having left Sullivan's camp, they were hidden and studying Chenussio carefully.[396] Boyd was very pleased with what they saw. The village was enormous, but there was no great force of Indians waiting for them. The very few Indians in the town were busily loading things on horses and preparing to move away, as they had moved away from each town in advance of the Sullivan army's approach. The night was clear and bright under a good moon and viewing the village from fairly close by was not difficult, aided by the several large fires the Indians had burning to see what they were doing as they loaded their horses.

At this point Boyd sent Jehoiakim and three of his privates back with this information to Sullivan and to inform the general that Boyd and his remaining men would continue watching from hiding for another hour or more and then start back also. He did so and, at daybreak, withdrew and began to move back toward the army. As they came within sight of Coshequa again, they saw four mounted Indians just enter the tiny town and disappear into one of the few houses. Because he still had twenty-four men plus himself, Boyd decided to take them. It was the second area where he exceeded authority and let his ambition lead him to disobey orders deliberately.

"No engagement with the enemy unless absolutely necessary to protect yourself," Sullivan had warned, but Boyd ignored it now.

The lieutenant selected eight men, headed by Private Timothy Murphy, a well-known Indian fighter from New York. Through the years Murphy had already killed thirty-two Indians. He had the reputation of having a charmed life and being able to squeeze out of any kind of a scrape with the Indians, no matter how dire.

Murphy's party, Boyd instructed, was to try to take the four Indians prisoner. If they were unable to do that, they were to kill them. The eight men left at once . . . and promptly botched the job. The horses of the Indians, seeing the eight soldiers sneaking up, whinnied in fear and immediately the Indians burst out of the house and fled. Rifles barked and one of the Indians was wounded, another one killed. The wounded man escaped with his companions along the trail leading toward Conesus.

Boyd's eight men returned, grinning, the scalp of the dead Indian in Murphy's hand — his thirty-third.[397] Lieutenant Boyd put his whole little force in motion again, heading for the army. After traveling about a mile more they paused to rest and Boyd once again exceeded his orders. Now, instead of planning to continue back to the encampment, he reasoned that the army would soon be coming toward him, and it was a bit ridiculous to move all his men back there only to turn right around and return here with them. After all, they'd been up all night and on the go and were tired. They'd earned a rest and certainly General Sullivan would understand. So now he dispatched another two men to go back to Sullivan with word of where he was, of what had happened, and of his intention now to rest in place until the army reached him.

Within ten minutes of their leaving, the two men hastily returned. They were excited and said they had just seen the wounded Indian on the road ahead, along with the other two, plus a couple more who had joined them. They were sitting beside the trail. Boyd grinned at this chance for another coup and mounted his men again to go after the Indians.

He completely forgot about the old, and very effective, Indian battle strategy of decoying an enemy into ambush.

[*September 13, 1779 — Monday, Early Morning*]

Only a few hours ago, when darkness was still full upon the land, the three hundred Indians under Brant had taken their position on the crest and side of the high hill at the southwestern end of Conesus Lake.[398] Here they overlooked, to the southeast, the encampment of General Sullivan and, beyond that, the abandoned Seneca town of Conesus — the village where for so many years Chief Big Tree had been leader.

Big Tree was with them now, watching what was occurring below and saying little. His house, built entirely of cedar planks, was the finest of the near twenty homes in Conesus. Beside Big Tree was standing Captain Sunfish, a black man who had many years before joined the Senecas and risen in prominence to become second chief of Conesus.

The Indians, mostly very young warriors hot for battle, had come here during the night on a swift march from Canawaugus. They had moved soundlessly all night and, as luck would have it, their trail unknowingly crossed that of the Boyd party less than an hour after Boyd and his men had passed en route to Chenussio. It was too dark to read trail and so there was no clue that the military party had gone by. Continuing southward, the Indians, and the few whites accompanying them, stopped at the point where the inlet of Conesus Lake passed closest to the hill and positioned themselves on the hill above this.[399] This was at a point where, after crossing the inlet and turning north toward Chenussio, the army would be tightly pinched between creek and hill and, thus, where they would be extremely vulnerable to the gunfire that would be directed at them from the hill above. The Indians knew they could not defeat the army, but they intended leaving this country of theirs with a great many soldiers lying dead behind them.

Long before daylight they had settled themselves in the ambush and waited. Then, with the coming of dawn, the complexion of matters changed. At first light Sullivan's army was active and the town of Conesus was soon being reduced to ashes by the raging fires that had been set.

As Big Tree and Captain Sunfish wordlessly watched the destruction of their village below, Brant and Colonel Butler, along with a few Tory Rangers, moved up and stood beside them. Butler glanced at Big Tree and his jaw muscles bunched some; he did not like the Seneca nor trust him. Big Tree was not long returned from his extended stay with General George Washington. Now, when Butler spoke, there was an edge of sarcasm to his voice.

"You said when you returned, Chief Big Tree, that General Washington was your friend and had promised that you would not be troubled by the war." He pointed toward the fires lighting the gray of dawn with a false sunrise glow. "You see how the Americans treat their friends."

Big Tree did not look at Butler but merely shook his head faintly and spoke so softly that his words were barely audible. "What I see is only the common fate of wars. It cannot logically be supposed," he added, now turning to look at the commander of the Rangers, "that the Americans can distinguish my property from yours, who are their enemy."

It was not the burning of Conesus that changed the complexion of the ambush plans. Rather, it was the movement at first light of the detachment of surveyors and soldiers sent out by Sullivan to look at, measure and more or less lay out the road they would take during this day's march. The path this group took from Conesus followed the existing trail, as Boyd had done earlier, to where it crossed the Conesus Lake inlet, where the bridge had been badly damaged by the Senecas when they abandoned the town. The ground was extremely marshy and it was obvious that the bridge would have to be repaired for the army to cross. Sullivan put his skilled engineers to work on this right away. But the surveying detachment, instead of turning north on the trail immediately

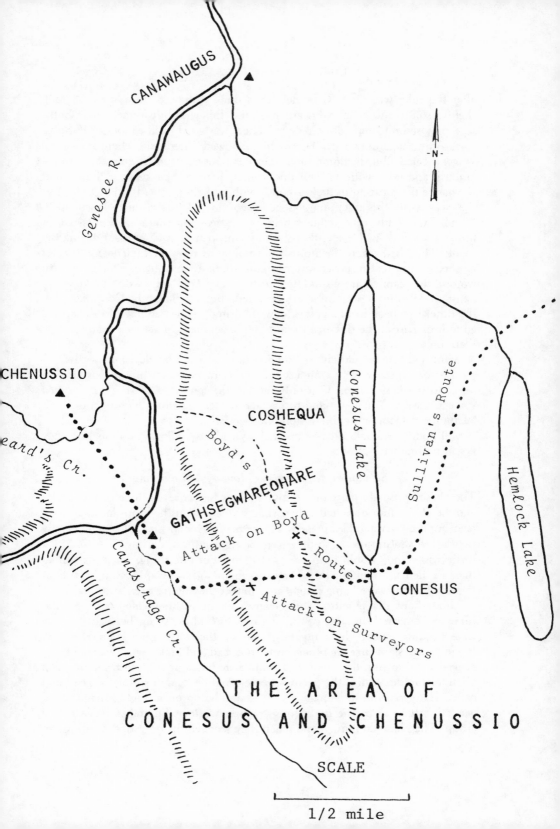

CANAWAUGUS

Genesee R.

CHENUSSIO

eard's Cr.

COSHEQUA

Boyd's

Conesus Lake

Sullivan's Route

Hemlock Lake

GATHSEGWAREOHARE

Attack on Boyd

Route

Canaseraga Cr.

Attack on Surveyors

CONESUS

-N-

THE AREA OF
CONESUS AND CHENUSSIO

SCALE

1/2 mile

after the inlet was crossed, as Boyd had done, followed the old trail, going slightly south and then westward over the hill, heading directly for Goth-segwarohare on Canaseraga Creek.[400] There was good justification for it: Sullivan's only map, drawn in 1770, which showed Chenussio where it was no longer located. But, by doing such, they were not going to fall into the planned ambush and now, with daylight upon them, there was no way for the Indians to change the location of their ambush without being sighted.

It was while this dilemma was being considered that runners raced up to Joseph Brant with some rather startling news. A detachment of twenty-five or thirty Americans had evidently been sent out to spy on Chenussio during the night. They had taken the north trail and were now on their way back. At Coshequa they had surprised four of Brant's Indians en route to Chenussio with word of the planned ambush. The four had been fired upon with one killed — Sah-nah-dah-yah — and another wounded, but the latter had escaped with the other two back to this party. Now the three, with a couple of others, had gone back part of the distance toward the detachment to act as a decoy to lure them on.

Brant had listened closely, nodding, and now made his decision swiftly.

"There is no way we can attack the main army now without exposing ourselves to needless danger. Our only satisfaction can be in striking the advance surveyors with a small hit-and-run attack but center our attention mostly on taking the detachment coming from Coshequa."

Still undetected by Sullivan's army, busy with its bridge-building below, they began pulling back at once.

[September 13, 1779 — Monday Midmorning]

The chase by Boyd's party of the four Indians had covered three or four miles and the soldiers were excited. Their shots at the Indians had thus far had no effect, but they weren't discouraged. The retreating Indians had also ineffectually fired a few shots at them, so they were being careful in closing the gap, but it was obvious they would soon be upon them. For one thing, not much more than a mile or so remained now between them and Sullivan's camp, so the retreating Indians were being caught in a pincer they didn't even know existed.

Throughout the pursuit, Chief Hanyerry's nervousness increased. Several times he remarked that this could be a ruse to lead them on, but because they were heading toward the army Boyd refuted the possibility. Then Hanyerry began seeing signs that the others could not read and he knew he was right. He begged Boyd to stop the chase and immediately detour back to the army by a circuitous route. At this the twenty-two-year-old lieutenant simply laughed and called Hanyerry an old woman who was simply too old to fight anymore and wanted only to sit by the fire. Stung, Hanyerry bit his lip and stayed with the group. The chase continued and when they reached the crest of the hill where the trail turned directly east and descended to the lake valley,[401] the pursued Indians continued straight southeastward. Within a quarter mile they came to the head of a ravine and paused, seemingly confused. Instantly Boyd moved with his men into a gallop to strike.

Instead, *they* were struck.

They had fallen into the ambush perfectly and now upward of three hundred Indians poured a fire toward them from cover on both sides. Realizing his mistake, Boyd froze for a horrified moment and then ordered them to break through the lines. They could not. He then ordered a retreat. It was too late. They were cut off behind and now almost completely boxed in.[402] He ordered them to plunge for a group of trees, which they did, and some of them followed his lead as they reached it successfully and leaped from their horses to take cover and try to hold position until a reinforcement from Sullivan could arrive. Part of the men, following the lead of Private Timothy Murphy, continued astride their horses, broke through a weak place in the Indian lines and plunged into a steep ravine. Here they left their horses and scattered afoot and eight of them, including Murphy, whose charm seemed still to be working, escaped.[403]

They were the extremely lucky ones. Above, it became a massacre.

Overwhelmed by sheer weight of numbers, all remaining of Boyd's detachment, with the exception of himself and Sergeant Parker, were killed. Fifteen men dead in a matter of moments and no indication that any of the enemy had been killed or even hurt.[404]

Boyd had taken a rifleball through the flesh of his side but nothing vital was hit. Recognized as the leader of these men, he was taken alive, as was Parker.[405] The dead were all scalped, stripped of weapons and valuables and their bodies badly mangled by knives and tomahawks, as all the Indians seemed eager to get their blows in to relieve the great pent-up anger that had been so long within them. The greatest excess of mutilation was committed upon the body of Hanyerry. When he was recognized a great cry went up from the Indians and a great anger was evident that he had cheated them, by being killed by a bullet, out of a vengeance they had long desired. When they finished with his body, it was hardly recognizable as having belonged to a human. The only thing identifiable was the scalped head, which had been impaled on a broken branch nearby.

With their burst of energy used up in the massacre and ensuing desecrations, the Indians now took their two captives with them and set out for Chenussio.

They had very special plans for Boyd and Parker.

[*September 14, 1779 — Tuesday*]

"Surely," Major General John Sullivan remarked generally to the officers clustered behind him, "this has to be considered as being one of the most beautiful places in all of America."

He was speaking of the great valley stretched out before them, where for as far as one could see were great waving fields of grass and grain, small clumps of fruit trees and expansive gardens; the valley through which meandered the Genesee River in a series of extreme undulations. And there, in the midst of all, lay the largest and finest Indian village any of them had ever seen — Chenussio.

The last miles here from Conesus had taken a couple of days, not because of distance but because of events. Shortly following the beginning of the burning of Conesus at dawn yesterday, there came the arrival of Jehoiakim and the three privates from Lieutenant Boyd, reporting on his whereabouts and his plans to remain in place and observe for a while longer before returning to the army. Sullivan was glad to get the intelligence but his expression darkened as he learned how many men Boyd had taken with him and how he was now, on his own, blandly ignoring the order to return here by sunrise. Such disobedience was often a prelude to disaster.

The destruction of the town and its crops was a four-hour job, with much of the army employed in the work. At the same time, the bridge over the mucky lake inlet was being repaired and a corduroy road of logs being cut and laid on the approach to the bridge so the army could cross. The surveying party under Lieutenant Benjamin Lodge, as it had been doing ever since leaving Easton, had crossed the inlet early and was out in front of the army by about a mile and a half with chain and compass, measuring the distances and recording this information and determining the route the army should travel.[406] With Lodge were four chain carriers and Corporal Robert Calhawn.

Because of intervening trees and hills, the surveying party had been unable to hear the gunfire accompanying the attack on the Boyd party somewhat over half a mile north of them. A very short time later, a small group of warriors rushed them and in the first firing Corporal Calhawn took a bullet through the body. Badly hurt, he nevertheless shot and killed an Indian chasing Lieutenant Lodge just as the Indian was catching up and raising his tomahawk to strike the officer.

Lodge ran to Calhawn and put an arm around him to help him while one of the chain carriers, Private Thomas Grant, rushed up and did the same on the other side. Together they ran back toward the bridge with the wounded man between them, leaving the surveying tools where they had fallen. They made it back to the main army without further incident, but now a flurry of activity was occurring.

A few survivors of the attack on Boyd — men who had escaped with Timothy Murphy — had already come in and told their story. General Sullivan immediately ordered General Hand to send out his light troops to attack. Though it was done without delay, it was too late. The Indians were already gone. Four or five bodies had been sighted at the spot where the attack had occurred, but the troops did not go there specifically. They followed the trail of the retreating enemy until it was clear they were heading for Chenussio and then they returned to the main army and reported to Sullivan.

Sullivan was furious at the loss of the men, especially since it was so unnecessary and had only occurred, in his way of looking at it, because of Boyd's ambition and disobedience. But the damage was done and so it was pointless to gnash one's teeth. He ordered the destruction of Conesus and its crops to be speeded up and the same with the work on the bridge and its approaches. By two in the afternoon the whole of the army was in motion again, still going by way of the old route rather than by the new trail that had resulted in Boyd's downfall. By late afternoon they had reached the valley of Canaseraga Creek and were approaching Gothsegwarohare.[407] The town itself was deserted, but well over a hundred of the warriors who had been a part of the attack on Boyd had drawn themselves up here with the idea of opposing the army. They were all young warriors and essentially leaderless, since Brant had gone on with the others. Sullivan at once ordered battle formation, fired the howitzer a few times and it was all over. The Indians thrashed across Canaseraga Creek in the gathering dusk and disappeared into the heavy cover on the other side. No attempt was made to pursue them. They entered the town and once more found, as they had on previous occasions, two white dogs hung as sacrifices to the spirits.

Gothsegwarohare was beautifully situated in the valley and surrounded by fine cornfields and orchards and vegetable patches. However, there was no way these could be destroyed in what remained of the last of daylight and so, the night guard tripled, the army camped here all last night. Early this morning the destruction was begun. It took until nearly noon. It was during that period that the wounded Corporal Calhawn died and was buried.

The twenty-five houses in Gothsegwarohare were fairly new and well built, but all were without chimneys, a small hole in the middle of the roof serving this purpose. Fruit trees — mainly peaches — were felled or girdled and vegetables trampled where they grew. There was so much corn to destroy — and it was in such an advanced state that simply cutting the stalks was no longer sufficient — that the ears were pulled off and tossed into the creek, the efficacy of which a number of the officers questioned among themselves.

As soon as the town's destruction was completed, the march was resumed for Chenussio. Within an hour or so they crossed the Genesee, nearly a hundred feet wide here and, though not over waist deep, still so swift that the men had to cross by platoons with arms interlocked to avoid being swept off their feet. On the west side of the river they had climbed to the plateau above and then almost universally gasped at the beauty of what lay before them. As Sullivan himself had just said, this had to be considered one of the most beautiful places in all America.

Fully ten to fifteen thousand acres of superb grasslands and cornfields stretched out before them. There were no bushes or scrubby growths anywhere — only occasional islands of stately trees rising here and there as if they were dark green ships on a bright green sea. A mile and a half ahead lay Chenussio, positioned between the large folds of the Genesee River on the east and the smaller folds of Little Beard's Creek on the west.[408] The great Seneca longhouse dominated the center of the town — an enormous building of peeled logs, two stories high, with gabled roof and painted bright red. Surrounding it were one hundred and twenty-eight of the most elegant houses yet encountered, with fine fruit trees growing near them and expansive orchard areas all around the town. It was an incredible sight. In the Seneca tongue, Chenussio meant "The Beautiful Valley" and it was certainly not misnamed.[409]

Almost as impressive was the sight the army itself made as it moved immediately into battle formation and advanced toward the town. In all of its marching on this campaign, this was the first time that the entire army was visible all at once in its complete formation. Battle flags were flying, fifers piping and drums rattling, and there was a deeply stirring sense about the whole picture of this army wading through deep grass toward its destination in the warm glow of the sunset.

The only living people in the town were a white woman and her eight-month-old baby. Her name was Sara Lester. She and her husband had been captured near Nanticoke, Pennsylvania, the previous November 7 and she had lived here ever since with the Indians. Her husband had been killed in the attack. She told them that two days before, all the squaws and children and old people had been sent off toward Niagara and only a few of the warriors had remained. Now, even they were gone. Beyond that she knew nothing. She was dazed and acted strangely; little more information could be gained from her. At length she and her child, both suffering malnutrition, were turned over to the care of Dr. Campfield.[410]

Carefully, moving from building to building slowly and guarding against being shot at from unexpected quarter, the army infiltrated the town and searched it. An abundance of furniture and belongings had been left behind and whole buildings were filled with husked and unhusked ears of corn. There were animal skins and lanterns, moccasins and jackets and leggings, even a few blankets and broken weapons. But there were no Indians.

Two soldiers of General Clinton's brigade — Moses Van Campen and Paul Sanborn — found the remains of Lieutenant Thomas Boyd and Sergeant Michael Parker. The sight never left their minds after that, nor the minds of any others who saw them. General Sullivan was informed before anything was touched and he came to the spot quickly and even he paled at what he saw and only through great will power was he able to restrain himself from vomiting.

The physical damage done to the pair was practically beyond belief and reconstruction of how it must have occurred indicated that both men had lived for a long time through the torture. Except for one major difference, the injuries suffered by both men were alike. Each had been stripped and tied to a post and severely whipped until the back was badly welted and bruised. Then the torturing had evidently begun with the ears being cut off, followed by the noses. All the nails of fingers and toes had been pulled out. The right eye was gone, apparently simply gouged out with a thumb and thrown away. Chunks of flesh were cut off the shoulders. Then the tongue was cut out. It seemed apparent that the men had still been alive at this point, but how much longer they lived with what followed there was no way of knowing. Certainly it couldn't have been too long and it was clear that many more outrages had been perpetrated after their deaths. The genital organs had been severed and hung pendulously from a mere strip of tissue a foot below where they belonged. Boyd's chest had been opened and his heart had been cut out and then fastened into his right hand. Both bodies had been stabbed repeatedly by spears, as many as twenty times each, and practically every major area of flesh was severely lacerated. The skin and flesh of the chest had been stripped away so that the bare ribs were exposed. A knife was still projecting from near the center of Boyd's back. The one major difference in the treatment of the bodies was that the head of Sergeant Parker was missing and could not be found. Boyd's head had been cut off, too, but it was scalped and then almost completely skinned and positioned on a log with its mouth open.[411]

Immediately upon having viewed the remains, General Sullivan ordered that the two men be buried at once with full military honors. A detail from Captain Simpson's company of riflemen dug the grave nearby and the remains were placed inside as well as could be done. The grave was located just to the side of a clump of wild plums beside Little Beard's Creek where it was crossed by the main trail.[412] A brief eulogy was spoken by Simpson and the captain then thrust his own sword into the head of the grave as a marker.[413]

For those who had viewed the bodies and attended the burial, a distinct pall had descended, but not for those who had not. Among that latter number, which included the majority, there was a tremendous feeling of buoyancy and relief. This was Chenussio! This was the final destination!

Tomorrow this gorgeous valley and beautiful town would be ravaged and once that was completed, every step taken would become a step closer to home.

[September 25, 1779 — Saturday]

The march of the Sullivan army back to the Chemung River was accomplished with a great elevation of spirits and without sight of a single hostile person, white or Indian. In some areas they had passed on the way out to Chenussio, destruction was not complete, but that was seen to on the return trip, with firmness. It began with the greatest single destruction of all — that of Chenussio.

It was no easy task. The entire army was employed at that job and yet, though it was begun at 6:00 A.M. on September 15, it was not completed until 2:00 P.M. The corn crop was the biggest problem, since it was conservatively estimated at twenty thousand bushels. Some of the ears were twenty-three inches in length and in many areas the stalks grew to a height of eighteen feet. Some of this corn was cut and burned on fires in the field, those fires fueled with lumber from the houses. Some was stacked deeply in the houses before the houses were themselves burned. In some cases, individual ears were simply thrown into the river. The same was true for the abundant crops of vegetables. Hundreds of fruit trees were girdled and felled.

When at last the work was finished and the smoke rising from the great council longhouse and the one hundred and twenty-eight fine homes formed an obscene smudge in the clear blue sky, the entire army was formed into ranks and a proclamation by General Sullivan was read aloud in the great booming voice of Adam Hubley:

"The commander in chief informs this brave and resolute army that the immediate objects of this expedition are accomplished, viz.: total ruin of the Indian settlements and destruction of their crops, which were designed for the support of those inhuman barbarians while they were desolating the American frontiers. He is by no means insensible to the obligations he is under to those brave officers and soldiers whose virtue and fortitude have enabled him to complete the important designs of this expedition, and he assures them he will not fail to inform America at large how much they stand indebted to them."

Hubley paused and looked back and forth across the hundreds of faces before him, then smiled slightly as he looked again at the paper and completed reading it. "The army will this day commence its march for Tioga."

Instantly a wild cheering erupted from the men. They thumped one another on the backs and did little jigs where they stood or simply grinned with overwhelming pleasure at the news. Home! They were going home *today!*

Within the hour the march was begun and by sunset the great expanse of the lush valley had been crossed and the army was just finishing its fording of the Genesee near the mouth of Canaseraga Creek. They moved a couple of miles more up that creek and camped where they had been the night before last, at Gothsegwarohare.

On the morning of September 16 there was more crop destruction in that area to complete what had not previously been finished and at 10:00 A.M. the army moved on again. A detail under Captain William Henderson of the 4th Pennsylvania Regiment was sent out to bury the bodies of Lieutenant Boyd's men, including Hanyerry, where they had fallen. The fifteen bodies, badly mangled, were located and buried with honors.[414]

Little of any real significance occurred on the remainder of the march back. When they arrived at Honeoye they found Fort Cummings still in good shape, along with its inhabitants, which was a relief to Sullivan, who had feared that Boyd, under questioning, might have revealed the weakness of the place and thus inspired an attack to be made against it. The fortification was destroyed as they left it and progressed toward Tioga.

The packhorses now began faltering very badly and each day more of them died or could not go on and had to be shot lest they fall into the hands of the enemy. Some days the loss was as low as fifteen or twenty animals, some days much higher. The worst was when between three hundred and four hundred had to be destroyed on the same day because they simply could not go on.[415]

At Canandaigua the army was met by a contingent of four Oneidas. Their leader was the minor chief Blue Back, whom Sullivan had sent back to his people on the journey north to solicit their assistance in the campaign. Blue Back reported that the Oneidas had raised themselves in arms and were en route to join Sullivan when they encountered a group of Indians allegedly coming from the army who said their presence was no longer required and sent them back. Blue Back said he had tried to dissuade them but had been unsuccessful. He was deeply distressed at learning of the death of Hanyerry and now, on behalf of his people, he begged Sullivan to spare the Cayuga settlements from destruction. Thus far those settlements had been largely untouched, lying as they did westward of the Mohawk, yet eastward of the line of march of the army northward from Shequaga to Kanadasaga. Blue Back said his people were related to the Cayugas through ties of intermarriage and he was worried that if the Cayuga towns were destroyed, the Cayugas would then come to the Oneidas for subsistence; and the burdens the Oneidas already had, he said, were too heavy to bear. Besides, Blue Back had continued, the Cayugas were neutral and had been so since the war began. Sullivan shook his head at this.

"The whole course of the Cayugas," he told the Oneida, "is marked with duplicity and hostility, for which they are to be chastized, and I will not turn from this purpose."

Nor did he. As they reached Kanadasaga he ordered that two large detachments — one led by Lieutenant Colonel Henry Dearborn and the other by Lieutenant Colonel William Butler — go farther eastward and ravage the villages and crops of the Cayugas. Dearborn's detachment was to march up the west side of Cayuga Lake and meet at its head the detachment of Butler, marching up the east side of the lake. Having completed their destruction, they were to rejoin the main army at Shequaga, or, should the army have passed that point by then, follow it to the supply depot at Kanawaholla.

Two other detachments were sent out while the army stopped at Kanadasaga.

Lieutenant Colonel William Smith was sent with his detachment up the west side of Seneca Lake to complete the crop destruction at Kashong, which had been incomplete on the outward journey. The other detachment, under Colonel Peter Gansevoort, was sent directly eastward to strike the Mohawk River at Fort Stanwix and descend that river, pausing at the Lower Mohawk Castle — Teantontalago — to arrest every male Mohawk there and take them prisoner to Albany.[416]

These matters seen to, Sullivan then turned his army southward on the same route originally traveled northward, along the east shore of Seneca Lake. They had arrived at Shequaga the day before yesterday, September 23, and finding neither Dearborn's nor Butler's detachment waiting, continued toward the Chemung.

It was there, where Newtown Creek joins the Chemung River, at the site of the village of Kanawaholla, which they had destroyed on the trip north, that Captain Reed was to have established an advance post to await their return. They were not disappointed. Reed's detachment had arrived at Fort Sullivan with the sick and lame from Kanadasaga on September 14 and immediately he had returned with boats and stores and set up the fortification — a small palisaded works the men were calling Fort Reed — near where Kanawaholla had been. It was a tremendously welcome sight to Sullivan's army as they neared it yesterday.

There was great joy on both sides. The cannon at Fort Reed split the air with a salute of thirteen shots and this was echoed by thirteen from the lead cannon in Proctor's artillery. The reunion was an extremely happy one and for the first time in weeks the men were permitted to eat all the beef they wanted. As a further bonus, whiskey was distributed — a gill to each soldier, a half-pint to each officer.

General Sullivan made the decision to remain here at Kanawaholla until the detachments of Butler, Dearborn and Smith rejoined the army and, in the meanwhile, he sent two more detachments out — one under Lieutenant Colonel William D'Hart and the other under Colonel Philip Van Cortlandt — to go up the Chemung as far as Painted Post and destroy the last of the villages there.

It was here, too, that Chief Blue Back of the Oneidas came to General Sullivan and spoke long and earnestly as he presented a special request.

"We, the Oneidas, against the traditions and wishes of our own Iroquois League, have supported the Americans generally and this army specifically, since the beginning of the troubles between you and England. Our principal chief, Hanyerry, guided you and served you faithfully and eventually gave up his life. Now, because of the stand we have made, we Oneidas are apart from the rest of the tribes and we face a winter of hunger. We therefore request that official permission be given to us to hunt in the lands which were, but are no longer, the lands of the Iroquois. We will do no harm — only hunt for the meat we need to sustain us."

Sullivan shook his head sadly. "I'm sorry," he said, "but I cannot give you such permission. I do not have the authority to do so. I see no reason for this to be denied to you, but I suggest you apply to Congress and I feel sure that, in view of the Oneidas' friendly conduct, you will be granted your request."

Not especially pleased, Blue Back shook his head and looked at Sullivan narrowly. "Perhaps," he murmured, as he turned and left, "the Oneida really *were* wrong in what they did."

In the meanwhile, today was a day of great celebration at Fort Reed. The army rested and ate and drank and was very happy. During the day Colonel Smith's detachment rejoined them. Excellent news was waiting in regard to the war. Spain had allied herself to the United States and declared war on England and now the fortunes of the Revolution were definitely on the upswing for the Americans. More immediately of moment, Congress had passed the pay increase for all soldiers and officers. Letters from wives and sweethearts, families and friends, were waiting for practically everyone.

This morning General Sullivan, more animated and high-spirited than anyone had ever seen him act before, ordered that all rifles be fired, which was done. He then had blank cartridges issued to every man and gave the order for a *feu de joie* to be lighted at five o'clock in the evening. At this time, he said, he wanted the lines of troops drawn up and a running fire of musketry made.

This was done. Just prior to the lighting of the huge bonfire, the cannon boomed out with thirteen earth-vibrating blasts and then the flames of the bonfire leaped high into the air. The running fire of muskets from right to left was done, but it was ragged and poorly accomplished and Sullivan, with pretended gruffness, said it was not good enough and they would do it again.

"We'll do it right this time, by God!" he said loudly. "A right-to-left firing again, but not a man to fire till I come abreast him."

With this he leaped grinning into the saddle of his horse and, to the cheers of his men, moved far to the right of the line. As soon as all were ready, he kicked his mount into a gallop and rode with whip and spur at full tilt before the line. This time, with the running fire exploding as he passed, it all went off very well, and as he reached the end he wheeled his steed about and as it pranced nervously back before the troops he shouted loudly:

"Now that was very grand! It went just like a great hallelujah! You're good men, all of you! I'm ordering up for the men of each regiment five gallons of spirits and also for each regiment the finest fattest ox to be roasted!"

Now, as evening came on, the merriment and pleasure of eating and drinking and companionship continued, perhaps not so loudly, but certainly no less enthusiastically. The officers of each brigade dined together and the most elaborate of these individual celebrations was that of General Hand's brigade. A large bower was constructed and illuminated with thirteen small fires of pine knots. All the officers attended and sat in a double row on the ground facing one another, with Brigadier General Edward Hand at one end and Colonel Thomas Proctor at the other, all dining heartily on bread and beef and then turning their attention to drinking the spirits that the commander in chief had provided.

No less inspired than Major General John Sullivan had been a few hours before, General Hand now led his officers in thirteen toasts.

"To the thirteen sisters," he shouted, holding his cup high and referring to the thirteen united states, "and to their sponsors!"

"Hear! Hear!" came the response and the drinks were quaffed.

Hand had only begun. Once again the cup raised and once again the toast: "To the honorable, the American Congress!"

Again they drank, and over and again as Hand continued his toasts, never pausing, never at a loss for whom to toast next and seemingly becoming more inspired with each toast.

"To General Washington and the American army!

"To the Commander in Chief of the Western Expedition!

"To the American navy!"

The sixth toast was to France, the first foreign nation to ally itself to the United States and support it in its audacious Revolution: "To our faithful allies, the united Houses of Bourbon!"

Edward Hand began to wax more eloquent as he became flushed with the drinks. "May the American Congress and all her legislative representatives be endowed with virtue and wisdom and may her independence be as firmly established as the pillars of time!

"May the citizens of America, and her soldiers, be ever unanimous in their reciprocal support of each other and in support of American Liberty!

"May altercations, discord and every degree of fraud be totally banished from the peaceful shores of America!"

The tenth toast caused the levity, though not the enthusiasm, to be diminished somewhat: "May the memory of the brave Lieutenant Boyd, and the soldiers under his command who were horribly massacred by the inhuman savages, or by their more barbarous and detestable allies, the British and Tories, on the thirteenth instant, be ever dear to their country!

"An honorable peace or perpetual war to the enemies of America!

"May the Kingdom of Ireland merit a stripe in the American standard!"

Of all the toasts General Hand offered, however, none other was so inspired as the last, none other so joyfully drunk to, none other created such laughter and none other was so memorable. Weaving somewhat now and with liquor beginning to slosh over the lip of his cup, Hand held the vessel high and spoke with the slow, strong precision of a man feeling his liquor who wishes to state his remarks clearly and without fuzziness or misinterpretation.

"May the enemies of America," he shouted, "be metamorphosed into pack-horses and sent on a western expedition against the Indians!"

The cries of "Hear! Hear!" were positively deafening.

The festivities then became general as Hand led the men in the performance of several Indian dances and Irish jigs. On the whole, it was an uncommonly memorable evening.

[*September 30, 1779 — Thursday*]

It was over. All over.

The greatest expedition ever to be mounted against the Indians of North America to this time was finished. It ended today as the army of Major General John Sullivan returned at last to its starting point, Fort Sullivan at Tioga.

Lieutenant Colonel Henry Dearborn's detachment had returned to the main army at Kanawaholla four days ago, having burned six more Indian towns and destroyed much more corn and vegetable crops. Two days later, Lieutenant Colonel William Butler's detachment also returned, his force having burned five more towns and destroyed two hundred acres of corn and over fifteen hundred fruit trees. Neither detachment had encountered any hostile Indians and neither had suffered any loss except for a private in Butler's detachment who, almost in sight of Fort Reed, had died of a heart attack.

Yesterday the palisaded Fort Reed had been demolished and the army had started down the Chemung. Late today they arrived at Tioga and the welcome to the victorious army given by Colonel Israel Shreve at Fort Sullivan surpassed even that which the army had experienced at Fort Reed. The very hills resounded with the thunderous boomings of the artillery in salute and the fifes and drums and Proctor's regimental band lent a lively aspect to the arrival. Celebration was rampant and even though they were still a long way from Wyoming and even farther yet from Easton and the more civilized life of the East, yet they knew that now the expedition was truly over; there would be no more fighting, no more concern for lives, no more expectation of attack, no more destruction to be carried out. It was over!

Late in the day hundreds of letters and reports were being written by soldiers and officers, but none more important than the long document being penned by Major General John Sullivan as his official report to General George Washington and the Congress of the United States of America. He had begun writing it in the afternoon and now, at close to midnight, with fifteen or twenty pages already completed, he was just finishing, summing up in his final paragraphs the accomplishments of the expedition. In the flickering light of the lantern in his quarters within Fort Sullivan, his hand moved steadily back and forth across the pages, making precise lines of his writing:

It is with pleasure I inform Congress that this army has not suffered the loss of forty men in the action or otherwise since my taking command, though perhaps few troops have experienced a more fatiguing campaign. Besides the difficulties which naturally attend marching through an enemy's country abounding in woods, creeks, rivers, morasses and defiles, we found no small inconvenience from the want of proper guides; and maps of the country are so exceedingly erroneous that they serve not to enlighten but to perplex. We had not a single person who was sufficiently acquainted with the country to conduct a party out of the Indian path by day, or scarcely in it by night; though they were the best I could possibly procure. Their ignorance arose, doubtless, from the Indians having ever taken the best measures in their power to prevent their country's being explored. We had much labor in clearing out the roads for the artillery, notwithstanding which the army moved from twelve to sixteen miles every day when not detained by rains or employed in destroying settlements.

I feel myself much indebted to the officers of every rank for their unparalleled exertions, and to the soldiers for the unshaken firmness with which they endured to toils and difficulties attending the expedition. Though I had it not in command, I should ventured to have paid Niagara a visit, had I been supplied with fifteen days' provisions in addition to what I had, which I am persuaded from the bravery and ardor of our troops, would have fallen into our hands.

I forgot to mention that the Oneida sachem requested me to grant them liberty to hunt in the country of the Five Nations, as they would never think of settling again in a country once subdued and where their settlements must ever be in our power. I, in answer, informed him that I had no authority to grant such a license, that I could not at present see reason to object to it, but advised them to make application to Congress who, I believed, would, in consideration of their friendly conduct, grant them every advantage of this kind that would not interfere with our settlement of the country, which I believed would soon take place. The Oneidas say that as no Indians were discovered by Colonel Butler at Cayuga, they are of the opinion that they are gone to their castle and that their chiefs will persuade them to come in to surrender themselves on the terms I have proposed.

The army began its march from Kanawaholla yesterday and arrived here this evening. After leaving the necessary force for securing the frontiers in this area, I shall move on to join the main army.

It would have been very pleasing to this army to have drawn the enemy to a second engagement, but such a panic seized them after the first action that it was impossible, as they never ventured themselves in reach of the army, nor have they fired a single gun at it on its march or in its quarters, though in a country exceedingly well calculated for ambuscades. This circumstance alone would sufficiently prove that they suffered severely in their first effort.

Congress will be pleased to pardon the length of this narration, as I thought a

*particular and circumstantial detail of facts would not be disagreeable, espe-
cially as I have transmitted no accounts of the progress of this army since the action of the 29th of August. I flatter myself that the orders with which I was entrusted are fully executed, as we have not left a single settlement or field of corn
in the country of the Five Nations, or is there even the appearance of an Indian
on this side of Niagara. Messengers and small parties have been constantly passing, and some imprudent soldiers who straggled from the army mistook the route
and went back almost to Chenussio without discovering even the trace of an Indian.*

*I trust that the steps I have taken with respect to the Oneidas, Cayugas and
Mohawks will prove satisfactory. And here I beg leave to mention that on
searching the house of those pretended neutral Cayugas, a number of scalps were
found which appeared to have been lately taken, which Colonel Butler showed to
the Oneidas, who said they were then convinced of the justice of the steps I had
taken. The promise made to the soldiers in my address at Newtown, I hope will
be thought reasonable by Congress and flatter myself that the performance of it
will be ordered.*

Colonel Bruin [417] *will have the honor of delivering these dispatches to your
Excellency. I beg leave to recommend him to the particular notice of Congress as
an officer who, on this as well as several other campaigns, has proved himself an
active, brave and truly deserving officer.*

*I have the honor to be, with the most exalted sentiments of esteem and re-
spect, Your Excellency's most obedient and very humble servant,*

JOHN SULLIVAN [418]

Yes, it was all over. Even those officers who had been most critical of the
manner in which it was being carried out and most biting in their journal comments now reconsidered and had to concede that perhaps the Sullivan Campaign, as it would ever afterward be called, was not quite so badly handled as
initially believed.

Reaching Tioga today marked not only the end of the campaign. [419] It also
marked the end of many of the journals that had been kept by various officers
until now. Significant among these was the journal of Major Jeremiah Fogg,
the self-appointed conscience and severest critic of the expedition. He ended his
journal with this day's entry, finishing, though he didn't know it, at almost exactly the same time General Sullivan was finishing his official report.

Fogg dipped his quill pen and wrote his final words with a firm hand:

*30th. Arrived at Tioga about 3 o'clock, where we were saluted by thirteen
cannon from the fort. From hence we have water carriage to Wyoming, a most
fortunate affair, as our horses are worn down and our men naked.*

Although we are, now, one hundred and twenty miles from peaceful inhabitants, yet we consider ourselves at home and the expedition ended; having fulfilled the expectations of our country by beating the enemies and penetrating and destroying their whole country. The undertaking was great and the task arduous. The multiplicity of disappointments, occasioning a long delay at the beginning, foreboded a partial, if not total, frustration of our design; but the unbounded ambition and perseverance of our commander and the army led him to the full execution, contrary to our most sanguine expectations.

The army marched from Tioga with twenty pounds of beef and twenty-seven pounds of flour per man, with which they marched twenty days out through an enemy's country yet unexplored, with five pieces of artillery; having a road to clear through swamps and over mountains a hundred and fifty miles, after having marched three hundred from their winter quarters; a cruel, subtle and desultory foe to contend with; void of hospital stores and conveniences for the sick and wounded; scarcely able to move for want of means of transportation, one battle at the extent of our route must have been attended with consequences such as nothing but the event itself could ascertain; yet a march of three hundred miles was performed, a battle was fought and a whole country desolated in thirty days.

But let us not arrogate too much, for "The battle is not to the strong," is a proverb fully verified in this expedition; the special hand and smiles of Providence being so apparently manifested, that he who views the scene with indifference is worse than an infidel. The dimmest eye must observe through the whole, a succession of most fortunate events. The very evils that at first predicated a defeat, were a chain of causes in our favor. (I mean our delay.) Had we marched when we wished, we could not have had a general engagement; for a great scarcity, amounting almost to a famine, the preceding year had prevented their embodying until the growth of the present crop, and we must therefore have been harassed daily by small parties, much to our disadvantage. The artillery, which at first seemed a clog and totally useless, served a noble purpose; the action being general, their total rout together with the thunder of our artillery impressed them with such a terrific idea of our importance that a universal panic struck both the sachem and the warrior, each finding full employment in removing his little ones from threatening danger. The place of action was likewise remarkable, having water carriage for our wounded. Not a single gun was fired for eighty miles on our march out, or an Indian seen on our return. Then, when we expected the greatest harassment, a hundred might have saved half their country by retarding us until our provisions were spent; and a like number hanging on our rear on the return would have occasioned the loss of much baggage and taught us an Indian dance. Their corn and vegetables were half our support, which we should have been deprived of, had our march been earlier. And to say no more, the extraordinary continuance of fine weather has infinitely facilitated our expectations — having never been detained a single day, nor has there been an hour's rain since the thirtieth day of August.

The question will naturally arise, what have you to show for your exploits? Where are your prisoners? To which I reply that the rags and emaciated bodies of our soldiers must speak for our fatigue; and when the querist will point out a mode to tame a partridge, or the expedience of hunting wild turkey with light horse, I will show them our prisoners. The nests are destroyed, but the birds are still on the wing.

EPILOGUE

[*Spring — 1780*]

T*HE nests are destroyed, but the birds are still on the wing.*

It was true. The Indians themselves were not destroyed. Only a mere handful had been killed in the campaign, but other things were destroyed that were of immeasurable importance to them:

Their towns were destroyed; nearly fifty of them, consisting of about twelve hundred houses, in each of which two or three or even more families had lived.

Their corn was destroyed; nearly two hundred thousand bushels of the grain they most needed to subsist.

Their vegetables were destroyed; nearly fifty thousand bushels of the crops they had to have to live — potatoes, peas, beans, pumpkins, squash, watermelons, cucumbers, cabbages, carrots, parsnips.

Their fruit was destroyed; upward of ten thousand trees girdled or felled — apples, plums, peaches.

Their burial places were destroyed; the graves of their fathers and sons, mothers and daughters, had been opened and ransacked and the bones scattered; the sepulchers of their chiefs had been vandalized, pushed over, broken apart and the spirits disturbed.

Their health was destroyed; without proper food and shelter they became susceptible to famine and disease; the ensuing winter was the coldest on record and many of the Indians froze and starved and died of disease.[420]

Their League was destroyed; the powerful Iroquois League that had existed for over a quarter of a millennium, the League that had ruled by conquest the tribes of a quarter of the continent, the League that had struck fear into the hearts of the tribes of over half the continent, the League that was mightier than any other confederation of Indians in North America had ever been or would ever be.

Their *will* was destroyed; the will to carry on, to hold their land or perish in the effort to do so.

They had been very powerful and now their power was but a travesty of what had been. They had been fierce and strong, warriors with a reputation for great ferocity in battle, great cunning in strategy, great cruelty in torture; but they did not do what the Americans had done — they did not destroy growing things and living things other than enemies. They did not ruin the gardens and crops and fruit trees of their foes. Did the precepts of the Great Spirit in some magical, mystical, occult manner coincide with those of Moses, who forbade the destruction of all meat-bearing trees, or with those of the Koran, which dictates that no palm tree or fruit tree should be cut down, no field of corn burned, no mischief done to livestock; and was the elemental rule that "Only may you kill to eat" something they knew inherently?

The nests are destroyed, but the birds are still on the wing.

Yes, it was true. There would be more fights, more skirmishes, more battles. Joseph Brant — War Chief Thayendanegea — would lead them still and there would be more border warfare. But the fortunes of such war were going to the Americans and the Iroquois had thrown their lot with those who would be vanquished, and so it could not last. They would fight a little longer and diminish themselves a little more each time. And bit by bit all they ever had would dissolve until finally nothing was left.[421]

It remained to Red Jacket — Sagoyewatha — to articulate what all the other warriors and chiefs of the Iroquois feared to admit:

"We are encircled — we are encompassed. The Evil Spirit rides the blast. The waters are disturbed. They rise. They press upon us and the waves settle over us. We disappear forever. Who, then, lives to mourn us? None! What marks our extermination? Nothing! We are mingled with the common elements."

The Six Nations — the Iroquois League — had been a mighty empire . . . but they had fought their last wilderness war and this was the twilight of that empire.

AMPLIFICATION NOTES

THE following notes are keyed to consecutively corresponding numbers throughout the text.

PROLOGUE

1. Shenango was also known by the names of Shengo, Shingo, Shingo's Town and Mingo Town. It was located on the right bank of the Ohio River below present Pittsburgh, Pennsylvania, on the upstream side of the mouth of Little Sewickley Creek near present Leetsdale. Inhabited by Indians of a variety of tribes, it was one of a handful of villages called Mingo Town, after the loose confederation of Indians who coexisted peacefully. The Mingo was a poorly organized confederation based primarily in the area of western Pennsylvania and eastern Ohio, consisting almost entirely of Delawares, Shawnees and Cayugas, but sometimes including Senecas and Mohawks. Mingoes were never a tribe, although they are often mistaken as such. Probably the most famous Mingo was the Cayuga chief Tal-ga-yee-ta, better known as Chief Logan. The Mingo Confederation, if such it can be termed, began falling apart of its own volition following Lord Dunmore's War late in 1774.

2. This village of Shenango, which disappeared about 1748, should not be confused with the village of Logstown, which was so important in the Indian/English trade at this period. Logstown was situated another eleven miles downstream from Shenango, also on the north bank of the Ohio, at the mouth of Beaver River, approximately at the site of present Rochester, Pennsylvania.

3. The mother's name, meaning Where-the-Bird-Sits, has also been recorded as Owondaugh or Owandagh; the father's name, a shortening of Teho-waghwen-garagh-kwin (also spelled Teho-waghwen-garagh-win), means He-Buries-His-Face-in-the-Fur. It has been recorded in numerous sources that he was a member of the powerful Wolf Clan of the Mohawks, but this is probably an error. Though there is no reason why he could not have been a member of the Wolf Clan, the misconception that he definitely was probably stems from the fact that the baby's illustrious stepfather and step-grandfather were both important figures in the Wolf Clan of the Mohawks.

4. It was customary not to name a newborn child until at least ten days had passed. There were three reasons for this: First, infant mortality was high during the initial ten days and the baby

was not considered to be an existing individual until that crucial period was past; if it died during that period, the body was discarded and there was no acceptance that it had ever existed. Second, it was considered bad luck to name a baby before the passage of the ten days because something might occur during that interval that could be interpreted as a suggestion from the Great Spirit in regard to what the child should be called; thus, it is likely that during Owandah's own initial ten days of life, a chicken or some other bird had perched on or near her, and that Teho-wa, during his first ten days, had probably rubbed his face in the fur in which he was swaddled. A renowned example was Tecumseh, the great Shawnee chief, whose name was bestowed because at the moment of his birth a comet passed over, and Tecumseh means Shooting-Star or The-Panther-Passing-Across (with the Panther in Shawnee tradition being a comet). The third reason for delaying the naming of a child was the belief that if the child were named before the tenth day and then, in fact, died during that period, the person after whom the baby might have been named would also die. For this reason, if the child was to be named after someone, that possibly intended name was never even spoken until the naming time had come.

5. Although not at this time given the name by which he would become so notorious on the frontier, Joseph would be given a second name in English — Brant. His Mohawk name, Thayendanegea, means "Strength." His sister's name, Degonwadonti, means "Several Against One," but why she came to be called this is not known. Like Joseph, she too was given the surname of Brant, but the name Mary was later corrupted to Molly and she gained renown under the name of Molly Brant. Most authorities claim that Joseph Brant — Thayendanegea — was born in 1742, but this is an error. An early biographer of Brant, William L. Stone, made the mistake initially and it was then accepted as fact by subsequent historians. It was not the custom for Indian youths to be introduced to adult warfare until their fifteenth year. Brant, under the tutelage of the famous Mohawk chief Tiyanoga (Hendrik), was introduced to warfare in the Battle of Lake George (N.Y.) in September of 1755, when he was only mere days away from being fifteen. That he would have been taken into such devastating battle at age thirteen is extremely unlikely. Further, the Reverend John Strachan's *Memoirs* quotes Bishop James Strachan as saying in *Visit to Upper Canada*) that Brant was definitely fifteen when he went on the warpath for the first time. Lyman C. Draper, an authority on Brant, concurred that this was by far the more probable. There is also some historical allegation that Joseph Brant was Shawnee by birth and Mohawk by adoption. This is without foundation, arising from the fact that at the time of his birth, Shawnees made up more of the population of Shenango than other tribes, and that later, when his Mohawk mother married yet another Mohawk, that man did in fact adopt both Joseph and Mary as his own children.

6. Canajoharie was located on the site of present Canajoharie, New York, about twenty miles upstream from Amsterdam, New York. It was sometimes called the Mohawk Castle because it was the seat of the Mohawk tribe.

7. Brant was one of the four Indian "kings" who, in 1710, had been taken to England by Mayor Peter Schuyler, whom the Indians called Brother Quedor, and presented to Queen Anne, creating a sensation not only in her court but throughout all of London. These four men represented the Six Nations — another name for the Iroquois League — which was the longest-lived, most powerful and most feared Indian confederacy ever to occur in North America. In addition to Brant (whose Indian name was Saga-yean-qua-rash-tow), the other chiefs who had visited Queen Anne were John (Teyee-hoga-prow), Elow Occam (also spelled Elow Oh-kaom, Ohnee-yeath-tonno-prow), and Tiyanoga (Etawa Causne), who was called Hendrik by the Dutch and English settlers in New York.

8. Turner's *Traits of Indian Character* (II, 12) states that Joseph Brant "derived his name from a Dutch foster father who took care of the little savage while a child." This, of course, was not correct, since Brant's stepfather and step-grandfather were also named Brant. Another long-standing story, no doubt apocryphal, states that Owandah, after moving back to Canajoharie, married an Indian whose Christian name of Brant was corrupted from Barnet or Bernard, the name of a white man who had befriended him. His little stepson allegedly became known as Brant's Joseph, but this name was later reversed to become Joseph Brant. This does not take

into account, however, that Degonwadonti became Molly Brant and that the father of Nichus Brant was also named Brant. Nichus Brant was known by a number of different names. As well as Carrihoga, he was called Arrogy-hiadecker and Taicati-hago, these names roughly translating to Newscarrier, by which English name he has sometimes been called. He has also been recorded as Nichus Hance, Nichus Hans, Nichus Hance Brant and Old Nicholas. Even the Nichus was variously spelled Nickus, Nickos and Nickas.

9. For complete details on the adoption of Johnson, see the author's *Wilderness Empire*, 48–55.

10. To avoid confusion, further reference to her will be by the name Molly rather than Mary.

11. It has been suggested in some accounts that Joseph Brant was really the bastard son of William Johnson, but this statement has no basis whatever in fact. The belief of Johnson's parentage of Joseph Brant seems to stem from a comment to this effect made, without foundation, by General Philip Schuyler in a letter to General George Washington.

CHAPTER I

12. The then Lebanon, Connecticut, is now Columbia. The school was also called Wheelock's Indian School. It was the forerunner of Dartmouth College.

13. Three other Indians about Brant's age were accepted into the school at the same time. One was David Hill of Canajoharie, who eventually became a Mohawk chief and who remained friends with Brant all their lives, who signed treaties along with Brant and who eventually resided at Grand River with him. Hill died in October, 1790. Another was a young man called Center, who sickened and died while at the school. The third was a youth named Negyes, who became captivated by a young Connecticut woman and married her.

14. Extract of a letter from Sir William Johnson to Eleazar Wheelock:

Fort Johnson, Nov. 17, 1761

Reverend Sir, —
    . . . I am pleased to find ye lads I sent have merited your good opinion of them. I expect they will return, and hope will make such progress in the English language, and their learning, as may prove to your satisfaction and the benefit of the Indians, who are really much to be pitied. . . . I have given in charge to Joseph [Brant] to speak in my name to any good Boys he may see, and encourage 'em to accept the Generous offer now made them, which he promised to do, and return as soon as possible, and that without horses.

WM. JOHNSON

15. This involved problem is the principal theme of *Wilderness Empire*.

16. Mohawk, Oneida, Onondaga, Cayuga, Seneca. Later, as the sixth nation, the Tuscaroras.

17. All of the principal Iroquois villages have been known as castles, as well as have many less important villages. Some of these included both the Lower Mohawk Castle (Teantontalago) and Upper Mohawk Castle (Canajoharie), Onondaga Castle, Chenussio Castle (or Genesee Castle) and Kanadasaga of the Senecas, Oneida Castle and Cayuga Castle. This reference to castles is sometimes confusing to the reader unfamiliar with the historical context.

18. North Carolina.

19. As the years passed after the formation of the Iroquois League, the tribes spread out considerably; but when the League was formed the tribes were indeed in a relatively straight line, beginning with the Mohawks between present Albany and Utica and ending with the Senecas in the Genesee valley and later as far west as Niagara and Buffalo.

20. Wampum belts were not money, as generally believed, but a form of record-keeping used for recording treaties, speeches, war declarations, etc. As such, they were highly valued, but not in a monetary sense.

21. The site of present Syracuse, New York.

22. The whites who were versed in government and politics at this time had every reason to marvel at this form of Indian government, which had withstood the test of time and which recognized the individual tribes as independent entities yet united for mutual offense and defense. Actually, so admirably democratic was the League's form of government that in 1744, when Connecticut and Pennsylvania were negotiating with the Indians to adjust land claims, an Oneida chief suggested to the colonial delegates that the Colonies ought to establish a similar form of government. This suggestion was reiterated in Albany in 1755 and Benjamin Franklin is reputed to have become a strong advocate of adapting the Iroquois League's form of government to the needs of the Colonies when they were making their initial efforts to form an independent union and later to frame a constitution.

23. Since there is no recorded instance of an earthquake having occurred in the area, the story of the Tyadaghtons and their silver mine is probably apocryphal, yet the Iroquois evidently did have a good source of silver, which has never been located. Dr. Lyman C. Draper, who investigated this just after the Civil War, kept notes that indicated that the mine was located "near Elmira, New York, on Pine Creek where it is joined by Elk Run."

24. Details of this battle and of the death of Tiyanoga are presented in their entirety in *Wilderness Empire*.

25. Polly was actually Mary Johnson, but she was rarely referred to by her Christian name. It was William Johnson's habit to nickname his daughters; thus, Mary became Polly and Anne became Nancy.

26. Molly Brant had, in September, 1759, given birth to a son sired by Sir William Johnson and they had named him Peter Warren Johnson after Sir William's uncle Peter Warren, who had been William's original benefactor in America. Then, on October 21, 1761, Molly had given birth to Johnson's daughter, whom they named Elizabeth Johnson. During their years together, Molly and William Johnson eventually had eight children.

27. Out of a total of 1,950 able warriors in the Iroquois League at this time, the Senecas alone claimed to have 1,050. Yet there is ample evidence to indicate that the Senecas still considered the Mohawks to be virtually their equals in strength and thus were unwilling either to separate from the League or to breach openly the alliance with the Mohawks, which would have disrupted the structure of the League.

28. In large measure this was due to the postures taken by Sir Jeffrey Amherst, governor-general of the North American colonies. His hatred of *all* Indians was poorly concealed and his policies against them were outrageous. It was he who actually advocated decimation of the Indians by distributing to them as gifts the blankets taken from the corpses of soldiers that had died of smallpox. The resulting epidemic took many Indian lives. Details of this and other Amherst policies that provoked Pontiac's war are provided in the author's *The Conquerors*, 467, 480, especially regarding smallpox.

29. The site of present Franklin, Pennsylvania, southeast of Erie.

30. Teedyscung, a self-proclaimed prophet of some note, was also widely known under the name of Captain Bull.

31. Extract of an article in the Boston *Gazette*, April 30, 1764:

    . . . And as the Senecas will now join with the Five Nations (since they have entered into a peace with Sir William, and made large concessions for the performance of which they have left several hostages) there is great reason to think our enemies will be overtaken and justly chastised for their defection.

32. Now State Street in Boston.

33. Both factions were to some degree to blame for the incident, which assumed far more importance than it should have. The soldiers had acted without orders in firing on the crowd, but there was a considerable degree of provocation. Two of the soldiers were found guilty of manslaughter in the subsequent trial and both were branded on the hand as punishment and then released. The conviction among the colonists was reinforced that the King's men had butchered wholly unoffending Americans. Massacre Day, as it was called, was observed among

the colonists as a patriotic holiday until a more glorious one superseded it on July 4, 1776.

34. No record has been found to indicate that any names other than Isaac and Christina were ever bestowed on these two of Brant's children, although logic and custom suggest that they did have Indian names. Isaac was always a great disappointment to his father. In 1795 Isaac, who had become an alcoholic, attacked Brant and tried to kill him. Brant fought back and it was Isaac who was killed. It was a situation that weighed heavily on Brant, who surrendered himself to authorities but who was exonerated on grounds of self-defense.

35. Tuberculosis.

36. Quoted in the New York *Daily Tribune*, Saturday, May 31, 1879.

37. The congress at Fort Stanwix, the site of present Rome, New York, was organized by Sir William Johnson in an effort to protect Indian lands from increasing white settlement. This was especially important since it had become obvious that the Indian trade could not adequately be controlled. The congress had been set up as a result of Sir William's long, explicit correspondence with the Earl of Shelburne in London regarding the wrongs done the Indians. The boundary line between the whites' and the Indians' hunting grounds, which had been fixed in 1768, was, by the Fort Stanwix Treaty, extended to the Cherokee River (now Tennessee River) by a concession of the Six Nations. For this the Iroquois received the royal payment. In coming to attend the treaty congress, Sir William had arrived with thirty bateaux (cargo boats) of presents and food, including sixty barrels of flour, fifty barrels of pork, six barrels of rice and seventy barrels of miscellaneous provisions. Provided with this, the Indians met every request that Johnson made of them. However, there was strong disapproval from Lord Hillsborough, Secretary for the Colonies, because of the inclusion of the Kentucky/Tennessee area against the instructions of the Lords of Trade. He held up the proceedings until finally overruled. It was also at the Fort Stanwix Congress that the Penns purchased a considerable extension to their Pennsylvania holdings. The Fort Stanwix Treaty cost the Crown £10,000 and the barriers it established were quickly ignored by the westward-expanding white settlers, but it did represent a final strong effort to preserve lands for the Indians.

38. Present Herkimer, New York.

39. This speech given by Brant to the entire assemblage of Indians and whites before Johnson Hall was one of the final speeches of the congress. It accomplished little, but it was important in that it proves Brant was not a chief at this time and had not inherited any sort of chieftainship from his mother, since he spoke as a warrior and for the warriors.

40. This area was in the Wyoming Valley, the center of which was the area of present Wyoming, across the Susquehanna River from present Wilkes-Barre, Pennsylvania.

41. The site of present Stroudsburg, the seat of Monroe County, Pennsylvania, on the Delaware River.

42. The marriage took place in a log cabin at the corner of what is now River and South streets in Wilkes-Barre, Pennsylvania.

43. Lazarus Stewart was born in the Paxton District of Pennsylvania in 1733 and had commanded a company of Rangers of the Scottish and Irish Regiment in the French and Indian War. In 1763 he came with his company and another company under Captain Clayton to bury the dead New England settlers at the massacre that occurred at Wyoming on October 15. Stewart was notorious on the frontier and a man with whom not to trifle. Hotheaded and impetuous, it was he who, in retaliation for such frontier raids by the Indians, led a gang of ruffians called the Paxton Boys on horseback into Lancaster, Pennsylvania, on December 27, 1763, burst into the jail and killed fourteen peaceful Indians who were being held there for their own protection. This incident was the impetus for near riots occurring in Philadelphia shortly afterward. For more complete details, see *The Conquerors*.

44. She was the former Martha Espy of Trenton and Philadelphia.

45. The new county named Tryon embraced the whole of New York westward of a north-south line extending through nearly the center of present Schoharie County.

46. Near the site of present Canoga in Seneca County, New York. Despite the fact that Otetiana was without doubt a Seneca, because of his mother's lineage the village of Canoga was a Cayuga village. On some older maps it is shown as Ganogah.

47. Daniel Claus and "Miss Nancy" — Anne Johnson, Sir William's eldest daughter — were married early in the spring of 1762, when Claus was thirty-five and Nancy twelve years younger. It was perhaps the difference in age that first made Sir William take a dim view of the union, although he was probably also angry with himself for having failed to recognize that love had developed between them. A sort of quiet courtship had been engaged in by the couple, although it was sporadic at best, since Claus was headquartered at Montreal where, under Johnson, he was in charge of Indian affairs for the nine Canadian nations. The only time Claus and Miss Nancy saw one another was when he periodically came to Johnson Hall to confer with his supervisor.

48. Sir John subsequently named his second son Adam Gordon Johnson and this son became the third baronet in the Johnson line.

49. The eight children Sir William Johnson sired through Molly Brant included Peter, who was born in 1759 and who was killed in a duel at a fairly early age; Elizabeth, born in 1761, who married Robert Kerr and died at age thirty-three in 1794; Magdalene, born in 1763, who married Colonel John Ferguson and died at age fifty-four in January, 1818; Margaret, who was born in 1765 and married George Farley and who died after 1835; George, born in 1767, who died at age fifty-five in 1822; Mary, born in 1769, who never married and died at age forty-four on October 10, 1813; Susannah, born in 1771, who married Lieutenant Henry Lemoine and who died at age twenty-four on December 19, 1795; and Anne, born February 14, 1773, who married Hugh Earle and died at age forty-five on February 17, 1818.

50. The Executive Council of New York, upon receiving the report and conducting some further investigations on its own, concurred with Sir William Johnson's findings and the matter was officially closed.

51. A tradition without support or really much likelihood says that John Johnson rode a horse to death between Fort Johnson and Johnson Hall in his haste to arrive before his father died.

52. On the resignation in 1772 of Lord Hillsborough, Lord Dartmouth, Secretary of Colonial Affairs, had assumed the presidency of the Board of Trade.

53. The actual figure was 25,420 men. The total figure included all the tribes of the Northern District. Of this, the Iroquois numbered 10,000, of which 2,000 were fighting men. The entire population of New York Province at this time was 182,251, with the provincial militia strength at 32,000 men. This latter figure dropped sharply at the outbreak of the Revolution, as those remaining loyal to the Crown fled New York.

54. Brant always referred to the Americans as Bostonians, as mentioned earlier, but for less confusion, further such reference will be as "Americans."

55. Because of the use of "Tory" as derived from the original Irish as an epithet to tack onto the Loyalists, the term has now the established parallel meaning as one who is a strong advocate of conservative principles and opposed to reform or radicalism.

56. In a letter from the Reverend Samuel Kirkland to the Albany Committee dated June 9, 1775, Kirkland states the only reason he knows for his removal from office by Johnson:

> Colonel Johnson has orders from government (British) to remove the dissenting minister from the Six Nations till the difficulties between Great Britain and the Colonies are settled. . . . All he has against me I suppose to be this: A suspicion that I have interpreted to the Indians the doings of the Continental Congress, which has undeceived and too much opened the eyes of the Indians for Colonel Johnson's purposes. I confess to you, gentlemen, that I have been guilty of this, if it be any transgression. . . . I apprehend my interpreting of the doings of the Continental Congress to their sachems has done more real service to the cause of this country, or the cause of truth and justice, than £500 in presents would have effected.

57. The total number of British participating in the twenty-hour series of skirmishes beginning with Lexington and ending at the crossing to Charlestown was approximately 1,800 men, of which there were 73 killed, 174 wounded and 26 missing. During that same period, the Americans had 3,763 men engaged in the fighting, though never all of them at the same time, and they had 49 killed, 41 wounded and 5 missing.

58. Johnson called them Scotch, which was accepted usage at that time, although presently natives of Scotland are preferentially referred to as Scots or Scottish.

59. Not to be confused with the Mohegans of Connecticut, even though the names are variations of the same word. The Iroquois called them Akochakanen, meaning Those-Who-Speak-a-Strange-Tongue. They were also called Loups by the French, River Indians by the Dutch and Canoe Indians by the English, although Cadwallader Colden in 1747 called them Uragees.

60. Present Hoosic River.

61. Even though he was called colonel — a rank he subsequently achieved — John Butler was at this time only a major in the Tryon County Militia.

62. The reference here was to the gunpowder, which the province of New York had heretofore supplied to the Indians through the superintendent as a partial means of keeping them satisfied and which, being withheld now as a result of the revolutionary unrest, was causing extreme dissatisfaction and unrest among them, for which the Indians were justly blaming the Americans, not the British authorities.

63. Nevertheless, after Johnson and his little army left Guy Park and before they'd departed from Cosby's Manor, an alarm swept the populace. The rumor was that Johnson intended to attack Little Falls with about 900 Indians and then move on down the Mohawk, ravaging the country below. The militia was ordered to arms and placed on alert, while expresses were sent for reinforcements from Schenectady and Albany. No such attack by Johnson came.

64. The site of present Rome, New York. Fort Stanwix was built by General John Stanwix on orders from General James Abercromby in the summer of 1758 close to where, in an earlier day, an insubstantial fortification called Fort Williams had stood.

65. Now Oswego River.

66. Fort Oswego was sometimes called Old Oswego or Fort Pepperell. It was initially erected by the British in 1746 on the left (west) bank of the mouth of the Onondaga (Oswego) River on the site of present Oswego, New York. Later, directly across the river mouth on the right (east) bank, Fort Ontario was built. While under the command of Colonel Hugh Hercer in 1756, Fort Oswego was captured by the French under the Marquis de Montcalm. Another smaller fortification in the area was Fort George. The French burned Fort Oswego on August 14, 1756, but it was later rebuilt by the British and remained a vital link in the communication between the Great Lakes and the Mohawk/Hudson valleys of New York, as well as an important stopping place on the communication between Montreal and Niagara.

67. Pronounced *Rah*-zin-oh-gy-*yah*-tah.

68. His name is pronounced Goo-*singe*, a shortening of the full name, Gu-cingerachton, pronounced Goo-*singe*-uh-*rack*-ton. The meaning of the name is unclear.

CHAPTER II

69. Although the Americans were working in this direction with the Indians on a number of different fronts, no such alliance or arming had yet occurred. The report of such, which Dartmouth had received a week earlier, was obviously a statement of fact for that which was merely a potential.

70. The "large assortment of presents" spoken of by Dartmouth was, indeed, a substantial initial payment for securing the desired Indian alliance. It consisted of £2,500 worth of goods, including hundreds of fine rifles "with blue barrels, walnut stocks, trimmings of wrought brass and silver sights," plus a multitude of excellent tomahawks, scalping knives, brass kettles, gold-laced hats, ruffled shirts, pipes, tobacco, greatcoats, hundreds of pots of blue, rose, yellow and vermilion war paints, and scores of kegs of gunpowder and lead.

71. See the full account of the surrender and following atrocity in *Wilderness Empire*, 471–476.

72. Oswego.

73. Montreal.

74. The breakdown of warrior strength committed by each of the Six Nations to Guy Johnson against the colonists at this time was as follows: 400 Senecas, 300 Mohawks, 300 Onondagas, 230 Cayugas, 200 Tuscaroras and 150 Oneidas (of a possible 410) for a total from the League of 1,580 warriors and chiefs.

75. Because of his actions, Skenando after this time became known as "The Friend of the Whites" — the whites in this case meaning the Americans.

76. Allen, at this time thirty-seven, had been born in a log cabin in Litchfield, Connecticut, in 1738. He'd begun his schooling under a clergyman with the aim of entering Yale, but the death of his father required him to forgo college and help support his mother and her other seven children. In 1768, at last free of this burden, he moved to the New Hampshire grants — now Vermont — and soon became colonel of his own colorful militia called the Green Mountain Boys. This force was subsequently absorbed into the army and Allen, who had grave personality problems and had come to be disliked even by his own men, lost his command.

77. Peter Warren Johnson had always lived as an Indian and, in honor of the capture of Ethan Allen, was made a minor chief among the Iroquois. However, not long after this incident he was killed in a duel.

78. The storm continued until the evening of November 13, at the conclusion of which Arnold's army crossed the St. Lawrence and laid siege to Quebec.

79. Montreal was essentially undefensible and so as soon as Carleton heard that Montgomery's Americans were at La Prairie, he put on shipboard the most valuable equipment and supplies and destroyed the residue. The ships carried him to Sorel. Montreal still held for a short while longer under the inhabitants, but finally surrendered to General Montgomery on November 13. The Americans attacked the ships at Sorel, including the ship in which Carleton had taken refuge, the *Gaspé*. Finally, disguised as an ordinary laborer and accompanied by only two of his officers, Carleton escaped in a rowboat with muffled oars through a channel in the islands opposite Sorel and managed to reach Quebec safely. Eight small boats, two armed vessels and the *Gaspé*, with their cargoes, crews and the soldiers of the Montreal garrison, surrendered to the Americans.

80. The Continental companies involved were those of Brigadier General Abraham Ten Broeck and Colonel Richard Varick, although several other officers accompanied Schuyler.

81. Present Fonda, New York.

82. It is said that when Johnson made an effort to recover his buried papers three or four years later, they had all been ruined.

83. George Washington, when he took command of the Continental Army the previous June, had said, "I abhor the idea of American independence." He was generally supported in this view by the patriots.

84. Brant never did remove the ring. At his death in 1807, it was kept by his widow, Catherine, until somehow she lost it in 1811. The same ring was found twenty-three years later by a little girl in a plowed field near Wellington Square, Ontario, Canada.

85. Burgoyne sailed from London to America to become second-in-command to Governor General Guy Carleton in Canada. The fleet was composed of fifteen ships carrying seven Irish regiments, one English regiment and 2,000 Hessian mercenaries hired by George III. The flagship was under the command of Captain Pennell of the Royal Navy and was named the *Blonde*, after the in-vogue saying that "soldiers and sailors prefer blondes."

86. There are numerous accounts that Brant led the Indians in this battle and that, after it was over, he exerted himself enormously to prevent the massacre of the captured Americans. Such accounts evidently were first inspired by an error on the part of Colonel William Stone, whose *Life of Brant* states that the Mohawk chief was active in this Battle of the Cedars. Many other historians have accepted Stone's account as factual when, in truth, it is not. Brant was at this time still in England and did not leave there until June 3, arriving back at New York City on July 29, ten weeks after the Battle of the Cedars had been fought. Further, a story grew out of this battle, entirely fallacious, which attributed to Brant an act of mercy of an unusual nature. An American officer in Major Sherburne's party, Captain John McKinis-

try, was captured. The story alleges that he was stripped and prepared for death at the stake when Brant came upon the scene. Through some mysterious set of circumstances that no historian satisfactorily explains, McKinistry, bound at the stake, somehow realized that Joseph Brant was a Mason (a questionable matter to begin with) and gave him a secret signal. Brant, recognizing the signal, thereupon exerted himself in behalf of the prisoner among the other Indians and, because of his power among them, effected McKinistry's release and good treatment thereafter and he and Brant remained good friends throughout the years. So popular did this fable become that others adopted it and there are recorded no less than a dozen cases in the next few years where Brant allegedly saved the lives of white prisoners because they gave the secret Masonic sign. In no case has the author been able to verify any such account and Brant himself, who in certain instances *did* help to save certain individuals and later in life used to tell of it, never mentioned or attested to the accuracy of any story having him save a Masonic brother because of a secret signal being exchanged. McKinistry, who actually was captured at the Battle of the Cedars, afterward became a colonel in the New York Regiment and died at Livingston, New York, on June 9, 1822.

87. Once again, even though Brant is at this time still in London, there are numerous accounts of his being with Sir John Johnson at this time and that it was he who led Sir John and his party by the difficult but safe route to Montreal. To reinforce this story, it is said that only moments before their departure from Johnson Hall, Brant took the time to race up the massive main staircase and then come down more slowly, pausing every few feet to chop a mark in the balustrade rails with his tomahawk. These, he allegedly explained to Sir John, were his marks; they would be seen and recognized and respected by any Indians who might come here in their absence. His mark of protection would therefore prevent destruction of the house. Even today, in guided tours of the mansion, these marks are pointed out to visitors and this story told. It is likely that the marks were put there in the manner described and for the purpose intended, but they definitely were not put there by Brant. Johnson Hall survived the Revolution virtually unscathed.

88. Variously spelled Onouaquago, Oquaga, Ouguaga, Oquagaa and Onoquago, the town was on the west bank of the Susquehanna, about fifteen miles east of Binghamton, New York, on the site of present Ouaquaga.

89. The fort was built on a slight eminence about 150 yards from the site of the present courthouse of Herkimer, New York.

90. This was the site of Rome, New York, in Oneida County, on the very important early portage between the Mohawk River and Wood Creek leading toward Oswego. In many of the documents of the time the names Fort Stanwix and Fort Schuyler are used interchangeably, creating some degree of confusion, especially because during the French and Indian War twenty years earlier there had been a Fort Schuyler named after General Philip Schuyler's uncle, built at the site of present Utica, but which at this time no longer existed. Also, the name of Fort Schuyler, which Colonel Dayton placed on the rebuilt fortification, was subsequently changed back to Fort Stanwix. Therefore, to avoid some of the confusion that generally results, the author has taken the liberty of referring to this fortification only as Fort Stanwix. The village here was ultimately named Rome after the heroic defense of the Republic made here.

91. Herkimer, born in 1726, was the eldest son of Johan Yost Erghemar, one of the original patentees of Burnetsfield, Herkimer County, New York. At some point during the boyhood of Nicholas, his father began calling himself Han Jost Herchheimer and later yet the surname was changed to Herkimer. The elder Herkimer was said to be "a mighty man, astonishing the Mohawks by his prodigious strength." His was a German family of considerable wealth and Nicholas had also become influential in the Mohawk Valley in his manhood. He had been commissioned a lieutenant in Captain Wormwood's militia company in 1758 and was appointed colonel of the first battalion of the Militia of Tryon County in 1775.

92. Diarrhea; usually dysenteric.

93. Located at the head of Lake Ontario at the mouth of the Niagara River where it enters the lake. The fort was positioned on the right (or east) point of land there.

94. It is the view of some historians that Germain's hatred for Guy Carleton stemmed from Carleton having been a witness against him at Germain's court-martial many years previously at Minden, but this is without foundation, as Carleton was not called to testify on that occasion. More likely Germain had been insulted by Carleton and the grudge within him had grown disproportionately, to the point where Germain's judgment was impaired. This becomes obvious in the heated correspondence he engaged in at this time with Carleton. Obviously, by what transpired in those letters, Germain's concern was wholly for General Sir William Howe, at Carleton's expense. Germain had been court-martialed in March, 1760, for disobedience of orders on the battlefield. His name at that time was Lord George Sackville — a name he later changed to Germain upon inheriting some property. In that court-martial, the final judgment was: "It is the opinion of this court that the said Lord George Sackville is, and is hereby ajudged, unfit to serve His Majesty in any military capacity whatever." It was remarkable that he was not sentenced to be executed. It is miraculous that he surfaced again in 1775 as Secretary of State for the American colonies and for the Revolutionary War in America.

95. It is a rather remarkable example of prescience that during the preceding summer, when Burgoyne was at Lake Champlain, George Washington remarked on July 4: "It seems beyond question that the enemy will attempt to unite their two armies, that under General Burgoyne, and the one here."

96. This oversight on the part of Lord George Germain has been held by some authorities to have been the incident that eventually lost the war for the British. F. J. Huddleston, librarian of the British War Office in 1927 and author of *Warriors in Undress* and *Gentleman Johnny Burgoyne*, calls Germain "a poltroon . . ." and "an incompetent ass," adding that "we have in London no statue of Lord George Germain. He did so much to lose the American War that there surely ought to be one of him in the United States, with emblematical figures of Cowardice and Stupidity on either side of him as supporters."

97. July 17, 1775.

98. March 1, 1776.

99. On receipt of Carleton's letter, Germain quickly took refuge behind the King and replied to Carleton on July 25 only with the comment: ". . . *It would ill become my situation to enter into an ill-humored altercation with you. . . . I think it proper to assure you that whatever reports you may have heard of my having any personal dislike for you are without the least foundation.*"

100. It has never been determined fully who was responsible on the British side for turning over the war plans to the enemy, or who on the American side received them and spread the news. Informed speculation narrows it down to none other than George Germain himself for reasons understood by himself only. There is, however, no concrete evidence to corroborate such an allegation. There is also speculation that it might have been Sir Guy Carleton, done to cause a campaign from which he had been excluded to fail and so improve his own chances for recognition in the next. As with Germain, such allegations have never been substantiated with anything more than the most dubious and flimsy of circumstantial evidence.

101. The 8,000 consisted of 4,000 British regulars of the 9th, 20th, 21st, 24th, 47th, 53rd and 62nd regiments, plus 3,000 Hessians, 150 Canadians, 500 Indians and a large artillery train with requisite personnel.

102. "Family," in this case, refers to his staff.

103. The deputy British secretary of state, William D'Oyley.

104. A Lieutenant Edgar Anburey, serving at this time as an aide-de-camp to Burgoyne, wrote to a friend, saying:

> We have more dangerous enemies at home than we have to encounter abroad; for all transactions that are to take place are fully known before they are given out in orders, and I make no doubt you will be as much surprised as the General was when I tell you that the whole operations of the ensuing campaign were canvassed for several days before he arrived, while he supposed he was communicating an entire secret.

105. In some early accounts the settlement is called De-u-na-dillo, but it was referred to by Brant himself as Unadilla.

106. This Unadilla settlement was approximately five miles downstream from the site of present Unadilla in Otsego County, New York.

107. Scalps were purchased at the equivalent of $10 each. Adult male prisoners ordinarily brought the equivalent of $15 each.

108. One account states that the blue came from the camlet cloak of Captain Swartout, a cloak first captured from the British at Peekskill.

109. It is believed that this flag of the United States, even if not entirely accurate in its design, was the first to be flown in battle in the history of the United States.

110. Because of the bounties placed on scalps, the taking of people of all ages and sexes soon became something of a business on the frontier. In some cases the colonists — or, later on, the Americans — offered bounties on Indian scalps, but the greatest trafficking in scalps came as a result of the wide range of bounties placed on them by the British. Because different age and sex scalps brought different prices, the scalps had to be marked for proper payment to be given. Such bundles of scalps ordinarily were shipped in large lots of eight to twenty bundles, comprised of eighty-eight to one hundred scalps per bundle, or no less than seven hundred scalps per shipment. Scalps taken for British bounties were ordinarily shipped in these bundles to the governor of Canada in Quebec. Each scalp was stretched on a painted willow hoop and further painted on the inside of the skin. The colors and markings were used in a wide combination so that all of the necessary information about any particular scalp could be had at a glance. The basic hoop and scalp markings denoted the following:

Four-inch hoop painted black	Soldier
Four-inch hoop painted red	Man other than soldier
Four-inch hoop painted green	Old person
Four-inch hoop painted blue	Woman
Two-inch hoop painted green	Boy
Two-inch hoop painted yellow....	Girl
Two-inch hoop painted white	Infant
Skin painted red	Officer
Skin painted brown	Farmer killed in house
Skin painted green	Farmer killed in field
Skin painted white	Infant
Skin painted yellow	Girl
Skin painted white with red tears ..	Small boy
Skin painted half white, half red ..	Older boy
Skin painted yellow with red tears .	Mothers
Hair braided...................	Wives
Black spot in center of skin	Killed by bullet
Red hoe in center of skin	Farmer
Black ax in center of skin	Settler
Black tomahawk in center of skin .	Killed by tomahawk
Black scalping knife in center of skin	Killed by knife
Black war club in center of skin...	Beaten to death
Yellow flames in center of skin ...	Tortured to death
Black circle all around	Killed at night
White circle all around with yellow spot	Killed by day
Small red foot	Died fighting

111. Captain Laurence Gregg was one of the very small percentage of soldiers and settlers on the American frontier who survived being scalped. Occasionally scalping victims would remain

alive for a short while after such an ordeal, but even among these the mortality rate was high due to infection.

112. St. Leger had changed his mind about the battle route he would follow after entering Lake Ontario. He landed his force at the mouth of the Little Salmon River near present Texas, New York, and proposed to follow that river and its South Branch upstream to the area of present West Amboy, then southward through the areas of present Gayville, West Monroe and Constantia to Oneida Lake. This would have been a much more difficult route over which to take his artillery and supplies and almost surely the entire expedition would have become bogged down in the area between present West Amboy and Constantia.

113. The cohorn, or "royal," was a small, portable mortar for lobbing grenades, a very useful instrument for dropping explosive charges into forts or encampments and causing injury from bursting shrapnel among the troops. Its great weakness was a very limited range.

114. Estimates of the size of St. Leger's force have ranged from as few as 1,200 to as many as 2,500, with the greatest variable being the number of Indians present. Gordon's *History* (London, 1787), II, 477, says for example that the whole of St. Leger's force probably did not exceed 800 men, yet on page 529 he credits St. Leger with having at least 700 Indian warriors alone.

115. Sometimes he was called Colonel Louis . . . the name, in either case, pronounced Loo-eee.

116. Present Whitehall, New York.

117. At the time of its abandonment, Fort Ticonderoga was under command of Major General Arthur St. Clair. It was in disreputable condition. The key to the American northern region, it guarded Lake Champlain where it narrows sharply. Reinforcements wouldn't help because there was no food available for them. Tents were bad and powder magazines were so rotten that 50 pounds of powder weekly was getting ruined. There was also no paper for making cartridges. What bateaux they had would not float for lack of pitch and tar for repairing the leaks. St. Clair averred that to defend the place would require 10,000 men and of the 4,000 he had, many were merely boys and only one in ten even had a bayonet.

118. The site of present Deerfield, New York, directly across the Mohawk River from Utica.

119. The banquette is a platform inside the parapets, about five feet below the sharpened picket points, built so defenders can stand on it, look past the tops of the upright log pickets and shoot from there, yet with their bodies protected from enemy fire.

120. A redoubt is a small independent earthwork, usually square or polygonal, completely enclosed.

121. The site of present Utica, New York.

122. Johannes Yost Herkimer was one of the Tory refugees of the Mohawk Valley who had fled the area with Guy Johnson.

123. The work of clearing Wood Creek and opening the temporary road was undertaken by detachments under Captain Bouville and Lieutenant Lundy.

CHAPTER III

124. What induced the Oneidas not only to go against the ruling of the Iroquois League, of which they were an integral part, but to set themselves up actually to attack the brother tribes of the Iroquois League has never been satisfactorily ascertained. They could not have been ignorant of the awful consequences such treachery would bring about, yet they acted as if they were oblivious to it.

125. The site of present Whitesboro, New York.

126. That road followed almost exactly the course of present New York State 69.

127. Oriska was the Mohawk name for "The Place of the Nettles." In various accounts and on various maps the name has been given as Oriska (by St. Leger), Eriska (by Colonel Willett), Orisco (by Captain Deygart), Oriske (in London Documents), Ochriscany (on the Chronological Map of the Province of New York, London, 1779), Ochriskeney (map of 1790 in Vol. I, *Documentary History of New York*), O-his-heh (by the Senecas), O-his-ha (by the

Cayugas), O-his-ka (by the Onondagas), Olehisk (by the Oneidas), Ole-his-ka (by the Tus-caroras).

128. This is the present Battle Brook of Whitestown Township.

129. Colonel Isaac Paris was reportedly tortured to death by the Indians on August 24, eighteen days after the battle. Eight other officers who had been captured were allegedly killed running the gauntlet.

130. This spot is a little rise of ground just west of the center of the ravine at the Oriskany Memorial Battle Park, about where the flagstaff is located.

131. So many of the Oneidas were killed in this action that the event has forever since been mourned at the tribe's important feasts and dances.

132. Major Stephen Watts subsequently lost his leg as a result of his wound.

133. Some accounts, without any known justification or authentication, reported that as the Indians became afraid, they suspected that Sir John's Greens and Colonel Butler's and Major Watts's Rangers were shooting Indians. At this they — the Indians — allegedly began killing Rangers and Greens. In England it was believed that as many of the British force were killed by Brant's Indians as by the Tryon Militia. This, of course, is patently ridiculous. For one thing, had it occurred, Brant and his Indians would never have fought beside these forces again.

134. Some accounts say that Sir John Johnson was the one who was driven from his tent in shirtsleeves, but that is incorrect. Because it was Johnson's camp and much of his property was confiscated in the raid, and because Bird ran from the camp in shirtsleeves, the erroneous conclusion was made that Bird was Johnson. Such was not the case. Johnson was still close to the Oriskany battle site at this time.

135. Willett's officers on this sortie included Lieutenant Stockwell, Captain Allen and Major Badlam.

136. When first brought captive to the St. Leger camp, John Frey was seen by his own brother, a radical Tory in St. Leger's command. The brother, Robert, allegedly rushed at John Frey and had to be physically restrained from killing him.

137. A common torture of the Iroquois Indians was to prepare a great quantity of wooden splinters about the thickness of a pencil at one end and tapering to a sharp point at the other, each about five inches long. These would be soaked in turpentine or pitch and then stuck into the naked body of a bound captive at random until he might take on the appearance of a pincushion. The pain of the turpentine or pitch in the wounds alone was excruciating, but these splinters would then be set afire. Some victims were able to remain alive in such condition for three hours or more.

138. The name was pronounced *Hahn You*. He was not related to Major General Philip Schuyler.

139. Incredibly, the American officers were claiming a victory at the Battle of Oriskany on the ground that Herkimer's army still "held the field" at the close of that inglorious day.

140. The British army was wholly stupefied by Howe's movement south instead of north. General Clinton wrote: "*I owe it to the truth to say there was not, I believe, a man in the army except Lord Cornwallis and General Grant, who did not reprobate the movement to the southward and see the necessity of cooperation with General Burgoyne.*" The Secretary for War for the United States wrote: "*The people here are very puzzled by General Howe's conduct.*" Perhaps the most sanctimonious reaction was that of Lord George Germain, whose error it was that Lord Howe was never informed in full of Burgoyne's plan. Germain commented: "*I am sorry the Canada army will be disappointed in the junction they expect with Sir William Howe, but the more honour for Burgoyne if he does his business without any assistance from New York.*"

141. Incidents of cannibalism are not common in the history of American Indian tribes, but they do exist. Ordinarily the cannibalism, when it occurred, was ritualistic, in which usually the heart of an enemy — sometimes cut from his chest while still beating — was eaten raw. In this way the strength of the enemy was believed to be absorbed by the victor. There were, however, occasional cases, especially during times of famine or when returning from war with prisoners and the march was long and difficult, when captives were slain and eaten as a food source. Such was the case here with Pickering. At such times the Indians were choosy

about the physical condition of the to-be-devoured victim and either chose an adult in relatively good — and plump — physical condition or, more often, a small child or baby. At no time was such cannibalism an ordinary occurrence.

142. Located in present Bradford County, Pennsylvania, not far from the site of present Wyalusing near the mouth of Wyalusing Creek, this town began its existence in 1754 with the establishment of a large Indian village by the Monsey chief named Papunhank. In 1763 a Moravian village was established here and the entire town soon became Christianized. The mission removed to Ohio in 1772. At the outbreak of the American Revolution, there were forty homes here.

143. An intensive search of the documents of this period indicates that this letter of Schuyler's advocating an expedition into the Indian country to destroy their towns was the first mention of it anywhere by anyone and so, in fairness, this may be said to constitute the inception of what eventually became the important campaign launched to this end a year later under the leadership of Major General John Sullivan. Unfortunately, Philip Schuyler was never given due credit for having originated the plan.

144. This journey, traced on a modern map, was about 300 miles in length, carrying them from Fort Niagara at the mouth of the Niagara River on Lake Ontario to present Rochester, upstream on the Genesee to present Geneseo, then overland along trails past the foot of Conesus Lake and through the present village of Conesus, then essentially along the course of present U.S. 15 through Springwater to Cohocton, then down the Cohocton to Painted Post and present Corning, past Shwe-do-wah — present Elmira — and then across the border into Pennsylvania to Tioga — present Athens — at the junction of the Chemung River with the Susquehanna. The journey then went upstream on the Susquehanna, northward into New York again, then eastward past Ahwaga — present Owego — past present Endicott, and Oochenang — present Binghamton — then southward and eastward again, taking a brief swing down into Pennsylvania through Great Bend and Susquehanna and then almost directly northward into New York again, past present Windsor and finally to Oquaga — also then called Ahquaga and Onuh-huh-quau-geh — which was on the site of present Ouaquaga.

145. Andrustown was located in what is presently the northern section of the little town of Warren, New York, near the head of Otsego Lake, some 14 miles southeast of present Herkimer.

146. This oversight was partially rectified — poorly and with some difficulty — during the next few weeks.

147. The site of present Canandaigua, Ontario County, New York, at the foot of Canandaigua Lake.

148. The site of present Geneva, New York, at the foot of Seneca Lake.

149. Shequaga — also known as Catherine's Town — was located on the west bank of the inlet creek to Seneca Lake at its head.

150. Also known as Skwe-do-wah, Kanawaholla was on the site of present Elmira, New York, in Chemung County.

151. Newtown was also known as New Chemung, located a mile upstream from present Wellsburg, New York; Chemung was located near the site of present Chemung, New York, both in Chemung County.

152. Tioga — also called Tioga Point — was at the site of present Athens, Bradford County, Pennsylvania.

153. Although Gu-cinge had been passed over in favor of Brant as war chief, he was now war chief of the Senecas and a powerful man. He was also known by the name Giengwahtol.

154. The Indian trail taken by Gu-cinge and his party moved down the west bank of the Susquehanna to the site of present Milan, Pennsylvania, then westward through present East Smithfield and Springfield to near present Columbia Crossroads. From there, basically following the course of Pennsylvania Route 14, it moved through the areas of present Troy and Canton to the headwaters of Lycoming Creek at Leolyn, then down that stream to its junction with the West Branch at present Williamsport. From here the force moved downstream, destroying all minor settlements as far south as present Milton, Pennsylvania.

155. York and Fitch were not as lucky as Jenkins believed. Fitch, still suffering from a fever that had attacked him at Fort Niagara, died during the voyage and was buried at sea. York was able eventually to reach the home of his father-in-law, Manassah Miner, in Voluntown, Connecticut, at which time he learned of the massacre at Wyoming. He and his father-in-law were convinced that York's wife and children had perished in that massacre. York, only a few weeks later, contracted smallpox. Because of his weakened state due to imprisonment he died. Only eleven days later, York's wife and children, refugees from the Wyoming attack, arrived in Voluntown. They had believed since his capture the preceding November that he had been killed by the Indians.

156. Present Judds Falls.

157. Some accounts say that it was Brant himself who killed Lieutenant Wormwood, but there is no firsthand account of it. There is also a tradition that Wormwood was a personal friend of Brant's but no justification can be found for this claim either. Wormwood was much younger than Brant and so they would not have been boys together. Also, though Wormwood spent much time in Canajoharie, especially at Fort Plank, it was primarily after Brant had left the area. It is almost certain, however, that Wormwood recognized Brant by having seen him on occasion, as Brant worked for Sir William Johnson. Brant was recognizable to many people he did not know personally.

158. This tube, still containing its partially legible messages, was found in the wooded ravine between some rocks thirty years later, in 1808, by a ten-year-old boy named Herbert Van Deusen.

159. The site of present Cobleskill, New York. This settlement was also referred to at this time as Cover's Kill, Cover's Creek, Cobus Kill, Cobus Creek and Cobuskill Creek.

160. The site of Lawyersville on New York Route 145.

161. The site of present Warnersville on New York Route 7.

162. As occurs so many times in battles in which Brant was involved — or purportedly involved when he was not — there are some reports from this one of lives being spared by Brant when his enemies made the Masonic sign. Oddly enough, though both Maynard and Patrick were killed in this engagement, some reports stated that Patrick, only wounded, was saved by Brant when he made a Masonic sign that Brant recognized; and that Maynard, captured, was saved by Brant when the Indian war chief discovered Masonic symbols marked on Maynard's arms in India ink. Both claims are, of course, false. Neither man survived the skirmish. Why this Masonic rescue fable began and persisted all throughout Brant's wartime career and even later in his life remains a mystery, but there is hardly a frontier battle fought wherein someone does not claim having been saved from death by Brant, who heard a Masonic word uttered, saw a Masonic sign given, or saw a Masonic symbol drawn.

163. All the dead were scalped and it is reported that Captain Patrick, who was evidently not killed by the bullet he took through the groin, was stabbed several times in the body before being scalped. Lieutenant Maynard is also said to have had one of his breasts cut off and burned between his legs, along with his genitals.

164. The army detachment from Schoharie had 22 of its 40 men killed. Three of the militia were killed. Six residents of Cobleskill, who were unable to flee in time, were killed. Three regular soldiers and three militiamen were wounded. All of the dead were buried in a common grave near the George Warner residence on June 6 by Colonel Vrooman with his troops from Schoharie.

165. Jenkins Fort, at what was then Exeter, was located just above the west end of the present Pittston Bridge (U.S. 11) on the west bank of the Susquehanna at present West Pittston, Pennsylvania, five miles above the strongest installation of the Wyoming Valley, Forty Fort, and seven miles above present Wilkes-Barre, Pennsylvania.

166. Wysockton, at the site of present Wysox in Bradford County (then Westmoreland County), Pennsylvania, was first established as Wes-sau-ken, an Indian village. The Sebastian Strope family settled there in 1773. There are detailed accounts of what subsequently happened to the Strope family during its captivity, but much of it is in error or distorted.

167. That flat is the site of the present Skyhaven Landing Field directly south across the river from present Tunkhannock, Pennsylvania.

168. This village was also called Kanagsaws and was located near the head of Conesus Lake in Livingston County, New York.
169. Wilkes-Barre Fort was located at the site of present Wilkes-Barre, Pennsylvania, just above the mouth of present Mill Creek, where it had been erected to protect the mill on that stream. Forty Fort, so named because Susquehanna Township, in which it was located, had originally been settled by forty proprietors, was an acre or more in extent on the west bank of the river.
170. Wyoming Fort was located within the present limits of Wilkes-Barre near the river's edge at South Street.
171. Wintermoot Fort was located at the site of the northern edge of present Exeter, adjacent to the southern edge of Happy Valley.
172. Pittston Fort was located within the limits of present Pittston, Pennsylvania.
173. This island, now known as LaGrange Island, is directly opposite the mouth of Mill Run, which enters the Susquehanna from the east at the site of the present little community of Osterhout.
174. Those who were on hand for the wedding of Bethiah Harris and John Jenkins, inside Jenkins Fort, included: Lieutenant John Jenkins, commander of Jenkins Fort; Bethiah Harris Jenkins, his wife; Private Stephen Jenkins, his brother; Private John Murphy; his wife, Elizabeth Murphy, who was pregnant; Captain Stephen Harding; Private Benjamin Harding; Private Stukeley Harding; Private Stephen Harding, Jr.; Private James Hadsall; Private James Hadsall, Jr.; John Hadsall, a boy; Peter Rogers, a boy; Private Ebenezer Reynolds; his wife, Sarah Hadsall Reynolds, daughter of James Hadsall; Private Daniel Carr; Rachel Hadsall Carr, daughter of James Hadsall and wife of Daniel Carr; Private Daniel Wallen; Private William Martin; Private Quocko Martin, Negro slave of William Martin; Private Samuel Morgan; Private Ichabod Phelps; Private Joel Phelps; the Reverend James Whittlesey.
175. Less than a mile above the present town of Nordmont, Pennsylvania.
176. The mountain they crossed was North Mountain and their path took them along the north shores of both Canoga Lake and Lake Jean. They reached the headwaters of Bowman Creek in present Rickett's Glen State Park in northwestern Luzerne County, Pennsylvania.
177. There is a report that states that Butler's force during this descent of the river engaged in "several robberies and murders" and that this included, by mistake, the massacre of the wife and five children of one of the Tories earlier rounded up by the Wyoming Valley Americans and sent to Connecticut for trial. No verification or supportive evidence can be located for this claim.
178. This place is presently known as Keeler's Eddy and is approximately a half mile south of Upper Exeter and just slightly upstream from the present village of Ransom on the east bank of the Susquehanna.
179. Presently known as Sutton Creek.
180. Present Lewis Creek.
181. Sutton Creek.
182. On the morning of July 4, following the Wyoming battle of July 3, Gardner, who was the father of five children, was permitted to see his wife and children a final time. He was then chained to a log and given a large burden of plunder to carry. After the farewell, he had a rope tied around his neck and was led away. He survived until the party reached the vicinity of Kanadasaga (present Geneva, New York) at the foot of Seneca Lake on July 15. There, still carrying his great load, he collapsed. He was handed over to squaws and as his fellow prisoner, Daniel Carr, watched, they piled brush around him, stuck him full of turpentine splinters and burned him to death.
183. There was no blood relationship whatsoever between Colonel John Butler of the British and Colonel Zebulon Butler of the Americans.
184. Sheshaquin, built about 1765, was probably established by Eghobund. It was located on the site of present Ulster on the west bank of the Susquehanna in Bradford County, Pennsylvania. There is, at present, a community called Sheshaquin on the east bank of the Susquehanna, opposite present Ulster, but this was not — as is generally supposed — where Eghobund's village was located, although at one point some Senecas from the village did establish

a smaller village of sorts on or about the site of present Sheshaquin. The name of Chief Eghobund is sometimes found erroneously spelled Echobund. It is believed that he died of smallpox in about 1773.

185. Scovell Mountain was originally named after Elisha Scovell, who settled near the foot of it. Scovell, however, was a Tory who aided Butler on his arrival at Wyoming and so later the mountain was given its present name of Peterson Mountain. There is, however, still a Scovell Island in the Susquehanna River at the southeastern foot of the mountain.

186. They left present Sutton Creek in about the vicinity of Exeter Township School.

187. This was present Lewis Creek, which was crossed just a hundred yards or so north of Mount Zion Church.

188. Present Hicks Creek.

189. That site was approximately one-half mile almost due south of the present Lookout Tower.

190. Of the original garrison of nineteen at Fort Jenkins, this was their status on the evening of July 1, 1778:

Killed:	Miner Robbins, Benjamin Harding, Stukeley Harding, Quocko Martin, James Hadsall, Jr., James Hadsall, Sr.
Wounded:	Joel Phelps, Ebenezer Reynolds
Sick:	Samuel Morgan
Captive:	John Gardner, Daniel Carr
Lame:	Ichabod Phelps
On Duty at	
Forty Fort:	Stephen Harding, Jr., Stephen Harding, Sr.
Able-bodied:	John Jenkins, William Martin, John Murphy (who had not gone to Forty Fort because his wife, in Jenkins Fort, was on the point of going into labor)

CHAPTER IV

191. This bridge was at approximately the spot where the present U.S. 11 crosses Abraham Creek at the eastern edge of present Swoyersville.

192. No record has ever been found that gives the identity of this first American killed at the Wyoming battle.

193. The halt to form battle lines was made on what is the present property of the Wilkes-Barre Wyoming Valley Airport, just south of U.S. 11, but north of the present terminal building.

194. Oddly, Dana's name has sometimes been reversed and recorded as Dana Anderson instead of Anderson Dana. Also, in all accounts he is listed as a private, yet he also served as Colonel Zebulon Butler's adjutant, although there were many commissioned officers in Butler's wing. Dana, who had a wife and a thirteen-year-old son, Anderson Dana, Jr., had settled in the Wyoming Valley in 1772. He was a native of Ashford, Connecticut.

195. This was present Hicks Creek, which originated atop what is presently Peterson Mountain and flowed down from between that hill and Mount Lookout to the west of it, entering the Wyoming Valley just east of the present community of Happy Valley. Here the stream turned east and meandered past Wintermoot's to eventually empty into the Susquehanna just opposite the western point of triangular Scovell Island. Much of the former marsh area became a strip-mined sector.

196. Tawannears — pronounced *Ta-wa-ne-ars* — was known to the whites as Black Snake. He was chief of the village of Kershong on the west shore of Seneca Lake about seven miles south of present Geneva, New York. It is said that at six and a half feet in height, he was one of the tallest of the Senecas.

197. Isaac was killed in a field here the following November and David, who in this Wyoming battle escaped the Indians by hiding in the river, contracted pneumonia and died.

198. Later in the day Lieutenant Elisha Blackman, father of Lavinia, who was at this time at Wilkes-Barre Fort with his family, sent his wife and children, including Lavinia, out into the

wilderness to make their way as best they could to a place of safety while he stayed to help in the defense. The family survived, eating whortleberries, and on the third day of their flight, famished and exhausted, arrived at the German settlements at Northampton.

199. Lieutenant Obediah Gore, Jr., the eldest brother, was in the regular army serving under George Washington in New Jersey at this time.

200. Lieutenant Shoemaker's body was washed ashore near Forty Fort, where it was recovered by the Americans and buried.

201. In these early accounts the island is frequently referred to as Monocasy Island; however, the present spelling of Monocanock is used here.

202. Slocum remained hidden until nightfall and then went back to the west shore of the Susquehanna, where he encountered another refugee, Nathan Carey, and the two of them made it safely together to Forty Fort.

203. One version has Colonel Zebulon Butler being the officer to rescue Bennett, but it was actually Denison who did so. Zebulon had by this time reached Forty Fort and had taken command from Lieutenant Jenkins.

204. Joseph Elliott later escaped with the Wilkes-Barre Fort refugees and survived.

205. There were, at this time, three paths leading eastward from Wyoming. The southernmost was called the Warrior's Path, which went via Fort Allen and along the Lehigh River to the Delaware at Easton. The northernmost went by way of the Lackawanna River at Capouse Meadows, through Cobbs's Gap and the Lackawaxen, to the Delaware and Hudson. The middle path, along which General Sullivan's military road was constructed the next year, led through the Wind Gap to Easton. Most of the refugees were now using the central trail. Many succumbed to exposure, fatigue and excitement, and many became lost and perished. However, the total loss figure is not likely to be the "thousands" which so many accounts say without foundation.

206. That swamp was soon afterward named The Shades of Death and the area bears that same name today. The journals are filled with hundreds of tales of the escape or fate of the refugees from Wyoming.

207. The rock, still visible, is a landmark known today as Queen Esther's Rock.

208. The battle statistics quoted here seem to be reasonably accurate, although close study of numerous documents relating to the battle show an abnormally wide divergence of casualty totals. Colonel John Butler himself claimed to have only 7 men wounded and that 2 of these 7 eventually died of their wounds. Personal accounts of other participants, however, both English and American, as well as a few Indian accounts, indicate that no less than 9 Indians were killed on the battle site and that at least 2 others died later of their wounds. The disparity is especially great in regard to the American casualties, both in British and American sources. Colonel Zebulon Butler said that about 200 were killed. Colonel John Butler said his Indians took 227 scalps (but this does not account for many who were shot while swimming the river and whose bodies were swept away by the current, nor does it include the many wounded who subsequently died). The two most accurate recorders of the conflict in almost every respect — Colonel Nathan Denison and Lieutenant John Jenkins — are probably closest to the truth in their report of the death toll among the Americans. Jenkins states that about 300 were killed, which included 268 privates, 11 ensigns, 13 lieutenants, 7 captains, 2 majors and a colonel (actually a lieutenant colonel, George Dorrance). In addition, it has been alleged that another 200 noncombatants, primarily women, children and the elderly, perished in the wilderness while trying to escape. In some accounts this figure escalates into the thousands, which is nonsense. Even the estimate of 200 appears, under close scrutiny, to be a considerable exaggeration, perhaps deliberately blown out of proportion for propaganda value.

209. The terms of the capitulation were quite generous under the circumstances. The vanquished Americans were to give up their arms, surrender their public stores and remain neutral during the remainder of the war. Continental officers and soldiers were to be delivered up as prisoners of war. Colonel John Butler was to use his influence to prevent the plunder of their property. Butler was unable to effect the latter, but Denison thwarted the surrender of the Continentals. When Denison complained to Butler of the plundering being done by the In-

dians, Butler shook his head regretfully and said, "To tell you the truth, I can do nothing with them."

210. At one point when Colonel Butler and Colonel Denison were discussing the terms of the capitulation, it is reported that an Indian entered the room and demanded to have the hunting frock that Denison was wearing. When Denison resisted, the Indian seized the frock and raised his tomahawk threateningly. Then Denison complied, although it is reported that he first cleverly backed up toward a woman sitting behind him so she could get his purse out of his pocket before he surrendered his clothes. She did so. There is no record of the identity of either the Indian or the woman who helped Denison.

211. Because it was feared that the Continentals, including Zebulon Butler and John Jenkins, as well as those members surviving of Captain Dethick Hewitt's company, would be executed, Colonel Denison had stalled for time and gave those men the opportunity they needed to escape. Colonel Zebulon Butler, as noted, fled eastward with his wife, on horseback, across the mountains to Lehigh. John Jenkins crossed the river and set out to meet and escort to Wyoming the relief column under Captain Simon Spalding. The residue of Captain Hewitt's company fled downriver to the fort at Sunbury.

212. Two very great and long-lasting distortions have come down through history in regard to the Wyoming battle. The fact that Colonel John Butler strove continuously to prevent the Indians from committing atrocities has largely been overlooked and extremely distorted and sensationalized accounts of atrocities have been accepted as truth when they were not. Throughout the frontier the Americans accepted as fact every wild story that sprang up about the Wyoming battle; accepted such stories without reservation or question if they portrayed Butler and the Indians in a bad light. It was declared that he hounded the women and children until they had to flee into the wilderness and that many hundreds, perhaps even as many as two thousand, died of hunger and exposure in that wilderness. That, of course, is complete fabrication. A few of the elderly and sick who panicked and fled did, in fact, succumb, but the number was relatively small. Had they not fled at all but remained in their homes or with Colonel Denison's force, they would undoubtedly have received the same generous treatment that the Wyoming Militia prisoners received. Once the terms of the capitulation were accepted by Denison and his men laid down their arms, every inmate of the fort (except the deserter, Boyd) was permitted to march away unharmed. The stories that whole families were taken aside and butchered are not true. The stories that individuals or groups were herded into houses and then these houses set afire are not true. No evidence exists that any American man, woman or child was killed after the surrender. Colonel Nathan Denison himself reported that Colonel John Butler controlled his Indians and, on his part, abided by the terms of the capitulation without exception. The fall of Wyoming was, in fact, one of those rare cases of warfare involving Indians against whites where the Indians were prevented from perpetrating atrocities after a capitulation. Yet, despite his concern in this direction and his successful efforts to prevent loss of life, Butler quickly became reviled everywhere as a monster who had permitted or even encouraged all manner of atrocities to occur. Instead of being referred to as the Battle of Wyoming Valley, which in fact it was, it became known as the Wyoming Massacre — and is referred to by that name to this day. Colonel John Butler did not receive credit for a significant victory against a military force as he had anticipated he would. Rather, he was scorned and abused by practically everyone, including even his own countrymen, who believed the wild reports of monstrous atrocities having occurred. It was undoubtedly because of this that Colonel John Butler was not knighted and why his own personal reputation was ever afterward tainted by the fallacious acts attributed to him and his Indians.

The second matter of distortion is that the alleged atrocity-committing Indians were led by Thayendanegea — Joseph Brant. Although modern accounts are generally in agreement now that Brant was nowhere near the Wyoming Valley during its destruction on July 3–5, 1778, throughout much of the frontier history of America he is reviled as having been the leader of the Indians on this occasion. In point of fact, he was about 70 miles away at the time. Documents prove that Brant was at his headquarters village of Oquaga and that the day after the Wyoming battle he was en route from Oquaga upstream to Unadilla where, on July 5, he signed a receipt for some corn and other provisions he procured there while Colonel John Butler and his Indians were still destroying Wyoming. As late as July 9, 1778, Brant had still not even heard of the Wyoming destruction, as is evident from a letter he wrote from Oquaga on this date to a Mr. Carr, as follows:

Sir — I understand by the Indians that was at your house last week, that one Smith lives near you and has a little more corn to spare. I shall be much obliged to you if you will be so kind as to get me as much corn as Smith can spare; he sent me five skipples already, of which I am obliged to him and will see him paid, and I would be very glad to see him, and I wish you could send me as many guns as they have, as I know you have no use for them if you have any; as I now mean to fight the cruel Rebels as well as I can. Whatever you will be able to send me you must send by bearer.

I am your sincere friend and
humbler servant,
JOSEPH BRANT
To: MR CARR
P.S. I hear that Cherry Valley people is very bold, and intend to make nothing of us. They call us wild geese, but I known the contrary.   JOS. B.

213. When Pittston Fort was taken and destroyed, Bethiah Jenkins and Elizabeth Murphy, who had earlier taken refuge there from Jenkins Fort, left together for safety eastward. Two days into the wilderness, Elizabeth Murphy had her baby, which Bethiah Jenkins delivered. Together they then had continued eastward to Stroudsburg and arrived safely. Mother and child were doing well. Unfortunately, Private John Murphy had been killed in the Wyoming Valley. The Murphy baby was only one of several babies born in the wilderness during this difficult time. One of the more poignant stories in this genre was that of the Ebenezer Marcy family. Marcy was one of the fortunate ones who survived the battle unharmed and managed to get across the river to his family, which included his pregnant wife and five children. They began their walk eastward at once. They subsisted on berries picked along the way by able children. Mostly, Mrs. Marcy walked along, aiding herself in the difficult task with a staff. The entire family suffered much from hunger. On the evening of July 7, the fourth day of their wilderness trek, Mrs. Marcy gave birth to a baby girl. The next day, with Ebenezer Marcy carrying the newborn child, they all walked another sixteen miles and finally reached some habitation. Marcy bought a used wagon and a broken-down horse so his wife, the baby and the smaller children could now ride. They continued their trek and on the evening of July 11, the eighth day of their journey, they arrived at Fishkill on the Hudson River, 100 miles from the Wyoming Valley. The next day Mrs. Marcy spent the whole day repairing the tattered garments of the children. Toward evening Ebenezer and his wife abruptly realized they had not yet even named the baby and so, to commemorate their narrow escape, they named her Thankful Marcy.
214. Andrustown was on the site of present Springfield, New York.
215. Fort Herkimer had been constructed through the fortification of the residence of the late General Herkimer and was so much better and more defensible an installation than Fort Dayton, the latter had all but been abandoned in favor of the former. Though still occasionally used at this time, Fort Dayton was now in a sad state of disrepair.
216. The two Tories accompanying Brant's party were George House, from what was then Young's Settlement — now Little Lakes — and John Powers, who was himself a resident of Andrustown but who had been treated badly by his neighbors because of his being a Tory. Some accounts state that House and Powers led the Brant party to the area, but this is ridiculous, since Brant knew quite well where Andrustown was and had been there many times. He certainly needed no guide to get there, though he may have been encouraged to hit Andrustown as an act of retaliation against Powers's neighbors.
217. One account, evidently erroneous, states that Mary Reese was just outside her house when the attack occurred and, being thinly clad, stepped back into the house and was reaching under the bed for a skirt to put on when she was tomahawked and scalped.

218. In some accounts the name of the Sheappermans is given as Shireman.
219. Actually ten, but George Staring burned to death a short time later when the houses were fired.
220. Actually the British paid for a *total* of 294 scalps as a result of these forays, accounted for as follows: 22 from Cobleskill by Brant's force; 45 from West Branch Susquehanna by Gucinge's force; 227 from Wyoming Valley by Butler's force. For these scalps, the British government paid $2,940 in gold and silver.
221. Fort Laurens was the first American fort located within the present limits of Ohio. It was situated on the west bank of the Tuscarawas River about a half mile below Bolivia, Ohio, near the north line of Tuscarawas County.
222. The Nanticoke settlement, the site of present Nanticoke, Pennsylvania, was named after a small tribe of Indians who had settled nearby but who had originally lived near the mouth of Choconut Creek (the site of present Endicott, New York), about 14 miles above Owego on the Susquehanna. As with the Tuscarawas, the Nanticokes were from the South and had become wards of the Iroquois but without voice or representation in the Iroquois councils. In return for protection by the Iroquois League, they paid an annual tribute of furs and produce.
223. In the days and weeks to come, numerous other remains of dead were found and these, too, were buried on or near the spot where discovered. The 96 that had been buried in the one mass grave were exhumed and reinterred on July 4, 1832, when a commemorative monument was erected at the site.
224. Actually, the target named was Karightongegh, meaning "The Oak Woods," the Seneca name for Cherry Valley.
225. Pronounced *Sack-uh-yen-ware-rah-don*. Because of the difficulty of pronunciation, the English version of his name is being used.
226. The Tioga here means the Chemung River. In addition to being called the Tioga, it was also not infrequently referred to as the Cayuga.
227. The first scouting party followed the road that has since been supplanted by U.S. 20. The second followed the road toward a tiny community called Beaver Dam, located on Cherry Valley Creek several miles below Cherry Valley. The town no longer exists but it was close to the location of present Rosebloom. The road this latter patrol took is the course of present New York 166, which runs to Milford, 19 miles from Cherry Valley.
228. The old Indian path that came up from the southwest followed the main trail until reaching the vicinity of present Milford. At Milford the main trail — present New York 166 — followed the course of Cherry Valley Creek northeast directly into Cherry Valley. The old Indian trail, however, continued generally to follow the course of the Susquehanna River along its east bank up to the river's source at Otsego Lake. Just east of present Cooperstown the trail followed the Red Creek Valley essentially along the course of the present county road that runs through Whig Corners, Lentsville and Middlefield Center to the area of Stanley School and then, still following the path of this county road, slightly southeast from there to the Cherry Valley Creek. However, unlike the present county road, which joins the present New York 166 a mile and a half southwest of Cherry Valley, the old trail, screened by trees and brush, paralleled the main road on the side of the hills rising westward from Cherry Valley and leading to a marsh west of the town through which runs one of the uppermost brook tributaries of Cherry Valley Creek.
229. Some accounts give his name as Hamble or Hamelin. Hamlin appears to be the most consistently recorded.
230. The Hill brothers, Mohawks who had been raised in Canajoharie, were lifelong friends of Brant and both had been educated, as had Brant, in English schools through the influence of Sir William Johnson. Kanonaron — Little Aaron or Aaron Hill — had been village chief of Oquaga until its recent destruction.
231. Colonel William Stacy's name has also been spelled, frequently and erroneously in past historical writings, Stacey, Stacie and Stacia. Stacy is correct. A native of Salem, Massachusetts, his family engaged in seafaring businesses and William became something of a black sheep because he broke that mold and moved to New Salem in Hampshire County to become a

farmer. At the outbreak of the Revolution he gained the praise and support of his fellows by publicly tearing up his lieutenant's commission from the King and denouncing George III as a tyrant. He was thereupon chosen as captain in his district and led his band to Cambridge to help support the actions against His Majesty's troops. In May, 1776, he became major of Woodbridge's Regiment and on January 1, 1777, he was commissioned lieutenant colonel of Alden's 6th Massachusetts Regiment, the position he had held ever since.

232. Here once again we encounter the carefully nurtured story that Stacy was not killed because he gave a secret Masonic sign to Brant, who allegedly recognized him as a brother Freemason and spared him. Another story says it was later, when Stacy was stripped naked and tied to a post to be killed, that he gave the sign that caused Brant to save his life. There seems to be much more romance than fact to the stories.

233. The destruction of the Wells family brought great infamy to Walter N. Butler, including even the strong criticism of his own father, Colonel John Butler. The Wells family at the time of the massacre was headed by Robert Wells, but his deceased father had been a Tryon County court judge and, as one of the justices of the quorum, had been on intimate terms with Sir William Johnson and his family who, along with Brant in tow, had frequently visited this house. He was also a close acquaintance of Colonel John Butler, who was a fellow judge of the Tryon County courts. The Wells family had not been active in the war, preferring to remain neutral so far as they could. Later, in a conversation relative to them, Colonel John Butler said, "I would have gone miles on my hands and knees to have saved that family, and why my son did not do it, God only knows." Ironically, Walter N. Butler was shot and wounded and then tomahawked and scalped by an Oneida Indian on October 24, 1781, in the last important engagement connected with the Revolutionary War. Pursued after the Battle of Johnstown, he was shot a few miles above Herkimer as he crossed West Canada Creek.

234. There has been some historical dispute over who killed Colonel Alden. Gould's *History of Delaware County* (215–216) states that a Tory by the name of Nathan Foster claimed to have done it, but this proves to be mere braggadocio. William Campbell in his *Annals of Tryon County* simply says it was an Indian who threw the fatal tomahawk and who scalped the colonel; but the most informed source, *The Letters of J. N. Clyde*, and Mr. Clyde's own statement assert that without any doubt it was most certainly Joseph Brant who killed and scalped Colonel Alden in the manner related here.

235. In most cases, the known "mark" of a chief is an absolute protection from danger by other Indians.

236. Because they were Moore's family and he one of their principal enemies here, these two were not released with the other women and children prisoners. Instead, they were taken to Fort Niagara. There, Miss Moore was courted by an English officer and married him at the fort in February, 1780, followed by Joseph Brant being married to his third wife in the same place, by Colonel John Butler.

237. Catherine Wasson Clyde was from Worcester, Massachusetts, where she had been born on April 5, 1737. When she was a young girl, her family had moved near Johnson Hall and she had become closely acquainted with the Johnsons as well as with Joseph Brant.

238. Gilbert Newbury was the same man who had deliberately bashed out the brains of old Richard Fitzpatrick at Tunkhannock on the Susquehanna when Lieutenant John Jenkins was taken captive there almost exactly a year before.

239. One hundred and eighty-two residents escaped death or captivity.

240. The obstinacy, stupidity and pomposity of Colonel Ichabod Alden was undoubtedly the greatest cause for the loss of life and property at Cherry Valley. In the *Memorial of the Life and Times of John Wells*, which was privately printed in 1874, its author said of Colonel Alden: "... *for his plentitude of stupidity he had won the immortal execration of those interested in this distressing period of our history. In a time replete with alarms and dangers and pregnant with warning, deficient in the sagacity and vigilance of a soldier, he proved himself in every way unworthy of the sacred trust reposed in him. Honorable fame is the reward of the brave, but infamy must wait upon the memory of him whose neglect was treachery*" (Lyman C. Draper Manuscript Collection, D-5-F:102–103).

241. No further mention is made in any of the records of Abigail Clyde and it is presumed that she did not survive.
242. Letter of Colonel Jacob Klock to General Edward Hand from Klock's position four miles from Cherry Valley:

> *November 12, 1778*
>
> *Sir — I arrived here with upwards of 300 with an intent to march to Cherry Valley tomorrow by break of day. I have information that the enemy were about the fort at 12 o'clock today, and fired against it with small arms. Colonel Alden is killed and Colonel Stacia [Stacy] and a number of other officers are missing; a great number of the inhabitants, men, women and children, murdered in a most horrible manner — all the buildings burnt. This is the best information I can get at present.*
>
> > *I am, Sir, your humble Servant,*
> > JACOB KLOCK

Lieutenant Colonel William Stacy was taken some 200 miles to the Seneca village of Kanadasaga (the site of present Geneva, New York) and there sentenced to death. Once again the tired old story is given of a life saved by a Masonic sign being given. Allegedly Stacy, under sentence of death, gave the Freemason sign to Brant, who then saved him. Apart from other considerations, Brant held little sway over the Senecas and a prisoner condemned to death in their principal village could not have been saved by Brant.

243. When Shankland and his son reached Fort Alden in the small hours of the morning, almost dead from exhaustion and exposure, they were provided with food, warmth and clothing. Soon after daylight they were back on their feet and went into the woods as Brant had directed them and Shankland called out for his wife. His voice was hoarse from a cold he had developed from the exposure suffered and it did not sound normal. Katy several times heard him call but because his voice sounded so strange she was afraid to reply for fear it was a trick. Four-year-old Nancy, however, said she knew it was her daddy and if he called again she would answer him. Before Katy could tell her not to, Shankland called again and, oddly, this time he called Nancy's name and she responded immediately. They were rescued. Three days later they left for Schenectady and then moved to Bethlehem near Albany. There, Henry and Katy Shankland lived out the rest of their lives and this is where they are buried (account of Nancy Shankland's daughter in the Lyman C. Draper Manuscript Collection, D-5:F-112–112^1–113).

244. Mrs. Samuel Campbell and her four children were taken to the Seneca capital of Kanadasaga by the Senecas. The children were taken from her there and given to different families in different tribes. Mrs. Campbell herself was given to a family to fill a vacancy caused by the death of one family member. It was originally intended that her Kanadasaga residence be only temporary and that she be taken to the village of Chenussio (present Geneseo) the following spring. However, Chief Grahta, principal chief of the Senecas, interceded on her behalf and she was exchanged back to the Americans. When she left, Grahta said to her, "You are now about to return to your home and friends. I rejoice. You live a great way; many days' journey from here. I am an old man and do not know that I shall live to see the end of this war. If I do, when the war is over, I will come and see you." That never occurred.

245. This, of course, was a patently false statement. Oquaga was essentially a Mohawk village under the chieftainship of Kanonaron. It was the headquarters of Brant. Yet it was Brant and Kanonaron and their Mohawks who tried hardest to temper the destruction and death being caused at Cherry Valley by the Tory Rangers and the Senecas under Chief Little Beard. It is also interesting to note that the *Law Reporter* for the State of New York exonerated Brant from any acts of cruelty that occurred at the destruction of Cherry Valley.

CHAPTER V

246. A large number of prisoners, from both Wyoming and Cherry Valley, were being held at Fort Niagara at this time. One report, without seeming foundation, states that Molly Brant, who was also here at this time, demanded the head of Lieutenant Colonel William Stacy of Cherry Valley, but the request was denied.

247. In his letter of April 14, 1779, to the president of congress, George Washington wrote, in this respect: "*This command, according to all present appearances, will probably be of the second, if not of the first, importance of the campaign. The officer conducting it has a flattering prospect of acquiring more credit than can be expected by any other this year; and he has the best reason to hope for success.*"

248. Later on, Washington strongly de-emphasized the taking of prisoners, considering it not really of the value he had originally anticipated it would be. His original plan was to hold them as hostages, which he initially told Sullivan was "the only kind of security to be depended upon for the good behavior of the Six Nations." As time passed, Washington came to realize that having Indian hostages not only might have the reverse effect, it was also unnecessary in view of what the other objectives of the campaign would accomplish.

249. In his diary entry for April 6, 1779, Lieutenant John Jenkins had written: "*Waited on General Washington and had a long interview with him in relation to the Indian country, on the headwaters of the Susquehanna and around the Lakes, and the facilities for an expedition into that country.*"

250. Onondaga was located on the site of present Syracuse, New York. Actually, three towns were known collectively as Onondaga: the first located at the southwest corner of the lake in the area of the present sewage disposal plant where it is crossed by Hiawatha Boulevard; the second and largest in the area of the present State Fairgrounds parking area just south of Lakeview Point; and the third just north of the mouth of Ninemile Creek in the area of present Lakeland.

251. The New York government had long wished to punish the Onondagas for their repeated treachery and cruelty. General Schuyler, with George Washington's approval, directed Brigadier General James Clinton, brother of the governor, to send out a strong detachment for that purpose. It is of interest to note that General Clinton, in giving Van Schaick his orders, also warned him not to let his men violate any Indian women who might be taken. Clinton wrote him: "*Bad as the savages are, they never violate the chastity of any woman, their prisoners. . . .*" After a timely and forceful admonition to Van Schaick, he added, "*It would be well to take measures to prevent a stain on our army.*" While rape of Indian women had occurred in the past and would again in the future, it did not occur now. Van Schaick's detachment went up the Mohawk and made preparations at Fort Schuyler (Stanwix) and then made its lightning strike. The force consisted of the 1st New York Regiment under Van Schaick, with a detachment from the 3rd New York Regiment under Lieutenant Colonel Marinus Willett and Major Roger Cochrane, together with several detached companies from other regiments. The officers of the 1st New York Regiment included its commander, Colonel Goos Van Schaick, Lieutenant Colonel Cornelius Van Dyck, Major John Graham, Captains John H. Wendell, Andrew Finck, Benjamin Hicks, Nicholas Van Rensselaer and Charles Parsons, Captain-Lieutenant Guy Young, Lieutenants Barent S. Salisbury, John C. Ten Broeck, Adiel Sherwood, Peter B. Tearse, Nathaniel Henry, Abraham Hardenbergh and Ephraim Snow, and Ensigns Bartholomew Van Valkenbergh, Christopher Muller, Henry Van Woert, Abraham Ten Eyck, Jacob Henry Wendell, Wilhelmus Ryckman and Benjamin Gilbert.

252. Brigadier General William Maxwell, commander of the Jersey Line, was described as being a gentleman of refinement and an officer of high character, yet little is known of his personal history. It is believed he was born in Ireland, brought to America at an early age by his parents and raised in New Jersey. He entered military service when quite young and at the outbreak of the Revolution was appointed colonel of the 2nd Battalion of the 1st Establishment. He was with General Montgomery in the Canadian Campaign and was promoted to brigadier in October, 1776. He commanded the Jersey Brigade in the battles of Brandywine

and Germantown and in all other battles in which the Jersey Brigade was engaged until he resigned his commission in July, 1780. He died in November, 1798.

253. A lover of fine horses and himself an excellent horseman, Edward Hand was one of George Washington's favorite subordinates. Born in Ireland on the last day of December, 1744, he entered the British army as an ensign and served two years in his regiment in America. He then resigned his commission and settled in Pennsylvania, becoming increasingly disenchanted with British colonial policies. At the onset of the Revolution he entered the Continental Army as a lieutenant colonel. In 1776 he was colonel of a rifle corps and was engaged in the Battles of Long Island and Trenton. He acquired good knowledge of the Indian country and modes of Indian warfare during the summer and autumn of 1777 when he commanded Fort Pitt. George Washington consulted him frequently in regard to the Sullivan campaign while it was in the planning stages and relied heavily on his knowledge and strategic talent. In 1780, Hand succeeded Alexander Scammel as adjutant general of the United States Army. He died in Lancaster County, Pennsylvania, on September 3, 1802, at the age of fifty-seven.

254. Brigadier General Enoch Poor was born in Andover, Massachusetts, on June 21, 1736, but mostly he lived in or claimed as his residence Exeter, New Hampshire. His death was very nearly the cause of an international incident and, as a result, its true cause was held secret for many years. Immediately after the Battle of Lexington, three companies were raised by New Hampshire and Poor was placed in command of their third. On February 21, 1777, he was promoted to brigadier general. His brigade was so closely engaged at the Stillwater Battle that of the total American loss of killed, wounded and missing, two-thirds were from his brigade. He led the attack at the Battle of Saratoga and the vigor of his charge, supported by Colonel Morgan, broke the British line. In 1780, two brigades of light infantry chosen from the whole army were formed and, on recommendation of General Lafayette, Poor was given command of one of them. He was extremely popular and his death on September 9, 1780, at a camp in Hackensack, New Jersey, was attributed to "a fever" when in actuality he was killed in a duel with a French officer. However, so beloved was he that it was felt if it were known that he was killed by a French officer, a tide of resentment would rise against the French allies of the United States to the detriment of the war effort. Not until after the Revolution was the true cause of his death brought to light.

255. Corduroy roads were so called because of their riblike structure. In areas where ordinary roadbuilding was impossible due to natural conditions of bogginess, shifting earth, etc., felled trees would be trimmed of branches and their trunks laid side by side (perpendicular to the flow of traffic) to form a substantial base for wheeled vehicles. The jolting and jarring caused in traversing such a road was terrible, but bone-shaking as it was, in many cases this was the only type of road an army could build by which to maintain its supply and communication lines to the front.

256. James Clinton, son of Colonel Charles Clinton, was born in Orange County, New York, on August 9, 1736. At the age of twenty he was an officer in the French and Indian War under General Bradstreet and distinguished himself at the capture of Fort Frontenac. He commanded the troops raised in Orange and Ulster Counties, New York, in 1763, to defend the frontiers from Indian ravages. He was a colonel under General Montgomery in the invasion of Canada in 1775. He was promoted to brigadier general on his fortieth birthday, August 9, 1776. He was commander of Fort Clinton when it was attacked by British Sir Henry Clinton in October, 1777. At this same time his brother George, who soon became New York's governor, was commanding at Fort Montgomery. Both forts were carried by storm after a spirited defense and General Clinton was said to be last to leave the works. During most of 1778 he was stationed at West Point. His occupation as engineer and surveyor was largely responsible for the remarkable action he took at Lake Otsego during the Sullivan Campaign in 1779. He was present at both the siege of Yorktown and the surrender of Cornwallis. Later he held civil positions in the New York State Legislature and was a member of the New York State Constitutional Convention. He was also one of the original members of the Society of Cincinnatus. The father of DeWitt Clinton, who also became governor of New York, James Clinton died on December 22, 1812, at Little Britain, Orange County, New York.

257. That trail is presently followed from Easton northward through Stockertown and Belfast to Wind Gap, then to Bartonsville.

258. That trail passes through the present townships of Pocono, Tunkhanna, Tobyhanna, Buck, Bear Creek and Wyoming. Much of it is still in use and is known as the Old Sullivan Trail.

259. Meaning Newtown on the Chemung River.

260. Sullivan's reference here is to the verbal instructions he had received from Washington to time his movements so that he could destroy the enemy's crops before they could be harvested, but also to be late enough so there was no time to replant. The commander in chief also had instructed Sullivan not to hasten too much his march from Easton until it was known what the Comte Charles d'Estaing, then in the West Indies, would do. Washington said he expected d'Estaing to sail north very soon and he wanted to cooperate with him in striking a particularly decisive blow to the enemy.

261. Colonel Zebulon Butler, present commander of the rebuilt Wilkes-Barre Fort.

262. Colonel John Butler of the British Rangers.

263. The bateaux were the workhorses of river traffic and extremely important in frontier movement of men and supplies. They could be constructed in varying sizes, but the individual bateau was of a basically fundamental design — a flat-bottomed, shallow-drafted boat with a raked bow and stern and a rockered interior bottom for added strength. The bateau was not only a very stable craft, it was strong enough to take severe poundings when colliding with rocks and other obstructions in rapids or treacherous river passages. Its stability and carrying capacity were its great attributes. Its liabilities included its poor maneuverability and its considerable weight when portages had to be made.

264. The terminus of this route was 1¾ miles south of present Springfield Center at a firm dry area of shoreline at the northeastern base of the 1,800-foot hill presently known as Mount Wellington.

265. The other two companies of Morgan's Partisan Corps that were detached under Major Parr at this time were those of Captain Gabriel Long of Maryland and Captain Michael Simpson of Pennsylvania.

266. Upon learning of the execution, General Schuyler commended General Clinton, writing to him: *"In executing Hare, you have rid the State of the greatest villain in it."*

267. The site of Cooperstown, New York.

268. Sullivan, at Easton, already had with him a few of the Stockbridge Indians under Chief Jehoiakim.

269. That total includes noncombatant bateaumen.

270. This passage is 1½ miles north of the present town of Wind Gap, Pennsylvania, west of Stroudsburg.

271. Larned's Tavern — not Learns's — was the last house on the frontier and from this point the army moved mostly westward. The camp at this last "civilized" spot was near the grounds of present Grace Church on the banks of Pocono Creek, about a half mile north of present Tannersville, Pennsylvania.

272. In a letter to Sullivan on June 21, George Washington wrote: *"A body of troops under the command of Lieut. Col. Pawling will still be ready for the proposed co-operation. Two hundred of these being engaged for a more permanent service, affecting the first object, will meet General Clinton at Onoquaga [Oquaga] and proceed with him to join you. . . . Lieut. Colo. Pawling is a very good officer."* Pawling turned out to be not quite as good as Washington had believed, as was indicated by his subsequent failure without good cause to make the rendezvous.

273. Lieutenant Colonel Henry Dearborn, the youngest regimental commander in Sullivan's army, was at this time commanding the 3rd New Hampshire (Scammel's) Regiment. At twenty-eight he was a very dashing and energetic officer with an impressive background already in military matters. Born in Hampton, New Hampshire, in March, 1751, he had studied medicine and settled in Nottingham, New Hampshire. Unmarried and quite handsome, he was considered an especially eligible bachelor and was the target of many an otherwise demure young lady. In 1774–75 he started drilling local townsmen in military arts and after Lexington became a captain in Stark's Regiment. He was a captain at the Battle of Bunker

Hill and took part in Arnold's 1775 campaign to Quebec, where he was taken prisoner. He was exchanged early in 1779 and appointed major of Scammel's Regiment. In both battles of Saratoga he commanded separate battalions and received special commendation from General Gates. At Monmouth he distinguished himself and the regiment by leading a gallant charge. When Colonel Scammel became acting adjutant general of the army in 1779, Dearborn was placed in command of the regiment and was its leader at the time of the Sullivan Campaign. Dearborn was at the siege of Yorktown in 1781 and afterward on garrison duty at Saratoga and West Point until 1784. He served two years in Congress and was for eight years Secretary of War under President Thomas Jefferson. In the War of 1812 he was senior major general of the army. From 1822 to 1824 he was minister to Portugal. He died at the age of seventy-eight in Roxbury, Massachusetts, June 6, 1829.

274. Present Port Jervis, New York.

275. That ambush took place at Minisink Ford, New York, in then Orange County, now Sullivan County. This is almost directly across the river from present Lackawaxen, Pennsylvania, at the mouth of the Lackawaxen River. So terrified were the inhabitants at the time and so difficult to get to was the hill upon which the ambush took place that the bodies of the dead went uncollected and unclaimed for an incredible forty-three years! Finally, in April, 1822, the bones were collected by Henry W. Denton and Daniel and Benjamin Dunning, along with one of the few survivors of the battle, Jonathan Bailey. These remains were then interred with proper ceremonies at Goshen, New York, in present Orange County. A Minisink Battlefield Memorial now exists on a site where part of the battle took place. The line of the mile-long funeral procession at that time was led by West Point cadets.

276. As early as July 9 the lake level had risen two feet. By late July the level was up three feet. On July 9 Clinton had written to his brother, Governor George Clinton: "*I have thrown a dam across the outlet, which I conceive will be of infinite importance, as it has raised the lake at least two feet, by which the boats may be taken down with less danger than otherwise, although from the intricate winding of the channel, I expect to meet some difficulties on the way.*" Had not Clinton early on seen the advisability of constructing the dam, it would have taken his force much longer to reach Sullivan's and with considerably fewer supplies. That could have resulted in an aborted campaign or a resounding defeat.

277. The artillery, all of it brass, consisted of two six-pounders, four three-pounders, two five-and-one-half-inch howitzers, and a small cohorn mounted on a wooden block with two handles for hand carrying when necessary. This latter piece had legs built under it by Proctor and was placed in the bow of one of the lead boats to precede the fleet. Because it tended to jump backward when fired, Proctor had dubbed it "The Grasshopper."

278. The Lackawanna River flows into the Susquehanna from the northeast, entering at present Upper Pittston, opposite the southern tip of Scovell Island and the northern edge of West Pittston. The name of the river derives from the Delaware Indian name for it, Lechau-Hanneck, signifying the forks of a river or stream. The Iroquois tribes referred to this river as Hazirok. Long before the Wyoming Valley settlements existed, an Indian town named Adjouquay existed on the site of where Pittston is now located, just a mile below the mouth of the Lackawanna.

279. Sergeant Thomas Roberts, a resident of Middletown Point, Monmouth County, New Jersey, was a shqemaker by trade. For almost a hundred years after the Sullivan campaign his journal disappeared from view. Then it reappeared, much faded and almost illegible, at a Nassau Street bookstall in New York City. It was purchased and subsequently presented to the New-York Historical Society on February 10, 1886, by Alexander Campbell.

280. Falling Springs originates from never-failing springs atop the mountain presently known as Campbell Ledge. Flowing from an elevation of 1,200 feet at the summit, it drops in a cascade. One of the three falls is fully 90 feet. The Susquehanna at this point is at an elevation of 535 feet.

281. Present Gardner Creek, running between the present Ransom-Newton State Hospital and the village of Ransom.

282. Quilutimunk is an Indian word that translates literally to "We came unawares upon them."

Tradition has it that in the dim past Indian forces fought one another here. The Sullivan campsite was about a half mile above the present community of Wyoanna. It was evidently then a beautiful area. Hubley wrote of it in his journal: *"Quilutimunk is a good spot of ground situate on the river; fine, open and clear; quantity, about 1,200 acres; soil very rich, timber fine, grass in abundance, and contains several exceedingly fine springs."* It is significant of our "progress" that this area is now an extensive gravel pit.

283. This crossing was made opposite the present community of West Falls.

284. Those four small mountains in succession were those presently known as Post Hill, Greenwood Hill, Osterhout Mountain and Avery Mountain.

285. Sullivan's camp this night of August 3, 1779, was on the site of present Tunkhannock, Pennsylvania.

286. The hill after Teague's Creek was Russell Hill, with the Warrior's Path after Russell's Hill being the same route as present U.S. 6 past Florey Knob, through present Meshoppen, then along the severe cut on the side of Blue Ridge Mountain overlooking the Susquehanna and finally to the night's campsite near the mouth of present Black Walnut Creek.

287. Frederick Vanderlip had been the first settler above the Lackawanna. At the outbreak of hostilities between Britain and her American colonies, he had remained loyal to the King and, as a Tory, was forced to flee his homestead. He never returned and afterward died in Canada.

288. The line of march on August 5 to Wyalusing is over present Doolittle Hill, which divides Black Walnut from Skinner's Eddy (also known as DePews, in honor of John DePew, pre–Revolutionary War settler here). The army crossed Tuscarora Creek at its mouth through the river plain area of present Laceyville and then went over Indian Hill — so named because of the slight skirmish had there with the Indians by Colonel Hartley on his return from the expedition against Tioga the preceding fall. A human skull was found hung on a bush there as if to mock or warn them. The army's march then followed the route of present U.S. 6 again a little way on Tuscarora Creek and all the way into Wyalusing.

289. Nathan Kingsley, a fairly prominent settler, had been captured by the Indians near Wyoming in October, 1777, and taken prisoner to Canada. He eventually escaped and reached General Schuyler at Saratoga with some important intelligence on July 24, 1779. He was afterward a justice of the Quorum.

290. The Wyalusing camp was at the site of present Wyalusing in Bradford County, Pennsylvania. Its history seems to stretch into remote antiquity. In *Cammerhoff's Journal*, 1750, it is written:

Passing up the river we came to a place called by the Indians, Gohontoto, which is Wyalusing. Here, they tell us, in early times was an Indian town, traces of which are still noticeable; e.g., corn pits, &c., inhabited by a distinct nation (neither Iroquois nor Delaware) who spoke a peculiar language and were called Tehotitachase; against these the Five Nations warred, and rooted them out. The Cayugas for a time held a number of them, but the nation and their language are now exterminated and extinct. This war, said the Indian, fell in the time when the Indians fought in battles with bows and arrows, before they had guns and rifles.

Wyalusing was also the site of the Friedenshutten Moravian Mission, which was established in 1765 and abandoned in 1772. The Indian town of Gohontoto was located above present Wyalusing, the Moravian town below. The most considerable white settlement on the Susquehanna above Wyoming, Wyalusing was destroyed by Indians and Tories in the winter of 1777–78.

291. The hill crossed was present Vaughan Hill and the army's route took them through present Limehill. They encountered the river again at present Rummerfield (the unnamed creek now Rummerfield Creek) and camped at the site of the present village of Standing Stone.

292. Approximately one mile south of present Wysox, Pennsylvania, near where U.S. 6 crosses the creek.

293. Present Laning Creek. Their route took them essentially along the course of present Hillside Drive and Fifth Avenue at the base of the hill to avoid the swamp that was covering the

whole flat from about the area of present Central School in Wysox to East Towanda. They then turned up present Laning Creek along the course of what is now Laning Creek Road and followed it to its source at Black Lake.

294. That creek is present Sugar Creek and the hill is the one that overlooks the present small community of Quarry Glen.

295. A messenger was sent to inform Colonel Proctor's boatmen coming up below and those cattle that were killed in the fall were gathered up and dressed for their meat.

296. The creek bears the same name today. On the west shore of the Susquehanna at this point, as previously noted, was where the village of Sheshaquin had been located, which had been established about 1765 by Chief Eghobund, the Seneca, husband of Queen Esther. That village had been destroyed by Colonel Hartley the previous year. There is a present village of Sheshaquin on the east bank of the Susquehanna, just north of Deer Lick Creek.

297. This area of islands was just opposite the present city of Towanda, Pennsylvania.

298. The area of Newtychanning and the town itself have an interesting history. The exact location of the village was on the side of the slight rise of land just west of present Sugar Creek where present York Avenue, U.S. 6 and U.S. 220 cross it. There is some discrepancy as to its size. Colonel Proctor said it had about 30 houses; Gifford himself and Dr. Campfield said 28, and Sullivan said 22. Canfield said it had been built the preceding year and had "fifteen to twenty houses." This village was approximately on the site of an earlier village called Oscalui, which had been built by a tribe called the Carantouannais about the year 1600. It was called Ogehage on Captain Hendricksen's map of 1616. At odds with the Iroquois League, the Carantouannais were driven out by the Five Nations prior to 1650 and the village destroyed. Tradition has it there was a silver mine in the area, but its location has never been discovered.

299. The reinforcement crossed at the encampment and moved directly across the river to join Gifford at the site of present Ulster, Pennsylvania, where the original village of Sheshaquin had been until its destruction the previous fall by Colonel Hartley.

300. The Indian path followed by the west bank detachment was essentially the route of present U.S. 220 and ran at that time from Sheshaquin to Queen Esther's Town.

301. The place is today a flood plain called Tioga Point, directly south of the city of Athens, Pennsylvania. The name Tioga derives from the Iroquois Ta-ye-o-ga which translated by Red Jacket was "the point of land where the waters meet," but which more literally translated is "an interval or anything between two other things." The Red Jacket interpretation, of course, means that the addition of Point after Tioga is superfluous. The Oneidas called this place Te-ah-o-ge, the Mohawks called it Te-yo-ge-ga, and the Cayugas called it Da-a-o-ga. Tioga had been, from time immemorial, one of the most strategic points of the Iroquois League. Zeisberger passed through here in 1750 and said that "at Tioga, or The Gate, Six Nations Indians were stationed for the purpose of ascertaining the character of all persons who crossed over into their country, and that whoever entered their territory by any other way than through the Gate, or by way of the Mohawk, was suspected by them of evil purpose and treated as a spy or enemy." The earliest known account of the place is found in Champlain, who sent out one of his interpreters, named Steven Brulé, in 1615, to arrange with the Carantouannais for a force of 500 warriors to cooperate with him in an attack on the Onondaga stronghold, then located on the site of the subsequent town of Fenner in Madison County, New York. Brulé, with a small party of Hurons, passed through the country of the Five Nations to the great town of Carantouan, containing over eight hundred warriors, then located on the so-called Spanish Hill near Waverly. Brulé returned to Carantouan after the expedition and the next year, 1616, went down the Susquehanna to the sea where he "found many nations that are powerful and warlike."

302. Chemung was located only a half mile west of the present village of Chemung, New York. The reasons for its abandonment by the Indians are not clear, but thought attributable to the attack the preceding autumn by Colonel Hartley that had resulted in the destruction of Tioga and Queen Esther's Town. The new village of Chemung had been relocated approximately two miles farther upriver on the north bank of the Chemung and was more protected from

downstream attack than Old Chemung because of the very large hill between the two. This hill ran steeply down to the river, 800 feet below, from its 1,654-foot summit. This hill, the Indians believed, would impede the progress of an army. The present name of this hill is Narrow Hill.

303. A gill is one-quarter of a pint.

304. At this point the army had reached the base of the hill on the top of which is the present municipal golf course of Waverly, New York, only a few hundred yards above the New York–Pennsylvania border. The path hereupon began following what is basically the route of Chemung Street, New York Route 17.

305. Here the path was still following the trace of present New York Route 17 — Chemung Street — on the side of the very steep mountain presently called Glory Hill, on the summit of which is located St. John of the Cross Monastery. This precipitous slope is almost a thousand feet from summit to riverbank.

306. The first creek crossed here was Dry Brook; the second was Wynkoop Creek, at the southeastern edge of the present town of Chemung, New York.

307. This was present Narrow Hill and Old Chemung, the Indian village, was located at about the same site now occupied by the oval track off Neason Road at the western edge of present Chemung, New York.

308. Known locally as the Hogback at present, just a short distance east of present Hoffman Hollow Road, 2½ miles southeast of the Newtown Monument.

309. Oddly, in the multitude of accounts and official reports of this incident, the six men who were killed instantly are never referred to by name. Their identity remains unknown. The only private of the six who were wounded whose name is known is John McDowell, who cited this wound through his body in his petition to Pennsylvania for a pension, record of which is in *Pennsylvania Archives XIV*.

310. Franklin, commander of the thirty-five-man Salem and Huntington Company of the Wyoming Militia, was a rather remarkable man of northern Pennsylvania. Among the early immigrants to Wyoming, he was made captain of the militia raised by order of Congress on March 16, 1778. He survived this wound received at Chemung and was afterward a justice of the peace. Following his recovery, he reentered the service and continued therein until the close of the war. In land controversies, he espoused the Connecticut side with such fervor that he was arrested for high treason but released without trial after being confined for thirteen months. In 1792 he was elected high sheriff of Luzerne County, Pennsylvania, and held this post for three years. After that he was a member of the assembly, 1795–1805. He finally settled at Athens (Tioga), Pennsylvania, where he died at home March 1, 1831, at the age of eighty-two.

Carbury, commander of the 8th Company, 11th Pennsylvania, had been promoted from lieutenant the preceding November 30. He was in command of a troop of light horse that had been dismounted by General Sullivan. Surviving his wound, he retired from the service in January, 1781. He was concerned in the riot of soldiers of the Pennsylvania Line and fled to Maryland, where he disappeared from record.

Of the 7th Company, 11th Pennsylvania, William Huston was commissioned an ensign, but was at this time doing duty as adjutant, with rank and pay of lieutenant, to which he was promoted the following February 24.

311. There is no record of the Indian casualties except for guesses made by participants, such guesses being based on blood found on the ground. All Indian wounded (and dead, if any) were carried off in their retreat. Some accounts say, without foundation, three Indians were killed and a few wounded. An example of the statistical conclusions reached by some, most likely incorrect, is seen in a typical one by an officer of the campaign who wrote in his journal on August 15: "*I forgot to mention the supposed loss of the enemy in the battle on Friday. A jacket of one of them was picked up, bloody and shot through. Also a hat. One or two were seen to fall and afterwards to be carried off by the others. From these circumstances it is imagined they had seven or eight killed and wounded.*"

312. Later, there is another diary entry of a nature very similar to this, describing in almost the

same way a strange icon found in another village. Unfortunately, with such an intriguing entry, no further description or explanation is given anywhere in this journal or any of the others.

313. A very puzzling and intriguing journal entry about this incident was penned that night by one of the most accurate and informative of journal-keepers of this campaign, Major Jeremiah Fogg, who wrote: *"One man was killed and several wounded, but it is uncertain whether by the enemy or by our own men, as the fire was very irregular."* No other journal account of the incident carries any inference that the Americans may have been shot by their own people.

314. The wounded, including Carbury, Franklin and Huston, remained at Tioga until August 28, when they were taken by boat to Wyoming where they could receive somewhat better care.

315. All seven dead were buried in a common grave the next morning, with the Reverend William Rogers officiating.

316. Lieutenant John Jenkins makes an error in his journal for this date when he says, *"The Indians killed three men, scalped young Elliott and wounded another."*

317. Present Oaks Creek.

318. This village was located three miles below the site of the present city of Oneonta in Otsego County, New York. There is a present village called Otego downstream approximately three miles from the mouth of Otego Creek, but this village is not the site of the Indian village of that name.

319. This camp was on the U-curve of the Susquehanna where it swings around the southernmost bluffs of the ridge presently known as Calder Hill, a mile above present Otego.

320. Some accounts called the settlement Albout. The creek that empties into the Susquehanna below the site is presently called Ouleout Creek. Most of the Scottish settlers went to Canada at the beginning of the war, but those few who remained were more in sympathy with the British than with the Americans.

321. It should be noted that the Indian village of Unadilla was not located on the site of present Unadilla, New York, but rather five miles farther down the Susquehanna at the site of present Sidney, New York, where the Unadilla enters from the north. It was situated on both sides of the river at that point.

322. Conihunto was located on the west bank of the Susquehanna just a mile below the center of present Afton, New York, almost directly opposite the T-intersection of present Ives Hill Road with State Route 41 on the east side of the river.

323. The similarity in name between Conihunto and Gunna Gunter is probably because both stem from the same Indian root. Gunna Gunter Island was the largest and farthest downstream of the island cluster, a mile and three-quarters northwest of the present community of Bettsburg, Chenango County, New York.

324. Approximately the site of present Ouaquaga, New York.

325. Some of the passenger pigeon flocks in America at this time were comprised of more than five million birds each and they did, indeed, have the ability to darken the skies as they flew. Hunting pressure and diminishing habitat caused this lovely bird to become extinct, the last wild bird being killed in 1900 and the last captive bird — Martha — dying in the Cincinnati Zoological Gardens in 1914. The story of that bird and its extinction are told in the author's book *The Silent Sky.*

326. It is not known what delayed Lieutenant Colonel William Pawling's detachment or when he actually arrived at the Oquaga rendezvous. The only mention in this context is in a letter from George Washington to General Sullivan dated September 3, 1779, in which the commanding general wrote: *"Colo. Pawling, not having been able to reach Anaquaga [Oquaga] at the appointed time, and upon his arrival there finding that General Clinton had passed by, has returned to the settlement [Wawasing] with the men under his command, which were about two hundred."*

327. The site of present Windsor in Broome County, New York.

328. Ingaren was located at approximately the site of present Great Bend, Susquehanna County, Pennsylvania, only a few miles below the New York border.

329. The site of present Binghamton, New York, but many years previously of a Tuscarora village

called Oochenang — or sometimes Oochanang-goah — which was supposedly destroyed by a flood and never rebuilt.

330. Also called Chenango and Zeninge, Otsiningo was a Tuscarora village of twenty fairly substantial buildings located about midway between present Port Dickinson and Chenango Bridge on the west side of the river. A number of past accounts have incorrectly located the site of Otsiningo as Binghamton.

331. That camp was located approximately at the grounds of the present St. Patrick's Cemetery on the riverbank in Binghamton, opposite present Crocker Island.

332. Another name both these villages went by is Chuggnut. The smaller of the two was located on the east bank of the Susquehanna at the mouth of Choconut Creek near present Vestal, New York. The second, three miles upstream, was located at approximately the foot of present Hooper Road in Endwell, New York. Both villages had substantial grain and vegetable crops, which were also destroyed.

333. Owego was located on Owego Creek about a mile above its junction with the Susquehanna, near the present city of Owego in Tioga County, New York. General Poor had camped at this same place on his way upstream on August 17.

334. This was the site of some ancient Indian ruins that were still vaguely visible at the time Clinton and Poor stopped here but that have since disappeared. Located at the site of present Barton, New York, on the north bank of the Susquehanna, it was also referred to in some of the journals by the name of Red Brook. This may have been because present Ellis Brook, which runs through Barton, is sometimes stained reddish from mud. It was also called Mauckatawangum by Captain Jenkins and Mawkautowouguh by Major Fogg.

CHAPTER VI

335. They consisted of Captain McDonald, a sergeant, a corporal and twelve privates. Some accounts have placed either or both Colonel Guy Johnson and Sir John Johnson at the battle, but this is not supported by any evidence, and there is much evidence that discounts it. Both Johnsons were out of touch by this time with the mainstream of Indian matters, although Sir John was still, at this time, in title, commander of the Royal Greens. Colonel Guy Johnson soon after this time went to London, where he finally died on March 5, 1788, broken in health, spirit and estate. Sir John Johnson died at the age of eighty-eight in 1830.

336. Present Sullivan Hill.

337. Actually, at the time of the battle, the number was about 1,250.

338. Two six-pounders, four three-pounders, one 8-inch howitzer, one 5½-inch howitzer, plus the cohorn, were taken. Two six-pounders were left with the garrison to help defend Fort Sullivan. A number of the officers considered it ludicrous to attempt to take along nine such pieces of artillery. Major Fogg wrote of this: *". . . the army got in motion toward Kanadasaga with nine pieces of artillery and their appendages; the transportation of which, to Genesee, appears to the army in general as impractical and absurd as an attempt to level the Allegheny Mountains."*

339. Colonel Shreve's subordinate company commanders at Fort Sullivan were to include Captains Isaiah Wools of the artillery, George Tudor of the 4th Pennsylvania, John Myers of the 2nd New Jersey, Benjamin Weatherby of Spencer's New Jersey, Moody Dustin of the 1st New Hampshire, Amos Morrell of the 1st New Hampshire, Nathaniel Norton of the 4th New York, Luke Day of the 6th Massachusetts, and John McEwen of Spencer's New Jersey.

340. It was this march that alerted the Indians spying from nearby that the army was on its way upstream again and the relay system of runners set out to warn Brant.

341. The camp was close to the river on the line of the present western terminus of Broad Street in Waverly, New York, just north of Spanish Hill.

342. That defile was, again, Glory Hill, northwest of present Waverly, atop which is located the monastery of St. John of the Cross.

343. The advance party under Lieutenant Thomas Boyd was encountering Baldwin Creek at the site of the present community of Lowman, directly across the river and about a mile north of present Wellsburg, New York.

344. The line of fortifications the Brant force had erected was at about the 950-foot level of present Sullivan Hill, running from its closest point to the river, just below Newtown, southeastward in a great U-shape to the Lowman area, then following the Baldwin Creek valley upward about a mile. A small observation party was on the summit of the hill, where the present monument is located. A larger observation party was near the summit of the hill almost exactly opposite Sullivan Hill, on the east side of the creek a mile distant.

345. Present New York Route 17.

346. At this time the main army had advanced to about the point of the present gravel pit one-half mile west of Roberts Hollow Road on the north side of New York 17.

347. The route of present New York 17.

348. A British account of the battle says, without confirmation, that a further stand and skirmish occurred above Newtown when Colonel Butler stood his ground and tried to stop Poor, Clinton and Ogden, but in vain. However, no details of this are given in the British account and nothing even remotely like it is suggested by any of the journals or reports of the Americans involved, making the whole thing seem implausible. Additionally, the British and Indians were pretty much in a state of terror at this time, many having lost their weapons and goods, and it is most unlikely that with such frightened and ill-equipped forces, Butler would have made any attempt to stand against four full regiments and a large detachment.

349. The American dead include the mortally wounded who later died. Those eleven Americans were: Captain John Combs of Spencer's New Jersey Regiment; Captain Elijah Clayes of the 2nd New Hampshire; Lieutenant Nathanial McCauley of the 1st New Hampshire, whose leg was amputated the night of the battle and who died before morning; Ensign Thomas Callis; Sergeant Oliver Thurston; Corporal Adam Hunter; Private Abner Dearborn; Private Joshua Mitchell; Private Sylvester Wilkins; plus two unnamed privates.

350. Allegedly, in one account, Indians were seen dumping bodies of their dead in the river, which they would never do, and, in another account, that nineteen more Indian bodies were discovered hidden in the bushes, which was a fabrication. Brant himself said twelve Indians were killed.

351. The name Kanawaholla signifies A-Head-Stuck-On-a-Pole. Red Jacket referred to this town as Canaweola. A variety of English spellings has been associated with the name of this town. Most of the men in Sullivan's army who were keeping journals referred to it as Knaw-a-holee. Some spelled it Kanawaloholla or Knawaholla. The town was located at the site of present Elmira, New York, just above the junction of Newtown Creek on the east edge of town with the Chemung River where it turns westward, directly above Jones Island, approximately on the site of East Water Street (New York 352), about 500 yards east of its junction with New York 17.

352. Teaoga was located near present Painted Post, New York.

353. That creek was the stream presently known as Seeley Creek, which empties into the Chemung about three miles southeast of present Elmira.

354. This village was referred to by Butler as Caracolina and was located at approximately the site where New York 427 from Wellsburg to Elmira crosses Seeley Creek.

355. These wounded and sick reached Wyoming on September 3.

356. Of the American casualties of 11 dead and 32 wounded, all but four had been of Colonel Reid's regiment in General Poor's brigade.

357. A few of the officers rather strongly criticized this morning and evening cannon firing by Sullivan from this point on in the campaign as being "unsoldierly and unwise." However, there is some evidence that indicates that Sullivan instituted this practice on direct orders of George Washington, whose chief concern was not in fighting other battles but in destroying crops and villages and thus, in the process, destroying the Indians' ability for waging any further warfare against the frontier.

358. This village, on the east bank of the Chemung, was located a mile above the mouth of Seeley Creek, opposite present Big Island.

359. Colonel Elias Dayton should not be confused with General Sullivan's aide-de-camp, Captain Jonathan Dayton. Elias Dayton was born in Elizabethtown, New Jersey, in 1735. In 1774 he represented Elizabethtown in the Committee of Safety. In 1775 he was involved in the capture of a British prison ship off the Jersey coast. A prominent Freemason and first president of the Society of Cincinnati of New Jersey, he was made colonel of the 3rd Jersey Battalion on February 9, 1776, and subsequently of the 3rd Regiment. He commanded the Jersey Brigade as of July 25, 1780, following the death of General Maxwell. He was promoted to brigadier general on January 7, 1783. Said to have cool judgment and sound discretion, he died in Philadelphia in June, 1807, at the age of seventy-two.

360. Shequaga meant The-Place-with-the-Smell-of-Onions and this was essentially the same name as that of another Indian village hundreds of miles to the west at the foot of Lake Michigan — a name that gradually became corrupted to Chicago.

361. This campsite was on the very ground occupied at present by the courthouse and post office of the city of Horseheads, Chemung County, New York.

362. The creek was present Sing Sing Creek, which they encountered about a mile above present Harris Mill Manor.

363. The village of Runonvea was located on the flat ground just east of present Carpenter Road, a mile southeast of present Big Flats village. It was at the junction of present Cuthrie Run with Sing Sing Creek.

364. The creek bears the same name today.

365. It was a place that would have been exceptional for the Indians to have ambushed the army; the place where Brant would have liked to have done so; a place where a skilled handful could have held off hundreds and where a force the size of Brant's could possibly have annihilated the army. Practically everyone was aware of this and it increased the apprehension and frustration of the day. Even such of those as unskilled in military tactics as Dr. Campfield marveled at the situation and its deadly potential. He wrote: "*The Indians and Tories under Butler, certainly, are destitute of the spirit of soldiers, or they would not suffer us to progress without any resistance. I am sure a few men of spirit might here exceedingly retard our movement.*"

366. Hand's advance broke free of the swamp at approximately the point where present Wigwam Road meets present New York 14, the Sullivan Trail, one mile south of the center of present Montour Falls. It was as they were between the present Cook Cemetery and Catherine Creek that they were seen by the Indian rear guard, which then fled.

367. With his usual flair for descriptive writing, Major Jeremiah Fogg wrote in his journal that night:

> Early this morning we found in a bark hut an awful object and upon examination it appeared to be Madame Sacho, one of the Tuscarora [actually Cayuga] tribe, whose silvered locks, wrinkled face, dim eyes and curvitude of body denoted her to be a full-blooded antideluvian hag!

368. Catherine Montour was the daughter of French Margaret and the granddaughter of Madame Montour, who was aged and blind in 1749 and probably died prior to 1752. Catherine's husband was Thomas Hudson, a Seneca chief, whose Indian name was Telenemut. She had a son named Amochol who was living in Salem, Massachusetts, in 1788 and, in a report dated 1779, it is stated that she had two daughters, but they are not identified. Catherine was the sister of Queen Esther, who was killed at the Battle of Newtown. There was also another sister, named Mary, who became the wife of John Cook, who settled first on the Allegheny and then later on the Ohio. John Cook was a Seneca chief named Kanaghragait, who was sometimes called White Mingo by frontiersmen. He died at Fort Wayne in 1790. Catherine had a son, Roland, and nephews John and Andrew. Roland married the daughter of the then principal chief of the Senecas, Grahta, who was also called Siangorachti. Catherine never returned to Shequaga but remained in Canada and in 1791 it was reported that she was living "over the lake, not far from Niagara." It is not recorded where or when she died.

369. Colonel Tusten was killed at the Battle of Minisink.

370. Kanadasaga was located on the western edge of present Geneva, New York, a mile and a half

west of City Hall, where present Castle Creek (then Kanadasaga Creek) is crossed by present Pre-emption Road on the grounds of the New York State Agricultural Experiment Station. The town was located on both sides of the creek in this area. Though Kanadasaga was sometimes referred to as the Seneca Castle, meaning capital, it should not be confused with the present town of Seneca Castle, located 4½ miles west of the Kanadasaga site, on Flint River.

371. Grahta was also known as Old Smoke, Old King, Guyanguahta, Siangorachti, and King of Kanadasaga.

372. At present Hector Falls Point, Schuyler County, New York.

373. The stream was present Sawmill Creek and the delta is now known as Peach Orchard Point.

374. Present Valois Point at Valois, New York.

375. This was present Indian Creek just north of the Willard State Hospital grounds at Willard, Seneca County, New York.

376. Kendaia (sometimes Kaendae) was located on both sides of a stream at the northern boundary of the U.S. Naval Training Station just south of Pontius Point in Seneca County, New York. Situated in what is present Romulus Township, Lot 79, it should not be confused with the present community of Kendaia, which is in the same area but a mile and a half inland from the lake.

377. Swah-ya-wanna was located near the site of present McDuffie Town, two miles northeast of Romulus, New York.

378. This site was where present U.S. 20 and New York 5 and the New York Central Railroad cross the brook, approximately one-half mile east and slightly north of the city hall of Geneva, New York.

379. Major Fogg was disgusted by the ridiculousness of the idea of catching the Indians by surprise. As he later, rather caustically, wrote in his journal:

Notwithstanding the occult and evasive qualities of the savages with which our general must before this time have been acquainted, he made a disposition of his troops thinking to surround and surprise the town, after having been five hours within three miles of it.

380. Machin, a captain in Colonel John Lamb's 2nd New York Regiment of artillery, did in fact, make an unsuccessful effort to find the parents of the boy. He thereupon took him home with him to North River and adopted him, christening him Tom. However, the boy was stricken with smallpox two years later and died at Kingston, New York. Machin himself was born in England on March 20, 1744, settled in America in 1772, and took an early and active interest in the Revolution. He was made second lieutenant of the New York Artillery on January 18, 1776, and captain lieutenant in the second battalion of artillery on January 1, 1777. He held this rank during the expedition against Onondaga under Colonel Goose Van Schaick. He was employed as an engineer in constructing and placing the chain across the Hudson in the Highlands and after the war was for a time engaged in coining money for the States before the adoption of the federal Constitution, his works being at the outlet of a pond, five miles back from Newburgh. He enjoyed the confidence of Governor George Clinton, General James Clinton, George Washington and Lafayette, as well as that of many other distinguished men of his day. He obtained patents of large tracts of land in the northern part of Oneida County, was a member of the New York State Society of Cincinnati, and was succeeded by his son, General Thomas Machin of Albany. He died at Charleston, Montgomery County, New York, on April 3, 1816.

381. Pimps, in this context, mean scoundrels, sneaks and informers.

382. Skoyase, also called Skoiyase, Skolyase, Scawyase and Shaiyus, was located on the site of present Waterloo, New York. It was important because it was located on the main east-west road through Indian country. It was also called Large Falls and Long Falls, due to the rapids located in the river there.

383. As nearly as can be determined, this is the first recorded instance of fish being held alive by American Indians as a food source to be tapped later.

384. Kashong was also variously called Kershong, Shenawaga, Gaghsiungua, Gothsinquea, and Gothseunquean. It was located at the mouth of present Kashong Creek at Kashong Point,

east of the junction of Kashong Road and New York 14 in Ontario County, at the edges of Seneca and Yates counties.

385. Canawaugus was a Seneca village located very nearly on the site of present Avon, New York.

386. Present Flint River. Their route was basically along the route of present U.S. 20.

387. No identification has been found of the soldier who died.

388. The Seneca town of Canandaigua was located on the west side of the present town of that name, just east of present Sucker Brook, partly on the grounds of the present West Avenue Cemetery.

389. Not the same location as present Honeoye, which is on the west side of the outlet. The line of march was southwest from Canandaigua through Bristol and then along the route of present U.S. 20A to Honeoye Lake. The Seneca town of Honeoye was located approximately one-half mile east of present Honeoye, along the north bank of Mill Creek. Honeoye means "the loss of a finger," and evidently refers to some occurrence the Indians had here.

390. They marched directly west and crossed the outlet of present Hemlock Lake on the line where present Rix Hill Road crosses it, one-half mile west of Glenville.

391. Conesus was also known as Conighsas, Kanagsaws and Adjuton. It was located one mile northwest of the site of the present town of Conesus. The army camped on present Henderson's Flats northwest of present Union Corners and southwest of present Foot's Corners, on the crest of the rise above present North McMillan Creek.

392. Along the present route of West Lake Road.

393. First along the route of present Gray Hill Road, and then along the route of present Maple Beach Road and Groveland Road and then due west.

394. Along the present Jones Bridge Road.

395. Coshequa, also called Sqatekak, was located just over two miles northwest of present East Groveland, New York, and three miles southeast of the center of present Geneseo, New York, on the headwaters of Fall Brook at the junction of present Groveland Road (sometimes called Geneseo Road) and Jones Bridge Road.

396. Chenussio, also called Chinefee, Beardstown, Genesee and Geneseo, was not located at the site of present Geneseo, New York, but rather 2½ miles southwest of there, on the west side of the Genesee River, one mile east of present Cuylersville, between Boyd-Parker State Park and eastward to just east of the junction of present Barrett Road with U.S. A-20.

397. This Indian was a Seneca warrior named Sahnahdahyah.

398. Some accounts say Brant at this time had 800 men with him, but this is incorrect. The route from Canawaugus (Avon, New York) had brought Brant's force straight south on the route of present U.S. 15 and New York 256 along the west shore of Conesus Lake.

399. This was at a point approximately one-half mile south of the junction of present Gray Hill Road with West Lake Road (New York 256.)

400. The route of this road was approximately along the route of present Turner Road to Groveland Hills Road, then southward to Groveland Corners and westward on present Bennett Road to the Canaseraga Creek valley. Here the trail turned northward (present New York 63) and paralleled Canaseraga Creek to its junction with the Genesee River. Two miles above the mouth of Canaseraga Creek was where Gothsegwarohare was located. This was close to where present Swain Hill Road meets New York 63, one mile south of present Hampton Corners.

401. Present course of Gray Hill Road.

402. This occurred at the head of the first ravine south of Lakeview Cemetery at Gray Corners.

403. Also among the escaped were men identified only as Elerson, McDonald, Garrett Putnam of Fort Hunter, and a French Canadian.

404. A few of the accounts say that numerous Indians were seen to fall as Boyd's detachment fought bravely from cover for a while and that the Indian deaths had to at least equal those of the detachment. Such accounts are wholly without foundation. None of Boyd's party on hand during the final stand survived to tell the details. No Indian bodies were discovered, nor any evidence to indicate that any Indians were wounded or killed. Of the fifteen dead here of Boyd's detachment, only nine have been positively identified. They were the Oneida chief, Hanyerry, Sergeant Nicholas Hungerman of Captain Mears's company, and Privates John

Conrey, William Faughey, William Harvey, James McElroy and John Miller, all of the Pennsylvania Brigade, and John Putnam of Fort Hunter (brother of Garrett Putnam who escaped with Timothy Murphy) and Benjamin Curtin (or Custin) of Schoharie, New York.

405. We encounter once again the story of Masonic symbol salvation. One of the accounts has it that Boyd, recognizing Brant, gave the Masonic sign and when Brant came to him at once, he begged Brant to save him. Brant thereupon allegedly put Boyd under his protection. However, it was said that Brant later on was "called away on other business" and Boyd was then devoid of Brant's protection. The whole story is rather ridiculous.

406. The surveying party was at this time at approximately the present intersection of Barber Hill Road and Turner Road.

407. The town was also known by the name of Cassawaughloughly. The meaning of the Indian name, loosely translated, is "a spear laid up."

408. Named after Chenussio's Chief Little Beard, the creek has since become known simply as Beards Creek.

409. So deeply moved by the scene were so many of the soldiers of this army that, as soon as it was opened to settlement, many of these same soldiers returned here at once and claimed land as their own.

410. Two days after this, Mrs. Lester's infant died. She subsequently remarried, becoming the wife of Captain Roswell Franklin, and they became part of the first party that settled the town of Aurora on Cayuga Lake.

411. It is alleged that the torturing was done at the direction of Colonel John Butler, to extract information from Boyd and Parker about the strength of the Sullivan army and its commander's plans in regard to coming farther than Chenussio, perhaps even to Niagara. However, that thesis doesn't hold up well. All that information was already known to Butler and the idea of his subjecting the two prisoners to such torture simply to corroborate what he already knew is not very plausible, especially if the previous generally humane character of the man is considered. It has also been suggested, and perhaps with more of an element of truth (certainly with more believability), that the questioning was not done by Butler but by his son, Captain Walter N. Butler, whose streak of cruelty was already well established with what had transpired at Cherry Valley. Finally, the manner of the indignities ultimately resulting in death are reasonably characteristic of the torture deaths the Iroquois sometimes subjected captives to and it may be that, following questioning, the two captives were simply turned over to the Indians to do with as they wished. This is the most likely reconstruction of events, all things considered. A letter dated September 19, 1779, to Robert Hamilton from Niagara, but unsigned, reports:

The Lieutenant [Boyd] was examined, and told that there were about five thousand, consisting of Continental troops, with fifteen hundred riflemen, with four six and three-pounders, and a small mortar, Commanded by General Sullivan and two other general officers — one regiment of 500 men left at Tioga, and another at Genesee [Honeoye], which completed the whole six thousand; and that they had only one month's provisions with them and intended to destroy the Indian country and then return.

From this it may be deduced that Boyd did reveal relatively accurate information to the enemy, but whether or not because of being tortured is not known. Colonel John Butler, after this time, fades somewhat in prominence. He finally died on May 13, 1796.

412. The mound of this grave was visible for many years along that road. The remains of Boyd and Parker were reinterred at Mount Hope Cemetery, Rochester, New York, in August, 1842. The Boyd-Parker State Park now marks the place where they died.

413. On March 27, 1780, a party of Indians captured Thomas Bennett and others in the Wyoming Valley. The leader of the Indians had a fine sword that he said had belonged to Boyd, adding: "Boyd brave man!" During the night the prisoners rose up and fell on the captors and slew them, then returned to Wyoming with the sword.

414. A view of the spot where they were buried is provided in *History of Livingston County*. In 1841 this grave was opened and some of the bones removed and reinterred at the Mount

Hope Cemetery in Rochester. As part of the occasion, a historical address was given by S. Treat at Geneseo to an audience of an estimated 5,000 people at the formal delivery of the remains by the citizens of Livingston County to the Committee of Rochester. At Rochester, the Honorable William H. Seward delivered a patriotic address and a number of Sullivan's soldiers were present, including the two men who found Boyd's and Parker's remains, Moses Van Campen and Paul Sanborn.

415. The area where this occurred later became known by a name that referred to the incident. The bleached bones of the horses in later years were strewn all about and for some peculiar reason of their own, the Indians who drifted back to the area the following year and found the skeletons took all the skulls and placed them in rows along the trail. From that it became known as the Valley of the Horseheads. In 1886 it was known simply as Horseheads, and today Horseheads is a section of what is presently North Elmira, New York.

416. Gansevoort's detachment followed the main east-west Indian trail eastward, the line of which was afterward substantially adopted for the Seneca Turnpike, passing through Auburn and Onondaga Hill to Rome. They reached Fort Stanwix on September 25, 1779, without any untoward incident. On September 27, Gansevoort, as ordered, took all the male Mohawks at Teantontalago prisoner and brought them on to Albany for incarceration. They were later released.

417. This was Colonel Bryan Bruen, private secretary to Major General John Sullivan.

418. Shortly after his return to the East, John Sullivan resigned his commission and the following summer he was elected to the Congress.

419. Fort Sullivan was demolished as the army left Tioga on October 3, 1779. They marched to Morristown, New Jersey, and entered winter quarters there.

420. The winter of 1779–80 was so cold that cannon from Staten Island were transported to New York City by pulling them across the ice with teams of horses.

421. When the British entered into the Treaty of Paris with the United States in 1783, they signed away all claims which they *or the Indians* had to "the ancient Iroquois lands," despite their promises previously given to the Indians. Brant finally, after another trip to England, managed to get for the Mohawks a grant of land six miles wide on each side of the Grand River of Ontario, from its mouth on Lake Erie to its headwaters. Here Brant remained until his death, November 24, 1807. His final words (to an adopted nephew) were: "Have pity on the poor Indians. If you can get any influence with the great, endeavor to do them all the good you can."

PRINCIPAL SOURCES

PROLOGUE

Allen, W. L., *Allen's Biographical Dictionary* (Burlington, Vt.), 187–189.
American Museum Reports, Series V, 226.
Coffin, C. L., *Old Times in the Colonies* (Philadelphia, 1841), 384.
Draper, Lyman C., Draper Manuscript Collection, State Archives, Madison, Wisconsin.

  D-1-F: 1–22, 28, 31–33, 83, 98, 98a–b–99, 119.
  D-13-F: 118.
  D-2-G: 2, 7, 100, 108³, 108¹⁴.
  D-3-G: 26–27, 224.

Flexner, James Thomas, *Mohawk Baronet* (New York, 1959), 22, 104, 185–186.
Parkman, Francis, *The Conspiracy of Pontiac* (Boston, 1894), I, 117.
Pound, Arthur, *Johnson of the Mohawks* (New York, 1930), 438.
Rupp, Israel, *History of Western Pennsylvania* (Harrisburg, 1846), Appendix XIV, XVI.
Strachan, James (Bishop), *Visit to Upper Canada* (Albany, 1819), 152.
Strachan, John (Reverend), *Memoirs* (Albany, 1846), 71.
Swanton, John R., *Indian Tribes of North America* (Washington, D.C., 1953), 38–39.
Turner, E. F., *Traits of Indian Character* (New York, 1920), II, 12.
Weekly Expositor, Brantford, Ontario, October 15, 1886.
Weiser, Conrad, *Journal* (New York, 1806), 28.

CHAPTER I

Allen, W. L., *Allen's Biographical Dictionary* (Burlington, Vt.), 219–223, 740.
American Archives, II, 1542, 1641, 1747; III, 12, 18, 26.
American Historical Record, October, 1874, 461–462.
Bailey, Thomas A., *The American Pageant* (Boston, 1956), 98.
Belknap, Jeremy, *History of New Hampshire* (Concord, 1902), II, 353.
Boston Gazette, April 30, 1764.
Campbell, William W., *Annals of Tryon County* (New York, 1831).

Colonial History of New York (Albany, 1850), VII, 955.
Columbian Magazine, 1792, Part Second, 410.
Documentary History of New York (Albany, 1850), I, 141–142, 153–155, 165, 269; II, 582; IV,
    201, 203, 207–207f–208, 211.
Drake, Samuel A., *Events in the Life of Brant* (Boston, 1881), 2–3.
Draper, Lyman C., Draper Manuscript Collection, State Archives, Madison, Wisconsin.

D-1-F: 5, 16–17, 17a, 18, 26, 28, 32–33, 35–36, 40, 72–76, 78–79, 83–85, 98b–d, 99[111],
          105[3–15], 115–116, 119–120.
D-2-F: 6–8, 9–14, 21–22, 25, 27–29, 29[1], 31, 40, 43[1], 44–45, 48, 50–53, 60, 72, 80, 120.
D-4-F: 135, 137b, 137r, 138.
D-5-F: 232, 121.
D-7-5:   21–21[1].
D-13-F: 181.
D-14-F: 28, 40.
D-18-F: 313.
D-1-G: 1[4–5], 3, 3[32–40], 3, 7–8, 12[11], 12[46], 15[171–173], 16[90–91], 22[69 f], 27[309].
D-2-G: 2, 3, 101, 105, 105[3–5], 108[14], 108[16–17], 183, 189.
D-3-G: 3, 26–27, 31, 224[27].
D-4-H: 138.

Flexner, James Thomas, *Mohawk Baronet,* 186–187, 215, 223, 231, 258–259, 261–264, 266–267,
    282–283, 290–292, 324–331.
Gladwin Manuscripts and Bouquet Papers, Ann Arbor, 1884, 41, 198, 242, 654.
Graham, Lloyd, *Niagara Country* (New York, 1949), 15, 22–23.
Hall & McKenney, *Indian Tribes* (Washington, D.C., 1963), I, 88.
Harper's Magazine, August, 1858, 309; July, 1877, 326.
Hough, Franklin B., *Diary of the Siege of Detroit* (Albany, 1860), 19, 72–73, 75n5, 79, 86, 91.
Howe, Henry, *Historical Collections of Ohio* (Cincinnati, 1904), I, 310, 963.
Huddleston, F. J., *Gentleman Johnny Burgoyne* (New York, 1927), 123–124.
Indian Charity School, 1762–65: 4, 21–22; 1766: 32, 35–36; 1769: 45, 71.
Johnson, William, *Papers,* Albany Archives, III, 371–372, 381–382, 481–482, 515; VII, 5.
Jones, R., *Annals of Oneida County* (New York, 1876), 852.
Journal of the New York Provincial Congress, II, 33.
Kirkland, Samuel, *Life of Samuel Kirkland* (privately printed, n.d.), 233, 241.
Maryland *Gazette,* March 22, 1764; May 3, 1764.
Massachusetts Historical Collections, 5th Series, VIII, 227–228.
New York Colonial Documents (Albany, 1850), I, 322, 352–353; IV, 73, 994; VI, 512, 520,
    720–721; VII, 180, 609–611, 624–625, 629, 648–649, 652, 655–656, 671, 685; VIII, 78–79,
    94, 183, 227–228, 303, 473, 477–478, 490, 499–500, 507–508, 515–520, 524–525, 534.
New York *Daily Tribune,* May 31, 1879.
Oneonta *Herald and Democrat,* October 18, 1878.
Parkman, Francis, *The Conspiracy of Pontiac and the Indian War after the Conquest of Canada*
    (Boston, 1894), II, 20, 40n, 72–73, 77–79, 101–102, 113–114, 124–125n, 127, 164–168,
    171, 174, 200–200n, 271, 307, 315–316, 319–320, app. A, B.
———, *Frontenac and New France* (Boston, 1894), 128, 146, 149, 153.
———, *Montcalm and Wolfe* (Boston, 1894), I, 288, 357; II, 407.
Peckham, Howard, *Pontiac and the Indian Uprising* (Princeton, 1947), 224–225, 229–230.
Pennsylvania *Gazette,* July 5, 1775.
Pennsylvania *Journal,* September 8, 1773.
Pennsylvania *Ledger,* July 1, 1775.
Pennsylvania Records, IX, 171.
Pound, Arthur, *Johnson of the Mohawks* (New York, 1930), 388, 406, 420–421, 430–439,
    521–522, 538[L]–539.
Schoolcraft, Henry R., *Indian Tribes* (New York, 1847), V, 519–521.

Sterling, James, *Letters*, mss., Ann Arbor, 7.
Stone, William L., *Life of Joseph Brant* (New York, 1838), I, 19–20, 72–80, app. 73; II, 408, 488, 489.
Stone, William L., Jr., *Life and Times of Sir William Johnson* (Albany, 1865), I, 25–26, 353, 409–410; II, 173–175, 214–215, 224, 379–381, 409–410, 430–431, 448, 503.
Ward, Christopher, *The War of the Revolution* (New York, 1952), II, 32–40, 480.
Wheelock, Eleazar, *Memoirs* (Dartmouth, 1847), 27, 227–228.
Wood, Norman, *Lives of Famous Indian Chiefs* (Aurora, 1906), 144–146, 163, 241.

CHAPTER II

Allen, W. L., *Allen's Narrative* (Burlington, Vt., 1846), 37–40.
Almon's Remembrancer, 1776 (New York), II, 60–63, 105–107, 137, 221; III, 205.
American Archives, 5th Series, I, 394, 814, 835, 839; II, 1193; III, 485, 492–493, 526, 548–549, 605, 681–682, 705, 739, 754, 797–798, 827, 839–840, 926, 1029, 1217, 1232, 1245, 1291, 1476–1477, 1500, 1996, 1999; IV, 821–822; V, 416, 527, 767, 770–772, 818; VI, 400, 729–731, 1046; VII, 395–396, 715, 814, 835, 865; VIII, 125.
Burgoyne, John, *State of the Expedition from Canada* (London, 1780).
———, *Thoughts on Conducting the War from the Side of Canada* (London, 1780).
Campbell, William W., *Annals of Tryon County* (New York, 1831), 49–50, 54–55, 59–65, 68, 71–75, 92–93, 97–99, app. 67, 78.
Colonial History of New York (Albany, 1850), VIII, 713, 727.
Draper, Lyman C., Draper Manuscript Collection, State Archives, Madison, Wisconsin:

D-1-F: 16a, 26, 55, 98d, 98e, 98f, 99, 100a–e, 115, 117, 120–121.
D-2-F: 51, 61–65, 67, 69, 71, 73^2, 76–79, 81–82, 85–89, 93–94, 102–105, 113–125.
D-3-F: 1, 3^7, 4, 7–8, 17, 17^1, 18–20.
D-4-F: 4, 95.
D-5-F: 121–122, 127.
D-7-F: 39, 39^1, 65^{1-2}.
D-11-F: 29.
D-12-F: 109.
D-14-F: 14^{21}, 41.
D-20-F: 7, 52.
D-21-F: 39.
D-1-G: 1^5, 3^{6-11}, 3^{36-38}, 3^{40}, 3^{42-44}, 7^7, 12^{8-13}, 12^{15-17}, 12^{44-50}, 12^{59-61}, $13^{642-643}$, $13^{645-646}$, 14^{22-23}, 14^{25}, 14^{27}, 15, $15^{172-173}$, $15^{175-176}$, 22^{67-68}, 22^{70-72}, 24, $24^{102-104}$, 51.
D-2-G: 4–5, 108, 108^{5-6}, 109, 109^{16}, 109^{28}, 110^2, 111^1, 111^{29}.

Gentleman's Magazine, February, 1776, 86, 89.
Graham, Lloyd, *Niagara County* (New York, 1949), 23, 246.
Hamilton, Edward P., *Fort Ticonderoga* (Boston, 1964), 137–138.
Historical Magazine, April, 1859, vol. 3, no. 4.
House of Representatives, 25th Cong., 3rd Sess. U.S., doc. 203, February 18, 1839.
Huddleston, F. J., *Gentleman Johnny Burgoyne* (New York, 1927), 105–106, 109–110, 113–118, 121, 124, 126–128, 128n, 129, 134–138, 138n, 147–148, 152–155, 158–159.
Journal of the New York Provincial Congress, I, 96, 170, 202, 357, 377, 761, 777–780, 968, 976, 997, 1001–1002, 1004, 1007, 1010–1011, 1017; II, 31, 59, 96, 278, 300–301, 340; III, 340.
Journals of John Sullivan (Auburn, N.Y., 1887), 237n, 238, 337–338, 337n, 339n, 341n, 369n.
London Magazine, July, 1776.
Lossing, S., *Life and Times of Philip Schuyler* (New York, 1883), I, 252, 352; II, 69, 107, 270; V, 388.
Magazine of American History, vol. I, no. 11, November, 1877; vol. II, no. 1, January, 1878.
Moore, Lee, *Diary of the Revolution* (Boston, 1846), I, 290–291, 303.

New England *Chronicle*, August 17, 1775, 2; September 14, 1775, 3; September 21, 1774, 2; October 5, 1775, 3; March 28, 1776, 4.

New York Colonial Documents, VIII, 596, 605, 619, 621, 630, 636–637, 654–655, 657, 660–662, 667, 670, 678, 683, 687–688, 699, 711–718, 720–725, 813, 815.

New York *Herald*, August 14, 1878, "Cherry Valley."

Pennsylvania *Evening Post*, September 19, 1776; July 17, 1777.

Pennsylvania *Gazette*, August 7, 21, 28, September 11, November 6, 1776.

Pennsylvania *Journal*, August 14, 1776.

Pennsylvania *Ledger*, August 17, 1776.

Political Magazine, December, 1780, 757.

Pound, Arthur, *Johnson of the Mohawks* (New York, 1930), 337–337n, 366, 431–434, 439.

Salisbury and Winston Journal, England, December 2, 1776; February 16, 1778.

Schoolcraft, Henry R., June 19, 1845, speech, "Historical Considerations on the Siege and De-
———, "Schoolcraft's Addenda" 1846, 27–28.

Sibley, John L., letter, Harvard University Library, July 2, 1877.

Smith, William, *Treatise on Indian Warfare* (New York, 1829), 58.

Sparks, L., *Life of George Washington* (Boston, 1846), III, 110.

Stone, William L., *Life of Joseph Brant* (New York, 1838), I, 144, 147, 147n, 150–151, 170, 186, 228; II, 3n, 411.

Ward, Christopher, *War of the Revolution* (New York, 1952), 60, 66–71, 143–145, 150–162, 168–201, 386, 417, 430, 480–484, 897–898, 898n, 930, 931.

Wood, Norman, *Lives of Famous Indian Chiefs* (Aurora, 1906), 241.

CHAPTER III

Burnett, Edmund C., *Letters of Members of the Continental Congress* (Washington, D.C., 1921–26), II, 405–406.

Campbell, William W., *Annals of Tryon County* (New York, 1831), 83–85, 88–89, 109.

Cobleskill (N.Y.) *Index*, May 23, 1878.

Continental Journal, September 3, 1778.

Draper, Lyman C., Draper Manuscript Collection, State Archives, Madison, Wisconsin.

D-1-F: 98g–h.
D-2-F: 82.
D-3-F: 4, 6–7, 18–19$^{1-3}$, 66, 89–90.
D-4-F: 3, 4, 113, 118.
D-5-F: 15, 15^1, 52, 70, 85, 95, 122, 123, 128, 177–177$^{1-2}$, 178–179, 180, 183^1, 185.
D-7-F: 64^1, 65^2.
D-14-F: 12, 12^2, 13.
D-18-F: 313.
D-20-F: 8–8^1, 52.
D-21-F: 39.
D-1-G: 1^5, 3$^{10-16}$, 3$^{18-19}$, 3$^{21-28}$, 3$^{44-45}$, 3^{310}, 4$^{1-2}$, 12$^{12-13}$, 12^{15}, 12$^{17-28}$, 12^{22}, 12^{44}, 12^{47}, 12$^{49-53}$, 12$^{58-63}$, 12^{109}, 13$^{641-643}$, 13$^{646-648}$, 14$^{22-26}$, 15$^{177-179}$, 15$^{181-183}$, 15^{189}, 16$^{89-90}$, 17$^{123-124}$, 18^{218}, 22$^{69-70}$, 22^{70c}, 22$^{71-80}$, 316–317.
D-2-G: 108^6, 108$^{23-24}$, 108$^{29-30}$, 109$^{17-18}$, 109$^{22-33}$, 111^{19}, 111^{25}, 111$^{29-33}$, 111^{19}, 111^{25}, 111$^{29-33}$.
D-3-G: 7–8, 27, 33.

Flexner, James Thomas, *George Washington in the American Revolution* (Boston, 1968), II, 194–195.

Harper's Magazine, August, 1858, 310.

Hatcher, Harlan, *Lake Erie* (New York, 1945), 53–54.

Historical Magazine, July, 1877, 420.

Howe, Henry, *Historical Collections of Ohio* (Cincinnati, 1888), II, 467, 910.
Huddleston, F. J., *Gentleman Johnny Burgoyne* (New York, 1927), 154, 156–156n, 157, 161–162, 164–166, 177, 179–180, 184, 186, 192–193, 195, 204, 208.
Jones, R., *Annals of Oneida County* (New York, 1876), 361.
Journal of the Congress of the United States, IV, 113.
Journals of John Sullivan (Auburn, N.Y., 1887), 338–339, 341n, 349n.
Lossing, Benson J., *Pictorial Field Book of the American Revolution* (New York, 1883), I, 242, 256.
————, *Trip, 1860* (New York, 1872), VIII, 19, 69, 71, 115.
Magazine of American History, vol. I, no. 11, November, 1877.
New York Colonial Documents, VIII, 725, 727, 741, 752.
New York Historical Magazine, II, 160–161.
New York Provincial Congress, II, 422.
New York *Tribune*, August 16, 1878.
Pennsylvania *Evening Post*, August 16, 19, 21, 1777.
Schoolcraft, Henry R., *Notes of the Iroquois* (New York, 1840), 141, 440–441.
Stedman, Charles, *British History of the American Revolution* (London, 1794), 353.
Stone, William L., *Life of Joseph Brant* (New York, 1838), I, 209, 239–240, 364–366, 461.
Utica *Daily Republican*, July 19, 1878.
Utica *Herald*, July 27, 1877.
Van Der Beet, Richard, *Held Captive by the Indians* (Knoxville, 1972), 237–237n30, 238–239.
Ward, Christopher, *War of the Revolution* (New York, 1952), 485–490, 496–498, 634.
Washington's Writings, ed. John C. Fitzpatrick, (Washington, D.C., 1931–34), VII, 100n, 133; VIII, 161n.

CHAPTER IV

Bradford, Alden, *Alden Bradford's History of Massachusetts* (Boston, 1892), II, 167–168.
Campbell, William W., *Annals of Tryon County* (New York, 1831), app. 60, 104, 107–109, 112, 160–161.
Continental Journal, September 3, 1778; October 29, 1779.
Draper, Lyman C., Draper Manuscript Collection, State Archives, Madison, Wisconsin.

  D-3-D: 8.
  D-1-F: 1^5, 98H, 111b.
  D-2-F: 64.
  D-4-F: 1, 5, 113–114, 117–118, 121–122, 135, 135^{a-b}, 171, 177–184, 186, 187, $189–189^{a-c}$, 192, 198–199.
  D-5-F: $5–5^1$, 8, 11, $33–33^{1-3}$, $35–35^{1-2}$, 36, 37–39, 40–41, $43–44–44^1–45$, 48–49, $50–52–52^{1-2}$, 60, 70–71, 88–89, 95–96, $102–107–107^2$, 108–109, $111–112–112^1–113$, 118, 122–124, 128–129, 136^2, 137–138.
  D-7-F: 39^1.
  D-12-F: 109.
  D-13-F: 132–133.
  D-14-F: 12^{2-3}, 41.
  D-1-G: 1^5, 1^{10}, $4–4^{1-3}$, 16^{89}, $17^{124-125}$, 17^{128}, 17^{315}, 18^{219}, $18^{212-213}$, 19^{247}, 23^{26}, 23^{128}, 25^{297}, $27^{310-315}$.
  D-2-G: 108^{6-7}, 109^{26-49}, 109^{50-54}, $109^5 42$, $109^{55,58-59}$, $109^{60-63,70-71}$, 110^6, 111^{12-25}, 111^{27}, 111^{31-33}, $114^{456-457}$.
  D-3-G: 7–10, 27, 37, 224^{28}.
  D-5-G: 51, 149.

Elmira *Daily Advertiser*, July 3, 1878.
Graham, Lloyd, *Niagara Country* (New York, 1949), 15.

Howe, Henry, *Historical Collections of Ohio* (Cincinnati, 1888), II, 693.
History Magazine, April, 1858, 128; October, 1861, 297.
History of Sullivan County, New York, 275, 459.
Journals of John Sullivan (Auburn, N.Y., 1887), 118–118n, 240–240n, 288–289, 339–340–340n, 349n, 350n, 353–355, 364, 371, 414.
Lossing, Benson S., *Pictorial History of the United States*, (Hartford, 1868), 291.
Lossing, S., *Life and Times of Philip Schuyler* (New York, 1883), II, 397.
————, *Field Book*, I, 266.
————, *Trip, 1860* (New York, 1872), VII, 63–64, 135–138, 142; VIII, 124–126, 133–136.
"Mary Jemison," pamphlet, 1856, 31, 189.
Maryland Journal, September 1, 1778; September 8, 1778.
Memorial of the Life and Character of John Wells (privately printed, Cherry Valley, N.Y., 1874), 31.
Methodist Quarterly Review, July, 1846, 456.
Mohawk Independent, November 26, 1878.
Moore, Lee, *Diary of the American Revolution* (Boston, 1846), II, 104–105.
Oneonta *Herald and Democrat*, October 18, 1878.
Pennsylvania Archives, New Series, X, 484, report to General Stark.
Pennsylvania Archives, Old Series, 1778–79, 15, 63.
Pennsylvania *Packet*, October 31, 1778; September 29, 1778.
Pound, Arthur, *Johnson of the Mohawks* (New York, 1930), 422–423, 544[4].
St. Nicholas Magazine, vol. I, no. 4, July, 1853.
Stone, William L., *Life of Joseph Brant* (New York, 1838), I, 312, 336n, 367, 370; II, 245, 377.
Susquehanna *Journal*, Binghamton, N.Y., March 1, 1855.
Utica *Daily Republican*, July 19, 1878.
Utica *Morning Herald & Gazette*, July 19, 1878.
Van Der Beets, Richard, *Held Captive by the Indians* (Knoxville, 1972), 209–210, 237n31, 239n33, 240n34, 242n36.
Ward, Christopher, *War of the Revolution* (New York, 1952), 633–635.

CHAPTER V

Amory, Thomas C., *Military Services and Public Life of Major General John Sullivan* (Boston, 1868), 104.
Brooks, Edward, *George Washington* (Stamford, 1897), XV, 139n, 189n, F.v, 57.
Campbell, William W., *Annals of Tryon County* (New York, 1831), 114.
Continental Journal, May, 1779.
Dawson, Henry, *Battles of the United States* (New York, 1858), I, 471.
Delaware Gazette, Delhi, Delaware County, N.Y., October 21, 1879.
Draper, Lyman C., Draper Manuscript Collection, State Archives, Madison, Wisconsin.

D-1-F:	98H–I.
D-4-F:	6, 10.
D-5-F:	37–38, 39^1, 70, 123–124, 129, 174–175, 175^1, 176.
D-6-F:	61^1, 61^{6-7}.
D-7-F:	$1-1^2$, 2–3, $39-39^1$, 40, 55, 55^{1-5}, 55^{6-7}, 72^2-73, 77, 95–96.
D-8-F:	22, 104, 111, 124, 149, 150–151, 153^2, 155.
D-9-F:	8^L-18, 22–23, $50-50^{1-3}$, 109..
D-10-F:	5.
D-14-F:	12.
D-18-F:	319.
D-1-G:	1^9, 3^8, 4^{6-9}, 4^{15}, 5^2, 7^{2-3}, 16^{87}, 20^{408}, 20^{412}, $27^{318-319}$.
D-2-G:	108^7, 109^{63}, 111^{26-27}.
D-3-G:	37–38, 181, 194–195, 224^{28-31}.

Flexner, James Thomas, *George Washington in the American Revolution* (Boston, 1967), II, 104–106, 120, 326–327, 329, 346, 350.

Howe, Henry, *Historical Collections of Ohio* (Cincinnati, 1888), I, 467; II, 693–694.

Journals of John Sullivan (Auburn, N.Y., 1887), 3–7, 16, 20–24, 38–39, 52–55, 63–71, 80–87, 92–93, 102–109, 116–118, 118n, 119, 120, 120n, 121–126, 137–140, 146–153, 168–171, 178–185, 192–194, 198–203, 214–215, 224–230, 237–243, 245–263, 267–270, 276–278, 285–286, 339–340, 340n, 341–344, 344n, 345–346, 346n, 347–348, 348n, 349–349n, 350, 350n, 351, 351n, 352–354, 354n, 356, 416–417, 426–427, app. 5.

Land, Robert, *Sullivan County* (Albany, 1870), 190–198.

Lossing, Benson S., *Books of the Red*, bk. 5; bk. 1, 262; bk. 50, 251.

Magazine of American History, May 1, 1878.

Pennsylvania Archives, New Series, IV, 557.

Pennsylvania *Gazette*, April 21, 1779.

Sullivan County History, 191, 195, 198.

Van Der Beets, Richard, *Held Captive by the Indians* (Knoxville, 1972), 207–210.

Vermont Historical Collections, I, 10.

Virginia *Gazette*, August 28, 1779.

Ward, Christopher, *War of the Revolution* (New York, 1952), 602, 636–641, 645.

Wood, Norman, *Lives of Famous Indian Chiefs* (Aurora, 1906), 241.

CHAPTER VI AND EPILOGUE

Craft, David, Historical Address, Elmira Centennial Celebration, Elmira, New York, August 29, 1879.

Draper, Lyman C., Draper Manuscript Collection, State Archives, Madison, Wisconsin.

D-1-F: 98i.

D-7-F: 1^{2-3}, 21^2, 22, 42^1, 55, 55^{5-10}, 60^6, 66, 70^{2-6}, 71, 73, 75, 84, 96^{7-9}, 96^{11}, 96^{18-19}, 96^{20-22}.

D-10-F: 2, 4.

D-12-F: 109.

D-14-F: 12, 12^3.

D-1-G: 1^{9-10}, 4^4, 4^{9-16}.

D-2-G: 109^{64}, 114^{458}.

D-3-G: 3, 20–26, 32–39, 52–53.

Elmira *Daily Advertiser*, August 30, 1879.

Flexner, James Thomas, *George Washington in the American Revolution* (Boston, 1967), II, 353.

Galloway, William A., *Old Chillicothe* (Xenia, Ohio, 1934), 13–14, 41, 56, 61–62, 180–181.

Graham, Lloyd, *Niagara Country* (New York, 1949), 15–16, 23–24.

Howe, Henry, *Historical Collections of Ohio* (Cincinnati, 1888), II, 693.

Hughes, Rupert, *George Washington* (New York, 1926–30), XVI, 306–307, 377–378, 395–396, 399, 464.

Journals of John Sullivan (Auburn, N.Y., 1887), 7–15, 26–37, 39–41, 43–50, 55–61, 71–78, 87–91, 93–101, 105–106, 109–114, 126–130, 132–135, 140–143, 153–166, 171–177, 185–190, 203–208, 216–219, 230–237, 243–245, 264–265, 270–273, 278–282, 286–287, 354n, 356–361, 361n, 362, 362n, 363–379, 382–383, 414–416, 473, 475–476.

Lossing, Benson S., *Trip, 1860* (New York, 1872), VII, 65–66; VIII, 15–16, 24–25.

Rickey, Don, Jr., "Firearms in the Indian Wars" (Ph.D. diss., Oklahoma A & M, 1966), V, 136.

Tracy, William, "Indian Eloquence," in *Appleton's Journal* (1871), 543n.

Van Der Beets, Richard, *Held Captive by the Indians* (Knoxville, 1972), 204n3, 205n5, 209, 209n8.

Ward, Christopher, *War of the Revolution* (New York, 1952), 644–646, 650.

Wood, Norman, *Lives of Famous Indian Chiefs* (Aurora, 1906), 241.

SPECIFIC MILITARY JOURNALS OF THE OFFICERS INVOLVED IN
THE SULLIVAN CAMPAIGN AGAINST THE INDIANS

Journal of Lieutenant William Barton, June 8–October 9, 1779, *Proceedings of the New Jersey Historical Society*, vol. II, 1846–1847.

Journal of Lieutenant Erkuries Beatty, unpub., New York Historical Society Archives, New York City, April 6–October 22, 1779.

Journal of Lieutenant Thomas Blake, in Frederick Kidder and Joel Munsell, *History of the First New Hampshire Regiment in the War of the Revolution*, (Albany, 1868).

Journal of Major John Burrowes, unpub., New-York Historical Society archives, Buffalo.

Journal of Dr. Jabez Campfield, in *Proceedings of the New Jersey Historical Society*, III, IV, 1873, 115–136.

Journal of Lieutenant Colonel Henry Dearborn, unpub., Waterloo Library and Historical Society of Waterloo, Seneca County, New York.

Journal of Dr. Ebenezer Elmer, in *Proceedings of the New Jersey Historical Society*, II, 43–50; original in the Lyman C. Draper Manuscript Collection, State Archives, Madison, Wisc.

Journal of Sergeant Moses Fellows, unpub., in possession of the estate of A. Tiffany Norton, Lima, N.Y.

Journal of Major Jeremiah Fogg (Exeter, New Hampshire News Letter Press, 1879).

Journal of Ensign Daniel Gookin, in *New England Historical and General Register*, XVI (1), January 1862.

Journal of Sergeant Major George Grant, in *Hazard's Register* (Pa.), XIV, 72–76.

Journal of Thomas Grant, Surveyor, published in *Historical Magazine*, 1862, VI, 233–273.

Journal of Lieutenant John L. Hardenbergh, in *Cayuga County Historical Society Collections*, 1879, no. 1.

Journal of Lieutenant Colonel Adam Hubley, in the appendix of *Miner's History of Wyoming*, Pennsylvania Archives, New Series, vol. XI, vol. II of the American Revolution.

Journal of Lieutenant John Jenkins, estate of Steuben Jenkins, Wyoming, Pennsylvania; Pennsylvania Archives.

Journal of Captain Daniel Livermore, in *New Hampshire Historical Collections*, Vol. VI.

Journal of Captain Thomas Machin, in *Magazine of American History*, November, 1879.

Journal of Lieutenant William McKendry, in *Proceedings of the Massachusetts Historical Society*, 2nd Series, II, 436–438, October, 1886.

Journal of Lieutenant Charles Nukerck, in estate of General John S. Clark, Auburn, New York.

Journal of Major James Norris, in *Hill's New Hampshire Patriot*, Portsmouth, September 16, 1843.

Journal of Sergeant Thomas Roberts, unpub., New-York Historical Society, procured February 16, 1886.

Journal of Reverend William Rogers, D.D., in Sidney S. Rider, the *Rhode Island Historical Tracts*, no. 7, (Providence, 1879).

Journal of Sergeant William Rogers, unpub., estate of B. L. Rogers, Newark, New Jersey.

Journal of Lieutenant Samuel Shute, unpub., in estate of Williams E. Potters, Princeton, New Jersey.

Journal of Lieutenant Rudolphus Van Hovenburgh, unpub., in estate of Franklin B. Hough, Albany, New York.

Journal of Sergeant Nathaniel Webb, unpub., Lyman C. Draper Manuscript Collection, State Archives, Madison, Wisconsin.

INDEX